THE ANNALS
OF
AMERICA

THE ANNALS OF AMERICA

Volume 5

1821 - 1832

Steps Toward Equalitarianism

ENCYCLOPÆDIA BRITANNICA, INC.

Chicago London New Delhi Paris Sydney Taipei Tokyo Seoul

The editors wish to express their gratitude for permission to reprint
material from the following sources:

The Arthur H. Clark Company for Selections 15, 30,
48, 49, 57, 58, 63, 72, 82, from *A Documentary History of American Industrial Society,* ed. by John R. Commons *et al.*

J. P. Mayer for Selection 99, from *Journey to America,*
by Alexis de Tocqueville, ed. by J. P. Mayer, tr. by
George Lawrence.

The University of Chicago Press for Selection 109,
from *A Documentary History of American Higher Education,* ed. by Richard Hofstadter and Wilson Smith,
Vol. I, © 1961 by The University of Chicago.

CODED SOURCES IN THIS VOLUME

Colton

The Works of Henry Clay Comprising His Life, Correspondence and Speeches. Edited by Calvin Colton. In 10 vols. New York, 1904.

Commons

A Documentary History of American Industrial Society. Edited by John R. Commons *et al.* In 10 vols. Cleveland, 1910-1911.

Debates

[Annals of Congress] *The Debates and Proceedings in the Congress of the United States with an Appendix Containing Important State Papers and Public Documents and All the Laws of a Public Nature; with a Copious Index.* In 42 vols. Washington, 1834-1856.

H. A. Washington

The Writings of Thomas Jefferson: Being his Autobiography, Correspondence, Reports, Messages, Addresses and Other Writings, Official and Private. Edited by H. A. Washington. In 9 vols. Washington, 1853-1854. Vol. 7, New York, 1884.

MHSP

Proceedings of the Massachusetts Historical Society. Boston, 1791 *et seq.*

OSL

Old South Leaflets. Published by the Directors of the Old South Work, Old South Meeting House. In 8 vols. (Documents 1-200). Boston, n.d.

5 Peters 1

Reports of Cases Argued and Adjudged in the Supreme Court of the United States. Edited by Richard Peters. Vol. 5, Philadelphia, 1845, pp. 1ff.

Richardson

A Compilation of the Messages and Papers of the Presidents 1789-1897. Edited by James D. Richardson. In 10 vols. Washington, 1896-1899.

6 Wheaton 264
9 Wheaton 1

Reports of Cases Argued and Adjudged in the Supreme Court of the United States. Edited by Henry Wheaton. Vol. 6, New York, 1883, pp. 264ff. Vol. 9, pp. 1ff.

Contents

Index of Authors, *595*

STEPS TOWARD EQUALITARIANISM

In Pictures

Urban America 41-56

Under the impact of increasing industrialization, the large
cities of the Northeast, in particular New York, Boston, and
Philadelphia, were growing rapidly. Steam travel and the Erie Canal
stimulated growth in the Hudson Valley and Upstate New York,
while high society expanded to include the newly wealthy.

The Second Revolution 143-154

With the completion of the Erie Canal and the spread of the factory
system and the steamboat, the economy turned irrevocably to
industrialization and internal development. The first experimental
railroads foreshadowed the next stage of expansion.

Moving Westward 191-202

In the decade following the War of 1812, five western states entered the
Union and the first "great migration" flooded the Midwest and Deep South
with homesteaders. Commerce on the western rivers and discovery of ore
deposits attracted others not interested in farming, while, in the
South, the plantation system spread west to the Mississippi.

New Political Dimensions 243-252

The Monroe Doctrine and the first flourish of Jacksonian Democracy
defined America's commitment to democratization at home and hegemony
in the Western Hemisphere. Sectional differences and conflict over the
spread of slavery threatened the Union, while Jackson's fiscal and
tariff policies angered both the South and the Northeast.

New Life in the Arts 337-346

While Cooper and Irving shaped a native school of literature,
and the theater flourished, portrait painting was in its last
years as the dominant mode in American art.

"The Trail of Tears" 453-462

Removal of British influence in the West during the War of 1812
and the death of Tecumseh left the American government free
to deal with the Indians as it saw fit. By the early 1830s most
of the Southern and Midwestern nations had been removed west of
the Mississippi. The pace of resettlement expressed the force
and impatience of America's drive westward.

1821

1.

JOHN MARSHALL: *Cohens* v. *Virginia*

Chief Justice John Marshall was a strong nationalist, a number of whose decisions helped establish the authority of the federal government at the expense of the states. He felt that the Constitution should be liberally interpreted, even though its actual provisions for a national government were both limited and specific. The case of Cohens v. Virginia *arose when two men were convicted under a state law for selling tickets in a national lottery permitted by federal law. The issues before the Supreme Court were basically two: the supremacy of federal law over a state law; and the appellate jurisdiction of the Court in a case where the parties were a state and citizens of that state. Marshall's decision of February 1821, reprinted in part below, was based largely on the Eleventh Amendment and Section 25 of the Judiciary Act of 1789.*

Source: 6 Wheaton 264.

THE GENERAL GOVERNMENT, though limited as to its objects, is supreme with respect to those objects. This principle is a part of the Constitution; and if there be any who deny its necessity, none can deny its authority.

To this supreme government, ample powers are confided; and if it were possible to doubt the great purposes for which they were so confided, the people of the United States have declared that they are given "in order to form a more perfect union, establish justice, ensure domestic tranquillity, provide for the common defense, promote the general welfare, and secure the blessings of liberty to themselves and their posterity."

With the ample powers confided to this supreme government, for these interesting purposes, are connected many express and important limitations on the sovereignty of the states which are made for the same purposes. The powers of the Union, on the great subjects of war, peace, and commerce, and on many others, are in themselves limitations of the sovereignty of the states; but, in addition to these, the sovereignty of the states is surrendered, in many instances, where the surrender can only operate to the benefit of the people, and where, perhaps, no other power is conferred on Congress than a conservative power to maintain the principles established in the Constitution. The maintenance of these principles in their purity is certainly among the great duties of the government.

One of the instruments by which this duty may be peaceably performed is the Judicial Department. It is authorized to decide all cases of every description arising under the Constitution or laws of the United States. From this general grant of jurisdiction, no exception is made of those cases in which a state may be a party. When we consider the situation of the government of the Union and of a state, in relation to each other; the nature of our Constitution; the subordination of the state governments to that Constitution; the great purpose for which jurisdiction over all cases arising under the Constitution and laws of the United States is confided to the Judicial Department, are we at liberty to insert in this general grant an exception of those cases in which a state may be a party? Will the spirit of the Constitution justify this attempt to control its words? We think it will not. We think a case arising under the Constitution or laws of the United States is cognizable in the courts of the Union, whoever may be the parties to that case. . . .

The Constitution gave to every person having a claim upon a state a right to submit his case to the Court of the nation. However unimportant his claim might be, however little the community might be interested in its decision, the framers of our Constitution thought it necessary, for the purposes of justice, to provide a tribunal as superior to influence as possible in which that claim might be decided. . . . The judicial power of every well-constituted government must be coextensive with the legislative, and must be capable of deciding every judicial question which grows out of the Constitution and laws. . . .

In many states, the judges are dependent for office and for salary on the will of the legislature. The Constitution of the United

David B. Ogden (1775-1849) appeared in defense of Cohens; painting by Trumbull

States furnishes no security against the universal adoption of this principle. When we observe the importance which that Constitution attaches to the independence of judges, we are the less inclined to suppose that it can have intended to leave these constitutional questions to tribunals where this independence may not exist, in all cases where a state shall prosecute an individual who claims the protection of an act of Congress. These prosecutions may take place even without a legislative act. A person making a seizure under an act of Congress may be indicted as a trespasser if force has been employed, and of this a jury may judge. How extensive may be the mischief if the first decisions in such cases should be final! . . .

A constitution is framed for ages to come, and is designed to approach immortality as nearly as human institutions can approach it. Its course cannot always be tranquil. It is exposed to storms and tempests, and its framers must be unwise statesmen indeed if they have not provided it, so far as its nature will permit, with the means of self-preservation from the perils it may be destined to encounter. No government ought to be so defective in its organization as not to contain within itself the means of securing the execution of its own laws against other dangers than those which occur every day. Courts of justice are the means most usually employed; and it is reasonable to expect that a government should repose on its own courts rather than on others. . . .

It is very true that whenever hostility to the existing system shall become universal, it will be also irresistible. The people made the Constitution, and the people can unmake it. It is the creature of their will, and lives only by their will. But this supreme and irresistible power to make or to unmake resides only in the whole body of the people, not in any subdivision of them. The attempt of any of the parts to exercise it is usurpation and ought to be repelled by those to whom the people have delegated their power of repelling it.

The acknowledged inability of the government, then, to sustain itself against the public will and, by force or otherwise, to control the whole nation is no sound argument in support of its constitutional inability to preserve itself against a section of the nation acting in opposition to the general will. . . .

That the United States form, for many and for most important purposes, a single nation has not yet been denied. In war, we are one people. In making peace, we are one people. In all commercial regulations, we are one and the same people. In many other respects, the American people are one; and the government which is alone capable of controlling and managing their interests in all these respects is the government of the Union. It is their government,

and, in that character, they have no other. America has chosen to be, in many respects and to many purposes, a nation; and for all these purposes her government is complete; to all these objects, it is competent. The people have declared that in the exercise of all powers given for these objects it is supreme. It can, then, in effecting these objects, legitimately control all individuals or governments within the American territory. The constitution and laws of a state, so far as they are repugnant to the Constitution and laws of the United States, are absolutely void. These states are constituent parts of the United States; they are members of one great empire — for some purposes sovereign, for some purposes subordinate.

In a government so constituted, is it unreasonable that the judicial power should be competent to give efficacy to the constitutional laws of the legislature? That department can decide on the validity of the Constitution or law of a state if it be repugnant to the Constitution or to a law of the United States. Is it unreasonable that it should also be empowered to decide on the judgment of a state tribunal enforcing such unconstitutional law? Is it so very unreasonable as to furnish a justification for controlling the words of the Constitution?

We think it is not. We think that in a government, acknowledgedly supreme, with respect to objects of vital interest to the nation, there is nothing inconsistent with sound reason, nothing incompatible with the nature of government, in making all its departments supreme, so far as respects those objects and so far as is necessary to their attainment. The exercise of the appellate power over those judgments of the state tribunals which may contravene the Constitution or laws of the United States is, we believe, essential to the attainment of those objects.

2.

Debate on Property and Suffrage

Property ownership as a qualification for voting had seldom been challenged before the 1820s. However, as merchants, manufacturers, craftsmen, and small plot farmers became more numerous, as the large estates that had been associated with the propertied class were divided into smaller holdings, many pressed for universal suffrage. In September 1821 the New York State constitutional convention met and formed a committee to review the electoral laws of the state. The discussion that ensued revealed a wide range of viewpoints, which are represented in the following speeches made during a long month of debate. Nathan Sanford introduced and defended a resolution, ultimately adopted, that extended suffrage to all white taxpayers. Other liberal committee members who supported Sanford or, in the case of Peter Jay, presented an argument for black suffrage as well, were P. R. Livingston, John Cramer, David Buel, Jr., and John Ross. These relatively unknown figures were opposed by two men who already had acquired national reputations and who, as defenders of the status quo, were passionately admired by some of the greatest political and legal thinkers of the time: the renowned jurist, Chancellor James Kent, and Martin Van Buren, a U.S. senator, who was later to become the eighth President of the United States.

Source: *Reports of the Proceedings and Debates of the Convention of 1821, Assembled for the Purpose of Amending the Constitution of the State of New-York*, Albany, 1821, pp. 178-185, 219-225, 235-244, 255-258, 366-368.

I.

Speech by NATHAN SANFORD

THE QUESTION BEFORE US is the right of suffrage — who shall or who shall not have the right to vote. The committee have presented the scheme they thought best; to abolish all existing distinctions and make the right of voting uniform. Is this not right? Where did these distinctions arise? They arose from British precedents. In England they have their three estates, which must always have their separate interests represented. Here there is but one estate — the people. To me the only qualifications seem to be the virtue and morality of the people; and if they may be safely entrusted to vote for one class of our rulers, why not for all?

In my opinion, these distinctions are fallacious. We have the experience of almost all the other states against them. The principle of the scheme now proposed is that those who bear the burdens of the state should choose those that rule it. There is no privilege given to property as such; but those who contribute to the public support we consider as entitled to a share in the election of rulers. The burdens are annual, and the elections are annual, and this appears proper. To me, and the majority of the committee, it appeared the only reasonable scheme that those who are to be affected by the acts of the government should be annually entitled to vote for those who administer it.

Our taxes are of two sorts, on real and personal property. The payment of a tax on either, we thought, equally entitled a man to a vote, and thus we intended to destroy the odious distinctions of property which now exist. But we have considered personal service, in some cases, equivalent to a tax on personal property, as in work on the high roads. This is a burden and should entitle those subject to it to equivalent privileges. The road duty is equal to a poll tax on every male citizen of twenty-one years, of 62½ cents per annum, which is about the value of each individual's work on the road. This work is a burden imposed by the legislature — a duty required by rulers, and which should entitle those subject to it to a choice of those rulers.

Then, sir, the militia next presents itself; the idea of personal service, as applicable to the road duty, is, in like manner, applicable here; and this criterion has been adopted in other states. In Mississippi mere enrollment gives a vote. In Connecticut, as is proposed here, actual service, and that without the right of commutation, is required. The duty in the militia is obligatory and onerous. The militiaman must find his arms and accouterments and lose his time. But, after admitting all these persons, what restrictions, it will be said, are left on the right of suffrage? (1) The voter must be a citizen. (2) The service required must be performed within the year, on the principle that taxation is annual, and election annual; so that when the person ceases to contribute or serve, he ceases to vote.

A residence is also required. We propose the term of six months, because we find it already in the constitution; but we propose this residence in the state and not in the county or town, so that, wherever a voter may be at the time of election, he may vote there if he has been a resident of the state for six months. The object of this was to enable those who move, as very many do, in the six months preceding an election, out of the town or ward in which they have resided, to retain the right of voting in their new habitations. The term of six months is deemed long enough to qualify those who come into our state from abroad to understand and exercise the privileges of a citizen here.

Now, sir, this scheme will embrace almost the whole male population of the state. There is, perhaps, no subject so purely matter of opinion as the question how far the right of suffrage may be safely carried. We propose to carry it almost as far as the male population of the state. The Convention may perhaps think this too broad. On this subject we have much experience; yet there are respectable citizens who think this extension of suffrage unfavorable to the rights of property. Certainly this would be a fatal objection, if well founded; for any government, however constituted, which does not secure property to its rightful owners is a bad government. But how is the extension of the right of suffrage unfavorable to property? Will not our laws continue the same? Will not the administration of justice continue the same? And, if so, how is private property to suffer? Unless these are changed, and upon them rest the rights and security of property, I am unable to perceive how property is to suffer by the extension of the right of suffrage. . . .

The course of things in this country is for the extension and not the restriction of popular rights. I do not know that in Ohio or Pennsylvania, where the right of suffrage is universal, there is not the same security for private rights and private happiness as elsewhere. Every gentleman is aware that the scheme now proposed is derived from the law calling this Convention, and in the constitution of this body we have the first fruits of the operation of the principle of extensive suffrage; and will anyone say that this example is not one evincing the discretion with which our people exercise this right? In our town meetings, too, throughout the state, we have the same principle. In our town elections we have the highest proof of the virtue and intelligence of our people; they assemble in town meetings as a pure democracy and choose their officers and local legislatures, if I may so call them; and if there is any part of our public business well done, it is that done in town meetings. Is not this a strong practical lesson of the beneficial operation of this principle? . . .

II.

Reported Speech of
MARTIN VAN BUREN

FROM DATA TO BE OBTAINED in the comptroller's office, it might with safety be stated that the personal property in the state, which was the subject of taxation, amounted to about $150 million; and that the real estate was valued at $256 million. The true question, then, presented to the committee by this amendment, was whether this $150 million of personal property, which annually contributed to defray the public burdens and to promote public improvements, and which was not now directly represented in any branch, should be wholly excluded from representation in one branch of the legislature; and that the one possessed of most power, and by far the most important of the two. But this was not all.

By the census of 1814, it appeared that of 163,000 electors in this state, upwards of 75,000 were freeholders, under $250, and all of them householders, who may possess any amount of personal property — men who have wives and children to protect and support, and who have everything but the mere dust on which they trod to bind them to the country. And the question was whether, in addition to those who might,

by this Convention, be clothed with the right of suffrage, this class of men, composed of mechanics, professional men, and small landholders, and constituting the bone, pith, and muscle of the population of the state, should be excluded entirely from all representation in that branch of the legislature which had equal power to originate all bills, and a complete negative upon the passage of all laws; from which, under the present constitution, proceeded the power that had the bestowment of all offices, civil and military, in the state. And, above all, which, in the language of an honorable member from Albany, as a court of *dernier* resort, was entrusted with the life, liberty, and property of every one of our citizens. This, said he, is, in sober truth, the question under discussion; and it would seem to him to be only necessary that it should be fairly stated and correctly understood to secure its rejection. This was the grievance under which so great a portion of the people of this state had hitherto labored. It was to relieve them from this injustice and this oppression that the Convention had been called; and it was, and always had been, a matter of astonishment to him that a reformation in this particular had been so long delayed. . . .

In whose name, and for whose benefit, he inquired, were they called upon to disappoint the just expectations of their constituents, and to persevere in what he could not but regard as a violation of principle? It was in the name and for the security of "farmers" that they were called upon to adopt this measure. This, he said, was, indeed, acting in an imposing name; and they who used it knew full well that it was so. It was . . . the boast, the pride, and the security of this nation that she had in her bosom a body of men who, for sobriety, integrity, industry, and patriotism, were unequalled by the cultivators of the earth in any part of the known world; nay, more, to compare them with men of similar pursuits in other countries was to degrade them. And woeful must be our degeneracy, before anything which might be supposed to affect the interests of the farmers of this country could be listened to with indifference by those who governed us.

He could not, he said, yield to any man in respect for this invaluable class of our citizens, nor in zeal for their support. But how did this matter stand? . . . Was the allegation that they were violating the wishes and tampering with the security of the farmers founded in fact, or was it merely colorable? Who, he asked, had hitherto constituted a majority of the voters of the state? The *farmers* — who had called for, and insisted upon, the Convention. *Farmers and freeholders!* Who passed the law admitting those who were not electors to a free participation in the decision of the question of *Convention* or *No Convention,* and also in the choice of delegates to that body? A legislature, a majority of whom were farmers, and probably every one of them freeholders, of the value of $250 and upwards! The farmers of this state had, he said, by an overwhelming majority, admitted those who were not freeholders to a full participation with themselves in every stage of this great effort to amend our constitution, and to ameliorate the condition of the people. Could he, then, ought he to be told, that they would be disappointed in their expectations when they found that, by the provisions of the constitution as amended, a great proportion of their fellow citizens were enfranchised, and released from fetters which they themselves had done all in their power to loosen? He did not believe it.

Again, inquired Mr. V. B., who are we that have been chosen to perform this great, and he could not but think, good work? A great majority of us are practical farmers; all *freeholders,* and of no small amounts. Were they their own worst enemies? Could they be suspected of a want of fidelity to the freehold interest? No! The farmers had

looked for such an event; they earnestly desired it. Whatever ravages the possession of power might have made in the breasts of others, they at least had shown that they could "feel power without forgetting right." If anything (said Mr. Van Buren) could render this invaluable class of men dearer and more estimable than they were, it was this magnanimous sacrifice which they had made on the altar of principle, by consenting to admit those of their fellow citizens, who, though not so highly favored as themselves by fortune, had still enough to bind them to their country, to an equal participation in the blessings of a free government. . . .

Mr. Van Buren said that as the vote he should now give on what was called the highway qualification would be different from what it had been on a former occasion, he felt it a duty to make a brief explanation of the motives which governed him. The qualifications reported by the first committee were of three kinds, viz.: the payment of a money tax; the performance of military duty; and working on the highway. The two former had met with his decided approbation; to the latter he wished to add the additional qualification that the elector should, if he paid no tax, performed no militia duty, but offered his vote on the sole ground that he had labored on the highways, also be a *householder;* and that was the only point in which he had dissented from the report of the committee. To effect this object, he supported a motion . . . to strike out the highway qualification, with a view of adding "householder." That motion, after full discussion, had prevailed by a majority of twenty. But what was the consequence? The very next day, the same gentlemen who thought the highway tax too liberal a qualification voted that every person of twenty-one years of age, having a certain term of residence, and excluding actual paupers, should be permitted to vote for any officer in the government, from the

Pencil and watercolor drawing of Martin Van Buren by J. Vanderlyn

highest to the lowest — far outvieing, in this particular, the other states in the Union, and verging from the extreme of restricted to that of universal suffrage.

The Convention, sensible of the very great stride which had been taken by the last vote, the next morning referred the whole matter to a select committee of thirteen, whose report was now under consideration. That committee, though composed of gentlemen, a large majority of whom had voted for the proposition for universal suffrage, had now recommended a middle course, viz., the payment of a money tax, or labor on the highway, excluding militia service, which had, however, been very properly reinstated. The question then recurred; shall an attempt be again made to add that of householder, to the highway qualification, and run the hazard of the reintroduction of the proposition of the gentleman from Washington, abandoning all qualifications, and throwing open the ballot boxes to everybody — demolishing at one blow the distinctive character of an elector, the proudest and most invaluable attribute of freemen?

Mr. Van Buren said he had, on the motion of the gentleman from Columbia, this day hinted at the numerous objections which he had to the proposition, which the other day passed the Convention, in regard to the right of suffrage — objections which he intended to make had the committee reported in favor of that vote; and by which, when fully urged, he knew that he would be able to convince every member of this committee of the dangerous and alarming tendency of that precipitate and unexpected prostration of all qualifications. At this moment, he would only say that among the many evils which would flow from a wholly unrestricted suffrage, the following would be the most injurious, viz.:

First, it would give to the city of New York about 25,000 votes; while, under the liberal extension of the right on the choice of delegates to this Convention, she had but about 13,000 or 14,000. That the character of the increased number of votes would be such as would render their elections rather a curse than a blessing, which would drive from the polls all sober-minded people; and such, he was happy to find, was the united opinion, or nearly so, of the delegation from that city.

Second, it would not only be injurious to them but that injury would work an equally great one to the western and northern parts of the state. It was the present consolation of our hardy sons of the west that, for their toils and their sufferings in reducing the wilderness to cultivation, they were cheered by the conviction, not only that they would be secure in the enjoyment of their dear bought improvements, in consequence of their representation in the legislature, but that any increase of that represention gave them a still greater influence there. That as far as it respected this state, their march and the march of empire kept pace.

This arose from the circumstance of the representation in the state being founded on the number of electors; and because almost every man in a new county was an elector, under the existing and contemplated qualifications; while in the old counties, and especially in cities, there were great numbers who would not be embraced by them. So great was this effect that the city of New York alone would, under the vote of the other day, have become entitled to additional voters, over those who voted at the election of delegates, equal, or nearly so, to the whole number of votes of Ontario or Genesee. The direct consequence of which would be that the additional representation of fourteen members, which are next year to be distributed among the counties, would, instead of going principally to the west, be surrendered to the worst population of the old counties and cities.

And, third, the door would have been entirely closed against retreat, whatever might be our after conviction, founded on experience, as to the evil tendency of this extended suffrage.

The just equilibrium between the rights of those who have and those who have no interest in the government could, when once thus surrendered, never be regained, except by the sword. But, according to the present report, if experience should point out dangers, from the very extensive qualifications we were about to establish, the legislature might relieve against the evil by curtailing the objects of taxation. By the establishment of turnpikes, the making of canals, and the general improvements of the country, the highway tax would naturally be lessened, and might, if the legislature thought proper, be hereafter confined to property, instead of imposing it, as they now do, on adult male citizens. For one hundred years at least, this would afford a sufficient protection against the evils which were apprehended. He would, therefore, notwithstanding his desire to have the qual-

ification of *householder* added to the electors of the third description remain unchanged, accept the report of the committee as it was, with the addition of the military qualification, which he thought ought to be adopted for the sake of principle, if for no other reason.

III.

Speech by JAMES KENT

I AM IN FAVOR of the amendment which has been submitted by my honorable colleague from Albany; and I must beg leave to trespass for a few moments upon the patience of the committee while I state the reasons which have induced me to wish that the Senate should continue, as heretofore, the representative of the landed interest and exempted from the control of universal suffrage. I hope what I may have to say will be kindly received, for it will be well intended. But, if I thought otherwise, I should still prefer to hazard the loss of the little popularity which I might have in this house, or out of it, than to hazard the loss of the approbation of my own conscience.

I have reflected upon the report of the select committee with attention and with anxiety. We appear to be disregarding the principles of the constitution, under which we have so long and so happily lived, and to be changing some of its essential institutions. I cannot but think that the considerate men who have studied the history of republics, or are read in lessons of experience, must look with concern upon our apparent disposition to vibrate from a well-balanced government to the extremes of the democratic doctrines. Such a broad proposition as that contained in the report, at the distance of ten years past, would have struck the public mind with astonishment and terror, so rapid has been the career of our vibration.

Let us recall our attention, for a moment,

to our past history. This state has existed for forty-four years under our present constitution, which was formed by those illustrious sages and patriots who adorned the Revolution. It has wonderfully fulfilled all the great ends of civil government. During that long period we have enjoyed, in an eminent degree, the blessings of civil and religious liberty. We have had our lives, our privileges, and our property protected. We have had a succession of wise and temperate legislatures. The code of our statute law has been again and again revised and corrected, and it may proudly bear a comparison with that of any other people. We have had, during that period (though I am, perhaps, not the fittest person to say it), a regular, stable, honest, and enlightened administration of justice. All the peaceable pursuits of industry, and all the important interests of education and science, have been fostered and encouraged. We have trebled our numbers within the last twenty-five years, have displayed mighty resources, and have made unexampled progress in the career of prosperity and greatness.

Our financial credit stands at an enviable height; and we are now successfully engaged in connecting the Great Lakes with the ocean by stupendous canals, which excite the admiration of our neighbors and will make a conspicuous figure even upon the map of the United States.

These are some of the fruits of our present government; and yet we seem to be dissatisfied with our condition, and we are engaged in the bold and hazardous experiment of remodeling the constitution. Is it not fit and discreet — I speak as to wise men — is it not fit and proper that we should pause in our career and reflect well on the immensity of the innovation in contemplation? Discontent in the midst of so much prosperity, and with such abundant means of happiness, looks like ingratitude and as if we were disposed to arraign the goodness of Providence. Do we not expose

New York Historical Society

James Kent (1763-1847) favored retaining property requirements; portrait by S. F. B. Morse

ourselves to the danger of being deprived of the blessings we have enjoyed? When the husbandman has gathered in his harvest, and has filled his barns and his granaries with the fruits of his industry, if he should then become discontented and unthankful, would he not have reason to apprehend that the Lord of the harvest might come in His wrath and with His lightning destroy them?

The Senate has hitherto been elected by the farmers of the state, by the free and independent lords of the soil, worth at least $250 in freehold estate, over and above all debts charged thereon. The governor has been chosen by the same electors, and we have hitherto elected citizens of elevated rank and character. Our assembly has been chosen by freeholders, possessing a freehold of the value of $50, or by persons renting a tenement of the yearly value of $5, and who have been rated and actually paid taxes to the state. By the report before us, we propose to annihilate, at one stroke, all those property distinctions and to bow before the idol of universal suffrage. That extreme democratic principle, when applied to the Legislative and Executive departments of government, has been regarded with terror by the wise men of every age, because in every European republic, ancient and modern, in which it has been tried, it has terminated disastrously and been productive of corruption, injustice, violence, and tyranny. And dare we flatter ourselves that we are a peculiar people who can run the career of history, exempted from the passions which have disturbed and corrupted the rest of mankind? If we are like other races of men, with similar follies and vices, then I greatly fear that our posterity will have reason to deplore, in sackcloth and ashes, the delusion of the day.

It is not my purpose at present to interfere with the report of the committee, so far as respects the qualifications of electors for governor and members of assembly. I shall feel grateful if we may be permitted to retain the stability and security of a Senate, bottomed upon the freehold property of the state. Such a body, so constituted, may prove a sheet anchor amid the future factions and storms of the republic. The great leading and governing interest of this state is, at present, the agricultural; and what madness would it be to commit that interest to the winds. The great body of the people are now the owners and actual cultivators of the soil. With that wholesome population we always expect to find moderation, frugality, order, honesty, and a due sense of independence, liberty, and justice. It is impossible that any people can lose their liberties by internal fraud or violence so long as the country is parceled out among freeholders of moderate possessions, and those freeholders have a sure and efficient control in the affairs of the government. Their habits, sympathies, and employments necessarily inspire them with a correct spirit of freedom and justice; they are the safest guardians of property and the laws.

We certainly cannot too highly appreciate the value of the agricultural interest. It is the foundation of national wealth and power. According to the opinion of her ablest political economists, it is the surplus produce of the agriculture of England that enables her to support her vast body of manufacturers, her formidable fleets and armies, and the crowds of persons engaged in the liberal professions and the cultivation of the various arts.

Now, sir, I wish to preserve our Senate as the representative of the landed interest. I wish those who have an interest in the soil to retain the exclusive possession of a branch in the legislature as a stronghold in which they may find safety through all the vicissitudes which the state may be destined, in the course of Providence, to experience. I wish them to be always enabled to say that their freeholds cannot be taxed without their consent. The men of no property, together with the crowds of dependents connected with great manufacturing and commercial establishments, and the motley and undefinable population of crowded ports, may, perhaps, at some future day, under skillful management, predominate in the assembly, and yet we should be perfectly safe if no laws could pass without the free consent of the owners of the soil. That security we at present enjoy; and it is that security which I wish to retain.

The apprehended danger from the experiment of universal suffrage applied to the whole Legislative Department is no dream of the imagination. It is too mighty an excitement for the moral constitution of men to endure. The tendency of universal suffrage is to jeopardize the rights of property and the principles of liberty. There is a constant tendency in human society, and the history of every age proves it; there is a tendency in the poor to covet and to share the plunder of the rich; in the debtor, to relax or avoid the obligation of contracts; in the majority, to tyrannize over the minority and trample down their rights; in the indolent and the profligate, to cast the whole burdens of society upon the industrious and the virtuous; and *there is a tendency in ambitious and wicked men to inflame these combustible materials.*

It requires a vigilant government and a firm administration of justice to counteract that tendency. "Thou shalt not covet," "Thou shalt not steal" are divine injunctions induced by this miserable depravity of our nature. Who can undertake to calculate with any precision how many millions of people this great state will contain in the course of this and the next century, and who can estimate the future extent and magnitude of our commercial ports? The disproportion between the men of property and the men of no property will be in every society in a ratio to its commerce, wealth, and population.

We are no longer to remain plain and simple republics of farmers like the New England colonists or the Dutch settlements on the Hudson. We are fast becoming a great nation, with great commerce, manufactures, population, wealth, luxuries, and with the vices and miseries that they engender. One-seventh of the population of the city of Paris at this day subsists on charity, and one-third of the inhabitants of that city die in the hospitals; what would become of such a city with universal suffrage? France has upward of 4 million, and England upward of 5 million of manufacturing and commercial laborers without property. Could these kingdoms sustain the weight of universal suffrage? The radicals in England, with the force of that mighty engine, would at once sweep away the property, the laws, and the liberties of that island like a deluge.

The growth of the city of New York is enough to startle and awaken those who are pursuing the *ignis fatuus* [will o' the wisp] of universal suffrage. In 1773 it had 21,000 souls; in 1801 it had 60,000; in 1806 it had 76,000; in 1820 it had 123,000. It is rapidly swelling into the unwieldly population, and with the burdensome pauperism, of a European metropolis. New York is destined to become the future London of America; and in less than a century that city, with the operation of universal suffrage and under skillful direction, will govern this state.

The notion that every man that works a day on the road, or serves an idle hour in the militia, is entitled as of right to an equal participation in the whole power of the government is most unreasonable and has no foundation in justice. We had better at once discard from the report such a nominal test of merit. If such persons have an equal share in one branch of the legislature, it is surely as much as they can in justice or policy demand. Society is an association for the protection of property as well as of life, and the individual who contributes only one cent to the common stock ought not to have the same power and influence in directing the property concerns of the partnership as he who contributes his thousands. He will not have the same inducements to care, and diligence, and fidelity. His inducements and his temptation would be to divide the whole capital upon the principles of an agrarian law.

Liberty, rightly understood, is an inestimable blessing, but liberty without wisdom and without justice is no better than wild and savage licentiousness. The danger which we have hereafter to apprehend is not the want but the abuse of liberty. We have to apprehend the oppression of minorities and a disposition to encroach on private right; to disturb chartered privileges; and to weaken, degrade, and overawe the administration of justice; we have to apprehend the establishment of unequal and, consequently, unjust systems of taxation and all the mischiefs of a crude and mutable legislation. A stable Senate, exempted from the influence of universal suffrage, will powerfully check these dangerous propensities, and such a check becomes the more necessary since this Convention has already determined to withdraw the watchful eye of the Judicial Department from the passage of laws.

We are destined to become a great manufacturing as well as commercial state. We have already numerous and prosperous factories of one kind or another, and one master-capitalist, with his 100 apprentices, and journeymen, and agents, and dependents, will bear down at the polls an equal number of farmers of small estates in his vicinity who cannot safely unite for their common defense. Large manufacturing and mechanical establishments can act in an instant with the unity and efficacy of disciplined troops. It is against such combinations, among others, that I think we ought to give to the freeholders, or those who have interest in land, one branch of the legislature for their asylum and their comfort. Universal suffrage, once granted, is granted forever and never can be recalled. There is no retrograde step in the rear of democracy. However mischievous the precedent may be in its consequences, or however fatal in its effects, universal suffrage never can be recalled or checked but by the strength of the bayonet. We stand, therefore, this moment, on the brink of fate, on the very edge of the precipice. If we let go our present hold on the Senate, we commit our proudest hopes and our most precious interests to the waves.

It ought further to be observed that the Senate is a court of justice in the last resort. It is the last depository of public and private rights, of civil and criminal justice. This gives the subject an awful consideration and wonderfully increases the importance of securing that house from the inroads of universal suffrage. Our country freeholders are exclusively our jurors in the administration of justice, and there is equal reason that none but those who have an interest in the soil should have any concern in the composition of that court. As long as the Senate is safe, justice is safe, property is safe, and our liberties are safe. But when the wisdom, the integrity, and the independence of that court is lost, we may be certain that the

freedom and happiness of this state are fled forever.

I hope, sir, we shall not carry desolation through all the departments of the fabric erected by our fathers. I hope we shall not put forward to the world a new constitution as will meet with the scorn of the wise and the tears of the patriot.

IV.

Reported speech of P. R. LIVINGSTON

HE WAS WELL PERSUADED that every member of the Convention was a friend to property and to the landed interest. But he thought that the views of some gentlemen, if adopted, were not calculated to advance the cause of civil liberty.

Allusions had been made to the formation of the constitution under which we live; and what was the first feature in our remonstrance against the usurpations of Britain? Was it not that taxation and representation were reciprocal; and that no imposition could be laid upon us without our consent? Was it the paltry tax on tea that led to the Revolution? No, sir; it was the *principle* for which we contended; and the same principle, in my judgment, requires a rejection of the proposition now on your table. But we are asked what evidence we have that the people want this extension of suffrage. Sir, 74,000 witnesses testified last spring that they wanted it. Meetings and resolutions, public prints, and conversation have united to require it.

It is concluded, however, that the measure proposed by the original amendment jeopardizes the landed interest. Sir, it is the landed interest, in common with others, that have demanded this measure at our hands; and will they resort to projects which are calculated to injure ourselves? France has been alluded to. The French Revolution, sir, has produced incalculable

Portrait of Colonel Peter R. Livingston (1766-1847)
by William H. Powell

blessings to that country. Before that Revolution, one-third of the property of the kingdom was in the hands of the clergy; the rest in the hands of the nobility. Where the interest of one individual has been sacrificed, the interests of thousands have been promoted. After dining with that friend of universal liberty, the patriotic Lafayette, he once invited me to a walk upon the top of his house, that commanded a view of all the surrounding country. Before the Revolution, said he, all the farms and hamlets you can see were mine. I am now reduced to 1,000 acres, and I exult in the diminution, since the happiness of others is promoted by participation.

This, sir, is the language of true patriotism; the language of one whose heart, larger than his possessions, embraced the whole family of man in the circuit of its beneficence. And shall we, with less ample domains, refuse to our poorer neighbors the common privileges of freemen?

But, sir, we are told and warned of the rotten boroughs of England. By whom are they owned? By men of wealth. They confer the right of representation on the few, to the exclusion of the many. They are always found in the views of the monarch; and while aristocracy is supported by the House of Lords, the House of Commons is borne down by the boroughs.

It is said that wealth builds our churches, establishes our schools, endows our colleges, and erects our hospitals. But have these institutions been raised without the hand of labor? No, sir; and it is the same hand that has leveled the sturdy oak, the lofty pine, and the towering hemlock, and subdued your forests to a garden. It is not the fact, in this country, that money controls labor; but labor controls money. When the farmer cradles his wheat and harvests his hay, he does not find the laborer on his knees before him at the close of the day, solicitous for further employment; but it is the farmer who takes off his hat, pays him his wages, and requests his return on the morrow.

Apprehensions are professed to be entertained that the merchant and manufacturer will combine to the prejudice of the landed interest. But is not agriculture the legitimate support of both? And do gentlemen really suppose that they will madly combine to destroy themselves? If the title to land contributed to the elevation of the mind, or if it gave stability to independence, or added wisdom to virtue, there might be good reason for proportioning the right of suffrage to the acres of soil. But experience has shown that property forms not the scale of worth, and that character does not spring from the ground. It seems, indeed, to be thought that poverty and vice are identified. But look to the higher classes of society. Do you not often discover the grossest abuse of wealth? Look to the republics of Greece. They were all destroyed by the wealth of the aristocracy bearing down the people.

And how were the victories of Greece achieved in her better days? By the militia. How were the liberties of Rome sustained?

By her militia. How were they lost? By her standing armies. How have we been carried triumphantly through two wars? By the militia; by the very men whom it is now sought to deprive of the inestimable privilege of freemen. And whom do you find in your armies in time of war? The miser? The monied Shylock? The speculator? No, sir; it is the poor and hardy soldier who spills his blood in defense of his country; the veteran to whom you allow the privilege to fight but not to vote. If there is value in the right of suffrage, or reliance to be placed upon our fellow citizens in time of war, where, I ask, is the justice of withholding that right in times of peace and safety?

V.

Speech by JOHN CRAMER

I HAD SUPPOSED that the great fundamental principle that all men were equal in their rights was settled, and forever settled, in this country. I had supposed, sir, that there was some meaning in those words, and some importance in the benefits resulting from them. I had supposed, from the blood and treasure which its attainment had cost, that there was something invaluable in it; and that in pursuance of this principle it ought to be the invariable object of the framers of our civil compact to render all men equal in their political enjoyments, as far as could be consistent with order and justice. But, sir, this, the honorable gentleman from Albany, for whose opinion on such subjects I have entertained a profound respect, and who has presented the amendment now under consideration, has informed us with great assurance and emphasis is a most egregious mistake, and that in it consists the very essence of aristocracy. However, he has the charity to suppose that the mistake arose in the committee of which I had the honor of being a member, and who presented the report on your ta-

ble, not from design, but from ignorance, and that a careful examination of proper authorities, on this subject, would convince any person of the correctness of his position; and as a lawyer and a distinguished jurist, he has referred us to certain authorities which I shall endeavor to examine as to their bearing on the subject under discussion, in the same order in which they were presented.

And, first, the 62nd Number of *The Federalist,* said to be written by the venerated Hamilton; I have read it, and it contains no such principles, it advocates no such sentiments as are contained in the amendment of the honorable gentleman from Albany; for the author is there describing the necessary qualifications of the *elected,* not of the *electors.* But, the gentleman has said that whatever had fallen from the pen of that distinguished statesman is entitled to great consideration, and is to be considered as a political textbook to the framers of free government, and has also said that he entertains the most profound veneration for all his political writings. I have read, sir, other productions of that venerable gentleman, in the secret debates of the Convention which formed the Constitution of the United States; I have read there, sir, the plan which he submitted to that Convention in which he recommends a president for life, a senate for life, and that the president should have the power of appointing the state executives.

Is this the political textbook which the gentleman from Albany so much admires? Is this the form of government which this gentleman wishes to see adopted? I presume not. I, too, sir, have a high estimation of the character of the departed Hamilton; he had talents, he had integrity of a superior, I had almost said, of a celestial order; but he was mortal and subject to the frailties of our nature. He had entertained too degrading an opinion of his fellowman; his political opinions, therefore, I never did respect, and I will not. I cannot play the hypocrite by pretending to revere, now he is no more, what I condemned in him while living.

Next, sir, we were referred to the opinion of that champion of the rights of man, Mr. Jefferson, whom I consider of all others in this country as having done the most in the establishment and maintenance of civil and religious liberty; that man who will of all others in this country occupy the seat in the temple of fame, and the most exalted place in the affections of his countrymen. And we were told, and gravely told, that this distinguished individual, in his *Notes on Virginia*, had advocated a freehold distinction as to the qualifications of electors. But it would have been fair, it would have been candid, and was due to the character of that truly great man, to have stated one further fact, which I presume the gentleman from Albany was conversant with, which is, that Mr. Jefferson had retracted that opinion, and that some years since, when a convention was contemplated in Virginia for new modeling the constitution of that state, Mr. Jefferson presented an entire new plan, in which he did not recognize the right or the necessity of any freehold distinction in the electors, and that in fact he recommended almost universal suffrage.

Next, sir, we were invited by the honorable gentleman to take a sail across the Atlantic and witness the blessed effect of his system of exclusive rights and privileged orders in the great city of Paris, where, we were told, there are fifty poor persons to one man of fortune, so that each landed nabob, there, can have fifty menial servants, subject to his nod, to administer to his comfort and to supply his wants. Next, we were invited to behold the glorious inequality in property and in the civil privileges of the people of England, and among other causes it was ascribed, and justly so, to their system of borough elections, the very system which the gentleman would by his

amendment adopt here; for as in that, so in his system, territory and not population is the basis of representation. There, sir, many little deserted villages and boroughs, which do not contain fifty families, have the right to elect two representatives to the House of Commons. And are equal rights and equal enjoyments recognized there? No, sir, privileged orders and a landed aristocracy, the natural effects of a monarchical government, are, and ever have been, the order of the day.

Thus much for the authorities of the gentleman; and in turn I would refer him, and this committee, to a few plain, practical, modern commentators on the rights of man and on civil government, in our own country; namely, the constitutions of the several states. True, they have nothing of royalty nor much of antiquity to recommend them. First, sir, I will mention the state of Connecticut, that land of steady habits, that very *peculiar* people. That state, sir, in 1818, had a convention for the purpose of forming a constitution consisting of her most distinguished civilians and her most profound jurists, and they did not think it necessary, in order to protect the landed interest of that state, that a principle of this kind should be engrafted in their constitution. No, sir, freehold distinctions among the electors had not an advocate in that venerable assembly, and they extended this right to nearly all their male adult population. In Rhode Island, also, which has something of antiquity to recommend it to the consideration of this committee, the civil rights obtained under a charter from Charles II in 1663 continue to be enjoyed; and no property test whatsoever is required in the elector; there, too, are old cities and dense population, and who has ever yet heard that any of these evils have been there realized, which will at some future period, as is prognosticated, subvert the foundation of your government, if the report of the committee should be adopted? Who has ever yet heard of a combination of their poor, of their profligate poor, as they have been denominated on this floor, to steal the farms of their more wealthy neighbors?

In fact, but two states in the Union, with the exception of this state, have any freehold distinction as to electors; which are Virginia and North Carolina; and the constitutions of those states were adopted at an early period of the Revolutionary War, when the rights of man were little understood, and the blessings of a free government had not been realized. And when in opposition to these we find that all the different constitutions which have been formed or amended within the last thirty years have discarded this odious, this aristocratical, this worse than useless feature from their political charts, will any gentleman of this committee say that all this affords no evidence to his mind of the impropriety of retaining this freehold distinction? To me, it is satisfactory and conclusive. . . .

I shall now take notice of what was said by my venerable friend from Albany (Mr. Van Vechten), who last addressed this committee; and as he took an extensive range and traveled over a wide field of conjecture into which his fertile imagination and extensive information generally lead him, I must be excused should I only touch on *some* of the frightful specters which he has painted to terrify and alarm this community. He affected to be ignorant of public sentiment on this subject, and doubted whether the very men who have been heretofore excluded from the exercise of this right would be so unreasonable as to wish its exercise in the election of members to that branch of the legislature heretofore consecrated to the soil. I have heard much on this subject for several years past, and so far as I have been able to judge, there is but one sentiment among the intelligent and virtuous, which is "grant universal suffrage to all, except those excluded by crime, and abolish the distinction in regard to electors which now prevails be-

cause of one man's possessing more of the soil than another."

He knew nothing of any public meetings, entitled to any weight, in sanctioning this alteration! There were some, sir, of which I have heard, held on the last Tuesday of April last, in every town and county in this state, and at which a majority of 70,000 demanded an alteration in this feature of our constitution. There was, sir, another meeting, in June last, of the people on this subject, and they, by their ballots, elected the members of this Convention, and demanded, at their hands, the extension of equal rights and equal enjoyments, without distinction as to property. This was one of the great objects which induced the people to call a Convention; but for this, sir, and for the purpose of having your government made cheaper and more economical in all its departments, this Convention would not have been called by the honest yeomanry of the country; and it was not for the paltry, contemptible consideration of disposing of the loaves and fishes, as stated by a gentleman from New York in debate a few days since.

But it has been said that the landed interest of this state bears more than its equal proportion of the burdens of taxation. This, sir, I deny. All property, real and personal, is equally taxed, and bears its just proportion of the public burdens: but, sir, is not life and liberty dearer than property, and common to all, and entitled to equal protection? No, sir. That gentleman appeared to be impressed with the idea that the *turf* is of all things the most sacred, and that for its security you must have thirty-two grave turf senators from the soil, in that *sanctum sanctorum*, the Senate chamber, and then all your rights will be safe. No matter whether they possess intelligence, if they are selected by your rich landholders, all is well.

But it is alleged by gentlemen, who have spoken on that side of the house, that the poor are a degraded class of beings, have no will of their own, and would not exercise this high prerogative with independence and sound discretion if entrusted with it; and, therefore, it would be unwise to trust them with ballots. This, sir, is unfounded; for more integrity and more patriotism are generally found in the laboring class of the community than in the higher orders. These are the men who add to the substantial wealth of the nation in peace. These are the men who constitute your defense in war. Of such men consisted your militia, when they met and drove the enemy at Plattsburgh, Sacket's Harbor, Queenston, and Erie; for you found not the rich landholder or speculator in your ranks; and are we told that these men, because they have no property, are not to be trusted at the ballot boxes! Men, who in defense of their liberties, and to protect the property of this country, have hazarded their lives; and who, to shield your wives and children from savage brutality, have faced the destructive cannon and breasted the pointed steel! All this they could be trusted to do. They could, without apprehension, be permitted to handle their muskets, bayonets, powder, and balls; but, say the gentlemen, it will not answer to trust them with tickets at the ballot boxes.

I would admonish gentlemen of this committee to reflect who they are about to exclude from the right of suffrage, if the amendment under consideration should prevail. They will exclude your honest industrious mechanics and many farmers, for many there are who do not own the soil which they till. And what for? Because your farmers wish it? No, sir, they wish no such thing; they wish to see the men who have defended their soil participate equally with them in the election of their rulers. Nay, now you exclude most of the hoary headed patriots who achieved your independence, to whom we are indebted for the very ground we stand upon and for the liberties we enjoy. But for the toil and sufferings of these men, we should not now be here debating as to forms of government. No, sir, the legitimates would soon have disposed of all this business. And why are these men to be excluded? Not because they are not virtuous, not because they are not meritorious, but, sir, because they are poor and dependent, and can have no will of their own, and will vote as the man who feeds them and clothes them may direct, as one of the honorable gentlemen has remarked. I know of no men in this country who are not dependent. The rich man is as much dependent upon the poor man for his labor as the poor man is upon the rich for his wages. I know of no men who are more dependent upon others for their bread and raiment than the judges of your Supreme Court are upon the legislature, and who will pretend that this destroys their independence, or makes them subservient to the views of the legislature.

Let us not, sir, disgrace ourselves in the eyes of the world, by expressing such degrading opinions of our fellow citizens. Let us grant universal suffrage, for after all it is upon the virtue and intelligence of the people that the stability of your government must rest. Let us not brand this constitution with any odious distinctions as to property, and let it not be said of us, as has been truly said of most republics, that we have been ungrateful to our best benefactors.

VI.

Speech by DAVID BUEL, JR.

IT IS SAID by those who contend that the right, of voting for senators should be confined to the landholders that the framers of our constitution were wise and practical men, and that they deemed this distinction essential to the security of the landed property; and that we have not encountered any evils from it during the forty years' experience which we have had. To this I answer that, if the restriction of the right of suffrage has produced no positive evil, it cannot be shown to have produced any good results.

The qualifications for Assembly voters, under the existing constitution, are as liberal as any which will probably be adopted by this Convention. Is it pretended that the Assembly, during the forty-three years' experience which we have enjoyed under our constitution, has been, in any respect, inferior to the Senate? Has the Senate, although elected exclusively by freeholders, been composed of men of more talents, or greater probity, than the Assembly? Have the rights of property, generally, or of the landed interests in particular, been more vigilantly watched and more carefully protected by the Senate than by the Assembly? I might appeal to the journals of the two houses, and to the recollections and information of the members of the committee on this subject; but it is unnecessary, as I understand the gentlemen who support the amendment distinctly admit, that hitherto the Assembly has been as safe a depository of the rights of the landed interest as the Senate. But it is supposed that the framers of our constitution must have had wise and cogent reasons for making such a distinction between the electors of the different branches of the government. May we not, however, without the least derogation from the wisdom and good intentions of the framers of our constitution, ascribe the provision in question to circumstances which then influenced them, but which no longer ought to have weight?

When our constitution was framed, the domain of the state was in the hands of a few. The proprietors of the great manors were almost the only men of great influence; and the landed property was deemed worthy of almost exclusive consideration. Before the Revolution, freeholders only were allowed to exercise the right of suffrage. . . . The tendency of this system, it is well understood, was to keep the lands of the state in few hands. But since that period, by the operation of wiser laws, and by the prevalence of juster principles, an entire revolution has taken place in regard to real property. Our laws for regulating descents, and for converting entailed estates into fee-simple, have gradually increased the number of landholders. Our territory has been rapidly divided and subdivided. And although the landed interest is no longer controlled by the influence of a few great proprietors, its aggregate importance is vastly increased, and almost the whole community have become interested in its protection. In New England, the inhabitants, from the earliest period, have enjoyed the system which we are progressively attaining to. There, the property of the soil has always been in the hands of the *many*. The great bulk of the population are farmers and freeholders, yet no provision is incorporated in their constitutions excluding those who are not freeholders from a full participation in the right of suffrage. . . .

It is supposed, however, by the honorable member before me (Chancellor Kent) that landed property will become insecure under the proposed extension of the right of suffrage, by the influx of a more dangerous population. That gentleman has drawn a picture from the existing state of society in European kingdoms, which would be indeed appalling if we could suppose such a state of society could exist here. But are arguments drawn from the state of society in Europe applicable to our situation? . . . It is conceded by my honorable friend that the great landed estates must be cut up by the operation of our laws of descent; that we have already seen those laws effect a great change; and that it is the inevitable tendency of our rules of descent to divide up our territory into farms of moderate size. The real property, therefore, will be in the hands of the *many*. But in England, and other European kingdoms, it is the policy of the aristocracy to keep the lands in few hands. The laws of primogeniture, the entailments and family settlements, all tend to give a confined direction to the course of descents. Hence, we find in Europe the landed estates possessed by a few rich men; and the great bulk of the population poor, and without that attachment to the government which is found among the owners of the soil. Hence, also, the poor envy and hate the rich, and mobs and insurrections sometimes render property insecure.

Did I believe that our population would degenerate into such a state, I should, with the advocates for the amendment, hesitate in extending the right of suffrage; but I confess I have no such fears. I have heretofore had doubts respecting the safety of adopting the principles of a suffrage as extensive as that now contemplated. I have given to the subject the best reflection of which I am capable; and I have satisfied myself that there is no danger in adopting those liberal principles which are incorporated in almost all the constitutions of these United States.

There are, in my judgment, many circumstances which will forever preserve the people of this state from the vices and the degradation of European population, besides those which I have already taken notice of. The provision already made for the establishment of common schools will, in a very few years, extend the benefit of education to all our citizens. The universal diffusion of information will forever distinguish our population from that of Europe. Virtue and intelligence are the true basis on which every republican government must rest. When these are lost, freedom will no longer exist. The diffusion of education is the only sure means of establishing these pillars of freedom. I rejoice in this view of the subject, that our common school fund will (if the report on the Legislative Department be adopted) be consecrated by a constitutional provision; and I feel no apprehension for myself, or my posterity, in confiding the

right of suffrage to the great mass of such a population as I believe ours will always be.

The farmers in this country will always outnumber all other portions of our population. Admitting that the increase of our cities, and especially of our commercial metropolis, will be as great as it has been hitherto, it is not to be doubted that the agricultural population will increase in the same proportion. The city population will never be able to depress that of the country. New York has always contained about a tenth part of the population of the state, and will probably always bear a similar proportion. Can she, with such a population, under any circumstances, render the property of the vast population of the country insecure? It may be that mobs will occasionally be collected, and commit depredations in a great city; but, can the mobs traverse our immense territory, and invade the farms, and despoil the property of the landholders? And if such a state of things were possible, would a senate, elected by freeholders, afford any security? It is the regular administration of the laws by an independent judiciary that renders property secure against private acts of violence. And there will always be a vast majority of our citizens interested in preventing legislative injustice.

But the gentleman who introduced the proposition now before the committee has predicted dangers of another kind to the landed interest, if their exclusive right of electing the Senate shall be taken away. He supposes that combinations of other interests will be formed to depress the landholders by charging them exclusively with the burden of taxation. I cannot entertain any apprehension that such a state of things will ever exist. Under any probable extension of the right of suffrage, the landed interest will, in my view of the subject, always maintain a vast preponderance of numbers and influence.

From what combinations of other interests can danger arise? The mercantile and manufacturing interests are the only ones which can obtain a formidable influence. Are the owners of manufacturing establishments, scattered through the state, as they always must be, likely to enter into a confederacy with the merchants of the great cities for the purpose of depressing the yeomanry and landholders of this great state? Has our past experience shown any tendency in those two great interests to unite in any project, especially for such a one as that which I have mentioned? We usually find the merchants and manufacturers acting as rivals to each other; but both feel a community of interest with the landholders; and it will ever be the interest of the farmers, as it ever has been, to foster and protect both the manufacturing and mercantile interests. The discussions which the tariff has undergone, both in and out of Congress, have demonstrated the feelings of rivalship which exist between our manufacturers and our merchants. But who has ever heard, in this or any other country, of a combination of those two classes of men to destroy the interest of the farmers? No other combination, then, can be imagined but that of the poor against the rich. Can it be anticipated that those who have no property can ever so successfully combine their efforts as to have a majority in both branches of the legislature, unfriendly to the security of property?

One ground of the argument of gentlemen who support the amendment is that the extension of the right of suffrage will give an undue influence to the rich over the persons who depend upon them for employment; but if the rich control the votes of the poor, the result cannot be unfavorable to the security of property. The supposition that, at some future day, when the poor shall become numerous, they may imitate the radicals of England, or the Jacobins of France; that they may rise, in the majesty of their strength, and usurp the property of the landholders is so unlikely to be realized that we may dismiss all fear arising from that source. Before that can happen,

wealth must lose all its influence; public morals must be destroyed; and the nature of our government changed; and it would be in vain to look to a Senate, chosen by landholders, for security in a case of such extremity. I cannot but think that all the dangers which it is predicted will flow from doing away the exclusive right of the landholders to elect the senators are groundless.

I contend that by the true principle of our government, property, as such, is not the basis of representation. Our community is an association of persons — of human beings — not a partnership founded on property. The declared object of the people of this state in associating was to "establish such a government as they deemed best calculated to secure the rights and liberties of the good people of the state, and most conducive to their happiness and safety." Property, it is admitted, is one of the rights to be protected and secured; and although the protection of life and liberty is the highest object of attention, it is certainly true that the security of property is a most interesting and important object in every free government. Property is essential to our temporal happiness, and is necessarily one of the most interesting subjects of legislation.

The desire of acquiring property is a universal passion. I readily give to property the important place which has been assigned to it by the honorable member from Albany (Chancellor Kent). To property we are indebted for most of our comforts, and for much of our temporal happiness. The numerous religious, moral, and benevolent institutions which are everywhere established owe their existence to wealth; and it is wealth which enables us to make those great internal improvements which we have undertaken. Property is only one of the incidental rights of the person who possesses it; and, as such, it must be made secure; but it does not follow that it must therefore be represented specifically in any branch of the government. It ought, indeed, to have an influence — and it ever will have, when properly enjoyed. So ought talents to have an influence. It is certainly as important to have men of good talents in your legislature as to have men of property; but you surely would not set up men of talents as a separate order, and give them exclusive privileges.

The truth is that both wealth and talents will ever have a great influence; and without the aid of exclusive privileges, you will always find the influence of both wealth and talents predominant in our halls of legislation.

VII.

Speech by JOHN ROSS

MR. CHAIRMAN: In assigning the reasons which influenced the select committee in making the report now under consideration, I shall rely much on the honorable gentlemen with whom I had the pleasure to be associated on that committee. But, sir, feeling a responsibility in common with the members of that committee, I may perhaps be permitted to state, as concisely as I can, in addition to the views just submitted by the honorable chairman of that committee (Mr. N. Sanford) some of the motives which led to the provisions contained in that report.

The subject now submitted may be viewed as one of deep and interesting importance, inasmuch as it discriminates who among our fellow citizens shall be allowed to exercise the high privilege of designating, by their votes, who shall represent them in their wants and their wishes in the various and multiplied concerns of legislation and civil government. In every free state, the electors ought to form the basis, the soil from which everything is to spring, relating to the administration of their political concerns. Otherwise, it could not be denominated a government of the people. This results from the immutable principle that civil government is instituted for the benefit of the governed. Consequently, all, at least, who contribute to the support or defense of the state have a just claim to exercise the elective privilege, if consistent with the safety and welfare of the citizens. It is immaterial whether that support or defense of the state be by the payment of money or by personal service, which are precisely one and the same thing, that of taxation.

Assuming this, then, as the basis, as being the least objectionable of any other, we are furnished with certain data by which the right to vote can be determined. By entering them in a register, we are able to test the qualification of electors, without resorting to the multiplication of oaths, which under the present constitution had grown into a most corrupting and alarming evil. After the most full and attentive consideration of the subject, the committee were led to the conclusion that this would be the most simple and practical mode of ascertaining, with certainty, who are entitled to the privilege of electors. At the same time, it gives a liberal extension to that privilege which, unquestionably, a vast majority of our constituents will demand at our hands, and which we can have no wish to withhold, unless to perpetuate those odious distinctions which have hitherto so long and so justly been complained of.

This is one of the crying evils for which we were sent here to provide a remedy. It is not to be expected, sir, that any general rules can be devised that will extend to every possible case that it would be desirable to include, nor is it possible to exclude all who might abuse the privilege. Where evils must necessarily exist, the great object of this Convention, I trust, will be to choose the least — to settle down on such general principles as will result in conferring on the people of this state the greatest possible sum of happiness and prosperity.

That all men are free and equal, according to the usual declarations, applications, applies to them only in a state of nature, and not after the institution of civil government; for then many rights, flowing from a natural equality, are necessarily abridged, with a view to produce the greatest amount of security and happiness to the whole community. On this principle the right of suffrage is extended to white men only. But why, it will probably be asked, are blacks to be excluded? I answer, because they are seldom, if ever, required to share in the common burdens or defense of the state. There are also additional reasons; they are a peculiar people, incapable, in my judgment, of exercising that privilege with any sort of discretion, prudence, or independence. They have no just conceptions of civil liberty. They know not how to appreciate it, and are, consequently, indifferent to its preservation.

Under such circumstances it would hardly be compatible with the safety of the state to entrust such a people with this right. It is not thought advisable to permit aliens to vote, neither would it be safe to extend it to the blacks. We deny to minors this right, and why? Because they are deemed incapable of exercising it discreetly, and therefore not safely, for the good of the whole community. Even the better part of creation, as my honorable friend from Oneida (Mr. N. Williams) styles them, are not permitted to participate in this right.

In nearly all the Western and Southern states, indeed many others, even in Connecticut, where steady habits and correct principles prevail, the blacks are excluded. And gentlemen have been frequently in the habit of citing the precedents of our sister states for our guide; and would it not be well to listen to the decisive weight of precedents furnished in this case also?

It is true that in many of the states the black population is more numerous than in ours. Then, sir, if the exclusion be unjust or improper, that injustice would be of so much greater extent. The truth is, this ex-clusion invades no inherent rights, nor has it any connection at all with the question of slavery. The practice of every state in the Union is to make such exceptions, limitations, and provisions in relation to the elective privilege, under their respective constitutions, as are deemed to be necessary or consistent with public good — varied in each according to the existing circumstances under which they are made. It must, therefore, necessarily rest on the ground of expediency. And, sir, I fear that an extension to the blacks would serve to invite that kind of population to this state, an occurrence which I should most sincerely deplore. The petition presented in their behalf, now on your table, in all probability has been instigated by gentlemen of a different color, who expect to control their votes. But whether this be so or not, next the blacks will claim to be represented by persons of their own color in your halls of legislation. And can you consistently refuse them? It would be well to be prepared for such a claim.

On the whole, sir, let your constitution, at a proper period, declare their emancipation; exempt them from military service as the United States government directs, and from other burdens as heretofore; give them the full benefits of protection; and there, in mercy to themselves and to us, let us stay our hands.

VIII.

Speech by Peter Jay

THE CHAIRMAN OF THE SELECT COMMITTEE has given a fair and candid exposition of the reasons that induced them to make the report now under consideration, and of the motives by which they were governed. He has clearly stated why they were desirous of extending the right of suffrage to some who did not at present enjoy it, but he has wholly omitted to explain why they deny it to others who actually possess it. The omission, however, has been supplied by one of his colleagues, who informed us that all who were not white ought to be excluded from political rights, because such persons were incapable of exercising them discreetly, and because they were peculiarly liable to be influenced and corrupted. These reasons, sir, I shall notice presently.

When this Convention was first assembled, it was generally understood that provisions would be made to extend the right of suffrage, and some were apprehensive that it might be extended to a degree which they could not approve. But, sir, it was not expected that this right was in any instance to be restricted, much less was it anticipated, or desired, that a single person was to be disfranchised. Why, sir, are these men to be excluded from rights which they possess in common with their countrymen? What crime have they committed for which they are to be punished? Why are they, who were born as free as ourselves, natives of the same country, and deriving from nature and our political institutions the same rights and privileges which we have, now to be deprived of all those rights, and doomed to remain forever as aliens among us?

We are told, in reply, that other states have set us the example. It is true that other states treat this race of men with cruelty and injustice, and that we have hitherto manifested toward them a disposition to be just and liberal. Yet, even in Virginia and North Carolina, free people of color are permitted to vote, and, if I am correctly informed, exercise that privilege. In Pennsylvania, they are much more numerous than they are here, and there they are not disfranchised, nor has any inconvenience been felt from extending to all men the rights which ought to be common to all. In Connecticut, it is true, they have, for the last three years, adopted a new constitution, which prevents people of color from acquiring the right of suffrage in future, yet even there they have preserved the right of all those who previously possessed it.

Mr. Chairman, I would submit to the consideration of the committee whether the proposition of the gentleman from Saratoga is consistent with the Constitution of the United States. That instrument provides that "citizens of each state shall be entitled to all the privileges and immunities of citizens in the several states." No longer ago than last November, the legislature of this state almost unanimously resolved that "if the provisions contained in any proposed constitution of a new state deny to any citizens of the existing states the privileges and immunities of citizens of such new state, that such proposed constitution should not be accepted or confirmed; the same in the opinion of this legislature being void by the Constitution of the United States." Now, sir, is not the right of suffrage a privilege? And can you deny it to a citizen of Pennsylvania, who comes here and complies with your laws, merely because he is not six feet high, or because he is of a dark complexion?

But we are told by one of the select committee that people of color are incapable of exercising the right of suffrage. I may have misunderstood that gentleman; but I thought he meant to say that they labored under a physical disability. It is true that some philosophers have held that the intellect of a black man is naturally inferior to that of a white one; but this idea has been so completely refuted, and is now so universally exploded, that I did not expect to have heard of it in an assembly so enlightened as this, nor do I now think it necessary to disprove it.

That in general the people of color are inferior to the whites in knowledge and in industry, I shall not deny. You made them slaves, and nothing is more true than the ancient saying, "The day you make a man a slave takes half his worth away." Unaccustomed to provide for themselves, and habituated to regard labor as an evil, it is no wonder that when set free, they should be improvident and idle, and that their children should be brought up without education, and without prudence or forethought. But will you punish the children for your own crimes; for the injuries which you have inflicted upon their parents? Besides, sir, this state of things is fast passing away. Schools have been opened for them, and it will, I am sure, give pleasure to this committee to know that in these schools there is discovered a thirst for instruction, and a progress in learning, seldom to be seen in the other schools of the state. They have also churches of their own, and clergymen of their own color, who conduct their public worship with perfect decency and order, and not without ability.

This state, Mr. Chairman, has taken high ground against slavery and all its degrading consequences and accompaniments. There are gentlemen on this floor who, to their immortal honor, have defended the cause of this oppressed people in Congress, and I trust they will not now desert them. Adopt the amendment now proposed, and you will hear a shout of triumph and a hiss of scorn from the Southern part of the Union, which I confess will mortify me — I shall shrink at the sound because I fear it will be deserved. But it has been said that this measure is necessary to preserve the purity of your elections. I do not deny that necessity has no law, and that self-preservation may justify in states, as well as in individuals, an infringement of the rights of others. Were I a citizen of one of the Southern states, I would not (much as I abhor slavery) advise an immediate and universal emancipation.

But where is the necessity in the present instance? The whole number of colored people in the state, whether free or in bondage, amounts to less than a fortieth part of the whole population. When your numbers are to theirs as forty to one, do

New York Hospital

Peter Augustus Jay (1776-1843) argued against color discrimination; he was the son of John Jay

you still fear them? To assert this would be to pay them a compliment, which, I am sure, you do not think they deserve. But there are a greater number in the city of New York. How many? Sir, in even that city, the whites are to the blacks as ten to one. And even of the tenth which is composed of the black population, how few are there that are entitled to vote? It has also been said that their numbers are rapidly increasing. The very reverse is the fact. During the last ten years, in which the white population has advanced with astonishing rapidity, the colored population of the state has been stationary. This fact appears from the official returns of the last and the preceding census, and completely refutes the arguments which are founded upon this misstatement. Will you, then, without necessity, and merely to gratify an unreasonable prejudice, stain the constitution you are about to form, with a provision equally odious and unjust, and in direct violation of the principles which you profess, and upon which you intend to form it? I trust, I am sure, you will not.

3.

John Quincy Adams: A Pessimistic View of Relations with Latin America

The revolutions that broke out in Latin America after the Napoleonic Wars were hailed by Henry Clay as a "glorious spectacle of eighteen millions of people struggling to burst their chains and to be free." To the dismay of Secretary of State John Quincy Adams, who believed that the United States should pursue a policy of nonintervention in the affairs of other nations, Clay called for immediate diplomatic recognition of these countries. Four or five years later, by 1821, most of Latin America had achieved full independence. The two adversaries, Clay and Adams, once again discussed the future of these new nations and their relation to the United States. In the following selection from his Memoirs, Adams related their talk of March 9, 1821, in which Clay admitted that his demands for recognition had been premature. Adams, though now ready to accept the new governments, nevertheless retained his pessimistic outlook about their future.

Source: *Memoirs of John Quincy Adams, Comprising Portions of his Diary from 1795 to 1848,* Charles Francis Adams, ed., Vol. V, Philadelphia, 1875, pp. 324-325.

He [Clay] said he regretted that his views had differed from those of the administration in relation to South American affairs. He hoped, however, that this difference would now be shortly over. But he was concerned to see indications of unfriendly dispositions toward the South Americans in our naval officers who were sent to the Pacific, and he was apprehensive they would get into some quarrel there which might alienate the minds of the people in the two countries from each other.

I said the instructions to the naval officers were as positive and pointed as words could make them to avoid everything of that kind. I hoped no such event would occur, as we could have no possible motive for quarreling with the South Americans. I also regretted the difference between his views and those of the administration upon South American affairs. That the final issue of their present struggle would be their entire independence of Spain I had never doubted. That it was our true policy and duty to take no part in the contest I was equally clear. The principle of neutrality to *all* foreign wars was, in my opinion, fundamental to the continuance of our liberties and of our Union.

So far as they were contending for independence, I wished well to their cause; but I had seen, and yet see, no prospect that they would establish free or liberal institutions of government. They are not likely to promote the spirit either of freedom or order by their example. They have not the first elements of good or free government. Arbitrary power, military and ecclesiastical, was stamped upon their education, upon their habits, and upon all their institutions. Civil dissension was infused into all their seminal principles. War and mutual destruction was in every member of their organization, moral, political, and physical. I had little expectation of any beneficial result to this country from any future connection with them, political or commercial. We should derive no improvement to our own institutions by any communion with theirs. Nor was there any appearance of a disposition in them to take any political lesson from us.

As to the commercial connection, I agreed with him that little weight should be allowed to arguments of mere pecuniary interest; but there was no basis for much traffic between us. They want none of our productions, and we could afford to purchase very few of theirs. Of these opinions, both his and mine, *time* must be the test; but, I would candidly acknowledge, nothing had hitherto occurred to weaken in my mind the view which I had taken of this subject from the first.

4.

ANONYMOUS: Motives for Stopping the Domestic Slave Trade

Although smuggling of slaves persisted until about 1860, the importation of slaves into the United States had been strictly forbidden by legislation passed during the first two decades of the century. These regulations did not prohibit the slave trade within the U.S. borders, and, consequently, the domestic slave business boomed. Opposition to commerce in slaves was frequently based on other than humanitarian motives. Many Southerners, such as the anonymous author of the following piece, were fearful of slave insurrections and believed that it was in the best interest of slave owners to regulate the interstate slave trade. This letter by a "Citizen" to the editor of a Georgia newspaper appeared in early December 1821.

Source: *Journal* (Milledgeville, Ga.), December 4, 1821.

THE POLICY OF PROHIBITING the further introduction of slaves for the purpose of speculation is so obvious that it seems almost preposterous to attempt its proof. The arguments in its support are so numerous and so strong as almost to overwhelm us. We scarcely know where to begin or where to end them. It is difficult to imagine a clearer

truth than that it is inexpedient to increase an acknowledged evil. The following are some of the considerations which forbid the introduction of slaves for the purpose of speculation.

Every man knows that speculators would constantly introduce into the state the dregs of the colored population of the states north of us; that the jails of North and South Carolina, Maryland, and Virginia would be disgorged upon this deluded state. Negro speculators, many of whom would come from other states, and would fear none of the calamities they might bring on us, would naturally introduce among us Negroes of the worst character, because, in many instances, they would purchase them for half price; and the villain who might attempt the assassination of his master, the rape of his mistress, or the conflagration of a city, might, in a few days, be transported to Georgia and sold to an unsuspecting citizen for the hard earnings of his honest labor. To the dealer in human flesh, it would be a matter of little consequence if the next day he perpetrated any or all those crimes!

But not only would speculators constantly introduce firebrands among our colored people; but they would, in very many instances, inveigle and run off the slaves of our fellow citizens north of us; they would, by fraud and violence, tear from the dearest associations and sell among us persons as much entitled to personal liberty by the laws of the land as the reader who kindly gives me his attention while I endeavor to show him the magnitude of one of the greatest calamities which would afflict this state; I mean, an unrestricted domestic slave trade! It is perhaps needless to detail instances of the stealing of Negroes, bond and free, which might easily be cited. The reader's memory will easily supply them; as well as some notable instances in which men from the South have expiated these offenses by the most ignominious punishments in the North; thus casting the blackness of their character on the section of country to which they belonged.

Who sees not the progress of society? Who sees not the spirit of the age? Can anyone be insensible of the increasing disposition of Virginia, Maryland, and some other states to throw off their colored population? When they have made any considerable advance toward this object, will they not assume the tone of the Northern states? Will they not join in the imposition of "restrictions" upon the slaveholding states? May they not promote *abolition* in the South? Insensible as they may become in process of time to the difficulties and dangers of the South, may they not pursue a course of conduct tending to produce a state of things too horrible to contemplate? It is clearly incumbent on Georgia to persevere in her countervailing policy; it is clearly incumbent on her to refuse to receive in her bosom the colored population of states who, after relieving themselves of the greatest weight that presses on them, may, at some remote period, join in a general crusade against the South.

We should forbear to increase the aggregate amount of investments in property, which, by the progress of society, by the operations of a spirit which is evidently gone abroad in Christendom, may become not only worthless but dangerous. Nor ought it to destroy the force of this reasoning, that these consequences may be remote. He who confines his views to the present moment, he who endeavors not to avert from future generations the calamities which threaten them, is alike unworthy of the name of a parent and of a politician.

The late discussions on the subject of slavery with reference to Missouri shook our political fabric to its foundations. Will the citizens of Georgia consent to increase an evil which so lately threatened a dissolution of the Union and the annihilation of the best hopes of man? . . .

We know the vast excess of colored people in the West Indies. Within a few years, we have seen a government established in one of the largest of them, which is constantly increasing in numbers and intelligence in physical and moral and political importance and which portends the most terrible convulsions in the West Indies. Constituted and situated as the Southern states are, can they hope to remain entirely undisturbed by those convulsions? And is it not one of the plainest dictates of policy, nay, of *common sense*, not to *increase* the numbers of an enemy already too numerous! I say, *enemy;* for such, in the nature of man, they necessarily are; and let it be remembered, too, *that they overspread our entire country and occupy the most commanding positions.* . . .

If the great state of South Carolina has pursued an oscillating policy in relation to the slave trade, it may furnish ground for regret, but certainly furnishes no matter for the imitation of other states. It remains for Georgia, placed as she is between the old and the new slaveholding states, to exhibit an example of steady and enlightened policy; which, while it shall prevent the increase of an acknowledged evil by suppressing *the speculation* in slaves, shall yet allow to citizens and to emigrants the right to introduce them for their own use, or the use of their children; and shall extend to our colored population all the comfort that is consistent with their situation and the good of the community. In this way, she might, from her circumstances and her local situation, exert the most benign influence on the fate of unborn millions of both colors: She might secure the applause and the benedictions of the world.

But, it may possibly be supposed that an increase of the number of our slaves is necessary on account of the late acquisitions and of further contemplated acquisitions of territory. This is denied. We have already laborers enough to cut down and exhaust our territory as fast as we can extinguish the Indian title. But suppose an increase of laborers necessary; citizens and emigrants already have the right to make this increase for their own use. And though the permanent interests of the community might perhaps require an adoption of the Virginia policy, yet, perhaps, for the blindness of our mind and the hardness of our heart, it might be better to continue, for the present, the policy of permitting citizens or real emigrants to introduce slaves for their own use, and only to direct our efforts against the colossal evil of the *speculation* in slaves.

Yet the Virginia policy may demand consideration. They have closed every avenue to the further introduction of slaves; and they afford every facility gradually to drain off a population, for whose introduction they now reproach the memory of their ancestors — a population which has exhausted their soil, deteriorated their morals, and endangered their repose. This policy is sanctioned by their Washingtons and Henrys and Jeffersons and Monroes. It is not for me to decide whether a policy adapted to the situation of Virginia is suited to the circumstances of Georgia; or whether the great principles which constitute the best support of her policy are equally applicable to all nations, all times, and all circumstances.

1822

5.

THOMAS JEFFERSON: On Sectarian Rivalry

For Thomas Jefferson, education was indispensable for the preservation of a free society. Writing to William Roscoe in 1820, he said of the University of Virginia: "This institution will be based on the illimitable freedom of the human mind. For here we are not afraid to follow truth wherever it may lead, nor to tolerate any error so long as reason is left free to combat it." Independence of thought and action would be the mark of a man educated in an atmosphere free of the pressures of preconceived ideologies, whether political, social, or religious. It was to the role of established religion in the university that Jefferson devoted this letter of November 2, 1822, to Dr. Thomas Cooper. The relationship of the several denominations to the public universities in the twenty-first century is along the lines suggested by Jefferson.

Source: H. A. Washington, VII, pp. 266-268.

YOUR FAVOR OF OCTOBER THE 18TH came to hand yesterday. The atmosphere of our country is unquestionably charged with a threatening cloud of fanaticism, lighter in some parts, denser in others, but too heavy in all. I had no idea, however, that in Pennsylvania, the cradle of toleration and freedom of religion, it could have arisen to the height you describe. This must be owing to the growth of Presbyterianism. The blasphemy and absurdity of the five points of Calvin, and the impossibility of defending them, render their advocates impatient of reasoning, irritable, and prone to denunciation. In Boston, however, and its neighborhood, Unitarianism has advanced to so great strength, as now to humble this haughtiest of all religious sects; insomuch that they condescend to interchange with them and the other sects, the civilities of preaching freely and frequently in each others' meetinghouses. In Rhode Island, on the other hand, no sectarian preacher will permit a Unitarian to pollute his desk. In our Richmond there is much fanaticism, but chiefly among the women. They have their night meetings and praying parties, where, attended by their priests, and sometimes by a henpecked husband, they pour forth the effusions of their love to Jesus, in terms as amatory and carnal as their modesty would permit them to use to a mere earthly lover.

In our village of Charlottesville, there is a good degree of religion, with a small spice only of fanaticism. We have four sects, but without either church or meetinghouse. The courthouse is the common temple, one Sunday in the month to each. Here, Episcopalian and Presbyterian, Methodist and Baptist, meet together, join in hymning their Maker, listen with attention and devotion to each others' preachers, and all mix in society with perfect harmony. It is not so in the districts where Presbyterianism prevails undividedly. Their ambition and tyranny would tolerate no rival if they had power. Systematical in grasping at an ascendancy over all other sects, they aim, like the Jesuits, at engrossing the education of the country, are hostile to every institution which they do not direct, and jealous at seeing others begin to attend at all to that object. The diffusion of instruction, to which there is now so growing an attention, will be the remote remedy to this fever of fanaticism; while the more proximate one will be the progress of Unitarianism. That this will, before long, be the religion of the majority from north to south, I have no doubt.

In our university you know there is no professorship of divinity. A handle has been made of this, to disseminate an idea that this is an institution, not merely of no religion, but against all religion. Occasion was taken at the last meeting of the visitors, to bring forward an idea that might silence this calumny, which weighed on the minds of some honest friends to the institution. In our annual report to the legislature, after stating the constitutional reasons against a public establishment of any religious instruction, we suggest the expediency of encouraging the different religious sects to establish, each for itself, a professorship of their own tenets, on the confines of the university, so near as that their students may attend the lectures there, and have the free use of our library, and every other accommodation we can give them; preserving, however, their independence of us and of each other. This fills the chasm objected to ours, as a defect in an institution professing to give instruction in *all* useful sciences. I think the invitation will be accepted, by some sects from candid intentions, and by others from jealousy and rivalship. And by bringing the sects together, and mixing them with the mass of other students, we shall soften their asperities, liberalize and neutralize their prejudices, and make the general religion a religion of peace, reason, and morality.

The time of opening our university is still as uncertain as ever. All the pavilions, boardinghouses, and dormitories are done. Nothing is now wanting but the central building for a library and other general purposes. For this we have no funds, and the last legislature refused all aid. We have better hopes of the next. But all is uncertain. I have heard with regret of disturbances on the part of the students in your seminary. The article of discipline is the most difficult in American education. Premature ideas of independence, too little repressed by parents, beget a spirit of insubordination, which is the great obstacle to science with us, and a principal cause of its decay since the Revolution. I look to it with dismay in our institution, as a breaker ahead, which I am far from being confident we shall be able to weather. The advance of age, and tardy pace of the public patronage, may probably spare me the pain of witnessing consequences.

6.

William Duane: Pennsylvania Common Schools

Education, "the great equalizer of men," as public education advocate Horace Mann once called it, was far from being available equally to all in the early nineteenth century. Private institutions existed where wealthy parents could be assured that their children would find a competent faculty and adequate facilities, but the public schools, for the most part, lacked both. As common people spoke out for equal economic opportunities, they also sought better educational opportunities for their children. The following selection, dated July 12, 1822, and written by the Pennsylvania journalist and politician William Duane, was his response to a questionnaire sent to him by the Kentucky Assembly. In it, he joined perceptive observations of the Pennsylvania common school system with educational theories much advanced for the times. Many of the views of the great Swiss educational reformer Johann Pestalozzi, whose programs were widely copied in America, are reflected in Duane's commentary.

Source: *Journal of the Senate of the Commonwealth of Kentucky,* Frankfort, 1822, pp. 204-211.

There is, in Pennsylvania, a general but very imperfectly executed system for the instruction of the children of poor persons, and there is a particular law which embraces the children of the District of Philadelphia, county and city. The former I cannot from memory describe, and only know generally that it is not effective, owing in a principal measure to its want of vigorous and systematic prosecution, the insufficiency of the means either to reward competent teachers and thereby secure their zeal and the accordant want of any definite method by which the progress or the elementary instruction. could be suitably inculcated. Another circumstance which probably might be overcome if there was any effective or coherent system is the reaction of two kinds of pride; that of the opulent who are repugnant to the idea of schools, or education in anything like a school that has the denomination or attribute of being for the poor, or as their ideas associate it with charity. This unfortunate pride extends to the actually poor themselves; by which I mean that

class of men who acquire their subsistence by useful labors in all the arts, agricultural, mechanical, and liberal.

That a good system would remove this obstacle of pride is manifest from the solicitude of all classes to educate their children at the Academy of West Point, where education is conducted with a degree of success, the most flattering and honorable to the country. There is one other school on a similar system founded by Captain Patridge, who formerly superintended the Military Academy. It is established at Norwich, in Vermont, and I speak of it from experience as equally efficient as that of the Military Academy. I know of no other institution for education in the United States, besides these two, deserving of the name of a liberal institution for education; for I know of no college or other institution that is not conducted upon a system that appears to me barbarous and adverse to the development of the intellect of the species. I know of no female school but one, and that is confined to a few pupils. It is conducted by a Madame Fitegeot of this city, who is a disciple of Pestalozzi of Switzerland, and teaches in his method, somewhat modified to the prejudices of society. . . .

The schools of a public foundation are in townships, but they are not general, and, I believe, very few. The schools in this district have, within three years, been assimilated to the forms of mutual instruction of the celebrated English teacher Lancaster; a system that has the common defect of all modern systems, that of a method of *rote*, communicated and confirmed *orally;* but which confines its impressions to the mere accumulation of words, and appears to leave out of view the only important part of education, that of acquiring and comprehending ideas or facts.

This system, however benevolent the views of the founder, is connected with the most unfortunate of all prejudices — that is, *cheapness.* The mercenary spirit is one of the most fatal of all the causes that injure morals, knowledge, and education. In a society where the population is cut up into castes and orders, this poverty-stricken system may have its uses because, there, every other, or better, is hopeless. But it is not adapted to unfold human faculties, nor to form or to confirm sound minds. As far as it can render services, probably it does so here; but it is a lamentable evidence of the imperfection or the perversion of the most generous intentions.

In the counties, the county commissioners have, I think, the direction or control; and the persons chosen to such offices are not exactly the description of men, nor do the pecuniary objects for which such stations are sought tend to promote the purposes of the laws or of public beneficence. In this district, a number of benevolent men volunteer under a special law and give a certain degree of attention to the prosecution of the undertaking. But even here, the want of conformity of sentiments and aptitude of men of different sects to give predominance to their own peculiar tenets or theories have

a pernicious influence; and then the stipends are such that it is the extreme of false economy to waste money where no man who has faculties can obtain even a commonly comfortable subsistence for his labors. Incompetent teachers are, therefore, taken from necessity; and it would be disingenuous not to declare the consequence. The children are taught to be ignorant, and this must ever be the result of a mercenary penury, where there should not only be the best capacities employed, and rewards adequate to that most important of all branches of social institutions. . . .

No intelligent and upright man can approve of the present state of education; a great portion of the population appear to be insensible or indifferent; and, among the opulent, the improvement of the understanding and the heart enters very little into the consideration. "My son, make money," is the order of the day. But this is only a necessary effect of the social state in which money is the substitute and the criterion of every virtue, to which human rights, human liberty, social virtue, and public character are all sacrificed. There is nothing sacred or revered which is not sacrificed to money. When the government and the laws, and the habits of thinking, are thus radically vitiated, it is not to be expected that any other effect can be produced. . . .

In my own opinion, the prevailing systems of education are all wrong, from the first to the last stage. Education begins where it should terminate; and youth, instead of being led to the development of their faculties by the use of their senses, are made to acquire a great quantity of words, expressing the ideas of other men, instead of comprehending their own faculties, or becoming acquainted with the words they are taught or the ideas that the words should convey. There is only one system of education in existence fit for a country that is free, or for a people to whom intellectual knowledge is essential, in an age where *knowledge is power* and ignorance is weak-

William Duane

ness. And perhaps you may be surprised to learn that there is only one man in this country, and that one man in Kentucky, who is powerfully qualified to teach and to enable others to teach it. But such is the fact, and I shall not hesitate to name him to you, and to give you my ideas of his system; as I know it and saw it, I can warrant the perfection of its practice.

There is, living near Frankfort, a German of the name of Joseph Neef. He was a coadjutor of Pestalozzi, in Switzerland. He was offered every rich temptation to go to Russia; he preferred coming to the United States, and he was mistaken. He is the most disinterested man I ever saw, and most capable. No science is to him difficult or strange, because his method is such that he can analyze them all. In short, his system is expressed by the word "analytic"; for as all knowledge consists of the comprehension of facts, and the ideas of which that knowledge is composed, he is a teacher of facts.

To afford a very imperfect idea of his system, I will just invite your attention to one branch of it. He makes his pupil his equal, and the knowledge of sensible objects forms the topics of discourse and investigation. There are two primary ideas that belong to all our early perceptions. We see *forms* of things — trees, houses, hills, rivers, animals; and we perceive they have shapes or forms; but that the diversity of things have a diversity of forms and that like things have similarity of forms; and as there must be some principle both to express and to define the discrimination, that principle is to be sought.

It is the first law of sensible things, which all perceive, though they do not distinctly distinguish how until the idea is revealed by analysis. How do you describe the difference between an oak and a horse or a house? It is by its form! But how is that form composed? By lines; by the outline of each form. The lines drawn to represent a tree is first the outline, or the line which circumscribes its outer bound, as it is erect in space. Draw this outline accurately, and whoever has seen a tree recognizes in the outline the resemblance and the idea of a tree. So of a horse or a house; and so of all other sensible objects. Every visible thing has a form, and that is described by lines. This fact explains the motto which Plato placed on the entrance of the Academy, "Let no man enter here who is ignorant of geometry," for, in fact, geometry is the science of forms; and the knowledge which should be first acquired is that first and most universally felt. Hence, Mr. Neef would teach his pupil the study and the practice of forms; he would teach him geometry before he taught him to read or to write. But in teaching him to draw forms, he would also teach him to draw letters and to apply the power of letters to articulate sounds.

As next to forms, the first inchoate idea we perceive is individuality, number, or multitude; as we see one parent in our mother, another in our father, so the succession of number accumulates and requires terms to class quantities or equal or unequal numbers. So that as all things have forms, so all things are of number, either one or more in a class; there is one or more trees, horses, houses; and number expresses as naturally this classification as forms did that of sensible objects; and these two principles are the keys of science. Particular forms and quantities compose the detail; then come in the varieties of colors to fill the outline; then the sense of feeling is brought to comprehend other properties besides form, number, color; objects are hard or soft, as a rock or as water. Then another sense determines a property of taste; and hearing and smelling complete the chain of sensation, and the brief principles of all human knowledge and ideas, because there are no ideas apàrt from these sensations. All ideas belong to them directly, or are referable to them by analogy.

This is a very imperfect sketch of the fundamental principles of an accurate education, and by which more knowledge of any science or all the sciences may be obtained between the ages of six and fourteen years, than is, or, can be, obtained in any college to the twentieth year. I speak knowingly in what I say, and if Kentucky be resolved to establish education as it should be, and to possess the ablest and wisest men, the men of truest science, and the most correct and comprehensive knowledge, it is in their power; and at an expense so trivial compared with the extravagance of their Colleges of Freshmen, Sophomores, and all the trumpery of the remains of Aristotelian schools, that posterity would hold them in perpetual gratefulness, and they would give a signal and proud example of wisdom, which would live after them.

7.

ZERAH HAWLEY: Frontier Schools

Easterners, when comparing their own region with the less advanced frontier areas, were frequently content to focus on the obvious shortcomings of the West without regard for what the new states might one day become. Certainly the average Easterner could find much to criticize in the crude way of life on the frontier, if his standards were the conveniences and comforts of New England towns and cities. One such critic was Connecticut physician Zerah Hawley, who traveled to Ashtabula County, Ohio, in 1820, where he spent about a year. His observations on life in Ohio were collected in Journal of a Tour, *published in 1822. The following selection comprises excerpts from two letters written in the spring of 1821.*

Source: *A Journal of a Tour Through Connecticut, Massachusetts, New-York, the North Part of Pennsylvania and Ohio, etc., etc.*, New Haven, 1822, pp. 64-73.

SCHOOLS IN THIS PART OF THE COUNTRY are necessarily very indifferent. Young men and women, in many cases, can read and write, but very badly.

I knew two young men, one of nineteen, the other twenty-one years old, conversing with each other respecting the points used in writing. One remarked to the other that "that is a comma," "the semicolon is the pause of two syllables," etc., which, by their manner of speaking, they appeared to have just learned, and expressed as much pleasure in knowing these things, as children of eight years old would have done. These were sons of one of the most wealthy farmers in the town where they resided.

If you inquire of the people if they have seen or read such and such books which are most common in New England, they will reply in most cases that they have never heard of them; and the library of most families consists of (at most) three or four volumes. . . .

Schools in this part of the country are taught (if kept up at all), by females, about three months for the summer term, who teach merely the rudiments of reading, writing, and plain sewing. In many cases these schools are not taught more than eight weeks, and some not more than six, and compensation for teaching is made in almost all cases in such articles as the country affords, and not in money; so that teachers of much erudition cannot be prevailed upon to undertake the business of teaching the rising generation.

In the winter term, men teach the same branches as are taught by the females in the summer, with the addition of a little arithmetic and the exclusion of sewing, during about three months.

From this method of teaching, the short time the schools are kept, and the long intervals that intervene between the terms, it will readily be conceived that the children forget nearly as much as they learn, and it is very common to meet with young men and women who cannot read better than children in Connecticut of six years of age, and even with less propriety than some with which I am acquainted.

Their knowledge of geography, grammar, etc., is confined to a few who may have the privilege of occasionally attending the few academies which are established here; or to those very few who have property sufficient to send their children abroad. Those who have property sufficient to give their children a good education, and are disposed so to do, cannot at this time procure cash sufficient to pay the expense of such an education.

On the subject of religion and religious education, much might be said; but I shall make but few remarks on this head.

In a few towns on the Reserve, clergymen are settled for four or six months in the year, and the remainder of the time they ride as missionaries, through the townships which lie contiguous to them. In a *very* small number of towns, ministers are settled for the whole year.

These remarks apply to Presbyterians and Episcopalians. The other preachers are illiterate Baptist elders and still more illiterate itinerant Methodists. From this view of the subject it will easily be seen that the situation of the inhabitants of this country is most deplorable with regard to religious privileges.

It may further be remarked that many families are without the Word of God, and are groping in almost heathenish darkness, and are unable to procure the word of life to make them wise unto salvation. This is not all; at least eleven months in twelve, the great body of the people have no better oral instruction than what they receive from the most uninformed and fanatical Methodist preachers, who are the most extravagant ranters of which anyone can form an idea, who bawl forth one of their incoherent rhapsodies in one township in the morning, in another township in the afternoon, and a third in a third place in the evening. Thus they run through the country, "leading captive at their will, silly women," and men equally unwise. . . .

Their sermons are without plan or system, beginning with *ignorance* and ending in *nonsense*, interlarded with something nearly approaching blasphemy in many cases.

Many of the inhabitants in this part of our country are very sensible of their want of religious privileges, and earnestly desire to enjoy the rationally preached gospel, and say, "come over and help us." Missionaries are, as appears to me, almost as much needed here as in the Islands of the Seas; and as these people are our own brethren according to the flesh, there appears to be a duty incumbent on those who possess the means, an *urgent necessity,* to send them well-instructed teachers who may lead them in the way of Heaven.

This state (with the exception of a few towns) is still thinly settled, many townships remaining in the same situation, or nearly so, as they were when possessed by the savages of the forest.

The average number of inhabitants in the various townships may be 150, which is 6 to every square mile. In some towns, however, there is four-sixths of a person to a square mile. One of these is Millsford, which lies southeast of Jefferson, cornering on that town; south of Denmark and east of Lenox, which is directly south of Jefferson. Millsford contains two families, composed of six individuals. This township began to be settled about as early as any in the country; but has never contained but one family at a time, till this spring, when a second moved into the township. In this township, about eight acres of land are cleared, and the remainder is in a state of nature, covered with huge forest trees, such as white oak, white wood, beech, sugar maple, ash, etc., loaded with an abundant foliage of the most beautiful green imaginable.

The township is low and covered with water most of the year; the soil as good as the neighboring townships.

8.

RICHARD FURMAN: A Religious Defense of Slavery

Slavery was defended in the South not only on economic but also on religious grounds, and many preachers found justification for the "peculiar institution" in the Bible. They pointed out that the Old Testament told, apparently without censure, of the ownership of slaves by the patriarchs, and they cited passages in the New Testament that seemed to support slavery in the Roman Empire. To clergymen such as Richard Furman, the Bible, which was the book of the highest law, gave divine sanction to the American practice. Representing the South Carolina Baptists, Furman in 1822 wrote and presented the following declaration to the governor of the state, who responded with unqualified praise. The significant portions of the declaration appear below.

Source: Rev. Dr. Richard Furman's Exposition of the Views of the Baptists, Relative to the Coloured Population of the United States, in a Communication to the Governor of South-Carolina, Charleston, 1823, pp. 7-16.

ON THE LAWFULNESS OF HOLDING SLAVES, considering it in a moral and religious view, the convention think it their duty to exhibit their sentiments on the present occasion before Your Excellency, because they consider their duty to God, the peace of the state, the satisfaction of scrupulous consciences, and the welfare of the slaves themselves as intimately connected with a right view of the subject. The rather, because certain writers on politics, morals, and religion, and some of them highly respectable, have ad-

Furman University
Portrait of Richard Furman

vanced positions and inculcated sentiments very unfriendly to the principle and practice of holding slaves; and, by some, these sentiments have been advanced among us, tending in their nature *directly* to disturb the domestic peace of the state, to produce insubordination and rebellion among the slaves, and to infringe the rights of our citizens; and *indirectly* to deprive the slaves of religious privileges by awakening in the minds of their masters a fear that acquaintance with the Scriptures and the enjoyment of these privileges would naturally produce the aforementioned effects; because the sentiments in opposition to the holding of slaves have been attributed by their advocates to the Holy Scriptures and to the genius of Christianity.

These sentiments, the convention, on whose behalf I address Your Excellency, cannot think just or well-founded; for the right of holding slaves is clearly established in the Holy Scriptures, both by precept and example. In the Old Testament, the Israelites were directed to purchase their bondmen and bondmaids of the heathen nations; except they were of the Canaanites, for

these were to be destroyed. And it is declared that the persons purchased were to be their "bondmen forever," and an "inheritance for them and their children." They were not to go out free in the year of jubilee, as the Hebrews, who had been purchased, were; the line being clearly drawn between them. . . .

Had the holding of slaves been a moral evil, it cannot be supposed that the inspired apostles, who feared not the faces of men and were ready to lay down their lives in the cause of their God, would have tolerated it for a moment in the Christian Church. If they had done so on a principle of accommodation, in cases where the masters remained heathen, to avoid offenses and civil commotion, yet, surely, where both master and servant were Christian, as in the case before us, they would have enforced the law of Christ and required that the master should liberate his slave in the first instance. But, instead of this, they let the relationship remain untouched as being lawful and right, and insist on the relative duties.

In proving this subject justifiable by scriptural authority, its morality is also proved; for the Divine Law never sanctions immoral actions.

The Christian Golden Rule of doing to others as we would they should do to us has been urged as an unanswerable argument against holding slaves. But surely this rule is never to be urged against that order of things which the Divine Government has established; nor do our desires become a standard to us, under this rule, unless they have a due regard to justice, propriety, and the general good. . . .

If the holding of slaves is lawful, or according to the Scriptures, then this scriptural rule can be considered as requiring no more of the master, in respect of justice (whatever it may do in point of generosity) than what he, if a slave, could consistently wish to be done to himself, while the relationship between master and servant should be still continued.

In this argument, the advocates for emancipation blend the ideas of injustice and cruelty with those which respect the existence of slavery, and consider them as inseparable. But, surely, they may be separated. A bondservant may be treated with justice and humanity as a servant; and a master may, in an important sense, be the guardian and even father of his slaves. . . .

That Christian nations have not done all they might, or should have done, on a principle of Christian benevolence for the civilization and conversion of the Africans; that much cruelty has been practised in the slave trade, as the benevolent Wilberforce and others have shown; that much tyranny has been exercised by individuals, as masters over their slaves, and that the religious interests of the latter have been too much neglected by many cannot, will not be denied. But the fullest proof of these facts will not also prove that the holding men in subjection, as slaves, is a moral evil and inconsistent with Christianity. Magistrates, husbands, and fathers have proved tyrants. This does not prove that magistracy, the husband's right to govern, and parental authority are unlawful and wicked. The individual who abuses his authority and acts with cruelty must answer for it at the Divine Tribunal, and civil authority should interpose to prevent or punish it; but neither civil nor ecclesiastical authority can consistently interfere with the possession and legitimate exercise of a right given by the Divine Law. . . .

It appears to be equally clear that those, who by reasoning on abstract principles, are induced to favor the scheme of general emancipation, and who ascribe their sentiments to Christianity, should be particularly careful, however benevolent their intentions may be, that they do not by a perversion of the scriptural doctrine, through their wrong views of it, not only invade the domestic and religious peace and rights of our citizens on this subject but, also by an intemperate zeal, prevent indirectly the religious improvement of the people they design, professedly, to benefit; and, perhaps, become, evidently, the means of producing in our country scenes of anarchy and blood. And all this in a vain attempt to bring about a state of things which, if arrived at, would not probably better the state of that people; which is thought by men of observation to be generally true of the Negroes in the Northern states who have been liberated.

To pious minds it has given pain to hear men, respectable for intelligence and morals, sometimes say that holding slaves is indeed indefensible, but that to us it is necessary and must be supported. On this principle, mere politicians, unmindful of morals, may act. But surely, in a moral and religious view of the subject, this principle is inadmissible. It cannot be said that theft, falsehood, adultery, and murder are become necessary and must be supported. Yet there is reason to believe that some of honest and pious intentions have found their minds embarrassed, if not perverted, on this subject by this plausible but unsound argument. From such embarrassment the view exhibited above affords relief.

The convention, sir, are far from thinking that Christianity fails to inspire the minds of its subjects with benevolent and generous sentiments; or that liberty, rightly understood or enjoyed, is a blessing of little moment. The contrary of these positions they maintain. But they also consider benevolence as consulting the truest and best interests of its objects; and view the happiness of liberty as well as of religion as consisting not in the name or form but in the reality. While men remain in the chains of ignorance and error, and under the dominion of tyrant lusts and passions, they cannot be free. And the more freedom of action they have in this state, they are but the more qualified by it to do injury both to themselves and others. It is, therefore, firmly believed that general emancipation to the Negroes in this country would not, in present circumstances, be for their own happiness, as a body; while it would be extremely injurious to the community at large in various ways; and, if so, then it is not required even by benevolence.

But acts of benevolence and generosity must be free and voluntary; no man has a right to compel another to the performance of them. This is a concern which lies between a man and his God. If a man has obtained slaves by purchase, or inheritance, and the holding of them as such is justifiable by the law of God, why should he be required to liberate them, because it would be a generous action, rather than another, on the same principle, to release his debtors or sell his lands and houses and distribute the proceeds among the poor? These also would be generous actions. Are they, therefore, obligatory? Or, if obligatory, in certain circumstances, as personal, voluntary acts of piety and benevolence, has any man or body of men, civil or ecclesiastic, a right to require them? Surely those who are advocates for compulsory or strenuous measures to bring about emancipation should duly weigh this consideration.

Should, however, a time arrive when the Africans in our country might be found qualified to enjoy freedom, and, when they might obtain it in a manner consistent with the interest and peace of the community at large, the convention would be happy in seeing them free. And so they would, in seeing the state of the poor, the ignorant, and the oppressed of every description and of every country meliorated; so that the reputed free might be free, indeed, and happy. But there seems to be just reason to conclude that a considerable part of the human race, whether they bear openly the character of slaves or are reputed freemen,

will continue in such circumstances, with mere shades of variation, while the world continues. . . .

And here I am brought to a part of the general subject which, I confess to Your Excellency, the convention, from a sense of their duty as a body of men to whom important concerns of religion are confided, have particularly at heart, and wish it may be seriously considered by all our citizens: This is the religious interests of the Negroes. For though they are slaves, they are also men; and are with ourselves accountable creatures, having immortal souls and being destined to future eternal award. Their religious interests claim a regard from their masters of the most serious nature; and it is indispensable. Nor can the community at large, in a right estimate of their duty and happiness, be indifferent on this subject. To the truly benevolent it must be pleasing to know that a number of masters, as well as ministers and pious individuals of various Christian denominations among us, do conscientiously regard this duty; but there is great reason to believe that it is neglected and disregarded by many.

The convention are particularly unhappy in considering that an idea of the Bible's teaching the doctrine of emancipation as necessary, and, tending to make servants insubordinate to proper authority, has obtained access to any mind; both on account of its direct influence on those who admit it, and the fear it excites in others, producing the effects before noticed. But it is hoped it has been evinced that the idea is an erroneous one, and that it will be seen that the influence of a right acquaintance with that Holy Book tends directly and powerfully, by promoting the fear and love of God, together with just and peaceful sentiments toward men, to produce one of the best securities to the public for the internal and domestic peace of the state.

"Packet Row," South Street, New York from Maiden Lane, 1828; aquatint by William Bennett

URBAN AMERICA

Rapid expansion of manufacturing and trade after the War of 1812 spurred a tremendous growth in the cities where these activities were centered. The diversity and scope of economic expansion was also changing the nature of American commercial enterprise. In shipping, long a source of wealth, the merchant trader, who owned both ship and cargo, was giving way to the common carrier, who transported goods bought and sold by others. By 1828, Congress had eliminated most of the special duties protecting American shipping from foreign competition in domestic ports. The shipping industry was thought to be so strong that these protections were not needed. Removing them would benefit other sectors of the economy by stimulating international trade. At the same time the manufacturers began to seek protection from foreign competition. The migrations west, the development of canals, and the growth of manufac-

turing all contributed to a vast growth in domestic trade and commerce. In all of this, the first beneficiaries were the cities, particularly New York. The Erie Canal, connecting the Hudson River with Lake Erie, was opened in 1825. It linked the farms and cattle-raising lands of the West with the markets and manufacturing of the East and gave New York a singular advantage in East-West trade. In a short time the city was the unchallenged commercial heart of the nation. With a population of 33,000 in 1790, New York City had grown to almost 200,000 by 1830. While outstripped by New York, two other great commercial centers grew rapidly, Philadelphia and Boston. The textile and whaling industries growing up in near-by towns particularly profited Boston, which continued its traditional involvement in international trade. Philadelphia began to find new profit from coal mining in the mountains.

Smith and Dimon shipyard, East River, New York City; painting by James Pringle, 1833

Business Capital

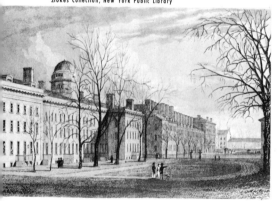

As with every important city, land became a great source of wealth to speculators in New York City. The building boom meant the rise of tenements as well as stately mansions, banks and exchanges, factories and offices, shops, theaters, schools, and all the other structures that mark a city. It also meant the removal of old landmarks. Suburbanites took refuge in Brooklyn, commuting to Manhattan by ferry boat. These boats could ply the waters surrounding the city on reasonably regular schedules. Columbia College was training men for the professions and business.

(Above) Columbia College in 1830; drawing by A. J. Davis; (right) view of the offices of "The New York Mirror" in 1830

THE NEW-YORK MIRROR:

A REPOSITORY OF POLITE LITERATURE AND THE ARTS.

VOLUME VIII.   NEW-YORK, SATURDAY, SEPTEMBER 4, 1830.   NUMBER 9.

View of a section of Ann and Nassau streets—taken from the south corner.

Drawn by Davis and engraved by Anderson, expressly for this work.

New York property auction in the 1830s; from the "Mirror"

Ruins of the Stuyvesant House in 1830; from the "Mirror"

Philip Hone, mayor of New York in 1825

House raising in New York; painting by William Chappel

View of the bay and harbor of New York from the Battery; engraving in the "Mirror"

Park Row, New York; engraving from the "Mirror," 1830

View of Wall Street engraved for the "New York Mirror," 1830

View of New York from Weehawken, New Jersey

(Above) "Winter Scene in Brooklyn" by Francis Guy; (left) the ferry at Brooklyn

(Above) Patent drawing for a revolving washing machine. Clothes were worked around a roller inside the cylinder drum; (right) fanning device operated by system of weights and gears

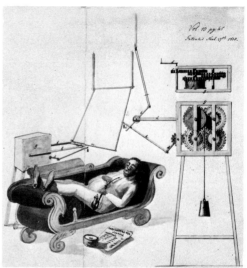

"The Good Life"

Demands for time- and labor-saving devices brought impractical as well as practical inventions. It is a far cry from Whitney's cotton gin to the frivolous fanning device shown here. The Patent Office received dozens of schemes for "improved" washing machines, most of which were harder on clothes than on dirt. Leisure meant music lessons and dancing for the young and formal or informal gatherings for "society."

Two patent drawings for washing machines: (above) model in which clothes were moved between two sets of rollers by a vibrating frame; (right) model which agitates clothes by four hammers attached to a crankshaft

(Above) "The Dinner Party" by Henry Sargent; (top right) drawing from an advertisement for Duboise Piano-forte and Music Store; (center right) Waltz Dance; engraving by Alexander Anderson; (below) "The Tea Party"; also by Sargent

The resort hotel at Saratoga Springs, N.Y., 1828

Hudson Valley

New York's prosperity spread up the Hudson and led to the growth of resorts where the well-to-do could leave the urban scenes behind. Excursions to nearby points were popular. A visit to West Point on the Hudson meant a chance to see the new military academy. Further afield, the elite could enjoy the healthful waters of the baths at Saratoga Springs, not yet a racing center. Steamboat travel made these and other journeys outside the city practical.

Schoolhouse at Tappan, N.Y. engraved for the "Mirror," 1832, from a painting by R. W. Wier

View of the Military Academy at West Point, painted by George Catlin, 1828

View of Albany, N.Y., 1828, lithograph from a drawing by Jacques Milbert

Albany

The capital of New York State was moved to Albany in 1797. New York was typical in this respect, as many states moved their capitals out of the large coastal cities to be nearer the centers of their shifting populations. Land speculation and political jockeying between rural and city interests also played a role. The political and social life of Albany, still a town of only 24,000 in 1830, was dominated by descendents of the Dutch patroons and was a main way-station for people traveling west.

(Above) Stephen Van Rensselaer, 1764-1839, congressman, member of the New York Board of Regents and founder of Rensselaer Polytechnic Institute; (left) home of the first Dutch governors in the center of Albany, 1828, also by Milbert

New York

The opening of the Erie Canal stimulated migration into central and western New York. The solitude of the Mohawk River Valley, through which the canal ran, was broken by the bawling of drivers as mule teams hauled barges up and down the canal. Villages grew into towns and towns into cities. Buffalo, at the western end of the canal, was an authentic boom town with cheap hotels and taverns thrown up to serve the freight-handlers and mule-skinners. Cargoes were transferred at Buffalo from lake steamers to canal barges.

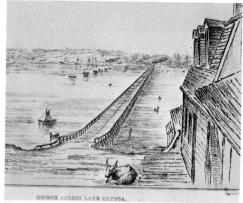

Bridge across Lake Cayuga; etching by Basil Hall using camera lucida, 1829

Rochester, New York, in 1829; etching by Basil Hall

"Road and Bridge over the Mohawk"; lithograph from a painting by J. Milbert, 1828

(Above) Charles Carroll by Harding; (above right) Thomas Jefferson by Sully

An Era Passes

When the Marquis de Lafayette visited America in 1824, only a handful of his Revolutionary War associates were still alive. He was given a tumultuous welcome amidst a general patriotic revival of the Revolutionary era. In a symbolic coincidence Adams and Jefferson died on the same day two years later, July 4, 1826, leaving Charles Carroll as the surviving signer of the Declaration of Independence.

(Above) John Adams and (right) Lafayette, by Morse; (below) James Madison by Longacre

Boston

The traditional resources of Boston, international trade and Harvard, remained central to the economic and cultural life of the city in the 1820s. At the same time, new industries, textile and shoe manufacturing, were centered on the port of Boston, and the products of near-by whaling towns flowed across the city's docks. Molasses from the West Indies was distilled into rum and ships from the Orient arrived with cargoes of silks, tea and spices. Most of Boston's Far East trade, however, went directly from the East to European markets.

Faneuil Hall, being used as a warehouse (top); (left) Josiah Quincy, who became president of Harvard in 1829 after a term as mayor of Boston; (below) Harvard College in 1821, by Alvin Fisher

"The Boston Light House, July 4, 1832," watercolor painted by Karl Bodmer

(Above) A view of Boston and the waterfront from the South Boston Bridge, 1828, by Milbert; (below) "Boston Harbor" by Robert Salmon. A warship is being towed by a group of rowboats

Philadelphia

By 1830, Philadelphia had relinquished its status as the largest city and major port in the country to New York. In addition, the nation's financial center shifted to New York at this time, under the impact of that city's growth and Jackson's dissolution of the United States Bank, which had been located in Philadelphia. On the other hand, industry, based on coal from the Lehigh Valley, was flourishing. A canal was underway to connect Philadelphia with Pittsburgh and other inland areas. In spite of these activities, Quaker and German traditions remained strong and Philadelphia retained its distinctive character among American cities.

(Top) The Delaware River shore looking toward the waterfront, sketched in 1824 by Charles Lesueur; (above) Philadelphia had spread along the River but Penn's original grid plan can be seen

View of Philadelphia from Fairmount, looking down the Schuylkill, 1836

Philadelphia waterworks on the Schuylkill, by Milbert; (below) Market Square in Germantown, by William Britton; (bottom) the large open pit coal mine at Mauch Chunk, Pa., 1825, sketched by Lesueur

(Above) **Ephraim McDowell (1771-1830), prac-
ticed in Ky. after attending medical school in
Edinburgh; (above right) Philip Syng Physick
(1768-1837), leading surgeon and teacher in
Philadelphia; (below) David Hosack (1769-
1835) painted by Rembrandt Peale; (bottom
right) woodcut of the hole in Alexis St. Martin's abdomen, from William Beaumont's "Experiments and Observations on the Gastric
Juice"**

Medicine

Philadelphia remained the center of medical education and practice in the early 19th
century, although excellent medical schools
had been founded at Columbia and Harvard. Philip Syng Physick made numerous
contributions to surgical technique and medical education and came to be known as
the "father of American surgery." David
Hosack, a pioneer surgeon, founded Belle-
vue Hospital in New York and the Rutgers
Medical School. Ephraim McDowell pio-
neered in the removal of tumors, gall stones
and in other abdominal surgery. William
Beaumont, experimenting on a man with a
bullet wound in his stomach, revolutionized
understanding of the digestive process.

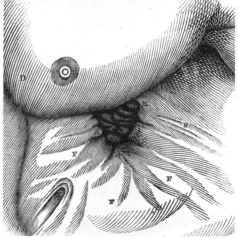

1823

9.

John Quincy Adams: The Caribbean and Our National Interest

By 1822, all of the Spanish colonies in Central and South America except Bolivia had proclaimed themselves independent, but certain key islands in the Caribbean remained under Spain's control. Because of their proximity to the North American continent, they were of strategic and commercial importance to the United States. When France invaded Spain in April 1823, rumors spread that Cuba or Puerto Rico would be ceded to France, or that Britain would relinquish her neutrality and come to Spain's aid, in which case the islands could come under British control. Either possibility seemed ominous to Secretary of State John Quincy Adams, who sent the following letter, dated April 28, 1823, to Hugh Nelson, the American foreign minister to Spain.

Source: *Writings of John Quincy Adams*, Worthington C. Ford, ed., Vol. VII, New York, 1917, pp. 369-421.

It has been a maxim in the policy of these United States, from the time when their independence was achieved, to keep themselves aloof from the political systems and contentions of Europe. To this principle it is yet the purpose of the President to adhere, and in the war about to commence, the attitude to be assumed and maintained by the United States will be that of neutrality.

But the experience of our national history has already shown that, however sincerely this policy was adopted, and however earnestly and perseveringly it was maintained, it yielded ultimately to a course of events by which the violence and injustice of European powers involved the immediate interests and brought in conflict the essential rights of our own country.

Two of the principal causes of the wars between the nations of Europe since that of our own Revolution have been, indeed, the same as those in which that originated — civil liberty and national independence. To these principles, and to the cause of those who contend for them, the people of the United States can never be indifferent. A feeling of sympathy and of partiality for every nation struggling to secure or to defend these great interests has been and will be manifested by this Union; and it is among the most difficult and delicate duties of the general government, in all its branches, to indulge this feeling so far as it may be compatible with the duties of neutrality, and to withhold and restrain from encroaching upon them. So far as it is indulged, its tendency is to involve us in foreign wars, while the first and paramount duty of the government is to maintain *peace* amidst all the convulsions of foreign wars, and to enter the lists as parties to no cause other than our own.

In the *maritime* wars of Europe, we have, indeed, a direct and important interest of our own; as they are waged upon an element which is the common property of all; and as our participation in the possession of that property is perhaps greater than that of any other nation. The existence of maritime war itself enlarges and deepens the importance of this interest; and it introduces a state of things in which the conflict of neutral and belligerent rights becomes itself a continual and formidable instigation to war. To all maritime wars Great Britain can scarcely fail of becoming a party; and from that moment arises a collision between her and these states, peculiar to the situation, interests, and rights of the two countries, and which can scarcely form a subject of discussion between any other nation and either of them.

This cause then is peculiarly our own; and we have already been once compelled to vindicate our rights implicated in it by war. It has been, too, among the dispensations of Providence that the issue of that war should have left that question unsettled for the future; and that the attempts which on the part of the United States have been repeatedly made since the peace for adjusting it by amicable negotiation, have in like manner proved ineffectual. There is therefore great reason to apprehend that if Great Britain should engage in the war now just kindled in Europe, the United States will again be called to support by all their energies, not excepting war, the rights of their national independence, enjoyed in the persons of their seamen.

But in the war between France and Spain now commencing, other interests, peculiarly ours, will in all probability be deeply involved. Whatever may be the issue of this war, as between those two European powers, it may be taken for granted that the dominion of Spain upon the American continents, North and South, is irrecoverably gone. But the islands of Cuba and of Puerto Rico still remain nominally and so far really dependent upon her, that she yet possesses the power of transferring her own dominion over them, together with the possession of them, to others. These islands, from their local position, are natural appendages to the North American continent; and one of them, Cuba, almost in sight of our shores, from a multitude of considerations has become an object of transcendent importance to the political and commercial interests of our Union. Its commanding position with reference to the Gulf of Mexico and the West India seas; the character of its population; its situation midway between our southern coast and the island of San Domingo; its safe and capacious harbor of Havana, fronting a long line of our shores destitute of the same advantage; the nature of its productions and of its wants, furnishing the supplies and needing the returns of a commerce immensely profitable and mutually beneficial; give it an importance in the sum of our national interests with which that of no other foreign territory can be compared, and little inferior to that which binds the different members of this Union together.

Such indeed are, between the interests of that island and of this country, the geographical, commercial, moral, and political relations, formed by nature, gathering in the process of time and even now verging to maturity, that in looking forward to the probable course of events for the short period of half a century it is scarcely possible to resist the conviction that the annexation of Cuba to our federal republic will be indispensable to the continuance and integrity of the Union itself. It is obvious, however, that for this event we are not yet prepared. Numerous and formidable objections to the extension of our territorial dominions beyond the sea present themselves to the first contemplation of the subject. Obstacles to the system of policy by which it alone can be compassed and maintained are to be foreseen and surmounted, both from at home and abroad. But there are laws of political as well as of physical gravitation; and if an apple severed by the tempest from its native tree cannot choose but fall to the ground, Cuba, forcibly disjoined from its own unnatural connection with Spain, and incapable of self-support, can gravitate only toward the North American Union, which by the same law of nature cannot cast her off from its bosom.

In any other state of things than that which springs from this incipient war between France and Spain, these considerations would be premature. They are now merely touched upon to illustrate the position that, in the war opening upon Europe, the United States have deep and important interests involved, peculiarly their own. The condition of Cuba cannot but depend upon the issue of this war. As an integral part of the Spanish territories, Cuba has been formally and solemnly invested with the liberties of the Spanish constitution. To destroy those liberties and to restore in the stead of that constitution the dominion of the Bourbon race is the avowed object of this new invasion of the Peninsula. There is too much reason to apprehend that in Spain itself this unhallowed purpose will be attended with immediate, or at least with temporary, success; the constitution of Spain will be demolished by the armies of the Holy Alliance; and the Spanish nation will again bow the neck to the yoke of bigotry and despotic sway.

Whether the purposes of France, or of her continental allies, extend to the subjuga-

tion of the remaining ultramarine possessions of Spain or not has not yet been sufficiently disclosed. But to confine ourselves to that which immediately concerns us, the condition of the island of Cuba, we know that the republican spirit of freedom prevails among its inhabitants. The liberties of the constitution are to them rights in possession; nor is it to be presumed that they will be willing to surrender them because they may be extinguished by foreign violence in the parent country. As Spanish territory the island will be liable to invasion from France during the war; and the only reasons for doubting whether the attempt will be made are the probable incompetency of the French maritime force to effect the conquest, and the probability that its accomplishment would be resisted by Great Britain. In the meantime and at all events, the condition of the island in regard to that of its inhabitants is a condition of great, imminent, and complicated danger. And without resorting to speculation upon what such a state of things must produce upon a people so situated, we know that its approach has already had a powerful effect upon them, and that the question what they are to do upon contingencies daily pressing upon them and ripening into reality, has for the last twelve months constantly excited their attention and stimulated them to action.

Were the population of the island of one blood and color, there could be no doubt or hesitation with regard to the course which they would pursue, as dictated by their interests and their rights. The invasion of Spain by France would be the signal for *their* Declaration of Independence. That even in their present state it will be imposed upon them as a necessity is not unlikely; but among all their reflecting men it is admitted as a maxim fundamental to all deliberation upon their future condition, that they are not competent to a system of permanent self-dependence. They must rely for the support of protection upon some force from without; and as, in the event of the overthrow of the Spanish constitution, that support can no longer be expected from Spain, their only alternative of dependence must be upon Great Britain, or upon the United States. . . .

The transfer of Cuba to Great Britain would be an event unpropitious to the interests of this Union. This opinion is so generally entertained that even the groundless rumors that it was about to be accomplished, which have spread abroad and are still teeming, may be traced to the deep and almost universal feeling of aversion to it, and to the alarm which the mere probability of its occurrence has stimulated. The question both of our right and our power to prevent it, if necessary, by force, already obtrudes itself upon our councils, and the administration is called upon, in the performance of its duties to the nation, at least to use all the means within its competency to guard against and forefend it.

It will be among the primary objects requiring your most earnest and unremitting attention to ascertain and report to us any movement of negotiation between Spain and Great Britain upon this subject. We cannot, indeed, prescribe any special instructions in relation to it. We scarcely know where you will find the government of Spain upon your arrival in the country; nor can we foresee with certainty by whom it will be administered. Your credentials are addressed to Ferdinand, the king of Spain under the constitution. You may find him under the guardianship of a Cortes, in the custody of an Army of Faith, or under the protection of the invaders of his country. So long as the *constitutional* government may continue to be administered in his name, your official intercourse will be with his ministers; and to them you will repeat what Mr. Forsyth has been instructed to say, that the wishes of your government are that Cuba and Puerto Rico may continue in

connection with independent and constitutional Spain. You will add that no countenance has been given by us to any projected plan of separation from Spain which may have been formed in the island.

This assurance becomes proper, as, by a late dispatch received from Mr. Forsyth, he intimates that the Spanish government have been informed that a revolution in Cuba was secretly preparing, fomented by communications between a society of Free Masons there and another of the same fraternity in Philadelphia. Of this we have no other knowledge; and the societies of Free Masons in this country are so little in the practice of using agency of a political nature on any occasion that we think it most probable the information of the Spanish government in that respect is unfounded. It is true that the Free Masons at the Havana have taken part of late in the politics of Cuba; and, so far as it is known to us, it has been an earnest and active part in favor of the continuance of their connection with Spain.

While disclaiming all disposition on our part, either to obtain possession of Cuba or of Puerto Rico ourselves, you will declare that the American government had no knowledge of the lawless expedition undertaken against the latter of those islands last summer. . . .

You will not conceal from the Spanish government the repugnance of the United States to the transfer of the island of Cuba by Spain to any other power. The deep interest which would to them be involved in the event gives them the right of objecting against it; and as the people of the island itself are known to be averse to it, the right of Spain herself to make the cession, at least upon the principles on which the present Spanish constitution is founded, is more than questionable. Informal and verbal communications on this subject with the Spanish minister of foreign affairs will be most advisable.

In casual conversation, and speaking as from your own impressions, you may suggest the hope that if any question of transferring the island to any other power is or shall be in agitation, it will not be withheld from your knowledge, or from ours; that the condition of Cuba cannot be changed without affecting in an eminent degree the welfare of this Union, and consequently the good understanding between us and Spain; that we should consider an attempt to transfer the island, against the will of its inhabitants, as subversive of their rights, no less than of our interests; and that, as it would give them the perfect right of resisting such transfer by declaring their own independence, so if they should, under those circumstances, resort to that measure, the United States will be fully justified in supporting them to carry it into effect.

10.

JOHN QUINCY ADAMS: Russia and the Pacific Northwest

When Americans began to move into the Mississippi Valley in large numbers, many farsighted men envisioned a United States of continental dimensions. Entrepreneurs in fur and lumber had established commercial and trading outposts along the Northwest Pacific Coast. However, American interests were not uncontested — Russia and Great Britain had also explored this area — and the need for an expression of United States policy to head off colonization by other powers seemed imperative. On July 17, 1823, Secretary of State John Quincy Adams informed Baron Tuyl, Russian minister at Washington, of the policy that later was announced in the Monroe Doctrine. The substance of this talk, as recorded by Adams in his Memoirs, *appears as the first of the following selections. The second is a dispatch in which Adams emphatically affirmed United States rights to specified areas in the Northwest. It was sent on July 22 to the American minister in England, Richard Rush.*

Source: *Memoirs of John Quincy Adams, Comprising Portions of his Diary from 1795 to 1848,* Charles Francis Adams, ed., Vol. VII, Philadelphia, 1875, p. 163.

58 Congress, 2 Session, Senate Document No. 162, Vol. I, pp. 52-56.

I.

Memo of July 17

AT THE OFFICE, Baron Tuyl came, and inquired if he might inform his government that instructions would be forwarded by Mr. Hughes to Mr. Middleton for negotiating on the Northwest Coast question. I said he might. He then manifested a desire to know as much as I was disposed to tell him as to the purport of those instructions. I told him as much as I thought prudent, as he observed that it was personally somewhat important to him to be so far confided in here as to know the general purport of what we intended to propose. I told him specially that we should contest the right of Russia to *any* territorial establishment on this continent, and that we should assume distinctly the principle that the American continents are no longer subjects for *any* new European colonial establishments. We had a conversation of an hour or more, at the close of which he said that although there would be difficulties in the negotiation, he did not foresee that they would be insurmountable.

II.

Letter to RICHARD RUSH

AMONG THE SUBJECTS of negotiation with Great Britain which are pressing upon the attention of this government is the present condition of the northwest coast of this continent. This interest is connected, in a manner becoming from day to day more important, with our territorial rights; with the whole system of our intercourse with the Indian tribes; with the boundary relations between us and the British North American dominions; with the fur trade; the fisheries in the Pacific Ocean; the commerce with the Sandwich Islands and China; with our boundary upon Mexico; and, lastly, with our political standing and intercourse with the Russian Empire.

By the 3rd Article of the convention between the United States and Great Britain of October 20, 1818, it is agreed that any "country that may be claimed by either party on the northwest coast of America, westward of the Stony Mountains, shall, together with its harbors, bays, and creeks, and the navigation of all rivers within the same, be free and open for the term of ten years from the date of the signature of the convention, to the vessels, citizens, and subjects of the two powers; it being well understood that this agreement is not to be construed to the prejudice of any claims which either of the two high contracting parties may have to any part of the said country, nor shall it be taken to affect the claims of any other power or state to any part of the said country, the only object of the high contracting parties in that respect being to prevent disputes and differences amongst themselves."

On the 6th of October, 1818, fourteen days before the signature of this convention, the settlement at the mouth of Columbia River had been formally restored to the United States by order of the British government. (Message of the President of the United States to the House of Representatives, April 15, 1822, p. 13. Letter of Mr. Prevost to the secretary of state of November 11, 1818.)

By the treaty of amity, settlement, and limits between the United States and Spain of February 22, 1819, the boundary line between them was fixed at the 42° latitude, from the source of the Arkansas River to the South Sea [Pacific Ocean]; by which treaty the United States acquired all the rights of Spain north of that parallel.

The right of the United States to the Columbia River and to the interior territory washed by its waters rests upon its discovery from the sea and nomination by a citizen of the United States; upon its exploration to the sea by Captain Lewis and Clarke; upon the settlement of Astoria, made under the protection of the United States, and thus restored to them in 1818; and upon this subsequent acquisition of all the rights of Spain, the only European power who prior to the discovery of the river had any pretensions to territorial rights on the northwest coast of America.

The waters of the Columbia River extend by the Multnomah to the latitude 42°, where its source approaches within a few miles of those of the Platte and Arkansas, and by Clarke's River to the latitude 50° or 51°; thence descending southward, till its sources almost intersect those of the Missouri.

To the territory thus watered, and immediately contiguous to the original possessions of the United States, as first bounded by the Mississippi, they consider their right to be now established by all the principles which have ever been applied to European settlements upon the American hemisphere.

By the ukase of the Emperor Alexander of the 4th (16th) of September, 1821, an exclusive territorial right on the northwest coast of America is asserted as belonging to

Russia and as extending from the northern extremity of the continent to latitude 51°, and the navigation and fishery of all other nations are interdicted by the same ukase to the extent of one hundred Italian miles from the coast.

When Mr. Poletica, the late Russian minister here, was called upon to set forth the grounds of right conformable to the laws of nations which authorized the issuing of this decree, he answered in his letters of February 28 and April 2, 1822, by alleging first discovery, occupancy, and uninterrupted possession.

It appears upon examination that these claims have no foundation in fact. The right of discovery on this continent claimable by Russia is reduced to the probability that in 1741 Captain Tchirikoff saw from the sea the mountain called St. Elias, in about the latitude 59° N. The Spanish navigators as early as 1582 had discovered as far north as 57°30'.

As to occupancy, Captain Cook in 1779 had the express declaration of Mr. Ismaeloff, the chief of the Russian settlement at Onalashka, that they knew nothing of the continent in America; and in the Nootka Sound controversy between Spain and Great Britain it is explicitly stated in the Spanish documents that Russia had disclaimed all pretension to interfere with the Spanish exclusive rights to beyond Prince Williams Sound, latitude 61°. No evidence has been exhibited of any Russian settlement on this continent south and east of Prince Williams Sound to this day, with the exception of that in California, made in 1816.

It never has been admitted by the various European nations which have formed settlements in this hemisphere that the occupation of an island gave any claim whatever to territorial possessions on the continent to which it was adjoining. The recognized principle has rather been the reverse, as, by the law of nature, islands must be rather considered as appendages to continents than continents to islands.

The only color of claim alleged by Mr. Poletica which has an appearance of plausibility is that which he asserts as an authentic fact: "That in 1789 the Spanish packet *St. Charles,* commanded by Captain Haro, found in the latitude 48° and 49° Russian settlements to the number of 8, consisting, in the whole, of 20 families and 462 individuals." But more than twenty years since, Heurieu had shown, in his introduction to the voyage of Marchaud, that in this statement there was a mistake of at least ten degrees of latitude, and that instead of 48° and 49° it should read 58° and 59°. This is probably not the only mistake in the account. It rests altogether upon the credit of two private letters — one written from San Blas and the other from the city of Mexico, to Spain — there communicated to a French consul in one of the Spanish ports, and by him to the French minister of marine. They were written in October 1788 and August 1789. We have seen that, in 1790, Russia explicitly disclaimed interfering with the exclusive rights of Spain to beyond Prince Williams Sound in latitude 61°; and Vancouver, in 1794, was informed by the Russians on the spot that their most eastern settlement there was on Hitchinbrook Island, at Port Etches, which had been established in the course of the preceding summer, and that the adjacent continent was a sterile and uninhabited country.

Until the Nootka Sound contest, Great Britain had never advanced any claim to territory upon the northwest coast of America by right of occupation. Under the treaty of 1763 her territorial rights were bounded by the Mississippi.

On the 22nd of July, 1793, Mackenzie reached the shores of the Pacific by land from Canada, in latitude 52°21' N, longitude 128°2' west of Greenwich.

It is stated in the 52nd number of the *Quarterly Review,* in the article upon Kotzebue's voyage, "that the whole country, from latitude 56°30′ to the boundary of the United States, in latitude 48° or thereabouts, is now and has long been in the actual possession of the British Northwest Company". . . .

It is not imaginable that, in the present condition of the world, any European nation should entertain the project of settling a colony on the northwest coast of America. That the United States should form establishments there, with views of absolute territorial right and inland communication, is not only to be expected but is pointed out by the finger of nature, and has been for many years a subject of serious deliberation in Congress. A plan has for several sessions been before them for establishing a territorial government on the borders of the Columbia River. It will undoubtedly be resumed at their next session, and even if then again postponed there cannot be a doubt that in the course of a very few years it must be carried into effect.

As yet, however, the only useful purpose to which the northwest coast of America has been or can be made subservient to the settlements of civilized men are the fisheries on its adjoining seas and trade with the aboriginal inhabitants of the country. These have hitherto been enjoyed in common by the people of the United States, and by the British and Russian nations. The Spanish, Portuguese, and French nations have also participated in them hitherto, without other annoyance than that which resulted from the exclusive territorial claims of Spain, so long as they were insisted on by her.

The United States and Great Britain have both protested against the Russian imperial ukase of September 4 (16), 1821. At the proposal of the Russian government, a full power and instructions are now transmitted to Mr. Middleton, for the adjustment, by amicable negotiation, of the conflicting claims of the parties on this subject.

We have been informed by the Baron de Tuyl that a similar authority has been given

on the part of the British government to Sir Charles Bagot.

Previous to the restoration of the settlement at the mouth of Columbia River in 1818, and again upon the first introduction in Congress of the plan for constituting a territorial government there, some disposition was manifested by Sir Charles Bagot and by Mr. Canning to dispute the right of the United States to that establishment, and some vague intimation was given of British claims on the northwest coast. The restoration of the place and the convention of 1818 were considered as a final disposal of Mr. Bagot's objections, and Mr. Canning declined committing to paper those which he had intimated in conversation.

The discussion of the Russian pretensions in the negotiation now proposed necessarily involves the interests of the three powers, and renders it manifestly proper that the United States and Great Britain should come to a mutual understanding with respect to their respective pretensions, as well as upon their joint views with reference to those of Russia. Copies of the instructions to Mr. Middleton are, therefore, herewith transmitted to you, and the President wishes you to confer freely with the British government on the subject.

The principles settled by the Nootka Sound Convention of October 28, 1790, were —

1. That the rights of fishery in the South Seas, of trading with the natives of the northwest coast of America, and of making settlements on the coasts itself for the purpose of that trade, north of the *actual* settlements of Spain, were common to all the European nations, and of course to the United States.

2. That so far as the actual settlements of Spain had extended, she possessed the exclusive rights, territorial and of navigation and fishery, extending to the distance of ten miles from the coasts so actually occupied.

3. That on the coasts of South America, and the adjacent islands south of the parts

already occupied by Spain, no settlement should thereafter be made either by British or Spanish subjects, but on both sides should be retained the liberty of landing and of erecting temporary buildings for the purposes of the fishery. These rights were also, of course, enjoyed by the people of the United States.

The exclusive rights of Spain to any part of the American continents have ceased. That portion of the convention, therefore, which recognizes the exclusive colonial rights of Spain on these continents, though confirmed as between Great Britain and Spain by the first additional article to the treaty of the 5th of July, 1814, has been extinguished by the fact of the independence of the South American nations and of Mexico. Those independent nations will possess the rights incident to that condition, and their territories will of course be subject to no exclusive right of navigation in their vicinity, or of access to them by any foreign nation.

A necessary consequence of this state of things will be that the American continents henceforth will no longer be subjects of colonization. Occupied by civilized independent nations, they will be accessible to Europeans and to each other on that footing alone, and the Pacific Ocean in every part of it will remain open to the navigation of all nations, in like manner with the Atlantic.

Incidental to the condition of national independence and sovereignty, the rights of anterior navigation of their rivers will belong to each of the American nations within its own territories.

The application of colonial principles of exclusion, therefore, cannot be admitted by the United States as lawful upon any part of the northwest coast of America or as belonging to any European nation. Their own settlements there, when organized as territorial governments, will be adapted to the freedom of their own institutions and, as constituent parts of the Union, be subject to the principles and provisions of their constitutions.

The right of carrying on trade with the natives throughout the northwest coast they cannot renounce. With the Russian settlements at Kodiak, or at New Archangel, they may fairly claim the advantage of a free trade, having so long enjoyed it unmolested, and because it has been and would continue to be as advantageous at least to those settlements as to them. But they will not contest the right of Russia to prohibit the traffic, as strictly confined to the Russian settlement itself, and not extending to the original natives of the coast.

If the British Northwest and Hudson's Bay companies have any posts on the coast, as suggested in the article of the *Quarterly Review* above cited, the 3rd Article of the convention of October 20, 1818, is applicable to them. Mr. Middleton is authorized by his instructions to propose an article of similar import to be inserted in a joint convention between the United States, Great Britain, and Russia for a term of ten years from its signature. You are authorized to make the same proposal to the British government, and, with a view to draw a definite line of demarcation for the future, to stipulate that no settlement shall hereafter be made on the northwest coast or any of the islands thereto adjoining by Russian subjects south of latitude 55°, by citizens of the United States north of latitude 51°, or by British subjects either south of 51° or north of 55°. I mention the latitude of 51° as the bound within which we are willing to limit the future settlement of the United States because it is not to be doubted that the Columbia River branches as far north as 51°, although it is most probably not the Taconesche Tesse of Mackenzie. As, however, the line already runs in latitude 49° to the Stony Mountains, should it be earnestly insisted upon by Great Britain, we will consent to carry it in continuance on the same parallel to the sea.

11.

RICHARD RUSH: The Affinity of British and American Interests

Although the United States had recognized the new republics in Latin America in 1822, Great Britain had cautiously refrained from any such public recognition. Secretly, however, she had been aiding the rebels. Spain herself was in the throes of revolution, and, when France crossed the Pyrenees to quell the uprisings, it was with King Ferdinand VII's approval. Britain and the United States suspected that the Spanish monarch had agreed to form a Franco-Spanish expedition to retake Spain's American colonies. Fearing the British commercial interests were at stake, Foreign Minister George Canning spoke to Richard Rush, the U.S. minister to Great Britain, about the possibility of an Anglo-American declaration against any foreign intervention in Spanish America. The substance of their conversation was communicated to Secretary of State John Quincy Adams via the following letter, written on August 19, 1823, three days after the interview took place.

Source: MHSP, XV, pp. 412-415.

WHEN MY INTERVIEW with Mr. Canning on Saturday was about to close, I transiently asked him whether, notwithstanding the late news from Spain, we might not hope that the Spaniards would get the better of all their difficulties. I had allusion to the defection of Ballasteros in Andalusia, an event seeming to threaten with new dangers the constitutional cause. His reply was general, importing nothing more than his opinion of the increased difficulties and dangers with which, undoubtedly, this event was calculated to surround the Spanish cause.

Pursuing the topic of Spanish affairs, I remarked that should France ultimately effect her purposes in Spain, there was at least the consolation left that Great Britain would not allow her to go further and lay her hands upon the Spanish colonies, bringing them, too, under her grasp. I here had in my mind the sentiments promulgated upon this subject in Mr. Canning's note to the British ambassador at Paris of the 31st of March, during the negotiations that pre-

ceded the invasion of Spain. It will be recollected that the British government says in this note that time and the course of events appeared to have substantially decided the question of the separation of these colonies from the mother country. Although their formal recognition as independent states by Great Britain might be hastened or retarded by external circumstances, as well as by the internal condition of those new states themselves; and as His Britannic Majesty disclaimed all intention of appropriating to himself the smallest portion of the late Spanish possessions in America, he was also satisfied that no attempt would be made by France to bring any of them under her dominion, either by conquest or by cession from Spain.

By this we are to understand, in terms sufficiently distinct, that Great Britain would not be passive under such an attempt by France, and Mr. Canning, on my having referred to this note, asked me what I thought my government would say to going hand in hand with this, in the same sentiment; not, as he added, that any concert in action under it could become necessary between the two countries, but that the simple fact of our being known to hold the same sentiment would, he had no doubt, by its moral effect put down the intention on the part of France, admitting that she should ever entertain it. This belief was founded, he said, upon the large share of the maritime power of the world which Great Britain and the United States shared between them, and the consequent influence which the knowledge that they held a common opinion upon a question on which such large maritime interests, present and future, hung, could not fail to produce upon the rest of the world.

I replied that in what manner my government would look upon such a suggestion I was unable to say but that I would communicate it in the same informal manner in which he threw it out. I said, however, that I did not think I should do so with full advantage, unless he would at the same time enlighten me as to the precise situation in which His Majesty's government stood at this moment in relation to those new states, and especially on the material point of their own independence.

He replied that Great Britain certainly never again intended to lend her instrumentality or aid, whether by mediation or otherwise, toward making up the dispute between Spain and her colonies, but that, if this result could still be brought about, she would not interfere to prevent it. Upon my intimating that I had supposed that all ideas of Spain ever recovering her authority over the colonies had long since gone by, he explained that he did not mean to controvert that opinion, for he, too, believed that the day had arrived when all America might be considered as lost to Europe, so far as the tie of political dependence was concerned. All that he meant was that if Spain and the colonies should still be able to bring the dispute, not yet totally extinct between

them, to a close upon terms satisfactory to both sides, and which should at the same time secure to Spain commercial or other advantages not extended to other nations that Great Britain would not object to a compromise in this spirit of preference to Spain. All that she would ask would be to stand upon as favored a footing as any other nation after Spain. Upon my again alluding to the improbability of the dispute ever settling down now even upon this basis, he said that it was not his intention to maintain such a position and that he had expressed himself as above rather for the purpose of indicating the feeling which this cabinet still had toward Spain in relation to the controversy than of predicting results.

Wishing, however, to be still more specifically informed, I asked whether Great Britain was at this moment taking any step or contemplating any, which had reference to the recognition of these states, this being the point in which we felt the chief interest.

He replied that she had taken none whatever, as yet, but was upon the eve of taking one, not final, but preparatory, which would still leave her at large to recognize or not, according to the position of events at a future period. The measure in question was to send out one or more individuals under authority from this government to South America, not strictly diplomatic, but clothed with powers in the nature of a commission of inquiry and which in short he described as analogous to those exercised by our own commissioners in 1817, and upon the result of this commission much might depend as to the ulterior conduct of Great Britain. I asked whether I was to understand that it would comprehend all the new states, or which of them, to which he replied that for the present it would be limited to Mexico.

Reverting to his first idea, he again said that he hoped that France would not, should even events in the Peninsula be favorable to her, extend her views to South America for the purpose of reducing the colonies, nominally, perhaps, for Spain, but in effect to subserve ends of her own; but that in case she should meditate such a policy, he was satisfied that the knowledge of the United States being opposed to it, as well as Great Britain, could not fail to have its influence in checking her steps. . . .

I again told him that I would convey his suggestions to you for the information of the President and impart to him whatever reply I might receive. My own inference rather is that his proposition was a fortuitous one; yet he entered into it, I thought, with some interest and appeared to receive with a corresponding satisfaction the assurance I gave him that it should be made known to the President. I did not feel myself at liberty to express any opinion unfavorable to it and was as careful to give none in its favor.

Mr. Canning mentioned to me, at this same interview, that a late confidential dispatch which he had seen from Count Nesselrode to Count Lieven, dated, I think, in June, contained declarations respecting the Russian ukase relative to the northwest coast that were satisfactory; that they went to show that it would probably not be executed in a manner to give cause of complaint to other nations and that, in particular, it had not yet been executed in any instance under orders issued by Russia subsequently to its first promulgation.

12.

America and Europe

Following a discussion between Richard Rush, the U.S. minister at London, and George Canning, the British foreign minister, concerning a joint Anglo-American declaration of nonintervention in Latin America, the latter sent a formal proposal to the American minister on August 20, 1823. Without committing his country, Rush forwarded the proposal to President Monroe. Receiving the dispatch on October 9, the President consulted his political mentors, the retired Presidents Jefferson and Madison, as to their feelings on the subject. The first of the following selections is Monroe's letter of October 17 to Jefferson, in which Monroe expressed an inclination at variance with the action he eventually took in spelling out the Monroe Doctrine. Jefferson's reply of October 24 is also reprinted here. For the nation's security, he advised Monroe to accept Canning's proposal, a notable decision considering that he had done as much as anyone else to define the traditional American foreign policy of avoiding "entangling alliances."

Source: MHSP, XV, p. 375.   H. A. Washington, VII, pp. 315-317.

I.

MONROE TO JEFFERSON

I TRANSMIT TO YOU TWO DISPATCHES which were received from Mr. Rush while I was lately in Washington which involve interests of the highest importance. They contain two letters from Mr. Canning, suggesting designs of the Holy Alliance against the independence of South America and proposing a cooperation between Great Britain and the United States in support of it against the members of that alliance.

The project aims in the first instance at a mere expression of opinion, somewhat in the abstract, but which, it is expected by Mr. Canning, will have a great political effect by defeating the combination. By Mr. Rush's answers, which are also enclosed, you will see the light in which he views the subject and the extent to which he may have gone.

Many important considerations are involved in this proposition. (1) Shall we entangle ourselves, at all, in European politics and wars, on the side of any power, against others, presuming that a concert by agreement, of the kind proposed, may lead to that result? (2) If a case can exist in which a sound maxim may and ought to be departed from, is not the present instance precisely that case? (3) Has not the epoch arrived when Great Britain must take her stand, either on the side of the monarchs of Europe or of the United States and, in consequence, either in favor of despotism or of liberty, and may it not be presumed that, aware of that necessity, her government has seized on the present occurrence as that which it deems the most suitable to announce and mark the commencement of that career.

My own impression is that we ought to meet the proposal of the British government and to make it known that we would view an interference on the part of the European powers, and especially an attack on the colonies by them, as an attack on ourselves, presuming that, if they succeeded with them, they would extend it to us. I am sensible, however, of the extent and difficulty of the question and shall be happy to have yours, and Mr. Madison's opinions on it. I do not wish to trouble either of you with small objects, but the present one is vital, involving the high interests for which we have so long and so faithfully and harmoniously contended together. Be so kind as to enclose to him the dispatches, with an intimation of the motive.

II.

JEFFERSON TO MONROE

THE QUESTION PRESENTED by the letters you have sent me is the most momentous which has ever been offered to my contemplation since that of independence. That made us a nation; this sets our compass and points the course which we are to steer through the ocean of time opening on us. And never could we embark upon it under circumstances more auspicious.

Our first and fundamental maxim should be never to entangle ourselves in the broils of Europe; our second, never to suffer Europe to intermeddle with cis-Atlantic affairs. America, North and South, has a set of interests distinct from those of Europe and particularly her own. She should therefore have a system of her own, separate and apart from that of Europe. While the last is laboring to become the domicile of despotism, our endeavor should surely be to make our hemisphere that of freedom.

One nation, most of all, could disturb us in this pursuit; she now offers to lead, aid, and accompany us in it. By acceding to her proposition, we detach her from the bands of despots, bring her mighty weight into the scale of free government, and emancipate a continent at one stroke, which might otherwise linger long in doubt and difficulty. Great Britain is the nation which can do us the most harm of anyone, or all on earth; and with her on our side we need not fear the whole world. With her, then, we should most sedulously cherish a cordial friendship; and nothing would tend more to knit our affections than to be fighting once more, side by side, in the same cause. Not that I would purchase even her amity at the price of taking part in her wars.

But the war in which the present proposition might engage us, should that be its consequence, is not her war, but ours. Its object is to introduce and establish the American system of keeping out of our land all foreign powers — of never permitting those of Europe to intermeddle with the affairs of our nations. It is to maintain our own principle, not to depart from it. And if, to facilitate this, we can effect a division in the body of the European powers, and draw over to our side its most powerful member, surely we should do it.

But I am clearly of Mr. Canning's opinion that it will prevent instead of provoking war. With Great Britain withdrawn from their scale and shifted into that of our two continents, all Europe combined would not undertake such a war, for how would they propose to get at either enemy without superior fleets? Nor is the occasion to be slighted which this proposition offers of declaring our protest against the atrocious violations of the rights of nations by the interference of anyone in the internal affairs of another, so flagitiously begun by Bonaparte, and now continued by the equally lawless Alliance calling itself Holy.

But we have, first, to ask ourselves a question. Do we wish to acquire to our own confederacy any one or more of the Spanish provinces? I candidly confess that I have ever looked on Cuba as the most interesting addition which could ever be made to our system of states. The control which, with Florida point, this island would give us over the Gulf of Mexico and the countries and the isthmus bordering on it, as well as all those whose waters flow into it, would fill up the measure of our political well-being. Yet, as I am sensible that this can never be obtained, even with her own consent but by war, and its independence which is our second interest (and especially its independence of England), can be secured without it, I have no hesitation in abandoning my first wish to future chances,

and accepting its independence, with peace and the friendship of England, rather than its association, at the expense of war and her enmity.

I could honestly, therefore, join in the declaration proposed that we aim not at the acquisition of any of those possessions, that we will not stand in the way of any amicable arrangement between them and the mother country; but that we will oppose with all our means, the forcible interposition of any other power, as auxiliary, stipendiary, or under any other form or pretext, and most especially their transfer to any power by conquest, cession, or acquisition in any other way. I should think it, therefore, advisable that the executive should encourage the British government to a continuance in the dispositions expressed in these letters by an assurance of his concurrence with them as far as his authority goes; and that, as it may lead to war, the declaration of which requires an act of Congress, the case shall be laid before them for consideration at their first meeting and under the reasonable aspect in which it is seen by himself.

I have been so long weaned from political subjects, and have so long ceased to take any interest in them, that I am sensible I am not qualified to offer opinions on them worthy of any attention. But the question now proposed involves consequences so lasting, and effects so decisive, of our future destinies as to rekindle all the interest I have heretofore felt on such occasions and to induce me to the hazard of opinions, which will prove only my wish to contribute still my mite toward anything which may be useful to our country. And, praying you to accept it at only what it is worth, I add the assurance of my constant and affectionate friendship and respect.

13.

John Quincy Adams: On America and the Holy Alliance

*Early in November 1823, President Monroe's Cabinet met to discuss the proposal
of George Canning, the British foreign minister, to issue a joint Anglo-American
declaration against foreign intervention in Latin America. During the course of the
discussion, Secretary of State John Adams, who was suspicious of Britain's motives
for seeking such an alliance, expressed his skepticism about Canning's friendly
overture. Instead, he proposed that the time was ripe for a unilateral declaration by
the United States that would include a denunciation of any foreign attempts to intervene
in the Western Hemisphere. Adams reported the proceedings of this meeting of
November 7, 1823, in his* Memoirs, *from which the following is taken.*

Source: *Memoirs of John Quincy Adams, Comprising Portions of his Diary from 1795 to 1848,*
Charles Francis Adams, ed., Vol. VI, Philadelphia, 1875, pp. 177-181.

CABINET MEETING AT THE PRESIDENT'S from half-past one till four. Mr. Calhoun, secretary of war, and Mr. Southard, secretary of the navy, present. The subject for consideration was the confidential proposals of the British secretary of state, George Canning, to Richard Rush, and the correspondence between them relating to the projects of the Holy Alliance upon South America. There was much conversation, without coming to any definite point. The object of Canning appears to have been to obtain some public pledge from the government of the United States, ostensibly against the forcible interference of the Holy Alliance between Spain and South America; but really or especially against the acquisition to the United States themselves of any part of the Spanish-American possessions.

Mr. Calhoun inclined to giving a discretionary power to Mr. Rush to join in a declaration against the interference of the Holy Allies, if necessary, even if it should pledge us not to take Cuba or the province of Texas; because the power of Great Britain being greater than ours to seize upon them, we should get the advantage of obtaining from her the same declaration we should make ourselves.

I thought the case not parallel. We have no intention of seizing either Texas or Cuba. But the inhabitants of either or both may exercise their primitive rights, and solicit a union with us. They will certainly do no such thing to Great Britain. By joining with her, therefore, in her proposed declaration, we give her a substantial and perhaps inconvenient pledge against ourselves, and really obtain nothing in return. Without entering now into the inquiry of the expediency of our annexing Texas or Cuba to our Union, we should at least keep ourselves free to act as emergencies may arise, and not tie ourselves down to any principle which might immediately afterward be brought to bear against ourselves.

Mr. Southard inclined much to the same opinion.

The President was averse to any course which should have the appearance of taking a position subordinate to that of Great Britain, and suggested the idea of sending a special minister to protest against the interposition of the Holy Alliance.

I observed that it was a question for separate consideration, whether we ought in any event, if invited, to attend at a congress of the Allies on this subject.

Mr. Calhoun thought we ought in no case to attend.

The President, referring to instructions given before the Congress at Aix-la-Chapelle declaring that we would, if invited, attend no meeting relative to South America of which less than its entire independence should be the object, intimated that a similar limitation might be assumed now.

I remarked that we had then not recognized the South American independence ourselves. We would have been willing to recognize it in concert with the European Allies and therefore would have readily attended, if invited, a meeting of which that should have been the object. We could not now have the same motive. We *have* recognized them. We are very sure there will be now no meeting of the Allies with that object. There would, therefore, be no use or propriety in resorting to the same limitation. Our refusal to attend should be less explicit and unqualified.

To this the President readily assented.

I remarked that the communications recently received from the Russian minister, Baron Tuyl, afforded, as I thought, a very suitable and convenient opportunity for us to take our stand against the Holy Alliance, and at the same time to decline the overture of Great Britain. It would be more candid, as well as more dignified, to avow our principles explicitly to Russia and France, than to come in as a cockboat in the wake of the British man-of-war.

This idea was acquiesced on all sides. . . .

I remained with the President, and observed to him that the answer to be given to Baron Tuyl, the instructions to Mr. Rush relative to the proposals of Mr. Canning,

those to Mr. Middleton at St. Petersburg, and those to the minister who must be sent to France must all be parts of a combined system of policy and adapted to each other; in which he fully concurred. I added that as Baron Tuyl had made one part of his communications written and another verbal, if I should answer the whole in one written note it might place him personally in an awkward predicament. My official intercourse with the Baron had always been of the friendliest character, and I was desirous of observing with him all the forms of courtesy and kindness.

The President then proposed that I should confine my written answer to the purport of the Baron's written note and see the Baron again upon the verbal part of his communication. This course I shall accordingly take. I told the President I would see the Baron before sending him my written answer. I would then say that, having informed the President of what had passed between us at our recent conferences, he had approved the verbal answer that I had given to the Baron, and had directed me to add that, receiving in friendly part the expression of the Emperor's wish that the United States may continue to observe the neutrality announced on their recognition of the South American governments, he wished the Baron to state to his government, in return, the desire of that of the United States that the Emperor, on his part, should continue to observe the same neutrality. The Baron would make this the subject of a dispatch to his government, which I presume he would, according to his custom, show me before sending it off; and I could commit the substance of all these conferences to writing in the form of a report to the President. Of all this he approved.

The discussion at the cabinet meeting took a wide range. It was observed that Mr. Canning had not disclosed to Mr. Rush the special facts upon which he expected there would be a congress to settle the affairs of South America; and Mr. Calhoun expressed some surprise that Mr. Rush did not appear to have made of him any inquiries on that point.

I observed that I was rather glad of the objection of the British government to the *preliminary* recognition, as I should be sorry that we should be *committed* upon Canning's propositions, even so far as we might have been, by Mr. Rush on his own responsibility.

Calhoun wondered what could be the objection of Great Britain to the recognition.

I said there were two reasons: one, the aversion to fly directly in the face of the Holy Alliance; and, second, the engagements of her treaties with Spain, particularly that of July 5, 1814.

Calhoun and Southard thought that Great Britain would in no event take a stand against the Holy Alliance on South American affairs unless sure of our cooperation. She could not be belligerent leaving us neutral, because it must throw the whole commerce of the adverse party into our hands. It was the opinion of us all that a minister must immediately be sent to France.

14.

JAMES MONROE: The Monroe Doctrine

The Monroe Doctrine comprised some general remarks on foreign policy that President James Monroe included in his annual message to Congress on December 2, 1823. The first draft of the message included a reproof to the French for their invasion of Spain, an acknowledgment of Greek independence in the revolt against Turkey, and some further indications of American concern in European affairs. Secretary of State John Quincy Adams argued for the better part of two days against such expressions, which were finally eliminated from the message. "The ground that I wish to take," Adams noted in his Diary, *"is that of earnest remonstrance against the interference of the European powers by force in South America, but to disclaim all interference on our part with Europe; to make an American cause, and adhere inflexibly to that." Despite the ambiguities that have surrounded the application of this policy since its inception, one theme was clear: There were two worlds, the Old and the New; each must lead its separate existence, always aware of a bond between them, but never intervening in the affairs of the other.*

Source: Richardson, II, pp. 207-220.

A PRECISE KNOWLEDGE of our relations with foreign powers as respects our negotiations and transactions with each is thought to be particularly necessary. . . .

At the proposal of the Russian Imperial government, made through the minister of the emperor residing here, full power and instructions have been transmitted to the minister of the United States at St. Petersburg to arrange by amicable negotiation the respective rights and interests of the two nations on the northwest coast of this conti-

(Left) First page of the draft version of Monroe's State of the Union message, 1823, outlining to Congress the policies of the "Monroe Doctrine"; (center) conclusion of the Monroe Doctrine speech; (above) portrait of James Monroe by Gilbert Stuart

nent. A similar proposal had been made by His Imperial Majesty to the government of Great Britain, which has likewise been acceded to. The government of the United States has been desirous, by this friendly proceeding, of manifesting the great value which they have invariably attached to the friendship of the emperor and their solicitude to cultivate the best understanding with his government.

In the discussions to which this interest has given rise and in the arrangements by which they may terminate the occasion has been judged proper for asserting, as a principle in which the rights and interests of the United States are involved, that the American continents, by the free and independent condition which they have assumed and maintain, are henceforth not to be considered as subjects for future colonization by any European powers. . . .

It was stated at the commencement of the last session that great effort was then making in Spain and Portugal to improve the condition of the people of those coun-

tries and that it appeared to be conducted with extraordinary moderation. It need scarcely be remarked that the result has been so far very different from what was then anticipated. Of events in that quarter of the globe with which we have so much intercourse and from which we derive our origin, we have always been anxious and interested spectators. The citizens of the United States cherish sentiments the most friendly in favor of the liberty and happiness of their fellowmen on that side of the Atlantic. In the wars of the European powers in matters relating to themselves we have never taken any part, nor does it comport with our policy so to do. It is only when our rights are invaded or seriously menaced that we resent injuries or make preparation for our defense.

With the movements in this hemisphere we are of necessity more immediately connected, and by causes which must be obvious to all enlightened and impartial observers. The political system of the allied powers is essentially different in this respect from that of America. This difference proceeds from that which exists in their respective governments; and to the defense of our own, which has been achieved by the loss of so much blood and treasure, and matured by the wisdom of their most enlightened citizens, and under which we have enjoyed unexampled felicity, this whole nation is devoted. We owe it, therefore, to candor and to the amicable relations existing between the United States and those powers to declare that we should consider any attempt on their part to extend their system to any portion of this hemisphere as dangerous to our peace and safety.

With the existing colonies or dependencies of any European power we have not interfered and shall not interfere. But with the governments who have declared their independence and maintained it, and whose independence we have, on great consideration and on just principles, acknowledged, we could not view any interposition for the purpose of oppressing them, or controlling in any other manner their destiny, by any European power in any other light than as the manifestation of an unfriendly disposition toward the United States. In the war between those new governments and Spain we declared our neutrality at the time of their recognition, and to this we have adhered, and shall continue to adhere, provided no change shall occur which, in the judgment of the competent authorities of this government, shall make a corresponding change on the part of the United States indispensable to their security.

The late events in Spain and Portugal show that Europe is still unsettled. Of this important fact no stronger proof can be adduced than that the allied powers should have thought it proper, on any principle satisfactory to themselves, to have interposed by force in the internal concerns of Spain. To what extent such interposition may be carried, on the same principle, is a question in which all independent powers whose governments differ from theirs are interested, even those most remote, and surely none more so than the United States.

Our policy in regard to Europe, which was adopted at an early stage of the wars which have so long agitated that quarter of the globe, nevertheless remains the same, which is not to interfere in the internal concerns of any of its powers; to consider the government de facto as the legitimate government for us; to cultivate friendly relations with it, and to preserve those relations by a frank, firm, and manly policy, meeting in all instances the just claims of every power, submitting to injuries from none. But in regard to those continents, circumstances are eminently and conspicuously different. It is impossible that the allied powers should extend their political system to any portion of either continent without endangering our peace and happiness; nor can anyone believe that our southern brethren, if left to themselves, would adopt it of their own accord.

It is equally impossible, therefore, that we should behold such interposition in any form with indifference. If we look to the comparative strength and resources of Spain and those new governments, and their distance from each other, it must be obvious that she can never subdue them. It is still the true policy of the United States to leave the parties to themselves, in the hope that other powers will pursue the same course.

15.

Anonymous: Fears About Prison Labor

Many early nineteenth-century prison systems focused on rehabilitative rather than punitive methods in dealing with prisoners, who in some institutions were encouraged to practise a trade. This system was valuable as a reform measure and also provided a source of revenue for the state when state prisons were involved. However, as prison labor was free and its products and services could be sold at lower prices than those of the regular labor force, workers began to complain. Organized unions did not exist, but the collective voice of craftsmen, mechanics, and others was raised against the effects of prison labor on the labor market. One such protest of 1823 is reprinted below.

Source: *New York Mechanics' Gazette*, May 17, 1823 [Commons, V, p. 51].

You SEE, SIR, what the employment of state prisoners in the mechanic trades will lead to. I presume you see it; for I cannot believe that any can be so blind as not to discover the dissatisfaction it creates in the minds of all those whose business happens to be introduced in the prison.

You now perceive that the cabinetmakers have had a meeting, and that they protest in strong language against the employment of prisoners in their art. The cabinetmakers now begin to feel alarmed; they now are awakened to a sense of their interest and their duty in endeavoring to put a stop to this vile business of manufacturing in the prison to the disadvantage of mechanics, and mechanics only. They now see that the brushmakers, combmakers, shoemakers, and others had cause to complain; and I hope they will also see, as well as all other mechanics, that the only way left for redress is for all the mechanics, whether their business be at present interfered with or not, to turn out at the next general election, and to elect or give their suffrages to such, and such only, as will pledge themselves to use their best endeavors to stop the evils of which we so justly complain.

Let no man who is a mechanic think himself safe because his business is not conducted in the prison; for he knows not how soon an attempt may be made to wrest from him what must be ever dear to him, a fair opportunity of supporting his wife and children by the labor of his hands and the profit of his trade.

16.

George Ticknor: Curriculum Reform at Harvard

Until the 1820s, American institutions of higher education had resisted the attempts of reformers to change their curriculum or their organizational structure both of which were based on a standard course in the classics. Faculties and facilities were inadequate owing to a lack of funds and of public interest; most Americans, including academics, viewed the college's function as mainly disciplinary and were seldom concerned with serious scholarship. George Ticknor, who assumed the Smith Chair of Modern Languages at Harvard in 1819, was disturbed by the condition of American education. He had recently been in Germany, where he had been particularly impressed by the university system of departmentalized courses of study. Ticknor believed in the feasibility of applying European educational procedures to Harvard, and on July 23, 1823, he presented a paper outlining his proposals to members of the Harvard faculty. Portions of his remarks are reprinted below.

Source: *Life, Letters, and Journals of George Ticknor*, 9th edition, Boston, 1878, Vol. I, pp. 356-359.

It is, I think, an unfortunate circumstance that all our colleges have been so long considered merely places for obtaining a degree of bachelor of arts to serve as a means and certificate whereon to build the future plans and purposes of life. Such a state of things was, indeed, unavoidable at the earlier period of our college, when there was only a president, who sometimes lived permanently in Boston, and a few tutors, who kept a school in Newton; for the number of scholars was so small that it was possible to teach only by classes, and each student, the number being also small, could pass through the hands of every one of them and receive from everyone all the instruction he could give.

But now the state of the case is reversed. There are 20 or more teachers, and 300 students, and yet the division into classes remains exactly the same, and every student is obliged to pass through the hands of nearly or quite every instructor. Of course, the recitations become mere examinations, and it cannot be attempted to give more than the most superficial view of very important subjects, even to those who would gladly investigate them thoroughly, because they must keep with the class to which they are bound and hurry on from a teacher and subject to which they have, perhaps, important reasons for being attached, to another teacher and another subject, wherein their present dispositions and final pursuits in life make it impossible for them to feel any interest.

But at the same time that we at once perceive this system . . . has been carried too far . . . we must still feel that it has in some respects its peculiar advantages. The majority of the young men who come to Cambridge should not be left entirely to

Copy of Thomas Sully's portrait of George Ticknor

themselves to choose what they will study because they are not competent to judge what will be most important for them; and yet no parent would wish to have his child pursue branches of knowledge which he is sure can never be of use to him in future life.

A beneficial compromise can, however, as it seems to me, be effected between the old system still in operation and the most liberal concessions that would be demanded by one of the merely free and philosophical universities of Europe. . . .

Now if this be the condition of the college, which I do not doubt, or if anything like it exist there, which nobody will deny, it is perfectly apparent that a great and thorough change must take place in its discipline and instruction; not to bring it up to the increasing demands of the community, but to make it fulfill the purposes of a respectable high school to which young men may be safely sent to be prepared for the study of a profession. . . .

Whenever the tribunal of three are satisfied that a young man does not fulfill the purposes for which he came to college, they should be required instantly to dismiss him, for his own sake, for the sake of his friends, and for the sake of the college, since from that moment he becomes a nuisance; for, if it be mere dullness, he is out of his vice, he is continually spreading mischief around him. . . . The longest vacation should happen in the hot season, when insubordination and misconduct are now most frequent, partly from the indolence produced by the season. There is a reason against this, I know: the poverty of many students, who keep school for a part of their subsistence. . . .

And it would be difficult to prove that it is always even poverty that is encouraged, for, of sixteen beneficiaries in the senior class, only nine were last winter so poor as to be compelled to resort to schoolkeeping; so that, on all accounts, I think it is apparent the college can fulfill all its duties to the poorer portion of the community without resorting to the winter vacation. . . .

For myself, I will gladly perform all the duties that fall to my office as Smith Professor and give besides a full twelfth of all the additional common instruction at college for the three next years, provided this reform may take place, and such branches be assigned to me as I can teach with profit to the school. I am persuaded every other teacher would be equally willing to pledge himself to extra labors in such a cause. . . .

But one thing is certain. A change must take place. The discipline of college must be made more exact, and the instruction more thorough. All now is too much in the nature of a show and abounds too much in false pretenses. . . . It is seen that we are neither a university, which we call ourselves, nor a respectable high school, which we ought to be, and that with "*Christo et Ecclesiae*" for our motto, the morals of great numbers of the young men who come to us are corrupted. We must therefore change, or public confidence, which is already hesitating, will entirely desert us. If we can ever have a university at Cambridge which shall lead the intellectual character of the country, it can be, I apprehend, only when the present college shall have been settled into a thorough and well-disciplined high school, where the young men of the country shall be carefully prepared to begin their professional studies, and where in medicine, law, and theology sufficient inducements shall have been collected around and within the college . . . to keep graduates there two years longer, at least, and probably three. . . .

We have now learned that as many years are passed in our schools and colleges and professional preparation as are passed in the same way, and for the same purpose, in the best schools in Europe, while it is perfectly apparent that nothing like the same results are obtained; so that we have only to choose whether the reproach shall rest on the talents of our young men, or on the instruction and discipline of our institutions for teaching them. Now, as there can be no doubt which of the two is in fault, our colleges, constituting as they do the most important portion of our means of teaching, must come in for their full share of the blame. There may be defects, and there are defects, I know, in the previous preparation of the young men, but the defects at college are greater and graver.

17.

Anonymous: On the Louisiana Penal Code

Until the nineteenth century, few states enacted statutory provisions in the field of criminal law, and most cases were tried on the basis of English common law. Under the leadership of pro-Jackson Democrats like Edward Livingston, a move toward definite and inclusive penal codes developed, although in most states common law continued to have force in the courts. Livingston, a newly elected representative in the Louisiana legislature, was commissioned to revise the state's penal code in 1821. Working within the framework of the theory that the final effect of criminal law should be preventative and reformative rather than punitive, he produced an eight-volume code in 1825. The following selection is an extract from a review published in 1823 of Livingston's preliminary plan. It is interspersed with quotations from his Report on the penal code, *presented to the legislature in 1822.*

Source: *North American Review*, October 1823.

MR. LIVINGSTON'S REPORT was made in consequence of an act of the General Assembly of Louisiana relative to the criminal laws of that state, passed in February 1820, which, after adverting in the Preamble to the primary importance of judicious criminal laws to every well-regulated state, and the defectiveness of those already existing there, proceeds to declare that a person should be chosen by the legislature to prepare and present to them the *projet* of a suitable penal code for Louisiana. This honorable task was accordingly assigned to Mr. Livingston, whom, with a confidence equally flattering to him and creditable to the state, the legislature appointed to carry their designs into execution; and to these proceedings we are indebted for the report.

As this is the first instance, we believe, in our country in which a radical reform of the criminal laws of a state has been systematically and deliberately undertaken, we rejoice that the attempt was commenced under such favorable auspices. We congratulate the state of Louisiana that so many propitious circumstances have conspired, in the present experiment, to give it a chance of fair and unembarrassed trial, so far as the intrinsic perfection of the code can minister to its successful operation in practice. And we consider it as not the least propitious of these circumstances that a jurist was selected to prepare the plan, whose personal qualities are an adequate pledge and guarantee of the excellence of whatever comes from beneath his hand, and whose public standing is such that he must move in a sphere far above the influence of any inducements but an ambition to promote the best good of his country and his species.

It was an advantage, also, of no inconsiderable weight, that only a single person was charged with this noble trust — that Mr. Livingston was not encumbered and shackled in the prosecution of his inquiries by a subjection to the opinions of associates in his important functions, but was wisely left to the guidance of his own individual intellect. Had the task of compiling a criminal code been committed to several persons instead of one alone, we believe the symmetry and excellence of the work would have been essentially impaired. . . .

The code is divided into six books. The first is composed of definitions of technical words and directions with regard to the promulgation of the code; the second contains a preamble and certain dispositions of a general and introductory nature; the third defines offenses and designates their punishment; the fourth establishes a system of criminal procedure; the fifth contains rules of evidence applicable to trials for the several offenses made punishable by the code; and the last relates to the establishment and government of a penitentiary. . . .

Mr. Livingston proposes, among other smaller changes, four principal deviations from the crimes designated by the common law, all which deviations are defended with great eloquence and with a cogency of reasoning which it is certainly difficult to withstand. The first of them is a modification of the law respecting complicity. Our juridical readers will recollect that, by the common law, any "person, who, knowing a felony to have been committed, receives, relieves, comforts, or assists the felon," is styled an accessory after the fact and, in most cases, subjected to the same punishment as the principal offender. By the provisions of the new code of Louisiana, such an act is to cease to be criminal in relations of the principal in the ascending or descending line, or in the collateral, as far as the first degree, or in persons united to him by marriage, or owing him obedience as a servant. . . .

Whatever doubt there may be, however, with respect to the expediency of this change, there can be none as to the two next proposed by Mr. Livingston. The reasons which induced him to expunge from his code the act of suicide and another, whose name ought never to pollute the laws of a civilized people, we think are unanswerable. . . .

The three changes on which we have commented are omissions of crimes recognized by the common law as it exists in England and is adopted in most of the United States. The last change in the enumeration of public offenses recommended by Mr. Livingston is the creation of a new class, against the freedom of the press. He remarks:

It has generally been thought a sufficient protection [of the liberty of the press] to declare that no punishment should be inflicted on those who legally exercise the right of publishing; but hitherto no penalties have been denounced against those who illegally abridge this liberty. Constitutional provisions are, in our republics, universally introduced to assert the right, but no sanction is given to the law. Yet do not the soundest principles require it? If the liberty of publishing be a right, is it sufficient to say that no one shall be punished for exercising it? I have a right to possess my property, yet the law does not confine itself to a declaration that I shall not be punished for using it; something more is done; and it is fenced round with penalties, imposed on those who deprive me of its enjoyment. . . .

All violence, or menace of violence, or any other of the means which are enumerated in the code; all exercise of official influence or authority which may abridge this valuable privilege is declared to be an offense. Nay, the project which will be presented to you goes further, and, considering the constitutional provision as paramount to any act of ordinary legislation, and consequently that all laws in derogation of it are void, it declares all those guilty of an offense who shall execute any law abridging or restraining the liberty of the press contrary to the privilege secured by the constitution.

We confess that this improvement strikes us as being rather fanciful, and, what is worse, as unnecessary and incapable of answering any useful purpose. Mr. Livingston cannot be more ardently attached to a free press than ourselves, nor more resolute to maintain it to the best of our ability, in its full integrity, at every hazard. Most fervently do we respond to the declaration of our own constitution, that "the liberty of the press is essential to the security of freedom in a state." But we think this liberty is sufficiently guarded by the removal of all restrictions on its legitimate use. From whom are we to apprehend any infringement of it, which a penal sanction in the laws could prevent? Not surely from persons in their private, individual capacity; because the liberty is of such a nature that no direct invasion of it can be made by private persons. It is not in the power of man to impede us in the mere publication of our sentiments by any immediate act for which the laws do not sufficiently provide.

In revenge of what we have published, or in anticipation of what we intend to publish, he may attack, seize, imprison our persons; he may denounce our principles and defame our characters; he may deface or destroy our manuscripts, or sheets, or scatter their fragments abroad to the winds of heaven; he may break up our apparatus for printing and disperse our types or shake them together into inextricable confusion; but who would pretend that either of these acts was, properly speaking, an invasion of the freedom of the press? They are all infringements of the rights of personal security, liberty, or property, for which the comprehensive remedies of the common law already afford adequate redress. No direct attack can be made on the freedom of the press *as such* but by some branch of the government.

Now, if the executive or judicial authorities attempt to debar a citizen from the free use of a privilege accorded him by the laws, the injured party may proceed against the wrongdoer as a private individual, amenable, like other individuals, to the municipal laws of his country; or he may pursue the constitutional remedy of an impeachment of such wrongdoer for the illegal act as perpetrated in his official capacity; or he may do both; and in this alternative, he certainly has most ample opportunity to obtain legal indemnification for his injury. In short, there is but one source in our republics from which any serious attack on the liberty of the press can be rationally apprehended and that is the legislature. Should our legislative halls ever become a field for the ambitious efforts of unprincipled men, it would evidently be for their interest and would probably be their endeavor to abridge and circumscribe the operations of the press, which, if free, could not fail to oppose the most formidable resistance to the execution of any project for subverting the constitution.

Now, if such a crisis in the affairs of Louisiana should hereafter occur, how is it that the penal denunciations in the new code can chain the hands of the General Assembly? They do not become incorporated in the constitution. The same power which enacts the code may repeal it. Nor do we think it sufficient to reply to this objection, as Mr. Livingston does, that "the repeal of this part of the code would be an acknowledgment, on the part of those who procured it, that they were hostile to the right secured by the constitution"; and that this no representative would dare to avow. If it were reasonable to suppose this would prevent the repeal of the provisions in question, still it could not prevent the execution of those insidious practices against the freedom of the press, which, our author very justly intimates, are much more to be dreaded than direct and open attacks.

Suppose some future legislature should endeavor to abridge and circumscribe the liberty of the press by passing a law to declare certain descriptions of writing libelous. If the law was incompatible with the constitution, it would be merely void and so could do no harm. If it was constitutional — if it was a law which it was fully within the authority of the legislature to enact — we see no way by which Mr. Livingston's plan could prevent its being executed; because the courts cannot have a right to animadvert on the legislature for the exercise of a strictly constitutional power. Furthermore, we do not conceive it to be necessary to protect the liberty of the press by penal laws against its infringement. It is no more requisite in this case than it is in order to protect the liberty of conscience — a liberty as dear, unquestionably, to freemen and to Americans as that of the press.

If the laws grant every man the right of enjoying perfect freedom in respect to his religious sentiments so long as the public safety or the corresponding right of his fellow citizens is not compromised, his freedom is secure, and he ought to ask for nothing more from the state. So it is, in our opinion, with regard to the liberty of the press. We do not deny that there are many very serious defects in the present law of libel; and we should rejoice to see the leading provisions in Mr. Brougham's famous bill for securing the liberty of the press and preventing its abuses adopted on this side the Atlantic; but we feel satisfied that our present system of laws, when so amended, would abundantly suffice to protect the exercise of this invaluable privilege in its full extent.

We have enlarged on this topic considerably, both because of its importance in itself and because we entertain such high respect for the judgment and opinions of Mr. Livingston that we were unwilling to differ from him materially without assigning our reasons at some length.

Mr. Livingston next proceeds to consider a portion of criminal law, which is undoubtedly the most important, namely, the means of securing obedience to its prohibitory and mandatory provisions, or the punishment of crimes. . . . Banishment, deportation, simple imprisonment or imprisonment in chains, confiscation of property, exposure to public derision, labor on public works, mutilation or other indelible marks of disgrace, stripes or the infliction of other bodily pain are all of them punishments which the good sense of the people of our country in general, no less than the sober conviction of men who make this a subject of philosophical inquiry, has almost universally condemned as alike inconsistent with the principles of justice and humanity, unsuited to the temper of the times, and hostile to the liberal spirit of all our laws, customs, habits, and institutions. Mr. Livingston has done, we apprehend, what the great mass of his countrymen will cordially approve, in throwing these altogether out of the question in the compilation of his code; and, in abolishing, at the same time, the punishment of death, he has ventured upon the trial of a system whose efficacy all humane men will rejoice to see thoroughly tried, whatever doubt may exist with regard to the issue.

For the reason just mentioned, as also that we have heretofore expressed our opinion very fully . . . on the subject of all the descriptions of punishment discarded by Mr. Livingston but death, we may pass over them here; but we crave the attention of our readers while we enter briefly into the examination of his remarks on this last head. While so many wise and excellent persons continue to think the exigencies of social order require us to stop, in the career of penal reform, at the point beyond which Mr. Livingston has dared to go, we do not feel prepared to urge unreservedly the expediency of abandoning capital punishments; but we desire to state why we rejoice, as we said, that the experiment is about to be tried in Louisiana, and why we wish it might be tried in her sister states. . . .

The advocates of the punishment of death in this country are not desirous, we believe, to extend it to more than five or six of the most flagitious crimes, such as treason, murder, robbery, arson of a dwellinghouse, and a few others of a like dangerous stamp, which, as they contend, the security of society demands should be thus rigorously punished. Now let us suppose that a misguided man, infatuated by the temporary madness of revengeful passions, raises his hand against the life of another; or, urged and goaded on by the stimulus of imperious want, seizes, with licentious rapacity, the gold which fortune has bestowed upon his more prosperous fellow. When the strong arm of the law has arrested the unhappy offender — who, if he deserves to be con-

demned for his guilt, deserves also to be pitied for his weakness — in what manner shall violated justice visit his crime?

Shall she array herself in wrath and pursue him with the sternness of private vengeance? No — she personates the majesty and integrity of the laws; it is not for her to indulge in those very passions which have troubled the world's peace. Shall she presume to scrutinize his heart and then hurl down her indignation upon the criminality which she imagines she can discover there? O, no — she herself does but speak the voice of poor fallible man; it is not for human justice to assume the attributes or arrogate the prerogatives of heaven. She has detected a member of the community in a daring attack upon its vital interests — she has apprehended him in arms against the public tranquillity — she has found him, if you please, throwing off the protection of the laws and overleaping the pale of the social compact. What then? Shall she serve him as was practised of old in England with outlawed felons, who, having renounced all law, were said to have *caput lupinum*; shall she declare that he may be hunted down and slain, wheresoever he can be caught, as a beast of prey?

This is what the advocates of capital punishment would have her do; but surely the national power is most unworthily used if it be wreaked thus terribly upon the wretch, whom it ought in the beginning to have withheld from committing crime, and whom, now that it is too late to prevent his guilt, it should endeavor to reclaim to society and enable to atone for his sin by passing the residue of his days in penitence and usefulness.

But we shall be told it is not enough to dispose of this single individual. The good of society requires, when the laws have been violated, that the offender should be so dealt with as by the salutary influence of his example to deter others from a repetition of his offense. Although as respects this individual himself, if he stood alone, it would be the right of the government to take measures only to secure his future obedience; yet, as some method must be devised to sanction the laws, the government has a further right to sacrifice him at the shrine of public justice for the benefit of the community, whose protection he has forfeited.

It is at this point — the comparative force of death as an example — that our author takes up the argument, which he chiefly confines to this consideration. He contends that the fear of the privation of life does not exert so powerful an influence on the mind as many other motives which are within the control of a legislator; and that, if you make the spectacle of the infliction of death common, it debases and brutalizes the public sentiment; if you make it rare, it converts the criminal into a martyr; and, in either alternative, does more evil than good. . . .

Our author next goes into a variety of considerations in support of his views, all tending to show that the infliction of death at any time as a punishment is unnecessary, impolitic, unjust, and hurtful to the good order of society. He concedes, however, and we think wisely, that governments have an undoubted right to inflict it, provided it can be proved necessary to the preservation of public and private peace. . . .

We have followed Mr. Livingston so closely thus far, that, for what remains of his code, where there is less of novelty and more of the uncontested principles of law, we content ourselves with referring to the pages of the report. We have been attracted to the discussion of the subject by the consideration that even at this day, widely and profoundly as the researches of philosophers have been pushed, there is still much to learn of a subject which embraces the entire range of man's actions, his physical and moral constitution, habits, feelings, propensities, destiny. . . . Where truths in the science of remedial law are so clearly demonstrated as to be fundamental axioms, still the improvements, which they dictate, remain to be adopted, and men yet obstinately and pertinaciously cling to their inveterate prejudices.

The names of two hundred capital offenses continue recorded in the statute book of England. In that country, ministerial influence has not yet ceased to elude, nor ministerial sophistry ceased to resist, the repeal of laws the most absurd in principle, the most pernicious in operation. But in America, all the most odious features in the penal laws of our fatherland, with but few exceptions, have yielded themselves up, and what remains cannot long maintain itself in opposition to the healthful influences of the young spirit of freedom.

Our emancipation from the tyranny of the feudal institutions is fast approaching its full accomplishment. And Mr. Livingston's code, although confined in the immediate sphere of its operation to Louisiana, will sensibly contribute, we doubt not, to the diffusion of an unexceptionably liberal system of criminal law throughout the United States.

18.

Felix Grundy: A Protest Against the Caucus System

Under the congressional caucus system, candidates for the offices of President and Vice-President were nominated by members of their party in Congress. The system was first used in 1796, when Washington retired from office and there was a difference of opinion over who should succeed him. The caucus system of nominating candidates was often attacked as undemocratic, and the attacks upon it became so frequent with the rise of the Jacksonian Democrats that after 1824 the congressional caucus ceased to exist. The following resolutions, proposed by Felix Grundy and adopted by the Tennessee legislature in 1823, show the reasons for the unpopularity of such a system for obtaining candidates for high office. With the demise of the caucus system came the rise of the political party convention.

Source: *Niles' Weekly Register*, November 1, 1823.

The General Assembly of the state of Tennessee has taken into consideration the practice which, on former occasions, has prevailed at the city of Washington, of members of the Congress of the United States meeting in caucus, and nominating persons to be voted for as President and Vice-President of the United States; and, upon the best view of the subject which this General Assembly has been able to take, it is believed that the practice of congressional nominations is a violation of the spirit of the Constitution of the United States.

That instrument provides that there shall be three separate and distinct departments of the government, and great care and caution seems to have been exercised by its framers to prevent any one department from exercising the smallest degree of influence over another; and such solicitude was felt on this subject, that, in the 2nd Section of the 2nd Article, it is expressly declared, "That no senator or representative, or person holding an office of trust or profit under the United States, shall be appointed an elector." From this provision, it is apparent that the Convention intended that the

members of Congress should not be the principal and primary agents or actors in electing the President and Vice-President of the United States; so far from it, they are expressly disqualified from being placed in a situation to vote for these high officers.

Is there not more danger of undue influence to be apprehended when the members of Congress meet in caucus and mutually and solemnly pledge themselves to support the individuals who may have the highest number of votes in such meeting than there would be in permitting them to be eligible to the appointment of electors? In the latter case, a few characters rendered ineligible by the Constitution might succeed; but, in the former, a powerful combination of influential men is formed, who may fix upon the American people their highest officers against the consent of a clear majority of the people themselves; and this may be done by the very men whom the Constitution intended to prohibit from acting on the subject.

Upon an examination of the Constitution of the United States, there is but one case in which the members of Congress are per-

Portrait of Felix Grundy

mitted to act, which is in the event of a failure to make an election by the electoral college; and then the members of the House of Representatives vote by states. With what propriety the same men, who, in the year 1825, may be called on to discharge a constitutional duty, can, in the year 1824, go into a caucus and pledge themselves to support the men then nominated, cannot be discerned, especially when it might so happen that the persons thus nominated could not, under any circumstances, obtain a single vote from the state whose members stand pledged to support them.

It is said that an election by the House of Representatives would be a dangerous occurrence which ought to be avoided. If so, let the Constitution be so changed as to avoid it; but so long as the Constitution directs one mode of electing officers, let not a different mode prevail in practice. When the history of the American government is looked into with an eye to this subject, the apprehended danger disappears. Experience long since pointed out the inconveniences of the original provision in the Constitution on this subject. An amendment, calculated, as was supposed, to remove every obstacle, was proposed by our wisest statesmen — it was adopted by the American people, and no difficulty has presented itself in subsequent practice. Shall a fear that the amendment made may fail to answer the end proposed by it induce us to adopt a course, or persist in a practice, which is manifestly an evasion of the Constitution and a direct infraction of the spirit of one of its most important provisions?

It has been said that the members of Congress in caucus only recommend to the people for whom to vote, and that such recommendation is not obligatory. This is true and clearly proves that it is a matter which does not belong to them — that, in recommending candidates, they go beyond the authority committed to them as members of Congress and thus transcend the trust delegated to them by their constituents. If their acts had any obligatory force, then the authority must be derived from some part of the Constitution of the United States and might be rightfully exercised; but when they say they only *recommend*, it is an admission, on their part, that they are acting without authority and are attempting, by a usurped influence, to effect an object not confided to them and not within their powers, even by implication.

It cannot be admitted that there is any weight in the argument drawn from the fact that both the parties, heretofore contending for the superiority in the United States, have, in former times, resorted to this practice. The actions of public or private men, heated by party zeal and struggling for ascendency and power, ought not to be urged as precedents when circumstances have entirely changed. All political precedents are of doubtful authority and should never be permitted to pass unquestioned, unless

made in good times and for laudable purposes. In palliation of the practice of resorting to caucus nominations in former times,
it was said that each party must of necessity
consult together in the best practicable way
and select the most suitable persons from
their respective parties so that the united efforts of all those composing it might be
brought to bear upon their opponents. It is
to be recollected that there is no danger of
a departure from or violation of the Constitution, except when strong temptations are
presented, and this will seldom occur, except when parties are arrayed against each
other and their feelings violently excited.

The state of things, however, in the United States is entirely changed; it is no longer
a selection made by members of Congress
of different parties, but it is an election by
the two houses of Congress, in which all
the members must be permitted to attend
and vote. It is not difficult to perceive that
this practice may promote and place men in
office who could not be elected were the
constitutional mode pursued. It is placing
the election of President and Vice-President
of the United States — an election in
which all the states have an equal interest
and equal rights — more in the power of a
few of the most populous states than was
contemplated by the Constitution. This
practice is considered objectionable on other
accounts: so long as Congress is considered
as composed of the individuals on whom
the election depends, the executive will is
subjected to the control of that body, and it
ceases, in some degree, to be a separate and
independent branch of the government; and
and expectation of executive patronage may
have an unhappy influence on the deliberations of Congress.

Upon a review of the whole question, the
following reasons which admit of much am-
plification and enlargement, more than has
been urged in the foregoing, might be conclusively relied on to prove the impolicy
and unconstitutionality of the congressional

nominations of candidates for the presidency and vice-presidency of the United States:
1. A caucus nomination is against the spirit
of the Constitution. 2. It is both inexpedient and impolitic. 3. Members of Congress
may become the final electors and therefore
ought not to prejudge the case by pledging
themselves previously to support particular
candidates. 4. It violates the equality intended to be secured by the Constitution to the
weaker states. 5. Caucus nominations may,
in time (by the interference of the states),
acquire the force of precedents and become
authoritative and, thereby, endanger the
liberties of the American people.

This General Assembly, believing that the
true spirit of the Constitution will be best
preserved by leaving the election of President and Vice-President to the *people themselves,* through the medium of electors chosen by them, uninfluenced by any previous
nomination made by members of Congress,
have adopted the following resolutions:

1. *Resolved,* that the senators in Congress
from this state be instructed, and our representatives be requested, to use their exertions to prevent a nomination being made
during the next session of Congress, by the
members thereof in caucus, of persons to fill
the offices of President and Vice-President
of the United States.

2. *Resolved,* that the General Assembly
will, at its present session, divide the state
into as many districts, in convenient form,
as this state is entitled to electoral votes, for
the purpose of choosing an elector in each
to vote for President and Vice-President of
the United States.

3. *Resolved,* that the governor of this state
transmit a copy of the foregoing preamble
and resolutions to the executive of each of
the United States, with a request that the
same be laid before each of their respective
legislatures.

4. *Resolved,* that the governor transmit a
copy to each of the senators and representatives in Congress from this state.

19.

John Taylor: An Interpretation of the Constitution

John Taylor of Caroline County, Virginia, had a distinguished career of public service from the Revolution to his death in 1824 and was also the theoretician of Jeffersonian democracy. He was a brilliant spokesman for states' rights, local government, and agrarian democracy against what he regarded as the pernicious tendency toward consolidation of power by the federal government. The following selection from Taylor's last book, New Views of the Constitution of the United States, *published in 1823, compares federal and national forms of government.*

Source: *New Views of the Constitution of the United States,* Washington, 1823, pp. 237-295.

THE GREAT QUESTION, whether a federal or a national system of government will best secure the liberty and happiness of the people, remains to be more fully considered; and though it must be referred to the better understandings which abound in our country, yet a few observations will be hazarded as to this point. . . .

Liberty and power are adverse pleaders, and the arguments or temptations offered by both have never failed to make proselytes. Between the tyranny of concentrated power and of unbridled licentiousness is a space filled with materials for computing effects produced by controlling both extremes, and estimating the chances for promoting human liberty and happiness. It seems to be nature's law that every species of concentrated sovereignty over extensive territories, whether monarchical, aristocratical, democratical, or mixed, must be despotic. In no case has a concentrated power over great territories been sustained, except by mercenary armies; and wherever power is thus sustained, despotism is the consequence. . . .

The geography of our country and the character of our people unite to demonstrate that the ignorance and partiality of a concentrated form of government can only be enforced by armies; and the peculiar ability of the states to resist promises that resistance would be violent; so that a national government must either be precarious or despotic. By dividing power between the federal and state governments, local partialities and oppressions, the common causes of revolution, are obliterated from our system.

This division is contrived, not only for avoiding such domestic evils but also for securing the United States against foreign aggression. For the attainment of both ends, it was equally necessary to bestow certain powers on a federal government and reserve others to the state governments. The two intentions point forcibly toward a genuine construction of the Constitution, and the theory is defended by the only principle capable of securing civil liberty. Communities possessed of sufficient knowledge to discriminate between liberty and slavery have uniformly labored to invest governments with a portion of power sufficient to secure social happiness, but insufficient for its destruction. The United States understood the discrimination and, in the formation of the federal government, endeavored, by limitations and prohibitions, to reserve and secure as many of their individual rights as might be retained without defeating the end of providing for their common interest. The two principles of a division or a concentration of power are the adversaries contending for preference. Every government must be of one or the other description. An absolute supremacy in one belongs to the concentrating principle, like an absolute supremacy in one man. Hence it has happened that an aristocratical or representative body of men, exercising supreme power, has been as tyrannical, or more so, than a single despot. The United States saw that any geographical interest, if invested with supremacy by the establishment of a consolidated national government, would oppress some other geographical interest, and made a new effort to avoid this natural malignity of a concentrated supreme power, though lodged in the representatives of the people. . . .

It is as impossible that politicians can extend the intellectual powers of men beyond their natural limits as that priests can turn bread and wine into flesh and blood. The incapacity of one mind for securing the liberty and happiness of an extensive country dictates the wisdom of dividing power; and the same natural incapacity in the representatives of one state to provide for the local good government of another more forcibly dictated the internal independency of each. A division of mechanical labor is so highly valuable that even a pin can be better made by many workmen than by one. In like manner it is at length happily discovered that a division of intellectual labors is equally necessary for the construction of the most perfect form of government. It would have been more preposterous to expect that

the representatives of Massachusetts could provide for the prosperity of Louisiana than that we might get to the moon in a balloon. The human mind can only act judiciously within the scope of its intelligence. Accordingly, those powers only are entrusted to the federal government as to which the intelligence and interest of the states are the same; and those are withheld as to which the similarity between the intelligence and interest of the states fail.

A uniformity in the operation of federal laws throughout the states is required to prevent these wise precautions from being defeated. This uniformity illustrates the independency of local rights, because, if these were liable to be regulated by federal laws, great inequalities would have ensued. The interest of one state is embraced by the intellectual powers of representatives chosen by counties, because the counties have a common interest, just as the intellectual powers of members of Congress will reach the common interests of the United States; but there would be no difference between requiring the county representatives of Virginia to regulate the local affairs of Massachusetts and requiring the representatives from Virginia in Congress to do the same thing.

Why would the first mode of governing Massachusetts be tyrannical and absurd? Because neither the sympathies nor intellectual powers of a resident in Virginia are adequate to the local government of Massachusetts. Are they rendered more adequate if he is chosen by the whole state, or by a district of it, instead of being chosen by a county? Will the mode of appointment revoke the laws of nature? A conviction that this could not happen, suggested the division of powers between the state and federal governments as being a preference of knowledge to ignorance. To expect from ignorance or an adverse interest the fruits of knowledge and a common interest would have been unnatural. Calamities or blessings are their respective consequences. Our system, therefore, draws upon federal knowledge and sympathy for federal prosperity, and upon state knowledge and sympathy for local prosperity. By reversing its drafts in either case, they would either be protested, or paid in very bad paper. . . .

Let us now turn our eyes toward the state sovereignties and consider whether they are like baronial or other concentrated supremacies, universally hostile to liberty. State governments are confined to local objects, as the powers of an individual are to his own domicile. They are excluded from declaring war, from keeping armies in time of peace, and from entering into foreign treaties or internal confederacies. They are restrained both by the principle of division and by their responsibility to the people. They are checked by the federal government, as the federal government is by them. They are controllable by three-fourths of the states. The principles of division and control are applied extensively to the state governments, whereas they are not applied at all, or ineffectually applied, to the concentrated baronial, monarchical, or mixed governments of Europe. This difference accounts for the exclusive blessings we have reaped from our modes of dividing and controlling power. If we should exchange them for a concentrated supremacy in the federal government, the internal divisions of the state governments would be rendered useless, and state elections for controlling state departments would dwindle into an idle ceremony. . . .

The division of local from federal interests was a fine idea for excluding geographical collisions, for effecting a lasting amity between federal interests, and for shielding the people against a concentrated supremacy, ignorant of their wants and incapable of providing for their happiness.

It is repeatedly urged that the division of powers between the federal and state governments will neither secure a mutual spirit of moderation nor control the ambition of either department. If not, what will? The objection only propounds the question of preference between a federal and a national government, or between divided and concentrated power, in a new form, and endeavors to defeat the best political principle by charging it with imperfection. In estimating this objection, we ought to consider that both these governments have, in a vast majority of instances, adhered to the Constitution and acted with moderation; and that both in cases comparatively few have exceeded their powers. Mutual moderation is therefore the general effect of our system, and occasional excess an inconsiderable exception. What produces the general effect but our division of powers, the moral coequality of the states, and a congeniality in the state and federal governments with the powers assigned to each? Ought this general effect to be surrendered because it is exposed to exceptions?

It is an axiom that the means must be commensurate to the end. If the moderation of power is the end, is its concentration, or its division, the best mode of effecting this end? But collision occurs when power is moderated by division. This is not a vice but the very virtue in the principle of dividing power, which gives it all of its efficacy and all its value; and the absence of collision from a concentrated supremacy is exactly the vice which engenders all its oppressions. The authors of *The Federalist* earnestly and frequently impressed the mutual control between the federal and state governments as the chief recommendation of the Constitution. Without collision, this control could not have any operation. Let us contrast this remedy against oppression, with the project for putting an end both to this admired control and the collisions it produces, by converting Congress or the Supreme Court into a council of censors, able by laws and judgments to abrogate state laws and to create constitutional laws.

Either censorial supremacy will put an end to the division of power, with all its controlling and moderating effects, so highly praised and so ably defended by *The Federalist*. . . .

The censorial supremacy exercised by the federal Court has been proposed to be transferred to the federal Senate by investing that body with a supervision of political judgments; but this would be an exchange of the mutual control between the state and federal governments, and of the mode prescribed for amending the Constitution, for the very principle which the Court is laboring to establish; namely, that of a national supremacy in the federal government, able to alter the Constitution by construction, without the concurrence of three-fourths of the states. . . . The proposition to invest the Senate with a power to supervise the political judgments of the Court is an admission that the judicial federal department may alter the Constitution by such judgments; and against this evil the remedy proposed is to transfer from the judicial department to the federal senatorial department the same supreme right of alteration. But both the admission and the remedy are equally contrary to the constitutional definition of the right of alteration, equally an acknowledgment of a supreme concentrated power and equally an obliteration of the division between state and federal powers.

If neither of the enumerated departments can alter the Constitution, the chief difficulty of my course of reasoning is removed, and the arguments by which it is assailed are surmounted. The word "Constitution" can no longer be construed to contain recondite powers, to be drawn from it by departments having no power to alter it. We have used it to express the formation of both the state and federal governments; but not with a design that it should furnish a pretext for altering the form or principles of either, without the sanction required in each case. If the word gives no authority to any department of state governments to alter state constitutions without the consent of the people, it can give no authority to any federal department to alter the federal Constitution without the consent of three-fourths of the states. Though we have obtained this undeniable truth, it is said to be inert for want of means to give it efficacy.

The Union is admitted to be constituted of state and federal powers, but it is contended that the Constitution has been inexplicit in dividing them. An apprehension of difficulty from this circumstance caused the supremacy over the Constitution to be deposited in three-fourths of the states and not in a majority of Congress nor in a majority of the Supreme Court. Even a majority of the states themselves was not entrusted with this power. But other precautions were necessary to prevent the state or federal department from altering the Constitution by construction. Among these, the chief must be a principle applicable to both departments, or it could not have any effect. Neither can alter the Constitution. What principle can enforce this truth, except that of a coequal right of construction and of self-preservation?

If no department throughout our whole system can, by any unconstitutional act, legislative or judicial, deprive a citizen of a constitutional right, it would be strange if either the federal or state governments could be thus deprived of constitutional rights. Modes are resorted to for securing the rights of individuals. As to the rights of these departments, they are first secured by their coequality. Neither or both can construe the Constitution. Neither or both can alter it by construction. Neither or both can exercise the power of usurping a right belonging to the other. Neither or both can defend its own rights. The Constitution gives no supremacy to either of these departments over the other. But the Constitution, aware that this mutual right of self-defense against unconstitutional construction might produce collisions, has provided a remedy to act in concert with the mutual check, as well devised for securing state and federal constitutional rights as any which has ever been devised for securing the rights of individuals. If these departments should differ as to the extent of their respective rights, the remedy provided is not that one should exercise dominion over the other. On the contrary, the Constitution contains a different, and probably the best, remedy which could have been devised, both to restrain and give effect to the salutary mutual check between the state and federal departments.

Two-thirds of Congress may appeal from an erroneous state construction and propose an amendment for controlling it to the tribunal invested with the right of decision. Why was this right of appeal limited to two-thirds of Congress, if a majority was invested with a supreme power of construction, or if the same majority could appeal to the federal Court? Can a majority evade this limitation, with or without the aid of its court? Two-thirds were required to prevent hasty and frivolous appeals, and to preserve the rights of the states against party majorities and geographical prepossessions. If two-thirds will not appeal against a state law, it is an admission of its constitutionality by the constitutional mode established for deciding the question. If this specified mode is defeated by transferring the supremacy of construction from two-thirds of Congress and three-fourths of the states to a majority of Congress and a majority of the Court, one of these majorities would be invested with a power of deciding collisions between the state and federal governments, although neither is invested with a right even to propose an alteration of the powers given to either department by the Constitution. The precision in the mode of amendment is the remedy provided against any want of precision in the division of powers,

which the licentiousness of construction might lay hold of. The security against unconstitutional or inconvenient state acts is deposited in two-thirds of Congress and three-fourths of the states as a provision for settling collisions between the state and federal governments amicably, and for avoiding the more dangerous conflicts which a supremacy of geographical majorities would produce, if invested with a supremacy liable to geographical fluctuations. In this provision the Constitution discloses an eminent superiority over every other division of power which has hitherto been invented. . . .

The division of local and federal interests united each allotment of powers with the strongest natural motive for their preservation. It was the interest of each state to manage its local affairs in its own way, and it was the interest of all the states to manage their common affairs by a mutual concert. Thus both interests were made to harmonize with both objects; they were not violated in either case; and a common interest was used as the cement both of local and federal powers.

To suppose that the state governments, operating within limited territorial lines, either would or could defeat our federal prosperity, and yet that a national government, operating without any limitation, would not or could not commit local partialities, is in theory a contradiction. A common federal interest prevents a state from attempting the first mischief; all the allurements of supreme power would invite a national government to commit the second. That these can get into a federal Congress has been practically proved, upon occasions both important and frivolous. Ought they to be multiplied by changing a federal into a national Congress? The geographical question about unsettled lands was so managed as to get them from some states and leave them to others. The funding and banking questions were decided by geographical motives. The Sedition Law was intended to operate geographically. The controversy for the presidency discloses geographical feelings, both in Congress and the states. The Missouri question displayed a more formidable geographical spirit in Congress than has ever appeared in a state government. The usurped supremacy over a federal treasury has cost the people many millions. These and other facts prove that a national supremacy would be only a perpetual lottery for distributing blanks and prizes to states and individuals, by the will of a geographical majority; and that excessive corruption and the keenest resentment would probably be produced by these geographical benefits and injuries.

The result of the practical testimony is that local interests, if left at home, will never hurt the federal Union; but that, if assembled in Congress, they will produce a government influenced by fraud, which must end in tyranny or destroy the Union. An exercise of local powers by Congress and the Supreme Court has already interrupted our federal harmony; and it is obvious that the division of powers between the state and federal governments must have been the true source of that share of prosperity which we have hitherto enjoyed. . . .

To prevent local interests from going to war with each other, they are incarcerated within the lines of a state, and if they should be let loose through the avenue of Congress, and the postern of the Supreme Court, the soundest security for the Union of the states and the liberty of the people will be lost. Local interests, instead of being confined within the boundary of each state, will go to war with each other in Congress, the causes of their hostility, intended to be removed by the Union, will be revived, victories will be gained and defeats suffered, and both will generate new battles. Repulsion and attraction, arising from the difference and similitude of geographical interests, would create combinations to commit local injuries or obtain local advantages by the laws of Congress; conflicts between states, intended to be prevented, would be excited, and multiplied; and a national supremacy over state rights would either produce a mass of fragments as materials for some new form of government or require the almighty power of despotism to enforce its fraudulent awards. Against this host of evils, the Constitution provides, by using the geographical interest of the United States to unite them against the geographical interest of other countries, and by leaving the internal geographical interest of each state undisturbed, that it may not destroy our internal tranquillity. . . .

In establishing the division of powers between the federal and state governments, another principle as important, and not less true than that of uniting sympathy with power, was kept in view by the Convention; namely, that great power is a great temptation to do wrong. The able expositors of the Constitution, having in *The Federalist* adverted to this axiom, united in an opinion that a greater share of power was reserved to the states than was delegated to the federal government; and, therefore, concluded that the danger of usurpation rested in that department. As neither their opinion nor inference could have any foundation, if the powers reserved to the states were controllable by the federal government, they must have believed, as they said, that each department was independent of the other within its own sphere; because, had the Constitution invested the federal with a supremacy over the state governments, the greatest share of power could not have been assigned to the latter. The anticipation of the comparative magnitude of the two primary divisions of power to ascertain which would be most sorely afflicted with the malady of usurpation was then chiefly conjectural; and the egregious mistake of these commentators is both a proof that their constructions are not infallible and also an admonition against destroying the mutual check which they commended.

If experience has ascertained that the superiority of power is in the federal government, they have proved that the disposition to encroach must go with it. The axiom that the least moderation is to be expected from the most power decides the comparative magnitude of these primary dividends, since there is as much difficulty in discovering an instance of the usurpation of a power delegated to the federal government by a state as in discovering a state reserved power, not usurped or threatened by federal precedents. The whole mass of state powers are attempted to be drawn within the federal sphere by a supremacy claiming a right to remove obstructions to its dominion; converting them, whatever may have been their constitutional magnitude, into ciphers, useful only to endow the federal sphere with an unlimited decimal increase of power. To transfer our jealousy from the encroaching sphere to that, experimentally weak, unassuming, and too submissive, would seem to violate common sense and would certainly defeat the mutual control, eulogized by *The Federalist*, and established by the Constitution, to ensure the moderation of power upon which it is agreed that all the benefits of civil liberty depend.

But the modern commentators, far from believing with *The Federalist* that the state governments possess a superiority of power, contend that it resides to such an extent in the federal government as to make it absurd for the states to struggle for rights which must be lost or to oppose an impetus which must prevail. Giving up the idea of checking power on account of its magnitude, they urge its magnitude as a reason for suppressing the check and submitting to its commands. Expounding the Constitution by Lord Shaftesbury's logic, they ridicule its attempt to reserve rights to the states in communion with the great power bestowed on the federal government; and laughing at its provisions, they yield to their subversion, because they are too feeble to withstand the usurpations of the federal government.

Should the contempt thus plenteously poured out upon the state governments unite them for the preservation of rights common to all, the barriers against the disposition of great power to usurp may prove stronger than these facetious gentlemen are disposed to believe. If the parties actuated by conflicting principles should happen to be described by proper names, such as consolidators and constitutionalists, or concentrators and federalists, it might induce the people to consider whether they would subscribe to the combined projects of laughing or coercing them out of their state rights, and they could easily make the charge of absurdity, urged against the Constitution, recoil upon the statesmen by whom it is advanced. But consolidation avows its patriotism by talking of the sovereignty of the people, while assailing their state rights, and of its loyalty to the Constitution, while appealing from it to the supremacy of construction.

Gentlemen, I refuse to sign any pledge. I never have been drunk, and, by the blessing of God, I never will get drunk, but I have a constitutional privilege to get drunk, and that privilege I will not sign away.
            CHANCELLOR KENT, *Memoirs*, when a temperance committee
            asked him to sign a pledge not to use intoxicating beverages

20.

Charles J. Ingersoll: The Influence of America on the Mind

During the early nineteenth century, intellectuals both in the United States and in Europe began to seek the cultural implications of America's unique experiment in self-government. That the United States lacked a significant cultural heritage, that her culture was imitative or, as some believed, nonexistent, was denied by men of nationalistic sentiments, who called for the production of art, architecture, and literature based on American themes. Charles Ingersoll, a Philadelphia lawyer, de-emphasized concern over American literature in the belief that America's greatness lay in her political, social, and educational institutions, and in her technological inventiveness. He expressed these sentiments in the annual oration to the American Philosophical Society at Philadelphia on October 18, 1823. "A Discourse Concerning the Influence of America on the Mind," portions of which are reprinted here, attracted worldwide attention and was often cited by those who wished to substitute functional for classical curriculums in the schools.

Source: *A Discourse Concerning the Influence of America on the Mind*, London, 1824.

In the United States . . . the arts and sciences are but of recent and spontaneous growth, scattered over extensive regions and a sparse population. . . .

By the Constitution of the United States it is the duty of government to promote the progress of science and the useful arts. Not one of the eleven new states has been admitted into the Union without provision in its constitution for schools, academies, colleges, and universities. In most of the original states large sums in money are appropriated to education, and they claim a share in the great landed investments which are mortgaged to it in the new states. Reckoning all those contributions, federal and local, it may be asserted that nearly as much as the whole national expenditure of the United States is set apart by laws to enlighten the people.

The public patronage of learning in this country, adverting to what the value of these donations will be before the close of the present century, equals at least the ostentatious bounties conferred on it in Europe. In one state alone, with but 275,000 inhabitants, more than 40,000 pupils are instructed at the public schools. I believe we may compute the number of such pupils throughout the United States at more than half a million. . . .

Nearly the whole minor population of the United States are receiving school education. Besides the multitudes at school, there are considerably more than 3,000 undergraduates always matriculated at the various colleges and universities authorized to grant academical degrees; not less than 1,200 at the medical schools; several hundred at the theological seminaries; and at least 1,000 students of law. Nearly all of these are under the tuition of professors without sinecure support, depending for their livelihood on capacity and success in the science of instruction. In no part of these extensive realms of knowledge is there any monastic prepossession against the modern improvements. . . .

The English language makes English reading American; and a generous, especially a parental, nationality, instead of disparaging a supposed deficiency in the creation of literature, should remember and rejoice that the idiom and ideas of England are also those of this country and of this continent, destined to be enjoyed and improved by millions of educated and thinking people, spreading from the Bay of Fundy to the mouth of the Columbia. Such is the influence of general education and self-government that already, over a surface of almost 2,000 miles square, there are scarcely any material provincialisms or peculiarities of dialect, much less than in any nation in Europe, I believe I might say than in any 100 miles square in Europe. And, what is perhaps even more remarkable, the German, Dutch, and French veins which exist in different sections are rapidly yielding to the English ascendancy by voluntary fusion, without any coercive or violent applications. Adverting to the great results from the mysterious diversity of the various languages of mankind, the anticipation is delightful in the effects of the American unity of tongue, combined with universal education throughout this vast continent — the home of liberty, at least, if not the seat of one great empire.

But speaking and writing the language of an ancient and refined people, whose literature preoccupies nearly every department, is, in many respects, an unexampled disadvantage in the comparative estimate. America cannot contribute in any comparative proportion to the great British stock of literature, which almost supersedes the necessity of American subscriptions. Independent of this foreign oppression, the American mind has been called more to political, scientific, and mechanical than to literary exertion. And our institutions, moreover, partaking of the nature of our government, have a leveling tendency. The average of intellect and of intellectual power in the United States surpasses that of any part of Europe. But the range is not, in general, so great, either above or below the horizontal line. In the literature of imagination, our standard is considerably below that of England, France, Germany, and, perhaps, Italy. The concession, however, may be qualified by a claim to a respectable production of poetry; and the recollection that American scenes and incidents have been wrought by American authors into successful romances, some of which have been republished and translated and are in vogue in Europe; and that even popular dramatic performances have been composed out of these incidents.

The stage, however, is indicative of many things in America, being engrossed by the English drama and English actors. But as a proof of American fondness, if not taste, for theatrical entertainment, I may mention here that an English comedian has lately received for performances before the audiences of four or five towns, whose united population falls short of 400,000 people, a much larger income than any of the actors of that country receive in which this sort of intellectual recreation is most esteemed. There would be no inducement for strolling across the Atlantic, if the largest capital in Europe afforded similar encouragement, taking emolument as the test and London, with 1,200,000 inhabitants, as the standard. As another remarkable proof of the state of the stage in the United States, I may add that an eminent American actor appears in the same season (and it is practicable within the same month) before audiences at Boston and New Orleans, compassing 2,000 miles from one to the other, by internal conveyance. Such is the philosophical, as well as natural, approximation of place and the unity of speech throughout that distance.

In the literature of fact, of education, of politics, and of, perhaps, even science, European preeminence is by no means so decided. The American schools, the church, the state, the bar, the medical profession, are, all but the last, largely, and all of them adequately, supplied by their own literature. Respectable histories are extant by American authors. . . . Our national histories, inferior in subordinate attractions to the romantic historical fictions of Europe, are composed of much more permanent and available materials. In biography, without equal means, have we not done as much since we began as our English masters? In the literature as well as the learning of the sciences, botany, mineralogy, metallurgy, entomology, ornithology, astronomy, and navigation, there is no reason to be ashamed of our proficiency. In mathematics and chemistry, our comparative deficiency is perhaps the most remarkable. In grammatical researches, particularly in the interesting elements of the Indian languages, American erudition has preceded that of Europe, where some of the most learned and celebrated of the German and French philologists have caught from American publications the spirit of similar inquiry. In natural and political geography our magnificent interior has produced great accomplishments, scientific and literary.

The maps of America have been thought worthy of imitation in Europe. Mr. Tanner's *Atlas*, lately published, is the fruit of a large investment of money and time, and reflects credit on every branch of art employed in its execution. The surveys of the coast now making by government will be among the most extensive, accurate, and important memorials extant. Several scientific expeditions have likewise been sent by the government, at different times, into the western regions, whose vast rivers, steppes, and deltas have been explored by learned men, whose publications enrich many departments of science and are incorporated with applause into the useful literature of the age. One of the most, copious and authentic statistical works in print is an American production which owes its publication to the patronage of Congress.

The public libraries . . . abound with proof and promise of the flourishing condition and rapid advances of literature and science throughout America. A single newspaper of this city contains advertisements, by a single bookseller, of more than 150 recent publications by American authors from the American press, comprehending romance, travels, moral philosophy, mineralogy, political and natural geography, poetry, biography, history, various scientific inquiries and discoveries, botany, philology, oratory, chemistry applied to the arts, statistics, agricultural and horticultural treatises, strategy, mechanics, and many other subjects. From this ample and creditable catalog, I may select for especial notice the *Journal of the Academy of Natural Sciences* as a work of uncommon merit; and the profound and elaborate report on *Weights and Measures* as a laudable specimen of official function.

The first and the present secretaries of the Department of State, who have both made reports on this important branch of scientific politics, rank among the foremost scholars of the age by their eminence in various literary and scientific attainments. The America state papers, generally, have received the homage of the most illustrious statesmen of England, for excellence in the principles and eloquence of that philosophy which is the most extensively applied to the affairs of men; and their publications afford large contributions to its literature. Whether any policy be preferable to another is generally a merely speculative topic. But I may with propriety assert that the United States have been the most steadfast supporters of maritime liberality, of international neutrality, and of the modern system of commercial equality. They were the first to outlaw the slave trade and the first to declare it piratical. Great Britain is imitating their example in commercial, colonial, navigation, penal, and even financial regulations. France, Spain, Italy, Portugal, parts of Germany, and South America have in part adopted their political principles. And in all the branches of political knowledge, the American mind has been distinguished.

The publication of books is so much cheaper in this country than in Great Britain that nearly all we use are American editions. . . . It is estimated that between $2 million and $3 million worth of books are annually published in the United States. . . .

It is to be regretted that literary property here is held by an imperfect tenure, there being no other protection for it than the provisions of an inefficient act of Congress, the impotent offspring of an obsolete English statute. The inducement to take copyrights is therefore inadequate, and a large proportion of the most valuable American books are published without any legal title. . . .

Among the curiosities of American literature, I must mention the itinerant book trade. There are, I understand, more than 200 wagons which travel through the country, loaded with books for sale. Many biographical accounts of distinguished Americans are thus distributed. Fifty thousand copies of Mr. Weems' *Life of Washington* have been published and mostly circulated in this way throughout the interior.

The modern manuals of literature and science, magazines, journals, and reviews abound in the United States, although they have to cope with a larger field of newspapers than elsewhere. The *North American Review*, of which about 4,000 copies are circulated, is not surpassed in knowledge or learning, is not equaled in liberal and judicious criticism, by its great British models, the *Edinburgh* and *Quarterly Reviews*, of which about 4,000 copies are also published in the United States. Written in a pure Old English style, and, for the most part, a fine American spirit, the *North American Review* superintends with ability the literature and science of America.

Not less than 1,000 newspapers, some of them with several thousand subscribers, are circulated in this country; the daily fare of nearly every meal in almost every family, so cheap and common that, like air and water, its uses are undervalued. But a free press is the great distinction of this age and country, and as indispensable as those elements to the welfare of all free countries. Abundant and emulous accounts of remarkable occurrences concentrate and diffuse information, stimulate inquiry, dispel prejudices, and multiply enjoyments. Copious advertisements quicken commerce; rapid and pervading publicity is a cheap police. Above all, the press is the palladium of liberty. An American would forego the charms of France or Italy for the luxury of a large newspaper, which makes every post an epoch and provides the barrenest corners of existence with a universal succedaneum. Duly to appreciate the pleasures of it, like health or liberty, we must undergo their temporary privation. Nor is our experience of the licentiousness of the press too dear a price to pay for its freedom. . . .

From literature the transition is natural to the arts, which minister to usefulness, comfort, and prosperity, individual and national. Under their authority to provide for the encouragement of the arts and sciences, the United States, in thirty years, have issued about 4,400 patent rights for new and useful inventions, discoveries, and improvements. By the prevailing construction of the acts of Congress, American patentees must be American inventors or improvers and are excluded from all things before known or used in any other part or period of the world. The English law allows English patentees to monopolize the inventions, discoveries, and improvements of all the rest of the world when naturalized in Great Britain. Notwithstanding this remarkable disadvantage, I believe the American list of discoveries is quite equal to the English. The specimens and models open to public inspection in the national repository at Washington are equal, I understand, to any similar collections in England or France, and superior to those of any other country. It will hardly be expected that I should undertake to mention even the most remarkable articles of this immense museum, containing every element of practical science, of mechanism, of refinement, and of skill.

I may be allowed, however, to say that the cotton gin has been of more profit to the United States than ten times all they ever received by internal taxation; that our grain-mill machinery, applied to the great staples of subsistence, is very superior to that of Europe; that there are in the Patent Office models of more than twenty different power looms, of American invention, operated on and weaving solely by extraneous power — steam, water, wind, animals, and otherwise; and that the English machines for spinning have been so improved here that low-priced cottons can be manufactured cheap enough to undersell the English in England after defraying the charges of transportation. Where American ingenuity has been put to trial, it has never failed. In all the useful arts and in the philosophy of comfort — that word which cannot be translated into any other language, and which, though of English origin, was reserved for maturity in America — we have no superiors. If laborsaving machinery has added the power of a hundred millions of hands to the resources of Great Britain, what must be the effect of it on the population and means of the United States? Steam navigation, destined to have greater influence than any triumph of mind over

matter, equal to gunpowder, to printing, and to the compass, worthy to rank in momentum with religious reformation, and civil liberty, belongs to America. . . .

Steam navigation was reserved for the genius of those rivers, on a single one of which there are already more than 100 steamboats, containing upward of 14,000 tons, and in whose single seaport 50 steamboats may be counted at one time. This was the meridian to reduce to practical results, whatever conceptions may have existed elsewhere on this subject. Necessity, the mother of this invention, was an American mother; born, perhaps, on the shores of the Potomac, the Delaware, or the Hudson, yet belonging to the Missouri, the Arkansas, the Mississippi, and the Pacific Ocean. . . .

The mechanics, artisans, and laborers of this country are remarkable for a disposition to learn. Asserted European superiority has been of great advantage to America in preventing habitual repugnance to improvement, so common to all mankind, especially the least informed classes. Superior aptitude, versatility, and quickness in the handicrafts are the consequences of this disposition of our people. A mechanic in Europe is apt to consider it almost irreverent and altogether vain to suppose that anything can be done better than as he was taught to do it by his father or master. A house or ship is built in much less time here than there. From a line-of-battle ship or a steam engine to a tenpenny nail; in everything, the mechanical genius displays itself by superior productions. The success of a highly gifted American mechanical genius now in England seems to be owing in part to his adapting his improvements, by a happy ingenuity, to the preservation of machinery, for which several English mechanics have been enriched and ennobled, but which would have been superseded as useless had it not been thus rescued.

If a ship, a plow, and a house be taken as symbols of the primary social arts of navigation, agriculture, and habitation, we need not fear comparisons with other people in any one of them. In the intellectual use of the elements, the combinations and improvements of the earth and its products, of water, of air, and of fire, no greater progress has been made in Europe within this century than in the United States. The houses, ships, carriages, tools, utensils, manufactures, implements of husbandry, conveniences, comforts, the whole circle of social refinement are always equal, mostly superior here, to those of the most improved nations. I do not speak of mere natural advantages — of being better fed, more universally housed, and more comfortably clothed than any other people; but, excepting the ostentatious and extravagant, if not degenerate and mischievous, luxuries of a few in the capitals of Europe merely; looking to the general average of civilization, where does it bespeak more mind or display greater advancement?

Internal improvements, roads, bridges, canals, waterworks, and all the meliorations of intercourse have been as extensively and as expensively made within the last ten years in the United States as in probably any other country; notwithstanding the sparseness of a population of which scarcely half a million is concentrated in cities and a slender capital. Five thousand post offices distribute intelligence throughout the United States with amazing celerity and precision over 80,000 miles of post roads. The mail travels 21,000 miles every day, compassing 8,000,000 miles in a year. There are 12,000 miles of turnpike roads. Our facilities and habits of intercourse are unequaled in Europe, almost annihilating the obstacles of space.

Within two years from this time, when all the great canals now in progress shall be completed, an internal navigation of 10,000 miles will belt this country from the great western valley to the waters of the Hudson and the Chesapeake. The New York canal and the Philadelphia waterworks are not surpassed, if equaled, by any similar improvements in Europe within the period of their construction.

The polite arts, painting, engraving, music, sculpture, architecture, the arts of recreation, amusement, and pageantry, flourish most in the seats of dense population. Few of them thrive without the forcing of great capitals, the reservoirs of the refinements of ancient, sometimes declining, empire. Architecture is an art of state whose masterworks are reserved for seats of government. . . .

To these imperfect views of education, literature, science, and the arts, I will add sketches of the American mind, as developed in legislation, jurisprudence, the medical profession, and the church; which, in this country, may be considered as the other cardinal points of intellectual exercise.

Representation is the great distinction between ancient and modern government. Representation and confederation distinguish the politics of America, where representation is real and legislation perennial. Thousands of springs, gushing from every quarter, eddy onward the cataract of representative democracy, from primary self-constituted assemblies to the state legislatures and the national Congress; 3,000 chosen members represent these United States in twenty-five legislatures. There are, moreover, innumerable voluntary associations under legislative regulations in their proceedings. I am within bounds in asserting, that several hundred thousand persons assemble in this country every year, in various spontaneous convocations, to discuss and determine measures according to parliamentary routine. From Bible societies to the lowest handicraft there is no impediment, but every facility, by law, to their organization; and we find not only harmless but beneficial those various self-created associations which in other countries give so much trouble and alarm. It is not my purpose to consider the political influences of these assemblies, nor even their political character. But their philosophical effect on the individuals composing them is to sharpen their wits, temper their passions, and cultivate their elocution; while this almost universal practice of political or voluntary legislation could hardly fail to familiarize a great number of persons with its proprieties. . . .

In their national capacity, the United States have no common law, but all the original states are governed by that of England, with adaptations. In one of the new states, in which the French, Spanish, and English laws happen to be all naturalized, an attempt at codification from all these stocks is making, under legislative sanction. In others, possibly all of the new states which have been carved out of the old, a great question is in agitation whether the English common law is their inheritance. . . . Notwithstanding . . . the law has been much simplified in transplantation from Europe to America, and its professional as well as political tendency is still to further simplicity. The brutal, ferocious, and inhuman laws of the feudists, as they were termed by the civilians (I use their own phrase), the arbitrary rescripts of the civil law, and the harsh doctrines of the common law have all been melted down by the genial mildness of American institutions. . . .

The education for the bar is less technical, their practice is more intellectual, the vocation is, relatively at least, more independent in the United States than in Great Britain. Here, as there, it is a much frequented avenue to political honors. All the chief justices of the United States have filled eminent political stations, both abroad and at home. Of the five Presidents of the United States, four were lawyers; of the several candidates at present for that office, most, if not all, are lawyers. But without any public promotion, American society has no superior to the man who is advanced in any of the liberal professions. Hence there are more accomplished individuals in pro-

fessional life here than where this is not the case. . . .

There are about 10,000 physicians in the United States and medical colleges for their education in Massachusetts, Rhode Island, Connecticut, New York, Pennsylvania, Virginia, and Ohio. There are also two medical universities in the state of New York, one in Pennsylvania, one in Maryland, one in Massachusetts, and one in Kentucky, containing altogether about 1,200 students. Under the impulses of a new climate and its peculiar distempers, the medical profession has been pursued and its sciences developed with great zeal and success in this country, whose necessities have called forth a bolder and more energetic treatment of diseases, more discriminating and philosophical, as well as decisive and efficient; a more scientific assignment of their causes and ascertainments of their nature. Many medical errors and prejudices, now abandoned in Europe, were first refuted here.

What is justly termed a national character has been given to the medical science of America, and American medical literature is circulated and read in Europe, where several American medical discoveries and improvements have been claimed as European. Anatomy, the most stationary of the medical sciences, is ardently cultivated and has been advanced by discoveries in the American schools. Valuable contributions have been made to physiology, and more rational views inculcated of animal economy. An American discovery in chemistry has distinguished its author throughout Europe. . . .

The American improvements in surgery are too numerous and, though not the less important, too minute and technical to be generalized in a summary. Its apparatus, mechanism, and operations have been improved by a theory and practice equal in science, skill, and success to any in the world. . . .

I shall conclude with some views of the American church. . . . In estimating the progress and condition of the mind in America . . . I have neither disposition nor occasion to deny that the condition of religion is one of the best tests of the general intellectual state. Independently of their help in the cure of souls, the clergy have always rendered the most important services to the human understanding. Learning and science were long in their exclusive care. In those periods when the mind was most depressed, the church was the chancery of its preservation. To it, we owe nearly all the best relics of ancient learning; from it, we still receive much of our education; for here, as elsewhere, most of our teachers are ecclesiastics. . . .

Segregation from political connection and toleration are the cardinal principles of the American church. . . . Both of these principles are not only fundamental political laws but ancient, deep-seated doctrines, whose bases were laid long before political sovereignty was thought of, when Williams, Penn, and Baltimore, by a remarkable coincidence, implanted them in every quarter and in every creed. American toleration means the absolute independence and equality of all religious denominations. American segregation means that no human authority can in any case whatever control or interfere with the rights of conscience. Adequate trial of these great problems, not less momentous than that of political self-government, has proved their benign solution. Bigotry, intolerance, bloodthirsty polemics waste themselves in harmless, if not useful, controversy, when government takes no part. We enjoy a religious calm and harmony, not only unknown but inconceivable in Europe. We are continually receiving accessions of their intolerance, which is as constantly disarmed by being let alone. Our schools, families, legislatures, society find no embarrassment from varieties of creed which in Europe would kindle the deadliest discord. . . .

Naturalists and statists, philosophers, historians, ambassadors, poets, priests, nobles, tourists, journalists — I speak with precision to this catalog — have in vain sentenced this country to degradation. It already ranks with communities highly refined before America was discovered. France and England were enjoying Augustan ages when the place where we are met to discourse of literature and science was a wilderness.

But 140 years have elapsed since the patriarch of Pennsylvania first landed on these shores and sowed them with the germs of peace, toleration, and self-government; since when a main employment has been to reclaim the forests for habitation. It is not yet half a century since the United States were politically emancipated; it is only since the late war that they have begun to be intellectually independent. Colonial habits and reverence still rebuke and counteract intellectual enterprise. Education, the learned professions, the arts — scientific and mechanical — legislation, jurisprudence, literature, society — the mind, in a word — require time to be freed from European pupilage.

It was not in a spirit of hostility to any other country that I undertook to show what has been already done in this; but by that review to encourage further and keener exertions.

To those who will inquire and reflect, the encouragement of philosophy is as strong as the instinct of patriotism. But the empire of habit and of prejudice is in strong opposition to the supremacy of thought and reason. There was a time when it was not considered disaffection to be ashamed of our country nor disloyalty to despair of it when we recolonized ourselves. But within the last ten years especially, the mind of America has thought for itself, piercing the veil of European *beau ideal*.

Still less, however, than national disparagement was national vanity the shrine of my sacrifice. Comparative views are indispensable. I might have compared America now with America forty years ago, which would have presented a striking and enlivening contrast. But I preferred the bolder view of America compared with Europe, disclaiming, however, invidious comparisons, which have been studiously avoided. The cause asserted is of too high respect to be defended by panegyric or avenged by invective. The truth is an ample vindication. Let us strive to refute discredit by constant improvement. Let our intellectual motto be that naught is done while aught remains to be done; and our study, to prove to the world that the best patronage of religion, science, literature, and the arts, of whatever the mind can achieve, is *self-government*.

21.

JOHN HOWARD PAYNE: "Home, Sweet Home"

The words of "Home, Sweet Home" were written by John Howard Payne in the late fall of 1822 or the early spring of 1823, when he and the British composer Sir Henry Rowley Bishop were preparing their opera Clari, or, The Maid of Milan *for its production, in London, on May 8. Payne is supposed to have poured out his homesickness for his charming cottage in East Hampton (Long Island), New York, in the famous refrain; in any event, the song was a hit, the* London Quarterly Musical Magazine and Review *affirming in its next issue that "never was any ballad so immediately and deservedly popular." It was as successful in America, where it was published the same year, as in England. It is hardly ever sung nowadays, but the words, at least, survive — if only on thousands of samplers on as many American walls.*

Source: *Library of Poetry and Song*, William Cullen Bryant, ed., New York, 1874, p. 133.

🎵 HOME, SWEET HOME

'Mid pleasures and palaces though we may roam,
Be it ever so humble, there's no place like home;
A charm from the sky seems to hallow us there,
Which, seek through the world, is ne'er met with elsewhere.

Refrain:
Home! Home! sweet, sweet home!
There's no place like home! there's no place like home!

An exile from home, splendor dazzles in vain;
O, give me my lowly thatched cottage again!
The birds singing gaily, that came at my call —
Give me them — and the peace of mind, dearer than all!

22.

Edward Everett: On Greek Independence

Revolutions in Europe and in the New World inspired a feeling of national consciousness in the Greeks, who had long been oppressed by Turkish rule. In March 1821 a major uprising occurred that was applauded and materially supported by liberal Europeans. The U.S. government, though in sympathy with the rebels' cause, refrained from active participation in the revolt. When on May 25, 1821, the Messenian Senate sent an appeal to the American people, many Americans, moved by a sense of moral responsibility to the cause of liberty, demanded that the United States support the Greeks. Edward Everett, editor of the North American Review, *expressed his sentiment in the magazine in October 1823. The article reprinted here was prefaced by the Greek Appeal of 1821, which was debated in Congress in 1824.*

Source: *North American Review*, October 1823.

To the Citizens of the United States of America:

Having formed the resolution to live or die for freedom, we are drawn toward you by a just sympathy; since it is in your land that liberty has fixed her abode, and by you that she is prized as by our fathers. Hence, in invoking her name, we invoke yours at the same time, trusting that, in imitating you, we shall imitate our ancestors, and be thought worthy of them if we succeed in resembling you.

Though separated from you by mighty oceans, your character brings you near us. We esteem you nearer than the nations on our frontiers; and we possess, in you, friends, fellow citizens, and brethren, because you are just, humane and generous; just because free, generous and liberal because Christian. Your liberty is not propped on the slavery of other nations, nor your prosperity on their calamities and sufferings. But, on the contrary, free and prosperous yourselves, you are desirous that all men should share the same blessings; that all should enjoy those rights, to which all are by nature equally entitled. It is you who

first proclaimed these rights; it is you who have been the first again to recognize them, in rendering the rank of men to the Africans degraded to the level of brutes. It is by your example that Europe has abolished the shameful and cruel trade in human flesh; from you that she receives lessons of justice, and learns to renounce her absurd and sanguinary customs. This glory, Americans, is yours alone, and raises you above all the nations which have gained a name for liberty and laws.

It is for you, citizens of America, to crown this glory in aiding us to purge Greece from the barbarians, who for 400 years have polluted the soil. It is surely worthy of you to repay the obligations of the civilized nations, and to banish ignorance and barbarism from the country of freedom and the arts. You will not assuredly imitate the culpable indifference or, rather, the long ingratitude of the Europeans. No, the fellow citizens of Penn, of Washington, and of Franklin will not refuse their aid to the descendants of Phocion, and Thrasybulus, of Aratus, and of Philopoemen. You have already shown them esteem and confidence in sending your children to their schools. You know with what pleasure they were welcomed, and the steady kindness and attentions which they received. If such has been their conduct when enslaved, what friendship and zeal will they not manifest to you when, through your aid, they shall have broken their chains. Greece will then furnish you advantages which you can in vain seek from her ignorant and cruel tyrants; and the bands of gratitude and fraternity will forever unite the Greeks and the Americans. Our interests are of a nature more and more to cement an alliance founded on freedom and virtue.

At Calamata, May 25, 1821
Signed, The Messenian Senate at
Calamata
Peter Mavromichalis, commander in chief

OUR READERS WILL OBSERVE that this proclamation is the act of the Senate of Calamata, one of those local assemblies which were organized in Greece at the commencement of the present struggle, and before the establishment of the general government. . . .

Though we do not consider the foregoing address to be in very good taste, nor in every part perfectly intelligible, it shows at least how soon and how spontaneously the eyes of Greece were turned to this country as the great exemplar of states in the agonies of contest for independence.

Such an appeal from the anxious conclave of self-devoted patriots, in the inaccessible cliffs of the Morea, must bring home to the mind of the least reflecting American the great and glorious part which this country is to act in the political regeneration of the world. It must convince us that what Burke originally said in eulogy of his own land is going into its literal fulfillment here; and in a wider sense than he dared to speak it. Wheresoever the chosen race, the sons of liberty, shall worship freedom, they will turn their faces to us.

We have seen, in our own days, the oldest and most splendid monarchy in Europe casting off its yoke, under the contagion of liberty caught from us; and why should the excesses of that awful crisis be ascribed to the new-found remedy rather than to the inveterate disease? Through France, the influence of our example has been transmitted to the other European states, and in the most enslaved and corrupted of them, the leaven of freedom is at work. Meantime, at one and the same moment, we perceive in either hemisphere the glorious work of emancipation going on; and the name and the example of the United States alike invoked by both. . . .

While the great states of Europe, which for centuries have taken the lead in the affairs of the world, stand aghast at this spectacle, and know not if they shall dare to sanction what they cannot oppose, our envoys have already climbed the Andes and reached the Pacific with the message of gratulation.

We devoutly trust that another season will find them on their way to Greece. The recognition of South American independence, in many respects of national policy a dubious measure, was adopted with the cheering unanimity of old revolutionary times; and the man who was not in his seat in Congress that day felt that he had done himself and his constituents a wrong in losing the opportunity to record his voice among those of his brethren. Not less popular, we venture to say, would be the recognition of the independence of Greece. We feel none of the scruples which perplex the cabinets of Europe. We see nothing but an enterprising, intelligent, Christian population struggling against a ghastly despotism, that has so long oppressed and wasted the land; and if an animating word of ours could cheer them in the hard conflict, we should feel that not to speak it were to partake the guilt of their oppressors.

Meantime, there is something for the people of this country, in their private capacity, to do for Greece. In Germany and in France, large numbers of enthusiastic young men have devoted themselves personally to the cause and flocked to Greece, as the same class of generous spirits did to this country in the Revolutionary War. Considerable sums of money have also been raised in those countries, and supplies of arms and ammunition sent to the Grecian armies. In England a benevolent association has been formed under the presidency of Lord Milton, a nobleman of one of the wealthiest and most powerful British families; and this association has entered into a correspondence with the Grecian authorities. Local political dissensions have unfortunately mingled themselves with the counsels adopted in England for the relief of the Grecians. Still, however, large subscriptions have been made and forwarded to that country.

We are sorry for the fact that America did not set this example also. The experience of our own Revolutionary War is so recent that we ought to have felt how precious would be any aid from a distant land, however insignificant in amount. Who does not know that there were times in our own Revolutionary War when a few barrels of gunpowder, the large guns of a privateer, a cargo of flour, a supply of clothing, yea, a few hundred pairs of shoes for feet that left in blood the tracks of their march would have done essential service to the cause of suffering liberty. We perceive that the writer of an article, already quoted, in the *Quarterly Review*, observes "that £ 200,000 would hardly afford a week's relief to the numerous applicants, and if laid out in the purchase of military stores, might be lost in the course of a single siege or battle."

America has done something for Greece. Our missionary societies have their envoys to the Grecian church, with supplies of Bibles and religious tracts for their benighted flocks. But in the present state of this unhappy people, this is not the only succor they require. They are laying the foundations of civil freedom, without which even the blessings of the Gospel will be extended to them in vain; and while they are cementing with their blood this costly edifice, they are in the condition of the returning Jews, of whom "everyone with one of his hands wrought at the work, and with the other hand held a weapon." We would respectfully suggest to the enlarged and pious minds of those who direct the great work of missionary charity that, at this moment, the cause of the Grecian church can in no way be so effectually served as by contributions directed to the field of the great struggle. . . .

In the few remarks which we have taken the liberty to make on this occasion, we have not insisted on the topic of the glorious descent of the Greeks; of the duty of hastening to the succor of those whose fathers were the masters of the world, in the school of civilization. It is not because we are not sensible of the power of this appeal, also, but because we think a much stronger appeal may be made. To take an interest in the fate of a people whose ancestors fill so important a place in the history of the world and of the human mind is certainly natural. The geographical names which fill the accounts from Greece excite an interest of themselves; and we feel a double eagerness to hear that the Turks have not only been beaten but beaten out of the Acropolis of Athens; and that Odysseus is still successful on the sides of Eta.

It is not merely the countrymen of Aristides, the fellow citizens of Phocion, the descendants of Aratus that are calling upon us. These glorious names are a dead letter to two-thirds of the community of Christendom. But it is Christians bowed beneath the yoke of barbarous infidels; it is fathers and mothers condemned to see their children torn from them and doomed to the most cruel slavery; it is men like ourselves bereft of all the bounties which Providence has lavished on their land, obliged to steal through life, as through the passes of a mountain before the bloodhounds of the pursuer. No exhilarating prospect of public honor; no cheering hope of private success in life; no thrill at the name of country; no protection at the fireside — but all one blank of leaden, dreary despotism, which turns the very virtues and excellencies of character into a crime. It is the great curse of a despotism like that of the Turks that it inverts the laws of conduct for its subjects, and connects suffering and death with those principles and actions to which Providence attaches the rewards of life in a healthy state of society.

We are able to pity individuals among us, so unfortunately born and bred as to be surrounded with corrupting examples and taught to find occupation and pleasure in vice. What a spectacle do not the Greeks present in this connection to the practical philanthropist! Are they zealous in the profession of their religion and in the observance of its rights, they jeopardize the continuance of the jealous and contemptuous toleration beneath which they live. Do they love and serve the land of their birth, they are guilty of treason against its barbarous master. Do they with industry and enterprise acquire wealth, it is necessary studiously to conceal it from unprincipled extortion, and to invest it in foreign countries. Do they found schools and make provision for education, they expose themselves to exaction and their children to outrage, and are obligated to proceed with greatest possible secrecy and circumspection. What a monstrous complication of calamity to have the best, the worthiest, the purest designs and actions, loaded with all the consequences of vice and crime; to be deprived not only of all that makes life joyous but to be punished for doing well, and to be forced to go privately about those good deeds, to which men in other countries are exhorted as to a source of praise and honor.

These things ought to be considered; and a reprehensible apathy prevails as to their reality. If liberty, virtue, and religion were not words on our lips, without a substance in our hearts, it would be hardly possible to pursue our little local interests with such jealousy; to be all on fire in one state, for fear Congress should claim the power of internal improvements, and up in arms in another against a change of the tariff, and carried away in all, with a controversy between rival candidates for an office, which all would administer in much the same way. If a narrow selfishness did not lie at the bottom of our conduct, we could not do all this, while men, Christians as good as we, who have nerves to smart, minds to think, hearts to feel, like ourselves, are waging unaided, single-handed, at perilous odds, a war of extermination against tyrants, who deny them not only the blessings of liberty but the mercies of slavery.

But we hope better things of our country. In the great Lancastrian school of the nations, liberty is the lesson which we are appointed to teach. Masters we claim not, we wish not, to be, but the monitors we are of this noble doctrine. It is taught in our settlement, taught in our Revolution, taught in our government; and the nations of the world are resolved to learn. It may be written in sand and effaced, but it will be written again and again, till hands now fettered in slavery shall boldly and fairly trace it, and lips that now stammer at the noble word shall sound it out in the ears of their despots, with an emphasis to waken the dead. Some will comprehend it and practise it at the first; others must wrestle long with the old slavish doctrines; and others may abuse it to excess, and cause it to be blasphemed awhile in the world. But it will still be taught and still be repeated, and must be learned by all; by old and degenerate communities to revive their youth; by springing colonies to hasten their progress. With the example before them of a free representative government — of a people governed by themselves — it is no more possible that the nations will long bear any other than that they should voluntarily dispense with the art of printing or the mariner's compass.

1824

23.

Debate on the Greek Revolution

Despite the noninterventionist sentiments of the Monroe Doctrine, some members of Congress favored an expression of sympathy by the United States for the Greek revolutionary cause. A resolution to that effect was presented to the House of Representatives on December 8, 1823, by Daniel Webster, a representative from Massachusetts. Speaking in support of his resolution the following January 19, Webster, though eschewing material support for Greece such as Edward Everett had urged in the North American Review, *demanded verbal support in the name of moral and humanitarian principles. The following day, John Randolph of Roanoke vigorously opposed Webster's position, pointing out the far-reaching implications the resolution would have for American foreign relations. Portions of both speeches are reprinted here.*

Source: *Debates,* 18 Cong., 1 Sess., pp. 1084-1099, 1182-1201.

I.

DANIEL WEBSTER: For a Resolution of Sympathy

I AM AWARE, SIR, that it is a very easy thing to run over commonplaces on the subject of this resolution; to call it a visionary and Quixotic measure, and to urge the good old maxim of its being the soundest policy for each one to take care of his own concerns. That maxim, sir, is very true, but very inapplicable to the present occasion. The question which is now to be discussed is the American question in relation to this affair — What is it best for us to do in the present aspect of things respecting Greece? And surely, sir, this is a question that comprehends something more than a mere pecuniary calculation. Whenever my mind turns to that question, I cannot forget the age I live in, as well as the peculiar position of our own country. . . .

The age . . . is a peculiar one — it has a marked and striking character, and the position and circumstances of our country are no less so. Had we enjoyed the option, in which period of the world's history as thus far disclosed our personal lot should be cast, none of us, surely, would wish to have been born in any other time, or in any other country. There has occurred no age that may be compared with the present, whether in the interest excited by what now is, or the prospects it holds out as to what shall be. The attitude of the United States, meanwhile, is solemn and impressive. Ours is now the great republic of the earth; its free institutions are matured by the experiment of half a century; nay, as a free government, it goes further back — the benefits of a free constitution have virtually been enjoyed here for two centuries. As a free government, as the freest government, its growth and strength compel it, willing or unwilling, to stand forth to the contemplation of the world. We cannot obscure ourselves, if we would; a part we must take, honorable or dishonorable, in all that is done in the civilized world.

Now, it will not be denied that, within the last ten years, there has been agitated, in that world, a question of vast moment — a question pregnant with consequences favorable or unfavorable to the prevalence, nay, to the very existence, of civil liberty. It is a question which comes home to us. It calls on us for the expression of our opinion on the great question now before us. Assuredly, if there is any general tendency in the minds and affairs of men which may be said to characterize the present age, it is the tendency to limited governments. The enlightened part of mankind have very distinctly evinced a desire to take a share, at least, in the government of themselves. The men of this age will not be satisfied even with kind masters. . . .

The age we live in, and our own active character, have connected us with all the nations of the world; and we, as a nation, have precisely the same interest in international law as a private individual has in the laws of his country. . . .

What do we not, as a people, owe to the principle of lawful resistance? to the principle that society shall govern itself? These principles have raised us to a state of prosperity, in which our course is rapid and irresistible. We are borne on as by a mighty current, and if we would stop long enough to take an observation that we may measure our national course before we can effect it, we find we have already moved a vast distance from the point at which it was commenced. This course we cannot check; it is the course of things and it will go on. Shall we not, thus situated, give to others who are struggling for these very principles the cheering aid of our example and opinion? . . .

A second question, however, may here be asked. What can we do? This thunder is at a distance; the wide Atlantic rolls between; we are safe — Would you have us go to war? Would you have us send armies into Europe? No, I would not. But this reasoning mistakes the age. Formerly, indeed, there was no making an impression on a nation but by bayonets and subsidies, by fleets and armies; but the age has undergone a change. There is a force in public opinion which, in the long run, will outweigh all the physical force that can be brought to oppose it. Until public opinion is subdued, the greatest enemy of tyranny is not yet dead. What is the soul, the informing spirit, of our institutions, of our entire system of government? Public opinion. While this acts with intensity and moves in the right direction, the country must ever be safe — let us direct the force, the vast moral force, of this engine to the aid of others.

Public opinion is the great enemy of the Holy Alliance. It may be said that public opinion did not succeed in Spain. Public opinion was never thoroughly changed there; but does any man suppose that Spain is not at this day nearer, nor merely in point of time but intellectually and politically nearer, to freedom than she was last spring? True, indeed, the Bourbon power did make an almost unresisted march from the Pyrenees to Cadiz, but is Europe satisfied? Public opinion is neither conciliated nor destroyed — like Milton's angels, it is vital in every part — and this followed back the Conqueror as he returned and held Europe in indignant silence. Let us, then, speak; let us speak well of what has done well for us. We shall have the thinking world all with us; and, be it remembered, it was a thinking community that achieved our Revolution before a battle had been fought. . . .

It may now be asked, will this resolution do them any good? Yes, it will do them much good. It will give them courage and spirit, which is better than money. It will assure them of the public sympathy, and will inspire them with fresh constancy. It will teach them that they are not forgotten by the civilized world, and to hope one day to occupy, in that world, an honorable station.

A further question remains. Is this measure pacific? It has no other character. It simply proposes to make a pecuniary provision for a mission, when the President shall deem such mission expedient. It is a mere reciprocation to the sentiments of his message; it imposes upon him no new duty; it gives him no new power; it does not hasten or urge him forward; it simply provides, in an open and avowed manner, the means of doing what would else be done out of the contingent fund. It leaves him at the most perfect liberty, and it reposes the whole matter in his sole discretion. . . .

Do gentlemen fear the result of this resolution in embroiling us with the Porte? Why, sir, how much is it ahead of the whole nation, or rather let me ask how much is the nation ahead of it? Is not this whole people already in a state of open and avowed excitement on this subject? Does not the land ring from side to side with one common sentiment of sympathy for Greece and indignation toward her oppressors? Nay, more, sir, are we not giving money to this cause? More still, sir, is not the secreta-

New York Historical Society

Daniel Webster favored taking a stand supporting the Greek revolution; portrait by G.P.A. Healy

ry of state in open correspondence with the president of the Greek Committee in London? The nation has gone as far as it can go, short of an official act of hostility. This resolution adds nothing beyond what is already done; nor can any of the European governments take offense at such a measure. But if they would, shall we be withheld from an honest expression of liberal feelings in the cause of freedom for fear of giving umbrage to some member of the Holy Alliance? We are not, surely, yet prepared to purchase their smiles by a sacrifice of every manly principle. Dare any Christian prince even ask us not to sympathize with a Christian nation struggling against Tartar tyranny? We do not interfere; we break no engagements; we violate no treaties — with the Porte we have none.

Mr. Chairman, there are some things which, to be well done, must be promptly done. If we even determine to do the thing that is now proposed, we may do it too late. Sir, I am not one of those who are for withholding aid when it is most urgently needed, and when the stress is past and the aid no longer necessary, overwhelming the sufferer with caresses. I will not stand by and see my fellowman drowning without stretching out a hand to help him, till he has by his own efforts and presence of mind reached the shore in safety, and then encumber him with aid. With suffering Greece, now is the crisis of her fate — her great, it may be, her last struggle. Sir, while we sit here deliberating, her destiny may be decided. The Greeks, contending with ruthless oppressors, turn their eyes to us, and invoke us by their ancestors, by their slaughtered wives and children, by their own blood, poured out like water, by the hecatombs of dead they have heaped up as it were to heaven, they invoke, they implore of us some cheering sound, some look of sympathy, some token of compassionate regard. They look to us as the great republic of the earth; and they ask us, by our common faith, whether we can forget that they are struggling as we once struggled for what we now so happily enjoy?

I cannot say, sir, that they will succeed; that rests with Heaven. But for myself, sir, if I should tomorrow hear that they have failed — that their last phalanx had sunk beneath the Turkish scimitar, that the flames of their last city had sunk in its ashes, and that naught remained but the wide melancholy waste where Greece once was — I should still reflect, with the most heartfelt satisfaction, that I have asked you, in the name of 7 million freemen, that you would give them at least the cheering of one friendly voice.

II.

JOHN RANDOLPH: Against Moral Crusading in Foreign Policy

IT APPEARS TO ME that the bearings and consequences of the measure proposed by this resolution have not yet been traced to their utmost extent. . . . It is with serious concern and alarm . . . that I have heard doc-

trines broached in this debate, fraught with consequences more disastrous to the best interests of this people, than any that I ever heard advanced during the five-and-twenty years since I have been honored with a seat on this floor. They imply, to my apprehension, a total and fundamental change of the policy pursued by this government, *ab urbe condita* — from the foundation of the republic to the present day. Are we, sir, to go on a crusade in another hemisphere for the propagation of two objects as dear and delightful to my heart as to that of any gentleman in this or in any other assembly — liberty and religion — and, in the name of those holy words, by this powerful spell, is this nation to be conjured and beguiled out of the highway of heaven — out of its present comparatively happy state into all the disastrous conflicts arising from the policy of European powers, with all the consequences which flow from them? . . .

Sir, what are we now asked to do? To stimulate the executive to the creation of embassies. And what then? That we, or our friends, may fill them. Sir, the sending ambassadors abroad is one of the great prerogatives, if you will, of our executive authority; and we are, I repeat, about to stimulate the President to the creation of a new, and, I must be permitted to say, an unnecessary embassy — a diplomatic agency to Greece — that we, or our friends, may profit by it. . . .

But it is urged that we have sent and received ministers from revolutionary France. True . . . we have; but what was revolutionary France? Our own ancient and very good ally; a substantive power, if any such exist on the continent of Europe, whose independent existence no one could doubt or dispute, unless, indeed, the disciples of Berkeley, who deny that there is any such thing as matter. But, sir, have the United States always received the ministers that are sent to them from foreign powers? How long did the person who was appointed diplomatic agent here from Spain (Don

Onis) linger in your antechambers before he was acknowledged? And is it said that the situation of Greece approaches more nearly to independence than that of Spain when Don Onis came here as her minister? Sir, let these Greeks send a minister to us, and then we will deliberate on the question whether we will accredit him or not. If, indeed, there was a minister of Greece knocking at the door of the President's antechamber for admittance, and that admittance was denied, the question of Grecian independence would be more legitimately before us; but I greatly doubt if even that case would be sufficient to call for the interference of this House.

But . . . there [is] one aspect of this question which . . . ought to be conclusive on the minds of all, viz: That Russia, whose designs on Turkey have been unremittingly prosecuted ever since the days of Peter the Great for more than a century; that Russia, allied to the Greeks in religious faith, identified in that respect; that Russia, unassailable territorially, and dividing with us . . . the dread and apprehension of the Allied Powers — even Russia, in "juxtaposition" . . . to Turkey — even Russia dare not move. But we, who are separated first by the Atlantic Ocean, and then have to traverse the Mediterranean Sea to arrive at the seat of conflict — we, at the distance of 5,000 miles, are to interfere in this quarrel — to what purpose? To the advantage solely of this very colossal power which has been held up as the great object of our dread, and of whom it is difficult to say whether it is more to be dreaded for its physical force or its detestable principle.

Permit me, sir, to ask why, in the selection of an enemy to the doctrines of our government, and a party to those advanced by the Holy Alliance, we should fix on Turkey? She, at least, forms no party to that alliance; and, I venture to say, that, for the last century, her conduct, in reference to her neighbors, has been much more Christian than that of all the "Most Christian," "Most Catholic," or "Most Faithful" majesties of Europe — for she has not interfered, as we propose to do, in the internal affairs of other nations.

But, sir, we have not done. Not satisfied with attempting to support the Greeks, one world, like that of Pyrrhus or Alexander, is not sufficient for us. We have yet another world for exploits; we are to operate in a country distant from us 80° of latitude, and only accessible by a circumnavigation of the globe, and to subdue which we must cover the Pacific with our ships, and the tops of the Andes with our soldiers. Do gentlemen seriously reflect on the work they have cut out for us? Why, sir, these projects of ambition surpass those of Bonaparte himself.

It has once been said of the dominions of the king of Spain — thank God! it can no longer be said — that the sun never set upon them. Sir, the sun never sets on ambition like this; they who have once felt its scorpion sting are never satisfied with a limit less than a circle of our planet. . . .

I never expected that, of all places in the world (except Salem), a proposition like this should have come from Boston!

Sir, I am afraid that, along with some most excellent attributes and qualities — the love of liberty, jury trial, the writ of habeas corpus, and all the blessings of free government — that we have derived from our Anglo-Saxon ancestors, we have got not a little of their John Bull, or rather John Bulldog spirit — their readiness to fight for anybody and on any occasion. Sir, England has been for centuries the gamecock of Europe. It is impossible to specify the wars in which she has been engaged for contrary purposes; and she will, with great pleasure, see us take off her shoulders the labor of preserving the balance of power. We find her fighting now, for the queen of Hungary — then, for her inveterate foe the king of Prussia — now at war for the restoration of the Bourbons — and now on the eve of war with them for the liberties of Spain. These lines on the subject were never more applicable than they have now become:

> Now Europe's balanced, neither side
>   prevails;
> For nothing's left in either of the scales.

If we pursue the same policy, we must travel the same road, and endure the same burdens, under which England now groans. . . .

No, sir. Let us abandon these projects. Let us say to those 7 million Greeks: "We defended ourselves when we were but 3 million against a power, in comparison to which the Turk is but as a lamb. Go and do thou likewise." . . .

Let us adhere to the policy laid down by the second as well as the first founder of our republic — by him who was the Camillus as well as the Romulus of the infant state — to the policy of peace, commerce, and honest friendship with all nations, entangling alliances with none; for to entangling alliances we must come if you once embark in projects such as this. . . . We were sent here . . . to attend to the preservation of the peace of this country, and not to be ready, on all occasions, to go to war whenever anything like what in common parlance is termed a turnup takes place in Europe. . . .

What . . . is our situation? We are absolutely combating shadows. The gentleman would have us to believe his resolution is all but nothing; yet again it is to prove om-

John Randolph argued against American intervention in others' internal affairs; portrait by Harding

nipotent, and fills the whole globe with its influence. Either it is nothing, or it is something. If it is nothing, let us lay it on the table and have done with it at once; but if it is that something which it has been on the other hand represented to be, let us beware how we touch it. For my part, I would sooner put the shirt of Nessus on my back than sanction these doctrines — doctrines such as I never heard from my boyhood till now. They go the whole length. If they prevail, there are no longer any Pyrenees; every bulwark and barrier of the Constitution is broken down; it is become *tabula rasa* — a carte blanche for everyone to scribble on it what he pleases.

Three or four times I thought my temples would burst with the gush of blood . . . When I came out I was almost afraid to come near him. It seemed to me as if he was like the mount that might not be touched and that burned with fire. I was beside myself, and am so still.

GEORGE TICKNOR, *Journal*, after hearing a speech by Daniel Webster

24.

Henry Clay: The Protective Tariff

The Tariff of 1824 raised duties generally and increased the number of commodities that were subject to tax. Its passage was largely owing to the efforts of Henry Clay, who was motivated by a dual purpose. First, in order to make the nation economically independent, Clay felt that a high tariff was necessary to reduce foreign competition and thus to strengthen the domestic market. At the same time that the home market would be protected, the national government would gain a source of revenue that could be applied to the internal improvements that, in his view, were necessary. Second, as a candidate for the presidency, Clay hoped to win votes in the manufacturing states of the northeast by his so-called American System, in which the Tariff was an essential element. He outlined his views and defended the Tariff in a speech in Congress on March 31, 1824, from which the following is taken.

Source: Colton, VI, pp. 254-294.

THE POLICY OF ALL EUROPE is adverse to the reception of our agricultural produce so far as it comes into collision with its own; and, under that limitation, we are absolutely forbid to enter their ports, except under circumstances which deprive them of all value as a steady market. The policy of all Europe rejects those great staples of our country which consist of objects of human subsistence. The policy of all Europe refuses to receive from us anything but those raw materials of smaller value, essential to their manufactures, to which they can give a higher value, with the exception of tobacco and rice, which they cannot produce. Even Great Britain, to which we are its best customer, and from which we receive nearly one half in value of our whole imports, will not take from us articles of subsistence produced in our country cheaper than can be produced in Great Britain. . . .

Is this foreign market, so incompetent at present, and which, limited as its demands are, operates so unequally upon the productive labor of our country, likely to improve in future? If I am correct in the views which I have presented to the committee, it must become worse and worse. What can improve it? Europe will not abandon her own agriculture to foster ours. We may even anticipate that she will more and more enter into competition with us in the supply of the West India market. . . .

Our agriculture is our greatest interest. It ought ever to be predominant. All others should bend to it. And, in considering what is for its advantage, we should contemplate it in all its varieties, of planting, farming, and grazing. Can we do nothing to invigorate it; nothing to correct the errors of the past, and to brighten the still more unpromising prospects which lie before us? We have seen, I think, the causes of the distresses of the country. We have seen that an exclusive dependence upon the foreign market must lead to still severer distress, to impoverishment, to ruin.

We must, then, change somewhat our course. We must give a new direction to some portion of our industry. We must speedily adopt a genuine American policy. Still cherishing the foreign market, let us create also a home market to give further scope to the consumption of the produce of American industry. Let us counteract the policy of foreigners and withdraw the support which we now give to their industry and stimulate that of our own country. . . .

By creating a new and extensive business, then, we would not only give employment to those who want it, and augment the sum of national wealth by all that this new business would create, but we should meliorate the condition of those who are now engaged in existing employments. In Europe, particularly Great Britain, their large standing armies, large navies, large even on their peace arrangement, their established church afford to their population employments which, in that respect, the happier Constitution of our government does not tolerate but in a very limited degree. The peace establishments of our Army and our Navy are extremely small, and I hope ever will be. We have no established church, and I trust never shall have. In proportion as the enterprise of our citizens in public employments is circumscribed should we excite and invigorate it in private pursuits.

The creation of a home market is not only necessary to procure for our agriculture a just reward for its labors but it is indispensable to obtain a supply for our necessary wants. If we cannot sell, we cannot buy. That portion of our population (and we have seen that it is not less than four-fifths), which makes comparatively nothing that foreigners will buy, has nothing to make purchases with from foreigners. It is in vain that we are told of the amount of our exports supplied by the planting interest. They may enable the planting interest to supply all its wants; but they bring no ability to the interests not planting; unless, which cannot be pretended, the planting interest was an adequate vent for the surplus produce of the labor of all other interests.

It is in vain to tantalize us with the great-

er cheapness of foreign fabrics. There must be an ability to purchase, if an article be obtained, whatever may be the price, high or low, at which it is sold. And a cheap article is as much beyond the grasp of him who has no means to buy as a high one. Even if it were true that the American manufacturer would supply consumption at dearer rates, it is better to have his fabrics than the unattainable foreign fabrics; because it is better to be ill supplied than not supplied at all. A coarse coat which will communicate warmth and cover nakedness is better than no coat.

The superiority of the home market results, first, from its steadiness and comparative certainty at all times; second, from the creation of reciprocal interest; third, from its greater security; and, last, from an ultimate and not distant augmentation of consumption (and consequently of comfort) from increased quantity and reduced prices. But this home market, highly desirable as it is, can only be created and cherished by the *protection* of our own legislation against the inevitable prostration of our industry, which must ensue from the action of *foreign* policy and legislation. . . . The measure of the wealth of a nation is indicated by the measure of its protection of its industry; and . . . the measure of the poverty of a nation is marked by that of the degree in which it neglects and abandons the care of its own industry, leaving it exposed to the action of foreign powers. . . .

Having called the attention of the committee to the present adverse state of our country, and endeavored to point out the causes which have led to it; having shown that similar causes, wherever they exist in other countries, lead to the same adversity in their condition; and having shown that, wherever we find opposite causes prevailing, a high and animating state of national prosperity exists, the committee will agree with me in thinking that it is the solemn duty of government to apply a remedy to the evils which afflict our country, if it can apply one. Is there no remedy within the reach of the government? Are we doomed to behold our industry languish and decay yet more and more?

But there is a remedy, and that remedy consists in modifying our foreign policy, and in adopting a genuine *American system*. We must naturalize the arts in our country; and we must naturalize them by the only means which the wisdom of nations has yet discovered to be effectual — by adequate protection against the otherwise overwhelming influence of foreigners. This is only to be accomplished by the establishment of a tariff, to the consideration of which I am now brought.

And what is this tariff? It seems to have been regarded as a sort of monster, huge and deformed — a wild beast, endowed with tremendous powers of destruction, about to be let loose among our people, if not to devour them, at least to consume their substance. But let us calm our passions and deliberately survey this alarming, this terrific being. The sole object of the tariff is to tax the produce of foreign industry with the view of promoting American industry. The tax is exclusively leveled at foreign industry. That is the avowed and the direct purpose of the tariff. If it subjects any part of American industry to burdens, that is an effect not intended, but is altogether incidental and perfectly voluntary.

It has been treated as an imposition of burdens upon one part of the community, by design, for the benefit of another; as if, in fact, money were taken from the pockets of one portion of the people and put into the pockets of another. But is that a fair representation of it? No man pays the duty assessed on the foreign article by compulsion, but voluntarily; and this voluntary duty, if paid, goes into the common exchequer for the common benefit of all. . . .

But it is said by the honorable gentleman from Virginia that the South, owing to the character of a certain portion of its population, cannot engage in the business of man-

ufacturing. . . . What is to be done in this conflict? The gentleman would have us abstain from adopting a policy called for by the interest of the greater and freer part of our population. But is that reasonable? Can it be expected that the interests of the greater part should be made to bend to the condition of the servile part of our population? That, in effect, would be to make us the slaves of slaves. . . .

The existing state of things, indeed, presents a sort of tacit compact between the cotton grower and the British manufacturer, the stipulations of which are, on the part of the cotton grower, that the whole of the United States, the other portions as well as the cotton growing, shall remain open and unrestricted in the consumption of British manufactures; and, on the part of the British manufacturer, that in consideration thereof, he will continue to purchase the cotton of the South. Thus, then, we perceive that the proposed measure instead of sacrificing the South to the other parts of the Union seeks only to preserve them from being absolutely sacrificed under the operation of the tacit compact which I have described.

Supposing the South to be actually incompetent, or disinclined, to embark at all in the business of manufacturing, is not its interest, nevertheless, likely to be promoted by creating a new and an American source of supply for its consumption? Now, foreign powers, and Great Britain principally, have the monopoly of the supply of Southern consumption. If this bill should pass, an American competitor, in the supply of the South, would be raised up, and ultimately, I cannot doubt, that it will be supplied more cheaply and better. . . .

The second objection to the proposed bill is that it will diminish the amount of our exports. It can have no effect upon our exports, except those which are sent to Europe. Except tobacco and rice, we send there nothing but the raw materials. The argument is that Europe will not buy of us if we do not buy of her. The first objection to it is that it calls upon us to look to the question, and to take care of European ability in legislating for American interests. Now, if in legislating for their interests they would consider and provide for our ability, the principle of reciprocity would enjoin us so to regulate our intercourse with them as to leave their ability unimpaired. But I have shown that, in the adoption of their own policy, their inquiry is strictly limited to a consideration of their peculiar interests, without any regard to that of ours. . . .

The third objection to the tariff is, that it will diminish our navigation. This great interest deserves every encouragement, consistent with the paramount interest of agriculture. In the order of nature it is secondary to both agriculture and manufactures. Its business is the transportation of the productions of those two superior branches of industry. It cannot, therefore, be expected that they shall be molded or sacrificed to suit its purposes; but on the contrary, navigation must accommodate itself to the actual state of agriculture and manufactures. If, as I believe, we have nearly reached the maximum in value of our exports of raw produce to Europe, the effect hereafter will be, as it respects that branch of our trade, if we persevere in the foreign system, to retain our navigation at the point which it has now reached. . . . But, if I am mistaken in these views, and it should experience any reduction, the increase in our coasting tonnage resulting from the greater activity of domestic exchanges will more than compensate the injury. . . .

According to the opponents of the domestic policy, the proposed system will force capital and labor into new and reluctant employments; we are not prepared, in consequence of the high price of wages, for the successful establishment of manufactures, and we must fail in the experiment. We have seen that the existing occupations of our society, those of agriculture, commerce, navigation, and the learned professions, are overflowing with competitors, and that the want of employment is severely felt. Now what does this bill propose? To open a new and extensive field of business in which all that choose may enter. There is no compulsion upon anyone to engage in it. An option only is given to industry to continue in the present unprofitable pursuits, or to embark in a new and promising one. The effect will be to lessen the competition in the old branches of business and to multiply our resources for increasing our comforts and augmenting the national wealth. . . .

It is said that wherever there is a concurrence of favorable circumstances manufactures will arise of themselves, without protection; and that we should not disturb the natural progress of industry, but leave things to themselves. . . . Now, I contend that this proposition is refuted by all experience, ancient and modern, and in every country. If I am asked why unprotected industry should not succeed in a struggle with protected industry, I answer, the *fact* has ever been so, and that is sufficient; I reply that *uniform experience* evinces that it cannot succeed in such an unequal contest, and that is sufficient. . . .

The next objection of the honorable gentleman from Virginia which I shall briefly notice is that the manufacturing system is adverse to the genius of our government in its tendency to the accumulation of large capitals in a few hands; in the corruption of the public morals, which is alleged to be incident to it; and in the consequent danger to the public liberty. . . . The greatest danger to public liberty is from idleness and vice. If manufactures form cities, so does commerce. And the disorders and violence which proceed from the contagion of the passions are as frequent in one description of those communities as in the other.

There is no doubt but that the yeomanry of a country is the safest depository of public liberty. In all time to come, and under any probable direction of the labor of our population, the agricultural class must be much the most numerous and powerful, and will ever retain, as it ought to retain, a preponderating influence in our councils. The extent and the fertility of our lands constitute an adequate security against an excess in manufactures, and also against oppression, on the part of capitalists, toward the laboring portions of the community. . . .

Mr. Chairman, our Confederacy comprehends, within its vast limits, great diversity of interests: agricultural, planting, farming, commercial, navigating, fishing, manufacturing. No one of these interests is felt in the same degree and cherished with the same solicitude throughout all parts of the Union. Some of them are peculiar to particular sections of our common country. But all these great interests are confided to the protection of one government — to the fate of one ship — and a most gallant ship it is, with a noble crew. If we prosper and are happy, protection must be extended to all; it is due to all. . . .

If the promotion of those interests would not injuriously affect any other section, then everything should be done for them which would be done if it formed a distinct government. If they come into absolute collision with the interests of another section, a reconciliation, if possible, should be attempted, by mutual concession, so as to avoid a sacrifice of the prosperity of either to that of the other. In such a case, all should not be done for one which would be done, if it were separated and independent, but something; and, in devising the measure, the good of each part and of the whole should be carefully consulted. This is the only mode by which we can preserve, in full vigor, the harmony of the whole Union.

25.

Edward Everett: The Circumstances Favorable to the Progress of Literature in America

Speaking before the Harvard chapter of Phi Beta Kappa on August 26, 1824, Edward Everett, a highly accomplished orator, presented an analysis of American political and social conditions and their relation to the development of a national literature. Everett, who had political ambitions, took the opportunity publicly to express his nationalistic views, the favorable reception of which aided in his election to Congress the following November. His closing remarks about the Revolutionary hero Lafayette, who was sitting in the audience, were met with thunderous applause. Portions of Everett's address are reprinted here.

Source: *Orations and Speeches on Various Occasions,* 2nd edition, Boston, 1850, Vol. I, pp. 9-44.

THE FIRST CIRCUMSTANCE of which I shall speak, as influencing the progress of letters by furnishing the motives to intellectual effort among us, is the new form of political society established in the United States; viz., a confederacy of republics, in which, however, within the limits of the Constitution, the central government acts upon the individual citizen. It is not my purpose to detain you with so trite a topic as the praises of free political institutions; but to ask your attention to the natural operation of a system like ours on the literary character of a people. I call this a new form of political society. . . .

Here, for the first time, the whole direction and influence of affairs and all the great organic functions of the body politic are subjected, directly or indirectly (the executive and legislative functions directly), to free popular choice. Whatsoever quickening influence resides in public honors and trusts and in the cheerful consciousness of individual participation in the most momentous political rights is here for the first time exerted directly on the largest mass of men, with the smallest possible deductions; and as a despotism, like that of Turkey or Persia, is, by all admission, the form of government least favorable to the intellectual progress of a people, it would seem equally certain that the farther you recede from such a despotism in the establishment of a system of popular and constitutional liberty, the greater the assurance that the universal mind of the country will be powerfully and genially excited.

I am aware that it is a common notion that, under an elective government of very limited powers like that of the United States, we lose that powerful spring of action which exists in the patronage of strong hereditary governments and must proceed from the Crown. I believe it is a prevalent opinion abroad, among those who entertain the most friendly sentiments toward the American system, that we must consent to dispense with something of the favorable influence of princely and royal patronage on letters and the arts and find our consolation in the political benefits of a republican government. It may be doubted, however, whether this view be not entirely fallacious. For, in the first place, it is by no means true that a popular government will be destitute either of the means or the disposition to exercise a liberal patronage. No government, as a government, ever did more for

the fine arts than that of Athens. In the next place, it is to be considered in this connection that the evils of centralization are as evident, in reference to the encouragement of the general mind of the people, as they are in regard to a contented acquiescence in political administration. Whatever is gained, for those who enjoy it, by concentrating a powerful patronage in the capital and in the central administration, is lost in the neglect and discouragement of the distant portions of the state, and its subordinate institutions.

It must be recollected that our representative system extends far beyond the election of the high officers of the national and state governments. It pervades our local and municipal organizations, and probably exercises in them the most efficient and salutary parts of its influence. In the healthful action of this system, whatever virtue there is in patronage is made to pervade the republic like the air; to reach the farthest, and descend to the lowest. It is made not only to cooperate with the successful, and decorate the prosperous, but "to remember the forgotten, to attend to the neglected, to visit the forsaken." Hitherto, for the most part, men in need of patronage have had but one weary pilgrimage to perform — to travel up to court. . . .

But the beneficial effect of patronage, properly so called, is probably much overrated. This effect is not, on any system of distribution, to be sought in its direct application to the support of men of genius and learning. Its best operation is in the cheerful effect of kindly notice and intelligent audience. Talent, indeed, desires to earn a support, but not to receive a dole. It is rightfully urged, as the great advantage of our system, that the encouragements of society extend as widely as its burdens, and search out and bring forward whatsoever of ability and zeal for improvement are contained in any part of the land. I am persuaded that mainly in this equable diffusion of rights and privileges lies the secret of the astonishing development of intellectual energy in this country. Capacity and opportunity, the twin sisters who can scarce subsist happily but with each other, are brought together. These little local republics are schools of character and nurseries of mind. The people who are to choose, and from whose number are to be chosen by their neighbors, all those who, either in higher or lower stations, are entrusted with the management of affairs, feel the strongest impulse to mental activity. They read and think and form judgments on important subjects. In a special manner they are moved to make provision for education. With all its deficiencies our system of public schools — founded in the infancy of the country by the colonial legislature and transmitted to our own days — is superior to any system of public instruction (with possibly a single exception) which has ever been established by the most enlightened states of the Old World. . . .

From the first settlement of New England, and from an early stage of their progress in many of the other states, one of the most prominent traits of the character of our population has been to provide and to diffuse the means of education. The village schoolhouse and the village church are the monuments of our republicanism; to read, to write, and to discuss grave affairs in their primary assemblies are the licentious practices of our democracy.

But, in this acknowledged result of our system of government, another objection is taken to its influence, as far as literary progress is concerned. It is urged that, though it may be the effect of our system to excite the mind of the people, it excites it too much in a political direction; that the division and subdivision of the country into states and districts, and the equal diffusion of political privileges and powers among the whole population, with the constant recurrence of elections, however favorable to civil liberty, are unfriendly to learning; that they

kindle only a political ambition; and particularly, that they seduce the aspiring youth from the patient and laborious vigils of the student to plunge prematurely into the conflicts of the forum.

I am inclined to think that, as far as the alleged facts exist, they are the necessary result of the present stage of our national progress, and not an evil necessarily incident to representative government. Our system is certainly an economical one, both as to the number of persons employed and the compensation of public service. It cannot, therefore, draw more individuals from other pursuits into public life than would be employed under any other form or system of government. It is obvious that the administration of the government of a country, whether it be liberal or absolute or mixed, is the first thing to be provided for. Some persons must be employed in making and administering the laws, before any other human interest can be attended to. The Fathers of Plymouth organized themselves under a simple compact of government before they left the Mayflower. This was both natural and wise. Had they, while yet on shipboard, talked of founding learned societies, or engaged in the discussion of philosophical problems, it would have been insipid pedantry. As the organization and administration of the government are, in the order of time, the first of mere human concerns, they must ever retain a paramount importance. Everything else must come in by opportunity; this of necessity must be provided for, otherwise life is not safe, property is not secure, and there is no permanence in the social institutions. The first efforts, therefore, of men in building up a new state are of necessity political.

The peculiar relations of the colonies to the parent state, also, called into political action much of the talent of the country, for a century before the Revolution. But where else in the world did the foundation of the college ever follow so closely on that of the republic as in Massachusetts? In the early stages of society, when there is a scanty population, its entire force is required for administration and defense. We are receding from this stage, but have not yet reached, although we are rapidly approaching, that in which a crowded population produces a large amount of cultivated talent, not needed for the service of the state.

As far, then, as the talent and activity of the country are at present called forth in a political direction, it is fairly to be ascribed, not to any supposed incompatibility of popular institutions with the cultivation of letters, but to the precise point, in its social progress, which the country has reached. A change of government would produce no change in this respect. Can any man suppose, other things remaining the same, that the introduction of a hereditary sovereign, an order of nobility, a national church, a standing army, and a military police would tend to a more general and more fruitful development of mental energy or greater leisure on the part of educated men to engage in literary pursuits? It is obviously as impossible that any such effect should be produced as that the supposed producing cause should be put in action in this country. By the terms of the supposition, if such a change were made, the leading class of the community, the nobles, would be politicians by birth; as much talent would be required to administer the state; as much physical activity to defend it. If there were a class, as there probably would be, in the horizontal division of society which exists under such governments, not taking an interest in politics, it would be that which, under the name of the peasantry, fills, in most other countries, the place of perhaps the most substantial, uncorrupted, and intelligent population on earth — the American yeomanry. . . .

In thus maintaining that the tendency of our popular institutions, at the present stage of our national progress, to excite a diffusive interest in politics is in no degree unfriendly to the permanent intellectual improvement of the country, it is not intended to assert that the peculiar and original character of these institutions will produce no corresponding modification of our literature. The reverse is unquestionably the fact. It may safely be supposed that, with the growth of the people in wealth and population, as the various occasions of an enterprising and prosperous community placed on the widest theater of action ever opened to man call into strong action and vigorous competition the cultivated talent of the country, some peculiar tone, form, and proportion will be given to its literature by the nature of its political institutions and the social habits founded on them. Literature is but a more perfect communication of man with man and mind with mind. It is the judgment, the memory, the imagination; discoursing, recording, or musing aloud upon the materials drawn from the great storehouse of observation, or fashioned out of them by the creative powers of the mind. It is the outward expression of the intellectual man; or if not this, it is poor imitation.

What therefore affects the man affects the literature; and it may be assumed as certain that the peculiarity of our political institutions will be represented in the character of our intellectual pursuits. Government, war, commerce, manners, and the stage of social progress are reflected in the literature of a country. No precedent exists to teach us what direction the mind will most decidedly take under the strong excitements to action above described, unrestrained by the direct power of government, but greatly influenced by public sentiment throughout a vastly extensive and highly prosperous country into which the civilization of older states has been rapidly transfused.

This condition of things is evidently substantially new, and renders it impossible to foresee what garments our native muses will weave to themselves. To foretell our literature would be to create it. . . .

It would be equally impossible to mark out beforehand the probable direction in which the intellect of this country will move under the influence of institutions as new and peculiar as those of Greece, and so organized as to secure the best blessings of popular government without the evils of anarchy. But if, as no one will deny, our political system brings more minds into action on equal terms, and extends the advantages of education more equally throughout the community; if it provides a prompter and wider circulation of thought; if, by raising the character of the masses, it swells to tens of thousands and millions those "sons of emulation, who crowd the narrow strait where honor travels," it would seem not too much to anticipate new varieties and peculiar power in the literature, which is but the voice and utterance of all this mental action. The instrument of communication may receive improvement, the written and spoken language acquire new vigor; possibly, forms of address wholly new will be devised. Where great interests are at stake, great concerns rapidly succeeding each other, depending on almost innumerable wills, and yet requiring to be apprehended in a glance and explained in a word; where movements are to be given to a vast population, not so much by transmitting orders as by diffusing opinions, exciting feelings, and touching the electric chord of sympathy; there language and expression will become intense, and the old processes of communication must put on a vigor and a directness adapted to the condition of things.

Our country is called, as it is, practical; but this is the element for intellectual action. No strongly marked and high-toned literature, poetry, eloquence, or philosophy, ever appeared, but under the pressure of great interests, great enterprises, perilous risks, and dazzling rewards. Statesmen, and warriors, and poets, and orators, and artists start up under one and the same excitement. They are all branches of one stock. They form, and cheer, and stimulate, and what is worth all the rest, understand each other; and it is as truly the sentiment of the student in the recesses of his cell as of the soldier in the ranks, which breathes in the exclamation.

> To all the sons of sense proclaim,
> One glorious hour of *crowded life*
> Is worth an age without a name,

crowded with emotion, thought, utterance, and achievement. . . .

The next circumstance worthy of mention as peculiarly calculated to promote the progress of improvement and to furnish motives to intellectual exertion in this country is the extension of one government, one language, and substantially one character over so vast a space as the United States of America. Hitherto, in the main, the world has seen but two forms of political government — free governments in small states, and arbitrary governments in large ones. Though various shades of both have appeared at different times in the world, yet, on the whole, the political ingenuity of man has never before devised the method of extending purely popular institutions beyond small districts, or of governing large states by any other means than military power. The consequence has been that the favorable effect of free institutions on intellectual progress has never been developed on a very large scale. But, though favorable to the improvement of the mind under any circumstances, it is evident that in order to their full effect in bringing forth the highest attainable excellence, they must be permanently established in an extensive region and over a numerous people.

Such is the state of things existing in this country, and for the first time in the world, and for which we are indebted to the peculiar nature of our government as a union of confederated republics. Its effect upon literature must eventually be to give elevation, dignity, and generous expansion to every species of mental effort. . . .

This necessary connection between the extent of a country and its intellectual progress was, it is true, of more importance in antiquity than it is at the present day, because at that period of the world, owing to political causes on which we have not time to dwell, there was, upon the whole, but one civilized and cultivated people at a time upon the stage; and the mind of one nation found no sympathy and derived no aid from the mind of another. . . .

A charm which nothing can borrow, and for which there is no substitute, dwells in the simple sound of our mother tongue. Not analyzed, nor reasoned upon, it unites the simplest recollections of early life with the maturest conceptions of the understanding. The heart is willing to open all its avenues to the language in which its infantile caprices were soothed; and, by the curious efficacy of the principle of association, it is this echo from the faint dawn of intelligence which gives to eloquence much of its manly power, and to poetry much of its divine charm.

What a noble prospect presents itself, in this way, for the circulation of thought and sentiment in our country! Instead of that multiplicity of dialect by which mental communication and sympathy between different nations are restrained in the Old World, a continually expanding realm is opened to American intellect by the extension of one language over so large a portion of the continent. The enginery of the press is here, for the first time, brought to bear with all its mighty power on the minds and hearts of men in exchanging intelligence and

Edward Everett by Stuart, 1820; at the time of this portrait he was editor of the "North American Review"

circulating opinions, unchecked by diversity of language, over an empire more extensive than the whole of Europe. . . .

If it should be objected that the permanent and prosperous existence of a commonwealth so extensive is not to be hoped for, I reply that by the wise and happy partition of powers between the national and state governments, in virtue of which the national government is relieved from all the odium of internal administration, and the state governments are spared the conflicts of foreign politics, all bounds seem removed from the possible extension of our country but the geographical limits of the continent. Instead of growing cumbrous as it increases in size, there never was a moment since the first settlement in Virginia when the political system of America moved with so firm and bold a step as at the present day. Should our happy Union continue, this great continent, in no remote futurity, will be filled up with the mightiest kindred people known in history; our language will acquire an extension which no other ever possessed; and the empire of the mind, with nothing to resist its sway, will attain an expansion of which, as yet, we can but partly conceive. The vision is too magnificent to be fully borne; a mass of two or three hundred million not chained to the oar like the same number in China by a stupefying despotism but held in their several orbits of nation and state by the grand representative attraction; bringing to bear on every point the concentrated energy of such a host; calling into competition so many minds; uniting into one great national feeling the hearts of so many freemen, all to be guided, moved, and swayed by the master spirits of the time!

Let me not be told that this is a chimerical imagination of a future indefinitely removed; let me not hear repeated the poor jest of an anticipation of "2,000 years," of a vision that requires for its fulfillment a length of ages beyond the grasp of any reasonable computation. It is the last point of peculiarity in our condition to which I invite your attention as affecting the progress of intellect that the country is growing with a rapidity hitherto without example in the world. For the 200 years of our existence, the population has doubled itself in periods of less than a quarter of a century. In the infancy of the country, and while it remained within the limits of a youthful colony, a progress so rapid as this, however important in the principle of growth disclosed, was not yet a circumstance strongly to fix the attention. But, arrived at a population of 10 million, it is a fact of extreme interest that within less than twenty-five years, these 10 million will have swelled to 20 million; that the younger members of this audience will be citizens of the largest civilized state on earth; that in a few years more than one century, the American population will equal the fabulous numbers of the Chinese empire.

This rate of increase has already produced the most striking phenomena. A few weeks after the opening of the revolutionary drama at Lexington, the momentous intelligence that the first blood was spilled reached a party of hunters beyond the Alleghenies, who had wandered far into the western wilderness. In prophetic commemoration of the glorious event, they gave the name of Lexington to the spot of their encampment in the woods. That spot is now the capital of a state as large as Massachusetts; from which, in the language of one of her own citizens, one of the brightest ornaments of his country, the tide of emigration still farther westward is more fully pouring, than from any other in the Union.

I need not say that this astonishing increase of numbers is by no means the best measure of the country's growth. Arts, letters, agriculture, all the great national interests, all the sources of national wealth are growing in a ratio still more rapid. In our cities, the intensest activity is apparent; in the country, every spring of prosperity, from the smallest improvement in husbandry to the construction of canals and railroads across the continent, is in vigorous action. Abroad, our vessels are beating the pathways of the ocean white; on the inland frontier, the nation is moving forward with a pace more like romance than reality. . . .

We need not labor to contrast this state of things with the teeming growth and rapid progress of our own country. Instead of being shut up, as it were, in the prison of a stationary or a slowly progressive community, the emulation of our countrymen is drawn out and tempted on by a horizon constantly receding before them. New nations of kindred freemen are springing up, in successive periods, shorter even than the active portion of the life of man. "While we spend our time," says Burke on this topic, "in deliberating on the mode of governing 2 million in America, we shall find we have millions more to manage." Many individuals are in this house who were arrived at years of discretion when these words of Burke were uttered; and the 2 million which Great Britain was then to manage have grown into 10 million exceedingly unmanageable. The most affecting view of this subject is that it puts it in the power of the wise and good to gather, while they live, the ripest fruits of their labors. Where in human history is to be found a contrast like that which the last fifty years have crowded into the lives of those favored men, who, raising their hands or their voices when the feeble colonies engaged in a perilous conflict with one of the most powerful empires on earth, have lived to be crowned with the highest honors of the republic which they established? Honor to their gray hairs, and peace and serenity to the evening of their eventful days! . . .

This rapid march of the population westward has been attended by circumstances in some degree novel in the history of the human mind. It is a fact somewhat difficult of explanation that the refinement of the ancient nations seemed comparatively devoid of an elastic and expansive principle. . . . Though the colonies of Greece were scattered on the coasts of Asia, of Italy, of France, of Spain, and of Africa, no extension of their population far inward took place, and the arts did not penetrate beyond the walls of the cities where they were cultivated.

How different is the picture of the diffusion of the arts and improvements of civilization from the coast to the interior of America! Population advances westward with a rapidity which numbers may describe, indeed, but cannot represent with any vivacity to the mind. The wilderness, which one year is impassable, is traversed the next by the caravans of industrious emigrants, carrying with them the language, the institutions, and the arts of civilized life. It is not the irruption of wild barbarians sent to visit the wrath of God on a degenerate empire; it is not the inroad of disciplined banditti, put in motion by reasons of state or court intrigue. It is the human family, led out by Providence to possess its broad patrimony. The states and nations which are springing up in the valley of the Missouri are bound to us by the dearest ties of a common language, a common government, and a common descent. Before New England can look with coldness on their rising myriads, she must forget that some of the best of her own blood is beating in their veins; that her hardy children, with their axes on their shoulders, have been among the pioneers in this march of humanity; that, young as she is, she has become the mother of populous states.

What generous mind would sacrifice to a selfish preservation of local preponderance the delight of beholding civilized nations rising up in the desert; and the language, the manners, the principles in which he has been reared carried with his household gods to the foot of the Rocky Mountains? Who can forget that this extension of our territorial limits is the extension of the empire of all we hold dear; of our laws, of our character, of the memory of our ancestors, of the great achievements in our history? Whithersoever the sons of the thirteen states shall wander, to southern or western climes, they will send back their hearts to the rocky shores, the battlefields, the infant settlements of the Atlantic coast. These are placed beyond the reach of vicissitude. They have become already matter of history, of poetry, of eloquence.

Divisions may spring up, ill blood may burn, parties be formed, and interests may seem to clash; but the great bonds of the nation are linked to what is past. The deeds of the great men to whom this country owes its origin and growth are a patrimony, I know, of which its children will never deprive themselves. As long as the Mississippi and the Missouri shall flow, those men and those deeds will be remembered on their banks. The scepter of government may go where it will; but that of patriotic feeling can never depart from Judah. In all that mighty region which is drained by the Missouri and its tributary streams — the valley coextensive, in this country, with the temperate zone — will there be, as long as the name of America shall last, a father that will not take his children on his knee, and recount to them the events of the 22nd of December, the 19th of April, the 17th of June, and the 4th of July?

This, then, is the theater on which the intellect of America is to appear, and such the motives to its exertion; such the mass to be influenced by its energies; such the glory to crown its success. If I err in this happy vision of my country's fortunes, I thank Heaven for an error so animating. If this be false, may I never know the truth. Never may you, my friends, be under any other feeling than that a great, a growing, an immeasurably expanding country is calling upon you for your best services. The name and character of our alma mater have already been carried by some of our brethren hundreds of miles from her venerable walls; and thousands of miles still farther westward, the communities of kindred men are fast gathering whose minds and hearts will act in sympathy with yours. . . .

HERE, THEN, A MIGHTY work is to be performed, or never, by mortals. The man who looks with tenderness on the sufferings of good men in other times; the descendant of the Pilgrims who cherishes the memory of his fathers; the patriot who feels an honest glow at the majesty of the system of which he is a member; the scholar who beholds, with rapture the long-sealed book of truth opened for all to read without prejudice; these are they by whom these auspices are to be accomplished. Yes, brethren, it is by the intellect of the country that the mighty mass is to be inspired; that its parts are to communicate and sympathize with each other; its natural progress to be adorned with becoming refinements; its principles asserted and its feelings interpreted to its own children, to other regions, and to after ages.

Meantime, the years are rapidly passing away, and gathering importance in their course. With the present year will be completed the half century from that most important era in human history — the commencement of our Revolutionary War. The jubilee of our national existence is at hand. The space of time has elapsed since that momentous date has laid down in the dust, which the blood of many of them had already hallowed, most of the great men to whom, under Providence, we owe our national existence and privileges. A few still survive among us, to reap the rich fruits of their labors and sufferings; and *one* [General Lafayette, present at the delivery of this address] has yielded himself to the united voice of a people and returned in his age to receive the gratitude of the nation to whom he devoted his youth. It is recorded on the pages of American history that when this friend of our country applied to our commissioners at Paris in 1776 for a passage in the first ship they should dispatch to America, they were obliged to answer him (so low and abject was then our dear native land) that they possessed not the means, nor the credit, sufficient for providing a single vessel, in all the ports of France. "Then," exclaimed the youthful hero, "I· will provide my own." And it is a literal fact that, when all America was too poor to offer him so much as a passage to her shores, he left, in his tender youth, the bosom of home, of domestic happiness, of wealth, of rank, to plunge in the dust and blood of our inauspicious struggle!

Welcome, friend of our fathers, to our shores! Happy are our eyes that behold those venerable features! Enjoy a triumph such as never conqueror nor monarch enjoyed — the assurance that, throughout America, there is not a bosom which does not beat with joy and gratitude at the sound of your name! You have already met and saluted, or will soon meet, the few that remain of the ardent patriots, prudent counselors, and brave warriors with whom you were associated in achieving our liberty. But you have looked round in vain for the faces of many who would have lived years of pleasure on a day like this, with their old companion in arms and brother in peril. Lincoln, and Greene, and Knox, and Hamilton are gone; the heroes of Saratoga and Yorktown have fallen before the enemy that conquers all. Above all, the first of heroes and of men, the friend of your youth, the more than friend of his country, rests in the bosom of the soil he redeemed. On the banks of his Potomac he lies in glory and peace. You will revisit the hospitable shades of Mount Vernon, but him, whom you venerated as we did, you will not meet at its door. His voice of consolation, which reached you in the dungeons of Olmütz, cannot now break its silence to bid you welcome to his own roof. But the grateful children of America will bid you welcome in his name. Welcome! Thrice welcome to our shores! And whithersoever your course shall take you, throughout the limits of the continent, the ear that hears you shall bless you, the eye that sees you shall give witness to you, and every tongue exclaim, with heartfelt joy, Welcome! Welcome, La Fayette!

26.

Aldridge v. *The Commonwealth of Virginia*

Even when free, African Americans were second-class citizens in most states of the Union, as is evidenced by the following decision in a Virginia court case, Aldridge v. The Commonwealth of Virginia, *of June 1824. In the years before the Civil War the status and rights of citizens were regulated by the individual states, not guaranteed by the federal government.*

Source: *Judicial Cases Concerning American Slavery and the Negro,* Helen T. Catterall, ed., Vol. I, Washington, 1926, pp. 140-141.

THE PETITIONER WAS INDICTED as "a free man of color," for the larceny of banknotes of the value of $150. . . . He was convicted of the crime charged, and the jury ascertained the number of stripes to be inflicted on him to be thirty-nine. The Supreme Court pronounced judgment that he receive thirty-nine stripes on his bare back on June 26th next, and that after that day, he be sold as a slave, and transported and banished beyond the limits of the United States, in the manner prescribed by law.

Held: The act of February 21, 1823, is not contrary to the constitution of the state. The Bill of Rights . . . never was contemplated . . . to extend to the whole population of the state. Can it be doubted that it not only was not intended to apply to our slave population but that the free blacks and mulattoes were also not comprehended in it? The leading and most prominent feature in that paper is the equality of civil rights and liberty. And, yet, nobody has ever questioned the power of the legislature to deny to free blacks and mulattoes one of the first privileges of a citizen — that of voting at elections, although they might in every particular, except color, be in precisely the same condition as those qualified to vote.

The numerous restrictions imposed on this class of people in our statute book, many of which are inconsistent with the letter and spirit of the Constitution, both of this state and of the United States, as respects the free whites, demonstrate that, here, those instruments have not been considered to extend equally to both classes of our population. We will only instance the restriction upon the migration of free blacks into this state, and upon their right to bear arms.

As to the 9th Section of the Bill of Rights, denouncing cruel and unusual punishments, we have no notion that it has any bearing on this case . . . the best heads and hearts of the land of our ancestors had long and loudly declaimed against the wanton cruelty of many of the punishments practised in other countries; and this section in the Bill of Rights was framed effectually to exclude these, so that no future legislature, in a moment perhaps of great and general excitement should be tempted to disgrace our code by the introduction of any of those odious modes of punishment. In the decision of these points, the court is unanimous.

27.

John Marshall: *Gibbons v. Ogden*

With the invention of the steamboat, the boating trade along the waterways between the Eastern states became a profitable commercial enterprise. The New York legislature granted an exclusive right to operate steamboats in New York waters to Robert Livingston and Robert Fulton, who then assigned part of their rights to Aaron Ogden. A former partner of Ogden, Thomas Gibbons, entered the trade in violation of the monopoly grant, and Ogden sought redress through the courts. In holding the monopoly invalid, Chief Justice John Marshall first interpreted the commerce clause of the Constitution as extending the power of Congress to navigation between the states. He then held that the states, though having the power to police their internal affairs, could not infringe upon Congress' control over interstate commerce. Since a federal law existed that appeared to regulate "vessels employed in the coasting trade," New York could not constitutionally enact the monopoly regulation covering the same area. Marshall's broad interpretation of the commerce clause of the U.S. Constitution was strictly in accord with his strong nationalism.

Source: 9 Wheaton 1.

THE APPELLANT CONTENDS that this decree is erroneous because the laws which purport to give the exclusive privilege it sustains are repugnant to the Constitution and laws of the United States. They are said to be repugnant: first, to that clause in the Constitution which authorizes Congress to regulate commerce; second, to that which authorizes Congress to promote the progress of science and useful arts. . . .

As preliminary to the very able discussions of the Constitution which we have heard from the bar, and as having some influence on its construction, reference has been made to the political situation of these states, anterior to its formation. It has been said that they were sovereign, were completely independent, and were connected with each other only by a league. This is true. But, when these allied sovereigns converted their league into a government, when they converted their congress of ambassadors, deputed to deliberate on their common concerns, and to recommend measures of general utility, into a legislature, empowered to enact laws on the most interesting subjects, the whole character in which the states appear underwent a change, the extent of which must be determined by a fair consideration of the instrument by which that change was effected.

This instrument contains an enumeration of powers expressly granted by the people to their government. It has been said that these powers ought to be construed strictly. But why ought they to be so construed? Is there one sentence in the Constitution which gives countenance to this rule? In the last of the enumerated powers, that which grants, expressly, the means for carrying all others into execution, Congress is authorized "to make all laws which shall be necessary and proper" for the purpose. But this limitation on the means which may be used is not extended to the powers which are conferred; nor is there one sentence in the Constitution, which has been pointed out by the gentlemen of the bar, or which we have been able to discern, that prescribes this rule. We do not, therefore, think ourselves justified in adopting it.

What do gentlemen mean by a strict construction? If they contend only against that enlarged construction which would extend words beyond their natural and obvious import, we might question the application of the term, but should not controvert the principle. If they contend for that narrow construction which, in support of some theory not to be found in the Constitution, would deny to the government those powers which the words of the grant, as usually understood, import, and which are consistent with the general views and objects of the instrument; for that narrow construction, which would cripple the government, and render it unequal to the objects for which it is declared to be instituted, and to which the powers given, as fairly understood, render it competent; then we cannot perceive the propriety of this strict construction, nor adopt it as the rule by which the Constitution is to be expounded. As men whose intentions require no concealment generally employ the words which most directly and aptly express the ideas they intend to convey, the enlightened patriots who framed our Constitution, and the people who adopted it, must be understood to have employed words in their natural sense, and to have intended what they have said. . . .

If, from the imperfection of human language, there should be serious doubts respecting the extent of any given power, it is a well-settled rule that the objects for which it was given, especially when those objects are expressed in the instrument itself, should have great influence in the construction. We know of no reason for excluding this rule from the present case. The grant does not convey power which might be beneficial to the grantor, if retained by himself, or which can inure solely to the benefit of the grantee, but is an investment of power for the general advantage in the hands of agents selected for that purpose; which power can never be exercised by the people themselves, but must be placed in the hands of agents, or lie dormant. We know of no rule for construing the extent of such powers other than is given by the language of the instrument which confers them, taken in connection with the purposes for which they were conferred.

The words are: "Congress shall have power to regulate commerce with foreign nations, and among the several states, and

Gen. Aaron Ogden (1756-1839), at one time a governor of New Jersey, was ruined by the decision in "Gibbons v. Ogden"; portrait by A.B. Durand

can make no law prescribing what shall constitute American vessels, or requiring that they shall be navigated by American seamen.

Yet this power has been exercised from the commencement of the government, has been exercised with the consent of all, and has been understood by all to be a commercial regulation. All America understands, and has uniformly understood, the word "commerce" to comprehend navigation. . . .

The word used in the Constitution, then, comprehends, and has been always understood to comprehend, navigation within its meaning; and a power to regulate navigation is as expressly granted as if that term had been added to the word "commerce." To what commerce does this power extend? The Constitution informs us to commerce "with foreign nations, and among the several states, and with the Indian tribes." It has, we believe, been universally admitted that these words comprehend every species of commercial intercourse between the United States and foreign nations. No sort of trade can be carried on between this country and any other to which this power does not extend. It has been truly said that commerce, as the word is used in the Constitution, is a unit, every part of which is indicated by the term. If this be the admitted meaning of the word in its application to foreign nations, it must carry the same meaning throughout the sentence and remain a unit, unless there be some plain intelligible cause which alters it.

The subject to which the power is next applied is to commerce "among the several states." The word "among" means intermingled with. A thing which is among others is intermingled with them. Commerce among the states cannot stop at the external boundary line of each state, but may be introduced into the interior. It is not intended to say that these words comprehend that commerce which is completely internal,

with the Indian tribes." The subject to be regulated is commerce; and our Constitution being, as was aptly said at the bar, one of enumeration and not of definition, to ascertain the extent of the power it becomes necessary to settle the meaning of the word. . . .

Commerce, undoutedly, is traffic, but it is something more — it is intercourse. It describes the commercial intercourse between nations, and parts of nations, in all its branches, and is regulated by prescribing rules for carrying on that intercourse. The mind can scarcely conceive a system for regulating commerce between nations which shall exclude all laws concerning navigation, which shall be silent on the admission of the vessels of the one nation into the ports of the other, and be confined to prescribing rules for the conduct of individuals in the actual employment of buying and selling or of barter. If commerce does not include navigation, the government of the Union has no direct power over that subject, and which is carried on between man and man in a state, or between different parts of the same state, and which does not extend to or affect other states. Such a power would be inconvenient and is certainly unnecessary. Comprehensive as the word "among" is, it may very properly be restricted to that commerce which concerns more states than one. The phrase is not one which would probably have been selected to indicate the completely interior traffic of a state, because it is not an apt phrase for that purpose; and the enumeration of the particular classes of commerce to which the power was to be extended would not have been made had the intention been to extend the power to every description. The enumeration presupposes something not enumerated; and that something, if we regard the language or the subject of the sentence, must be the exclusively internal commerce of a state.

The genius and character of the whole government seem to be that its action is to be applied to all the external concerns of the nation and to those internal concerns which affect the states generally; but not to those which are completely within a particular state, which do not affect other states, and with which it is not necessary to interfere for the purpose of executing some of the general powers of the government. The completely internal commerce of a state, then, may be considered as reserved for the state itself.

But, in regulating commerce with foreign nations, the power of Congress does not stop at the jurisdictional lines of the several states. It would be a very useless power if it could not pass those lines. The commerce of the United States with foreign nations is that of the whole United States. Every district has a right to participate in it. The deep streams which penetrate our country in every direction pass through the interior of almost every state in the Union, and furnish the means of exercising this right. If Congress has the power to regulate it, that

power must be exercised whenever the subject exists. If it exists within the states, if a foreign voyage may commence or terminate at a port within a state, then the power of Congress may be exercised within a state.

This principle is, if possible, still more clear, when applied to commerce "among the several states." They either join each other, in which case they are separated by a mathematical line, or they are remote from each other, in which case other states lie between them. What is commerce "among" them, and how is it to be conducted? Can a trading expedition between two adjoining states commence and terminate outside of each? And if the trading intercourse be between two states remote from each other, must it not commence in one, terminate in the other, and probably pass through a third? Commerce among the states must, of necessity, be commerce with the states. In the regulation of trade with the Indian tribes, the action of the law, especially, when the Constitution was made, was chiefly within a state.

The power of Congress, then, whatever it may be, must be exercised within the territorial jurisdiction of the several states. The sense of the nation on this subject is unequivocally manifested by the provisions made in the laws for transporting goods by land between Baltimore and Providence, between New York and Philadelphia, and between Philadelphia and Baltimore.

We are now arrived at the inquiry — What is this power? It is the power to regulate, that is, to prescribe the rule by which commerce is to be governed. This power, like all others vested in Congress, is complete in itself, may be exercised to its utmost extent, and acknowledges no limitations other than are prescribed in the Constitution. These are expressed in plain terms and do not affect the questions which arise in this case, or which have been discussed at the bar. If, as has always been understood, the sovereignty of Congress, though limited to specified objects, is plenary as to those objects, the power over commerce with foreign nations and among the several states is vested in Congress as absolutely as it would be in a single government, having in its constitution the same restrictions on the exercise of the power as are found in the Constitution of the United States.

The wisdom and the discretion of Congress, their identity with the people, and the influence which their constituents possess at elections are, in this as in many other instances, as that, for example, of declaring war, the sole restraints on which they have relied to secure them from its abuse. They are the restraints on which the people must often rely solely in all representative governments. The power of Congress, then, comprehends navigation within the limits of every state in the Union so far as that navigation may be, in any manner, connected with "commerce with foreign nations, or among the several States, or with the Indian tribes." It may, of consequence, pass the jurisdiction line of New York, and act upon the very waters to which the prohibition now under consideration applies.

But it has been urged with great earnestness that, although the power of Congress to regulate commerce with foreign nations and among the several states be coextensive with the subject itself, and have no other limits than are prescribed in the Constitution, yet the states may severally exercise the same power within their respective jurisdictions. In support of this argument, it is said that they possessed it as an inseparable attribute of sovereignty before the formation of the Constitution, and still retain it, except so far as they have surrendered it by that instrument; that this principle results from the nature of the government, and is secured by the Tenth Amendment; that an affirmative grant of power is not exclusive, unless in its own nature it be such that the continued exercise of it by the former possessor is inconsistent with the grant, and that this is not of that description.

The appellant, conceding these postulates except the last, contends that full power to regulate a particular subject implies the whole power and leaves no residuum; that a grant of the whole is incompatible with the existence of a right in another to any part of it. Both parties have appealed to the Constitution, to legislative acts, and judicial decisions; and have drawn arguments from all these sources to support and illustrate the propositions they respectively maintain. . . .

In discussing the question, whether this power is still in the states, in the case under consideration, we may dismiss from it the inquiry, whether it is surrendered by the mere grant to Congress, or is retained until Congress shall exercise the power. We may dismiss that inquiry because it has been exercised, and the regulations which Congress deemed it proper to make are now in full operation. The sole question is — Can a state regulate commerce with foreign nations and among the states while Congress is regulating it?

The counsel for the respondent answer this question in the affirmative, and rely very much on the restrictions in the 10th Section as supporting their opinion. They say, very truly, that limitations of a power furnish a strong argument in favor of the existence of that power, and that the section which prohibits the states from laying duties on imports or exports proves that this power might have been exercised had it not been expressly forbidden; and, consequently, that any other commercial regulation, not expressly forbidden, to which the original power of the state was competent, may still be made. That this restriction shows the opinion of the Convention, that a state might impose duties on exports and imports, if not expressly forbidden, will be conceded; but that it follows, as a consequence from this concession, that a state may regulate commerce with foreign nations and among the states cannot be admitted. . . .

It has been contended by the counsel for the appellant that, as the word "to regulate" implies in its nature full power over the thing to be regulated, it excludes, necessarily, the action of all others that would perform the same operation on the same thing. That regulation is designed for the entire result, applying to those parts which remain as they were, as well as to those which are altered. It produces a uniform whole, which is as much disturbed and deranged by changing what the regulating power designs to leave untouched as that on which it has operated. There is great force in this argument, and the court is not satisfied that it has been refuted.

Since, however, in exercising the power of regulating their own purely internal affairs, whether of trading or police, the states may sometimes enact laws, the validity of which depends on their interfering with, and being contrary to, an act of Congress passed in pursuance of the Constitution, the court will enter upon the inquiry, whether the laws of New York, as expounded by the highest tribunal of that state, have, in their application to this case, come into collision with an act of Congress, and deprived a citizen of a right to which that act entitles him. Should this collision exist, it will be immaterial whether those laws were passed in virtue of a concurrent power "to regulate commerce with foreign nations and among the several states," or in virtue of a power to regulate their domestic trade and police.

In one case and the other the acts of New York must yield to the law of Congress; and the decision sustaining the privilege they confer against a right given by a law of the Union must be erroneous. This opinion has been frequently expressed in this court, and is founded as well on the nature of the government as on the words of the Constitution. In argument, however, it has been contended that, if a law passed by a state in the exercise of its acknowledged sovereignty comes into conflict with a law passed by Congress in pursuance of the Constitution, they affect the subject and each other like equal opposing powers.

But the framers of our Constitution foresaw this state of things and provided for it by declaring the supremacy not only of itself but of the laws made in pursuance of it. The nullity of any act inconsistent with the Constitution is produced by the declaration that the Constitution is supreme law. The appropriate application of that part of the clause which confers the same supremacy on laws and treaties is to such acts of the state legislatures as do not transcend their powers, but though enacted in the execution of acknowledged state powers, interfere with, or are contrary to, the laws of Congress, made in pursuance of the Constitution or some treaty made under the authority of the United States. In every such case, the act of Congress or the treaty is supreme; and the law of the state, though enacted in the exercise of powers not controverted, must yield to it. . . .

Decree . . . This court is of opinion that . . . so much of the several laws of the state of New York as prohibits vessels, licensed according to the laws of the United States, from navigating the waters of the state of New York, by means of fire or steam, is repugnant to the said Constitution and void. This court is, therefore, of opinion that the decree of the court of New York for the trial of impeachments and the correction of errors, affirming the decree of the chancellor of that state . . . is erroneous and ought to be reversed, and the same is hereby reversed and annulled. And this court doth further direct, order, and decree that the bill of the said Aaron Ogden be dismissed, and the same is hereby dismissed accordingly.

28.

The Beginning of Reform Judaism

*Reform Judaism began in Charleston, South Carolina, when a small group of Jewish
businessmen addressed the following memorial to their Congregation Beth Elohim on
December 23, 1824. Charleston had at the time the largest Jewish community in the
United States, but many of its members had grown lax in the observance of traditional
practices, a neglect partly attributable to their desire for closer ties with Christian
businessmen. Abraham Moise, who drafted the memorial, and the forty-seven who
signed it, sought not to weaken Orthodox Judaism but rather to reform it, with the intent
of thereby reviving the interest of Jews in their faith.*

Source: Lucius Moise, *Biography of Isaac Harby with an Account of the Reformed Society of
Israelites of Charleston, S.C., 1824-1833*, Columbia, 1931, pp. 52-59.

THE MEMORIAL OF THE UNDERSIGNED shows
unto your honorable body that they have
witnessed with deep regret the apathy and
neglect which have been manifested toward
our holy religion. As inheritors of the *true
faith*, and always proud to be considered by
the world as a portion of "God's chosen
people," they have been pained to perceive
the gradual decay of that system of worship
which, for ages past, *peculiarly* distinguished
us from among the nations of the earth.
Not unmindful, however, of the various
causes which regulate human conduct; and
at the same time unwilling to shield themselves from any censure to which their actions may justly entitle them, they have in-
genuously investigated the reasons which
may have led them from the synagogue,
and are now seriously impressed with the
belief that certain defects which are apparent in the present system of worship are the
sole causes of the evils complained of.

In pointing out these defects, however,
your memorialists seek no other end than
the future welfare and respectability of the
nation. As members of the great family of
Israel, they cannot consent to place before

their children examples which are only calculated to darken the mind and withhold
from the rising generation the more rational
means of worshiping the true God.

It is to this, therefore, your memorialists
would, in the first place, invite the serious
attention of your honorable body. By causing the *hasan*, or reader, to repeat in English such part of the Hebrew prayers as
may be deemed necessary, it is confidently
believed that the congregation generally
would be more forcibly impressed with the
necessity of divine worship, and the moral
obligations which they owe to themselves
and their Creator, while such a course
would lead to more decency and decorum
during the time they are engaged in the
performance of religious duties. It is not everyone who has the means, and many have
not the time, to acquire a knowledge of the
Hebrew language and consequently to become enlightened in the principles of Judaism. What then is the course pursued in all
religious societies for the purpose of disse-
minating the peculiar tenets of their faith
among the poor and uninformed? The principles of their religion are expounded to

them from the pulpit in the language that they understand; for instance, in the Catholic, the German, and the French Protestant churches. By this means the ignorant part of mankind attend their places of worship with some profit to their morals, and even improvement to their minds; they return from them with hearts turned to piety, and with feelings elevated by their sacred character. In this consists the beauty of religion — when men are invoked by its divine spirit to the practice of virtue and morality.

These results, it is respectfully submitted, would be sufficient of themselves to induce the alterations requested. But your memorialists cannot fail to impress upon the minds of your honorable body the singular advantages this practice would produce upon the habits and attention of the younger branches of the congregation; besides the necessity of good behavior, which the solemnity of the service should impose, they would become gradually better acquainted with the nature of our creed, the principal features which distinguish the Jew from every other religious denomination, and the meaning and the reason of our various forms and ceremonies. Believing, at the same time, that the above views of what is indispensable to the preservation of our faith will meet with the approbation of every reflecting and liberal mind, they repeat that they are actuated by no other motive than to see our synagogue in a better, a more wholesome, and a more respectable state of discipline; to see it elicit that regard from Jew and Gentile which its great character deserves and should always command; and finally, not to destroy long standing institutions, but to accommodate them to the progress of time and change of situation and circumstances.

With regard to such parts of the service as it is desired should undergo this change, your memorialists would strenuously recommend that the most solemn portions be retained, and everything superfluous excluded; and that the principal parts, and if possible all that is read in Hebrew, should also be read in English (that being the language of the country), so as to enable every member of the congregation fully to understand each part of the service. In submitting this article of our memorial to the consideration of your honorable body, your memorialists are well aware of the difficulties with which they must contend before they will be enabled to accomplish this desirable end; but while they would respectfully invite the attention of your honorable body to this part of their memorial, they desire to rest the propriety and expediency of such a measure solely upon the reason by which it may be maintained. Your memorialists would further submit to your honorable body whether, in the history of the civilized world, there can be found a single parallel of a people addressing the Creator in a language not understood by that people? It is indeed surprising that heretofore no innovation has even been *attempted*, although it is readily admitted your honorable body may boast of many very enlightened, liberal, and intelligent members.

Your memorialists would next call the particular attention of your honorable body to the absolute necessity of abridging the service generally. They have reflected seriously upon its present length, and are confident that this is one of the principal causes why so much of it is hastily and improperly hurried over. This must be evident to every reflecting mind when it is seen that, notwithstanding the evil complained of, the service of the Sabbath, for instance, continues until 12 o'clock, although usually commencing at 9. It is therefore manifest that, according to the prayer of your memorialists, should the service be in future conducted with due solemnity, and in a slow, distinct, and impressive tone, its length would certainly occupy the attention of the congregation until 2 o'clock, if not later.

The offerings will next command the attention of your honorable body; and upon this part of our memorial, we would respectfully crave the favor of a patient hearing while we clearly set forth the entire uselessness and impropriety of this custom. In the first place, your memorialists earnestly protest against the unwise and absurd practice of rendering in the Spanish language any offerings which may be intended to benefit the synagogue or which may be otherwise identified with our holy religion. Besides the free scope, which the practice of offering in a language understood by few affords to mischievous and designing men to pollute the holy altars by gratifying their evil intentions, we certainly think it highly inconsistent to select for this very purpose the language of a people from whom we have suffered and continue to suffer so much persecution.

But forgetting for a moment this consideration, your memorialists would further suggest to your honorable body whether the arrangement recently made in the financial transactions of the congregation would not altogether supersede the necessity of any offerings whatever? This is most seriously and strenuously desired by your memorialists, because they are prepared to show, by an act of your own body, that the practice of offering is not the result of any imperious necessity but merely intended as an idle and absurd indulgence. By the 11th Article of the constitution of your honorable body, it is provided that such offerings as are made by any member of the congregation shall, at the end of the year, be deducted out of the amount of his annual subscription, as well as that of his wife if he be a married man. According to this part of the constitution, a revenue is created independent of the offerings which are subsequently made and deducted out of the amount of subscription at the end of the year.

Your memorialists would, therefore, inquire wherein exists the necessity, under this arrangement, of any offerings whatever? How, and in what manner, the support of the congregation depends upon them? And, in a word, whether the above article is not a tacit admission by your constitution that so much of the offerings as may amount to the annual subscription of a member was never intended as a means of supporting the congregation, inasmuch as the whole amount is already anticipated long before a single offering is made! In fact, many persons, when their amount of assessment is exhausted in offerings, are induced to go out and remain in the synagogue yard to prevent being compelled to offer against their will — a practice irregular, indecorous, and highly to be censured, because it sets an ill example to our children and draws upon us the eyes of strangers.

According to the present mode of reading the Parasa [Parashah], it affords to the hearer neither instruction nor entertainment, unless he be competent to read as well as comprehend the Hebrew language. But if, like all other ministers, our reader would make a chapter or verse the subject of an English discourse once a week, at the expiration of the year the people would, at all events, know something of that religion which at present they so little regard.

It is also worthy of observation that a number of Israelites, whom it should be the special care of your honorable body to bring back under your immediate protection and influence, are now wandering gradually from the true God, and daily losing those strong ties which bind every pious man to the faith of his fathers! In these individuals, your honorable body have fair subjects for the holy work of reformation. By molding your present form of worship to suit their comprehensions, you will instantly receive them among you; they will collect under your special care and guardianship; they will aid in the pecuniary resources of your holy institutions; and if, from among the whole number now scattered about our city and state, either through irreligion, through disabilities imposed, or any other cause, you are enabled to make but one convert, it will add much to those laudable ends which it should be the principal desire of your honorable body to accomplish.

It should also be remembered that while other sects are extending the means of divine worship to the remotest quarters of the habitable globe — while they are making the most zealous efforts to bring together the scattered of their flock, offering the most flattering inducements to *all denominations* — we, who may be termed the mere remnant of a great nation, are totally disregarding the fairest opportunities of increasing our own numbers, and at the same time neglecting the brightest prospects of enlarging our resources and effectually perpetuating our national character.

Your memorialists trust that they have been perfectly understood by the foregoing observations that they entirely disclaim any idea of wishing to abolish such ceremonies as are considered landmarks to distinguish the Jew from the Gentile. They are wholly influenced by a warm zeal to preserve and perpetuate the principles of Judaism in their utmost purity and vigor, and to see the present and the future generations of Israelites enlightened on the subject of their holy religion, so as by understanding, they may learn the nature of its divine source and appreciate its holy precepts; that they would not wish to shake the firmness of any man's faith or take from his devotion toward it; that they will always fervently and zealously support it as the first and most ancient of religions.

The alterations above submitted being all your memorialists can in reason and moderation require, they would beg leave, in concluding, to bring to the notice of your honorable body the reformation which has been recently adopted by our brethren in Holland, Germany, and Prussia. The following is an extract from a German paper entitled the *Frankfort Journal*:

The functions relative to divine service, such as the rite of taking the Law out of the Ark, the promulgation of the Law, etc., shall no longer be sold by auction in the synagogue. The rabbis and the elders of the synagogue (the first in their discourses) must endeavor to put an end to the custom of seesawing during the prayers, and to that of repeating the prayers in too loud a voice; all profane tunes during divine service are prohibited. The ceremony of striking the impious Haman at the festival of Purim is most strictly prohibited. Children below the age of five years are not to be taken to the synagogue. All unsuitable pleasantries, in which the young people sometimes indulge in the synagogues on the eve of some festivals, or on the festivals themselves, as well as the distribution of sweetmeats by the women to each in the synagogues, are strictly forbidden. Some of the religious ceremonies must be accompanied by a German discourse [that being the vernacular] on a Hebrew text, in which the meaning of these solemnities shall be explained; and on the Sabbath a discourse shall be held in German in every synagogue after the reading of the prescribed passage of the Law and a chapter of the Prophets.

Thus, from the above extract, it appears that no climes, nor even tyranny itself, can forever fetter or control the human mind; and that even amidst the intolerance of Europe, our brethren have anticipated the free citizens of America in the glorious work of reformation. Let us then hasten to the task with harmony and good fellowship. We wish not to *overthrow* but to *rebuild;* we wish not to *destroy* but to *reform* and *revise* the evils complained of; we wish not to *abandon* the institutions of Moses but to *understand and observe them;* in fine, we wish to worship God, not as *slaves of bigotry and priestcraft* but as the enlightened descendants of that chosen race whose blessings have been scattered throughout the land of Abraham, Isaac, and Jacob.

1825

29.

John Quincy Adams: Inaugural Address

In the election of 1824, none of the four contenders for the presidency, John Quincy Adams, Andrew Jackson, William H. Crawford, and Henry Clay, received a majority of the electoral vote, and the choice fell to the House of Representatives. Clay, who had received the fewest votes, was eliminated from the contest, but he remained a powerful force in the House. With his support, Adams won the presidency. Adams' career in the White House was destined to be troubled from the beginning. His political adversaries, particularly the bitter Democrats whose hero Andrew Jackson had been defeated, launched attacks against most of his nationalistic policies and accused him of having aristocratic sentiments. However, Adams' Inaugural Address, in which he mentioned his designs for a nationally supported system of internal improvements, glowed with optimism for the future. The Address, reprinted below, was presented to the nation on March 4, 1825.

Source: Richardson, II, pp. 294-299.

IN COMPLIANCE WITH A USAGE coeval with the existence of our federal Constitution, and sanctioned by the example of my predecessors in the career upon which I am about to enter, I appear, my fellow citizens, in your presence and in that of Heaven to bind myself by the solemnities of religious obligation to the faithful performance of the duties allotted to me in the station to which I have been called.

In unfolding to my countrymen the principles by which I shall be governed in the fulfillment of those duties, my first resort will be to that Constitution which I shall swear to the best of my ability to preserve, protect, and defend. That revered instrument enumerates the powers and prescribes the duties of the executive magistrate, and in its first words declares the purposes to which these and the whole action of the government instituted by it should be invariably and sacredly devoted: To form a more perfect Union, establish justice, insure domestic tranquillity, provide for the common defense, promote the general welfare, and secure the blessings of liberty to the people of this Union in their successive generations.

Since the adoption of this social compact one of these generations has passed away. It is the work of our forefathers. Administered by some of the most eminent men who contributed to its formation, through a most eventful period in the annals of the world, and through all the vicissitudes of peace and war incidental to the condition of associated man, it has not disappointed the hopes and aspirations of those illustrious benefactors of their age and nation. It has promoted the lasting welfare of that country so dear to us all; it has, to an extent far beyond the ordinary lot of humanity, secured the freedom and happiness of this people. We now receive it as a precious inheritance from those to whom we are indebted for its establishment, doubly bound by the examples which they have left us and by the blessings which we have enjoyed as the fruits of their labors to transmit the same unimpaired to the succeeding generation.

In the compass of thirty-six years since this great national covenant was instituted, a body of laws enacted under its authority and in conformity with its provisions has unfolded its powers and carried into practical operation its effective energies. Subordinate departments have distributed the executive functions in their various relations to foreign affairs, to the revenue and expenditures, and to the military force of the Union by land and sea. A coordinate department of the judiciary has expounded the Constitution and the laws, settling in harmonious coincidence with the legislative will numerous weighty questions of construction which the imperfection of human language had rendered unavoidable. The year of jubilee since the first formation of our Union has just elapsed; that of the declaration of our independence is at hand. The consummation of both was effected by this Constitution.

Since that period a population of 4 million has multiplied to 12 million. A territory bounded by the Mississippi has been extended from sea to sea. New states have been admitted to the Union in numbers nearly equal to those of the first Confederation. Treaties of peace, amity, and commerce have been concluded with the principal dominions of the earth. The people of other nations, inhabitants of regions acquired not by conquest but by compact, have been united with us in the participation of our rights and duties, of our burdens and blessings. The forest has fallen by the ax of our woodsmen; the soil has been made to teem by the tillage of our farmers; our commerce has whitened every ocean. The dominion of man over physical nature has been extended by the invention of our artists. Liberty and law have marched hand in hand. All the purposes of human association have beeen accomplished as effectively as under any other government on the globe, and at a cost little exceeding in a whole generation the expenditure of other nations in a single year.

Such is the unexaggerated picture of our condition under a constitution founded upon the republican principle of equal rights. To admit that this picture has its shades is but to say that it is still the condition of men upon earth. From evil — physical, moral, and political — it is not our claim to be exempt. We have suffered sometimes by the visitation of heaven through disease; often by the wrongs and injustice of other nations, even to the extremities of war; and, lastly, by dissensions among ourselves, dissensions perhaps inseparable from the enjoyment of freedom, but which have more than once appeared to threaten the dissolution of the Union, and with it the overthrow of all the enjoyments of our present lot and all our earthly hopes of the future. The causes of these dissensions have been various, founded upon differences of speculation in the theory of republican government; upon conflicting views of policy in our relations with foreign nations; upon jealousies of partial and sectional interests, aggravated by prejudices and prepossessions which strangers to each other are ever apt to entertain.

It is a source of gratification and of encouragement to me to observe that the great result of this experiment upon the theory of human rights has, at the close of that generation by which it was formed, been crowned with success equal to the most sanguine expectations of its founders. Union, justice, tranquillity, the common defense, the general welfare, and the blessings of liberty — all have been promoted by the government under which we have lived. Standing at this point of time, looking back to that generation which has gone by and forward to that which is advancing, we may at once indulge in grateful exultation and in cheering hope. . . .

Of the two great political parties which have divided the opinions and feelings of our country, the candid and the just will now admit that both have contributed splendid talents, spotless integrity, ardent patriotism, and disinterested sacrifices to the formation and administration of this government, and that both have required a liberal indulgence for a portion of human infirmity and error. The revolutionary wars of Europe, commencing precisely at the moment when the government of the United States first went into operation under this Constitution, excited a collision of sentiments and of sympathies which kindled all the passions and embittered the conflict of parties till the nation was involved in war and the Union was shaken to its center. This time of trial embraced a period of five-and-twenty years, during which the policy of the Union in its relations with Europe constituted the principal basis of our political divisions and the most arduous part of the action of our federal government. With the catastrophe in which the wars of the French Revolution terminated, and our own subsequent peace with Great Britain, this baneful weed of party strife was uprooted. From that time no difference of principle, connected either with the theory of government or with our intercourse with foreign nations, has existed or been called forth in force sufficient to sustain a continued combination of parties or to give more than wholesome animation to public sentiment or legislative debate.

Our political creed is, without a dissenting voice that can be heard, that the will of the people is the source and the happiness of the people the end of all legitimate government upon earth; that the best security for the beneficence and the best guaranty against the abuse of power consists in the freedom, the purity, and the frequency of popular elections; that the general government of the Union and the separate governments of the states are all sovereignties of limited powers, fellow servants of the same masters, uncontrolled within their respective spheres, uncontrollable by encroachments upon each other; that the firmest security of peace is the preparation during peace of the defenses of war; that a rigorous economy and accountability of public expenditures should guard against the aggravation and alleviate, when possible, the burden of taxation; that the military should be kept in strict subordination to the civil power; that the freedom of the press and of religious opinion should be inviolate; that the policy of our country is peace and the ark of our salvation union are articles of faith upon which we are all now agreed.

If there have been those who doubted whether a confederated representative democracy were a government competent to the wise and orderly management of the common concerns of a mighty nation, those doubts have been dispelled; if there have been projects of partial confederacies to be erected upon the ruins of the Union, they have been scattered to the winds; if there have been dangerous attachments to one foreign nation and antipathies against another, they have been extinguished. Ten years of peace, at home and abroad, have assuaged the animosities of political contention and blended into harmony the most discordant elements of public opinion. There still remains one effort of magnanimity, one sacrifice of prejudice and passion, to be made by the individuals throughout the nation who have heretofore followed the standards of political party. It is that of discarding every remnant of rancor against each other, of embracing as countrymen and friends, and of yielding to talents and virtue alone that confidence which in times of contention for principle was bestowed only upon those who bore the badge of party communion.

The collisions of party spirit which originate in speculative opinions or in different views of administrative policy are in their nature transitory. Those which are founded on geographical divisions, adverse interests of soil, climate, and modes of domestic life are more permanent, and therefore, perhaps, more dangerous. It is this which gives inestimable value to the character of our government, at once federal and national. It holds out to us a perpetual admonition to preserve alike and with equal anxiety the rights of each individual state in its own government and the rights of the whole nation in that of the Union. Whatsoever is of domestic concernment, unconnected with the other members of the Union or with foreign lands, belongs exclusively to the administration of the state governments. Whatsoever directly involves the rights and interests of the federative fraternity or of foreign powers is of the resort of this general government. The duties of both are obvious in the general principle, though sometimes perplexed with difficulties in the detail. To respect the rights of the state governments is the inviolable duty of that of the Union; the government of every state will feel its own obligation to respect and preserve the rights of the whole.

The prejudices everywhere too commonly entertained against distant strangers are worn away and the jealousies of warring interests are allayed by the composition and functions of the great national councils annually assembled from all quarters of the Union at this place. Here the distinguished men from every section of our country, while meeting to deliberate upon the great interests of those by whom they are deputed, learn to estimate the talents and do justice to the virtues of each other. The harmony of the nation is promoted and the whole Union is knit together by the sentiments of mutual respect, the habits of social intercourse, and the ties of personal friendship formed between the representatives of its several parts in the performance of their service at this metropolis.

Passing from this general review of the purposes and injunctions of the federal Constitution and their results as indicating the first traces of the path of duty in the discharge of my public trust, I turn to the administration of my immediate predecessor as the second. It has passed away in a period of profound peace, how much to the satisfaction of our country and to the honor of our country's name is known to you all. The great features of its policy, in general concurrence with the will of the legislature, have been to cherish peace while preparing for defensive war; to yield exact justice to other nations and maintain the rights of our own; to cherish the principles of freedom and of equal rights wherever they were proclaimed; to discharge with all possible promptitude the national debt; to reduce within the narrowest limits of efficiency the military force; to improve the organization and discipline of the Army; to provide and sustain a school of military science; to extend equal protection to all the great interests of the nation; to promote the civilization of the Indian tribes; and to proceed in the great system of internal improvements within the limits of the constitutional power of the Union.

Under the pledge of these promises made by that eminent citizen at the time of his first induction to this office, in his career of eight years the internal taxes have been repealed; $60 million of the public debt have been discharged; provision has been made for the comfort and relief of the aged and indigent among the surviving warriors of the Revolution; the regular armed force has been reduced and its constitution revised and perfected; the accountability for the expenditure of public moneys has been made more effective; the Floridas have been peaceably acquired, and our boundary has been extended to the Pacific Ocean; the independence of the southern nations of this hemisphere has been recognized and recommended by example and by counsel to the potentates of Europe; progress has been made in the defense of the country by fortifications and the increase of the Navy, toward the effectual suppression of the African traffic in slaves, in alluring the aboriginal hunters of our land to the cultivation of the soil and of the mind, in exploring the interior regions of the Union, and in preparing by scientific researches and surveys for the further application of our national resources to the internal improvement of our country.

In this brief outline of the promise and performance of my immediate predecessor, the line of duty for his successor is clearly delineated. To pursue to their consummation those purposes of improvement in our common condition instituted or recommended by him will embrace the whole sphere of my obligations. To the topic of internal improvement, emphatically urged by him at his inauguration, I recur with peculiar satisfaction. It is that from which I am convinced that the unborn millions of our posterity who are in future ages to people this continent will derive their most fervent gratitude to the founders of the Union; that in which the beneficent action of its government will be most deeply felt and acknowledged. . . .

Some diversity of opinion has prevailed with regard to the powers of Congress for legislation upon objects of this nature. The most respectful deference is due to doubts originating in pure patriotism and sustained by venerated authority. But nearly twenty years have passed since the construction of the first national road was commenced. The authority for its construction was then unquestioned. To how many thousands of our countrymen has it proved a benefit? To what single individual has it ever proved an injury? Repeated, liberal, and candid discussions in the legislature have conciliated the sentiments and approximated the opinions of enlightened minds upon the question of constitutional power.

I cannot but hope that by the same process of friendly, patient, and persevering deliberation all constitutional objections will ultimately be removed. The extent and limitation of the powers of the general government in relation to this transcendently important interest will be settled and acknowledged to the common satisfaction of all, and every speculative scruple will be solved by a practical public blessing.

Fellow citizens, you are acquainted with the peculiar circumstances of the recent election, which have resulted in affording me the opportunity of addressing you at this time. You have heard the exposition of the principles which will direct me in the fulfillment of the high and solemn trust imposed upon me in this station. Less possessed of your confidence in advance than any of my predecessors, I am deeply conscious of the prospect that I shall stand more and oftener in need of your indulgence. Intentions upright and pure, a heart devoted to the welfare of our country, and the unceasing application of all the faculties allotted to me to her service are all the pledges that I can give for the faithful performance of the arduous duties I am to undertake. To the guidance of the legislative councils, to the assistance of the executive and subordinate departments, to the friendly cooperation of the respective state governments, to the candid and liberal support of the people so far as it may be deserved by honest industry and zeal, I shall look for whatever success may attend my public service; and knowing that "except the Lord keep the city the watchman waketh but in vain," with fervent supplications for His favor, to His overruling providence, I commit with humble but fearless confidence my own fate and the future destinies of my country.

Lifting Erie Canal barges through the five double locks at Lockport, New York

THE SECOND REVOLUTION

Pressure from textile and other manufacturing interests for protective tariffs signaled the coming of the Industrial Revolution to America. At the same time, the need for protection indicated that domestic production was not yet fully competitive with imports from abroad. A relative shortage of labor, with the impulse to mechanization that this created, increased the costs of industrial development. The size of the country and the dispersed population increased shipping costs. However, in the 1820s, both these factors were turned to advantage as American industry expanded from its base in textiles. Transportation needs stimulated development of the means to meet them. New foundries prospered in response to the intense demand for steam boilers, first for boats and then for locomotives. The needs of western farmers for strong, heavy plows and for labor-saving devices were reflected in efforts to develop farm machinery. Mechanization in Eastern factories was an important stimulus to technological innovation. Canals opened Western markets to Eastern manufacturing. New markets brought industrial growth and innovation. Cheaper transportation, itself a source of industrial incentive, made large-scale mechanized farming practical. Greater farm productivity lowered prices and stimulated demand. Greater demand required better and faster transportation. This ascending cycle of cause and effect was only beginning in the 1820s. Two major developments, the mechanical reaper and the railroad, were yet to come.

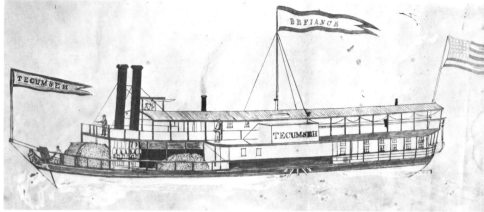

(Above) The "Tecumseh," early side-wheeler on the Ohio River; (left center) early New Orleans steamboat offering local service on Mississippi; (right center) Fulton's "Wm. Cutting"

Steamboats West

Steamboat transportation, which had proved its usefulness on the Hudson and other eastern rivers, soon spread west. Fulton launched a steamer at Pittsburgh in 1811. The first upstream voyage from New Orleans was made in 1817. The 25-day journey to Louisville cut the time for such a trip by three-fourths. At that time there were about a dozen steamboats operating on western rivers. Two years later there were 60 and by 1830, over 200. Most of these boats were built in Pittsburgh and Cincinnati and were owned by large freight companies. The growth of these lines and of commerce on western rivers was startling. By 1840, this commerce was nearly double that of United States foreign trade.

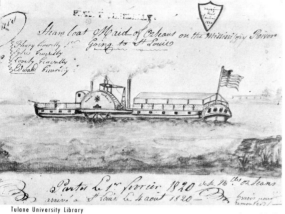

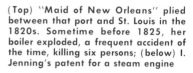

(Top) ''Maid of New Orleans'' plied between that port and St. Louis in the 1820s. Sometime before 1825, her boiler exploded, a frequent accident of the time, killing six persons; (below) I. Jenning's patent for a steam engine

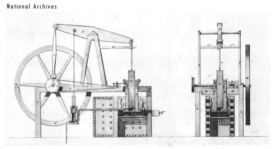

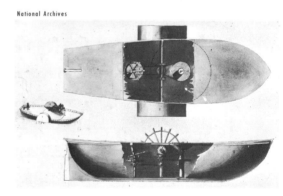

(Right) Even after steam power had proved itself, inventors worked on crude alternatives; (below) ''Walk-in-the-Water'' was the first steamboat on the Great Lakes. It was launched in 1818 and wrecked on a voyage to Detroit in 1821

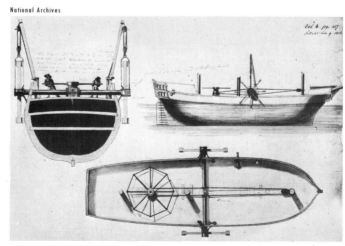

Manufacturing

The Eli Whitney Gun Works, near New Haven, Connecticut, 1821

Although the United States was still an agricultural nation in the 1820s, industrialization was firmly grounded. A number of characteristics distinguished American industrial development from the English model. Emphasis was placed on quantity production of standardized products. Labor shortages were overcome by early mechanization of as many phases of production as possible. The relative scarcity of capital led to the widespread adoption of the stock company. Throughout, the idea of interchangeable parts was important, whether in replaceable plowshares, gun parts, clockworks, or machine parts.

(Right) The West Point Foundry in New York was a key armament works during the War of 1812 and offered a full line of cast iron products; (bottom) factory in a New England village

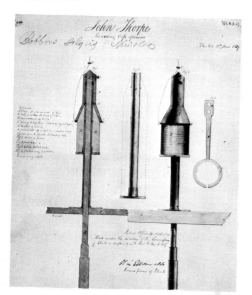

(Top) Mills on the Genesee River, at Rochester; (center) mills at Lowell, Mass. line the river, with the worker's cottages clustered nearby; (left) two patents by John Thorpe for improvements in the spinning process. The "cap" and "can" spinners insured an even flow of yarn, without tangling, and greatly speeded the process

Canals

The Erie Canal, connecting the Hudson Valley with the Great Lakes, was completed in 1825 at a cost of $7 million. It immediately brought economic gains to New York and stimulated development along its entire route. Greatly reduced shipping costs encouraged the exchange of goods with the West. An era of canal building followed and by 1840, 4,500 miles of canals had been built. Pittsburgh was connected with Philadelphia. The Chesapeake and Ohio Canal extended inland from Washington and Baltimore. A canal system was built in the Midwest, but all the later canals, unlike the Erie, experienced financial difficulties from the start, as competing railroads paralleled their routes.

(Top) Excavation of deep cut at Lockport; (center) view of New York Harbor during celebration marking completion of Erie Canal; (bottom) portrait of De Witt Clinton by Samuel Morse

(Top) Rural view of Erie Canal; (left center) view at western end of Canal; (right center) view of Buffalo before completion of Canal; (bottom) junction of Erie and Northern canals

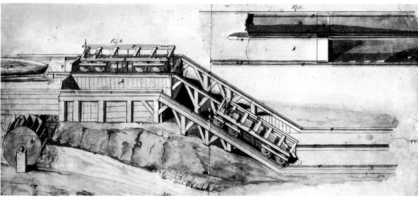

An inclined plane railway was proposed as an alternate to the canal lock. Locks were expensive to build and their lift capabilities were small. Pennsylvania's Portage Canal used successive stages of inclined plane railways to transport barges across the summit of the Alleghenies.

(Top) Archibald Tanner's double inclined plane railway powered by a locomotive; (center and bottom) Ephraim Morris' water-powered inclined plane railway

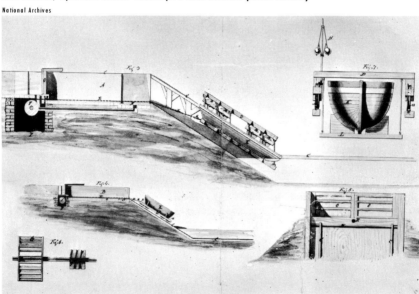

(Top) "Old Ironsides," first locomotive built by Baldwin; (right center) Matthias Baldwin; (lower center) race between Peter Cooper's "Tom Thumb" and horse-drawn carriage, (bottom) Peter Cooper

Railroads

In 1825, Col. John Stevens ran an experimental steam locomotive on his estate in New Jersey. Other experiments quickly followed. The Delaware and Hudson Canal Company ran an English engine called the "Stourbridge Lion" in 1829. Peter Cooper's "Tom Thumb" was the first to carry passengers, in 1830, and the first regular line was established in the same year in South Carolina. The early wood-burning engines showered passengers with sparks and public acceptance was slow in coming. Difficulties of terrain led to a distinct, American-type locomotive, which featured a rotatable front carriage and dual drive-wheels to improve traction. A major advance was the T-rail, which held the cars on the track. These and other innovations soon brought a rush of railroad development.

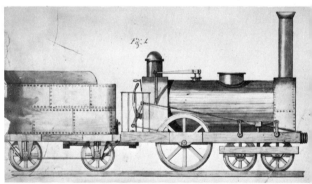

(Top) Railroad Jubilee on Boston Commons; (left center) Asa Whitney, early promoter of railroads; (right center) C. L. Miller's patent to increase driving wheel adhesion by throwing weight of tender on the locomotive; (bottom right) plan of Boston-Albany Railroad, surveyed in 1828

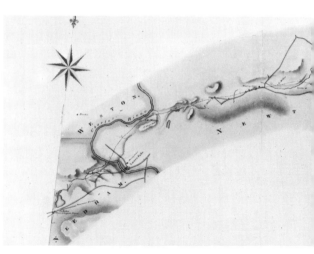

(Above) **Early railroad scene, Little Falls, New York; (below) railroad scene showing early type of passenger carriage and cow-catcher on locomotive**

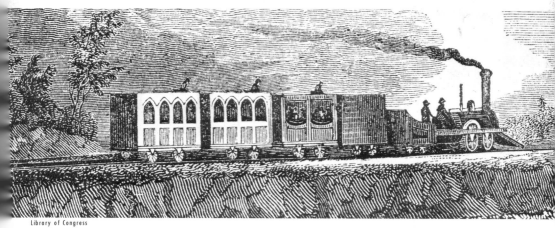

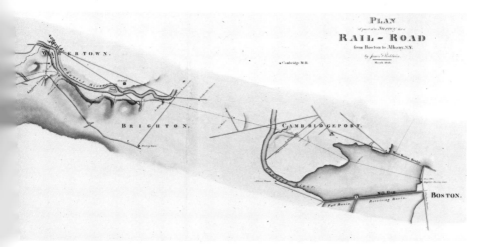

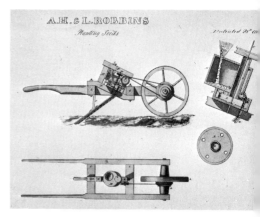

(Above) Wagon with a device for spreading lime or manure, 1830; (above right) seed planter, to drop the seed evenly as the spout is passed along a furrow, 1828; (below) threshing machine, with the machinery turned by horse power; (bottom) a machine, also turned by horse power, that was intended to thrash, separate, clean, and screen the wheat in one operation, 1822

Farm Machinery

The scarcity of labor and the large acreage of farms inevitably led to mechanization of agriculture. Mechanical seeders, fertilizers, reapers, and threshers appeared — each followed by a succession of improved versions. In 1819 Jethro Wood patented a cast-iron plow, previously developed by Charles Newbold. Popular in the East, it was unsuited to tough prairie sod. John Deere solved this problem with a steel plow in the late 1830s. Meanwhile Cyrus McCormick and Obed Hussey were developing the principles of the horse-drawn reaper.

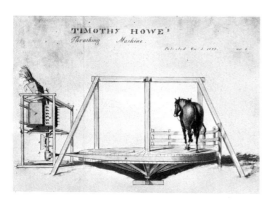

30.

Child Labor in Massachusetts

*Although primary schools were generally available to all children in the New England
area, the same was not true of secondary schools. Usually, a high school education
was only for children whose parents could afford it. Children of the poorer classes
worked on farms, in factories, as apprentices, or at home. The following report by the
Committee on Education of the Massachusetts legislature, issued on June 14, 1825, deals
with child labor in factories and the consequent neglect of the children's education. It
was not until 1827 that Massachusetts made legal provision for public high schools. And
it was not until many years later that the high school law was enforced. As the nineteenth
century wore on, child labor became even more prevalent.*

Source: *Legislative Files* (Massachusetts), 1825, Senate, No. 8074 [Commons, V, pp. 57-61].

THE COMMITTEE ON EDUCATION, to whom was referred so much of His Excellency's speech as related to that subject and to whom were also referred the returns made to the secretary's office by virtue of a resolve passed on February 26 last in relation to children employed in factories, have had the same under consideration and ask leave to report that they cordially unite in the sentiments expressed by His Excellency and solemnly recognized by our venerable ancestors in the charter of their rights — "that wisdom and learning as well as virtue, diffused generally among the people, are necessary to the preservation of their rights and liberties."

The importance of this sentiment cannot be too sensibly felt in a republic which depends for its annual organization, its existence, and efficiency on the ability of the people to understand, and their virtue to preserve the inestimable advantages of free government. Nor can it be doubted that our fellow citizens of the present day, imbibing the principles of a virtuous ancestry, will feel bound to "preserve, improve, and extend public provisions for the education of children and youth." The provisions already made for primary schools, the liberal grants for academies, and the generous donations bestowed on the university and colleges of this Commonwealth relieve the community from any apprehension that this great interest can for a moment be neglected.

The Committee are not aware that any interposition by the legislature at present is necessary in this regard, but they deem it important that its members in their private and public capacity should see that the requirements of existing laws are respected and enforced.

There are, however, two branches of the great business of education which have recently acquired consequence and in the opinion of this Committee well deserve very serious consideration. The first is the establishment of an institution for the education of the laboring classes in the practical arts and sciences.

On this subject the Committee are happy to find that commissioners appointed under a resolve of February 22 last are preparing a system embracing this extensive subject, which must necessarily require a very careful arrangement of detail; and that a report may be expected from them at an early day of the next session of this legislature.

It is not, however, to be doubted that private liberality and individual encouragement may do much for that part of the community engaged in pursuits of agriculture, and that the patronage of the legislature to enterprises of this kind, may, as they present themselves, be attended with advantage.

The other department referred to embraces the care of young persons engaged in manufacturing establishments, whose constant occupation in their daily tasks may gather round them a rust of ignorance as to all other concerns.

The Committee are happy to coincide with His Excellency that an "American sentiment" prevails throughout the country, to which these establishments are not exceptions, and which prevents them from being dangerous "to the moral habits and chaste manners" of the people. Still, however, this is a subject always deserving the parental care of a vigilant government, and the Committee are happy to find it has not escaped the attention of the legislature.

By the resolve of the last session of the General Court first above mentioned, the selectmen of every town in this Commonwealth and the mayor and aldermen of the city of Boston were instructed to send to the office of the secretary of the Commonwealth a statement of the number of persons under sixteen years of age employed by any incorporated manufacturing company within their town or city, setting forth the length of time during which they are usually kept at work and the opportunities allowed and means provided for their education. The returns made in pursuance thereof have been laid before this Committee and are very interesting documents. But inasmuch as the resolve related only to incorporated institutions, the returns do not present the full number of children engaged in manufactories.

It appears, however, that the time of employment is generally twelve or thirteen hours each day, excepting the Sabbath, which leaves little opportunity for daily instruction. Regard is paid to the instruction of these juvenile laborers as opportunity permits, but some further legislative provisions may hereafter become necessary, that the children who are at a future day to become proprietors of these establishments, or at least greatly to influence their affairs, may not be subjected to too great devotion to pecuniary interest at the risk of more than an equivalent injury in the neglect of intellectual improvement.

The Committee are not prepared to submit any specific propositions which could be acted upon at the present session; they therefore report that the further consideration of said returns be referred to the next session of this General Court.

31.

Philip Lindsley: Education for Every Child of the Republic

Until the 1820s, the inland states of the South, on the whole, were lacking in comprehensive and effective educational programs. Philip Lindsley, one of the most active and progressive educators of the nineteenth century, gave up the prestige and security of the Eastern schools to assume the presidency of a small and relatively backward school in Tennessee, Cumberland College (now the University of Nashville). In his inaugural address, Lindsley outlined his ideas on higher education, stressing particularly his belief that schooling should be made available to all citizens, poor as well as rich, in order to safeguard the republic. A part of his address, which was delivered on January 12, 1825, appears below.

Source: *An Address, Delivered in Nashville, January 12, 1825, at the Inauguration of the President of Cumberland College,* Nashville, 1825.

A FREE GOVERNMENT like ours cannot be maintained except by an enlightened and virtuous people. It is not enough that there be a few individuals of sufficient information to manage public affairs. To the people, our rulers are immediately responsible for the faithful discharge of their official duties. But if the people be incapable of judging correctly of their conduct and measures, what security can they have for their liberties a single hour?

Knowledge is power by whomsoever possessed. If the people would retain in their own hands that power which the Constitution gives them, they must acquire that knowledge which is essential to its safekeeping and rightful exercise. Otherwise, they will soon be at the mercy of the unprincipled aspiring demagogue who, for a time, may court and flatter them, but who will assuredly seize upon the first favorable crisis to bend their necks to his yoke and compel them to hail him as their lord and sovereign.

Give the people knowledge, therefore, and you give them power. Education must ever be the grand safeguard of our liberties — the palladium of our political institutions — of all our rights and privileges. In every country on the globe where the mass of the people are best instructed will be found the most liberty, the most virtue, and the most happiness. . . .

No greater foe to his country's dearest interests can be found than the enemy of education. Were it the purpose of any set of men to engross all the power, honors, and emoluments of official stations — to become a dominant aristocracy — an order of self-constituted nobility in the midst of the republic — their plan should be to discourage education, to frown upon every attempt to promote and extend it, to denounce colleges and schools of every kind, to put them down where they exist, and to prevent their establishment wherever desired. Their wealth would enable them to send their own sons abroad to be educated, while the great body of the people could not afford the expense, and would consequently be compelled to see their children become hewers of wood and drawers of water to their more fortunate and privileged neighbors.

Great is the mistake which is current on this subject that colleges are designed exclusively for the rich; that none but the rich can be benefited by them and, therefore, that the state ought not to patronize or endow them; that funds for their support ought not to be drawn from the public treasury or the people's purse, because this would be to tax the many for the advantage of a few. Nothing can be more groundless and fallacious than such a representation; no course more injurious to the people were it adopted. The direct contrary is their true policy and interest; for were a college established and maintained by an equitable tax upon the people, who would pay the tax? Not the poor — for no tax, or next to none, is ever levied on them. Men would contribute according to their means; and the principal burden would necessarily fall upon the rich, as in reason and justice it ought. The rich then would be taxed for the benefit of the whole community.

It is evident, as I before remarked, that the rich, at least the very rich, could easily educate their children at distant or foreign seminaries. And it would be greatly to their advantage to do so, at any expense, were there no seminaries at home or within everyone's reach. Suppose there were no college in Tennessee, and but twenty individuals wealthy enough to send their sons to a college out of the state; it would then be in the power of a score or two of persons to monopolize all the liberal professions and all the avenues to wealth and honor in the commonwealth. But raise up colleges among yourselves and you reduce the charges of a liberal education so considerably that hundreds and thousands can immediately avail themselves of their aid. Not only all the middling classes of citizens but enterprising youth of the poorest families may contrive to enter the lists of honorable competition with the richest, as is done every day in the Northern and Eastern states, where, indeed, the poor, more frequently than the rich, rise to eminence by their talents and learning.

Such is the peculiar genius and excellence of our republican institutions that moral and mental worth is the surest passport to distinction. The humblest individual, by the diligent cultivation of his faculties, may, without the aid of family or fortune, attain the most exalted stations within the reach or gift of freemen. What an encouragement to studious effort and enterprise! What an incentive to the generous aspirings and honorable ambition of our youth! Why should not the door be opened wide for their entrance upon this vast theater of useful action and noble daring?

But it may be said that common elementary schools are sufficient to answer every valuable purpose; that these ought chiefly to be encouraged by the state; that the great majority of the people, after all, must be content with a comparatively limited education; that it would be absurd to think of giving to all a liberal education even were it practicable, because, if acquired, it would be superfluous or injurious, inasmuch as only a small number, at best, can hope to succeed in the learned professions or to fill the public offices.

Far be it from me to utter a syllable in opposition to primary schools. They are indispensable and ought to be found in every neighborhood. But the best mode of encouraging and multiplying these is carefully to foster the higher seminaries, because the latter must or ought to furnish teachers to the former. The greater the number of the liberally educated, in any country, the better the chance of obtaining suitable instructors for the inferior institutions. Wherever colleges abound, there is no difficulty in providing teachers for all the academies and schools in their vicinity.

Witness the four universities of Scotland and the dozen colleges in New England. And what country can compare with these for the general diffusion of knowledge among the people? Where are common schools so numerous or so effective? Where can be found so many well-educated men — so many college graduates? Were there a like proportion in Tennessee, there would be no lack of village and country schools. They would grow up of course and from necessity.

As education extends, the desire and demand for it increase. Numbers will leave college every year compelled to gain a livelihood by their own exertions. Some will not have the means to prosecute the study of a profession immediately; some will not have the inclination or the proper qualifications; besides, many will despair of succeeding where the candidates are so numerous and therefore will be glad to teach as a regular business. Thus the gradual supply to the community of persons qualified and willing to instruct, and the constantly increasing thirst for knowledge among the people, will react upon each other — the latter making room and giving employment to the former, who, by their influence, example, and labors, will more and more extend and awaken the spirit of improvement. In this way, too, *teaching* would soon become what it ought to be, an honorable calling or profession. The advantages which would result to this state from such a policy are incalculable. And the individuals who shall succeed in introducing it will be hailed as public benefactors to the latest generations.

But there is another prevailing heresy on this subject which deserves exposure and condemnation. It is that superior learning is necessary only for a few particular professions and situations, such as we have been contemplating. Now, I affirm, in opposition, it may be, to all the learned faculties of all the learned professions and to all vulgar prejudices, that every individual who wishes to rise above the level of a mere laborer at taskwork ought to endeavor to obtain a liberal education. I use the term "liberal" in a liberal sense, without necessarily including every branch of literature or sci-

ence which usually constitutes a college course.

The farmer, the mechanic, the manufacturer, the merchant, the sailor, the soldier, if they would be distinguished in their respective callings must be educated. Should it be objected that well-educated youth will not *labor* for their support; that, if they become farmers or manufacturers, they will, at most, merely superintend and direct the labors of others, I answer, first, that we, at this moment, need thousands of such men. Would not every planter who cultivates the soil by slaves, and every farmer who does the same by hired laborers, be the better, the happier, the more useful with a good education than without it? May not the same be said of the directors of printing, mercantile, and manufacturing establishments, and, indeed, of every man who is above, or aspires to be above, the meanest drudgery of manual labor?

Here, then, are thousands in the community who, or whose children at least, might be liberally educated without diminishing the number of actual laborers; so that any increase of seminaries, upon any plan, is not likely very soon to affect the common concerns of productive industry, except by bringing to bear upon them the salutary influence of more light and knowledge, and so far greatly to improve and meliorate the character and condition of all classes of citizens.

But, in the second place, were it possible to give what might be styled a liberal education of a suitable kind to every child of the republic, so far from proving detrimental to industry and enterprise, it would produce a directly contrary effect. Differences in rank, station, and fortune would still exist. The pulpit, the bar, the healing art, the army, the navy, the legislative hall, the bench of justice, and all posts of honor and emolument would, of course, be occupied then as now by men of comparatively superior talents, learning, or address, while the remainder would be compelled, according to their abilities or necessities, to do what they best could for a livelihood. Though all would be learned to a certain extent, yet there would be various gradations of excellence. The competition for honorable distinction would range on a higher scale and among men of greater intellectual attainments than is now the case; but in reference to the whole body of the people, the principle and the result would be the same. All would find their level and every individual his appropriate place and sphere. Even supposing then, what is not likely soon to happen, that all were educated — and educated in the best manner — we need not apprehend that a famine would ensue from lack of industry.

In the third place, so far as the experiment has been made, we find that the educated poor do in fact become, in the same proportion, more industrious, useful, and happy. . . . Three centuries ago it was considered dangerous for the common people anywhere to be taught even the art of reading. And a mechanic who could then read his Bible was a greater rarity than would be, in our day, a mechanic who could read Homer in his native tongue. . . .

I have already shown how colleges of any kind must or may benefit the middling and poorer classes of the people, and that it is their special interest to wish them success. Here, however, a more direct chance for mental culture may be offered them — and for such culture as best befits their previous habits, their present circumstances, and their future prospects. As they cannot be expected to pay as liberally for their privileges as the rich, let them fare and dress according to the dimensions of their purses; let them supply any deficiency by their labor; or, when necessary, let them maintain themselves entirely by their own industry. . . .

Two hundred acres of land, more or less, in the vicinity of Nashville, divided into fields and gardens, under judicious management, would afford to many a youth not only a practical knowledge of farming and horticulture but the means of living while he is pursuing his studies at the college. Let some dozen or twenty mechanics of good moral character be duly authorized to open their shops for such as might prefer, or as might be better adapted to, this species of labor. Thus, many useful trades might be learned and the whole expense of their education be defrayed without any material loss of time — even if time, thus employed, could be accounted lost.

A youth, ardent in the pursuit of knowledge, would learn more in half his time than most of the indulged sons of affluence actually acquire in the whole. And there are few industrious young men who could not earn their living, and a little more, by laboring half of their time; especially in a town where so many profitable occupations would be at their option, and where the products of the field, the garden, and the workshop would ever find a ready market.

The most startling difficulty in the way of any plan of this kind would be suggested, probably, by the obvious inequality and apparently invidious distinctions which would obtain among the pupils of the same institution. But does not a similar inequality exist among our citizens and youth everywhere in society? The objection, however, is merely specious; for, in the first place, none but youth (poor youth, I mean) determined to have an education would resort to such an institution. These would soon learn to disregard or despise the *petits maitres* [petty schoolmasters] who might affect to be their superiors. They would in fact be as independent as the richest. How much more truly respectable and republican would be their condition while thus *laboring* for the food of body and mind than that of the student who is supported in luxurious ease by the charity of individuals or of the public? How vastly preferable to the situation of a Cambridge sizer or Oxford servitor — many of whom, nevertheless, have filled, and are filling, the highest stations in church and state?

In the second place, the *esprit de corps* which would prevail in the several ranks or classes of students would serve to keep each other in countenance and to render them indifferent to imaginary evils. Besides, they would be a regular component part of the establishment. They would be in the fashion. They would conform to established usage. They would have law and public sentiment in their favor. They would not form a sorry half dozen of pitiable exceptions to the reigning mode, as they would if found in any of our present colleges. They would constitute a respectable moiety — perhaps, a large majority of the whole. And they would be respectable, just in proportion to their modest, fearless, independent conformity to their actual condition. A poor youth of talents and becoming deportment will never be long despised anywhere. But here he would occupy a post of honor and have every motive and every encouragement to persevere, till he should be qualified to do honor to himself, his friends, and his country.

32.

Strike of Boston Carpenters

During the first four decades of the nineteenth century, almost all organized attempts on the part of labor to improve working conditions were considered illegal. An individual worker could legally bargain for higher wages and shorter hours, but any combination of workers to "regulate the value of labor" (which of course was far more effective than individual bargaining) was held to be a criminal conspiracy and was inveighed against by employers. The following three-part selection illustrates the situation as it was in 1825, when a group of Boston carpenters struck for higher wages. The first part of the selection is the resolutions of the journeymen carpenters, presented to the master carpenters; the second is the master carpenters' reply. Not surprisingly, the businessmen of Boston who were engaged in construction supported the master carpenters' rejection of the journeymen's demands, as the third part of the selection reveals.

Source: *Columbian Centinel*, April 20, 23, 1825.

I.

Resolutions of the Journeymen Carpenters

NOTICE TO HOUSE CARPENTERS and housewrights in the country. An advertisement having appeared in the papers of this city, giving information that there is at this time a great demand for workmen in this branch of mechanical business in this city, it is considered a duty to state for the benefit of our brethren of the trade that we are not aware of any considerable demand for labor in this business, as there is, at this time, a very considerable number of journeymen carpenters who are out of employ, and the probable inducement which led to the communication referred to arises from a disposition manifested on the part of the builders in this city to make their own terms as to the price of labor and the number of hours of labor which shall hereafter constitute a day's work.

It being a well-known fact that the most unreasonable requirements have been hitherto exacted with regard to the terms of labor of journeymen mechanics in this city; and it is further well known that in the cities of New York, Philadelphia, Baltimore, and most of the other cities a much more liberal and equitable course of policy has been adopted by the master builders on this subject, giving to their journeymen that fair and liberal support to which they are unquestionably entitled. It is an undoubted fact that on the present system, it is impossible for a journeyman housewright and house carpenter to maintain a family at the present time with the wages which are now usually given to the journeymen house carpenters in this city.

II.

Resolutions of the Master Carpenters

Resolved, that we learn with surprise and regret that a large number of those who are employed as journeymen in this city have entered into a combination for the purpose of altering the time of commencing and terminating their daily labor from that which has been customary from time immemorial, thereby lessening the amount of labor each day in a very considerable degree.

Resolved, that we consider such a combination as unworthy of that useful and industrious class of the community who are engaged in it; that it is fraught with numerous and pernicious evils, not only as respects their employers, but the public at large, and especially themselves; for all journeymen of good character and of skill may expect very soon to become masters and, like us, the employers of others; and by the measure which they are now inclined to adopt they will entail upon themselves the inconvenience to which they seem desirous that we should now be exposed!

Resolved, that we consider the measure proposed as calculated to exert a very unhappy influence on our apprentices by seducing them from that course of industry and economy of time to which we are anxious to inure them. That it will expose the journeymen themselves to many temptations and improvident practices from which they are happily secure while they attend to that wise and salutary maxim of mechanics, "Mind your business." That we consider idleness as the most deadly bane to usefulness and honorable living; and knowing (such is human nature that where there is no necessity, there is no exertion), we fear and dread the consequences of such a measure upon the morals and well-being of society.

Resolved, that we cannot believe this project to have originated with any of the faithful and industrious sons of New England but are compelled to consider it an evil of foreign growth, and one which, we hope and trust, will not take root in the favored soil of Massachusetts. And especially that our city, the early rising and industry of whose inhabitants are universally proverbial, may not be infested with the unnatural production.

Resolved, that if such a measure were ever to be proper and necessary, the time has not yet arrived when it is so; if it would ever be just, it cannot be at a time like the present, when builders have generally made their engagements and contracts for the season, having predicated their estimates and prices upon the original state of things in reference to journeymen. And we appeal therefore to the good sense, the honesty, and justice of all who are engaged in this combination, and ask them to review their doings, contemplate their consequences, and then act as becomes men of sober sense and of prudence.

Resolved, finally, that we will make no alteration in the manner of employing journeymen as respects the time of commencing and leaving work and that we will employ no man who persists in adhering to the project of which we complain.

III.

Resolutions of the Builders

Resolved, that we view with regret the late proceedings of a portion of the journeymen carpenters of this city terminating in a combination to curtail the usual number of working hours.

Resolved, that these proceedings are a departure from the salutary and steady usages which have prevailed in this city, and all New England, from time immemorial, by an adherence to which apprentices and journeymen, accustomed to industrious and temperate habits, have, in their turn, become thriving and respectable masters, and the great body of our mechanics have been enabled to acquire property and respectability, with a just weight and influence in society. That if this confederacy should be countenanced by the community, it must, of consequence, extend to and embrace all the working classes in every department in town and country, thereby effecting a most injurious change in all the modes of business, and in the operations of agriculture and commerce, opening a wide door for idleness and vice. It must finally commute the present condition of the mechanical classes, made happy and prosperous by frugal, orderly, temperate, and ancient habits, for that degraded state by which, in other countries, many of these classes are obliged to leave their homes, bringing with them their feelings and habits and a spirit of discontent and insubordination to which our native mechanics have hitherto been strangers.

Resolved, that while it is admitted every man is free to make such contract in respect to time and wages as he may think for his interest, it is also considered that all combinations by any classes of citizens intended to regulate or effect the value of labor by abridging its duration are in a high degree unjust and injurious to all other classes, inasmuch as they give an artificial and unnatural turn to business and tend to convert all its branches into monopolies. If the journeymen carpenters, by an example which other trades shall follow, effect an unnatural rise in the price of labor, their employers, who vend salt, sugar, and other necessaries, must indemnify themselves by similar combinations or suspend their employment.

Resolved, that we do highly approve of the firmness, temperance, and intelligence manifested by the master carpenters in their proceedings and indulge a strong hope that they will produce a due effect upon the well-disposed among the journeymen, and that those, upon reflection, will be satisfied that a perseverance in their present course will, in the end, produce a reaction ruinous only to themselves.

Resolved, that it is expedient for those concerned in building the present season to support the master carpenters, on the ground by them taken, at whatever sacrifice or inconvenience, and to this end extend the time for the fulfillment of their contracts, and even to suspend, if necessary, building altogether, and that we can foresee no loss or inconvenience arising from such suspensions equal to what must result from permitting such combinations to be effectual.

Resolved, that we cordially and sincerely invite and entreat the journeymen to retrace their steps and return to their business and to realize by their industry and perseverance in the good old way the fair advantages which are now promised by full employment and good wages to all who will embrace them, and we cannot doubt that all who think themselves worthy of becoming masters will perceive their true interest in conforming to this advice. But, if contrary to expectation they should persevere in the present determination, we hereby agree and pledge ourselves to each other not to employ any such journeymen or any other master carpenter who shall yield to their pretensions.

Voted, that the resolutions now adopted be published in the papers of this city and that Messrs. John Bellows, Josiah Marshall, John D. Williams, Samuel Perkins, and Amos Lawrence be a committee to present them to the Building Committee of Faneuil Hall Market for their concurrence and to deposit the same in convenient public places for the signatures of such citizens as may approve them and that fifty copies be printed for this purpose.

33.

WILLIAM CULLEN BRYANT: American Society as a Field for Fiction

By the age of thirty-one, when he wrote the review of a novel, Redwood, *by Catherine Maria Sedgwick, from which the following is taken, William Cullen Bryant had already made substantial contributions to the poetical literature of his country. It was not pride in his own accomplishments, however, that led him to make the points he makes here. Instead, he shared the widespread conviction of his contemporaries that America, heretofore unsung, offered the materials for literature, and particularly for great stories and novels. Whether or not Miss Sedgwick had told one was beside the point.*

Source: *North American Review*, April 1825.

THERE IS NOTHING paradoxical in the opinion which maintains that all civilized countries (we had almost said all countries whatever) furnish matter for copies of real life, embodied in works of fiction which shall be of lasting and general interest. Wherever there are human nature and society there are subjects for the novelist. The passions and affections, virtue and vice, are of no country. Everywhere love comes to touch the hearts of the young, and everywhere scorn and jealousy, the obstacles of fortune and the prudence of the aged, are at hand to disturb the course of love. Everywhere there exists the desire of wealth, the love of power, and the wish to be admired; courage braving real dangers, and cowardice shrinking from imaginary ones; friendship and hatred, and all the train of motives and impulses which affect the minds and influence the conduct of men. They not only exist everywhere but they exist, infinitely diversified and compounded, in various degrees of suppression and restraint, or fostered into unnatural growth and activity, modified by political institutions and laws, by national religions and subdivisions of those religions, by different degrees of refinement and civilization, of poverty or of abundance, by arbitrary usages handed down from indefinite antiquity, and even by local situation and climate. Nor is there a single one of all these innumerable modifications of human character and human emotion which is not, in some degree, an object of curiosity and interest.

Over all the world is human sagacity laying its plans, and chance and the malice of others are thwarting them, and fortune is raising up one man and throwing down another. In none of the places of human habitation are the accesses barred against joy or grief; the kindness of the good carries gladness into families, and the treachery of the false friend brings sorrow and ruin; in all countries are tears shed over the graves of the excellent, the brave, and the beautiful, and the oppressed breathe freer when the oppressor has gone to his account. Everywhere has nature her features of grandeur and beauty, and these features receive a moral expression from the remembrances of the past and the interests of the present. On her face, as on an immense theater, the passions and pursuits of men are performing the great drama of human existence.

At every moment, and in every corner of the world, these mighty and restless agents are perpetually busy, under an infinity of forms and disguises, and the great representation goes on with the majestic continuity and uninterrupted regularity which mark all the courses of nature. Who then will undertake to say that the hand of genius may not pencil off a few scenes acted in our vast country, and amid our large population, that shall interest and delight the world?

It is a native writer only that must and can do this. It is he that must show how the infinite diversities of human character are yet further varied by causes that exist in our own country, exhibit our peculiar modes of thinking and action and mark the effect of these upon individual fortunes and happiness. A foreigner is manifestly incompetent to the task; his observation would rest only upon the more general and obvious traits of our national character, a thousand delicate shades of manner would escape his notice, many interesting peculiarities would never come to his knowledge, and many more he would misapprehend.

It is only on his native soil that the author of such works can feel himself on safe and firm ground, that he can move confidently and fearlessly, and put forth the whole strength of his powers without risk of failure. His delineations of character and action, if executed with ability, will have a raciness and freshness about them which will attest their fidelity, the secret charm which belongs to truth and nature, and without which even the finest genius cannot invest a system of adscititious and imaginary manners. It is this quality which recommends them powerfully to the sympathy and interest even of those who are unacquainted with the original from which they are drawn, and makes such pictures from such hands so delightful and captivating to the foreigner. By superadding to the novelty of the manners described the interest of a narrative, they create a sort of illusion which places him in the midst of the country where the action of the piece is going on. He beholds the scenery of a distant land, hears its inhabitants conversing about their own concerns in their own dialect, finds himself in the bosom of its families, is made the depositary of their secrets and the observer of their fortunes, and becomes an inmate of their firesides without stirring from his own. Thus it is that American novels are eagerly read in Great Britain, and novels descriptive of English and Scottish manners as eagerly read in America.

It has been objected that the habits of our countrymen are too active and practical; that they are too universally and continually engrossed by the cares and occupations of business to have leisure for that intrigue, those plottings and counter-plottings, which are necessary to give a sufficient degree of action and eventfulness to the novel of real life. It is said that we need for this purpose a class of men whose condition in life places them above the necessity of active exertion, and who are driven to the practice of intrigue because they have nothing else to do.

It remains, however, to be proved that any considerable portion of this ingredient is necessary in the composition of a successful novel. To require that it should be made up of nothing better than the maneuvers of

New York Historical Society

Watercolor portrait of William Cullen Bryant by Henry Inman, 1827

those whose only employment is to glitter at places of public resort, to follow a perpetual round of amusements, and to form plans to outshine, thwart, and vex each other, is confining the writer to a narrow and most barren circle. It is requiring an undue proportion of heartlessness, selfishness, and vice in his pictures of society. It is compelling him to go out of the wholesome atmosphere of those classes, where the passions and affections have their most salutary and natural play, and employ his observations on that where they are the most perverted, sophisticated, and corrupt.

But will it be seriously contended that he can have no other resource than the rivalries and machinations of the idle, the frivolous, and the dissolute, to keep the reader from yawning over his pictures? Will it be urged that no striking and interesting incidents can come to pass without their miserable aid? If our country be not the country of intrigue, it is at least the country of enterprise; and nowhere are the great objects that worthily interest the passions and call forth the exertions of men pursued with more devotion and perseverance. The agency of chance,

too, is not confined to the shores of Europe; our countrymen have not attained a sufficient degree of certainty in their calculations to exclude it from ours.

It would really seem to us that these two sources, along with that blessed quality of intrigue which even the least favorable view of our society will allow us, are abundantly fertile in interesting occurrences for all the purposes of the novelist. Besides, it should be recollected that it is not in any case the dull diary of ordinary occupations or amusements that forms the groundwork of his plot. On the contrary, it is some event, or at least a series of events, of unusual importance, standing out in strong relief from the rest of the biography of his principal characters, and to which the daily habits of their lives, whatever may be their rank or condition, are only a kind of accompaniment.

But the truth is that the distinctions of rank and the amusements of elegant idleness are but the surface of society, and only so many splendid disguises put upon the reality of things. They are trappings which the writer of real genius, the anatomist of the human heart, strips away when he would exhibit his characters as they are, and engage our interest for them as beings of our own species. He reduces them to the same great level where distinctions of rank are nothing and difference of character everything. It is here that James I and Charles II and Louis IX and Rob Roy and Jeanie Deans and Meg Merrilies are, by the author of the *Waverley Novels,* made to meet. The monarch must come down from the dim elevation of his throne; he must lay aside the assumed and conventional manners of his station, and unbend and unbosom himself with his confidants before that illustrious master will condescend to describe him.

In the artificial sphere in which the great move, they are only puppets and pageants, but here they are men. A narrative, the scene of which is laid at the magnificent levees of princes, in the drawing rooms of nobles, and the bright assemblies of fashion, may be a very pretty, showy sort of thing, and so may a story of the glittering dances and pranks of fairies. But we soon grow weary of all this and ask for objects of sympathy and regard; for something the recollection of which shall dwell on the heart, and to which it will love to recur; for something, in short, which is natural, the unaffected traits of strength and weakness, of the tender and the comic, all which the pride of rank either removes from observation or obliterates.

If these things have any value, we hesitate not to say that they are to be found abundantly in the characters of our countrymen, formed as they are under the influences of our free institutions, and shooting into a large and vigorous, though sometimes irregular, luxuriance. They exist most abundantly in our more ancient settlements, and amid the more homogeneous races of our large populations, where the causes that produce them have operated longest and with most activity. It is there that the human mind has learned best to enjoy our fortunate and equal institutions, and to profit by them.

In the countries of Europe the laws chain men down to the condition in which they were born. This observation, of course, is not equally true of all those countries, but, when they are brought into comparison with ours, it is in some degree applicable to them all. Men spring up and vegetate and die without thinking of passing from the sphere in which they find themselves any more than the plants they cultivate think of removing from the places where they are rooted. It is the tendency of this rigid and melancholy destiny to contract and stint the intellectual faculties, to prevent the development of character and to make the subjects of it timid, irresolute, and imbecile. With us, on the contrary, where the proudest honors in the state and the highest deference in society are set equally before all our citizens, a wholesome and quickening impulse is communicated to all parts of the social system. All are possessed with a spirit of ambition and a love of adventure, an intense competition calls forth and exalts the passions and faculties of men, their characters become strongly defined, their minds acquire a hardihood and an activity which can be gained by no other discipline, and the community, throughout all its conditions, is full of bustle and change and action.

Whoever will take the pains to pursue this subject a little into its particulars will be surprised at the infinite variety of forms of character which spring up under the institutions of our country. Religion is admitted on all hands to be a mighty agent in molding the human character; and, accordingly, with the perfect allowance and toleration of all religions, we see among us their innumerable and diverse influences upon the manners and temper of our people. Whatever may be his religious opinions, no one is restrained by fear of consequences from avowing them, but is left to nurse his peculiarities of doctrine into what importance he pleases. . . .

It is in our country also that these differences of character, which grow naturally out of geographical situation, are least tampered with and repressed by political regulations. The adventurous and roving natives of our seacoasts and islands are a different race of men from those who till the interior, and the hardy dwellers of our mountainous districts are not like the inhabitants of the rich plains that skirt our mighty lakes and rivers. The manners of the Northern states are said to be characterized by the keenness and importunity of their climate, and those of the Southern to partake of the softness of theirs.

In our cities you will see the polished manners of the European capitals, but pass into the more quiet and unvisited parts of the country, and you will find men whom you might take for the first planters of our colonies. The descendants of the Hollanders have not forgotten the traditions of their fathers, and the legends of Germany are still recited, and the ballads of Scotland still sung in settlements whose inhabitants derive their origin from those countries. It is hardly possible that the rapid and continual growth and improvement of our country, a circumstance wonderfully exciting to the imagination and altogether unlike anything witnessed in other countries, should not have some influence in forming our national character. At all events, it is a most fertile source of incident. It does for us in a few short years what in Europe is a work of centuries.

The hardy and sagacious native of the Eastern states settles himself in the wilderness by the side of the emigrant from the British Isles; the pestilence of the marshes is braved and overcome; the bear and wolf and catamount are chased from their haunts; and then you see cornfields and roads and towns springing up as if by enchantment. In the meantime pleasant Indian villages situated on the skirts of their hunting grounds, with their beautiful green plats for dancing and martial exercises, are taken into the bosom of our extending population, while new states are settled and cities founded far beyond them. Thus a great deal of history is crowded into a brief space. Each little hamlet in a few seasons has more events and changes to tell of than a European village can furnish in a course of ages.

But if the writer of fictitious history does not find all the variety he wishes in the various kinds of our population, descended in different parts of our country, from ancestors of different nations, and yet preserving innumerable and indubitable tokens of their origin, if the freedom with which every man is suffered to take his own way in all things not affecting the peace and good order of society does not furnish him with a sufficient diversity of characters, employments, and modes of life, he has got other resources. He may bring into his plots men whose characters and manners were formed by the institutions and modes of society in the nations beyond the Atlantic, and he may describe them faithfully as things which he has observed and studied. If he is not satisfied with indigenous virtue, he may take for the model of his characters men of whom the Old World is not worthy, and whom it has cast out from its bosom. If domestic villainy be not dark enough for his pictures, here are fugitives from the justice of Europe come to prowl in America.

If the coxcombs of our own country are not sufficiently exquisite, affected, and absurd, here are plenty of silken fops from the capitals of foreign kingdoms. If he finds himself in need of a class of men more stupid and degraded than are to be found among the natives of the United States, here are crowds of the wretched peasantry of Great Britain and Germany, flying for refuge from intolerable suffering, in every vessel that comes to our shores. Hither, also, resort numbers of that order of men who, in foreign countries, are called the middling class, the most valuable part of the communities they leave, to enjoy a moderate affluence, where the abuses and exactions of a distempered system of government cannot reach them to degrade them to the condition of the peasantry.

Our country is the asylum of the persecuted preachers of new religions and the teachers of political doctrines which Europe will not endure; a sanctuary for dethroned princes and the consorts of slain emperors. When we consider all these innumerable differences of character, native and foreign, this infinite variety of pursuits and objects, this endless diversity and change of fortunes, and behold them gathered and grouped into one vast assemblage in our own country, we shall feel little pride in the sagacity or the skill of that native author who asks for a richer or a wider field of observation. . . .

The peculiarities in the manners and character of our countrymen have too long been connected with ideas merely low and ludicrous. We complain of our English neighbors for holding them up as objects simply ridiculous and laughable, but it is by no means certain that we have not encouraged them by our example. It is time, however, that they were redeemed from these gross and degrading associations. It is time that they should be mentioned, as they deserve to be, with something else than a sneer, and that a feeling of respect should mingle with the smile they occasion. We are happy to see . . . them as we find them connected in real life, with much that is ennobling and elevated, with traits of sagacity, benevolence, moral courage, and magnanimity. These are qualities, which by no means impair any comic effect those peculiarities may have; they rather relieve and heighten it. They transform it from mere buffoonery to the finest humor.

When this is done, something is done to exalt our national reputation abroad and to improve our national character at home. It is also a sort of public benefit to show what copious and valuable materials the private lives and daily habits of our countrymen offer to the writer of genius. It is as if one were to discover to us rich ores and gems lying in the common earth about us.

34.

Songs of the Erie Canal

The Erie Canal was opened to navigation in 1825. It had taken eight years to complete the 363 miles of inland waterway between Albany and Buffalo, New York, destined to become one of the most important routes to the West. Although the canal was a great improvement over the earlier rough roads, crewmen and passengers were still faced with many trials. Horses or mules, hauling the canal boats, progressed slowly along towpaths on the banks of the canal and were driven by men called "hoggies." The first song reprinted below, "Low Bridge, Everybody Down," uses as its refrain the warning cry of the hoggy to the passengers as the boat approached a bridge over the canal. It is usually thought of as a folk song, and maybe it is, but one scholar, at least, claims that it was first published in 1913. The second song, "E-RI-E," was a favorite song of the canal crews. In this imaginative evocation of a "terrible storm" they may have been responding to the haughty contempt of ocean sailors, who tended to discount the hazards of canal boating.

⛵ LOW BRIDGE, EVERYBODY DOWN

I've got a mule and her name is Sal,
Fifteen miles on the Erie Canal.
She's a good old worker and a good old pal,
Fifteen miles on the Erie Canal.
We've hauled some barges in our day,
Filled with lumber, coal, and hay,
And we know every inch of the way
From Albany to Buffalo.

Chorus:
Low bridge! Everybody down!
Low bridge! We're a-coming to a town.
You'll always know your neighbor,
        you'll always know your pal
If you've ever navigated on the Erie Canal.

We'd better get on our way, old pal,
Fifteen miles on the Erie Canal.
You can bet your life I'd never part with Sal,
Fifteen miles on the Erie Canal.
Get us there, Sal, here comes a lock;
We'll make Rome 'fore six o'clock.
One more trip and back we'll go,
Right back home to Buffalo.

E-RI-E

We were forty miles from Albany,
Forget it, I never shall;
What a terrible storm we had one night,
On the E-ri-e Canal.

Chorus:
Oh the E-ri-e was a-rising,
And the gin was a-getting low.
And I scarcely think we'll get a drink,
Till we get to Buffalo,-o-o,
Till we get to Buffalo.

We were loaded down with barley,
We were chock-up full on rye;
The captain he looked down on me
With his gol-durn wicked eye.

Two days out from Syracuse,
The vessel struck a shoal,
We like to all be foundered
On a chunk o' Lackawanna coal.

We hollered to the captain
On the towpath, treading dirt,
He jumped on board and stopped the leak
With his old red flannel shirt.

The cook she was a grand old gal,
She wore a ragged dress,
We hoisted her upon a pole
As a signal of distress.

The wind begin to whistle,
The waves begin to roll,
We had to reef our royals
On that raging canal.

When we got to Syracuse,
Off-mule he was dead,
The nigh mule he got blind staggers;
We cracked him on the head.

The captain, he got married,
The cook, she went to jail,
And I'm the only son-of-a-gun
That's left to tell the tale.

35.

Edward Livingston: On the Formation of New Laws

Legal reform was one of the primary objectives of the Jacksonian Democrats, who wished to codify the law, especially the common law, in order to dispel the ambiguities of conflicting legal codes and to abolish what they felt was the arbitrary power of the courts. The movement for codification dates back to the 1820s when Edward Livingston, at the request of the Louisiana state legislature, undertook a complete revision of Louisiana's system of penal law. A preliminary report of his plan was well received and, in 1825, Livingston submitted a new code. It comprised six books: a book of definitions; a preamble and other introductory remarks; a code of crimes and punishments; a code of procedure; a code of evidence; and a code of reform and prison discipline. The preamble is reprinted below. Although Louisiana failed to implement Livingston's reforms, his system received national and even international attention. The struggle for codification continued, and by 1835 successful code revisions had been made in New York, Ohio, and Pennsylvania.

Source: *A System of Penal Law, for the State of Louisiana,* Philadelphia, 1833, pp. 357-359.

No ACT OF LEGISLATION can be or ought to be immutable. Changes are required by the alteration of circumstances; amendments, by the imperfection of all human institutions; but laws ought never to be changed without great deliberation and a due consideration, as well, of the reasons on which they were founded, as of the circumstances under which they were enacted. It is therefore proper, in the formation of new laws, to state clearly the motives for making them, and the principles by which the framers were governed in their enactment. Without a knowledge of these, future legislatures cannot perform the task of amendment, and there can be neither consistency in legislation nor uniformity in the interpretation of laws.

For these reasons the General Assembly of the state of Louisiana declare that their objects in establishing the following code, are:

To remove doubts relative to the authority of any parts of the penal law of the different nations by which this state, before its independence, was governed.

To embody into one law and to arrange into system such of the various prohibitions enacted by different statutes as are proper to be retained in the penal code.

To include in the class of offenses acts injurious to the state and its inhabitants which are not now forbidden by law.

To abrogate the reference, which now exists, to a foreign law for the definition of offenses and the mode of prosecuting them.

To organize a connected system for the prevention as well as for the prosecution and punishment of offenses.

To collect into written codes, and to express in plain language, all the rules which it may be necessary to establish for the protection of the government of the country, and the person, property, condition, and reputation of individuals; the penalties and punishments attached to a breach of those rules; the legal means of preventing offenses, and the forms of prosecuting them when committed; the rules of evidence by which the truth of accusations are to be tested; and the duties of executive and judicial officers, jurors and individuals, in preventing, prosecuting, and punishing offenses, to the end that no one need to be ignorant of any branch of criminal jurisprudence, which it concerns all to know.

And to change the present penal laws, in all those points in which they contravene the following principles, which the General Assembly consider as fundamental truths, and which they have made the basis of their legislation on this subject, to wit:

Vengeance is unknown to the law. The only object of punishment is to prevent the commission of offenses: it should be calculated to operate:

First, on the delinquent, so as by seclusion to deprive him of the present means, and by habits of industry and temperance, of any future desire to repeat the offense.

Secondly, on the rest of the community, so as to deter them by the example, from a like contravention of the laws. No punishments, greater than are necessary to effect these ends, ought to be inflicted.

No acts or omissions should be declared to be offenses but such as are injurious to the state, to societies permitted by the laws, or to individuals.

But penal laws should not be multiplied without evident necessity; therefore, acts, although injurious to individuals or societies, should not be made liable to public prosecution when they may be sufficiently repressed by private suit.

From the imperfection of all human institutions, and the inevitable errors of those who manage them, it sometimes happens that the innocent are condemned to suffer the punishment due to the guilty. Punishments should, therefore, be of such a nature

that they may be remitted, and as far as possible compensated, in cases where the injustice of the sentence becomes apparent.

Where guilt is ascertained, the punishment should be speedily inflicted.

Penal laws should be written in plain language, clearly and unequivocally expressed, that they may neither be misunderstood nor perverted; they should be so concise as to be remembered with ease; and all technical phrases, or words they contain, should be clearly defined. They should be promulgated in such a manner as to force a knowledge of their provisions upon the people; to this end, they should not only be published but taught in the schools, and publicly read on stated occasions.

The law should never command more than it can enforce. Therefore, whenever from public opinion or any other cause, a penal law cannot be carried into execution, it should be repealed.

The accused, in all cases, should be entitled to a public trial, conducted by known rules, before impartial judges and an unbiased jury; to a copy of the act of accusation against him; to the delay necessary to prepare for his trial; to process to enforce the attendance of his own witnesses; and to an opportunity of seeing, hearing, and examining those who are produced against him; to the assistance of counsel for his defense; to free communication with such counsel, if in confinement, and to be bailed in all cases, except those particularly specified by law. No presumption of guilt, however violent, can justify the infliction of any punishment before conviction, or of any bodily restraint greater than is necessary to prevent escape; and the nature and extent of this restraint should be determined by law.

Perfect liberty should be secured of hearing and publishing a true account of the proceedings of criminal courts, limited only by such restrictions as morality and decency require; and no restraint whatsoever should be imposed on the free discussion of the official conduct of the judges and other ministers of justice in this branch of government.

Such a system of procedure, in criminal cases, should be established as to be understood without long study; it should neither suffer the guilty to escape by formal objections, nor involve the innocent in difficulties by errors in pleading.

For this purpose, amendments should be permitted in all cases, where neither the accused nor the public prosecutor can be surprised.

Those penal laws counteract their own effect, which, through a mistaken lenity, give greater comforts to a convict than those which he would probably have enjoyed while at liberty.

The power of pardoning should be only exercised in cases of innocence discovered, or of certain and unequivocal reformation.

Provision should be made for preventing the execution of intended offenses, whenever the design to commit them is sufficiently apparent.

The remote means of preventing offenses do not form the subject of penal laws. The General Assembly will provide them in their proper place. They are the diffusion of knowledge by the means of public education, and the promotion of industry and, consequently, of ease and happiness among the people.

Religion is a source of happiness here, and the foundation of our hopes of it hereafter; but its observance can never, without the worst of oppression, form the subject of a penal code. All modes of belief and all forms of worship are equal in the eye of the law; when they interfere with no private or public rights, all are entitled to equal protection in their exercise.

Whatever may be the majority of the professors of one religion or sect in the state, it is a persecution to force anyone to conform to any ceremonies, or to observe any festival or day, appropriated to worship by the members of a particular religious

Estate, John Ross Delafield; photo Frick

Portrait of Edward Livingston by J. W. Jarvis

persuasion. This does not exclude a general law establishing civil festivals or periodical cessations from labor for civil purposes unconnected with religious worship, or the appointment of particular days on which citizens of all persuasions should join, each according to the rites of his own religion, in rendering thanks to God for any signal blessing, or imploring His assistance in any public calamity.

The innocent should never be made to participate in the punishment inflicted on the guilty; therefore, no such effects should follow conviction as to prevent the heir from claiming an inheritance through or from the person convicted. Still less should the feelings of nature be converted into instruments of torture by denouncing punishment against the children to secure the good conduct of the parent.

Laws intended to suppress a temporary evil should be limited to the probable time of its duration, or carefully repealed after the reason for enacting them has ceased.

36.

John Bannister Gibson: Against Judicial Review

At a time when most of the nation's leading jurists had accepted the doctrine of judicial review as established by Marshall, Story, and others, a judge in the Pennsylvania Supreme Court, John Bannister Gibson, retained grave doubts about it. Always preferring to rest his decisions on principles rather than precedents, Gibson wrote the minority rather than the majority opinion in a number of cases. The opportunity to oppose the principles of judicial review handed down in Marbury v. Madison *(1803) presented itself in 1825, when the case of* Eakin v. Raub *appeared before the Supreme Court of Pennsylvania. Excerpts from Judge Gibson's dissenting opinion in this case appear below.*

Source: *Reports of Cases Adjudged in the Supreme Court of Pennsylvania,* 3rd edition, Philadelphia, 1874, Vol. XII, pp. 343-358.

It seems to me there is a plain difference, hitherto unnoticed, between acts that are repugnant to the constitution of the particular state and acts that are repugnant to the Constitution of the United States; my opinion being that the judiciary is bound to execute the former but not the latter. I shall hereafter attempt to explain this difference by pointing out the particular provisions in the Constitution of the United States on which it depends.

I am aware that a right to declare all unconstitutional acts void, without distinction as to either constitution, is generally held as a professional dogma; but I apprehend rather as a matter of faith than of reason. I admit that I once embraced the same doctrine, but without examination; and I shall, therefore, state the arguments that impelled me to abandon it, with great respect for those by whom it is still maintained. But I may premise that it is not a little remarkable that, although the right in question has all

along been claimed by the judiciary, no judge has ventured to discuss it, except Chief Justice Marshall (in *Marbury v. Madison*); and if the argument of a jurist so distinguished for the strength of his ratiocinative powers be found inconclusive, it may fairly be set down to the weakness of the position which he attempts to defend. . . .

I begin, then, by observing that in this country the powers of the judiciary are divisible into those that are *political* and those that are purely *civil.* Every power by which one organ of the government is enabled to control another, or to exert an influence over its acts, is a political power. The political powers of the judiciary are *extraordinary* and *adventitious;* such, for instance, as are derived from certain peculiar provisions in the Constitution of the United States, of which hereafter; and they are derived, by direct grant, from the common fountain of all political power. On the other hand, its civil are its *ordinary* and *appropriate* powers;

being part of its essence and existing independently of any supposed grant in the Constitution. But where the government exists by virtue of a *written* constitution, the judiciary does not necessarily derive from that circumstance any other than its ordinary and appropriate powers. . . .

With us, although the legislature be the depository of only so much of the sovereignty as the people have thought fit to impart, it is, nevertheless, sovereign within the limit of its powers and may relatively claim the same preeminence here that it may claim elsewhere. It will be conceded, then, that the ordinary and essential powers of the judiciary do not extend to the annulling of an act of the legislature. . . . I take it, therefore, that the power in question does not necessarily arise from the judiciary being established by a written constitution, but that this organ can claim, on account of that circumstance, no powers that do not belong to it at the common law; and that, whatever may have been the cause of the limitation of its jurisdiction, originally, it can exercise no power of supervision over the legislature without producing a direct authority for it in the Constitution, either in terms or by irresistible implication from the nature of the government; without which the power must be considered as reserved, along with the other ungranted portions of the sovereignty, for the immediate use of the people.

The constitution of Pennsylvania contains no express grant of political powers to the judiciary. But to establish a grant by implication, the constitution is said to be a law of superior obligation; and, consequently, that if it were to come into collision with an act of the legislature, the latter would have to give way; this is conceded. But it is a fallacy to suppose that they can come into collision *before the judiciary.*

What is a constitution? It is an act of extraordinary legislation by which the people establish the structure and mecha-

nism of their government; and in which they prescribe fundamental rules to regulate the motion of the several parts. What is a statute? It is an act of ordinary legislation by the appropriate organ of the government, the provisions of which are to be executed by the executive or judiciary, or by officers subordinate to them. . . .

The constitution and the *right* of the legislature to pass the act may be in collision; but is that a legitimate subject for judicial determination? If it be, the judiciary must be a peculiar organ, to revise the proceedings of the legislature and to correct its mistakes; and in what part of the constitution are we to look for this proud preeminence? Viewing the matter in the opposite direction, what would be thought of an act of assembly in which it should be declared that the Supreme Court had, in a particular case, put a wrong construction on the Constitution of the United States, and that the judgment should therefore be reversed? It would, doubtless, be thought a usurpation of judicial power. But it is by no means clear that to declare a law void, which has been enacted according to the forms prescribed in the Constitution, is not a usurpation of legislative power. . . .

But it has been said to be emphatically the business of the judiciary to ascertain and pronounce what the law is; and that this necessarily involves a consideration of the constitution. It does so; but how far? If the judiciary will inquire into anything besides the form of enactment, where shall it stop? There must be some point of limitation to such an inquiry; for no one will pretend that a judge would be justifiable in calling for the election returns, or scrutinizing the qualifications of those who composed the legislature. . . .

For instance, let it be supposed that the power to declare a law unconstitutional has been exercised. What is to be done? The legislature must acquiesce, although it may think the construction of the judiciary

Self-portrait of John Bannister Gibson

wrong. But why must it acquiesce? Only because it is bound to pay that respect to every other organ of the government which it has a right to exact from each of them in turn. This is the argument. But it will not be pretended that the legislature has not, at least, an equal right with the judiciary to put a construction on the constitution; nor that either of them is infallible; nor that either ought to be required to surrender its judgment to the other. . . .

Repugnance to the constitution is not always self-evident; for questions involving the consideration of its existence require for their solution the most vigorous exertion of the higher faculties of the mind, and conflicts will be inevitable, if any branch is to apply the constitution, after its own fashion, to the acts of all the others. I take it, then, the legislature is entitled to all the deference that is due to the judiciary; that its acts are, in no case, to be treated as *ipso facto* void, except where they would produce a revolution in the government; and that, to avoid them, requires the act of some tribunal competent, under the constitution (if any such there be), to pass on their validity. All that remains, therefore, is to inquire whether the judiciary or the people are that tribunal.

Now, as the judiciary is not expressly constituted for that purpose, it must derive whatever authority of the sort it may possess from the reasonableness and fitness of the thing. But, in theory, all the organs of the government are of equal capacity; or, if not equal, each must be supposed to have superior capacity only for those things which peculiarly belong to it. And as legislation peculiarly involves the consideration of those limitations which are put on the lawmaking power, and the interpretation of the laws when made involves only the construction of the laws themselves, it follows that the construction of the constitution, in this particular, belongs to the legislature, which ought, therefore, to be taken to have superior capacity to judge of the constitutionality of its own acts.

But suppose all to be of equal capacity, in every respect, why should one exercise a controlling power over the rest? That the judiciary is of superior rank has never been pretended, although it has been said to be coordinate. It is not easy, however, to comprehend how the power which gives law to all the rest can be of no more than equal rank with one which receives it and is answerable to the former for the observance of its statutes. Legislation is essentially an act of sovereign power; but the execution of the laws by instruments that are governed by prescribed rules and exercise no power of volition is essentially otherwise. The very definition of law, which is said to be "a rule of civil conduct, prescribed by the *supreme* power in the state," shows the intrinsic superiority of the legislature.

It may be said the power of the legislature, also, is limited by prescribed rules; it is so. But it is, nevertheless, the power of the people, and sovereign as far as it extends. It cannot be said that the judiciary is coordinate merely because it is established by the constitution; if that were sufficient, sheriffs, registers of wills, and recorders of deeds would be so too. Within the pale of their authority, the acts of these officers will have the power of the people for their support; but no one will pretend they are of equal dignity with the acts of the legislature. Inequality of rank arises not from the manner in which the organ has been constituted but from its essence and the nature of its functions; and the legislative organ is superior to every other, inasmuch as the power to will and to command is essentially superior to the power to act and to obey. It does not follow, then, that every organ created by special provision in the constitution is of equal rank. Both the executive, strictly as such, and the judiciary are subordinate; and an act of superior power exercised by an inferior ought, one would think, to rest on something more solid than implication.

It may be alleged that no such power is claimed, and that the judiciary does no positive act but merely refuses to be instrumental in giving effect to an unconstitutional law. This is nothing more than a repetition, in a different form, of the argument — that an unconstitutional law is *ipso facto* void; for a refusal to act under the law must be founded on a right in each branch to judge of the acts of all the others before it is bound to exercise its functions to give those acts effect. No such right is recognized in the different branches of the national government except the judiciary (and that, too, on account of the peculiar provisions of the Constitution), for it is now universally held, whatever doubts may have once existed, that Congress is bound to provide for carrying a treaty into effect, although it may disapprove of the exercise of the treaty-making power in the particular instance. A government constructed on any other principle would be in perpetual danger of standing still; for the right to decide on the constitutionality of the laws would not be peculiar to the judiciary, but would equally reside in the person of every officer whose agency might be necessary to carry them into execution. . . .

The negative which each part of the legislature may exercise in regard to the acts of the other was thought sufficient to prevent material infractions of the restraints which were put on the power of the whole; for, had it been intended to interpose the judiciary as an additional barrier, the matter would surely not have been left in doubt. The judges would not have been left to stand on the insecure and ever shifting ground of public opinion, as to constructive power; they would have been placed on the impregnable ground of an express grant; they would not have been compelled to resort to the debates in the convention, or the opinion that was generally entertained at the time. A constitution, or a statute, is supposed to contain the whole will of the body from which it emanated; and I would just as soon resort to the debates in the legislature, for the construction of an act of assembly, as to the debates in the convention, for the construction of the constitution. . . .

The grant of a power so extraordinary ought to appear so plain that he who should run might read. Now, put the Constitution into the hands of any man of plain sense, whose mind is free from an impression on the subject, and it will be impossible to persuade him that the exercise of such a power was ever contemplated by the convention. . . .

The oath to support the Constitution is not peculiar to the judges, but is taken indiscriminately by every officer of the government, and is designed rather as a test of the political principles of the man than to bind the officer in the discharge of his duty. Otherwise, it were difficult to determine what operation it is to have in the case of a recorder of deeds, for instance, who, in the execution of his office, has nothing to do with the Constitution. But granting it to relate to the official conduct of the judge, as well as every other officer, and not to his political principles, still, it must be understood in reference to supporting the Constitution, *only as far as that may be involved in his official duty;* and, consequently, if his official duty does not comprehend an inquiry into the authority of the legislature, neither does his oath. . . .

But do not the judges do a *positive* act in violation of the Constitution when they give effect to an unconstitutional law? Not if the law has been passed according to the forms established in the Constitution. The fallacy of the question is in supposing that the judiciary adopts the acts of the legislature as its own; whereas, the enactment of a law and the interpretation of it are not concurrent acts; and as the judiciary is not required to concur in the enactment, neither is it in the breach of the Constitution which may be the consequence of the enactment; the fault is imputable to the legislature, and on it the responsibility exclusively rests. . . . .

The constitution of this state has withstood the shocks of strong party excitement for thirty years, during which no act of the legislature has been declared unconstitutional, although the judiciary has constantly asserted a right to do so in clear cases. But it would be absurd to say that this remarkable observance of the constitution has been produced, not by the responsibility of the legislature to the people but by an apprehension of control by the judiciary. Once let public opinion be so corrupt as to sanction every misconstruction of the constitution, and abuse of power, which the temptation of the moment may dictate, and the party which may happen to be predominant, will laugh at the puny efforts of a dependent power to arrest it in its course.

For these reasons, I am of opinion that it rests with the people, in whom full and absolute sovereign power resides, to correct abuses in legislation by instructing their representatives to repeal the obnoxious act. What is wanting to plenary power in the government is reserved by the people for their own immediate use, and to redress an infringement of their rights in this respect would seem to be an accessory of the power thus reserved.

It might, perhaps, have been better to vest the power in the judiciary; as it might be expected that its habits of deliberation, and the aid derived from the arguments of counsel, would more frequently lead to accurate conclusions. On the other hand, the judiciary is not infallible; and an error by it would admit of no remedy but a more distinct expression of the public will, through the extraordinary medium of a convention; whereas, an error by the legislature admits of a remedy by an exertion of the same will in the ordinary exercise of the right of suffrage — a mode better calculated to attain the end, without popular excitement.

It may be said, the people would probably not notice an error of their representatives. But they would as probably do so as notice an error of the judiciary; and beside, it is a *postulate* in the theory of our government, and the very basis of the superstructure, that the people are wise, virtuous, and competent to manage their own affairs; and if they are not so, in fact, still, every question of this sort must be determined according to the principles of the constitution, as it came from the hands of its framers, and the existence of a defect which was not foreseen, would not justify those who administer the government, in applying a corrective in practice which can be provided only by a convention.

37.

The Courts and Public Opinion

In Kentucky, the Panic of 1819 precipitated a political struggle that almost grew into civil war. The banks had been forced to tighten their loan and credit policies and, in response to this action, the state legislature, which represented fewer lenders than borrowers, passed laws extending the time when payments would be due. A bitter fight ensued between two elements of the population organized as the Relief Party (debtors) and the Anti-Relief Party (creditors). The latter group fought the Relief Party's legislation, attempting to have it repealed and finally taking the issue to the Kentucky Court of Appeals, which decided in favor of the creditors. In 1824, a Relief governor and legislature tried to reorganize the court and appoint judges sympathetic to their cause. However, the original judges refused to relinquish their positions. The legislature, controlled by the Relief Party, contested the right of the courts to override laws that clearly represented prevailing public opinion. The following selection is taken from the legislature's resolution to that effect, passed on January 6, 1825.

Source: *Acts Passed at the First Session of the Thirty-Third General Assembly of the Commonwealth of Kentucky,* Frankfort, 1825, pp. 221-239.

THE JOINT COMMITTEE raised upon that part of the governor's communication which relates to the official conduct of the judges of the Court of Appeals have had that subject under consideration and beg leave to report: That the judges of that Court, at their last fall term, pronounced a decision in the cases of *Blair* v. *Williams* and *Lapsley* v. *Brashear* annulling, in effect, the laws of this state in relation to replevin bonds, to forthcoming bonds, to the valuation of property subjected to sale under execution, to the sale of property under execution upon a limited credit, and even to the occupying claimants of land, and circumscribing, by the reasoning which it employs and in the principles which it attempts to establish, the legislative power of the government within a compass too narrow to be exercised usefully or beneficially to the community.

The encroachment made by that opinion upon the constitutional and legitimate powers of the Legislative Department and upon the great principles of self-government by the people in the exercise, by that department, of its appropriate powers, and the afflicting degree in which it was calculated to disorder the social relations throughout the community, could not and did not escape the discernment and vigilance of our late excellent and patriotic chief magistrate, Gen. John Adair. In his communication to the legislature, at the last session of that body, he invited their attention to the import of that decision. The committee to whom that part of his communication was referred made a report sanctioning the decision and asserting the right of the judicial to *check* and *control* the Legislative Department in the exercise of its legislative powers.

The legislature, by appropriate preamble and resolutions, repelled the doctrine of the report, asserted the error of the principles of the opinion, and, in affirmance of their sentiment, superadded a cautionary enactment entitled "An Act to Regulate the Issuing of Executions," approved Jan. 2, 1824. Thus an issue was distinctly formed between the two departments and referred to the people, that august and paramount tribunal, from whose decision there can be no appeal by either party. They, it is believed, have made up their verdict, and it remains that their representatives should, at the present session, give it effect, and enroll it in the archives of state.

Their opinion is not the effervescence of popular excitement; it is the result of a deliberation, calm and dispassionate in a degree proportioned to the magnitude and importance of the question, viewed in all its aspects. They have not, in the consideration of this matter, been either ignorant or regardless of the boundaries which limit the rights and duties of the contending departments; nor have they overlooked the great political principles with which those rights and duties are respectively connected, and upon a just observance of which, by each, the welfare and repose of society essentially depend. They have not been convinced by reflection nor seduced or derided into the belief that the judiciary possess the *right*, by the constitution of the state or upon the natural and acknowledged principles of fitness, upon which all free governments are based, to check and control the Legislative Department. . . .

The limits prescribed in the constitution to the legislative power are but the modes in which the sovereign has ordained that that power shall be exerted; for the ordination of fundamental rules and the enaction of laws are alike the exercise of the sovereign power. It is from that consideration that both the constitution and the code derive their authority. The settled canons of our political rights and of sovereign agency are proclaimed in the constitution.

For our civil rights, we examine the code. The legislature, in supplying the code, display the will of the people, limited only by their own preordinations in the constitution, and that government only is free which knows no restraint upon the exercise of its legitimate faculties, which was not imposed by itself in its organization; and, among free governments, that is *freest* in which no restraint upon its legislative power is to be found in its constitution, which is not *essentially* necessary to its existence and wellbeing. It is by legislation only that an organized government can express its *will*, and as the freedom of an individual is diminished or extinguished by the partial or total control of his will, so is the freedom of government diminished or extinguished by the partial or total control of the legislative power.

Any people, therefore, which imposes in its constitution a restraint upon the exercise of the legislative power not necessary to the well-being of the government, so far uselessly diminishes its liberty; for . . . in the body politic, the power of legislation should be limited by that display only of *fixed will* in the constitution which is necessary to its living and healthful state.

But it is urged that the representatives of the people may err in the enaction of laws, and that, therefore, the exercise of legislative power should be subject to the check and control of the judiciary. Why should they be subject to the control of the judiciary rather than of the people, the only and legitimate sovereign? May not the judiciary err, also, in the exercise of the controlling power? Are they less liable to err than the legislature? But would not the skein of legislative power be strangely striped if the control of the legislature were taken from the people, to whom its members are immediately and directly responsible, and transferred to the judges, to whom they bear no responsible relation? And is it not strange that the power to control the legislature should be ascribed to the judges, who are, themselves, immediately responsible to that body as the organ of the people? But in controlling the only organ by which the people can express their will, would not the judges control the people themselves?

But the necessity of the control of the legislative power by the judiciary is not perceived. Does either reason or the experience of governments sanction it? It is believed not? The most solemn and eventful display of the legislative power which can be made by any people is made in the organization of their government, in the formation of their constitution; and yet, so far from their being availed in that interesting process, of the controlling wisdom of the judiciary, the judges are, by it, then only for the first time brought into existence, and that only in contemplation. It is reserved by that instrument, for the legislature, the very body whom they assert the right to control, to create them and prescribe their duties. And it would seem that if the people were wise and virtuous enough to be trusted with the organization of the government, and with the specification and recognition in the constitution of their great and essential rights, they ought to be supposed to be wise enough to enact laws for its administration — the latter as well without the control of the judiciary as the former. The same people that formed the constitution enact the laws; and if they were equal to the former, they ought not to be supposed to be incompetent to the latter.

Judicial control cannot be more necessary in the performance of the latter than of the former; but the people, it is admitted, are sovereign, and the legislature is the only organ by which they can express their will. To control, then, that only organ is to control the people. But they cease to be sovereign when they are controlled, and the judges who control them become the sovereign. This theory, then, of judicial control, eventuates in a curious spectacle — the creature controlling the creator — the subject, the sovereign; for the people, through their legislative organs, created the judges. . . .

The constitution is the people's; and when they cease to understand it, it ceases to be theirs. The general opinion of the import of the constitution is necessarily and alone the constitution. It is the deliberately expressed will of the majority; and to suppose that there is not in society intelligence enough to comprehend the purposes of its own deliberate will, in relation to the most essential rights of its members and to the rights, powers, and duties of its functionaries, is to assert that the people not only do not possess freedom but are incapable of enjoying it; for, to the enjoyment and maintenance of freedom, there must be a capacity to comprehend the principles upon which it depends. When, therefore, the judges have given an interpretation to the constitution which is contrary to the general understanding of it by the community, an interpretation in which they cannot acquiesce, a decent respect for public opinion, especially when that opinion is deliberately formed and expressed, ought to induce them to surrender it or their offices, for it is unsuitable and incongruous that public functionaries should wage war with public opinion.

They are trustees, and when they lose the confidence of the *cestui que trusts,* they should resign the trust. They are public *fiduciaries,* and they should not continue to be so without the public confidence and against the public opinion. They should not forget that public opinion is a tribunal of unlimited jurisdiction and correspondent power. There is nothing of which it does not take cognizance, from the most exalted to the humblest subject of human concern.

By what other standard do we settle claims to moral excellence or intellectual preeminence, to delicacy of taste or propriety of conduct, to distinction in arms or in arts? It is this tribunal which awarded epic preeminence to Homer, dramatic supremacy to Shakespeare, and immortality to Washington. It is to public opinion we submit our claims to reputation, which is dearer to us than life itself. What is excellent in painting or exquisite in music; what constitutes the grand, the beautiful, the sublime in nature, as well as all that charms in art, are settled and irreversibly too, by this august tribunal. Even the decencies and comities of life and of social intercourse are settled by the same arbitress. And shall public opinion be competent to all this and be unequal to the interpretation of an *article* in the constitution — be ignorant of what constitutes the *obligation* of a contract?

The attempt by the judges, in that decision, to prostrate the remedial system which the legislature had enacted in obedience to circumstances of peculiar and resistless pressure, by denying to society the power of accommodating its remedial enactions to its condition, and that too, upon subtle and metaphysical reasoning in relation to the obligation of a contract, by which to bring the power of legislation within the control of judicial discretion, in its exposition of the Constitution of the United States, must have, it is believed, the reprobation of public opinion to an unqualified extent; and that reprobation must be strengthened by the consideration that two of the judges (Judges Mills and Owsley) sanctioned, in their legislative capacities, anterior to their elevation to the bench, by their votes in the legislative hall, the very principle which, by their decision, they have attempted to vacate and annul.

Each of those gentlemen voted for the enaction of replevin laws, as the records of the Legislative Department evince. They have all, at various times and repeatedly, sanctioned by their decisions the principles upon which the right to enact them is asserted by the legislature and has been sanctioned in usage, almost time immemorial, by the people. As legislators, they believed with the rest of society that there existed in the *nature of things* a distinction between the *obligation* of a contract and the *remedy* furnished by the legislature for its enforcement; that the former consisted in the *consent of the parties, upon a valid consideration,*

to the import of the contract; that the latter consisted in that modification of the force of public will which the discretion of society, upon a just survey of its condition, chooses from time to time to afford in legislative enactment for remedial purposes; that the former consisted *essentially* in the exercise of the *volition of the parties,* displayed upon *valid consideration,* in their *assent* to the *contract;* the latter, in the *volition of the people,* displayed in remedial enactments.

The declaratory laws furnished the rules as to the competency of the parties to exercise their will in the formation of their contracts and as to the character of the consideration essential to their validity; the remedial laws provided for their enforcement only. But upon the *new theory* established by the judges, that the obligation of a contract consists alone in the remedy for its enforcement, legislative power must yield to judicial discretion. It must always be a matter of discretion with the judges whether the legislative remedy is conformable to their notion of the obligation of the contract, and their exposition of that clause of the Constitution which forbids the states to impair, by legislation, the obligation of contracts, and, consequently, the rights of the people must depend not upon law but upon judicial discretion.

That such has not been their opinion heretofore may be seen by their decisions in the cases of *Grubbs* v. *Harris* . . . of *Reardon* v. *Searcy's Heirs* . . . and of *Graves* v. *Graves' Executor.* In the first of those cases, that Court says:

Upon the propriety of the remedy by petition, etc., we can have no doubt. The statute is general as to the description of direct debts, whether they have commenced *before* or shall exist *after* the passage thereof. The statute does not change the *essence of the contract; it is the mode of recovery only which is changed.* If the proper distinction is observed between those laws which have reference to the *essence, nature, construction, or extent of the contract,* and those which have reference only to the *mode of enforcing the contract,* the question will be plain.

The *lex temporis,* etc., the means afforded by the law for enforcing a contract, in case of a breach or noncompliance, *make no part of the contract,* and the modes of bringing suit and of execution *are different from and make no part of the contract.* They do not enter into the *essence* of the contract. So the *forms of suit and of execution in our own country, at this time or that, make no part of a contract at one time or the other,* and the legislature are at liberty to *adopt this or that mode of enforcing contracts, which the circumstances of the country may suggest as expedient.*

The judges say, in the second case:

It is certainly a well-settled rule *that the law at the time the contract was made composes a part of it, so far as relates to the nature and construction of such contract;* but it is equally well settled that the *remedy* to enforce such contract must be according to the law in force at the time such remedy is sought. . . . Contracts are not made with an eye to the law that shall enforce them . . . but with an expectation of each party's performing, with good faith, what he has stipulated to do.

In the third case, they say:

With respect to the nature and validity of contracts, and the rights and obligations of the parties arising out of them, the principle is well settled that *the law of the place where the contract was made is to govern;* but with regard to the *remedy,* the principle is equally well established that the *law of the country where the contract is sought to be enforced ought to be the rule of decision.* The statute of limitations does not affect the validity of contracts, but the time of enforcing them; or, in other words, it does not *destroy the right* but *withholds the remedy.*

In the case of *Stanley* v. *Earl,* lately decided, they say that "the statute of limitations not only destroys the right but invests the adverse possessor of a slave with the right to recover him from the true and rightful owner."

The Supreme Court of the United States, in the case of the *Columbia Bank* v. *Oakley*

. . . say: "In giving this opinion, we attach no importance to the idea of this being a chartered bank. It is the *remedy* and not the right and as such we have no doubt of its being subject to the *will* of Congress. The *forms of administering justice,* and the duties and powers of courts . . . must forever be subject to legislative will, and the power over them is inalienable, so as to bind subsequent legislatures." And the same Court, in the case of *Crowninshield* v. *Sturges* . . . say: "The distinction between the *obligation* of a contract and the *remedy* given by the legislature to enforce that obligation has been taken at the bar and *exists in the nature of things.* Without *impairing* the obligation of contracts, the remedy may certainly be *modified,* as the wisdom of the nation may direct. . . ."

Here it is seen that the judges of the Court of Appeals have said, in three cases, that the *remedy* formed no part of the *obligation* of the contract and might be *altered, varied,* and *amended* without impairing the contract or its obligation. The Supreme Court of the United States has said the same thing, in strong and distinct terms. Yet the judges, in the cases of *Blair* v. *Williams* and *Lapsley* v. *Brashear,* say that the *remedy constitutes alone the obligation of the contract* and cannot be varied without impairing that obligation, and that any law varying the remedy is, on that account, void; that the statute of limitations, by taking away the *remedy,* extinguishes the *right.* They say that the *right* consists alone in the *remedy.* The Supreme Court says there is a distinction *in the nature of things* between *right* and *remedy.*

In the case of *Graves* v. *Graves' Executor,* Chief Justice Boyle says that the statute of limitations does not affect the validity of the contract; it does not destroy the *right,* it only withholds the *remedy.* In the late decision, they say that the replevin bond is void against the creditor but good against the debtor; that is, that the sovereign people of the state of Kentucky have not the power to pass a law giving validity to the bond; but a single creditor, whether citizen or alien, has the power to give it validity against the debtor and his securities. So that the same law, when enacted by the state, is unconstitutional and void and, when enacted by a *creditor*, is valid and binding; or, in other words, a replevin bond is void against the creditor, because it is a statutory bond and the statute was void; but it is valid against the debtor and his securities when the creditor shall choose to have it so and because he so chooses.

That Court has, in the case of *Stanley* v. *Earl* . . . pronounced at the last spring term, given an opinion in which they have employed the whole force of their intellect to sustain this new doctrine, that *right consists alone in remedy.* They apply, with much emphasis, the term "legal" to "right" and "remedy," and, by the adjunction of that term to the other two, arrive at a conclusion not very favorable to the good morals of society. The operation which they give to the new principle excites to the most flagrant dishonesty by the premium which it accords to its achievements; and they denounce as unfit to be reasoned with all who do not yield to the force of their reasoning.

The replevin principle had been sanctioned by successive enactments in Virginia and Kentucky, from the formation of the Constitution of the United States, and by the state of Virginia for near half a century anterior to the erection of Kentucky into a state. The valuation principle possessed the sanction of enactments by both states and by the Congress of the United States. Its practical sanction by the people and their functionaries, legislative and judicial, had, it is believed, become too inveterate to be disturbed, even if it had been erroneous; for there is an inveteracy of practical exposition, even of the Constitution itself, which cannot be disturbed.

But the principle, in its practical results, is calculated to convulse society. The sales which have been made of lands and slaves under execution have been, since the commencement of the government, in the ratio of at least ten to one, upon replevin and forthcoming bonds. If those bonds were all void, as they must be, according to the *new theory of obligation,* it would seem to result, obviously, that the executions were void; and, both being void, the sales would also be void and invest no title in the purchasers. For if there be a truth in the stores of philosophy, more accessible to common sense and more intelligible to common understanding than any other, it is that a lawless and void act can invest no right. Out of nothing, *nothing comes.*

But the first and most practical result of the opinion, if it had not been prevented by the cautionary enactment of the legislature before alluded to, must have been to strike dead at once upon the hands of society its entire paper medium, which then exceeded, and perhaps now exceeds, $2 million, and to subject the property of debtors to instant sale for gold and silver; for who would receive in payment of his debt a depreciated paper currency when he could force, without *replevin* and without *valuation,* the sale of his debtor's property, at whatever sacrifice, for gold and silver? The decision was calculated to afford to banking institutions a jubilee of exemption from legal restraints in the coercion of their debtors.

Society could not, it cannot now, bear the practical results of the new doctrine. It cannot live under them. It cannot surrender the right to exert, according to the limits prescribed in the constitution for their exertion, those remedial energies with which God and nature endowed it, for the avoidance and mitigation of human misery and the promotion of human happiness. It was for the right of exerting this power, that the blood of the Revolution was shed and independence achieved by the patriots of '76; it is for the exertion of this power that Greece is now prodigal of her blood and agonizing at every pore — the power of self-government by the people; of suiting, by their legislative enactments, their laws to their condition; and of varying them upon the same principle when their condition shall be varied.

Your committee, therefore, while they reverence appropriately the judicial functionaries of the government and applaud and admire that independence in that department, which, in giving effect to the laws, is regardless of every will but the deliberate will of the people, feel themselves constrained to report as follows:

Resolved by the General Assembly of the Commonwealth of Kentucky, that the principles asserted in the decisions pronounced by the judges of the Court of Appeals, in the cases of *Blair* v. *Williams* and *Lapsley* v. *Brashear,* are incompatible with the great principles upon which the rights, interests, and happiness of the good people of Kentucky depend; that they encroach upon the just and necessary exercise by the legislature of the powers accorded by the constitution to that department; that in narrowing the legislative power they encroach upon the freedom of the people, and the encroachment might, if acquiesced in, be carried to its utter extinction; *wherefore,* they do most deliberately and solemnly, again, in the name of the good people of this Commonwealth, protest against the obnoxious principles of those decisions as encroachments upon the fundamental principles of freedom and the inherent rights of the people.

38.

John Quincy Adams: A Policy for Internal Improvements

As the Northeastern states became increasingly oriented toward industry and commerce, and as the agricultural population expanded westward, improved systems of communication and transportation were more and more urgently needed. None disputed that, but the question was, who would finance such internal improvements. Unlike their opponents, John Quincy Adams and Henry Clay thought that the federal government should do it, and found in the Constitution sufficient authority for their belief. Both felt, in addition, that the economic growth of the country depended on having the federal government coordinate and control such projects, rather than local or state governments. In his first annual message to Congress, delivered on December 6, 1825, President Adams sought to gain support for his generally nationalistic policies, and in the section of the message reprinted here laid special emphasis on the need for internal improvements.

Source: Richardson, II, pp. 299-317.

THE APPROPRIATIONS made by Congress for public works, as well in the construction of fortifications as for purposes of internal improvement, so far as they have been expended, have been faithfully applied. Their progress has been delayed by the want of suitable officers for superintending them. An increase of both the corps of engineers, military and topographical, was recommended by my predecessor at the last session of Congress. The reasons upon which that recommendation was founded subsist in all their force and have acquired additional urgency since that time. It may also be expedient to organize the topographical engineers into a corps similar to the present establishment of the Corps of Engineers. The Military Academy at West Point will furnish from the cadets annually graduated there officers well qualified for carrying this measure into effect. . . .

It were, indeed, a vain and dangerous illusion to believe that, in the present or probable condition of human society, a commerce so extensive and so rich as ours could exist and be pursued in safety without the continual support of a military marine — the only arm by which the power of this confederacy can be estimated or felt by foreign nations, and the only standing military force which can never be dangerous to our own liberties at home. A permanent naval peace establishment, therefore, adapted to our present condition and adaptable to that gigantic growth with which the nation is advancing in its career, is among the subjects which have already occupied the foresight of the last Congress and which will deserve your serious deliberations. Our navy, commenced at an early period of our present political organization upon a scale commensurate with the incipient energies, the scanty resources, and the comparative indigence of our infancy, was even then found adequate to cope with all the powers of Barbary, save the first, and with one of the principal maritime powers of Europe. . . .

Upon this first occasion of addressing the legislature of the Union, with which I have been honored, in presenting to their view the execution so far as it has been effected of the measures sanctioned by them for promoting the internal improvement of our country, I cannot close the communication without recommending to their calm and persevering consideration the general principle in a more enlarged extent.

The great object of the institution of civil government is the improvement of the condition of those who are parties to the social compact, and no government, in whatever form constituted, can accomplish the lawful ends of its institution but in proportion as it improves the condition of those over whom it is established. Roads and canals, by multiplying and facilitating the communications and intercourse between distant regions and multitudes of men, are among the most important means of improvement. But moral, political, intellectual improvement are duties assigned by the Author of our existence to social no less than to individual man. For the fulfillment of those duties, governments are invested with power, and to the attainment of the end — the progressive improvement of the condition of the governed — the exercise of delegated powers is a duty as sacred and indispensable as the usurpation of powers not granted, is criminal and odious.

Among the first, perhaps the very first, instrument for the improvement of the condition of men is knowledge; and to the acquisition of much of the knowledge adapted to the wants, the comforts, and enjoyments of human life public institutions and seminaries of learning are essential. So convinced of this was the first of my predecessors in this office, now first in the memory, as living, he was first in the hearts, of our countrymen, that once and again in his addresses to the Congresses with whom he cooperated in the public service he earnestly recommended the establishment of seminaries of learning, to prepare for all the emergencies of peace and war: a national university and a military academy. With respect to the latter, had he lived to the present day, in turning his eyes to the institution at West Point, he would have enjoyed the gratification of his most earnest wishes; but in surveying the city which has been honored with his name he would have seen the spot of earth which he had destined and bequeathed to the use and benefit of his country as the site for a university still bare and barren.

In assuming her station among the civilized nations of the earth, it would seem that our country had contracted the engagement to contribute her share of mind, of labor, and of expense to the improvement of those parts of knowledge which lie beyond the reach of individual acquisition, and particularly to geographical and astronomical science. . . .

In inviting the attention of Congress to the subject of internal improvements upon a view thus enlarged, it is not my design to recommend the equipment of an expedition for circumnavigating the globe for purposes of scientific research and inquiry. We have objects of useful investigation nearer home, and to which our cares may be more beneficially applied. The interior of our own territories has yet been very imperfectly explored. Our coasts along many degrees of latitude upon the shores of the Pacific Ocean, though much frequented by our spirited commercial navigators, have been barely visited by our public ships. The River of the West, first fully discovered and navigated by a countryman of our own, still bears the name of the ship in which he ascended its waters, and claims the protection of our armed national flag at its mouth. With the establishment of a military post there or at some other point of that coast, recommended by my predecessor and already matured in the deliberations of the last Congress, I would suggest the expediency of connecting the equipment of a public ship for the exploration of the whole northwest coast of this continent.

The establishment of a uniform standard of weights and measures was one of the specific objects contemplated in the formation of our Constitution, and to fix that standard was one of the powers delegated by express terms in that instrument to Congress. . . .

Connected with the establishment of a university, or separate from it, might be undertaken the erection of an astronomical observatory, with provision for the support of an astronomer, to be in constant attendance of observation upon the phenomena of the heavens, and for the periodical publication of his observations. It is with no feeling of pride as an American that the remark may be made that on the comparatively small territorial surface of Europe there are existing upward of 130 of these lighthouses of the skies, while throughout the whole American hemisphere there is not one. . . .

The laws relating to the administration of the Patent Office are deserving of much consideration and perhaps susceptible of some improvement. The grant of power to regulate the action of Congress upon this subject has specified both the end to be obtained and the means by which it is to be effected, "to promote the progress of science and useful arts by securing for limited times to authors and inventors the exclusive right to their respective writings and discoveries." If an honest pride might be indulged in the reflection that on the records of that office are already found inventions, the usefulness of which has scarcely been transcended in the annals of human ingenuity, would not its exultation be allayed by the inquiry whether the laws have effectively insured to the inventors the reward destined to them by the Constitution — even a limited term of exclusive right to their discoveries? . . .

The spirit of improvement is abroad upon the earth. It stimulates the hearts and sharpens the faculties not of our fellow citizens alone but of the nations of Europe and of their rulers. While dwelling with pleasing satisfaction upon the superior excellence of our political institutions, let us not be unmindful that liberty is power; that the nation blessed with the largest portion of liberty must in proportion to its numbers be the most powerful nation upon earth; and that the tenure of power by man is, in the moral purposes of his Creator, upon condition that it shall be exercised to ends of beneficence, to improve the condition of himself and his fellowmen. While foreign nations less blessed with that freedom which is power than ourselves are advancing with gigantic strides in the career of public improvement, were we to slumber in indolence or fold up our arms and proclaim to the world that we are palsied by the will of our constituents, would it not be to cast away the bounties of Providence and doom ourselves to perpetual inferiority?

In the course of the year now drawing to its close, we have beheld, under the auspices and at the expense of one state of this Union, a new university unfolding its portals to the sons of science and holding up the torch of human improvement to eyes that seek the light. We have seen, under the persevering and enlightened enterprise of another state, the waters of our western lakes mingle with those of the ocean. If undertakings like these have been accomplished in the compass of a few years by the authority of single members of our confederation, can we, the representative authorities of the whole Union, fall behind our fellow servants in the exercise of the trust committed to us for the benefit of our common sovereign by the accomplishment of works important to the whole and to which neither the authority nor the resources of any one state can be adequate?

39.

John Quincy Adams: On Participating in a Congress of American Nations

The Latin American hero and liberator, Simon Bolívar, had long envisioned a league of American states, and to further this goal he called for a conference to meet at Panama in 1826. When the United States received an invitation to participate in the conference, President John Quincy Adams sought the opinion of Congress on the matter. Many congressmen and senators, including a majority of the Senate Foreign Affairs Committee, opposed U.S. participation for political reasons, but the President and those who sought more amicable hemisphere relations won congressional approval in the end. However, the U.S. delegation, composed of Richard C. Anderson and John Sergeant, did not reach Panama before the conference was completed. Adams' message to Congress on December 26, 1825, concerning the impending Panama Congress, appears below.

Source: Richardson, II, pp. 318-320.

In the message to both houses of Congress, at the commencement of the session, it was mentioned that the governments of the republics of Colombia, of Mexico, and of Central America had severally invited the government of the United States to be represented at the congress of American nations to be assembled at Panama to deliberate upon objects of peculiar concernment to this hemisphere, and that this invitation had been accepted.

Although this measure was deemed to be

within the constitutional competency of the executive, I have not thought proper to take any step in it before ascertaining that my opinion of its expediency will concur with that of both branches of the legislature; first, by the decision of the Senate upon the nominations to be laid before them; and, second, by the sanction of both houses to the appropriations, without which it cannot be carried into effect.

A report from the secretary of state and copies of the correspondence with the South American governments on this subject since the invitation given by them are herewith transmitted to the Senate. They will disclose the objects of importance which are expected to form a subject of discussion at this meeting, in which interests of high importance to this Union are involved. It will be seen that the United States neither intend nor are expected to take part in any deliberations of a belligerent character; that the motive of their attendance is neither to contract alliances nor to engage in any undertaking or project importing hostility to any other nation.

But the southern American nations, in the infancy of their independence, often find themselves in positions with reference to other countries with the principles applicable to which, derivable from the state of independence itself, they have not been familiarized by experience. The result of this has been that sometimes, in their intercourse with the United States, they have manifested dispositions to reserve a right of granting special favors and privileges to the Spanish nation as the price of their recognition. At others, they have actually established duties and impositions operating unfavorably to the United States, to the advantage of other European powers, and sometimes they have appeared to consider that they might interchange among themselves mutual concessions of exclusive favor, to which neither European powers nor the United States should be admitted.

In most of these cases their regulations unfavorable to us have yielded to friendly expostulation and remonstrance. But it is believed to be of infinite moment that the principles of a liberal commercial intercourse should be exhibited to them, and urged with disinterested and friendly persuasion upon them when all assembled for the avowed purpose of consulting together upon the establishment of such principles as may have an important bearing upon their future welfare.

The consentaneous adoption of principles of maritime neutrality, and favorable to the navigation of peace and commerce in time of war, will also form a subject of consideration to this congress. The doctrine that free ships make free goods and the restrictions of reason upon the extent of blockades may be established by general agreement with far more ease and perhaps with less danger by the general engagement to adhere to them concerted at such a meeting than by partial treaties or conventions with each of the nations separately. An agreement between all the parties represented at the meeting that each will guard by its own means against the establishment of any future European colony within its borders may be found advisable. This was more than two years since announced by my predecessor to the world as a principle resulting from the emancipation of both the American continents. It may be so developed to the new southern nations that they will all feel it is an essential appendage to their independence.

There is yet another subject upon which, without entering into any treaty, the moral influence of the United States may perhaps be exerted with beneficial consequences at such a meeting: the advancement of religious liberty. Some of the southern nations are even yet so far under the dominion of prejudice that they have incorporated with their political constitutions an exclusive church, without toleration of any other than the dominant sect. The abandonment of this last badge of religious bigotry and oppression may be pressed more effectually by the united exertions of those who concur in the principles of freedom of conscience upon those who are yet to be convinced of their justice and wisdom, than by the solitary efforts of a minister to any one of the separate governments.

The indirect influence which the United States may exercise upon any projects or purposes originating in the war in which the southern republics are still engaged, which might seriously affect the interests of this Union, and the good offices by which the United States may ultimately contribute to bring that war to a speedier termination, though among the motives which have convinced me of the propriety of complying with this invitation, are so far contingent and eventual that it would be improper to dwell upon them more at large.

In fine, a decisive inducement with me for acceding to the measure is to show by this token of respect to the southern repub-lics the interest that we take in their welfare and our disposition to comply with their wishes. Having been the first to recognize their independence and sympathized with them so far as was compatible with our neutral duties in all their struggles and sufferings to acquire it, we have laid the foundation of our future intercourse with them in the broadest principles of reciprocity and the most cordial feelings of fraternal friendship. To extend those principles to all our commercial relations with them and to hand down that friendship to future ages is congenial to the highest policy of the Union, as it will be to that of all those nations and their posterity.

In the confidence that these sentiments will meet the approbation of the Senate, I nominate Richard C. Anderson of Kentucky and John Sergeant of Pennsylvania to be envoys extraordinary and ministers plenipotentiary to the assembly of American nations at Panama, and William B. Rochester of New York to be secretary to the mission.

Thomas Jefferson still lives.
> JOHN ADAMS, last words. Jefferson had died a few hours earlier on the same day, July 4, 1826.

On the faces of the obelisk the following inscription, and not a word more
"Here was buried
Thomas Jefferson
Author of the Declaration of American Independence
of the Statute of Virginia for religious freedom
And Father of the University of Virginia."
because by these, as testimonials that I have lived, I wish most to be remembered.
> THOMAS JEFFERSON, directions for his tomb, found after his death in his own handwriting

The Delaware Water Gap leading into the Pennsylvania interior above Philadelphia

MOVING WESTWARD

The 1820s began the long period of large scale internal migration and immigration from abroad which populated the Midwest and the deep South. Each year brought greater numbers of settlers over the Appalachian Mountains into the Ohio Valley. Floating downstream from Pittsburgh or Wheeling, the migrants found land they could afford and set about carving farms from the wilderness. These were no longer pioneers but homesteaders. With them came almost equal numbers of tradesmen, merchants, and small businessmen. These men sold animals and farm implements, boots and cloth, glass and hardware. They established the shops, foundries, saw-mills, and the trading companies and steamboat lines that would grow as the towns grew. Litigation over land required lawyers. A growing population needed doctors and preachers, and of course, politicians. The names of Eastern Congressmen began to reappear, representing new constituencies in the West.

This westward rush was duplicated in the South, as plantation owners and small farmers alike moved into lands in Alabama and northern Mississippi that had been, or were being, acquired from the Indians.

During the ten years following the War of 1812 six states were admitted to the Union. In the next decade these new states in the South and Midwest more than doubled in population. Important river towns such as Louisville and Cincinnati held as many as 35,000 persons. For many the backbreaking labor of clearing, and planting the wilderness was over by the 1830s. The "frontier" was farther west. With plans underway for canals and railroads the new states were launched on a period of sustained growth.

The South

The demand for cotton to feed Northern textile mills and the soil depletion on the older plantations brought pressure for new land in the deep South. Migration of the plantation system into western Georgia, Alabama, and Mississippi was impeded by the presence of relatively civilized Indians with prior claims to the land. In some cases these Indians were plantation owners themselves. By the 1830s, however, white immigration had overwhelmed the Cherokees, Choctaws, and other tribes, and the plantation economy began to move west in full force. Some backcountry subsistence farmers joined the migration, but they found the new farmland no more suited to small-scale cultivation than the mountain valleys they had left behind.

(Top) Bolling's Dam, Petersburgh, Va.; (center) view of the Potomac at Harper's Ferry; (bottom) Spirit Creek, Augusta, Ga.

(Top) Columbus, Ga., on the Chatahoochie River, 1829; (right) Mick-e-no-pah, Seminole, painted by Catlin; (below) chiefs of the Creek nation; (bottom) family from the interior of Georgia

The Ohio Valley

For the majority of immigrants to the Midwest, the route led across the mountains to the Ohio River and then downstream. Regular steamboat service was operating on the Ohio by 1820, but most new settlers traveled by keelboat or raft. The numerous towns and cities that grew up along the river served as stopping points for travelers going inland and as commercial outlets for trade on the river. Louisville was situated where the Falls of the Ohio made a shipping halt necessary. Flatboats outfitted here for the trip downriver to the Mississippi.

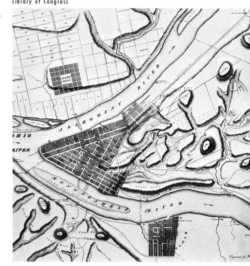

(Top) Workmen removing floating bridge from the Ohio River to allow a boat to pass; (above) plan for the development of Pittsburgh and the adjacent country; (left) passengers on a keelboat on the Ohio

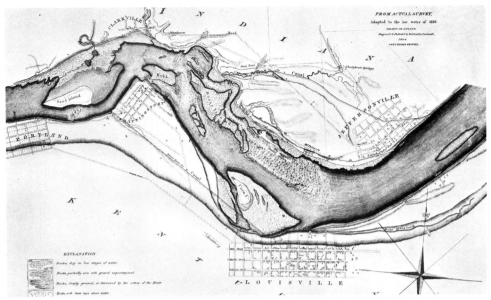

(Top) Map showing the Falls of the Ohio at low water and the town of Louisville, Ky., 1824; (left) Bland Ballard, early settler in Kentucky; (above) looking down the Ohio from dock at Louisville; (below) Plan of the proposed town of Hygeia

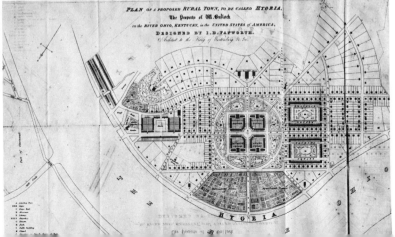

The Midwest

Moving inland from the Ohio and Mississippi river valleys, immigrants settled the farmlands of Indiana and Illinois. The first task was to clear the land for planting. The early settlers generally avoided the prairie grasslands until plows were developed to cut through the tough, deeply-rooted grass. Settlement in the Wisconsin and Michigan territories was limited largely to fur traders. However, the opening of the Erie Canal in 1825 brought increased immigration across the Great Lakes.

(Top) Detroit in 1820 with "Walk-in-the-Water" in the foreground, sketch by George H. Whistler; (center) American log house with snake fence, watercolor by John Halkett; (right) log tavern in Indiana, 1821

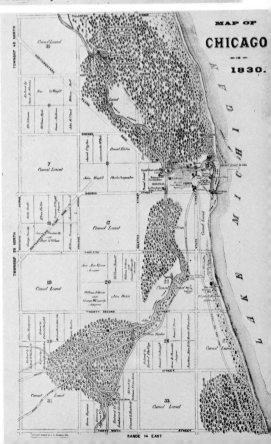

(Top) House on the bank of the Ohio River in Indiana, 1828; (center) view of Princeton, Indiana, 1827; (bottom left) Wolf's Point, Chicago, in 1830; (bottom right) map showing Chicago in 1830, with later streets and some of the early property lines superimposed

(Top) Milwaukee in 1820; (center left) Cassville, Wis., 1829; (center right) log cabin sketched by Victor Collot, 1826; (bottom) trading post at Fond du Lac, Wis.

Early Mining

In addition to rich farmland and the fur trade, early settlers in the Midwest found considerable profit in mining. Lead and zinc were discovered in southwest Wisconsin, northwest Illinois and Missouri. The ores were mined wherever they existed near enough to the rivers to make transportation possible. Copper in almost pure form and enormous iron ore deposits were found in Minnesota, upper Michigan and Wisconsin, but economic transportation for this ore was years away.

(Top) Herculanum, town on the left bank of the Mississippi in the lead mining region south of St. Louis; **(center)** view of LaMotte Village in Missouri, 1826; **(bottom)** lead mine at LaMotte

The Mississippi

Most of the products of the early settlers, the furs, lead, timber, and farm produce, were floated downstream on the Mississippi to New Orleans and then shipped by sea to markets in the East or overseas. At first flatboats, good only for floating with the current, were used in this long-distance shipping. By 1830, however, steamboats were numerous enough to take on much of the trade, and commerce on the Mississippi flourished. After 1825 the Erie Canal afforded an alternate route to the East.

(**Top to bottom**) Memphis, Tenn. in 1830; two flat boats carrying cotton, 1829. The long poles are rudders; steamboat tied up on the bank of the Mississippi to take on wood, 1829

(Top to bottom) Interior of a flatboat; steamboat landing and the lower town at Natchez, Miss., 1830. These sketches and several others in this section by Charles Lesueur; "Keelboat on the Mississippi River" by Felix A. St. Aulaire, 1832

California

View of the Presidio of San Francisco in the 1820s. It was one of a chain of military posts that served administrative centers for Spanish and Mexican rule

A continent away, the Spanish settlements in California continued their isolated existence based on small army posts and Franciscan missions. When Mexico achieved independence from Spain in 1821, California was a sparsely settled region of huge cattle ranches. Others, however, were becoming interested. The Russians had established an outpost north of San Francisco and the first Americans were crossing the Rockies into the unsettled areas of Northern California.

The presidio at Monterey, located on Monterey Bay south of San Francisco and for a time the capital of California

Mission San Carlos, near Monterey, was one of a series of missions along the California coast

1826

40.

Report on Executive Patronage

In the election of 1824, none of the four candidates had received a clear majority and thus the selection of a President was decided by the House of Representatives. Henry Clay, having the fewest electoral votes, was struck from the ballot; however, as one of the most influential members of the House, his support of John Quincy Adams helped to determine the election of a man who held political convictions similar to his own. When President Adams later appointed Clay secretary of state cries of "corrupt bargaining" and "executive patronage" were heard from the Jackson camp. Actually there is little historical evidence that Adams and Clay had arrived at a "deal." Adams himself wrote in his Diary, January 9, 1825, after a talk with Clay concerning the election, that the latter sought no "personal considerations for himself . . . and had no hesitation in saying that his preference would be for me." Nevertheless, the event precipitated a Senate committee study on the subject of executive patronage. Following is the committee's report.

Source: Thomas Hart Benton, *Thirty Years' View*, New York, 1886, Vol. I, pp. 80-81.

IN COMING TO THE CONCLUSION that executive patronage ought to be diminished and regulated on the plan proposed, the Committee rest their opinion on the ground that the exercise of great patronage in the hands of one man has a constant tendency to sully the purity of our institutions and to endanger the liberties of the country. This doctrine is not new. A jealousy of power and of the influence of patronage, which must always accompany its exercise, has ever been a distinguished feature in the American character. It displayed itself strongly at the period of the formation and of the adoption of the federal Constitution. At that time the feebleness of the old Confederation had excited a much greater dread of anarchy than of power — "of anarchy among the members than of power in the head"; and, although the impression was nearly universal that a government of more energetic character had become indispensably necessary, yet, even under the influence of this conviction, such was the dread of power and patronage that the states, with extreme reluctance, yielded their assent to the establishment of the federal government. . . .

Nothing could reconcile the great men of that day to a Constitution of so much power but the guards which were put upon it against the abuse of power. Dread and jealousy of this abuse displayed itself throughout the instrument. To this spirit we are indebted for the freedom of the press, trial by jury, liberty of conscience, freedom of debate, responsibility to constituents, power of impeachment, the control of the Senate over appointments to office, and many other provisions of a like character.

But the Committee cannot imagine that the jealous foresight of the time, great as it was, or any human sagacity could have foreseen and placed a competent guard upon every possible avenue to the abuse of power. The nature of a constitutional act excludes the possibility of combining minute perfection with general excellence. After the exertion of all possible vigilance, something of what ought to have been done has been omitted; and much of what has been attempted has been found insufficient and unavailing in practice. Much remains for us to do, and much will still remain for posterity to do — for those unborn generations to do on whom will devolve the sacred task of guarding the temple of the Constitution and of keeping alive the vestal flame of liberty.

The Committee believe that they will be acting in the spirit of the Constitution in laboring to multiply the guards and to strengthen the barriers against the possible abuse of power. If a community could be imagined in which the laws should execute themselves, in which the power of government should consist in the enactment of laws, in such a state the machine of government would carry on its operations without jar or friction. Parties would be unknown, and the movements of the political machine would but little more disturb the passions of men than they are disturbed by the operations of the great laws of the material world. But this is not the case. The scene shifts from this imaginary region where laws execute themselves to the theater of real life wherein they are executed by civil and military officers, by armies and navies, by courts of justice, by the collection and disbursement of revenue with all its train of salaries, jobs, and contracts; and in this aspect of the reality, we behold the working of *patronage* and discover the reason why so many stand ready, in any country and in all ages, to flock to the standard of *power*, wheresoever and by whomsoever it may be raised.

The patronage of the federal government at the beginning was founded upon a revenue of $2 million. It is now operating upon $22 million, and, within the lifetime of many now living, must operate upon $50 million. The whole revenue must in a few years be wholly applicable to subjects of patronage. At present about one half, say $10 million of it, are appropriated to the principal and interest of the public debt, which, from the nature of the object, involves but little patronage. In the course of a few years this debt, without great mismanagement, must be paid off. A short period of peace and a faithful application of the sinking fund must speedily accomplish that most desirable object. Unless the revenue be then reduced, a work as difficult in republics as in monarchies, the patronage of the federal government, great as it already is, must, in the lapse of a few years, receive a vast accession of strength. The revenue itself will be doubled, and, instead of one half being applicable to objects of patronage, the whole will take that direction. Thus, the reduction of the public debt and the increase of revenue will multiply in a fourfold degree the number of persons in the service of the federal government, the quantity of public money in their hands, and the number of objects to which it is applicable; but as each person employed will have a circle of greater or less diameter of which he is the center and the soul — a circle composed of friends and relations and of individuals employed by himself on public or on private account — the actual increase of federal power and patronage by the duplication of the revenue will be not in the arithmetical ratio but in geometrical progression, an increase almost beyond the power of the mind to calculate or to comprehend.

41.

Timothy Flint: Backwoodsmen

Timothy Flint, who was born in Massachusetts and educated at Harvard, lived as a missionary in the Ohio and Mississippi valleys from 1815 to 1825. His record of those years, published in Boston in 1826, is among the valuable firsthand accounts of frontier civilization. Flint's temper was confessedly romantic, and his experience of the rude West was disillusioning to him. Yet he learned much from the "backwoodsmen" with whom he associated, and he defended the region against criticisms by conservative Easterners such as Timothy Dwight. Flint's book is in the form of letters; the chapter reprinted here was written during the author's stay at St. Charles, Missouri.

Source: *Recollections of the Last Ten Years*, Boston, 1826, pp. 174-189.

THE PEOPLE IN THE ATLANTIC STATES have not yet recovered from the horror inspired by the term "backwoodsman." This prejudice is particularly strong in New England and is more or less felt from Maine to Georgia. When I first visited this country, I had my full share and my family by far too much for their comfort. In approaching the country, I heard a thousand stories of gougings and robberies and shooting down with the rifle. I have traveled in these regions thousands of miles under all circumstances of exposure and danger. I have traveled alone, or in company only with such as needed protection, instead of being able to impart it; and this too, in many instances, where I was not known as a minister, or where such knowledge would have had no influence in protecting me. I never have carried the slightest weapon of defense. I scarcely remember to have experienced anything that resembled insult, or to have felt myself in danger from the people. I have often seen men that had lost an eye. Instances of murder, numerous and horrible in their circumstances, have occurred in my vicinity. But they were such lawless encounters as terminate in murder everywhere, and in which the drunkenness, brutality, and violence were mutual. They were catastrophies in which quiet and sober men would be in no danger of being involved. When we look round these immense regions and consider that I have been in settlements 300 miles from any court of justice, when we look at the position of the men and the state of things, the wonder is that so few outrages and murders occur.

The gentlemen of the towns, even here, speak often with a certain contempt and horror of the backwoodsmen. I have read, and not without feelings of pain, the bitter representations of the learned and virtuous Dr. Dwight in speaking of them. He represents these vast regions as a grand reservoir for the scum of the Atlantic states. He characterizes in the mass the emigrants from New England as discontented cobblers, too proud, too much in debt, too unprincipled, too much puffed up with self-conceit, too strongly impressed that their fancied talents could not find scope in their own country to stay there. It is true there are worthless people here, and the most so, it must be confessed, are from New England. It is true there are gamblers, and gougers, and outlaws; but there are fewer of them than from the nature of things and the character of the age and the world we ought to expect. But it is unworthy of the excellent man in question so to designate this people in the mass.

The backwoodsman of the West, as I have seen him, is generally an amiable and virtuous man. His general motive for coming here is to be a freeholder, to have plenty of rich land, and to be able to settle his children about him. It is a most virtuous motive. And notwithstanding all that Dr. Dwight and Talleyrand have said to the contrary, I fully believe that nine in ten of the emigrants have come here with no other motive. You find, in truth, that he has vices and barbarisms peculiar to his situation. His manners are rough. He wears, it may be, a long beard. He has a great quantity of bear- or deerskins wrought into his household establishment, his furniture, and dress. He carries a knife or a dirk in his bosom and when in the woods has a rifle on his back and a pack of dogs at his heels. An Atlantic stranger, transferred directly from one of our cities to his door, would recoil from an encounter with him. But remember that his rifle and his dogs are among his chief means of support and profit. Remember that all his first days here were passed in dread of the savages. Remember that he still encounters them, still meets bears and panthers.

Enter his door and tell him you are benighted and wish the shelter of his cabin for the night. The welcome is indeed seemingly ungracious: "I reckon you can stay," or "I suppose we must let you stay." But this apparent ungraciousness is the harbinger of every kindness that he can bestow and every comfort that his cabin can afford. Good coffee, corn bread and butter, venison, pork, wild and tame fowls are set before you. His wife, timid, silent, reserved, but constantly attentive to your comfort, does not sit at the table with you, but, like the wives of the patriarchs, stands and attends on you. You are shown to the best bed which the house can offer. When this kind hospitality has been afforded you as long as you choose to stay, and when you depart and speak about your bill, you are most commonly told, with some slight mark of resentment, that they do not keep tavern. Even the flaxen-headed urchins will turn away from your money.

In all my extensive intercourse with these people, I do not recollect but one instance of positive rudeness and inhospitality. It was on the waters of the Cuivre of the Upper Mississippi; and from a man to whom I had presented Bibles, who had received the hospitalities of my house, who had invited me into his settlement to preach. I turned away indignantly from a cold and reluctant reception here, made my way from the house of this man, who was a German and comparatively rich, through deep and dark forests, and amidst the concerts of wolves howling on the neighboring hills. Providentially, about midnight, I heard the barking of dogs at a distance, made my way to the cabin of a very poor man, who arose at midnight, took me in, provided supper, and gave me a most cordial reception.

With this single exception, I have found the backwoodsmen to be such as I have described; a hardy, adventurous, hospitable, rough, but sincere and upright race of people. I have received so many kindnesses from them that it becomes me always to preserve a grateful and affectionate remembrance of them. If we were to try them by the standard of New England customs and opinions, that is to say, the customs of a people under entirely different circumstances, there would be many things in the picture that would strike us offensively. They care little about ministers, and think less about paying them. They are averse to all, even the most necessary, restraints. They are destitute of the forms and observances of society and religion; but they are sincere and kind without professions, and have a coarse but substantial morality which is often rendered more striking by the immediate contrast of the graceful bows, civility, and professions of their French Catholic neighbors, who have the observances of society and the forms of worship, with often but a scanty modicum of the blunt truth and uprightness of their unpolished neighbors. . . .

MISSOURI AND ILLINOIS have imported from abroad many men respectable for their talents and acquirements. Many more have come here from abroad expecting to eclipse everything of brightness that was already in the country, and who have very unexpectedly found themselves eclipsed. Of the itinerant preachers, I did not hear one who approached to mediocrity. They may have been pious men, but, for the most part, they defy all criticism. I heard one gentleman, who was for a while esteemed a great orator at St. Louis, twice use a figure which I think Swift would have selected as a fine example of bathos. Speaking of the love of God as naturally raising the soul to the object of that love, he illustrated the idea by saying that the stream would always rise as high as the fountain. He added that every lady had an explanation of this fact before her when she saw the water rising as high in the nose as in the body of the teapot! I heard him quote Greek to the Missourians, and his knowledge of Greek was of a piece with the figure of the teapot. . . .

There are a few preachers here, plain men, of sound instruction and good sense, who are respected for these qualifications, but are not popular as orators. These men are from New England and formed on the models of that country.

They have, also, some acute lawyers at the bar. It struck me as being superior to that of Ohio. . . . There was a young gentleman, Mr. B., who gave strong promise of future excellence. He was the only member of the bar whom I heard plead that showed in his manner the fruit of classical taste and discipline. He was happy in his arrangement and choice of words, and concise and condensed, and had a suavity in his manner. But these things were too often thrown away upon the jury, in a region where noise and flourish are generally mistaken for sense and reason.

THE PEOPLE HERE are not yet a reading people. Few good books are brought into the country. The few literary men that are here, seeing nothing to excite or reward their pursuits, seeing other objects exclusively occupy all minds, soon catch the prevailing feeling. The people are too busy, too much occupied in making farms and speculations, to think of literature.

America inherits, I believe, from England a taste for puffing. She has improved upon her model. In your quarter, as well as here, the people are idolators to the "golden calves." Some favorite man, fashion, or opinion sweep everything before them. This region is the paradise of puffers. One puffs up, and another down. As you draw near the influence of the "lord of the ascendant," you will find opinions graduated to his *dicta*. The last stranger that arrives from Kentucky or the Atlantic country is but poorly introduced to his new residence, if he have not one of these great men to puff a breeze in the sail of his skiff as he puts himself afloat.

I have been amused in reading puffing advertisements in the newspapers. A little subscription school, in which half the pupils are abecedarians, is a college. One is a Lancastrian school, or a school of *instruction mutuelle*. There is the Pestalozzi establishment, with its appropriate emblazoning. There is the agricultural school, the missionary school, the grammar box, the new way to make a wit of a dunce in six lessons, and all the mechanical ways of inoculating children with learning, that they may not endure the pain of getting it in the old and natural way. I would not have you smile exclusively at the people of the West. This ridiculous species of swindling is making as much progress in your country as here. The misfortune is that these vile pretensions finally induce the people to believe that there is a "royal road" to learning. The old and beaten track marked out by the only sure guide, experience, is forsaken. The parents are flattered, deceived, and swindled. Puffing pretenders take the place of the modest man of science, who scorns to compete with him in these vile arts. The children have their brains distended with the "east wind," and grow up at once empty and conceited.

These founders of new schools, for the most part, advertise themselves from London, Paris, Philadelphia, New York, Boston, and have all performed exploits in the regions whence they came, and bring the latest improvements with them. As to what they can do, and what they will do, the object is to lay on the coloring thick and threefold. A respectable man wishes to establish himself in a school in those regions. He consults a friend who knows the meridian of the country. The advice is: Call your school by some new and imposing name. Let it be understood that you have a new way of instructing children, by which they can learn twice as much in half the time as by the old ways. Throw off all modesty. Move the water, and get in while it is moving. In short, depend upon the gullibility of the people.

A school modeled on this advice was instituted at St. Louis, while I was there, with a very imposing name. The masters — professors, I should say — proposed to teach most of the languages and all the sciences. Hebrew they would communicate in twelve lessons; Latin and Greek, with a proportionate promptness. These men, who were to teach all this themselves, had read

Erasmus with a translation and knew the Greek alphabet; and in their public discourses — for they were ministers — sometimes dealt very abusively with the "King's English."

Town making introduces another species of puffing. Art and ingenuity have been exhausted in devising new ways of alluring purchasers to take lots and build in the new town. There are the fine rivers, the healthy hills, the mineral springs, the clear running water, the eligible mill seats, the valuable forests, the quarries of building stone, the fine steamboat navigation, the vast country adjacent, the central position, the connecting point between the great towns, the admirable soil, and, last of all, the cheerful and undoubting predictions of what the town must one day be. I have read more than a hundred advertisements of this sort. Then the legislature must be tampered with in order to make the town either the metropolis, or at least the seat of justice. In effect, we were told that, in Illinois, two influential men who both had Tadmors to be upreared, took a hand of cards to ascertain which should resign his pretensions to legislative aid in building his town in favor of the other.

A coarse caricature of this abomination of town making appeared in the St. Louis papers. The name was "Ne plus ultra." The streets were laid out a mile in width; the squares were to be sections, each containing 640 acres. The mall was a vast standing forest. In the center of this modern Babylon, roads were to cross each other in a meridional line at right angles, one from the South Pole to Symmes' Hole in the north, and another from Pekin to Jerusalem.

In truth, while traveling on the prairies of the Illinois and Missouri, and observing such immense tracts of rich soil of the blackness of ink and of exhaustless fertility; remarking the beautiful simplicity of the limits of farms, introduced by our government, in causing the land to be all surveyed in exact squares, and thus destroying here the barbarous prescription which has, in the settled countries, laid out the lands in ugly farms, and bounded them by zigzag lines; contemplating the hedge of verdure that will bound the squares on these smooth and fertile plains; remarking the beauty of the orchards and improvements that must ensue; being convinced that the climate will grow salubrious with its population and improvement; seeing the guardian genius, Liberty, hovering over the country; measuring the progress of the future only by the analogy of the past — it will be difficult for the imagination to assign limits to the future growth and prosperity of the country. Perhaps on one of these boundless plains, and contiguous to some one of these noble rivers, in view of these hoary bluffs, and where all these means of the subsistence and multiplication of the species are concentered in such ample abundance, will arise the actual "Ne plus ultra."

42.

ALBERT GALLATIN: The Land West of the Rockies

By 1825 the long-standing disputes concerning rights to the area west of the Louisiana Purchase had been resolved, at least to the extent that the United States and Great Britain, the only remaining contenders for the region, had signed a treaty by which they agreed to share its riches. Of particular interest to both nations was the Columbia River system, including its ports, the only usable ones on the Northwest coast. Neither country was yet ready to take effective possession of these valuable lands, but each looked forward to the time, obviously not far distant, when one of them would. Taking all of this into consideration, and pointing out that the main burden of exploration and settlement had so far been borne by Americans, Albert Gallatin put forward a claim in favor of U.S. ownership. In so doing, he outlined what has been called the "principle of contiguity": Lands adjacent to already settled territory could reasonably be claimed by the inhabitants of the settled territory. Gallatin's argument was an early, and relatively mild, version of the doctrine of "manifest destiny." Extracts from his statement at a meeting with British envoys on December 19, 1826, are reprinted below.

Source: 20 Congress, 1 Session, House Document No. 199.

IT MAY BE ADMITTED as an abstract principle that, in the origin of society, first occupancy and cultivation were the foundation of the rights of private property and of national sovereignty. But that principle, on which principally, if not exclusively, it would seem that the British government wishes to rely, could be permitted in either case to operate alone and without restriction, so long only as the extent of vacant territory was such, in proportion to population that there was ample room for every individual, and for every distinct community, or nation, without danger of collision with others. As in every society it had soon become necessary to make laws, regulating the manner in which its members should be permitted to occupy and to acquire vacant land within its acknowledged boundaries; so, also, nations found it indispensable for the preservation of peace and for the exercise of distinct jurisdiction to adopt, particularly after the dis-

A. Albert Gallatin, portrait by W. H. Powell

covery of America, some general rules which should determine the important previous question: "Who had a right to occupy?"

The two rules generally, perhaps universally, recognized and consecrated by the usage of nations, have flowed from the nature of the subject.

By virtue of the first, prior discovery gave a right to occupy, provided that occupancy took place within a reasonable time, and was ultimately followed by permanent settlements and by the cultivation of the soil.

In conformity with the second, the right derived from prior discovery and settlement was not confined to the spot so discovered or first settled. The extent of territory which would attach to such first discovery or settlement might not, in every case, be precisely determined. But that the first discovery and subsequent settlement within a reasonable time of the mouth of a river, particularly if none of its branches had been explored prior to such discovery, gave the right of occupancy and, ultimately, of sovereignty, to the whole country drained by such river and its several branches, has been generally admitted. And in a question between the United States and Great Britain,

her acts have, with propriety, been appealed to as showing that the principles on which they rely accord with her own.

It is, however, now contended that the British charters, extending in most cases from the Atlantic Ocean to the South Seas, must be considered as cessions of the sovereign to certain grantees, to the exclusion only of the other subjects, and as of no validity against the subjects of other states. This construction does not appear either to have been that intended at the time by the grantors, nor to have governed the subsequent conduct of Great Britain.

By excepting from the grants, as was generally the case, such lands as were already occupied by the subjects of other civilized nations, it was clearly implied that no other exception was contemplated, and that the grants were intended to include all the unoccupied lands within their respective boundaries to the exclusion of all other persons or nations whatsoever. In point of fact, the whole country drained by the several rivers emptying into the Atlantic Ocean, the mouths of which were within those charters, has, from Hudson's Bay to Florida and, it is believed, without exception been occupied and held by virtue of those charters. Not only has this principle been fully confirmed, but it has been notoriously enforced much beyond the sources of the rivers on which the settlements were formed. The priority of the French settlements on the rivers flowing westwardly from the Allegheny Mountains into the Mississippi was altogether disregarded; and the rights of the Atlantic colonies to extend beyond those mountains, as growing out of the contiguity of territory and as asserted in the earliest charters, was effectually and successfully enforced.

It is true that the two general rules which have been mentioned might often conflict with each other. Thus, in the instance just alluded to, the discovery of the main branch of the Mississippi including the mouth of that river, and the occupation of the intervening province of Louisiana by another nation, gave rise at last to a compromise of those conflicting claims and induced Great Britain to restrain hers within narrower limits than those originally designated.

But it is the peculiar character of the claim of the United States that it is founded on both principles, which in this case unite both in its support, and convert it into an incontestable right. It is in vain that in order to avert that conclusion, an attempt is made to consider the several grounds on which that right is urged, as incompatible one with the other, as if the United States were obliged to select only one and to abandon the others. In different hands the several claims would conflict one with the other; now united in the same power, they support each other. The possessors of Louisiana might have contended, on the ground of contiguity, for the adjacent territory on the Pacific Ocean with the discoveries of the coast and of its main rivers. The several discoveries of the Spanish and American navigators might separately have been considered as so many steps in the progress of discovery and giving only imperfect claims to each party. All those various claims, from whatever consideration derived, are now brought united against the pretensions of any other nation.

The actual possession and populous settlements of the valley of the Mississippi, including Louisiana, and now under one sovereignty, constitute a strong claim to the westwardly extension of that province over the contiguous vacant territory, and to the occupation and sovereignty of the country as far as the Pacific Ocean. If some trading factories on the shores of Hudson's Bay have been considered by Great Britain as giving an exclusive right of occupancy as far as the Rocky Mountains; if the infant settlements on the more southern Atlantic shores justified a claim then to the South Seas, and which was actually enforced to the Mississippi, that of the millions already within reach of those seas cannot consistent-ly be resisted. For it will not be denied that the extent of contiguous territory to which an actual settlement gives a prior right must depend, in a considerable degree, on the magnitude and population of that settlement, and on the facility with which the vacant adjacent land may, within a short time, be occupied, settled, and cultivated, by such population, as compared with the probability of its being thus occupied and settled from any other quarter. . . .

Louisiana having been acquired by the United States in 1803, an expedition was immediately ordered by the government to examine its western districts. In the course of this, Captains Lewis and Clarke ascended the Missouri to its source, crossed the Rocky Mountains, and explored the course of the Columbia from its most eastern sources to its mouth, where they arrived on November 6, 1805. There they erected the works called Fort Clatsop, and wintered in 1805-1806. And thus was the discovery of the river commenced and completed by the United States, before, as it is firmly believed, any settlement had been made on it, or any of its branches been explored by any other nation.

This is corroborated by the statement of the British plenipotentiaries. After having given as the date of Lewis and Clarke's exploration not the year 1805 but the years 1805-1806, they assert that, if not before, at least in the same and subsequent years, Mr. Thomson had already established a post on the headwaters of the northern or main branch of the Columbia. Had that post been established in 1805 before Lewis and Clarke's exploration, another and more distinct mode of expression would have been adopted. But it cannot be seriously contended that if Mr. Thomson had, in that year, reached one of the sources of the Columbia, north of latitude 50°, this, compared with the complete American exploration, would give to Great Britain "a title to parity, at least, if not priority of discovery, as opposed to the United States."

In the year 1810, Mr. Astor, a citizen of the United States, fitted out two expeditions for the mouth of the Columbia: one by sea and the other by land from the Missouri. In March 1811, the establishment of Astoria was accordingly commenced near the mouth of the river before any British settlement had been made south of the 49th parallel of latitude. From that principal post, several other settlements were formed, one of them (contrary to the opinion entertained by the British plenipotentiaries) at the mouth of the Wanahata, several hundred miles up, and on the right bank of the Columbia.

These establishments fell into the hands of the British during the war; and that of Astoria has since been formally restored in conformity with the Treaty of Ghent. On the circumstances of that restitution, it is sufficient to observe that, with the various dispatches from and to the officers of the British government, the United States have no concern; that it is not stated how the verbal communications of the British minister at Washington were received, nor whether the American government consented to accept the restitution with the reservation, as expressed in the dispatches to that minister from his government; and that the only written document affecting the restoration known to be in possession of that of the United States is the act of restoration itself, which contains no exception, reservation, or protest whatever.

It has thus been established that the Columbia River was first discovered by the United States, that that first discovery was attended by a complete exploration of the river from its most easterly source to the north, before any such exploration had been made by any other nation; by a simultaneous actual occupation and possession and by subsequent establishments and settlements made within a reasonable time and which have been interrupted only by the casualties of war.

This, it is contended, gives, according to the acknowledged law and usages of nations, a right to the whole country drained by that river and by its tributary streams, which could have been opposed only by the conflicting claim derived from the possession of Louisiana. Both, united and strengthened by the other Spanish and American discoveries along the coast (and, without reference to the cession of the pretensions of Spain, derived from other considerations), establish, it is firmly believed, a stronger title to the country above described, and along the coast as far north, at least, as the 49th parallel of latitude, than has ever at any former time been asserted by any nation to vacant territory.

Before the subject is dismissed, it may be proper to observe that the United States had no motive, in the year 1790, to protest against the Nootka Convention, since their exclusive right to the territory on the Pacific originated in Gray's discovery, which took place only in 1792. The acquisition of Louisiana and their last treaty with Spain are still posterior.

On the formality called "taking possession," though no actual possession of the country is taken, and on the validity of sales of land and surrender of sovereignty by Indians, who are for the first time brought into contact with civilized men; who have no notion of what they mean by either sovereignty or property in land; who do not even know what cultivation is; with whom it is difficult to communicate, even upon visible objects; the American plenipotentiary thinks that he may abstain from making any remarks.

While supporting their claim by arguments which they think conclusive, the United States have not been inattentive to the counterclaims of Great Britain.

They, indeed, deny that the trading posts of the Northwest Company give any title to the territory claimed by America, not only because no such post was established within the limits claimed when the first American settlement was made, but because the title of the United States is considered as having been complete before any of those traders had appeared on the waters of the Columbia. It is also believed that mere factories, established solely for the purpose of trafficking with the natives, and without any view to cultivation and permanent settlement, cannot, of themselves and unsupported by any other consideration, give any better title to dominion and absolute sovereignty, than similar establishments made in a civilized country.

But the United States have paid due regard to the discoveries by which the British navigators have so eminently distinguished themselves; to those, perhaps not less remarkable, made by land from the upper lakes of the Pacific; and to the contiguity of the possessions of Great Britain on the waters of Hudson's Bay to the territory bordering on that ocean. Above all, they have been earnestly desirous to preserve and cherish, not only the peaceful but the friendly relations which happily subsist between the two countries. And, with that object in view, their offer of a permanent line of demarcation has been made, under a perfect conviction that it was attended with the sacrifice of a portion of what they might justly claim.

Viewed as a matter of mutual convenience, and with equal desire on both sides to avert, by a definitive line of delimitation, any possible cause of collision in that quarter, every consideration connected with the subject may be allowed its due weight.

If the present state of occupancy is urged, on the part of Great Britain, the probability of the manner in which the territory west of the Rocky Mountains must be settled belongs also essentially to the subject. Under whatever nominal sovereignty that country may be placed, and whatever its ultimate destinies may be, it is nearly reduced to a certainty that it will be almost exclusively peopled by the surplus population of the United States. The distance from Great Britain, and the expense incident to emigra-

tion, forbid the expectation of any being practicable from that quarter but on a comparatively small scale. Allowing the rate of increase to be the same in the United States and in the North American British possessions, the difference in the actual population of both is such that the progressive rate which would, within forty years, add 3 million to these, would, within the same time, give a positive increase of more than 20 million to the United States. And if circumstances arising from localities and habits have given superior facilities to British subjects, of extending their commerce with the natives, and to that expansion which has the appearance, and the appearance only, of occupancy, the slower but sure progress and extension of an agricultural population will be regulated by distance, by natural obstacles, and by its own amount. The primitive right of acquiring property and sovereignty by occupancy alone, admitting it to be unlimited in theory, cannot extend beyond the capacity of occupying and cultivating the soil.

It may also be observed that, in reality, there were but three nations which had both the right and the power to colonize the territory in question: Great Britain, the United States, and Spain, or now the new American states. These are now excluded, in consequence of the treaty of 1819. The United States, who have purchased their right for valuable consideration, stand now in their place and on that ground, in the view entertained of the subject by the British government, are on a final partition of the country, fairly entitled to two shares.

Under all the circumstances of the case, as stated on both sides, the United States offer a line which leaves to Great Britain by far the best portion of the fur trade, the only object at this time of the pursuits of her subjects in that quarter, and a much greater than her proportionate share of the country with a view to its permanent settlement, if the relative geographical situation and means of colonizing of both parties are taken into consideration. From latitude 42° N to the Observatory Inlet, in about 55° 30′, there is a front on the Pacific of almost 14° of latitude, which the 49th parallel divides into two nearly equal parts. The mouth of the Columbia River, if accepted as a boundary, would leave less than one-third to the United States.

The offer of the free navigation of that river, when the whole territory, drained by all its tributary streams, including the northernmost branches, might have been justly claimed, would have also given to Great Britain, in time of peace, all the commercial advantages which it can afford to the Americans.

In the case of a war (which God forbid), whatever might be the result on shore, the line proposed by Great Britain, even with the addition of the detached and defenseless territory she offered, would leave the sea border at her mercy, and the United States without a single port; while the boundary proposed by them might, during that period, deprive Great Britain only of the use of the port at the mouth of the Columbia, and would leave [her] in the secure possession of numerous seaports, perhaps less convenient, but still affording ample means of communication with the interior. That line, indeed, with such slight reciprocal modifications as the topography of the country may indicate, would establish the most natural and mutually defensible boundary that can be found, and for that reason the least liable to collision and the best calculated to perpetuate peace and harmony between the two powers.

43.

Country Courting Songs

Some of the best loved American folk songs were originally sung in the southern hills of the Appalachians, which were settled by Scottish, Irish, and English immigrants. One of the most famous of their songs is a lover's lament, "On Top of Old Smoky," Old Smoky being a hill near Asheville, North Carolina. When the mountaineers joined the great Westward movement along the Southwest Trail, the tune gained wide popularity. "On Top of Old Smoky" and "Paper of Pins," another favorite song of backwoods lovers, are reprinted here.

Source: *American Broadside, c.* 1850-1870, Music Division, New York Public Library.

❧ ON TOP OF OLD SMOKY

On top of old Smoky, all covered with snow,
I lost my true lover from a-courting too slow.

For courting is pleasure and parting is grief,
And a false-hearted lover is worse than a thief.

A thief will just rob you and take what you have
But a false-hearted lover will lead you to the grave.

And the grave will decay you and turn you to dust;
Not one boy in a hundred a poor girl can trust.

They'll hug you and kiss you and tell you more lies
Than the cross-ties on the railroad or the stars in the skies.

So come all you young maidens and listen to me:
Never place your affection on a green willow tree.

For the leaves they will wither and the roots they will die;
You'll all be forsaken and never know why.

PAPER OF PINS

I'll give to you a paper of pins,
If you will tell me how our love begins,
If you marry, if you marry,
If you marry me.

I'll not accept a paper of pins,
To tell you how our love begins,
Nor I'll not marry, marry, marry,
Nor I'll not marry you.

I'll give to you a pink silk gown,
With golden laces hanging round,
If you marry, if you marry,
If you marry me.

I'll not accept the pink silk gown,
With golden laces hanging round,
Nor I'll not marry, marry, marry,
Nor I'll not marry you.

I'll give to you a dress of green,
That you may be my fairy Queen,
If you marry, if you marry,
If you marry me.

I'll not accept your dress of green,
That I may be your fairy queen,
Nor I'll not marry, marry, marry,
Nor I'll not marry you.

I'll give to you a little lap dog,
To take with you when you go abroad,
If you marry, if you marry,
If you marry me.

I'll not accept your little lap dog,
To take with me when I go abroad,
Nor I'll not marry, marry, marry,
Nor I'll not marry you.

I'll give to you the key of my heart,
That we may love and never part,
If you marry, if you marry,
If you marry me.

I'll not accept the key of your heart,
That we may love and never part,
Nor I'll not marry, marry, marry,
Nor I'll not marry you.

I'll give to you the key of my chest,
That you may have money at your request,
If you marry, if you marry,
If you marry me.

Yes! I'll accept the key of your chest,
That I'll have money at my request;
I will marry, I will marry,
I will marry you.

Ha! ha! ha! money is all,
Woman's love is none at all;
And I'll not marry, marry, marry,
And I'll not marry you.

1827

44.

First American High School Law

Publicly supported education was at first available only through grammar school. Those who could not afford to continue their education in private schools became apprentices or learned a trade in other ways. During the 1820s, Massachusetts led the movement toward public secondary education by establishing the first free high school on a voluntary basis at Boston in 1821. After further study by the state Board of Education, it was decided that all youths should be educated through the high school level, and to this end the law reprinted here was passed by the Massachusetts legislature in 1827.

Source: *The General Laws of Massachusetts,* Theron Metcalf, ed., Boston, 1832, Vol. III, pp. 179-184.

Section 1. *Be it enacted by the Senate and House of Representatives, in General Court assembled, and by the authority of the same,* that each town or district within this Commonwealth containing 50 families or householders shall be provided with a teacher or teachers, of good morals, to instruct children in orthography, reading, writing, English grammar, geography, arithmetic, and good behavior, for such term of time as shall be equivalent to six months for one school in each year. And every town or district containing 100 families or householders shall be provided with such teacher or teachers for such term of time as shall be equivalent to twelve months for one school in each year. And every town or district containing 150 families or householders shall be provided with such teacher or teachers as shall be equivalent to eighteen months for one school in each year. And

every city, town, or district containing 500 families or householders shall be provided with such teacher or teachers for such term of time as shall be equivalent to twenty-four months for one school in a year; and shall also be provided with a master of good morals, competent to instruct, in addition to the branches of learning aforesaid, the history of the United States, bookkeeping by single entry, geometry, surveying, and algebra; and shall employ such master to instruct a school, in such city, town, or district, for the benefit of all the inhabitants thereof, at least ten months in each year, exclusive of vacations, in such convenient place or alternately at such places in such city, town, or district as the said inhabitants, at their meeting in March or April, annually, shall determine. And in every city or town containing 4,000 inhabitants, such master shall be competent to instruct, in addition to all the foregoing branches, the Latin and Greek languages, history, rhetoric, and logic.

Section 2. *Be it further enacted,* that the several towns and districts in this Commonwealth be, and they hereby are, authorized and empowered, in town meetings to be called for that purpose, to determine and define the limits of school districts within their towns and districts. . . .

Section 3. *Be it further enacted,* that it shall be, and it hereby is, made the duty of the president, professors, and tutors of the university at Cambridge, and of the several colleges in this Commonwealth, preceptors and teachers of academies, and all other instructors of youth . . . to preserve and perfect a republican constitution and to secure the blessings of liberty, as well as to promote their future happiness, and the tendency of the opposite vices to slavery and ruin. And it shall be the duty of the resident ministers of the gospel, the selectmen, and school committees in the several towns in this Commonwealth to exercise their influence and use their best endeavors that the youth of their respective towns and districts do regularly attend the schools established and supported as aforesaid for their instruction.

45.

LEMUEL SHAW: Law as a Restraint on Power

American constitutional law reflected the prevailing mood of the Jacksonian period in its newfound concern with making "aristocracy" subservient to the interests of the people. The campaign against concentrated power took many forms: the rejection of property qualifications for voting, the transformation of appointive posts into elective ones, the recognition of the President as the principal repository of the popular will. Lemuel Shaw of the Massachusetts Supreme Court led his fellow jurists in adapting the common law to these new ideas, and in his thirty years as chief justice of that court, dealt with the major political and economic issues of the day. In the following selection from an address in May 1827 to the Suffolk Bar Association of Boston, on the "Profession of Law in the United States," Shaw discussed the use of law as a restraint on power.

Source: *American Jurist and Law Magazine,* January 1832.

LET US THEN, GENTLEMEN, proceed to consider the condition, the importance, and utility of the profession of the law in the actual situation and prospects of the United States. The proposition which I wish to maintain, and which I think may be fully established, is this; that in a free, representative government, founded upon enlarged and liberal views, designed to secure the rights, to promote the industry, and to advance the happiness of a great community, and adapted to a high state of civilization and improvement, it is of the highest importance that there should be a body of men, trained, by a well-adapted course of education and study, to a thorough and profound knowledge of the law, and practically skilled in its application, whose privilege and duty it is, in common with their fellow citizens, to exert a fair share of influence in the enactment of laws, and whose peculiar duty and exclusive occupation it is to assist in the application of them to practise in the administration of justice, in its various departments. May I not go further and add that the utility of this profession, the benefits which it is capable of conferring, and the respect in which it shall be held, in any community, will be in great measure proportioned to the degree in which the government and institutions of such community are founded upon free principles.

There are, obviously, two very different modes of governing mankind; the one, by the will of a superior, either absolute, as in the case of a naked despotism, or more or less modified and restrained, as in the case of a limited monarchy; the other, by laws fixed and certain, binding upon the whole people, being the will of the whole people, deliberately expressed in the mode established by fundamental laws, and openly promulgated, by which, and by which alone, every citizen is entitled to seek his rights, and bound to regulate his conduct. And this description applies not only to his civil rights but emphatically to those which in a much higher degree awaken the interest and engage the affections of freemen, because they are the only safe pledge and guaranty of all the rest — I mean his political rights. . . .

In asserting the absolute and entire supremacy of law as the distinguishing characteristic of free government, it may be interesting and important to trace somewhat more particularly the true distinction between the two systems. In practical operation, the difference, perhaps, may not be so striking, as in the theory and principle. An arbitrary government, whether it claims to derive its prerogatives from divine right, or from paternal authority, or from a right of conquest transmitted by hereditary descent, or whether it rest solely upon actual possession and enjoyment, is assumed to depend upon powers, extrinsic and superior to the authority and will of the people governed. The power of governing necessarily implies and presupposes an entire independence and supremacy on the one side, and subjection and obedience on the other. Hence the maxim, so apparently absurd to us, that the king can do no wrong. A sovereign amenable to his subjects is a solecism in the theory of arbitrary government. . . .

In all cases of great and trying emergency, in all cases not specifically provided for by the constitution, if there be one, or where its provisions are ill adapted to accomplish its objects, or its formal checks and balances are not maintained by adequate counteracting forces, all the derivative powers of government are supposed to revert to the source from which they flowed. Hence the perpetual and rapid tendency of arbitrary government, even under its most favorable forms, to that union and concentration of all powers — political, civil, military, and ecclesiastical — into one person or body, which constitutes the essential characteristic of despotism.

In the theory of free government, all this is exactly reversed. It regards men as by nature social and endowed with powers adequate to enable them, by the establishment of government, to provide for defining and securing their social rights, and under a natural obligation to respect those of others. And it presupposes that all power resides originally in the whole people as a social community, that all political power is derived from them, is designed to be exercised solely for the general good, and limited to the accomplishment of that object; that no powers are, or ought to be, vested in the government, beyond those which are necessary and useful to promote the general security, happiness, and prosperity; and that all powers not delegated remain with the people. The natural rights of persons, being equal, no natural distinctions are acknowledged, except those which flow from the disposition and ability to do good and to promote the general welfare, that inherent distinction which belongs to the possession and exercise of moral and intellectual powers.

As those who govern claim not to exercise an inherent power but simply to execute a delegated authority, created, regulated, and limited by law, there is no inconsistency in considering such authority as equally supreme over those who exercise it and those upon whom it operates. While it thus professes to derive its whole authority from the natural right and power of the people to provide for their own safety and happiness, and thus absolutely exclude the assumption of all arbitrary and extrinsic power, it guards with equal vigilance against the violence and encroachments of a wild and licentious democracy, by a well balanced constitution; such a constitution as at once restrains the violent and irregular action of mere popular will, and calls to the aid, and secures in the service of the government, the enlightened wisdom, the pure morals, the cultivated reason, and matured experience of its ablest and best members.

In thus pointing out the marked and radical distinction between the theory and principle of free and arbitrary forms of government, I am far from intimating that the one is wholly destitute of good, or the other free from imperfection. The existence of arbitrary government presupposes an entire control of the military strength of a country, the capacity to enforce a strict execution of the criminal law, and the most rigorous regulations of police, all calculated to secure an internal tranquility, which is not without its charms to the cautious, the timid, and the weak. On the other hand, a free government, whatever be its forms and however wisely framed, is still subject to the weakness and imperfection incident to all human productions. It depends essentially for its execution and utility upon the general intelligence of the people; upon public virtue

and moderation; a noble disregard of private, selfish, and personal interests; and a sincere respect for the equal rights of others and the best good of the whole. The unbounded latitude of public discussion, which its condition implies, upon all those subjects, which most deeply engage the passions and interests of men, may sometimes lead to a blind and enthusiastic zeal, which may be productive of great violence, oppression, and injustice.

But the true point of view in which the obvious distinction in the principle and practice of the two systems ought to be regarded by freemen, and which must always cherish the hopes and sustain the efforts of freemen, is this. Under an arbitrary government, the corrupting influence of uncontrolled power on the hearts of those who exercise it; the discouragement of education and general intelligence among the great body of the people; the debasing effect produced by the employment of physical force and coercion as the means and instrument of governing; the discouragement of patriotism and public virtue by rendering them useless or contemptible; the repression of enterprise, industry, and intellectual exertion by the establishment of artificial ranks — these circumstances produce a perpetual tendency on the part of the people to degradation, and on the part of the government to corruption and degeneracy.

While, under a free government, every advance in general intelligence and improvement adds something to the strength, security, and perfection of its institutions, all the aspirings of the most gifted minds are awakened and encouraged, all the efforts of enterprise are sustained by the assurance that its rewards are near and certain, that all the honors and privileges which society can confer are open to those who, by their virtues, talents, and public services, shall best deserve them. These circumstances have a constant tendency to advance society to the highest state of moral and intellectual improvement of which it is capable, and to ensure the greatest happiness of the greatest numbers.

Perhaps, gentlemen, in thus enlarging upon the nature and principles of government, it may appear that I am departing too widely from that range of topics which properly belong to the place and to the occasion. But, if I am not entirely mistaken, the practical consequences to be drawn from this view of the supremacy of law, in a free government, and the immediate and direct influence which this consideration must necessarily exert upon the character, condition, and duties of those who are professionally engaged in its actual administration, this must be a subject of deep and peculiar interest to the American lawyer. Our government, throughout its entire fabric, professes to be a free, representative government. It is peculiarly, exclusively, and emphatically a government of laws. The constitutions of the United States and of the several states, with all their provisions and limitations, are regarded, and very properly regarded, as part of the laws. Indeed, they possess this character in peculiar and eminent degree, because they are of general obligation, of a fixed and determinate character, controlling and modifying all the ordinary acts of legislation, binding and imperative upon all courts and tribunals of justice, and subject to be repealed or changed only by a peculiar and complicated mode in which the deliberate will of the whole people is cautiously expressed.

To these fundamental laws, every individual citizen has a right to appeal, and does constantly appeal, in the discussion and establishment of his rights, civil as well as political. In an equal degree, they regulate and control the highest functions of government, determine the just sources and limits, and regulate the distribution of all powers, executive, legislative, and judicial. These principles may, at any time, be drawn in question before the tribunals of justice, and are sub-

ject to the same rules of judicial interpretation, with all other legal provisions. It is difficult to conceive of the vast extent to which this consideration enlarges the field of American jurisprudence, and increases the functions and elevates the duties and character of the American lawyer. . . .

I have already remarked that in a free, representative government, our profession, as a body, if true to themselves, if they are characterized by learning, industry, moderation, disinterestedness, and genuine love of country, must always possess, in a great degree, the confidence and attachment of the people and enjoy a proportionate influence in their representative bodies. To the extent of this influence, they are unquestionably responsible for the character of the laws, particularly of all those which affect private rights and relate to the administration of justice.

In the multitude of legislators, among whom there is much learning, prudence, and experience mixed up with a great deal of ignorance, vanity, and pretension, it is not always easy to distinguish between a restless impatience of things as they are, a wanton love of innovation, and a sincere and ardent zeal for improvement. It is manifest, therefore, that with many propositions which would be really useful and beneficial, well adapted to existing principles, and conformable to the symmetry of the general system as a whole, many provisions calculated to extend the benefit of existing principles to the new relations which are perpetually arising in the complicated concerns of a most active community, there will also be multitudes of projects, founded upon crude and visionary notions, superficial views of the delicate and various relations which each particular provision bears to the whole system. Under these circumstances, it obviously requires great experience, sagacity and sound judgment to distinguish what is really useful and beneficial from what is useless or pernicious, great liberality in adopting all real ameliorations, and great firmness and decision in resisting the encroachments of innovation.

It is due to the spirit of the age that, while a rapid progress is making in every other department of knowledge, as much should be done for the science of law as the subject will admit. So far as this demands greater industry and perseverance, more thorough and exact knowledge, more enlarged, comprehensive, and liberal views of the law, and the various and incidental branches of knowledge with which it is connected, the duty of the American lawyer cannot be mistaken, and, unless I have entirely mistaken the spirit and character of our profession, will not be disregarded. . . .

In assigning to the law the character of a science, founded upon the principles of reason and natural justice, it would be a false and unreasonable conclusion to infer that natural reason is sufficient to furnish a rule in every particular case. I am aware that there are some persons who maintain that the law is a system of artificial and technical rules, having very little regard to principle, and that he is the best lawyer who has the most tenacious memory and who is most skillful and adroit in using the weapons furnished by these rules. Others, again, maintain that natural justice is sufficient to settle all controverted questions, and that every case may be well settled upon its own particular equities. Both of these views are unquestionably partial and erroneous. While the law is a science founded upon reason and principle, and no law can stand the test of strict inquiry which palpably violates the dictates of natural justice, yet it is also a system of precise and practical rules, adapted to regulate the rights and duties of persons in an infinite variety of cases in which natural law is silent or indifferent, and yet where it is of the utmost impor-

tance that there should be a fixed rule. . . .

The positive and practical rules of jurisprudence bear the same relation to the principles of natural law that a well-contrived constitution of government bears to the natural principles of society. It is a plain and manifest dictate of the social nature of man that there should be established government. But no natural principle requires that there should be a President, a Senate, or House of Representatives, or Supreme Court. In both cases, natural justice furnishes the general principle; positive or conventional law, the exact rule. But in both cases, when established, and because established, it is of the greatest importance that the exact rule be adhered to and enforced, because the general principle is consistent with reason and natural justice, and the precise practical rule is essential to the stability of the government, and the utility of the laws. This character of the law, therefore, as a science founded on principle, has no tendency to disparage the importance of positive enactment, nor to weaken the authority of judicial precedent.

Permit me, in conclusion, to express a hope that these views, hasty and superficial as they are, will not be without their practical utility. If the law be justly regarded as a liberal science, intimately connected with the existence and essential to the maintenance of free government, embracing an enlarged and profound study of the principles of moral and political philosophy, if its utility and importance be justly regarded by a free and enlightened community, these considerations cannot fail to excite the interest and industry of the student, to encourage the honorable exertions of the practitioner, and to awaken and cherish those feelings of sympathy and mutual respect which should ever characterize the associates and members of an honorable and liberal profession.

46.

SAMUEL CORNISH AND JOHN RUSSWURM: The First African American Newspaper

The Abolitionist movement of the 1830s was antedated by numerous organizations and newspapers dedicated not only to the emancipation of slaves in the Southern states but also to gaining equal opportunities and respect for free blacks in the Northern states. The first African American graduate of Bowdoin College, John Russwurm, joined with Samuel Cornish in founding the earliest newspaper written by and for African Americans. The first issue of Freedom's Journal *appeared on March 16, 1827, in New York City, and contained the following Abolitionist editorial. Though Russwurm and Cornish originally opposed efforts to establish a colony for American blacks in Africa, they finally succumbed to the unrelenting prejudices of U.S. society, writing in the end: "We consider it mere waste of words to talk of ever enjoying citizenship in this country." Russwurm himself later emigrated to Liberia.*

Source: *Freedom's Journal*, March 16, 1827.

To Our Patrons:

In presenting our first number to our patrons, we feel all the diffidence of persons entering upon a new and untried line of business. But a moment's reflection upon the noble objects which we have in view by the publication of this journal; the expediency of its appearance at this time, when so many schemes are in action concerning our people, encourage us to come boldly before an enlightened public. For we believe that a paper devoted to the dissemination of useful knowledge among our brethren, and to their moral and religious improvement, must meet with the cordial approbation of every friend to humanity.

The peculiarities of this journal render it important that we should advertise to the world our motives by which we are actuated and the objects which we contemplate.

We wish to plead our own cause. Too long have others spoken for us. Too long

has the public been deceived by misrepresentations in things which concern us dearly, though, in the estimation of some, mere trifles; for though there are many in society who exercise toward us benevolent feelings, still (with sorrow we confess it) there are others who make it their business to enlarge upon the least trifle which tends to the discredit of any person of color, and pronounce anathemas and denounce our whole body for the misconduct of this guilty one. We are aware that there are many instances of vice among us, but we avow that it is because no one has taught its subjects to be virtuous; many instances of poverty, because no sufficient efforts accommodated to minds contracted by slavery and deprived of early education have been made, to teach them how to husband their hard earnings and to secure to themselves comforts.

Education being an object of the highest importance to the welfare of society, we shall endeavor to present just and adequate views of it, and to urge upon our brethren the necessity and expediency of training their children, while young, to habits of industry, and thus forming them for becoming useful members of society. It is surely time that we should awake from this lethargy of years and make a concentrated effort for the education of our youth. We form a spoke in the human wheel, and it is necessary that we should understand our [de]-pendence on the different parts, and theirs on us, in order to perform our part with propriety.

Though not desirous of dictating, we shall feel it our incumbent duty to dwell occasionally upon the general principles and rules of economy. The world has grown too enlightened to estimate any man's character by his personal appearance. Though all men acknowledge the excellency of Franklin's maxims, yet comparatively few practise upon them. We may deplore, when it is too late, the neglect of these self-evident truths, but it avails little to mourn. Ours will be the task of admonishing our brethren on these points.

The civil rights of a people being of the greatest value, it shall ever be our duty to vindicate our brethren, when oppressed, and to lay the case before the public. We shall also urge upon our brethren (who are qualified by the laws of the different states) the expediency of using their elective franchise, and of making an independent use of the same. We wish them not to become the tools of party.

And as much time is frequently lost, and wrong principles instilled, by the perusal of works of trivial importance, we shall consider it a part of our duty to recommend to our young readers such authors as will not only enlarge their stock of useful knowledge but such as will also serve to stimulate them to higher attainments in science.

We trust, also, that through the columns of the *Freedom's Journal* many practical pieces, having for their bases the improvement of our brethren, will be presented to them from the pens of many of our respected friends, who have kindly promised their assistance.

It is our earnest wish to make our journal a medium of intercourse between our brethren in the different states of this great confederacy; that through its columns an expression of our sentiments on many interesting subjects which concern us may be offered to the public; that plans which apparently are beneficial may be candidly discussed and properly weighed; if worthy, receive our cordial approbation, if not, our marked disapprobation.

Useful knowledge of every kind and everything that relates to Africa shall find a ready admission into our columns; and as that vast continent becomes daily more known, we trust that many things will come to light proving that the natives of it are neither so ignorant nor stupid as they have generally been supposed to be.

And while these important subjects shall occupy the columns of the *Freedom's Journal*, we would not be unmindful of our brethren who are still in the iron fetters of bondage. They are our kindred by all the ties of nature; and though but little can be effected by us, still let our sympathies be poured forth, and our prayers in their behalf ascend to Him who is able to succor them.

From the press and the pulpit we have suffered much by being incorrectly represented. Men whom we equally love and admire have not hesitated to represent us disadvantageously without becoming personally acquainted with the true state of things, nor discerning between virtue and vice among us. The virtuous part of our people feel themselves sorely aggrieved under the existing state of things — they are not appreciated.

Our vices and our degradation are ever arrayed against us, but our virtues are passed by unnoticed. And what is still more lamentable, our friends, to whom we concede all the principles of humanity and religion, from these very causes seem to have fallen into the current of popular feeling and are imperceptibly floating on the stream — actually living in the practice of prejudice, while they abjure it in theory and feel it not in their hearts. Is it not very desirable that such should know more of our actual condition, and of our efforts and feelings, that in forming or advocating plans for our amelioration, they may do it more understandingly? In the spirit of candor and humility we intend by a simple representation of facts to lay our case before the public, with a view to arrest the progress of prejudice and to shield ourselves against the consequent evils. We wish to conciliate all and to irritate none, yet we must be firm and unwavering in our principles and persevering in our efforts.

If ignorance, poverty, and degradation have hitherto been our unhappy lot, has the eternal decree gone forth that our race alone are to remain in this state, while knowledge and civilization are shedding their enlivening rays over the rest of the human family? The recent travels of Denham and Clapperton in the interior of Africa, and the interesting narrative which they have published; the establishment of the republic of Haiti after years of sanguinary warfare; its subsequent progress in all the arts of civilization; and the advancement of liberal ideas in South America, where despotism has given place to free governments and where many of our brethren now fill important civil and military stations, prove the contrary.

The interesting fact that there are 500,000 free persons of color, one-half of whom might peruse, and the whole be benefited by the publication of the *Journal;* that no publication, as yet, has been devoted exclusively to their improvement; that many selections from approved standard authors, which are within the reach of few, may occasionally be made; and, more important still, that this large body of our citizens have no public channel — all serve to prove the real necessity, at present, for the appearance of the *Freedom's Journal.*

It shall ever be our desire so to conduct the editorial department of our paper as to give offense to none of our patrons, as nothing is further from us than to make it the advocate of any partial views, either in politics or religion. What few days we can number have been devoted to the improvement of our brethren; and it is our earnest wish that the remainder may be spent in the same delightful service.

In conclusion, whatever concerns us as a people will ever find a ready admission into the *Freedom's Journal,* interwoven with all the principal news of the day.

And while everything in our power shall be performed to support the character of our journal, we would respectfully invite our numerous friends to assist by their communications, and our colored brethren to strengthen our hands by their subscriptions, as our labor is one of common cause and worthy of their consideration and support. And we most earnestly solicit the latter, that if at any time we should seem to be zealous or too pointed in the inculcation of any important lesson, they will remember that they are equally interested in the cause in which we are engaged, and attribute our zeal to the peculiarities of our situation and our earnest engagedness in their well-being.

47.

Anonymous: On Educating African American Women

Freedom's Journal, the first African American newspaper, served not only as a forum for the Abolitionist sentiments of educated blacks, but also as an official sounding board for the average African American whose views heretofore had seldom been published. The August 10, 1827, issue of the paper carried the following letter, in which an anonymous author, "Matilda," made a humble plea for female education. It is noteworthy not only as one of the earliest entreaties for women's rights made by an African American but also because it was written when Emma Hart Willard and Catharine Beecher were just beginning their crusades for the educational rights of women.

Source: *Freedom's Journal*, August 10, 1827.

Messrs. Editors,

Will you allow a female to offer a few remarks upon a subject that you must allow to be all-important? I don't know that in any of your papers you have said sufficient upon the education of females. I hope you are not to be classed with those who think that our mathematical knowledge should be limited to "fathoming the dish-kettle," and that we have acquired enough of history if we know that our grandfather's father lived and died. It is true the time has been when to darn a stocking and cook a pudding well was considered the end and aim of a woman's being. But those were days when ignorance blinded men's eyes. The diffusion of knowledge has destroyed those degrading opinions, and men of the present age allow that we have minds that are capable and deserving of culture.

There are difficulties, and great difficulties, in the way of our advancement; but that should only stir us to greater efforts. We possess not the advantages with those of our sex whose skins are not colored like our own, but we can improve what little we have and make our one talent produce twofold. The influence that we have over the male sex demands that our minds should be instructed and improved with the principles of education and religion, in order that this influence should be properly directed. Ignorant ourselves, how can we be expected to form the minds of our youth and conduct them in the paths of knowledge? How can we "teach the young *idea* how to shoot" if we have none ourselves? There is a great responsibility resting somewhere, and it is time for us to be up and doing.

I would address myself to all mothers, and say to them that while it is necessary to possess a knowledge of cookery and the various mysteries of pudding making, something more is requisite. It is their bounden duty to store their daughters' minds with useful learning. They should be made to devote their leisure time to reading books, whence they would derive valuable information which could never be taken from them.

I will not longer trespass on your time and patience. I merely throw out these hints in order that some more able pen will take up the subject.

Matilda

48.

Anonymous: A Plea for Manufacturing in the South

Trends in the early nineteenth century toward political and social diversification in the three main geographic areas of the United States — the North, the West, and the South — were accompanied by increasing signs of economic sectionalism. The West was becoming a center for livestock, wheat, and other staples; and the industrial revolution was beginning in the Northeastern states, which were already the chief source of supply of manufactured goods. At the same time, the South was rapidly developing a one-crop economy based on cotton, which meant that she was increasingly dependent on the other regions. A number of Southerners, such as the anonymous author of this editorial in the Georgia Courier *of June 21, 1827, saw dangers in this situation and urged that the South should not concentrate on cotton alone, but instead diversify her economy.*

Source: *Courier* (Augusta, Ga.), June 21, 1827 [Commons, I, pp. 289-290].

WE SEE IN THE SOUTHERN PAPERS propositions to exclude Northern manufacturers and Western pork, beef, etc., and to manufacture and wear our own cloth, and eat pork and beef, etc., of our own raising. The object to be obtained by these suggestions all must approve, whatever they may think of the spirit which urges their adoption at this particular moment. That we have cultivated cotton, cotton, cotton, and bought everything else, has long enough been our opprobrium. It is time we should be roused by some means or other to see that such a course of conduct will inevitably terminate in our ultimate poverty and ruin. Let us manufacture, because it is our best policy. Let us go more on provision crops and less on cotton, because we have had everything about us poor and impoverished long enough. This we can do without manifesting any ill nature to any of the members of the same great family, all whose earnings go to swell the general prosperity and happiness.

Much of our chagrin and ill nature on this subject may be justly, because truly, ascribed to a sense of shame which we of the Southern states feel, that we have been so long behind our Northern neighbors in the production of everything that substantially administers to the elegance or the comforts of life. It has been our own fault — not theirs. If we have followed a ruinous policy and bought all the articles of subsistence instead of raising them, who is to blame? For what have we not looked to our Northern friends? From them we get not only our clothes, carriages, saddles, hats, shoes, flour, potatoes, but even our onions and horn buttons. The latter we wear on our undergarments, as if ashamed to acknowledge that we owed the manufacture of such a trifling article to others.

Let us change our policy, but without that spirit and those expressions which leave a festering sore in the hearts of those who should be brothers. Let our farmers make and wear their homespun; raise in greater plenty corn and wheat, which will enable them to raise their own hogs, cattle, and horses; and let those who have capital and enterprise manufacture on a more extensive scale. There is nothing to prevent us from doing it. We have good land, unlimited waterpower, capital in plenty, and a patriotism which is running over in some places. If the tariff drives us to this, we say, let the name be sacred in all future generations.

49.

A Union of Trade Associations

Both the status and the aspirations of the American worker of the 1820s are well depicted in the following Preamble of the (Philadelphia) Mechanics' Union of Trade Associations *Journeymen in the trades could see about them an increasing concentration of wealth and political power in the hands of a few. The price of labor was kept at subsistence level, while the rewards of labor went into the pockets of a few employers. All the while, the individual workingman had no bargaining power for higher wages and shorter hours, and associations of workers were looked upon as illegal conspiracies. In response to such conditions, the journeymen in several trades at Philadelphia in 1827 resolved to form an association to aid the individual worker in his struggle for a better life.*

Source: *Mechanics' Free Press*, October 25, 1828 [Commons, V, pp. 84-90].

WHEN THE DISPOSITION AND EFFORTS of one part of mankind to oppress another have become too manifest to be mistaken and too pernicious in their consequences to be endured, it has often been found necessary for those who feel aggrieved to associate for the purpose of affording to each other mutual protection from oppression.

We, the journeyman mechanics of the city and county of Philadelphia, conscious that our condition in society is lower than justice demands it should be, and feeling our inability, individually, to ward off from ourselves and families those numerous evils which result from an unequal and very excessive accumulation of wealth and power into the hands of a few, are desirous of forming an association which shall avert as much as possible those evils which poverty and incessant toil have already inflicted, and which threaten ultimately to overwhelm and destroy us. And, in order that our views may be properly understood, and the justness of our intention duly appreciated, we offer to the public the following summary of our reasons, principles, and objects.

If unceasing toils were actually requisite to supply us with a bare, and in many instances wretched, subsistence; if the products of our industry, or an equitable proportion of them, were appropriated to our actual wants and comfort, then would we yield without a murmur to the stern and irrevocable decree of necessity. But this is infinitely wide of the fact. We appeal to the most intelligent of every community and ask — Do not you, and all society, depend solely for subsistence on the products of human industry? Do not those who labor, while acquiring to themselves thereby only a scanty and penurious support, likewise maintain in affluence and luxury the rich who never labor?

Do not all the streams of wealth which flow in every direction and are emptied into and absorbed by the coffers of the unproductive exclusively take their rise in the bones, marrow, and muscles of the industrious classes? In return for which, exclusive of a bare subsistence (which likewise is the product of their own industry), they receive — not anything!

Is it just? Is it equitable that we should waste the energies of our minds and bodies, and be placed in a situation of such unceasing exertion and servility as must necessarily, in time, render the benefits of our liberal institutions to us inaccessible and useless, in order that the products of our labor may be accumulated by a few into vast pernicious masses, calculated to prepare the minds of the possessors for the exercise of lawless rule and despotism, to overawe the meager multitude and frighten away that shadow of freedom which still lingers among us? Are we who confer almost every blessing on society never to be treated as freemen and equals and never be accounted worthy of an equivalent, in return for the products of our industry? Has the Being who created us given us existence only with the design of making it a curse and a burden to us, while at the same time He has conferred upon us a power with which tenfold more of blessings can be created than it is possible for society either to enjoy or consume?

No! At the present period, when wealth is so easily and abundantly created that the markets of the world are overflowing with it, and when, in consequence thereof, and of the continual development and increase of scientific power, the demand for human labor is gradually and inevitably diminishing, it cannot be necessary that we, or any portion of society, should be subjected to perpetual slavery. But a ray of intelligence on this subject has gone forth through the working world, which the ignorance and injustice of oppressors, aided by the most powerful and opposing interests, cannot extinguish; and, in consequence thereof, the day of human emancipation from haggard penury and incessant toil is already dawning. The spirit of freedom is diffusing itself through a wider circle of human intellect; it is expanding in the bosoms of the mass of mankind and preparing them to cast off the yoke of oppression and servility, wherever and by whatever means it has been riveted upon them.

As freemen and republicans, we feel it a duty incumbent on us to make known our sentiments fearlessly and faithfully on any subject connected with the general welfare; and we are prepared to maintain that all who toil have a natural and unalienable right to reap the fruits of their own industry; and that they who by labor (the only source) are the authors of every comfort, convenience, and luxury are in justice entitled to an equal participation, not only in the meanest and the coarsest but likewise the richest and the choicest of them all.

The principles upon which the institution shall be founded are principles, alike, of the strictest justice and the most extended philanthropy. Believing that whatever is conducive to the real prosperity of the greatest numbers must in the nature of things conduce to the happiness of all, we cannot desire to injure nor take the smallest unjust advantage either of that class of the community called employers or of any other portion. It is neither our intention nor desire to extort inequitable prices for our labor; all we may demand for this shall not exceed what can be clearly demonstrated to be a fair and full equivalent. If we demand more, we wrong the society of which we are members, and if society requires us to receive less, she injures and oppresses us.

With respect to the relation existing between employers and the employed, we are prepared, we think, to demonstrate that it is only through an extremely limited view of their real interests that the former can be induced to attempt to depreciate the value of human labor. The workman is not more dependent upon his wages for the support of his family than they are upon the demand for the various articles they fabricate or vend. If the mass of the people were enabled by their labor to procure for themselves and families a full and abundant supply of the comforts and conveniences of life, the consumption of articles, particularly of dwellings, furniture, and clothing, would amount to at least twice the quantity it does at present, and of course the demand, by which alone employers are enabled either to subsist or accumulate, would likewise be increased in an equal proportion.

Each would be enabled to effect twice the quantity of sales or loans which he can effect at present, and the whole industry of a people, consisting of their entire productive powers, whether manual or scientific, together with all their capital, might be put into a full, healthful, and profitable action. The workman need not languish for want of employment, the vendor for sales, nor the capitalist complain for want of profitable modes of investment. It is therefore the real interest (for instance) of the hatter that every man in the community should be enabled to clothe his own head and those of his family with an abundant supply of the best articles of that description; because the flourishing demand thereby created, and which depends altogether on the ability of the multitude to purchase, is that which alone enables him to pay his rent and support his family in comfort.

The same may be said with respect to the tailor, the shoemaker, the carpenter, the cabinetmaker, the builder, and indeed of every other individual in society who depends for subsistence or accumulation upon the employment of his skill, his labor, or his capital. All are dependent on the demand which there is for the use of their skill, service, or capital, and the demand must ever be regulated by the ability or inability of the great mass of the people to purchase and consume. If, therefore, as members of the community, they are desirous to prosper, in vain will they expect to succeed unless the great body of the community is kept in a healthy, vigorous, and prosperous condition.

No greater error exists in the world than the notion that society will be benefited by depreciating the value of human labor. Let this principle (as at this day in England) be carried toward its full extent, and it is in vain that scientific power shall pour forth its inexhaustible treasures of wealth upon the world. Its products will all be amassed to glut the overflowing storehouses and useless hoards of its insatiable monopolizers, while the mechanic and productive classes, who constitute the great mass of the population, and who have wielded the power and labored in the production of this immense abundance, having no other resource for subsistence than what they derive from the miserable pittance which they are compelled by competition to receive in exchange for their inestimable labor, must first begin to pine, languish, and suffer under its destructive and withering influence.

But the evil stops not here. The middling classes next, vendors of the products of human industry, will begin to experience its deleterious effects. The demand for their articles must necessarily cease from the forced inability of the people to consume; trade must in consequence languish, and losses and failures become the order of the day.

At last the contagion will reach the capitalist, throned as he is in the midst of his ill-gotten abundance; and his capital, from the most evident and certain causes, will become useless, unemployed, and stagnant; himself the trembling victim of continual alarms from robberies, burnings, and murder, the unhappy and perhaps ill-fated object of innumerable imprecations, insults, and implacable hatred from the wronged, impoverished, and despairing multitude. The experience of the most commercial parts of the world sufficiently demonstrates that this is the natural, inevitable, and, shall we not say, righteous consequences of a principle whose origin is injustice and an unrighteous depreciation of the value and abstraction of the products of human labor — a principle which, in its ultimate effects, must be productive of universal ruin and misery and destroy alike the happiness of every class and individual in society.

The real object, therefore, of this association is to avert, if possible, the desolating evils which must inevitably arise from a depreciation of the intrinsic value of human labor; to raise the mechanical and productive classes to that condition of true independence and equality which their practical skill and ingenuity, their immense utility to the nation, and their growing intelligence are beginning imperiously to demand; to promote, equally, the happiness, prosperity, and welfare of the whole community; to aid in conferring a due and full proportion of that invaluable promoter of happiness, leisure, upon all its useful members; and to assist, in conjunction with such other institutions of this nature as shall hereafter be formed throughout the Union, in establishing a just balance of power, both mental, moral, political, and scientific, between all the various classes and individuals which constitute society at large.

1828

50.

James Hall: Letters from the West

James Hall was a pioneer in the Mississippi Valley region and a prolific chronicler of frontier history. As a circuit court judge, he knew well the society and customs and the emotions and beliefs of Western America. Traveling through small communities and isolated farm country, Hall gathered the material for his fictional tales and descriptive essays. The following selection is taken from his Letters from the West, *published in 1828, and is characteristic of his lucid observations of the region.*

Source: *Letters from the West*, London, 1828, pp. 166-174, 231-252, 306-345.

FRONTIER MANNERS

I HAVE REMARKED AT THE LITTLE TOWNS at which I have touched in this country that the appearance of a stranger does not excite the same degree of curiosity which we observe in the villages of the Eastern and Middle states, and particularly at those which are not on the great mail routes. In those places, the arrival of a well-dressed stranger is a matter of general interest, and peculiarly so, if his apparel or traveling equipage be a little finer than usual, or if he assume any airs of importance; the smith rests upon his anvil, the gossip raises her spectacles, and the pretty maidens thrust their rosy faces through the windows to gaze at the newcomer. This propensity has been impressed on my memory by the inconvenience it has sometimes produced and the pleasure it has frequently afforded me.

The pretty hamlets of New England as well as those which are more thinly scattered through the western part of the state of New York, or along the banks of the Delaware and the Susquehanna, in Pennsylvania, are distinguished for their rural beauty, neatness, and simplicity. On entering one of these at the close of a summer day, when the villagers sat about their doors and windows to enjoy the coolness of the evening breeze, I have checked my horse and, hanging carelessly on my saddle, have passed slowly along, gazing with delight at the blooming cheeks and sparkling eyes that have been directed toward me from every quarter. . . .

Would you not suppose that a well-dressed gentleman would be considered here as a natural curiosity, whose appearance would create a sensation as lively as that produced by the arrival of the elephant or the royal African tiger; and that a fashionable fair would rival the popularity of the Albiness or the waxen figure of the Boston beauty? As for a dandy, can you believe he would be suffered to run at large, and not encaged and exhibited as a monster? But such curiosity is here somewhat rare, and the absence of it is easily accounted for: the fact is that, insulated and lonesome as these spots appear, they are visited frequently by a great number and a great variety of people. The merchants who make their annual journeys to an Eastern city to purchase goods; the innumerable caravans of adventurers who are daily crowding to the West in search of homes; and the numbers who traverse these interesting regions from motives of curiosity produce a constant succession of visitors of every class and of almost every nation. English, Irish, French, and Germans are constantly emigrating to the new states and territories; and all the Eastern, Southern, and Middle states send them crowds of inhabitants; nor is it the needy and unfortunate alone who bury themselves among the shadows of the Western forests.

There was a time, indeed, when the word "emigration" carried with it many unpleasant sensations; and when we heard of a respectable man hieing to an unknown land, to seek a precarious existence among bears and mosquitoes, we fancied that we saw the hand of a land speculator beckoning him to destruction, and pitied his fate. . . . But this is not the fact now; whatever might have been the case a few years ago, we now find classes of people among the emigrants who would not be easily deluded. Gentlemen of wealth and intelligence, professional men of talents and education, and respectable farmers and artisans have, after dispassionate inquiry, determined to make this country their future abode. Like Lot, "they lifted up their eyes, and beheld all the plain of Jordan, that it was well watered everywhere"; fertile, "even as the Garden of Eden," and abounding in the choicest gifts of nature.

Thousands, it is true, have been driven here by want from countries less congenial to the needy; but though in some cases their poverty and not their wills consented to the change, they have generally found it an advantageous one. Thus it is that although in traveling you often meet the native woodsman with his hunting shirt and rifle, you as often encounter persons of a different character; and, on arriving at a cabin, it would be difficult to guess what may be the particular description of its inhabitant. It is natural, therefore, that the sight of a stranger should have ceased to be wonderful where it is no longer rare; and that no singularity of dress or appearance should excite the curiosity of those who are in the daily habit of seeing every variety of people.

For nearly the same reasons you will find few people in the West who are ignorant of the geography of their own country; they all know something of the general description of even the most distant parts of the Union. Many of them have emigrated from afar; some travel over an immense extent of country from mere curiosity, or in search of the most eligible place to settle; and others take long journeys on mercantile and other speculations. They are acute observers; and the most illiterate are seldom dull or ignorant. In the neighborhood of Pittsburgh you will meet but few persons who cannot give you some idea of the route to Detroit or to New Orleans, and a tolerably correct notion of the intermediate country. Such knowledge is more or less general throughout the Western country. All have traveled; and the information thus collected is communicated from one to another in their frequent discussions on the subject which is most common and most interesting to them — the comparative advantages of the different sections of the country. In short, you will scarcely meet an old woman who cannot tell you that Pittsburgh is full of coal and smoke; that in New Orleans the people play cards on Sunday; that living is dear at Washington City and codfish cheap at Boston; and that Irishmen are "plenty" in Pennsylvania and pretty girls in Rhode Island.

NATIONAL CHARACTER

IF IN THE LITTLE CIRCLE of my intellectual pleasures there is one which affords me more enjoyment than any other, it consists in tracing the varieties of character which exist in the different branches of our great national family. It is interesting to observe how soon every new country — nay, even every little colony — adopts some trait of habit or manners peculiar to itself. These may be ascribed to local circumstances: climate, soil, and situation all contribute to produce them. The keen blast that invigorates the frame, or the sultry beam that relaxes the system, induces a correspondent effect upon the mind; abundance leads to luxury; while the inhabitant of a niggard soil must be frugal and industrious. But there are a thousand other causes which produce particular customs in particular places; and this diversity, which to me is highly entertaining, affords an ample fund of vexation to the fastidious and makes room for innumerable sarcasms from those travelers who delight in ridiculing everything which does not exactly accord with their own habits or notions of propriety. . . .

The American colonies were peopled from Great Britain, and the Western states derive their inhabitants chiefly from New England and Virginia. Yet, when the American looks back at his British ancestor, he discovers few traits of similarity; and the backwoodsman is almost as far removed from his Eastern progenitor. In the great matters of religion and law, all of us in the United States are the same, as the children of one family, when they separate in the world, still preserve the impress of those

Library of Congress

James Hall (1793-1868) recorded and interpreted pioneer life and legend

principles which they imbibed from a common source; but, in all matters of taste and fancy, customs and exterior deportment, we find a variance. Those who live under the same government, participate in the same laws, and profess the same religion — whose representatives mingle in council, whose warriors rally under the same banner, who celebrate the same victories and mourn for the same disasters — must have many feelings and sentiments in common, though they may differ in their modes of evincing them. Thus, he who would attempt to portray the American character must draw, not a single portrait but a family-piece containing several heads. In each of these would be discovered some strong lines common to all: the same active, enterprising, and independent spirit; the same daring soul and inventive genius; and that aptitude or capacity to take advantage of every change, and subsist and flourish in every soil and situation.

But each would have a shade or cast of expression peculiar to itself; and at the first glance there would be seen no more resemblance between the Boston merchant, the Virginia planter, and the hunter of the West than if they had sprung from different sources. Observe them more closely, however, or rouse their energies into action, and you will still find, in each section of our country, the same American spirit which glowed in the breasts of Putnam, of Marion, and of Wayne. Show me a strong line in the South, and I will point out to you a kindred feature in the North; produce a Jackson from the West, and I will bring you a Perry from the East. In private life, the amiable, unassuming Rhode Islander might present a striking contrast to the fiery Tennessean; but the soul of the hero burned with not less ardor on Lake Erie — the light of the victory was not less brilliant than that which blazed at New Orleans.

Thence it is that foreigners err when they give a character to our whole population from observations made in a single seaport, or when they allow us no national character at all; because they discover traits in different places which seem to be the very antipodes of each other. In this latter sapient hypothesis, they evince, together with a good deal of ignorance, not a little of that insolence which distinguishes our foreign detractors. There are no people in the world whose national character is better defined or more strongly marked than our own. If the European theory on this subject be correct, is it not a little strange that our Yankee tars, whether on board of a frigate or a privateer, should always *happen* to play the same game when they come athwart an Englishman? Is it not a little singular that Brown in the North and Jackson in the South, who I suspect never saw each other in their lives, should always *happen* to handle Lord Wellington's veterans exactly after the same fashion? Accidents will happen in the best of families; but when an accident occurs in the same family repeatedly, we are apt to suspect that it runs in the blood.

In the different states there is certainly a great disparity in the manners of the people. In New England the soil is not rich, and the population is dense. The mass of the people are, of course, laborious, close, and frugal. The colonists were men of pure manners and religious habits. In all their municipal regulations, the suppression of vice and immorality, or rather the *exclusion* of them for they had none to suppress, formed a leading principle. Persons of this character would probably be inclined to lead domestic lives and be satisfied with cheap and innocent amusements. Thus every man, happy in the society of his family and his neighbors, preferred the little circle in which he found content and cheerfulness to all the world besides. Not sufficiently wealthy to be seduced by the siren song of pleasure nor so poor as to become debased by want, he neither spurned nor courted the stranger that approached his door. He was not unwilling to perform an act of charity or kindness, nor ashamed to offer what his humble board afforded; but he wished to know something of the character of the person whom he received into his friendship, whose vices might injure him in his substance, or whose licentiousness might contaminate the morals of his children.

The man whose home is thus the sphere of his usefulness and the scene of his enjoyments must feel deeply interested in every object around him; the conduct of his neighbors, the morals of his servants, and the minds of his children concern him too nearly to be neglected. Thus he is apt to become not only an industrious and virtuous citizen himself but a watchful observer of the conduct of others. Such were the manners of the primitive settlers in New England, and such they remain in many parts of it to this day.

But their local situation was not such as to allow them to retain their rural character in its pristine chastity. In repelling the hostile incursions which threatened to destroy eir infant settlements, they acquired confidence in their courage, and many of their outh imbibed a military spirit, which rendered their former avocations insipid. The tuation of their country, bounded by an xtensive seacoast indented with noble harors, presented commercial advantages too viting to be neglected; and the enterprising temper of the people soon rendered nem as conspicuous among the hardy sons f the ocean as they had been exemplary in nore peaceful scenes. The commercial spir-, thus engrafted upon the "steady habits" f these people, has given them a cast of haracter peculiar to themselves. Hardy and ndependent; ingenious in devising and inefatigable in executing any plan of which he end is gain; pursuing their designs with rdor and enthusiasm, yet adhering to them onstantly, conducting them prudently, and oncealing them artfully, if necessary, there re no people so versatile in their genius, nd none so universally successful in their ndertakings.

In their own country, there are no people nore domestic; yet, strange to tell, they are o be found scattered in the four corners of he earth, everywhere adopting the manners f those around them and flourishing even n the midst of ruin; so that it has become roverbial that a Yankee may live where nother man would starve. The poorest eople in that country receive the first rudinents of education; and from this source, erhaps, they derive a trait which is the reatest blemish in their character. "A little earning" has been said to be "a dangerous hing"; and from that source, I am inclined o believe, we derive that species of finesse ommonly called Yankee tricks.

The New Englanders are remarkable for heir shrewdness, or what the Irish call "mother wit"; and when such a man happens to have a bad heart or loose principles, 'a little learning" is really a dangerous accession of strength. He that has the ability to deceive, without the moral principle to control the evil propensities of human nature, or without sufficient weight of character to enlist pride as an auxiliary, must be exposed to temptations too strong for flesh and blood to resist. A man of colder temperament or less ingenuity would neither have the inclination to attempt, the wit to devise, nor the address to execute that which a Yankee undertakes with the utmost *sangfroid*. They are indeed, like Caleb Quotem, "up to everything," as the poet says. This, at first sight, appears to be a stigma on the character of our Eastern brethren; but when we recollect that it is confined to a portion of the population, and that portion among the lower classes, it would seem but fair to attribute it to the frailty of human nature, rather than to the want of national virtue.

In Virginia we find different manners. The white population is less dense and the country less commercial. Most of the gentlemen are *born gentlemen*; they are wealthy and receive liberal educations; from their cradles they despise money, because they are not in the habit of seeing those with whom they associate actively engaged in the pursuit of it. The slaves perform all the labor, leaving their masters at liberty to cultivate their minds and enjoy the society of their friends. The most numerous class is composed of the planters, and these are accomplished gentlemen, residing on their own estates, fond of pleasure, and princes in hospitality. Kentucky having been settled by Virginians, the manners of the people are nearly the same, except that the latter, living in a more fertile country, are perhaps more profuse in their generosity.

Now these two sections of our country have the same American character. The people in both are high-minded, spirited lovers of liberty, tenacious of their honor and quick in their resentments; they equally loathe everything in the shape of oppression, encroachment, or dictation; they claim the same right of instructing their officers and exercise the same power of dismissing them on the slightest provocation. But then these qualities, which are common to our country, display themselves differently in different situations; they are compressed or expanded by circumstances. In one section, the people are in the habit of curbing their passions and refraining from those pleasures which are inconvenient or expensive; in the other, they are more accustomed to indulge the propensities of their nature. They both have those generous feelings which must always form a part of the character of a free, brave, and enlightened people; but one has wealth and leisure to yield full play to all the impulses of the heart, which the other must restrain.

In New England, and still more in the Middle states, the want of servants is a great drawback upon social intercourse. Where the lady of the house, for instance, must go into her kitchen to superintend the preparation of a meal, or to dress herself, and, after hastily arranging her dress, return with a blowzed face to do the honors of her table, too much fatigued to enjoy its pleasures, the visit of a stranger must afford less pleasure than where such inconveniences do not occur. The New Englander, therefore, will be politely civil from a sense of duty, where the Virginian is profusely hospitable from generous feelings, and because he can enjoy the pleasures of society without its inconveniences.

But take the Virginian from his plantation, or the Yankee from his boat and harpoon, or from his snug cottage, his stone fences, his "neatly white-washed walls," his blooming garden and his tasteful grounds, and place him in a wilderness, with an axe in his hand or a rifle on his shoulder, and he soon becomes a different man; his *national character* will burst the chains of local habit. He does not, like the European in the same situation, languish for want of luxuries which he cannot procure or groan under hardships from which he cannot fly. His ingenuity supplies him with new sources of livelihood, his courage with new vigor; his hardy frame and versatile spirit easily accommodate themselves to new employments; and, though he has still the same heart, the same feelings, and the same principles, he is quite another person in his manners and mode of living.

In some of the Middle states the national character is not so well defined, as there is greater mixture of people. In the interior of Pennsylvania, there are large settlements of Irish and Dutch, or their immediate descendants, who have not yet inhaled our atmosphere long enough to acquire the peculiar characteristics of Americans; but there is no doubt that they, and even the English emigrants, when they have vegetated for a few generations in our happy country, will become estimable citizens.

This subject might be pursued with advantage, but having thrown out the hints, leave you to speculate upon them. My object is only to gather the raw material, which may be woven by more skillful hands; you must judge *ex pede Herculem*, or the whole from a part. Any person who is acquainted with the spirit of our Constitution and laws and the general description of our country, will be able to supply my defects from his own imagination, and to deduce a variety of inferences from the propositions which I have stated. That we have a national character cannot be denied; that that character is an estimable one will, I think, not be doubted; and that a part of it consists in loving our homes and cherishing our friends you will believe on [my] word. . . .

EMIGRATION

THE FOREIGNERS whom I met were in much worse circumstances than our own citizens. These arrive on our shores in a destitute condition, and undertake the journey without money enough to accomplish half the distance, and some without a cent to pay their entrance, confiding in the protection of heaven and the benefactions of the charitable. This confidence is not so often deceptive as might be expected, for an American is never seen to turn a houseless wanderer from his door or to refuse a morsel to the hungry. It is surprising to see to what a dreary plight some of these adventurers are reduced by their poverty or improvidence; and yet many of them will trudge along with light hearts and empty purses, apparently forgetful of the past and regardless of the future.

At Pittsburgh, where the emigrants generally embark on the Ohio, they may be seen in larger numbers than at any other place; and here may be remarked, not only their number but, in some degree, their various characters and as various expectations. Some arrive with furniture, farming utensils, and servants, and push forward, confident in their ability to overcome every obstacle; some come burdened with large families and but little worldly gear; and others, happy at such a time in their "single blessedness," come alone, errant knights, leaving all their cares behind them. Upon observing these motley collections, I have been reminded of the invitation in a camp-meeting song which I have heard, and which I think is about as follows:

Come hungry, come thirsty, come
  ragged, come bare,
Come filthy, come lousy, come just as
  you are.

For, to be brief, here you see all sorts of folks crowding to the West.

Those who are driven by misfortune from their homes go like exiles from the land, to which fond recollection attaches a thousand charms, to a wilderness, which fancy clothes with a thousand terrors. Every sympathy is awakened and every tender feeling thrilled with anguish, when they exchange the comforts of society, the scenes of their youth, and the friends of their hearts for the nameless and unknown difficulties which appear in the dark perspective. They dream of interminable forests and pestilential swamps, and at every step fancy themselves surrounded by noxious vermin and beasts of prey. Thus, anticipating no good and fearing every evil, they go into banishment with sorrowful hearts.

But there is a more sanguine class of emigrants to whom a different picture is presented. They have been allured by interest or ambition, or led by choice, to a new country, and hope arrays their future abodes with every charm. An *El Dorado* has been described to them, or they have created it, in which men are to be wooed to their happiness as a maiden to the bridal, and their only care is to determine with what grace they will accept the guerdon. The old men are to be blessed with wealth, the young men with honor, and the girls with husbands — and, I suppose, with wealth, and honor, and pleasure into the bargain; and, to crown all, the good folks of the West will feel so delighted and so flattered by their advent that they will crowd about them like the friends of Job, and everyone will give them "an earring and a piece of gold!"

All these are deceived, as well the desponding as the enthusiastic. The advantages of the Western country consist in the great fertility of the soil, the profusion of all the products of nature, whether of the animal, vegetable, or mineral kingdom, the cheapness of lands, and the newness of the country, which affords room and opportunity for enterprise. These, together with its commercial advantages, the total exemption from all taxes and political burdens, and the comparatively small portion of labor requisite to procure the necessaries of life, certainly render this a desirable home. But they who, like Ortogrul of Basra, desire the golden stream to be quick and violent, will, like him, discover a dry and dusty channel and will learn that slow and persevering industry is not less necessary here than elsewhere. Honors are the reward of personal popularity, which, we have been told, "may be gained without merit and lost without a fault," and in this respect the Western Hemisphere differs little from the rest of the world. Popular arts are the same in every country; but it is certain that few here are raised to eminent public stations without a long and intimate acquaintance with the people. In the West there is no jealousy or unfriendliness to strangers, who are generally received with open arms and treated with kindness and respect; but political honors are more sparingly bestowed and are seldom lavished upon foreigners, who, whatever may be their pretensions, can hardly be supposed to know or to feel the interests of the country.

The desponding emigrant, on the other hand, is agreeably surprised at finding every plain, substantial comfort which a reasonable man can wish; and, though he discovers no attempt at luxury or style, he sees hospitality, plenty, and intelligence. Instead of a vast wilderness he finds large settlements which, though thinly scattered, are now sufficiently dense to afford the comforts and civilities of life, to ensure protection, and to enforce municipal regulations. . . .

Well, and when the emigrant has reached his journey's end, what then? Why, then, my dear sir, he very often finds that he had better have stayed at home. Labor, labor, labor, hard, heavy, incessant labor, is the lot of him who proclaims war against the forest; but the victory is certain, and the conqueror's reward is rich and ample.

51.

Duke Bernhard: Observations by a German Visitor

During 1825 and 1826, Bernhard, duke of Saxe-Weimar Eisenach, visited America and made detailed observations on what he saw. The following selection is taken from two chapters of his Travels, *published in 1828. In the first chapter he recounts his impressions of New Orleans and its multiracial society. The second chapter deals with his visit to the Rapp community in Pennsylvania, one of the many semi-utopian religious societies that flourished in America during the nineteenth century.*

Source: *Travels Through North America During the Years 1825 and 1826,*
Philadelphia, 1828, Vol. II, pp. 57-63, 158-166.

Sunday is not observed with the puritanic strictness in New Orleans that it is in the North. The shops are open, and there is singing and guitar playing in the streets. In New York or Philadelphia, such proceedings would be regarded as outrageously indecent. On a Sunday we went for the first time to the French theater, in which a play was performed every Sunday and Thursday. The piece for this night was the tragedy of Regulus and two vaudevilles. The dramatic corps was merely tolerable, such as those of the small French provincial towns, where they never presume to present tragedies or comedies of the highest class. "Regulus" was murdered; Mr. Marchand and Madame Clozel, whose husband performed the comic parts very well in the vaudevilles, alone distinguished themselves.

The saloon is not very large, but well ornamented; below is the pit and parquet, a row of boxes each for four persons, and before them a balcony. The boxes are not divided by walls but only separated by a low partition, so that the ladies can exhibit themselves conveniently. Over the first row of boxes is a second, to which the free colored people resort, who are not admitted to any other part of the theater, and above this row is the gallery, in which slaves may go with the permission of their masters. Behind the boxes is a lobby where the gentlemen who do not wish to sit in a box stand or walk about, where they can see over the boxes.

The theater was less attended than we had supposed it would be; and it was said that the great shock felt in the commercial world on account of the bankruptcy of three of the most distinguished houses, in consequence of unfortunate speculations in cotton, and the failures of Liverpool was the cause of this desertion. . . .

There were subscription balls given in New Orleans, to which the managers had the politeness to invite us. These balls took place twice a week, Tuesdays and Fridays, at the French theater, where the masquerade had been, which I mentioned before. None but good society were admitted to these subscription balls. The first that we attended was not crowded, however, the generality of the ladies present were very pretty and had a very genteel French air. The dress was extremely elegant and after the latest Paris fashion. The ladies danced, upon the whole, excellently and did great honor to their French teachers. Dancing, and some instruction in music, is almost the whole education of the female Creoles.

Most of the gentlemen here are far behind the ladies in elegance. They did not remain long at the ball but hastened away to the Quadroon Ball, so called, where they amused themselves more and were more at their ease. . . .

A quadroon is the child of a mestizo mother and a white father, as a mestizo is the child of a mulatto mother and a white father. The quadroons are almost entirely white; from their skin no one would detect their origin; nay, many of them have as fair a complexion as many of the haughty Creole females. Such of them as frequent these balls are free. Formerly they were known by their black hair and eyes, but at present there are completely fair quadroon males and females. Still, however, the strongest prejudice reigns against them on account of their black blood, and the white ladies maintain, or affect to maintain, the most violent aversion toward them.

Marriage between the white and colored population is forbidden by the law of the state. As the quadroons on their part regard the Negroes and mulattoes with contempt and will not mix with them, so nothing remains for them but to be the friends, as it is termed, of the white men. The female quadroon looks upon such an engagement as a matrimonial contract, though it goes no further than a formal contract by which the "friend" engages to pay the father or mother of the quadroon a specified sum. The quadroons both assume the name of their friends, and, as I am assured, preserve this engagement with as much fidelity as ladies espoused at the altar.

Several of these girls have inherited property from their fathers or friends and possess handsome fortunes. Notwithstanding this, their situation is always very humiliating. They cannot drive through the streets in a carriage, and their "friends" are forced to bring them in their own conveyances after dark to the ball; they dare not sit in the presence of white ladies and cannot enter their apartments without especial permission. The whites have the privilege to procure these unfortunate creatures a whipping, like that inflicted on slaves, upon an accusation proved by two witnesses. Several of these females have enjoyed the benefits of as careful an education as most of the whites; they conduct themselves ordinarily with more propriety and decorum, and confer more happiness on their "friends," than many of the white ladies to their married lords. Still, the white ladies constantly speak with the greatest contempt, and even with animosity, of these unhappy and oppressed beings. The strongest language of high nobility in the monarchies of the Old World cannot be more haughty, overweening, or contemptuous toward their fellow creatures than the expressions of the Creole females with regard to the quadroons, in one of the much vaunted states of the free Union.

In fact, such comparison strikes the mind of a thinking being very singularly! Many wealthy fathers, on account of the existing prejudices, send daughters of this description to France, where these girls, with a good education and property, find no difficulty in forming a legitimate establishment. At the Quadroon Ball, only colored ladies are admitted; the men of that caste, be it understood, are shut out by the white gentlemen. To take away all semblance of vulgarity, the price of admission is fixed at two dollars, so that only persons of the better class can appear there.

As a stranger in my situation should see everything to acquire a knowledge of the habits, customs, opinions, and prejudices of the people he is among, therefore I accepted the offer of some gentlemen who proposed to carry me to this Quadroon Ball; and I must avow I found it much more decent than the masked ball. The colored ladies were under the eyes of their mothers; they were well and gracefully dressed and conducted themselves with much propriety

and modesty. Cotillions and waltzes were danced, and several of the ladies performed elegantly. I did not remain long there that I might not utterly destroy my standing in New Orleans, but returned to the masked ball and took great care not to disclose to the white ladies where I had been. I could not, however, refrain from making comparisons, which in nowise redounded to the advantage of the white assembly. . . .

RAPP'S SOCIETY, after leaving New Harmony, chose a new situation which they named Economy. This is eighteen miles from Pittsburgh. . . .

Having been prejudiced against Mr. Rapp and his society by what I had read, and more recently heard at New Harmony, I was much rejoiced at having visited this place, to be better informed by personal observation. Never have I witnessed a more truly patriarchal constitution than here, and men's actions speak best for their regulations and for the concord prevailing among them.

The elder Rapp is a large man of seventy years old, whose powers age seems not to have diminished; his hair is gray, but his blue eyes, overshadowed by strong brows, are full of life and fire; his voice is strong, and his enunciation full, and he knows how to give a peculiar effect to his words by appropriate gesticulation. He speaks a Swabian dialect, intermixed with a little English, to which the ear of a German in the United States must become accustomed; generally, what he says is clearly and plainly delivered.

Rapp's system is nearly the same as Owen's. Community of goods and all members of the society to work together for the common interest, by which the welfare of each individual is secured. Rapp does not hold his society together by these hopes alone, but also by the tie of religion, which is entirely wanting in Owen's community; and results declare that Rapp's system is the better. No great results can be expected

American Antiquarian Society

The Old Rappist Church in New Harmony, with the community hall in the background; May 1826

American Antiquarian Society

"Economi Town," Economy, Penn., a Rappist settlement downriver from Pittsburgh

from Owen's plan, and a sight of it is very little in its favor. What is most striking and wonderful of all is that so plain a man as Rapp can so successfully bring and keep together a society of nearly 700 persons, who, in a manner, honor him as a prophet.

Equally so, for example, in his power of government, which can suspend the intercourse of the sexes. He found that the society was becoming too numerous, wherefore the members agreed to live with their wives as sisters. All nearer intercourse is forbidden, as well as marriage; both are discouraged. However, some marriages constantly occur, and children are born every year, for whom there is provided a school and teacher. The members of the community manifest the very highest degree of veneration for the elder Rapp, whom they address and treat as a father.

Mr. Frederick Rapp is a large, good-looking personage, of forty years of age. He possesses profound mercantile knowledge and is the temporal, as his father is the spiritual, chief of the community. All business passes through his hands. He represents the society, which, notwithstanding the change in the name of their residence, is called the Harmony Society, in all their dealings with the world. They found that the farming and cattle raising, to which the society exclusively attended in both their former places of residence, were not sufficiently productive for their industry; they therefore have established factories, which in this country are very profitable, and have at present cotton and woolen manufactories, a brewery, distillery, and flour mill. They generally drink, during their good German dinners, uncommonly good wine, which was made on the Wabash and brought thence by them. They left the worst, as I have remarked, at New Harmony.

After dinner we visited the village, which is very regularly arranged, with broad, rectangular streets; two, parallel to the Ohio, and four, crossing them. On the 22nd of May it will be but two years since the forest was first felled upon which Economy is built; the roots still remaining in the streets are evidences of the short time that has elapsed. It is astonishing what united and regulated human efforts have accomplished in so short a time!

Many families still live in log houses, but some streets consist almost entirely of neat, well-built frame houses at proper distances from each other; each house has a garden attached to it. The four-story cotton and woolen factories are of brick; Mr. Rapp's dwelling house, not yet completed, and a newly begun warehouse are also to be of brick. The log houses stand in the rear of the line which the new houses are to occupy in the street, so that when, in time, they wish to erect brick buildings, it may be done without incommoding the tenants of the log dwellings. Mr. Rapp's residence speaks rather freely against the equality he preaches to his people, yet without exciting jealousy or becoming a stumbling block. It consists of a principal building, two stories high, with two lower wings standing in the same line, and is adorned with beautiful Philadelphia paper. . . .

In the cotton and woolen factories, all the machinery is set in motion by a high-pressure engine of seventy horsepower, made in Pittsburgh. The machine pumps the water from a well fifty feet deep, sunk for the purpose. The community possesses some fine sheep, among which are many Merino and Saxon; they purchase wool, however, from the surrounding farmers, who have already begun to raise it to bring to Economy. As soon as the wool is washed, it is picked by the old women of the community, who work in the fourth story, whence it is reconveyed by a sort of tunnel into the lower story. The wool is then separated according to its quality into four classes, dyed together in the dye house near the manufactory, returned to the mill, where it is combed, coarsely spun, and finally wrought into fine yarn by a machine similar to the spinning jenny.

As soon as spun, it is placed in the loom and wrought into cloth; this is placed in a steam fulling mill, so arranged that the steam from the engine is made to answer the purpose of soap and fuller's earth, which is a great saving. The cloth is shorn by means of a cylinder, upon which a strong piece of steel turns. There is a model of this shearing machine in the Patent Office at Washington. The woolen goods most in demand in this country are blue middling, gray mixed (principally used for pantaloons), and red and white flannel cloths. The red flannels are in great demand.

The cotton factory is employed in spinning and weaving. The printing of cottons has not yet been attempted, as the stamps cannot be procured without great expense and difficulty, and the fashions of printed calico are very changeable. The colored cottons woven here are blue and white, mixed; a stuff of this color much in demand in Tennessee is called cassinet, the chain of which is of cotton and the filling of wool.

The spinning machines are of the common kind, each of which have 150 spools at work. The first machine, which does the coarse spinning, has been much improved so as to save a great deal of manual labor. There are also some power looms here, though not many; neither have they at present but one dressing machine. Many of the machines are made in Pittsburgh; most of them, however, at Economy. As this establishment has been so recently founded, it is natural enough that but few machines should be prepared or in operation.

The factories and workshops are warmed during winter by means of pipes connected with the steam engine. All the workmen, and especially the females, have very healthy complexions and moved me deeply by the warm-hearted friendliness with which they saluted the elder Rapp. I was also much gratified to see vessels containing fresh, sweet-smelling flowers standing on all the machines. The neatness which universally reigns here is in every respect worthy of praise.

"The Old House of Representatives," by Samuel F. B. Morse, 1822

POLITICAL DIMENSIONS

The War of 1812, so inconclusive military, brought the United States the international respect that had been sought since independence. It was not so much the resort to war that achieved this, as the defeat of Napoleon and the end of European conflict. America's definition of the rights of neutrals had not been recognized by the peace treaty, but the French defeat removed the reasons for attacking American ships. European rulers were no more admiring of republicanism, but they were prepared to coexist peacefully with America so long as the notion of popular government did not spread. The monarchs of France, Austria, Prussia, and Russia joined in a "Holy Alliance" that was loosely dedicated to cooperative action against democratic movements, wherever they should appear. The intention of extending this policy to Spain's former colonies in Latin America was vaguely discussed. This and Russian interest in the west coast of North America impelled Monroe and his secretary of state, John Quincy Adams, to articulate a definitive policy that would meet the potential dangers posed by the Holy Alliance.

In domestic politics, the powerful surge westward and the vigorous resumption of Northern commerce quickly brought into focus a number of long-dormant problems. The great disputes over states' rights and central authority were revived. The issue of the expansion of slavery arose again and again as new states applied for admission to the Union.

Every decision, whether on tariffs or taxes or internal improvements, seemed to involve one or both of these issues and each controversy tested the ability of Congress to devise a compromise that would smooth over basic differences in the interest of union. Jackson's strong exercise of presidential powers and the infusion of a democratic spirit from the West added another dimension to political dissension.

(Above) **Note from Jefferson to Madison, commenting on Monroe's proposal, October 1823; (right) Monroe's letter to Jefferson, giving his thoughts on world affairs and asking comment**

The Monroe Doctrine

In 1822 the leaders of the Holy Alliance, meeting at the Congress of Verona, considered a plan to restore to King Ferdinand of Spain his former colonies in Latin America. This led George Canning, the British foreign secretary, to propose a joint British-American declaration opposing intervention. John Quincy Adams urged President Monroe to make a broad statement outlining an independent position. The assumption, which Monroe shared, was that Britain could never be aligned with the absolute monarchs and that, in the event of intervention, the British fleet would support the United States. The president's message to Congress in December 1823 outlined the principles that came to be called the Monroe Doctrine. It defined America's relationship to the Old World, while, by implication, assuming hegemony in the New.

(Above) Simon Bolivar; (below) Richard Rush, ambassador to Britain; (right) James Monroe

Oak hill october 19.th 1823

Dear sir

I transmit to you two despatches which was
rec'd from Mr Rush, while I was lately in Washington, which involve interests of the highest importance. They contain two letters from Mr Canning, supposing designs of the holy alliance, against the Independence
of So. America, & proposing a cooperation, between
G. Britain & the UStates, in support of it, against
the members of that alliance. The project, aims in the
first instance, at a mere expression of opinion, some
what in the abstract, but which it is expected by
Mr Canning, will have a great political effect, by
defeating the combination. By Mr Rush's answers,
which are also inclosed, you will see the light in which
he views the subject, & the extent to which he may have
gone. many important considerations are involved
in this proposition. 1st shall we entangle ourselves,
at all, in European politicks, & wars, on the side of
any power, against others, presuming that a concert
by agreement, of the kind proposed, may lead to that
result? 2.d If a case can exist in which a sound
maxim,
may, & ought to be departed from, is not the present
instance, precisely that case? 3.º Has not the epoch
arriv'd when G. Britain must take her stand.
on the side of the monarchs of Europe, or of the UStates,
& in consequence, either in favor of Despotism or of lib-
& may it not be presumed, that aware of that necessity,
her government, has seiz'd on the present occurrence, as
that, which it deems, the most suitable, to announce &
mark the commencement of that career.

My own impression is that we ought to meet the proposal of the British govt, & to make it known, that we
would view an interference on the part of the European
powers, and especially an attack on the Colonies, by
them, as an attack on ourselves, presuming that,
they succeeded with them, they would extend it to us. I

(Left) John Quincy Adams, portrait begun by Stuart and completed by Sully; (above) "Caucus Curs in Full Yell," an 1824 cartoon by James Akin, showing "Old Hickory" under attack from a pack of dogs, representing the opposition press

Election of 1824

The end of Monroe's administration also ended the consensus known as the "Era of Good Feeling." Five candidates sought the presidency. Calhoun settled for the vice-presidency, but Henry Clay, Andrew Jackson, William Crawford, and John Quincy Adams split the electoral votes and forced the decision into the House of Representatives, where Clay, as speaker, used his influence for Adams. Adams made Clay secretary of state, and Jackson denounced the "unholy bargain." He then organized, with Martin Van Buren, the "Jacksonian democracy."

(Left) Henry Clay; portrait by Samuel Osgood, and (right) William Crawford, engraved from a painting by Jarvis. Both were candidates in the election of 1824. Clay received 37 electoral votes and Crawford, 41

(Left) State Department, 1831; (right) Joel Poinsett, first minister to Mexico, by Sully

The Western Hemisphere

The Panama Congress of 1826 created a political storm in the United States. Black republics of the West Indies were invited — this antagonized the South, which blocked recognition of Haiti until 1862. Bolivar's call for the Congress of all Latin American republics indicated that slavery would be on the agenda. Moreover, a united Latin America was not conducive to U.S. expansion. The U.S. delegates to Panama never arrived at the Congress.

(Right) Philip Tilyard, first envoy from Santo Domingo and Richard Anderson, first ambassador to Columbia and delegate to Panama Conference; (below) the U.S. responded slowly to Bolivar's call to the Panama Conference, as the cartoon shows

Jackson Men,
Look out for the
SPURIOUS TICKET.

The Democratic Electoral Ticket, with *Forty Three* names on it, is circulated by the Opposition.

If you vote that Ticket, your Vote is lost to the Good Cause.

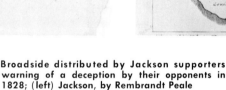

A NEW MAP OF THE
Exhibiting a View of

Broadside distributed by Jackson supporters warning of a deception by their opponents in 1828; (left) Jackson, by Rembrandt Peale

Anti-Jackson broadside, characteristic of the bitter campaign, refers to executions carried out by court martial under Jackson in 1815

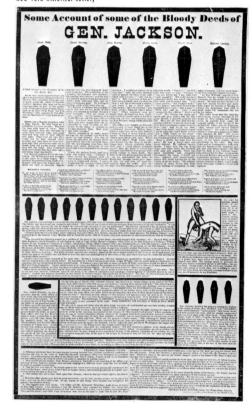

Jacksonian Democracy

Jackson was the first president from the West, and reflected the democratic aspirations of the leaner lands against the entrenched power of the East. Officeholders were turned out to be replaced by Jackson's supporters: opponents talked of the "spoils system," Jacksonians of "rotation in office."

(Above) Jackson rides the alligator with its eyes west, straining against the old "embargo" turtle, representing Eastern commercial interests; (below) the spoils system is lampooned as Jackson is shown administering political favors

JACKSON
AND A
STANDING ARMY

We are persuaded no man, not madly bent on disturbing the peace and putting in jeopardy the government of our country, can read the following correspondence, and not feel an increased dread of General Jackson, his principles, his disposition, and his notions of government. With a standing army of one hundred and twenty thousand men, and Jackson for its head, our liberties and republican government would be as unsubstantial as the "early dew."

To John Binns, Esq. Editor of the Democratic Press.

Sir...We send you for publication the enclosed correspondence, exhibiting features in the character of General Jackson which ought to be known to the citizens of the United States. We need only remark, that the law for reducing the army passed on the 2d of March, 1825, and the reduction was from about 12,000 men to 6,000.

There was a great majority in Congress in favor of the reduction, and we believe no law was ever more generally acceptable to the PEOPLE.

We are, respectfully,
Your ob't serv'ts,
Samuel Wetherill,   Jacob Mayland,
Richard Peters,   Edward Ingersoll,
D. W. Coxe,   Clement C. Biddle,
John Jennings,   Samuel Mifflin.
Philadelphia, 30th Sept. 1828.

(Above) Jackson's position favoring a large standing army brought charges of autocratic ambition; (below) Amos Kendall, an advisor and speech-writer, was a key member of Jackson's "Kitchen Cabinet" and later postmaster general

SEVENTH WARD BEGGARS.

The presidential campaign of 1828 was filled with envenomed personal abuse. Jackson men reminded the voters of the "corrupt bargain" between Adams and Clay. A skilled political coalition, headed by Martin Van Buren in New York and Calhoun in the South, swept into power with Jackson.

Amos Kendall
POSTMASTER GENERAL

**Cartoon during the nullification controversy shows the manu-
facturing North getting fat at Southern expense**

John C. Calhoun by Chester Harding

**Unknown primitive art-
ist expresses his view
of the nullification con-
troversey**

"Daniel Webster's Reply to Robert Y. Hayne" by G. P. A. Healy

States' Rights

The compromises that had created a Constitution in 1787 came back to haunt the republic in the 1820s. The Missouri Compromise made the slavery issue part of the political life-stream from then on. The 1828 tariff widened the breach: Calhoun became spokesman for the nullification doctrine adopted by South Carolina in 1832. Jackson broke with Calhoun, who resigned as vice-president; Jackson threatened federal invasion. A compromise patched up the tariff issue for the time, but the Senate chamber had already rung to the "great debate" between Daniel Webster and Robert Hayne on states' rights. A major issue of Jackson's two terms was the Bank of the United States, headed by Nicholas Biddle. Jackson vetoed a bill to renew the bank's charter, Biddle tightened credit, and Jackson withdrew all federal deposits.

Nicholas Biddle, president of the U.S. Bank

Jackson's nightmare, entitled "Political Quixotism," shows the President in frenzied battle with a monster; its chief head is labeled: U.S. Bank; (below) Jackson strikes down the bank by removing federal deposits. Caught in the rubble are numerous opposition papers and politicians. Biddle, the devil, flees

The 1832 Election

Increasing enfranchisement led in 1831 to the first political nominating convention in the land — that of the Anti-Masonic Party. Especially in New York, antagonism had grown to the control of public offices by the Freemasons, who elected numerous congressmen and state officials. The party nominated William Wirt as presidential candidate, though he himself had been a Mason. More serious issues by 1832 were banking, tariffs, and internal improvements. Jackson won easy re-election over Wirt and Henry Clay, supporter of the Bank of the United States.

BORN TO COMMAND.

OF VETO MEMORY.

HAD I BEEN CONSULTED.

KING ANDREW THE FIRST.

Library of Congress

Boston Athenaeum

Alexandria-Washington Lodge

(Left) 1832 cartoon accuses Jackson of monarchial ambitions; (above) William Wirt, portrait by Henry Inman; George Washington wearing his Mason's regalia

In 1826, William Morgan, author of an expose of Freemasonry, was abducted by Masons in up-state New York. Investigation revealed that most New York officeholders were Masons and Anti-Masonic sentiment gained considerable popular support. Woodcut from "Anti-Masonic Almanac," 1829

Granger Collection

| II. Month. | FEBRUARY. | 1829. |

New moon, 3d 9h 19m eve
First Quarter, 10d 2h 11m eve

Full moon, 18d 2h 3m eve
Last Quarter, 26d 3h 8m eve

52.

The Nashoba Community

Reformers and idealists in nineteenth-century America frequently felt that their aims were better served by withdrawing from society at large into semi-utopian communities. One such experiment that was of short duration was the Nashoba community, founded by Frances Wright in Tennessee in 1825. The purpose of Nashoba was to educate emancipated slaves to enable them to live in society. The following account of experiences at Nashoba is drawn from History of American Socialisms, *by John Humphrey Noyes, who was the founder of the Oneida community in New York State. The account is dated 1828, the year in which the Nashoba experiment terminated.*

Source: John Humphrey Noyes, *History of American Socialisms*, Philadelphia, 1870, pp. 66-72.

THIS EXPERIMENT WAS MADE in Shelby County, Tennessee, by the celebrated Frances Wright. The objects were to form a community in which the Negro slave should be educated and upraised to a level with the whites and thus prepared for freedom; and to set an example which, if carried out, would eventually abolish slavery in the Southern states; also to make a home for good and great men and women of all countries who might there sympathize with each other in their love and labor for humanity. She invited congenial minds from every quarter of the globe to unite with her in the search for truth and the pursuit of rational happiness. Herself a native of Scotland, she became imbued with these philanthropic views through a knowledge of the sufferings of a great portion of mankind in many countries, and of the condition of the Negro in the United States in particular.

She traveled extensively in the Southern states and explained her views to many of the planters. It was during these travels that she visited the German settlement of Rappites at Harmony, on the Wabash River, and after examining the wonderful industry of that community, she was struck with the appropriateness of their system of cooperation to the carrying out of her aspirations. She also visited some of the Shaker establishments then existing in the United States, but she thought unfavorably of them. She renewed her visits to the Rappites and was present on the occasion of their removal from Harmony to Economy on the Ohio, where she continued her acquaintance with them, receiving valuable knowledge from their experience and, as it were, witnessing a new village, with its fields, orchards, gardens, vineyards, flouring mills and manufactories, rise out of the earth beneath the hands of some 800 trained laborers. . . .

In the autumn of 1825 [when New Harmony was under full sail in the absence of Mr. Owen], Frances Wright purchased 2,000 acres of good and pleasant woodland, lying on both sides of the Wolf River in west Tennessee, about thirteen miles above Memphis. She then purchased several Negro families, comprising fifteen able hands, and commenced her practical experiment. . . .

We are informed that Frances Wright found in her new occupation intense and ever increasing interest. But ere long she was seized by severe and reiterated sickness, which compeled her to make a voyage to Europe for the recovery of her health. "During her absence," says her biographer, "an intriguing individual has disorganized everything on the estate, and effected the removal of persons of confidence. All her serious difficulties proceeded from her white assistants, and not from the blacks."

In December of the following year [1826] she made over the Nashoba estate to a board of trustees, by a deed commencing thus:

> I, Frances Wright, do give the lands after specified to General Lafayette, William Maclure, Robert Owen, Cadwallader Colden, Richardson Whitby, Robert Jennings, Robert Dale Owen, George Flower, Camilla Wright, and James Richardson, to be held by them and their associates and their successors in perpetual trust for the benefit of the Negro race.

By another deed she gave the slaves of Nashoba to the aforementioned trustees; and by still another she gave all her personal property.

In her appeal to the public in connection with this transfer, she explains at length her views of reform and her reasons for choosing the above-named trustees instead of the emancipation or colonization societies; and in respect to education says: "No difference will be made in the schools between the white children and the children of color, whether in education or any other advantage." After further explanation of her plans she goes on to say:

> It will be seen that this establishment is founded on the principle of community of property and labor: presenting every advantage to those desirous not of accumulating money but of enjoying life and rendering services to their fellow creatures; these fellow creatures, that is, the blacks here admitted, requiting these services by services equal or greater, by filling occupations which their habits render easy, and which, to their guides and assistants, might be difficult or unpleasing.

No life of idleness, however, is proposed to the whites. Those who cannot work must give an equivalent in property. Gardening or other cultivation of the soil, useful trades practised in the society or taught in the school, the teaching of every branch of knowledge, tending the children, and nursing the sick will present a choice of employment sufficiently extensive. . . .

In March 1828, the trustees published a communication in the *Nashoba Gazette* explaining the difficulties they had to contend with and the causes why the experience of two years had modified the original plan of Frances Wright. They show the impossibility of a cooperative community succeeding without the members composing it are superior beings; "for," say they, "if there be introduced into such a society thoughts of evil and unkindness, feelings of intolerance and words of dissension, it cannot prosper. That which produces in the world only commonplace jealousies and everyday squabbles is sufficient to destroy a community."

The society had admitted some members to labor, and others as boarders from whom no labor was required; and in this they confess their error, and now propose to admit those only who possess the funds for their support.

The trustees go on to say that "they desire to express distinctly that they have deferred, for the present, the attempt to form a society of cooperative labor; and they claim for the association only the title of a Preliminary Social Community."

After describing the moral qualifications of members, who may be admitted without regard to color, they propose that each one shall yearly throw $100 into the common fund for board alone, to be paid quarterly in advance. Each one was also to build for himself or herself a small brick house, with a piazza, according to a regular plan and upon a spot of ground selected for the purpose, near the center of the lands of Nashoba. . . .

It is probable that success did not further attend the experiment, for Frances Wright abandoned it soon after, and in June following removed to New Harmony, where, in conjunction with William Owen, she assumed for a short time the management of the *New Harmony Gazette,* which then had its name altered to the *New Harmony and Nashoba Gazette or Free Enquirer.*

Her biographer says that she abandoned, though not without a struggle, the peaceful shades of Nashoba, leaving the property in the charge of an individual who was to hold the Negroes ready for removal to Haiti the year following. In relinquishing her experiment in favor of the race, she held herself equally pledged to the colored families under her charge, to the Southern state in which she had been a resident citizen, and to the American community at large, to remove her dependents to a country free to their color. This she executed a year after.

53.

James Fenimore Cooper: On Popular Elections and on the American Girl

When Fenimore Cooper left the United States in 1826 for a seven-year sojourn in Europe, he was already renowned, at home and abroad, as America's first distinguished novelist. In France, Cooper befriended General Lafayette, who requested that he write a book commemorating his (Lafayette's) visit to the United States in 1824-1825. Cooper fulfilled Lafayette's request indirectly in an epistolary work, Notions of the Americans: Picked Up by a Traveling Bachelor *(1828), in which he posed as a European. While Lafayette's triumphal tour of the States was indeed discussed, it was Cooper's basic intention to write a book about America for Europeans in order to dispel the misconceptions that Europeans haughtily cherished about life in the New World.*

Source: *Notions of the Americans: Picked Up by a Traveling Bachelor,* London, 1828, Vol. I, pp. 344-363.
America and the Americans: Notions Picked Up by a Traveling Bachelor,
2nd edition, London, 1836, Vol. I, pp. 251-262.

I.

The Merits and Demerits of Popular Elections

THE DAY AFTER we had quitted Cooperstown, we saw a collection of people assembled in front of an inn, which was the principal edifice in a hamlet of perhaps a dozen houses. Cadwallader told me this was the first day of the state election, and that this spot was one of the polls, a name which answers in some degree to the English term "hustings." Fortunately, the stage changed horses at the inn, and I had an opportunity of examining the incipient step in that process which literally dictates all the national policy of this great republic.

Although each state controls its own forms, not only in the elections but in everything else, a description of the usages of one poll will be sufficiently near the truth to give a correct general idea of them all. I now speak literally only of the state of New

York, though, generally, of the whole Union. The elections occur once a year.[1] They last three days. In the large towns, they are stationary, there being no inconvenience in such an arrangement where the population is dense and the distances short. But in the country, they are held on each successive day at a different place in order to accommodate the voters. The state is divided into counties which cover, on an average, 900 square miles each. Some are, however, larger and some smaller. These counties are again subdivided into townships, covering, perhaps, 80 or 90 square miles. There is, also, great inequality in the size of these minor districts. These are the two great divisions of territory for all the ordinary purposes of government and police. The counties have courts of their own and a certain sort of legislative body which regulates many of their financial affairs.

In order that the whole subject, however, may be rendered as clear as possible, we will begin at the base and ascend to the superstructure of their government. The most democratic assemblage known to the laws, in which legal and binding resolutions can be enacted, are the town meetings. Any number of the people may assemble when and where they please to remonstrate, to petition, or even to plot, if they see fit; but their acts can only be recommendatory. The town meetings are held annually, and every citizen who has attained his majority can vote. A moderator (no bad name for a perfectly popular assembly) is chosen by acclamation to preside. The meeting is commonly held in some schoolhouse, but very often in the open air. In some places, though rarely, there are townhouses.

At these meetings, all the town officers

1. There is one state where they occur twice — the little state of Rhode Island, which is still governed by the form of its ancient charter, as granted by Charles II in 1663. As this is practically the most democratic state in the Union, it affords pretty good evidence that the experiment of a democratic government is not so new in America as some pretend.

are chosen. They consist of a supervisor; three assessors who apportion all the taxes on the individuals, whether imposed by town, county, state, or United States; collectors, who collect all the taxes, except those laid by the United States government, which, in time of peace, are just nothing at all; a town clerk, who keeps certain registers; constable, poor officers, overseers of highways, pathmasters, and a few others. The names of most of these officers indicate their duties. The overseers of the highway are the men who lay out the ordinary roads of the town and who say how much tax each individual shall contribute in work or in money; and the pathmasters inspect the labor. Men of property and education frequently seek the latter employment. The voting in this popular assembly may be by ballot, but it is generally done by acclamation. There is a penalty if an individual refuse to serve, though they are sometimes excused by the citizens if a good reason can be rendered.

The courts have also a discretionary power in imposing and in laying fines. I was present during the course of this excursion at one of these town meetings. There might have been 200 citizens assembled before the door of a large schoolhouse. Much good humor was blended with a sufficient dispatch of business. The Americans mingle with a perfect consciousness of their influence on the government, an admirable respect for the laws and institutions of their country. I heard jokes, and one or two open nominations of men of property and character to fill the humble offices of constable and poundkeeper; but the most perfect good sense and practical usefulness appeared to distinguish all their decisions. There was a contest for the office of supervisor, and it was decided by a close vote. The two candidates were present and on seemingly very good terms. They were respectable-looking yeomen, and he who lost told his rival that he thought the people had shown their judgment. There was no noise, no drinking, nor any excitement beyond that which one would feel in seeing an ordinary footrace.

One farmer observed that the crows had got the taste of his corn, and unless something was done, there could be little hope for the year's crop. He therefore would propose that a reward of six cents should be paid for every dozen that should be killed, within their town, for the next six months. The resolution was opposed by a hatter, who insisted that he could take care of his hats and that the farmers ought to take care of their corn. This logic was unsuccessful; the price was reduced a trifle, and the resolution was passed. It was then just as much a law as that which hangs a man for murder. The sum voted to meet the expense was to be apportioned with the other taxes, among the citizens by the assessors, collected by the collector, received and paid by another officer, etc. After this important act of legislation, the meeting adjourned.

The next body in the scale of the government is the board of supervisors. It is composed of the supervisors of each town in a county, who have a very similar legislative authority over the more familiar interests of the county as is possessed by their constituents in the towns themselves. They impose taxes for all objects connected with the expenses of the county. Their authority is, however, a good deal circumscribed, enactments by the state legislature being often necessary to enforce their recommendations. When the question involves an expense heavier than common, and its effects are entirely local, the question is often referred to a final decision of the people in their town meetings. This board audits the accounts, and I believe it appoints a treasurer for the county. So far, you see the process of government is exceedingly simple. The whole legislative duty is discharged in three or four days, and yet the decisions have great influence on the comfort and property of the people. The duties of the officers named

continue for one year, but the same incumbents are frequently continued for a whole life, especially the collectors, treasurers, constables, and clerks.

Each town is also subdivided into school districts and road districts. There are overseers of the schools, who regulate all that belongs to the familiar duties of the common schools of the country, to which anybody may go.

Each township is also a petty electoral district of itself, for all the ordinary purposes of the state and the United States' elections, which are held at the same time and place. The three stations taken for the convenience of the elections, as already mentioned, are selected by the inspectors of the poll, who are five or six of the town officers, named by law, and, of course, chosen annually by the people in their original capacity. Each county chooses its own representatives to the lower branch of the state legislature, the number being according to the amount of the population. The state is again divided into what are called senatorial districts, composed of several contiguous counties, each of which chooses a certain number of representatives, who sit in the upper body of the state legislature. Each state has a right to send to the lower house of Congress a number of representatives in proportion to its entire population. These representatives must be chosen by the people, but the states themselves may regulate the form. Some choose them by a general ticket; that is to say, each citizen votes for the whole number; and some choose them by districts, in which case each citizen votes for the member, or members, who represent his particular district. The latter is the course adopted by New York, and in most of the other large states, in which it is difficult for the characters of so many individuals to be intimately known to everybody.

Now, complicated as this system may seem in words, it is perfectly simple in practice. It is astonishing how clearly it is understood by those who exercise it, and how difficult it is to make a foreigner get a correct idea of its details. All the elections, except those which are made at the town meetings, where other duties necessarily assemble the citizens, are held at the same time and at the same place. Thus, an American in one of the more populous states can exercise all his constitutional rights at an expense commonly of a ride of four or five miles at the outside and of three hours of time.

The election on the present occasion embraced senators (always for the state), representatives in the Assembly, governor, lieutenant governor, etc. The inspectors were assembled in a quiet room of the inn, with the ballot boxes placed before them on a table. The voters entered at their leisure and delivered their different ballots to the officers who, holding them up as lottery numbers are usually exhibited, called the name of the voter aloud and then deposited the ballot in its proper box. "I challenge that vote," cried an individual, as the name of one man was thus proclaimed. It appeared there were doubts of its legality. An inquiry was instituted, an oath proffered, explanations were made, and the challenge was withdrawn. The vote was then received. Anyone who votes may challenge. Nothing could be more quiet and orderly than this meeting. A few handbills were posted around the house proclaiming the names and extolling the qualities of the different candidates, and I heard one or two men disputing the wisdom of certain public measures, rather in irony than in heat.

The election was not, however, esteemed a warm one, and perhaps quite one-third of the people did not attend the polls at all. Mr. Clinton, the governor, under whose administration the "canal policy," as it is called, has been fostered, had declined a reelection at the expiration of the official term preceding the one now in existence. His place had been filled by another. In the meantime, his political adversaries, profiting by a momentary possession of a legislative majority, had ventured to assail him in a manner the people were not disposed to relish. He was removed from a seat at the "canal board," a measure which was undoubtedly intended to separate him, as far as possible, from a policy that was already conferring incalculable advantage on the state. The instant Cadwallader was told of this ill-advised and illiberal measure, he exclaimed that the political adversaries of this gentleman had reseated him in the chair of the government. When asked for an explanation, my friend answered that the people, though they sometimes visited political blunders with great severity, rarely tolerated persecution. The event has justified his predictions. Although a popular candidate was selected to oppose him, Mr. Clinton has triumphed in this election by an immense majority, and, in a few days, he will become governor of the state for another term of two years.[2]

After quitting the poll, we familiarly discussed the merits and demerits of this system of popular elections. In order to extract the opinions of my friend, several of the more obvious and ordinary objections were started, with a freedom that induced him to speak with some seriousness.

"You see a thousand dangers in universal suffrage," he said, "merely because you have been taught to think so, without ever having seen the experiment tried. The Austrian would be very apt to say, under the influence of mere speculation, too, that it would be fatal to government to have any representation at all; and a vizier of the Grand Turk might find the mild exercise of the laws, which is certainly practised in Austria proper, altogether fatal to good order. Now, we know, not from the practice of fifty years only but from the practice of two centuries, that it is very possible to

2. No voter can put in two ballots, since all are compelled to place them in the hands of an inspector. In case two ballots are found rolled together, both are rejected. Thus fraud is impossible.

have both order and prosperity under a form of government which admits of the utmost extension of the suffrage. It is a never failing argument on these subjects that American order is owing to the morality of a simple condition of life, and that our prosperity is incidental to our particular geographical situation. There are many good men, and, in other respects wise men, even among ourselves, who retain so much of the political theory which pervades the literature of our language as to believe the same thing. For myself, I cannot see the truth of either of these positions. Our prosperity is owing to our intelligence, and our intelligence to our institutions. Every discreet man in America is deeply impressed with the importance of diffusing instruction among our people, just as many very well-meaning persons in your hemisphere honestly enough entertain a singular horror of the danger of schoolbooks, Thus it is our natural means of safety to do the very thing which must, of necessity, have the greatest possible influence on the happiness, civilization, and power of a nation.

"There can be no doubt that, under a bald theory, a representation would be all the better if the most ignorant, profligate, and vagabond part of the community were excluded from the right of voting. It is just as true that if all the rogues and corrupt politicians, even including those who read Latin and have well-lined pockets, could be refused the right of voting, honest men would fare all the better. But as it is very well known that the latter are not, nor cannot well be, excluded from the right of suffrage anywhere, except in a despotism, we have come to the conclusion that it is scarcely worthwhile to do so much violence to natural justice, without sufficient reason, as to disfranchise a man merely because he is poor. Though a trifling *qualification* of property may sometimes be useful, in particular conditions of society, there can be no greater fallacy than its *representation*. The most vehement declaimers in favor of the

justice of the representation of property overlook two or three very important points of the argument. A man may be a voluntary associate in a joint stock company and justly have a right to a participation in its management, in proportion to his pecuniary interest; but life is not a chartered institution.

"Men are born with all their wants and passions, their means of enjoyment, and their sources of misery, without any agency of their own, and frequently to their great discomfort. Now, though government is, beyond a doubt, a sort of compact, it would seem that those who prescribe its conditions are under a natural obligation to consult the rights of the whole. If men, when a little better than common, were anything like perfect, we might hope to see power lodged with safety in the hands of a reasonable portion of the enlightened, without any danger of its abuse. But the experience of the world goes to prove that there is a tendency to monopoly wherever power is reposed in the hands of a minority. Nothing is more likely to be true than that twenty wise men will unite in opinion in opposition to a hundred fools; but nothing is more certain than that, if placed in situations to control all the interests of their less-gifted neighbors, the chance is that fifteen or sixteen of them would pervert their philosophy to selfishness.

"This was at least our political creed, and we therefore admitted a vast majority of the community to a right of voting. Since the hour of the Revolution, the habits, opinions, laws, and, I may say, principles of the Americans are getting daily to be more democratic. We are perfectly aware that, while the votes of a few thousand scattered individuals can make no great or lasting impression on the prosperity or policy of the country, their disaffection at being excluded might give a great deal of trouble. I do not mean to say that the suffrage may not, in most countries, be extended too far. I only wish to show you that it is not here.

"The theory of representation of property

says that the man who has little shall not dispose of the money of him who has more. Now, what say experience and common sense? It is the man who has *much* that is prodigal of the public purse. A sum that is trifling in his account may constitute the substance of one who is poorer. Beyond all doubt, the government of the world, which is most reckless of the public money, is that in which power is the exclusive property of the very rich; and, beyond all doubt, the government of the world which, compared with its means, is infinitely the most sparing of its resources is that in which they who enact the laws are compelled to consult the wishes of those who have the least to bestow. It is idle to say that an enlarged and liberal policy governs the measures of the one, and that the other is renowned for a narrowness which has lessened its influence and circumscribed its prosperity. I know not, nor care not, what men who are dazzled with the glitter of things may choose to say; but I am thoroughly convinced from observation that, if the advice of those who were influenced by what is called a liberal policy had been followed in our country, we should have been a poorer and, consequently, a less important and less happy people than at present. The relations between political liberality and what is called political prodigality are wonderfully intimate.

"We find that our government is cheaper, and even stronger, for being popular. There is no doubt that the jealousy of those who have little often induces a false economy, and that money might frequently be saved by bidding higher for talent. We lay no claims to perfection, but we do say that more good is attained in this manner than in any other which is practised elsewhere. We look at the aggregate of advantage, and neither our calculations nor our hopes have, as yet, been greatly deceived.

"As to the forms of our elections, you see that they are beyond example simple and orderly. After an experience of near forty years, I can say that I have never seen a blow struck, nor any other violent proceeding, at a poll. These things certainly do happen but, in comparison with the opportunities, at remarkably long intervals. So far from the frequency of elections tending to disturb society, they produce an exactly different effect. A contest which is so soon to be repeated loses half its interest by familiarity. Vast numbers of electors are content to be lookers-on, rarely approaching a poll, except to vote on some question of peculiar concern. The struggle is generally whether A or B shall enjoy the temporary honor or the trifling emolument in dispute, the community seldom being much the better or the worse for the choice.

"People talk of the fluctuations which are necessarily the consequences of a popular government. They do not understand what they say. Every other enlightened nation of the earth is at this moment divided between great opposing principles, whereas here, if we except the trifling collisions of pecuniary interests, every body is of the same mind, except as to the ordinarily immaterial question of a choice between men. We have settled all the formidable points of policy by conceding everything that any reasonable man can ask. The only danger which exists to the duration of our Confederacy (and that is not a question of a form of government but one of mere policy) proceeds from the little that is aristocratical in our Union. The concentrated power of a state may become, like the overgrown power of an individual, dangerous to our harmony, though we think, and with very good reason, that, on the whole, even this peculiarity adds to the durability of the Union.

"It is unnecessary to say that so far as mere convenience goes, this method of election can be practised by 100 million people as easily as by 12. As to corruption, comparatively speaking, it cannot exist. No man can buy a state, a county, or even a town. In a hotly contested election, it is certainly sometimes practicable to influence votes enough to turn the scale; but, unless the question involve the peculiar interest of the less fortunate class of society, it is clear both parties can bribe alike, and then the evil corrects itself. If the question be one likely to unite the interests and the prejudices of the humbler classes, nine times in ten it is both more humane and wiser that they should prevail. That sort of splendid and treacherous policy which gives a fallacious luster to a nation by oppressing those who have the most need of support is manifestly as unwise as it is unjust. It violates the very principles of the compact, since governments are not formed to achieve but to protect. After a sufficient force has been obtained to effect the first great objects of the association, the governed, and not the governors, are the true agents in every act of national prosperity. Look at America. What people, or what monarch, if you will, has done half so much as we have done (compared to our means) in the last half century, and precisely for the reason that the government is obliged to content itself with protection, or, at the most, with that assistance which, in the nature of things, strictly requires a concentrated action.

"It is of far less importance, according to our notions, what the executive of a nation is called than that all classes should have a direct influence on its policy. We have no king, it is true, for the word carries with it, to our ears, an idea of expenditure; but we have a head who, for the time being, has a very reasonable portion of power. We are not jealous of him, for we have taken good care he shall do no harm.

"Though we are glad to find that principles which we have practised, and under which we have prospered so long, are coming more in fashion in Europe, I think you must do us the justice to say that we are not a nation much addicted to the desire of proselyting. For ourselves we have no fears, and as for other people, if they make some faint imitations of our system, and then felicitate themselves on their progress, we are well content they should have all the merit of inventors. That is a miserable rivalry which would make a monopoly of happiness. I think, as a people, we rather admire you most when we see you advancing with moderation to your object than when we hear of the adoption of sudden and violent means. We have ever been reformers rather than revolutionists. Our own struggle for independence was not in its aspect a revolution. We contrived to give it all the dignity of a war from the first blow. Although our generals and soldiers might not have been so well trained as those they fought against, they were far more humane, considerate, and, in the end, successful, than their adversaries.

"Our own progress has been gradual. It is not long since a trifling restriction existed on the suffrage of this very state. Experience proved that it excluded quite as many discreet men as its removal would admit of vagabonds. Now it is the distinguishing feature of our policy that we consider man a reasonable being, and that we rather court than avoid the struggle between ignorance and intelligence. We find that this policy rarely fails to assure the victory of the latter, while it keeps down its baneful monopolies. We extended the suffrage to include everybody, and, while complaint is removed, we find no difference in the representation. As yet, it is rather an improvement. Should it become an evil, however, we shall find easy and moderate means to change it, since we are certain that a majority will be sufficiently sagacious to know their own interests. You have only to convince us that it is the best government, and we will become an absolute monarchy tomorrow. It is wonderful how prone we are to adopt that which expectation induces us to think will be expedient, and to reject that which experience teaches us is bad.

"It must be confessed that, so far, all our experiments have been in favor of democracy. I very well know that you in Europe prophesy that our career will end in monarchy. To be candid, your prophecies excite but little feeling here, since we have taken up the opinion you don't very well understand the subject. But should it prove true, *à la bonne heure;* when we find that form of government best, depend on it, we shall not hesitate to adopt it. You are at perfect liberty, if you will, to establish a journal in favor of despotism under the windows of the capitol. I will not promise you much patronage at first, neither do I think you will be troubled with much serious opposition. At all events, there is nothing in the law to molest the speculation. Now look behind you at the 'poll' we have just left; reflect on this fact and then draw your conclusion of our own opinion, of the stability of our institutions. We may deceive ourselves, but you of Europe must exhibit a far more accurate knowledge of the state of our country before we shall rely on your crude prognostics rather than on our own experience."

I could scarcely assure myself that Cadwallader was not laughing at me during a good deal of the time he was speaking, but, after all, it must be confessed there is some common sense in what he said. There were three or four other passengers in the stage, men of decent and sober exterior, among whom I detected certain interchanges of queer glances, though none of them appeared to think the subject of any very engrossing interest. Provoked at their unreasonable indifference to a theme so delightful as liberty, I asked one of them if he did not apprehend there would be an end to the republic should General Jackson become the next President?

"I rather think not," was his deliberate, and somewhat laconic, answer.

"Why not? He is a soldier and a man of ambition." My unmoved yeoman did not care to dispute either of these qualities, but he still persevered in thinking there was not much danger, since he "did not know any one in his neighborhood who was much disposed to help a man in such an undertaking."

It is provoking to find a whole nation dwelling in this species of alarming security, for no other reason than that their vulgar and everyday practices teach them to rely on themselves, instead of trusting to the rational inferences of philanthropic theorists, who have so long been racking their ingenuity to demonstrate that a condition of society which has delusively endured for nearly 200 years has been in existence all that time in direct opposition to the legitimate deductions of the science of government.

II.

The American Girl

THE DISTINGUISHING FEATURE of American female manners is nature. The fair creatures are extremely graceful if left to exhibit their blandishments in their own way; but it is very evident that a highly artificial manner in those with whom they associate produces a blighting influence on the ease of even the most polished among them. They appear to me to shrink sensitively from professions and an exaggeration that form no part of their own politeness; and between ourselves, if they are wise, they will retain the unequaled advantage they now possess in carrying refinement no further than it can be supported by simplicity and truth.

They are decidely handsome: a union of beauty in feature and form being, I think, more common than in any part of Europe north of the Adriatic. In general, they are delicate; a certain feminine air, tone of voice, size, and grace being remarkably frequent. In the Northern, Eastern and Middle states, which contain much more than half the whole population of the country, the women are fair; though brunettes are not infrequent; and just as blondes are admired in France, they are much esteemed here, especially, as is often the case, if the hair and eyes happen to correspond. Indeed, it is difficult to imagine any creature more attractive than an American beauty between the ages of fifteen and eighteen. There is something in the bloom, delicacy, and innocence of one of these young things that reminds you of the conceptions which poets and painters have taken of the angels.

I think delicacy of air and appearance at that age, though perhaps scarcely more enchanting than what one sees in England, is even more common here than in the mother country, especially when it is recollected how many more faces necessarily pass before the eye in a given time in the latter nation than in this. It is often said that the women of this climate fade earlier than in the northern countries of Europe, and I confess I was, at first, inclined to believe the opinion true. That it is not true to the extent that it is commonly supposed, I am, however, convinced by the reasoning of Cadwallader, if indeed it be true at all.

Perhaps a great majority of the females marry before the age of twenty, and it is not an uncommon thing to see them mothers at sixteen, seventeen, or eighteen. Almost every American mother nurses her own infant. It is far more common to find them mothers of eight or of ten children, at fifty, than mothers of two or three. Now the human form is not completely developed in the northern moiety of this Union earlier than in France or in England. These early marriages, which are the fruits of abundance, have an obvious tendency to impair the powers of the female and to produce a premature decay. In addition to this cause, which is far more general than you may be disposed to believe, there is something in the customs of the country which may have a tendency not only to assist the ravages of time but to prevent the desire to conceal them.

There is no doubt that the animal as well as the moral man is far less artificial here than in Europe. There is thought to be something deceptive in the use of the ordinary means of aiding nature, which offends the simple manners of the nation. Even so common an ornament as rouge is denied, and no woman dares confess that she uses it. There is something so particularly soft and delicate in the color of the young females one sees in the streets here that at first I was inclined to give them credit for the art with which they applied the tints; but Cadwallader gravely assured me I was wrong. He had no doubt that certain individuals did, in secret, adopt the use of rouge; but within the whole circuit of his acquaintance he could not name one whom he even suspected of the practice. Indeed, several gentlemen have gone so far as to assure me that when a woman rouged, it is considered in this country as *prima facie* testimony that her character is frail.

It should also be remembered that when an American girl marries, she no longer entertains the desire to interest any but her husband. There is perhaps something in the security of matrimony that is not very propitious to female blandishments, and one ought to express no surprise that the wife who is content with the affections of her husband should grow a little indifferent to the admiration of the rest of the world. One rarely sees married women foremost in the gay scenes. They attend, as observant and influencing members of society, but not as the principal actors. It is thought that the amusements of the world are more appropriate to the young, who are neither burdened nor sobered with matrimonial duties, and who possess an inherent right to look about them in the morning of life in quest of the partner who is to be their companion to its close. And yet I could name, among my acquaintances here, a dozen of the youngest looking mothers of large and grown-up families that I remember ever to have seen.

The freedom of intercourse which is admitted between the young of the two sexes in America, and which undeniably is admitted with impunity, is to me, who have so long been kept sighing in the distance, perfectly amazing. I have met with self-sufficient critics from our side of the Atlantic, who believe, or affect to believe, that this intercourse cannot always be so innocent as is pretended. . . .

You will readily understand that the usages of society must always be more or less tempered by the circles in which they are exhibited. Among those families which can claim to belong to the elite, the liberty allowed to unmarried females, I am inclined to think, is much the same as is practised among the upper classes in England, with this difference, that, as there is less danger of innovation on rank through fortune hunters and fashionable aspirants, so is there less jealousy of their approaches. A young American dances, chats, laughs, and is just as happy in the saloon, as she was a few years before in the nursery. It is expected that the young men would seek her out, sit next her, endeavor to amuse her, and, in short, to make themselves as agreeable as possible. . . . But it is necessary to understand the tone of conversation that is allowed in order to estimate the dangers of this propinquity.

The language of gallantry is never tolerated. A married woman would conceive it an insult, and a girl would be exceedingly apt to laugh in her adorer's face. In order that it should be favorably received, it is necessary that the former should be prepared to forget her virtue, and to the latter, whether sincere or not, it is an absolute requisite that all adulation should at least wear the semblance of sincerity. But he who addresses an unmarried female in this language, whether it be of passion or only feigned, must expect to be exposed, and probably disgraced, unless he should be prepared to support his sincerity by an offer of his hand.

I think I see you tremble at the magnitude of the penalty! I do not mean to say that idle pleasantries, such as are mutually understood to be no more than pleasantries, are not sometimes tolerated; but an American female is exceedingly apt to assume a chilling gravity at the slightest trespass on what she believes, and, between ourselves, rightly believes, to be the dignity of her sex. Here, you will perceive, is a saving custom, and one, too, that it is exceedingly hazardous to infringe, which diminishes one-half of the ordinary dangers of the free communication between the young of the two sexes.

Without doubt, when the youth has once made his choice, he endeavors to secure an interest in the affections of the chosen fair by all those nameless assiduities and secret sympathies which, though they appear to have produced no visible fruits, cannot be unknown to one of your established susceptibility. These attractions lead to love; and love, in this country, nineteen times in twenty, leads to matrimony. But pure, heartfelt affection rarely exhibits itself in the language of gallantry. The latter is no more than a mask, which pretenders assume and lay aside at pleasure; but when the heart is really touched, the tongue is at best but a miserable interpreter of its emotions. I have always ascribed our own forlorn condition to the inability of that mediating member to do justice to the strength of emotions that are seemingly as deep as they are frequent.

54.

Thomas Dartmouth Rice: "Jump, Jim Crow"

"Jim Crow," the African American stereotype who was a famous minstrel show personality throughout the nineteenth century and whose name came later to stand for the segregation of blacks, is said to have been created in 1828 by the white showman, Thomas Dartmouth Rice. Rice blackened his face, wore old clothes, and performed a song and dance routine in which he imitated the jerky movements and unintelligible utterances of an elderly African American he claimed he had once seen. The act was immediately popular and was widely copied by other entertainers. Rice published a version of "Jump, Jim Crow" in 1830, but the song underwent numerous alterations, depending on the time or place of its performance. The version printed here makes reference to some political events of the Jacksonian period.

Source: Brown University, Harris Collection of American Poetry and Plays,
Series of Old American Songs, No. 15.

JUMP, JIM CROW

Come listen all you girls and boys
  I'm just from Tuckahoe;
I'm going to sing a little song —
  My name's Jim Crow.

  Chorus:
  Wheel about, turn about,
  Do just so;
  Every time I wheel about
  I jump Jim Crow.

I'm a roarer on the fiddle,
  And down in old Virginny,
They say I play the skientific
  Like Massa Pagganninny.

Then I go to Washington
  With bank memorial;
But find they talk such nonsense
  I spend my time with Sal.

Then I go to the President
  He ask me what I do;
I put the veto on the boot
  And nullify the shoe.

Then I go to New York,
  To put them right all there;
But find so many tick heads,
  I give up in despair.

I walk down to the Battery
  With Dina by my side;
And there we see Miss Watson,
  The Paganini bride.

She sing so lovely that my heart
  Go pit´ a pat just so;
I wish she'd fall in love with me,
  I'd let Miss Dina go.

55.

JEREMIAH DAY AND JAMES KINGSLEY: Curriculum Changes at Yale

Demands for reform in higher education to make it more relevant to the new American environment had been heard since the Revolution. By the third decade of the nineteenth century, opposition to the traditional course of classical studies was becoming intense. But the reform movement was not without its detractors. One of the strongest statements in favor of the classical system of college education was the Yale Report of 1828, written by Jeremiah Day, president of Yale, and James Kingsley, one of the faculty. Portions of the report, with a concluding statement by the Yale Corporation, are reprinted below.

Source: *American Journal of Science and Arts,* January 1829.

AT A MEETING of the president and fellows of Yale College, Sept. 11, 1827, the following resolution was passed:

> That His Excellency Governor Tomlinson, Rev. President Day, Rev. Dr. Chapin, Hon. Noyes Darling, and Rev. Abel McEwen be a committee to inquire into the expediency of so altering the regular course of instruction in this college as to leave out of said course the study of the *dead languages,* substituting other studies therefor; and either requiring a competent knowledge of said languages as a condition of admittance into the college, or providing instruction in the same for such as shall choose to study them after admittance; and that the said committee be requested to report at the next annual meeting of this corporation.

This committee, at their first meeting in April 1828, after taking into consideration the case referred to them, requested the faculty of the college to express their views on the subject of the resolution.

The expediency of retaining the ancient languages as an essential part of our course of instruction is so obviously connected with the object and plan of education in the college that justice could not be done, to the particular subject of inquiry in the resolution without a brief statement of the nature and arrangement of the various branches of the whole system. The report of the faculty was accordingly made out in two parts — one containing a summary view of the plan of education in the college; the other, an inquiry into the expediency of insisting on the study of the ancient languages.

This report was read to the committee at their meeting in August. The committee reported their views to the corporation at their session in September, who voted to accept the report, and ordered it to be printed, together with the papers read before the committee, or such parts of them as the prudential committee and the faculty should judge it expedient to publish.

REPORT OF THE FACULTY
PART I

WE ARE DECIDEDLY OF THE OPINION that our present plan of education admits of improvement. . . . The guardians of the college appear to have ever acted upon the principle that it ought not to be stationary but continually advancing. Some alteration has accordingly been proposed almost every year from its first establishment. It is with no small surprise, therefore, we occasionally hear the suggestion that our system is unalterable; that colleges were originally planned in the days of monkish ignorance; and that, "by being immovably moored to the same station, they serve only to measure the rapid current of improvement which is passing by them."

How opposite to all this is the real state of facts in this and the other seminaries in the United States. Nothing is more common than to hear those who revisit the college, after a few years absence, express their surprise at the changes which have been made since they were graduated.

Not only the course of studies and the modes of instruction have been greatly varied but whole sciences have, for the first time, been introduced — chemistry, mineralogy, geology, political economy, etc. By raising the qualifications for admission, the standard of attainment has been elevated. Alterations so extensive and frequent satisfactorily prove that if those who are entrusted with the superintendence of the institution still firmly adhere to some of its original features, it is from a higher principle than a blind opposition to salutary reform. Improvements, we trust, will continue to be made as rapidly as they can be without hazarding the loss of what has been already attained.

But perhaps the time has come when we ought to pause and inquire whether it will be sufficient to make *gradual* changes, as heretofore; and whether the whole system is not rather to be broken up and a better one substituted in its stead. From different quarters we have heard the suggestion that our colleges must be new-modeled; that they are not adapted to the spirit and wants of the age; that they will soon be deserted unless they are better accommodated to the business character of the nation.

As this point may have an important bearing upon the question immediately be-

fore the committee, we would ask their indulgence while we attempt to explain, at some length, the nature and object of the present plan of education at the college. We shall in vain attempt to decide on the expediency of retaining or altering our present course of instruction, unless we have a distinct apprehension of the *object* of a collegiate education. . . .

The two great points to be gained in intellectual culture are the *discipline* and the *furniture* of the mind; expanding its powers and storing it with knowledge. The former of these is, perhaps, the more important of the two. . . .

In laying the foundation of a thorough education, it is necessary that *all* the important mental faculties be brought into exercise. It is not sufficient that one or two be cultivated while others are neglected. . . . In the course of instruction in this college, it has been an object to maintain such a proportion between the different branches of literature and science as to form in the student a proper *balance* of character.

From the pure mathematics he learns the art of demonstrative reasoning. In attending to the physical sciences he becomes familiar with facts, with the process of induction, and the varieties of probable evidence. In ancient literature he finds some of the most finished models of taste. By English reading he learns the powers of the language in which he is to speak and write. By logic and mental philosophy he is taught the art of thinking; by rhetoric and oratory, the art of speaking. By frequent exercise on written composition he acquires copiousness and accuracy of expression. By extemporaneous discussion he becomes prompt and fluent and animated. It is a point of high importance that eloquence and solid learning should go together; that he who has accumulated the richest treasures of thought should possess the highest powers of oratory. . . .

No one feature in a system of intellectual education is of greater moment than such an arrangement of duties and motives as will most effectually throw the student upon the *resources of his own mind.* Without this, the whole apparatus of libraries and instruments and specimens and lectures and teachers will be insufficient to secure distinguished excellence. The scholar must form himself by his own exertions. . . .

A most important feature in the colleges of this country is that the students are generally of an age which requires that a substitute be provided for parental superintendence. When removed from under the roof of their parents and exposed to the untried scenes of temptation, it is necessary that some faithful and affectionate guardian take them by the hand and guide their steps. This consideration determines the *kind* of government which ought to be maintained in our colleges. . . .

The parental character of college government requires that the students should be so collected together as to constitute one family; that the intercourse between them and their instructors may be frequent and familiar. This renders it necessary that suitable buildings be provided for the residence of the students — we speak now of colleges in the country, the members of which are mostly gathered from a distance. In a large city, where the students reside with their parents, public rooms only are needed. This may be the case, also, in professional institutions in which the students are more advanced in age and, therefore, do not require a minute superintendence on the part of their instructors.

Having now stated what we understand to be the proper *object* of an education at this college, viz., to lay a solid *foundation* in literature and science, we would ask permission to add a few observations on the *means* which are employed to effect this object.

In giving the course of instruction, it is intended that a due proportion be observed between lectures and the exercises which are familiarly termed recitations; that is, examinations in a textbook. . . . But we are far

from believing that *all* the purposes of instruction can be best answered by lectures alone. They do not always bring upon the student a pressing and definite responsibility. He may repose upon his seat and yield a passive hearing to the lecturer without ever calling into exercise the active powers of his own mind. This defect we endeavor to remedy, in part, by frequent examinations on the subjects of the lectures. Still it is important that the student should have opportunities of retiring by himself and giving a more commanding direction to his thoughts than when listening to oral instruction. To secure his steady and earnest efforts is the great object of the daily examinations or recitations. In these exercises, a textbook is commonly the guide. . . .

Opportunity is given, however, to our classes for a full investigation and discussion of particular subjects, in the written and extemporaneous disputes, which constitute an important part of our course of exercises. So far as the student has time to extend his inquiries beyond the limits of his textbook, first faithfully studied, his instructor may aid him greatly by referring to the various authors who have treated of the more important points in the lessons; and by introducing corrections, illustrations, and comments of his own. . . .

We deem it to be indispensable to a proper adjustment of our collegiate system that there should be in it both professors and tutors. There is wanted, on the one hand, the experience of those who have been long resident at the institution, and, on the other, the fresh and minute information of those who, having more recently mingled with the students, have a distinct recollection of their peculiar feelings, prejudices, and habits of thinking. At the head of each great division of science, it is necessary that there should be a professor to superintend the department, to arrange the plan of instruction, to regulate the mode of conducting it, and to teach the more important and difficult parts of the subject. . . .

The collegiate course of study, of which we have now given a summary view, we hope may be carefully distinguished from several *other* objects and plans with which it has been too often confounded. It is far from embracing *everything* which the student will ever have occasion to learn. The object is not to *finish* his education but to lay the foundation and to advance as far in rearing the superstructure as the short period of his residence here will admit. If he acquires here a thorough knowledge of the principles of science, he may then, in a great measure, educate himself. He has, at least, been taught *how* to learn. . . .

The course of instruction which is given to the undergraduates in the college is not designed to include professional studies. Our object is not to teach that which is peculiar to any one of the professions but to lay the foundation which is common to them all. There are separate schools for medicine, law, and theology connected with the college, as well as in various parts of the country, which are open for the reception of all who are prepared to enter upon the appropriate studies of their several professions. With these, the academical course is not intended to interfere.

But why, it may be asked, should a student waste his time upon studies which have no immediate connection with his future profession? . . . Is a man to have no other object than to obtain a *living* by professional pursuits? Has he not duties to perform to his family, to his fellow citizens, to his country — duties which require various and extensive intellectual furniture?

Professional studies are designedly excluded from the course of instruction at college to leave room for those literary and scientific acquisitions which, if not commenced there, will, in most cases, never be made. They will not grow up spontaneously, amid the bustle of business. We are not here speaking of those giant minds which, by their native energy, break through the obstructions of a defective education and cut

their own path to distinction. These are honorable exceptions to the general law, not examples for common imitation. . . .

As our course of instruction is not intended to complete an education in theological, medical, or legal science, neither does it include all the minute details of mercantile, mechanical, or agricultural concerns. These can never be effectually learned except in the very circumstances in which they are to be practised. The young merchant must be trained in the counting room, the mechanic in the workshop, the farmer in the field. . . .

If suitable arrangements were made, the details of mercantile, mechanical, and agricultural education, might be taught at the college, to resident graduates. Practical skill would then be grounded upon scientific information. . . .

To bring down the principles of science to their practical application by the laboring classes is the office of men of superior education. It is the separation of theory and practice which has brought reproach upon both. Their union alone can elevate them to their true dignity and value. The man of science is often disposed to assume an air of superiority when he looks upon the narrow and partial views of the mere artisan. The latter, in return, laughs at the practical blunders of the former. The defects in the education of both classes would be remedied by giving them a knowledge of scientific principles preparatory to practice.

We are aware that a thorough education is not within the reach of all. Many, for want of time and pecuniary resources, must be content with a partial course. A defective education is better than none. This, we are well convinced, is far preferable to a *superficial* education. Of all the plans of instruction which have been offered to the public, that is the most preposterous which proposes to teach almost everything in a short time. In this way, nothing is effectually taught. The pupil is hurried over the surface so rapidly that scarce a trace of his steps remains when he has finished his course. . . .

But why, it is asked, should *all* the students in a college be required to tread in the same steps? Why should not each one be allowed to select those branches of study which are most to his taste, which are best adapted to his peculiar talents, and which are most nearly connected with his intended profession? To this we answer that our prescribed course contains those subjects only which ought to be understood, as we think, by everyone who aims at a thorough education. . . .

It is sometimes thought that a student ought not to be urged to the study of that for which he has no taste or capacity. But how is he to know whether he has a taste or capacity for a science before he has even entered upon its elementary truths? If he is really destitute of talent sufficient for these common departments of education, he is destined for some narrow sphere of action. But we are well persuaded that our students are not so deficient in intellectual powers as they sometimes profess to be, though they are easily made to believe that they have no capacity for the study of that which they are told is almost wholly useless.

When a class has become familiar with the common elements of the several sciences, then is the proper time for them to divide off to their favorite studies. They can then make their choice from actual trial. This is now done here, to some extent, in our junior year. The division might be commenced at an earlier period, and extended further, provided the qualifications for admission into the college were brought to a higher standard.

If the view which we have thus far taken of the subject is correct, it will be seen that the object of the system of instruction at this college is not to give a *partial* education consisting of a few branches only; nor, on the other hand, to give a *superficial* education containing a smattering of almost everything; nor to *finish* the details of either a professional or practical education; but to *commence* a *thorough* course and to carry it as far as the time of residence here will allow. It is intended to occupy to the best advantage the four years immediately preceding the study of a profession or of the operations which are peculiar to the higher mercantile, manufacturing, or agriculture establishments. . . .

Our institution is not modeled exactly after the pattern of European universities. . . . In this country, our republican habits and feelings will never allow a monopoly of literature in any one place. There must be in the Union as many colleges, at least, as states. Nor would we complain of this arrangement as inexpedient provided that starvation is not the consequence of a patronage so minutely divided. We anticipate no disastrous results from the multiplication of colleges if they can only be adequately endowed. We are not without apprehensions, however, that a feeble and stinted growth of our national literature will be the consequence of the very scanty supply of means to most of our public seminaries.

The universities on the continent of Europe, especially in Germany, have of late gained the notice and respect of men of information in this country. They are upon a broad and liberal scale, affording very great facilities for a finished education. But we doubt whether they are models to be copied in every feature by our American colleges. We hope, at least, that this college may be spared the mortification of a ludicrous attempt to imitate them while it is unprovided with the resources necessary to execute the purpose. . . .

One of the pleas frequently urged in favor of a partial education is the alleged *want of time* for a more enlarged course. We are well aware, as we have already observed, that a thorough education cannot be begun and finished in four years. But if three years immediately preceding the age

(Right) Jeremiah Day, portrait by Samuel F. B. Morse; (far right) James L. Kingsley, portrait by Nathaniel Jocelyn

of twenty-one be allowed for the study of a profession, there is abundant time previous to this for the attainment of all which is now required for admission into the college, in addition to the course prescribed for the undergraduates.

Though the limit of age for admission is fixed by our laws at fourteen, yet how often have we been pressed to dispense with the rule in behalf of some youth who has completed his preparation at an earlier period; and who, if compelled to wait till he has attained the requisite age, "is in danger of being ruined for want of employment"? May we not expect that this plea will be urged with still greater earnestness when the present improved methods of instruction in the elementary and preparatory schools are more and more accelerating the early progress of the pupil?

But suppose it should happen that the student, in consequence of commencing his studies at a later period, should be delayed a little longer before entering upon the duties of his profession; is this a sacrifice worthy to be compared with the immense difference between the value of a limited and a thorough education? Is a young man's pushing forward into business so indispensable to his future welfare that, rather than suspend it for a single year, he must forego all the advantage of superior intellectual discipline and attainments?

We well know that the whole population of the country can never enjoy the benefit of a thorough course of education. A large portion must be content with the very limited instruction in our primary schools. Others may be able to add to this the privilege of a few months at an academy. Others still, with higher aims and more ample means, may afford to spend two or three years in attending upon a partial course of study in some institution which furnishes instruction in any branch or branches selected by the pupil or his parents. The question is then presented, whether the college shall have all the variety of classes and departments which are found in academies; or whether it shall confine itself to the single object of a well-proportioned and thorough course of study.

It is said that the public now demand that the doors should be thrown open to all; that education ought to be so modified and varied as to adapt it to the exigencies of the country and the prospects of different individuals; that the instruction given to those who are destined to be merchants, or manufacturers, or agriculturalists should have a special reference to their respective professional pursuits.

The public are undoubtedly right in demanding that there should be appropriate courses of education accessible to all classes of youth. And we rejoice at the prospect of ample provision for this purpose in the improvement of our academies and the establishment of commercial high schools, gymnasia, lycea, agricultural seminaries, etc. But do the public insist that every college shall become a high school, gymnasium, lyceum, and academy? Why should we interfere with these valuable institutions? Why wish to take their business out of their hands? The college has its appropriate object and they have theirs. . . . No portion of our resources or strength or labor can be diverted to other purposes without impairing the education which we are attempting to give. . . .

But might we not, by making the college more accessible to different descriptions of persons, enlarge our numbers and in that way increase our income? This might be the operation of the measure for a very short time, while a degree from the college should retain its present value in public estimation — a value depending entirely upon the character of the education which we give. But the moment it is understood that the institution has descended to an inferior standard of attainment, its reputation will sink to a corresponding level. After we shall have become a college in *name only*, and in reality nothing more than an academy, or half college and half academy, what will induce parents in various and distant parts of the country to send us their sons, when they have academies enough in their own neighborhood? There is no magical influence in an act of incorporation to give celebrity to a literary institution which does not command respect for itself by the elevated rank of its education. . . .

The unexampled multiplication of schools and academies in this country requires that colleges should aim at a high standard of literary excellence. The conviction is almost universal that the former as well as the latter admit of great improvements. But who are to make these improvements, and give character and tone to our systems of instruction, if there are few men of thorough education in the country? He who is to arrange an extensive scheme of measures ought himself to stand on an eminence from which he can command a view of the whole field of operation. Superficial learning in our higher seminaries will inevitably

extend its influence to the inferior schools. If the fountains are shallow and turbid, the streams cannot be abundant and pure. Schools and colleges are not *rival* institutions. The success of each is essential to the prosperity of the other.

Our republican form of government renders it highly important that great numbers should enjoy the advantage of a thorough education. On the Eastern continent, the *few* who are destined to particular departments in political life may be educated for the purpose, while the mass of the people are left in comparative ignorance. But in this country, where offices are accessible to all who are qualified for them, superior intellectual attainments ought not to be confined to any description of persons. Merchants, manufacturers, and farmers, as well as professional gentlemen, take their places in our public councils. A thorough education ought, therefore, to be extended to all these classes. It is not sufficient that they be men of sound judgment who can decide correctly and give a silent vote on great national questions. Their influence upon the minds of others is needed — an influence to be produced by extent of knowledge and the force of eloquence. Ought the speaking in our deliberative assemblies to be confined to a single profession? If it is knowledge which gives us the command of physical agents and instruments, much more is it that which enables us to control the combinations of moral and political machinery. . . .

The active, enterprising character of our population renders it highly important that this bustle and energy should be directed by sound intelligence, the result of deep thought and early discipline. The greater the impulse to action, the greater is the need of wise and skillful guidance. When nearly all the ship's crew are aloft, setting the topsails and catching the breezes, it is necessary there should be a steady hand at helm. Light and moderate learning is but poorly fitted to direct the energies of a nation so widely extended, so intelligent, so powerful in resources, so rapidly advancing in population, strength, and opulence. Where a free government gives full liberty to the human intellect to expand and operate, education should be proportionably liberal and ample. When even our mountains and rivers and lakes are upon a scale which seems to denote that we are destined to be a great and mighty nation, shall our literature be feeble and scanty and superficial?

REPORT OF THE FACULTY
PART II

BY A LIBERAL EDUCATION, it is believed, has been generally understood such a course of discipline in the arts and sciences as is best calculated, at the same time, both to strengthen and enlarge the faculties of the mind, and to familiarize it with the leading principles of the great objects of human investigation and knowledge. . . . The subject of inquiry now presented is whether the plan of instruction pursued in Yale College is sufficiently accommodated to the present state of literature and science; and especially whether such a change is demanded as would leave out of this plan the study of the Greek and Roman classics and make an acquaintance with ancient literature no longer necessary for a degree in the liberal arts. . . .

The claims of classical learning . . . may be defended not only as a necessary branch of education in the present state of the world, but on the ground of its distinct and independent merits. . . . But the study of the classics is useful, not only as it lays the foundations of a correct taste and furnishes the student with those elementary ideas which are found in the literature of modern times, and which he nowhere so well acquires as in their original sources, but also as the study itself forms the most effectual discipline of the mental faculties. . . .

Classical discipline, likewise, forms the best preparation for professional study. The interpretation of language and its correct use are nowhere more important than in the professions of divinity and law. But in a course of classical education, every step familiarizes the mind with the structure of language and the meaning of words and phrases. In researches of an historical nature, and many such occur in the professions, a knowledge, especially of the Latin language, is often indispensable. The use of a thorough knowledge of Greek to a theologian no one will deny. . . .

In the profession of medicine, the knowledge of the Greek and Latin languages is less necessary now than formerly; but even at the present time it may be doubted whether the facilities which classical learning affords for understanding and rendering familiar the terms of science do not more than counterbalance the time and labor requisite for obtaining this learning. . . .

For these very obvious advantages which now attend the study of classical literature in the college, the course of study which, it is understood, would be proposed as a substitute, promises but few and partial equivalents. Instead of the poems of Homer, which have had so extensive and important an influence on the heroic poetry of all succeeding times, and which, it cannot be denied, are constantly appealed to as establishing many of the most important canons of criticism, we are presented, in several new courses, with the *Henriade* of Voltaire; and the history of Charles XII of the same author, in place of the historical writings of Livy and Tacitus. . . .

Or to make the inquiry more general — in order to understand the true spirit and genius of English literature, which is of the greatest practical use, the literature of France or the literature of Greece and Rome? The most superficial acquaintance with the principal authors in our language is sufficient to excite wonder that such questions should be seriously asked.

If the new course proposed, considered as an introduction to a knowledge of general literature, is altogether inferior to the old, and far less practical in its character, it will be found not less deficient for the purposes of mental discipline. . . .

Nor is this course of education which excludes ancient literature less objectionable as the foundation of professional study. The student who has limited himself to French, Italian, and Spanish is very imperfectly prepared to commence a course of either divinity or law. He knows less of the literature of his own country than if he had been educated in the old method; the faculties of his mind have been brought into less vigorous exercise; and the sources of the knowledge which he is now to acquire are less accessible. If it is said that the course of exclusive modern literature is intended for those who are not designed for professional life, the reply is that the number of those who obtain a liberal education without at first deciding whether they shall be professional men or not is far from inconsiderable. Many who originally suppose their minds determined on this subject alter their determinations from circumstances which they could not foresee. Adopt the course proposed, and many would enter upon it merely from its novelty; more from a persuasion that it would be attended with less labor; and the consequence would be that the college, so far as this cause should operate, would be the means of lowering the professional character of our country. . . .

To begin with the modern languages in a course of education is to reverse the order of nature. Modern languages, with most of our students, are studied and will continue to be studied as an accomplishment rather than as a necessary acquisition. . . . To suppose the modern languages more practical than the ancient to the great body of our students, because the former are now spoken in some parts of the world, is an obvious fallacy. The proper question is — What course of discipline affords the best mental culture, leads to the most thorough knowledge of our own literature, and lays

the best foundation for professional study? The ancient languages have here a decided advantage. . . .

No question has engaged the attention of the faculty more constantly than how the course of education in the college might be improved and rendered more practically useful. Free communications have at all times been held between the faculty and the corporation on subjects connected with the instruction of the college. When the aid of the corporation has been thought necessary, it has been asked; and by this course of proceeding the interests of the institution have been regularly advanced.

No remark is more frequently made by those who visit the college after the absence of some years than that changes have been made for the better; and those who make the fullest investigation are the most ready to approve what they find. The charge, therefore, that the college is stationary, that no efforts are made to accommodate it to the wants of the age, that all exertions are for the purpose of perpetuating abuses, and that the college is much the same as it was at the time of its foundation are wholly gratuitous. The changes in the country during the last century have not been greater than the changes in the college. These remarks have been limited to Yale College. . . . No doubt other colleges . . . might defend themselves with equal success.

REPORT OF THE COMMITTEE OF THE CORPORATION

THE COMMITTEE ARE MUCH GRATIFIED that the faculty, in the document herewith submitted, have taken a comprehensive view of the whole course of instruction, and developed the elements of a liberal education and the principles by which it should be regulated and administered; exhibiting forcibly the intimate connection which classical literature has with other learning and the sciences, and the facilities afforded by its preliminary study in their attainment. . . .

Fully convinced of the importance of the thorough study and an accurate knowledge of the ancient languages, and believing that much misconception regarding their utility has arisen from the fact that they have been but partially studied and acquired, the committee have seen with approbation that within the last twenty-five years those languages have here received increased attention, and that the classical and other attainments required as a qualification for admittance into the college have been considerably augmented. The effect of such augmentation has evidently been to elevate the character of the institution and the standard of scholarship. The period of academic preparation having been prolonged, and consequently the age at which students will ordinarily apply for admittance extended, they are enabled the more successfully to pursue the studies requiring maturity of intellect, and further to advance in learning and science.

Approving highly the course which has hitherto been pursued, the committee entertain the opinion that the terms of admission may very properly be gradually raised so as ultimately to render necessary, as a condition of admission, much greater acquirements, especially in the classics, than the laws of the college at present prescribe. The committee, however, do not deem it advisable that the corporation should act on this subject until they shall have availed themselves of the information and experience of the faculty, and received from them a specific recommendation.

56.

Hugh S. Legaré: On Limiting the Power of the Supreme Court

Hugh S. Legaré was a South Carolina lawyer of national reputation who divided his life between the study and practice of law and government service. Politically he espoused the doctrine of states' rights but in a less extreme form than John C. Calhoun, whom he opposed on the nullification issue. While serving as editor of a Southern periodical, Legaré in 1828 wrote a review of James Kent's Commentaries on American Law, *in which he set forth his position on states' rights. In the following selection from the review he criticized Supreme Court decisions such as that in* M'Culloch v. Maryland, *holding that they tended toward the formation of a consolidated government at the expense of the states.*

Source: *Southern Review*, August 1828.

If anything is taken for granted in this country, as a truth better established than all others, it is that in matters of government we have found out the philosopher's stone — and are now in possession of an infallible secret to make men free and happy, and to keep them so forever, even in spite of themselves. . . . Now, we are heterodox enough to think this not only an error but a most pernicious error. We believe that no constitution in the world is worth a straw but public opinion and national character, and that it is altogether impossible for mortal man to predict what is to be the result of any important change in the distribution of political powers. In a word, that no general principles in politics — except such as are too general to be of much practical utility — can be safely depended upon in the administration of affairs. . . .

If anyone wishes to be convinced how little even the wisest men are able to foresee the results of their own political contrivances, let him read the Constitution, with the contemporaneous exposition of it contained (even) in *The Federalist;* and then turn to this part of Chancellor Kent's work, to the inaugural speech of the present executive of the United States [John Quincy Adams], and to some of the records of Congress during the memorable session which is just past.

He will find that the government has been fundamentally altered by the progress of opinion; that instead of being any longer one of enumerated powers and a circumscribed sphere, as it was beyond all doubt intended to be, it knows absolutely no bounds but the will of a majority of Congress; that instead of confining itself in time of peace to the diplomatic and commercial relations of the country, it is seeking out employment for itself by interfering in the domestic concerns of society, and threatens, in the course of a very few years, to control, in the most offensive and despotic manner, all the pursuits, the interests, the opinions, and the conduct of men. He will find that this extraordinary revolution has been brought about in a good degree by the Supreme Court of the United States, which has applied to the Constitution — very innocently, no doubt, and with commanding ability in argument — and thus given authority and currency to such canons of interpretation as necessarily lead to these extravagant results. Above all, he will be perfectly satisfied that that high tribunal affords, by its own showing, no barrier whatever against the usurpations of Congress, and that the rights of the weaker part of this confederacy may, to any extent, be wantonly and tyrannically violated under color of law (the most grievous shape of oppression) by men neither interested in its destiny nor subject to its control, without any means of redress being left it except such as are inconsistent with all idea of order and government.

Perhaps, he will think with us, that the effect of a written constitution, interpreted by lawyers in a technical manner, is to enlarge power and to sanctify abuse rather to abridge and restrain them; perhaps, he will conclude that the American people have not been sufficiently careful at the beginning of their unprecedented experiment in politics what principles they suffered to be established; perhaps, he may look forward to the future with anxiety and alarm, as holding forth a prospect of a rapid accumulation of power in the hands of those who have already abused it, or, on the contrary, with a strong hope that experience will teach wisdom, and diversified interests and conflicting pretensions lead to moderation in conduct; perhaps (and surely nothing could be more rational), he might wish to see proper means adopted to bring back the government to its first principles, and put an end to the unhappy jealousies and heartburnings which are beginning to embitter one part of our people against another.

We do not undertake to anticipate his inferences, but we have no doubt in the world that he will agree with us as to the *fact;* that he will confess Congress to be, to all intents and purposes, omnipotent in theory, and that if, in practice, it prefer moderate counsels and a just and impartial policy, it will be owing, not to any check in the Constitution but altogether to the vigilance, the wisdom, and the firmness of a free people.

We are not, indeed, sure but that this conclusion will, in the end, be productive of much good, and that we ought rather to rejoice than complain that at so early a period of our history it has been forced upon the public mind — in one part at least of this Confederacy — by evidence too strong to be resisted, and with a depth and seriousness of conviction which promises to make it an active, permanent, and universal principle of conduct. Our political opinions, it appears to us, have been hitherto, in the last degree, wild and visionary. We have been so much accustomed to talk in a high-flown strain of the perfection — the faultless and unalterable perfection — of our institutions that we were beginning to think that everything had been done for us by our predecessors, and that it were impossible to mar their work by any errors of doctrine, or any defect in discipline among ourselves.

We do not sufficiently reflect what a rare and glorious privilege it is to be a free people (in the only proper sense of that term) and how difficult it is, even under the most favorable circumstances, to keep so. We have unbounded faith in forms, and look upon a written constitution as a sort of talisman, which gives to the liberties of a nation "a charmed life." In short, no people was ever so much addicted to abstractions.

It is really curious to look into the debates of Congress when measures pregnant with important consequences are the subject of discussion. The University of Paris, in the heyday of scholastic divinity, never excelled them in the thorny, unprofitable, and unintelligible subtleties of dialectics. Our statesmen are, in general, anything but practical men — a fact that may be, in some degree, accounted for by the vast predominance of mere professional lawyers (not of the first order) and the fact that we have a written Constitution to interpret by technical rules. We look in vain for that plain, manly, unsophisticated good sense — that

South Carolina Historical Society

Lithograph of Hugh Legaré by T. Doney

instinct of liberty, which characterizes the controversial reasoning of the great fathers of the English constitution — the Seldens, the Sidneys, the Prynnes — and their worthy descendants and disciples, the founders of our own Revolution.

A measure is proposed, revolting to the moral sense and the common sense of mankind — unequal and oppressive, inconsistent with the cardinal objects and the whole genius of the government. It is opposed by those upon whom it bears hardest as *unconstitutional;* that is to say, as unfit to be adopted by the rulers of a free people because it is unjust, and is not bona fide intended to fulfill the purposes of the federal compact. Immediately, a metaphysical disputation ensues, and if by such jargon as has immortalized the angelical and seraphic doctors, the constitutionality of the scheme be made to appear *very doubtful*, it is at once assumed by the majority as demonstrated, and, perhaps, acquiesced in by the minority, because the question, if it should be thought sufficiently important, can be tried again before the Supreme Court. The responsibility of those who pass the law is shifted upon those who interpret it; and thus the former venture a great deal further upon questionable ground than they would were their decision entirely without appeal.

If, again, when the law comes before the Supreme Court, that judicatory, from some defects in its constitution or its administration, will not or cannot pronounce it void — the will of the majority is at once considered as sanctified — its act is, of course, lawful, is just, is reasonable and proper. The people at large, after a few unheeded murmurs, submit to this imposing authority and think that their discontents must be unreasonable because their understandings have been puzzled by sophisters and awed by the learning of the bench! In short, the Constitution is made to have the effect of an estoppel (an odious thing in law) upon their just complaints, and they are expected to suffer, like poor Shylock, any hardship which a subtle interpretation can deduce from their "bond." . . .

We venture to predict that no act of the federal government (supposing it to have common discretion) will ever be pronounced unconstitutional in that Court for the simple reason that the principle of M'Culloch's case covers the whole ground of political sovereignty and consecrates usurpation in advance. . . .

M'Culloch's case established a doctrine sufficiently latitudinarian. It gave the government an unbounded discretion in the choice of "means" to effect its constitutional objects. Nor does it confine the exercise of this arbitrary power to cases of absolute necessity. It declares that Congress has the same latitude in matters even of the most doubtful character, by way of *standing policy:* in time of peace, for example, it may do what could only be justified by the pressing exigencies of war, when the urgency of the case creates its own law and supersedes all others. A national bank, is, no doubt, in many points of view an excellent institution, but did anyone ever before hear of such an establishment being founded for the purpose of collecting revenue? But whether as a *means*, "it is necessary and proper" it seems, is for the legislature to decide, and the Court has no right to look into that question.

What is this but to say that Congress may do anything, provided they declare that it is done with a view to effect something else — it is not material what — that is within their undoubted powers? Add to this, the rule laid down in *Fletcher* v. *Peck,* that the *motives* of the lawgiver cannot be looked into by the judges unless he vouchsafe to declare them, and this whole doctrine is as complete as the most ambitious political libertine could wish it to be. . . .

In a country extending over such an immense territory (already comprising a multitude of commonwealths, differing so widely in interests, in character, and in political opinions, and still going on to increase without any assignable limit) it is preposterous to expect that a central government, which shall attempt to meddle with the domestic concerns of society, can be tolerable to its subjects. It will be inevitably *societas mater discordiarum* [society, the mother of discord]; or if two sections should unite to give the law, it would be the most impracticable, impenetrable, and reckless tyranny that ever existed. At all events, whether we have pointed out the true causes of the evil, and whether there be any remedy for it or not, we are satisfied that no purity of character, no rectitude of intention, no superiority of judgment and capacity in the judges of the Supreme Court (and we can scarcely expect greater than it is already distinguished by) will ever enable that tribunal to answer its great end as an umpire between the states and the confederacy. The mischief has already been done — the first step is taken, and the whole *system* is radically wrong.

57.

A Petition for Free Use of Public Lands

The average citizen who wanted to move West to obtain land usually found that most land was either government owned or in the hands of speculators whose prices were too high. Petitions, such as the following of October 1828, were frequently sent to Congress urging that public lands be opened up for settlement without cost. "The settler," as Senator Thomas Hart Benton of Missouri said, "pays the value of the best land in the privations he endures . . . and the labor he performs." But opposition to free land was strong, both on the part of speculators and on the part of Eastern employers, who feared a labor shortage and the resultant high wages should land be offered free of charge to all who wanted it.

Source: *Mechanics' Free Press,* October 25, 1828 [Commons, V, pp. 43-45].

To the honorable the Senate and the House of Representatives of the United States, in Congress assembled:

The undersigned citizens of the United States respectfully suggest to Congress the propriety of placing all the public lands, without the delay of sales, within the reach of the people at large, by the right of a title of occupancy only.

Their reasonings on the case, to be brief, are as follows:

First, that until the public lands shall have been actually put under cultivation, it is clear they will be entirely useless.

Second, that they are fully satisfied that the present state of affairs must lead to the wealth of a few, and thus place within their reach the means of controlling all the lands of our country.

Third, that as all men must occupy a portion of the earth, they have, naturally, a birthright in the soil; and that while this right shall be subject to the control of others, they may be deprived of life, liberty, and the pursuit of happiness.

Fourth, that hence, it is perceived by them that a true spirit of independence cannot be enjoyed by the great body of the people, nor the exercise of freedom secured to them, so long as the use of the soil is withheld.

Fifth, that the general government can be under no necessity of holding these lands as an indemnity for existing appropriations nor for future expenditures. The national debt, within a very few years, will have been liquidated; and the necessary tendency of the revenue to the treasury will then demand more legislation in order to keep its surplus judiciously diffused for the purposes of an efficient circulating medium, than for those of any future constitutional disbursements.

Sixth, that the mere sale of these lands can give little ability to the people in sustaining national expenditures. As the relief thus to be derived could only arise from resources at that time extant, it is clear that this would be but the shifting of existing resources, however insufficient, from the people to the government. But by the widely extensive improvements of an agricultural nature which the general cultivation of these lands would induce, the people would against the hour of emergency, by large additions to the ordinary revenue, have absolutely created the means of meeting all the prospective expenditures of the most generous administration of the general government.

And, finally, that they deprecate every species of monopoly and exclusive privileges, and more especially all those which produce unnatural exclusions with relation to the public lands. . . .

That it is the opinion of your petitioners that (the people themselves being, de facto, the government), were the public lands thus perpetually held only to their use, it would be, perhaps, the only effectual prevention of future monopoly and the best safeguard of the American republic.

That your memorialists recommend to Congress that the public lands be reserved as a donation to the citizens of the United States in the character of perpetual leases, free from rent, and subject to revert to the government when the lessee or his heirs fail to cultivate or occupy it in proper person, for — years together; providing that, in the future location of towns, etc., for general or public purposes, the incidental possessor of the soil, besides a reasonable compensation for it, shall only share and share alike in the lots and other advantages thus to be derived.

That your petitioners therefore pray your honorable body to enact a law authorizing a grant to any individual who shall apply for it, of the free use of so much of the public lands (not less perhaps than twenty nor more than forty acres) as they in their wisdom shall deem sufficient, and limiting its conditions to the principles above suggested.

58.

Anonymous: Abuses of the Apprentice Labor System

The system of apprentices was of benefit both to the poor, who were unable to educate their children in expensive private institutions, and to the master, who gained a continuous and almost free supply of labor. An abundance of laws regulated the apprentice-master relationship during the tenure of service, but after that the master was not legally bound to retain his trainee, who had advanced to the rank of journeyman and could command higher wages. Consequently, many trained and experienced youths were unemployed, their jobs being taken by incoming apprentices. The following protest against this situation, signed "Candidus," was addressed on behalf of the journeymen to the editors of the Mechanics' Free Press, *in November 1828.*

Source: *Mechanics' Free Press,* November 29, 1828 [Commons, V, pp. 70-72].

THE PRACTICE OF MANY MASTER MECHANICS in this city, in employing none but apprentices in their manufacturing establishments, is an evil severely felt by the journeymen of all denominations; for whenever there is a greater number of mechanics than the demand of labor requires, it is evident the surplus must be thrown out of employ. There are men in this city who have from fifteen to twenty apprentices, who never or very seldom have a journeyman in their shops; but to supply the place of journeymen, and to monopolize to themselves trade and wealth, as one apprentice becomes free, another is taken to fill up the ranks. Let us for a moment view the bad effects of this monopolizing policy — I say bad effects because I conceive that whatever system shall be adopted to enrich one man at the expense of the many must be bad and destructive to the public good.

When we bind our sons for five, six, or seven years to learn a trade, it is with an idea that when they have faithfully served out the term of their apprenticeship, they will be enabled at least to find employment as journeymen. This reasonable expectation very often ends in disappointment, for the very moment they assume their independence their troubles begin: they are thrown out of employment by their parsimonious and ungenerous master, with whom no consideration of past services has any weight, and whose heart can melt at the sight of nothing but money.

Hence you see a young man of honest deportment and industrious habits thrown upon the wide world in the bloom of youth, without money, without friends, and without credit; and if he has friends, it often happens they are unable to help him. He applies to the man with whom he has faithfully served his time for employment, but finds none; he goes to others, and is frequently told they transact all their business by the aid of apprentices — here his spirits begin to droop, and his industrious habits and laudable ambition are nipped in the bud. He must now either turn his attention to some laborious work, to which he has not been accustomed, and which is at times difficult to obtain, or turn vaga-

bond at once. It is no wonder that so many young men, under such unfavorable circumstances, are ruined in their morals and reputations; and the world is too apt to throw all the blame upon the unfortunate, while they pass over with impunity the causes that produced it.

There are other master mechanics who are less fortunate than the former; they do much injury to society without enriching or benefiting themselves. These are men who manufacture goods altogether by apprentices, and sell them at so very low a rate that they can scarcely live by the profits.

One of the above description was selling some hats some time ago, and another of the trade asked him how he could afford to sell them so very low. His answer was that if he had not had them manufactured altogether by apprentices, he could not have afforded to have sold them for anything like the price. These men appear to me to injure others without benefiting themselves.

I hope, Messrs. Editors, that some philanthropic spirit will dictate some lawful means to eradicate and destroy such deadly poison circulated throughout the veins of society, and if it cannot be finally rooted out, let us employ the best antidote we can. Let us do good in our day and generation by establishing societies for the protection and help of such unfortunate young men as I have already sufficiently spoken of. If all were master mechanics, there would be no more labor performed than there is at present; but there would be a more equal distribution of the profits of that labor among the members of society, and consequently would destroy the powerful influence of monopolists.   CANDIDUS

———◆———

A Cent and a Half a Mile, a Mile and a Half an Hour.
Slogan (though not entirely complimentary) of the Erie Canal.
It took about six days to get from Albany to Buffalo.

59.

On the Unconstitutionality of the Protective Tariff

The so-called Tariff of Abominations of 1828 was passed at the instigation of Northern manufacturers, but it distressed many Southern planters who depended on foreign trade for their livelihood. Agriculture in South Carolina was undergoing grave difficulties owing to soil exhaustion, and many believed that the extraordinarily high tariffs would damage the state's economy irreparably. During 1828, protests were voiced through Southern newspapers and town meetings, and finally, on December 19, the state legislature issued "The South Carolina Exposition and Protest," which declared the tariff unconstitutional. Drafted by John C. Calhoun, the paper outlined the state's grievances and put forth the doctrine of nullification, according to which a state had the right to declare an act of the national government unconstitutional and void. The "Protest," which followed the "Exposition," appears below.

Source: *The Statutes at Large of South Carolina*, Thomas Cooper, ed., Columbia, Vol. I, 1836, pp. 244-245.

THE SENATE AND HOUSE OF REPRESENTATIVES of South Carolina now met and sitting in General Assembly, through the Hon. William Smith and the Hon. Robert Y. Hayne, their representatives in the Senate of the United States, do, in the name and on behalf of the good people of the said commonwealth, solemnly protest against the system of protecting duties, lately adopted by the federal government, for the following reasons:

First, because the good people of this commonwealth believe that the powers of Congress were delegated to it in trust for the accomplishment of certain specified objects which limit and control them, and that every exercise of them for any other purposes is a violation of the Constitution as unwarrantable as the undisguised assumption of substantive, independent powers not granted or expressly withheld.

Second, because the power to lay duties on imports is, and in its very nature can be, only a means of effecting objects specified by the Constitution; since no free government, and least of all a government of enumerated powers, can of right impose any tax, any more than a penalty, which is not at once justified by public necessity and clearly within the scope and purview of the social compact; and since the right of confining appropriations of the public money to such legitimate and constitutional objects is as essential to the liberties of the people as their unquestionable privilege to be taxed only by their consent.

Third, because they believe that the tariff law passed by Congress at its last session, and all other acts of which the principal object is the protection of manufactures or any other branch of domestic industry, if they be considered as the exercise of a power in Congress to tax the people at its own good will and pleasure, and to apply the money raised to objects not specified in the Constitution, is a violation of these fundamental principles, a breach of a well-defined trust, and a perversion of the high powers vested in the federal government for federal purposes only.

Fourth, because such acts, considered in the light of a regulation of commerce, are equally liable to objection. Since, although the power to regulate commerce may, like other powers, be exercised so as to protect domestic manufactures, yet it is clearly distinguishable from a power to do so *eo nomine* [by that name] both in the nature of the thing and in the common acception of the terms; and because the confounding of them would lead to the most extravagant results, since the encouragement of domestic industry implies an absolute control over all the interests, resources, and pursuits of a people and is inconsistent with the idea of any other than a simple, consolidated government.

Fifth, because, from the contemporaneous exposition of the Constitution in the numbers of *The Federalist* (which is cited only because the Supreme Court has recognized its authority), it is clear that the power to regulate commerce was considered by the Convention as only incidentally connected with the encouragement of agriculture and manufactures; and because the power of laying imposts and duties on imports was not understood to justify in any case a prohibition of foreign commodities, except as a means of extending commerce by coercing foreign nations to a fair reciprocity in their intercourse with us, or for some other bona fide commercial purpose.

Sixth, because, while the power to protect manufactures is nowhere expressly granted to Congress, nor can be considered as necessary and proper to carry into effect any specified power, it seems to be expressly reserved to the states by the 10th Section of the 1st Article of the Constitution.

Seventh, because even admitting Congress to have a constitutional right to protect manufactures by the imposition of duties, or by regulations of commerce designed principally for that purpose, yet a tariff of which the operation is grossly unequal and oppressive is such an abuse of power as is incompatible with the principles of a free government and the great ends of civil society — justice and equality, or rights and protection.

Eighth, finally, because South Carolina, from her climate, situation, and peculiar institutions, is and must ever continue to be wholly dependent upon agriculture and commerce, not only for her prosperity but for her very existence as a state; because the valuable products of her soil, the blessings by which Divine Providence seems to have designed to compensate for the great disadvantages under which she suffers in other respects, are among the very few that can be cultivated with any profit by slave labor; and if, by the loss of her foreign commerce, these products should be confined to an inadequate market, the fate of this fertile state would be poverty and utter desolation. Her citizens, in despair, would emigrate to more fortunate regions, and the whole frame and constitution of her civil polity be impaired and deranged, if not dissolved entirely.

Deeply impressed with these considerations, the representatives of the good people of this commonwealth, anxiously desiring to live in peace with their fellow citizens, and to do all that in them lies to preserve and perpetuate the union of the states and liberties of which it is the surest pledge, but feeling it to be their bounden duty to expose and resist all encroachments upon the true spirit of the Constitution, lest an apparent acquiescence in the system of protecting duties should be drawn into precedent — do, in the name of the commonwealth of South Carolina, claim to enter upon the journal of the Senate their protest against it as unconstitutional, oppressive, and unjust.

1829

60.

Richard M. Johnson: Sunday Observance and the Delivery of Mail

Several religious denominations formed national organizations in the 1820s and employed their combined strength to promote the idea that the United States was, both historically and constitutionally, a Christian nation. Among other things, they demanded that the government officially recognize Sunday as the Christian day of worship by suspending all government services, including delivery of mail. The Senate assigned the question to its Committee on Post Offices and Postal Roads, whose chairman, Richard M. Johnson of Kentucky, delivered the following report on January 19, 1829. The report, a defense of the separation of church and state, adopted the principle that the Constitution gave Congress no power to determine "what part of time, or whether any, has been set apart by the Almighty for religious exercises."

Source: 20 Congress, 2 Session, Senate Report No. 74.

THAT SOME RESPITE IS REQUIRED from the ordinary vocations of life is an established principle, sanctioned by the usages of all nations, whether Christian or pagan. One day in seven has also been determined upon as the proportion of time; and, in conformity with the wishes of the great majority of citizens of this country, the first day of the week, commonly called Sunday, has been set apart to that object. The principle has received the sanction of the national legislature, so far as to admit a suspension of all public business on that day, except in cases of absolute necessity or of great public utility. This principle the committee would not wish to disturb. If kept within its legitimate sphere of action, no injury can result from its observance. It should, however, be kept in mind that the proper object of government is to protect all persons in the enjoyment of their religious as well as civil rights and not to determine for any whether they shall esteem one day above another, or esteem all days alike holy.

We are aware that a variety of sentiment exists among the good citizens of this nation on the subject of the Sabbath day; and our government is designed for the protection of one as much as for another. The Jews, who in this country are as free as Christians, and entitled to the same protection from the laws, derive their obligation to keep the Sabbath day from the Fourth Commandment of their Decalogue, and, in conformity with that injunction, pay religious homage to the seventh day of the week, which we call Saturday. One denomination of Christians among us, justly celebrated for their piety, and certainly as good citizens as any other class, agree with the Jews in the moral obligation of the Sabbath and observe the same day. There are also many Christians among us who derive not their obligation to observe the Sabbath from the Decalogue but regard the Jewish Sabbath as abrogated. From the example of the Apostles of Christ, they have chosen the first day of the week instead of that day set apart in the Decalogue for their religious devotions. These have generally regarded the observance of the day as a devotional exercise, and would not more readily enforce it upon others than they would enforce secret prayer or devout meditations.

Urging the fact that neither their Lord nor His disciples, though often censured by their accusers for a violation of the Sabbath, ever enjoined its observance, they regard it as a subject on which every person should be fully persuaded in his own mind, and not coerce others to act upon his persuasion. Many Christians again differ from these, professing to derive their obligation to observe the Sabbath from the Fourth Commandment of the Jewish Decalogue, and bring the example of the Apostles, who appear to have held their public meetings for worship on the first day of the week, as authority for so far changing the Decalogue as to substitute that day for the seventh. The Jewish government was a theocracy which enforced religious observances; and though the committee would hope that no portion of the citizens of our country could willingly introduce a system of religious coercion in our civil institutions, the example of other nations should admonish us to watch carefully against its earliest indication.

With these different religious views the committee are of opinion that Congress cannot interfere. It is not the legitimate province of the legislature to determine what religion is true or what is false. Our government is a civil and not a religious institution. Our Constitution recognizes in every person the right to choose his own religion and to enjoy it freely, without molestation. Whatever may be the religious sentiments of citizens, and however variant, they are alike entitled to protection from the government, so long as they do not invade the rights of others.

The transportation of the mail on the first day of the week, it is believed, does not interfere with the rights of conscience. The petitioners for its discontinuance appear to be actuated from a religious zeal, which may be commendable if confined to its proper sphere; but they assume a position better suited to an ecclesiastical than to a civil institution. They appear, in many instances, to lay it down as an axiom that the practice is a violation of the law of God. Should Congress, in their legislative capacity, adopt the sentiment, it would establish the principle that the legislature is a proper tribunal to determine what are the laws of God. It would involve a legislative decision in a religious controversy, and on a point in which good citizens may honestly differ in opinion without disturbing the peace of society or endangering its liberties.

If this principle is once introduced, it will be impossible to define its bounds. Among all the religious persecutions with which almost every page of modern history is stained, no victim ever suffered but for the violation of what government denominated the law of God. To prevent a similar train of evils in this country, the Constitution has wisely withheld from our government the power of defining the divine law. It is a right reserved to each citizen; and while he respects the equal rights of others, he cannot be held amenable to any human tribunal for his conclusions.

Extensive religious combinations to effect a political object are, in the opinion of the

Col. Richard M. Johnson by John Neagle

committee, always dangerous. This first effort of the kind calls for the establishment of a principle, which, in the opinion of the committee, would lay the foundation for dangerous innovations upon the spirit of the Constitution, and upon the religious rights of the citizens. If admitted, it may be justly apprehended that the future measures of government will be strongly marked, if not eventually controlled, by the same influence. All religious despotism commences by combination and influence; and when that influence begins to operate upon the political institutions of a country, the civil power soon bends under it; and the catastrophe of other nations furnishes an awful warning of the consequence.

Under the present regulations of the Post Office Department, the rights of conscience are not invaded. Every agent enters voluntarily, and, it is presumed, conscientiously, into the discharge of his duties, without intermeddling with the conscience of another. Post offices are so regulated as that but a small proportion of the first day of the week is required to be occupied in official business. In the transportation of the mail on that day, no one agent is employed many hours. Religious persons enter into the business without violating their own consciences or imposing any restraints upon others. Passengers in the mail stages are free to rest during the first day of the week or to pursue their journeys, at their own pleasure. While the mail is transported on Saturday, the Jew and the Sabbatarian may abstain from any agency in carrying it, from conscientious scruples. While it is transported on the first day of the week, another class may abstain, from the same religious scruples. The obligation of government is the same to both of these classes; and the committee can discover no principle on which the claims of one should be more respected than those of the other, unless it should be admitted that the consciences of the minority are less sacred than those of the majority.

It is the opinion of the committee that the subject should be regarded simply as a question of expediency, irrespective of its religious bearing. In this light it has hitherto been considered. Congress have never legislated upon the subject. It rests, as it ever has done, in the legal discretion of the postmaster general, under the repeated refusals of Congress to discontinue the Sabbath mails. His knowledge and judgment in all the concerns of that department will not be questioned. His intense labors and assiduity have resulted in the highest improvement of every branch of his department. It is practised only on the great leading mail routes, and such others as are necessary to maintain their connections. To prevent this would, in the opinion of the committee, be productive of immense injury, both in its commercial, political, and in its moral bearings.

The various departments of government require, frequently in peace, always in war, the speediest intercourse with the remotest parts of the country; and one important object of the mail establishment is to furnish the greatest and most economical facilities for such intercourse. The delay of the mails one whole day in seven would require the employment of special expresses, at great expense, and sometimes with great uncertainty.

The commercial, manufacturing, and agricultural interests of our country are so intimately connected as to require a constant and the most expeditious correspondence between all our seaports, and between them and the most interior settlements. The delay of the mails during the Sunday would give occasion to the employment of private expresses, to such an amount that probably ten riders would be employed where one mail stage is now running on that day; thus diverting the revenue of that department into another channel, and sinking the establishment into a state of pusillanimity incompatible with the dignity of the government of which it is a department.

Passengers in the mail stages, if the mails are not permitted to proceed on Sunday, will be expected to spend that day at a tavern upon the road, generally under circumstances not friendly to devotion, and at an expense which many are but poorly able to encounter. To obviate these difficulties, many will employ extra carriages for their conveyance, and become the bearers of correspondence, as more expeditious than the mail. The stage proprietors will themselves often furnish the travelers with those means of conveyance; so that the effect will ultimately be only to stop the mail, while the vehicle which conveys it will continue, and its passengers become the special messengers for conveying a considerable proportion of what would otherwise constitute the contents of the mail.

Nor can the committee discover where the system could consistently end. If the observance of a holiday becomes incorporated in our institutions, shall we not forbid the movement of an army, prohibit an as-

sault in time of war, and lay an injunction upon our naval officers to lie in the wind while upon the ocean, on that day? Consistency would seem to require it. Nor is it certain that we should stop here. If the principle is once established that religion, or religious observances, shall be interwoven with our legislative acts, we must pursue it to its ultimatum. We shall, if consistent, provide for the erection of edifices for the worship of the Creator and for the support of Christian ministers, if we believe such measures will promote the interests of Christianity. It is the settled conviction of the committee that the only method of avoiding these consequences, with their attendant train of evils, is to adhere strictly to the spirit of the Constitution, which regards the general government in no other light than that of a civil institution, wholly destitute of religious authority.

What other nations call religious toleration, we call religious rights. They are not exercised in virtue of governmental indulgence but as rights, of which government cannot deprive any portion of citizens, however small. Despotic power may invade those rights, but justice still confirms them. Let the national legislature once perform an act which involves the decision of a religious controversy and it will have passed its legitimate bounds. The precedent will then be established and the foundation laid for that usurpation of the divine prerogative in this country, which has been the desolating scourge to the fairest portions of the Old World. Our Constitution recognizes no other power than that of persuasion for enforcing religious observances.

Let the professors of Christianity recommend their religion by deeds of benevolence; by Christian meekness; by lives of temperance and holiness. Let them combine their efforts to instruct the ignorant; to relieve the widow and the orphan; to promulgate to the world the gospel of their Savior, recommending its precepts by their habitual example. Government will find its legitimate object in protecting them. It cannot oppose them, and they will not need its aid. Their moral influence will then do infinitely more to advance the true interests of religion than any measures which they may call on Congress to enact.

The petitioners do not complain of any infringement upon their own rights. They enjoy all that Christians ought to ask at the hand of any government — protection from all molestation in the exercise of their religious sentiments.

Resolved, that the committee be discharged from the further consideration of the subject.

61.

Mrs. Samuel Harrison Smith: The Inauguration of Andrew Jackson

Andrew Jackson, successor to a long line of "patrician" presidents, was widely acclaimed as the "peoples' choice" and the symbol of the new "age of the common man." Jackson brought with him to the White House a reputation as a military hero and an image as a frontiersman. He had the support of Western farmers and Eastern workingmen, who flocked to Washington to celebrate his inauguration. Mrs. Samuel Harrison Smith, grande dame of Washington society, set down the following horrified eyewitness account of that tumultuous day in March 1829 in a letter to a friend written a few days after the event.

Source: *The First Forty Years of Washington Society,* Gaillard Hunt, ed., New York, 1906, pp. 290-298.

It [THE INAUGURATION] . . . was not a thing of detail or a succession of small incidents. No, it was one grand whole, an imposing and majestic spectacle, and, to a reflective mind, one of moral sublimity. Thousands and thousands of people, without distinction of rank, collected in an immense mass round the Capitol, silent, orderly, and tranquil, with their eyes fixed on the front of that edifice, waiting the appearance of the President in the portico. The door from the rotunda opens; preceded by the marshals, surrounded by the judges of the Supreme Court, the old man with his gray locks, that crown of glory, advances, bows to the people who greet him with a shout that rends the air. The cannons from the heights around, from Alexandria and Fort Warbur-

ton, proclaim the oath he has taken and all the hills reverberate the sound. It was grand; it was sublime! An almost breathless silence succeeded, and the multitude was still, listening to catch the sound of his voice, though it was so low as to be heard only by those nearest to him.

After reading his speech; the oath was administered to him by·the chief justice. Then Marshall presented the Bible. The President took it from his hands, pressed his lips to it, laid it reverently down, then bowed again to the people — yes, to the people in all their majesty. And had the spectacle closed here, even Europeans must have acknowledged that a free people, collected in their might, silent, and tranquil, restrained solely by a moral power, without

Library of Congress

"President's Levee or All Creation Going to the White House";
aquatint by Robert Cruickshank from the "Playfair Papers"

a shadow around of military force, was majesty rising to sublimity and far surpassing the majesty of kings and princes surrounded with armies and glittering in gold.

But I will not anticipate, but will give you an account of the inauguration in mere detail. The whole of the preceding day, immense crowds were coming into the city from all parts, lodgings could not be obtained, and the newcomers had to go to Georgetown, which soon overflowed, and others had to go to Alexandria. I was told the Avenue and adjoining streets were so crowded on Tuesday afternoon that it was difficult to pass.

A national salute was fired early in the morning, and ushered in March 4. By 10 o'clock, the Avenue was crowded with carriages of every description, from the splendid baronet and coach, down to wagons and carts, filled with women and children, some in finery and some in rags, for it was the people's President, and all would see him; the men all walked. . . .

The day was . . . delightful, the scene animating; so we walked backward and forward, at every turn meeting some new acquaintance and stopping to talk and shake hands. . . . We continued promenading here until near three, returned home unable to stand, and threw ourselves on the sofa.

Someone came and informed us the crowd before the President's house was so far lessened that they thought we might enter. This time we effected our purpose. But what a scene did we witness! The majesty of the people had disappeared, and a rabble, a mob, of boys, Negroes, women, children — scrambling, fighting, romping. What a pity, what a pity! No arrangements had been made, no police officers placed on duty, and the whole house had been inundated by the rabble mob. We came too late.

The President, after having been *literally* nearly pressed to death and almost suffocated and torn to pieces by the people in their eagerness to shake hands with Old Hickory, had retreated through the back way, or south front, and had escaped to his lodgings at Gadsby's. Cut glass and china to the amount of several thousand dollars had been broken in the struggle to get the refreshments. Punch and other articles had been carried out in tubs and buckets, but had it been in hogsheads it would have been insufficient; ice creams and cake and lemonade for 20,000 people, for it is said that number were there, though I think the estimate exaggerated. Ladies fainted, men were seen with bloody noses, and such a scene of confusion took place as is impossible to describe; those who got in could not get out by the door again but had to scramble out of windows.

At one time, the President, who had retreated and retreated until he was pressed against the wall, could only be secured by a number of gentlemen forming round him and making a kind of barrier of their own bodies; and the pressure was so great that Colonel Bomford, who was one, said that at one time he was afraid they should have been pushed down or on the President. It was then the windows were thrown open and the torrent found an outlet, which otherwise might have proved fatal.

This concourse had not been anticipated and therefore not provided against. Ladies and gentlemen only had been expected at this levee, not the people *en masse*. But it was the people's day, and the people's President, and the people would rule. God grant that one day or other the people do not put down all rule and rulers. I fear, enlightened freemen as they are, they will be found, as they have been found in all ages and countries where they get the power in their hands, that of all tyrants, they are the most ferocious, cruel, and despotic. The noisy and disorderly rabble in the President's house brought to my mind descriptions I had read of the mobs in the Tuileries and at Versailles. I expect to hear the carpets and furniture are ruined; the streets were muddy, and these guests all went thither on foot.

62.

FRANCES WRIGHT: Of Existing Evils and Their Remedy

Frances Wright first visited America around 1818. She returned in 1824 and remained to crusade for women's rights, labor, and education through lectures and coeditorship with Robert Dale Owen of the New Harmony Gazette *and the* Free Enquirer. *She invested much of her fortune in the ill-fated community of Nashoba, Tennessee, then became a leader of the equally short-lived New York Workingmen's Party. Undeterred by those failures, Miss Wright continued to advocate numerous reform measures, such as those mentioned in the following selection from her* Course of Popular Lectures, *delivered in Philadelphia, June 2, 1829.*

Source: *Course of Popular Lectures*, New York, 1829, pp. 150-170.

I SHALL NOW PRESENT a few observations on the necessity of commencing and gradually perfecting a radical reform in your existing outlays of time and money — [reforms] on and in churches, theological colleges, privileged and exclusive seminaries of all descriptions, religious Sabbath schools, and all their aids and adjuncts of Bibles, tracts, missionaries, priests, and preachers, multiplied and multiplying throughout the land, until they promise to absorb more capital than did the temple of Solomon, and to devour more of the first fruits of industry than did the tribe of Levi in the plentitude of its power; [reforms] on the necessity, I say, of substituting for your present cumbrous, expensive, useless, or rather pernicious, system of partial, opinionative, and dogmatical instruction one at once national, rational, and republican; one which shall take for its study our own world and our own nature; for its object, the improvement of man; and for its means, the practical development of truth, the removal of temptations to evil, and the gradual equalization of human condition, human duties, and human enjoyments, by the equal diffusion of knowledge without distinction of class or sect, both of which distinctions are inconsistent with republican institutions as they are with reason and with common sense, with virtue, and with happiness. . . .

And by whom and how are these changes to be effected? By whom! And do a free people ask the question? By themselves. By themselves — *the people.* . . .

We are fast traveling in the footsteps of Europe, my friends; for her principles of action are ours. We have in all our habits and usages the same vices and, with these same vices, we must have the same evils.

The great principles stamped in America's Declaration of Independence are true, are great, are sublime, and are *all her own.* But her usages, her law, her religion, her education are false, narrow, prejudiced, ignorant, and are the relic of dark ages — the gift and bequeathment of king-governed, priest-ridden nations, whose supremacy, indeed, the people of America have challenged and overthrown, but whose example they are still following.

[As] a foreigner, I have looked round on this land unblinded by local prejudices or national predilections; [as] a friend to humankind, zealous for human improvement, enamored to enthusiasm, if you will, of human liberty, I first sought in this country to

see in operation those principles consecrated in her national institutions, and whose simple grandeur had fired the enthusiasm and cheered the heart of my childhood, disgusted as it was with the idle parade and pride of unjust power inherent in European aristocracy. Delighted with the sound of political liberty, the absence of bayonets and constrained taxation, I spoke and published, as I felt, in praise of American institutions; and called and, I believe, first generally awakened, the attention of the European public to their study and appreciation.

Disappointed, in common with all the friends of liberty in Europe, by the issue of the well-imagined but ill-sustained revolutions of the old continent . . . I returned to this republic as to the last hope of the human family, anxious to inspect it through its wide extent and to study it in all its details.

The result of my observation has been the conviction that the reform commenced at the Revolution of '76 has been but little improved through the term of years which have succeeded; that the national policy of the country was then indeed changed but that its social economy has remained such as it was in the days of its European vassalage.

In confirmation of this, I will request you to observe that your religion is the same as that of monarchical England: taught from the same books, and promulgated and sustained by similar means, viz., a salaried priesthood, set apart from the people; sectarian churches, in whose property the people have no share, and over whose use and occupancy the people have no control; expensive missions, treasury funds, associations, and, above all, a compulsory power, compounded at once of accumulated wealth, established custom, extensive correspondence, and a system of education imbued with its spirit and all pervaded by its influence.

Again, in proof of the similarity between your internal policy and that of monarchical England, I will request you to observe that

Frances Wright (1795-1852), an early Feminist, was co-editor of the "New Harmony Gazette" and later in New York, editor of the "Free Enquirer"

her law is your law. Every part and parcel of that absurd, cruel, ignorant, inconsistent, incomprehensible jumble, styled the common law of England — every part and parcel of it, I say, not abrogated or altered expressly by legislative statutes, which has been very rarely done — is at this hour the law of revolutionized America.

Farther, in proof of the identity of your fabric of civil polity with that of aristocratical England, I will request you to observe that the system of education pursued in both countries is, with little variations, one and the same. There, you have endowed universities, privileged by custom, enriched by ancient royal favor, protected by parliamentary statutes, and devoted to the upholding, perpetuating, and strengthening [of] the power and privilege to which they owe their origin. There, too, you have parish schools under the control of the parish priest, and a press everywhere coerced by law, swayed, bribed, or silenced by ascend-

ant parties or tyrannous authority. And *here*, have we not colleges with endowments still held by the royal charters which first bestowed them, and colleges with lands and money granted by American legislatures, not for the advantage of the American people but for that of their rulers, for the children of privileged professions upon whom is thus entailed the privilege of their fathers, and that as certainly as the son of a duke is born to a dukedom in England?

Here, have we not also schools controlled by the clergy? Nay, have we not all our public institutions, scientific, literary, judicial, or humane, ridden by the spirit of orthodoxy, and invaded, perverted, vitiated, and tormented by opinionative distinctions? And *here*, have we not a press paralyzed by fear, disgraced by party, and ruled by loud-tongued fanaticism, or aspiring and threatening sectarian ambition? And more, my friends, see we not, in this nation of confederated freemen, as many distinctions of class as afflict the aristocracies of Britain, or the despotism of the Russias; and more distinctions of sect than ever cursed all the nations of Europe together, from the preaching of Peter the Hermit, to the trances of Madame Krudner, or the miracles of Prince Hohenlohe?

Surely all these are singular anomalies in a republic. . . . What then, is wanted here? What Sparta had: *a national education.* And what Sparta, in many respects, had not: *a rational education.*

Hitherto, my friends, in government as in every branch of morals, we have but too much mistaken words for truths and forms for principles. To render men free, it suffices not to proclaim their liberty; to make them equal, it suffices not to call them so. True, July 4, 1776, commenced a new era for our race. True, the sun of promise then rose upon the world. But let us not mistake for the fullness of light what was but its harbinger. Let us not conceive that man in signing the declaration of his rights secured their possession; that having framed the theory, he had not, and has not still, the practice to seek. . . .

Who speaks of liberty while the human mind is in chains? Who of equality while the thousands are in squalid wretchedness, the millions harassed with health-destroying labor, the few afflicted with health-destroying idleness, and all tormented by health-destroying solicitude? Look abroad on the misery which is gaining on the land! Mark the strife, and the discord, and the jealousies, the shock of interests and opinions, the hatreds of sect, the estrangements of class, the pride of wealth, the debasement of poverty, the helplessness of youth unprotected, of age uncomforted, of industry unrewarded, of ignorance unenlightened, of vice unreclaimed, of misery unpitied, of sickness, hunger, and nakedness unsatisfied, unalleviated, and unheeded. Go! Mark all the wrongs and the wretchedness with which the eye and the ear and the heart are familiar, and then echo in triumph and celebrate in jubilee the insulting declaration: *all men are free and equal!*

That evils exist, none that have eyes, ears, and hearts can dispute. That these evils are on the increase, none who have watched the fluctuations of trade, the sinking price of labor, the growth of pauperism, and the increase of crime will dispute. Little need be said here to the people of Philadelphia. The researches made by the public spirited among their own citizens have but too well substantiated the suffering condition of a large mass of their population. In Boston, in New York, in Baltimore, the voice of distress has, in like manner, burst the barriers raised, and so long sustained, by the pride of honest industry, unused to ask from charity what it has been wont to earn by the sweat of the brow.

In each and every city necessity has constrained inquiry; and in each and every city inquiry has elicited the same appalling facts: that the hardest labor is often without a re-

ward adequate to the sustenance of the laborer; that when, by overexertion and all the diseases, and often vices, which excess of exertion induces, the laborer, whose patient, sedulous industry supplies the community with all its comforts and the rich with all their luxuries, when he, I say, is brought to an untimely grave by those exertions which, while sustaining the life of others, cut short his own, when he is mowed down by that labor whose products form the boasted wealth of the state, he leaves a family, to whom the strength of his manhood had barely furnished bread, to lean upon the weakness of a soul-stricken mother and hurry her to the grave of her father. . . .

And what are the remedies suggested by our corporation, our newspaper editors, our religious societies, our tracts, and our sermons? Some have ordained facts, multiplied prayers, and recommended pious submission to a Providence who should have instituted all this calamity for the purpose of fulfilling the words of a Jewish prophet: "The poor shall never cease from the land." Some, less spiritual minded, have called for larger jails and more poorhouses; some, for increased poor rates and additional benevolent societies; others, for compulsory laws protective of labor and fixing a *minimum,* below which it shall be penal to reduce it; while others, and those not the least able to appreciate all the difficulties of the question, have sought the last resource of suffering poverty and oppressed industry in the humanity and sense of justice of the wealthier classes of society. . . .

Great reforms are not wrought in a day. Evils which are the accumulated results of accumulated errors are not to be struck down at a blow by the rod of a magician. A free people may boast that all power is in their hands; but no effectual power can be in their hands until knowledge be in their minds.

But how may knowledge be imparted to their minds? Such effective knowledge as shall render apparent to all the interests of all, and demonstrate the simple truths: that a nation to be strong, must be united; to be united, must be equal in condition; to be equal in condition, must be similar in habits and in feeling; to be similar in habits and in feeling, *must be raised in national institutions, as the children of a common family and citizens of a common country*. . . .

I know how difficult it is, reared as we all are in the distinctions of class, to say nothing of sect, to conceive of our interests as associated with those of the whole community. The man possessed of a dollar feels himself to be, not merely 100 cents richer but also 100 cents *better* than the man who is penniless; so on through all the gradations of earthly possessions — the estimate of our own moral and political importance swelling always in a ratio exactly proportionate to the growth of our purse. The rich man who can leave a clear independence to his children is given to estimate them as he estimates himself, and to imagine something in their nature distinct from that of the less privileged heirs of hard labor and harder fare. . . .

But it is first to the rich I would speak. Can the man of opulence feel tranquil under the prospect of leaving to such guardianship as existing law or individual integrity may supply the minds, bodies, morals, or even the fortune of their children? . . . Can, then, the rich be without solicitude when they leave to the mercy of a heartless world the beings of their creation? Who shall cherish their young sensibilities? Who shall stand between them and oppression? Who shall whisper peace in the hour of affliction? Who shall supply principle in the hour of temptation? Who shall lead the tender mind to distinguish between the good and evil? Who shall fortify it against the corruptions of wealth, or prepare it for the day of adversity? Such, looking upon life as it is, must be the anxious thoughts

even of the wealthy. What must be the thoughts of the poor man, it needs not that we should picture.

But, my friends, however differing in degree may be the anxiety of the rich and the poor, still, in its nature, is it the same. Doubt, uncertainty, apprehension are before all. We hear of deathbed affliction. My friends, I have been often and long on the bed of mortal sickness: no fear had the threatened last sleep for me, for *I was not a parent*.

We have here, then, found an evil common to all classes and one that is entailed from generation to generation. The measure I am about to suggest, whenever adopted, will blot this now universal affliction from existence; it will also, in the outset, alleviate those popular distresses whose poignancy and rapid increase weigh on the heart of philanthropy and crush the best hopes of enlightened patriotism. It must further, when carried into full effect, work the radical cure of every disease which now afflicts the body politic, and build up for this nation a sound constitution, embracing at once public prosperity, individual integrity, and universal happiness.

The measure, my friends, has been long present to my mind as befitting the adoption of the American people; as alone calculated to form an enlightened, a virtuous, and a happy community; as alone capable of supplying a remedy to the evils under which we groan; as alone commensurate with the interests of the human family, and consistent with the political institutions of this great confederated republic. . . .

The noble example of New England has been imitated by other states, until all not possessed of common schools blush for the popular remissness. But, after all, how can common schools, under their best form and in fullest supply, effect even the purpose which they have in view?

The object proposed by common schools [if I rightly understand it] is to impart to the whole population those means for the acquirement of knowledge which are in common use: reading and writing. To these are added arithmetic and, occasionally perhaps, some imperfect lessons in the simpler sciences. But I would ask: Supposing these institutions should even be made to embrace all the branches of intellectual knowledge, and thus, science offered gratis to all the children of the land, how are the children of the very class for whom we suppose the schools instituted to be supplied with food and raiment or instructed in the trade necessary to their future subsistence while they are following these studies? How are they, I ask, to be fed and clothed, when, as all facts show, the labor of the parents is often insufficient for their own sustenance and, almost universally, inadequate to the provision of the family without the united efforts of all its members?

In your manufacturing districts you have children worked for twelve hours a day; and in the rapid and certain progress of the existing system, you will soon have them, as in England, *worked to death*, and yet unable, through the period of their miserable existence, to earn a pittance sufficient to satisfy the cravings of hunger. At this present time, what leisure or what spirit, think you, have the children of the miserable widows of Philadelphia, realizing, according to the most favorable estimate of your city and county committee, $16 per annum for food and clothing? What leisure or what spirit may their children find for visiting a school, although the same should be open to them from sunrise to sunset? Or what leisure have usually the children of your most thriving mechanics, after their strength is sufficiently developed to spin, sew, weave, or wield a tool? It seems to me, my friends, that to build schoolhouses nowadays is something like building churches. When you have them, you need some measure to ensure their being occupied.

But, as our time is short, and myself somewhat fatigued by continued exertions, I must hasten to the rapid development of the system of instruction and protection which has occurred to me as capable, and alone capable, of opening the door to universal reform.

In lieu of all common schools, high schools, colleges, seminaries, houses of refuge, or any other juvenile institution, instructional or protective, I would suggest that the state legislatures be directed [after laying off the whole in townships or hundreds] to organize, at suitable distances and in convenient and healthy situations, establishments for the general reception of all the children resident within the said school district — these establishments to be devoted, severally, to children between a certain age. Say, the first, infants between two and four, or two and six, according to the density of the population, and such other local circumstances as might render a greater or less number of establishments necessary or practicable. The next to receive children from four to eight, or six to twelve years. The next, from twelve to sixteen, or to an older age if found desirable. Each establishment to be furnished with instructors in every branch of knowledge, intellectual and operative, with all the apparatus, land, and conveniences necessary for the best development of all knowledge; the same, whether operative or intellectual, being always calculated to the age and strength of the pupils.

To obviate, in the commencement, every evil result possible from the first mixture of a young population, so variously raised in error or neglect, a due separation should be made in each establishment; by which means those entering with bad habits would be kept apart from the others until corrected. How rapidly reform may be effected on the plastic disposition of childhood has been sufficiently proved in your houses of refuge, more especially when such establishments have been under *liberal* superintendence, as was formerly the case in New York. Under their orthodox directors, those asylums of youth have been converted into jails.

It will be understood that, in the proposed establishments, the children would pass from one to the other in regular succession, and that the parents, who would necessarily be resident in their close neighborhood, could visit the children at suitable hours, but, in no case, interfere with or interrupt the rules of the institution.

In the older establishments, the well-directed and well-protected labor of the pupil would, in time, suffice for and then exceed their own support; when the surplus might be devoted to the maintenance of the infant establishments.

In the beginning, and until all debt was cleared off, and so long as the same should be found favorable to the promotion of these best palladiums of a nation's happiness, a double tax might be at once expedient and politic.

First, a moderate tax per head for every child, to be laid upon its parents conjointly or divided between them, due attention being always paid to the varying strength of the two sexes and to the undue depreciation which now rests on female labor. The more effectually to correct the latter injustice, as well as to consult the convenience of the industrious classes generally, this parental tax might be rendered payable either in money or in labor, produce or domestic manufactures, and should be continued for each child until the age when juvenile labor should be found, on the average, equivalent to the educational expenses, which, I have reason to believe, would be at twelve years.

This first tax on parents to embrace equally the whole population, as, however moderate, it would inculcate a certain forethought in all the human family; more especially where it is most wanted — in young persons, who, before they assumed the responsibility of parents, would estimate their fitness to meet it.

The second tax to be on property, increasing in percentage with the wealth of the individual. In this manner I conceive the rich would contribute, according to their riches, to the relief of the poor and to the support of the state by raising up its best bulwark — an enlightened and united generation.

Preparatory to, or connected with, such measures, a registry should be opened by the state, with offices through all the townships, where, on the birth of every child or within a certain time appointed, the same should be entered, together with the names of its parents. When two years old, the parental tax should be payable, and the juvenile institution open for the child's reception; from which time forward it would be under the protective care and guardianship of the state, while it need never be removed from the daily, weekly, or frequent inspection of the parents.

Orphans, of course, would find here an open asylum. If possessed of property a contribution would be paid from its revenue to the common educational fund; if unprovided, they would be sustained out of the same.

In these nurseries of a free nation, no inequality must be allowed to enter. Fed at a common board; clothed in a common garb, uniting neatness with simplicity and convenience; raised in the exercise of common duties, in the acquirement of the same knowledge and practice of the same industry, varied only according to individual taste and capabilities; in the exercise of the same virtues; in the enjoyment of the same pleasures; in the study of the same nature; in pursuit of the same object — their own and each other's happiness. Say! Would not such a race, when arrived at manhood and womanhood, work out the reform of society; perfect the free institutions of America?

I have drawn but a sketch, nor could I presume to draw the picture of that which the mind's eye has seen alone, and which it is for the people of this land to realize.

In this sketch, my friends, there is nothing but what is practical and practicable; nothing but what you yourselves may contribute to effect. Let the popular suffrage be exercised with a view to the popular good. Let the industrious classes and all honest men of all classes unite for the sending to the legislatures those who will represent the real interests of the many, not the imagined interests of the few; of the people at large, not of any profession or class.

63.

Demand for a Ten-Hour Day

The New York Workingmen's Party was made up of skilled tradesmen and factory workers united in a short-lived political party in 1829-1830. One of the party's goals was the reduction of the work day to ten hours, as stated in the following remonstrance of April 28, 1829.

Source: *New York Morning Courier*, April 30, 1829 [Commons, V, pp. 147-148].

Resolved, that the Creator has made all equal.

Resolved, that in the first formation of government, no man gives up to others his original right of soil and becomes a smith, a weaver, a builder, or other mechanic or laborer without receiving a guaranty that reasonable toil shall enable him to live as comfortably as others.

Resolved, that the rights of the rich, or, in other words, the employer, are not greater now than they were then.

Resolved, that the rights of the poor or the employed are not less.

Resolved, that those who now undertake to exact an excessive number of hours of toil for a days work are aggressors upon the rights of their fellow citizens, invaders of their happiness, and justly obnoxious to the indignation of every honest man in the community.

Resolved, that we will not labor for any man more than the just and reasonable time of ten hours a day; and that if our employers are determined to make the experiment, which can longest be suspended, business with them, or with us the supply of the wants of nature for ourselves and families, we will hold them responsible, as we also hold ourselves, to the good sense of our fellow citizens, for the wrongs we may suffer at their hands.

Resolved, that a committee of fifty persons be appointed to devise the means of assisting those who may require it in consequence of fulfilling the foregoing resolutions and that they make report at a future meeting.

Resolved, that the same committee be authorized and instructed to call another meeting as soon as they shall deem it expedient.

Resolved, that the names of those who shall hereafter work more than ten hours a day, or require or receive it, shall be published in the public papers as soon as they shall be ascertained.

64.

THOMAS SKIDMORE: The Unequal Distribution of Property

*The Jacksonian Era was marked by two major reform movements: one, that of the
New England humanitarians, religious and philosophical in nature; the other, organized
among workingmen, secular and practical. Thomas Skidmore, a leader of the short-lived
New York Workingmen's Party, was deeply concerned with the plight of workers who, he
felt, were oppressed by the industrial and banking interests. Skidmore's major reform
treatise,* The Rights of Man to Property!, *analyzed the exploitation of workers and set
forth a program for the periodic redistribution of property and the abolition of monopolies
and inherited wealth. Portions of the book's concluding chapter are presented here.*

Source: *The Rights of Man to Property!*, New York, 1829, pp. 355-390.

IF A MAN WERE TO ASK ME to what I would
compare the unequal distribution of property which prevails in the world, and has ever
prevailed, I would say that it reminds me of
a large party of gentlemen who should have
a common right to dine at one and the
same public table; a part of whom should
arrive first, sit down and eat what they
chose, and, then, because the remaining part
came later to dinner, should undertake to
monopolize the whole and deprive them of
the opportunity of satisfying their hunger,
but upon terms such as those who had
feasted should be pleased to prescribe.

Such, now, is the actual condition of the
whole human race. Those who have gone
before us have been the first to sit down to
the table and to enjoy themselves without
interruption from those who came afterward; and, not content with this enjoyment,
they have disposed of the whole dinner in
such a manner that nine-tenths of the beings that now people this globe have not
wherewith to dine, but upon terms such as
these first monopolizers, or those to whom

they pretend they have conferred their own
power as successors, shall choose to dictate.
It is as if, after dining till they were satisfied, a general scramble ensued for what remained on the table; and those who succeeded in filling their pockets and other re-
ceptacles with provisions should have something to give to their children; but those
who should have the misfortune to get
none, or having got it, should lose it again,
through fraud, calamity, or force, should
have none for theirs, to the latest generation. . . .

Three hundred thousand freemen in this
state hold votes in their hands, which no
power that you can command can take out;
and of these freemen, more than 250,000
are men whom a preceding generation, together with yourselves and their own ignorance of their rights, have conspired to place
in situations such that they have no property in the state of which they are citizens;
although their title to such property is as
good as that of any man that breathes. . . .

Title to property exists for all, and for all

alike; not because others have been nor because they have *not* been; not because they had a certain being for a parent rather than another being; not because they appear later or earlier on the stage of life than others; not because of purchase, of conquest, of preoccupancy, or what not; *but because they are; because they exist. I am; therefore is property mine,* as much so as any man's, and that without asking any man's permission; without paying any man's price; without knowing or caring further than as my equal right extends, whether any other human being exists or not.

Such is the language of nature; such is the language of right; and such are the principles which will justify any people in pulling down any government which denies, even to a *single* individual of the human race, his possession, his real, tangible possession, of this inalienable right of nature or its unquestionable equivalent. How much more so, then, is it the duty of any such people to destroy their own government when *more than nine-tenths,* it may be, are deprived of rights which the Creator gave them when He gave them existence? . . .

Let the men of all nations be made equal among themselves in point of property, and then will wars be immediately self-extinguished forever. Keep up this unnatural inequality in wealth which now exists, and they will exist as long as two nations shall be found in existence. . . . It appears, then, that conquerors grow out of a state of unequal possession of property; and without such an unequal possession they would never have existed. It appears, also, that by destroying this inequality everywhere conquerors and warriors would be destroyed also. . . .

In all the principles of the rights of property which are . . . seen to have been almost insensibly adopted, *there is not one which has been adopted on any consideration, correct or otherwise, of its own merits.* Usage has done everything. Custom, practice, habit

has made all the law; and made it at times and under circumstances in which it was of no consequence to the generation then being, whether the principles involved in the custom were good in themselves or not; whether they would be productive of immense injury or not when they should come to have a dense population to act upon; whether they were consistent with the rigid rights of their own generation or not; whether they preserved the rights of posterity or sacrificed them with a most unsparing hand. . . .

How ridiculously absurd must those political physicians appear who shall oppose or attempt to postpone such enjoyment of their rights by the great mass of the people until they shall receive, as the phrase is, the benefit of education. If they be sincere in their belief that such education is so very indispensable as a previous step to this enjoyment, and that the people are not now sufficiently instructed, let me ask them how, under present circumstances, is it ever possible to give it? Is a family where both parents and children are suffering daily in their animal wants, where excessive toil is required to obtain the little they enjoy, where the unkind and the unfriendly passions generated by such a wretched condition of things reign with full sway — is such a family in a situation to receive instruction?

Even if the children attend public institutions of education as punctually as may be wished, where is that equality of rank and condition as well between their parents as between themselves, which is so necessary to banish even from among children those envious remarks on dress, etc., etc., which now render our public schools in a measure abortive?

Political dreamers! Reformers, if you prefer that I should call you so! Feed first the hungry; clothe first the naked or ill-clad; provide comfortable homes for all by hewing down colossal estates among us and equalizing all property; take care that the animal wants be supplied first, that even the *apprehension* of want be banished; and then will you have a good field and good subjects for education. Then will instruction be conveyed without obstacle; for the wants, the unsatisfied wants of the body, will not interfere with it.

In the meantime, let all remember that those who undertake to *hold back* the people from their rights of property . . . until education, as they call it, can first be communicated (though . . . they now know more of all that is valuable among men than those who attempt to teach them), either do not understand themselves or pursue the course they *are* pursuing for the purpose of diverting the people from the possession of these rights, that they may be held in bondage even yet longer. It becomes the people to consider and reflect how far it is proper for them to *suffer* themselves to be thus *decoyed* out of the enjoyment of their rights, even for a single hour, by any such fallacious pretexts. . . .

The truth is, all men are fitted for the enjoyment of their rights when they know what they are. And until that time they do not desire them. They languish in misery and wretchedness, every new day being a new day of sorrow to them, when they do not perceive them and seem rather disposed to charge their evil condition to some "bad luck," as they call it; to some imaginary decree of destiny; to some superstitious interference with their happiness than to any possession by others of property which belongs to *them*.

Thus is it the case with the poor and the rich passing now in review before us. The former does not imagine that it is the latter which renders his life miserable and wretched. He does not conceive that it is he who fills his cup with bitterness, and visits himself and his family with the afflictions of slavery. . . . In the same wandering and benighted spirit do both the poor and the rich, the proprietor and nonproprietor, he

who has everything and he who has nothing cheat themselves, daily, with self-delusions.

How came this to be your property? If I ask a man such a question, he immediately replies, "I bought it of such a one." "Well, then, I suppose he had *a right to sell it* to you?" "Certainly," he answers. "How came *he* by it?" I ask next. "He purchased of such a one." "And he, I suppose, had a right to sell, too?" "Undoubtedly." And so we go on inquiring, till we come even to the days of Adam. How came *he* by it? is the next question. And the true but hurried answer is, "God gave it to him!"

Here, for the first time, reason begins to awake and see where rights originate. What! And did God give rights to Adam which He has not given to you? Did God declare to the man of His first creation that *he* not only should have the *use* of this fair paradise, as it is said to have been, free of all charge, but should also have the power to say that no human being after him should have the use of it at all, forever? For, if Adam have the power to sell, so also has he power *not to sell*; he has power to deny its use to any or to all. Better, far better, for mankind if such is a correct foundation for our right to property that Adam had never been; for then we should have possessed it, without buying of him *who never bought himself* and to whom it was never *given* for the purpose of selling to others, but for the satisfaction of his wants, so long as he should have any; that is, so long as he should live. . . .

Thus does it appear that one generation cannot sell, give, or convey, even if it had the right, to another. The reason is that the one is dead; the other is living. The one is present; the other, absent. They do not and cannot *meet* to come to a treaty, to make delivery, to give or receive. He who is dying is present; so soon as he is dead, he is past, and is no nearer to us in an instant after life has departed, than if he had died a thousand centuries ago. Patience becomes exhausted in thus chasing away the phantoms on which possessors of property found their title to it; and on which, too, the poor yield their assent to the validity of such title. But it is useful to dispel such errors from the minds of both the one and the other; that one may not put up a claim which he shall see he cannot support; and that the other may not confirm it through a misunderstanding of its real character.

But if property thus derived does not give to its possessor title, how are debts to be founded upon it? How am I to purchase of another that which is already truly my own? How is a man truly to sell that which does not belong to him? If it does not belong to him, in unimpeachable right, he cannot give unimpeachable title; and unless he can give such title, he cannot have any just claim to receive consideration. If he *think* he has such title, he may be very honest in his opinions; but this would not make it the better for him. Title does not come into any man's possession merely by the force of imagination. It has other origin than this. To allow a man to sell that which is not his would be to compel someone to pay for that which, in true right, is already his own, without payment at all of any kind or of any amount.

Let no man, therefore, say that another owes him and ought to pay him; let him rather first inquire into the title by which he has held that which he pretends he has sold; let him inquire first if it was his own to sell. Let him ascertain if the pretended debtor, through his ignorance of his own rights, has not been placed, by his own government, in necessitous circumstances; and that himself has, by the same government, been placed in unjust affluent circumstances. If both of these suppositions are true, then there is no debt existing between them. He who is called the debtor has only received that which belonged to him of right; and he who calls himself the creditor has only

parted with that which he never had the right to possess or retain. Debts, therefore, and the same is also to be said of contracts, in the present order of society, are obligations having no moral force; especially as between rich and poor; and so long as it exists never can have any. . . .

Let society . . . be so modified as to give to each man his original right to property, at the proper season of his life, equal to that of any other man's, together with equal, early, and ample education; and then debts will have a good moral foundation on which to rest. At present, debt is little more or less than extortion, practised upon the needy, who have not and never have had what is their own, by those who have not only their own but also what belongs to those to whom they undertake to sell. It is like the thief selling his stolen goods to the true and original owner. . . .

What is called wealth, therefore, is nothing less than the power to make prisoners of our fellowmen; and to compel them to erect for its possessor a palace of marble, for example, when of his own equal or equivalent industry he could not erect it himself. But it is time that those who desire to be rich should desire to be so without enslaving their fellowmen. And it is altogether easier to do so without such a crying injustice than it is with it. . . .

Under the present unequal distribution of property, where labor is the sole resource the poor have by which to maintain their existence, degraded as it is by the slavery in which they are plunged, it is not wonderful that they have been found to be opposed to the introduction of improvements. Fruitless and unavailing as such opposition is, it is yet less unreasonable than at first sight it may appear to be. . . . May not improvement extend to such a degree that there will be no demand for his labor? Or if it does not reach this point, will it not approach so near it as to make him an extreme sufferer? Let it not be forgotten that while, on the one hand, laborsaving machinery is advancing in its march to perfection with rapid strides and diminishing demand for labor, so, on the other, are the numbers of the poor, among whom this demand is to be shared, augmenting in a fearful ratio.

It will be said, perhaps, that by reducing price, the direct and certain consequence of improvements (otherwise they do not deserve the name), consumption is augmented; and, therefore, the demand is increased. This is true only in a limited degree; for, as these improvements supersede, sooner or later, in a great measure, all demand for the labor of the poor, it dries up their resources faster than it multiplies them; this, in the end, diminishes rather than increases the demand; and the consequence is that, as inventions, any more than revolutions, never go backward, are never given up when their benefits are once tasted; that the whole laboring population must perish, as it were, in a sort of self-destruction, like useless beings on the earth, where, it would seem, they have no right to appear; or that they must avert such a calamity by the best means in their power.

That they cannot destroy the existence, and even increase, of laborsaving machines and processes is evident from this; that every one of those whose feelings are enlisted against the inutility to them, on account of their destroying demand for their labor, whenever he has occasion, purchases, because they come cheaper, the very productions afforded by the agents which he so much deprecates. Of what use, then, is it for a laboring man to cry out against improvements when he goes and buys a coat, for example, or rather the materials of it, at a low price, which these very improvements have made? It is reward that keeps these improvements in existence; and it is not a volley of hard words and abuse that will do them any injury. If, then, the poor themselves contribute, and as they do, by an unavoidable necessity, to the support of that which threatens their own destruction, what hope have they to escape? It is not the rich, certainly, that *will; even if it were right that they should;* and we see the poor *cannot* forego the advantages, individually speaking, of these inventions. How then, are they to avert so great a calamity?

The steam engine is not injurious to the poor when they can have the benefit of it; and this, on supposition, being *always* the case, instead of being looked upon as a curse, would be hailed as a blessing. If, then, it is seen that the steam engine, for example, is likely to greatly impoverish or destroy the poor, what have they to do but TO LAY HOLD OF IT AND MAKE IT THEIR OWN? LET THEM APPROPRIATE, ALSO, in the same way, THE COTTON FACTORIES, THE WOOLEN FACTORIES, THE IRON FOUNDRIES, THE ROLLING MILLS, HOUSES, CHURCHES, SHIPS, GOODS, STEAMBOATS, FIELDS OF AGRICULTURE, etc., . . . AS IS THEIR RIGHT. And they will never have occasion any more to consider that as an evil which never deserved that character; which, on the contrary, is all that is good among men; and of which we cannot, under these new circumstances, have too much. It is an equal division of property that MAKES ALL RIGHT, and an equal transmission of it to posterity KEEPS IT SO. . . .

In fine, let the people awake to their rights; let them understand in what they consist; let them see the course they must pursue to obtain them; let them follow up that course by informing, each as many as he can, his fellow citizens of the truth which this work contains; let all cooperate in the early and effectual accomplishment of the objects it recommends; and these objects will easily and speedily be achieved and none will have labored in vain.

65.

William Lloyd Garrison: The Dangers of Slavery

Antislavery movements had existed in the United States since the Revolution. They had even received occasional support in the South, on moral grounds; but the invention of the cotton gin in 1793 made slavery a seeming economic necessity. In addition, slave revolts like the Nat Turner uprising of 1831 stirred old fears among Southern whites, entangling the slavery question in a web of moral, social, and economic issues. As the South was uniting to defend and preserve slavery, William Lloyd Garrison began to preach a new kind of abolitionism in the North. Rejecting the efforts of colonization societies to deport freed slaves to Africa, Garrison insisted on the gradual emancipation of the slaves. (This position he was publicly to renounce in September 1829, when he became the most militant of crusaders for "abolition now.") Garrison delivered the following address on "The Dangers of the Nation" on July 4, 1829, when he was only twenty-four years old.

Source: OSL 180.

It is natural that the return of a day which established the liberties of a brave people should be hailed by them with more than ordinary joy; and it is their duty as Christians and patriots to celebrate it with signal tokens of thanksgiving.

Fifty-three years ago, the Fourth of July was a proud day for our country.. It clearly and accurately defined the rights of man; it made no vulgar alterations in the established usages of society; it presented a revelation adapted to the common sense of mankind; it vindicated the omnipotence of public opinion over the machinery of kingly government; it shook, as with the voice of a great earthquake, thrones which were seemingly propped up with atlantean pillars; it gave an impulse to the heart of the world, which yet thrills to its extremities. . . .

I speak not as a partisan or an opponent of any man or measures when I say that our politics are rotten to the core. *We* boast of our freedom, who go shackled to the polls, year after year, by tens and hundreds and thousands! *We* talk of free agency, who are the veriest machines, the merest automata, in the hands of unprincipled jugglers! *We* prate of integrity and virtue and independence, who sell our birthright for office, and who, nine times in ten, do not get Esau's bargain — no, not even a mess of pottage!

Is it republicanism to say that the majority can do no wrong? Then I am not a republican. Is it aristocracy to say that the people sometimes shamefully abuse their high trust? Then I am an aristocrat.

It is not the appreciation but the abuse of liberty to withdraw altogether from the polls, or to visit them merely as a matter of form, without carefully investigating the merits of candidates. The republic does not bear a charmed life; our prescriptions, administered through the medium of the ballot box — the mouth of the political body — may kill or cure, according to the nature of the disease and our wisdom in applying the remedy. It is possible that a people may bear the title of freemen who execute the work of slaves. To the dullest observers of the signs of the times, it must be apparent that we are rapidly approximating to this condition. . . .

But there is another evil which, if we had to contend against nothing else, should make us quake for the issue. It is gangrene preying upon our vitals, an earthquake rumbling under our feet, a mine accumulating materials for a national catastrophe. It should make this a day of fasting and prayer, not of boisterous merriment and idle pageantry; a day of great lamentation, not of congratulatory joy. It should spike every cannon and haul down every banner. Our garb should be sackcloth, our heads bowed in the dust, our supplications for the pardon and assistance of Heaven.

Last week this city was made breathless by a trial of considerable magnitude. The court chamber was inundated for hours, day after day, with a dense and living tide which swept along like the rush of a mountain torrent. Tiers of human bodies were piled up to the walls, with almost miraculous condensation and ingenuity. It seemed as if men abhorred a vacuum equally with nature; they would suspend themselves, as it were, by a nail and stand upon air with the aid of a peg. Although it was a barren, ineloquent subject, and the crowd immense, there was no perceptible want of interest, no evidence of impatience. The cause was important, involving the reputation of a distinguished citizen. There was a struggle for mastery between two giants, a test of strength in tossing mountains of law. The excitement was natural.

I stand up here in a more solemn court, to assist in a far greater cause; not to impeach the character of one man but of a whole people; not to recover the sum of $100,000 but to obtain the liberation of 2 million of wretched, degraded beings, who are pining in hopeless bondage, over whose sufferings scarcely an eye weeps or a heart melts or a tongue pleads either to God or man. I regret that a better advocate had not been found to enchain your attention and to warm your blood. Whatever fallacy, however, may appear in the argument, there is no flaw in the indictment; what the speaker lacks, the cause will supply.

Sirs, I am not come to tell you that slavery is a curse, debasing in its effect, cruel in its operation, fatal in its continuance. The day and the occasion require no such revelation. I do not claim the discovery as my own, that "all men are created equal," and that among their inalienable rights are "life, liberty, and the pursuit of happiness." Were I addressing any other than a free and Christian assembly, the enforcement of this truth might be pertinent. Neither do I intend to analyze the horrors of slavery for your inspection, nor to freeze your blood with authentic recitals of savage cruelty. Nor will time allow me to explore even a furlong of that immense wilderness of suffering which remains unsubdued in our land. I take it for granted that the existence of these evils is acknowledged, if not rightly understood. My object is to define and enforce our duty as Christians and philanthropists. . . .

I assume as distinct and defensible propositions:

1. That the slaves of this country, whether we consider their moral, intellectual, or social condition, are preeminently entitled to the prayers and sympathies and charities of the American people; and their claims for redress are as strong as those of any Americans could be in a similar condition.

2. That as the free states, by which I mean nonslaveholding states, are constitutionally involved in the guilt of slavery by adhering to a national compact that sanctions it, and in the danger by liability to be

called upon for aid in case of insurrection, they have the right to remonstrate against its continuance and it is their duty to assist in its overthrow.

3. That no justificative plea for the perpetuity of slavery can be found in the condition of its victims, and no barrier against our righteous interference in the laws which authorize the buying, selling, and possessing of slaves, nor in the hazard of a collision with slaveholders.

4. That education and freedom will elevate our colored population to a rank with the whites, making them useful, intelligent, and peaceable citizens.

In the first place, it will be readily admitted that it is the duty of every nation primarily to administer relief to its own necessities, to cure its own maladies, to instruct its own children, and to watch over its own interests. He is "worse than an infidel" who neglects his own household and squanders his earnings upon strangers; and the policy of that nation is unwise which seeks to proselyte other portions of the globe at the expense of its safety and happiness. . . .

The condition of the slaves, in a religious point of view, is deplorable, entitling them to a higher consideration, on our part, than any other race . . . higher than our red men of the forest, for we do not bind them with gyves [shackles] nor treat them as chattels.

And here let me ask — What has Christianity done, by direct effort, for our slave population? Comparatively nothing. She has explored the isles of the ocean for objects of commiseration; but, amazing stupidity, she can gaze without emotion on a multitude of miserable beings at home, large enough to constitute a nation of freemen, whom tyranny has heathenized by law. In her public services they are seldom remembered, and in her private donations they are forgotten. . . .

I have said that the claims of the slaves for redress are as strong as those of any

Americans could be in a similar condition. Does any man deny the position? The proof, then, is found in the fact that a very large proportion of our colored population were born on our soil and are therefore entitled to all the privileges of American citizens. This is their country by birth, not by adoption. Their children possess the same inherent and inalienable rights as ours; and it is a crime of the blackest dye to load them with fetters.

Every Fourth of July, our Declaration of Independence is produced, with a sublime indignation, to set forth the tyranny of the mother country and to challenge the admiration of the world. But what a pitiful detail of grievances does this document present in comparison with the wrongs which our slaves endure! In the one case, it is hardly the plucking of a hair from the head; in the other, it is the crushing of a live body on the wheel — the stings of the wasp contrasted with the tortures of the Inquisition. Before God, I must say that such a glaring contradiction as exists between our creed and practice the annals of 6,000 years cannot parallel. In view of it, I am ashamed of my country.

I am sick of our unmeaning declamation in praise of liberty and equality; of our hypocritical cant about the inalienable rights of man. I could not, for my right hand, stand up before a European assembly and exult that I am an American citizen, and denounce the usurpations of a kingly government as wicked and unjust; or, should I make the attempt, the recollection of my country's barbarity and despotism would blister my lips and cover my cheeks with burning blushes of shame.

Will this be termed a rhetorical flourish? Will any man coldly accuse me of intemperate zeal? I will borrow, then, a ray of humanity from one of the brightest stars in our American galaxy, whose light will gather new effulgence to the end of time. "This, sirs, is a cause that would be dishonored and betrayed if I contented myself with appealing only to the understanding. It is too cold and its processes are too slow for the occasion. I desire to thank God that, since He has given me an intellect so fallible, He has impressed upon me an instinct that is sure. On a question of shame and honor — liberty and oppression — reasoning is sometimes useless, and worse. I feel the decision in my pulse: if it throws no light upon the brain, it kindles a fire at the heart." . . .

I come to my second proposition, the right of the free states to remonstrate against the continuance and to assist in the overthrow of slavery.

This, I am aware, is a delicate subject, surrounded with many formidable difficulties. But if delay only adds to its intricacy, wherefore shun an immediate investigation? I know that we of the North affectedly believe that we have no local interest in the removal of this great evil; that the slave states can take care of themselves, and that any proffered assistance on our part would be rejected as impertinent, dictatorial, or meddlesome; and that we have no right to lift up even a note of remonstrance. But I believe that these opinions are crude, preposterous, dishonorable, unjust. Sirs, this is a business in which, as members of one great family, we have a common interest; but we take no responsibility, either individually or collectively. Our hearts are cold, our blood stagnates in our veins. We act, in relation to the slaves, as if they were something lower than the brutes that perish.

On this question I ask no support from the injunction of Holy Writ which says, "Therefore all things whatsoever ye would that men should do to you, do ye even so to them: for this is the law and the prophets." I throw aside the common dictates of humanity. I assert the right of the free states to demand a gradual abolition of slavery, because, by its continuance, they participate in the guilt thereof and are threatened with ultimate destruction; because they are bound to watch over the interests of the whole country without reference to territorial divisions; because their white population is nearly double that of the slave states, and the voice of this overwhelming majority should be potential; because they are now deprived of their just influence in the councils of the nation; because it is absurd and anti-republican to suffer property to be represented as men and vice versa; because it gives the South an unjust ascendancy over other portions of territory, and a power that may be perverted on every occasion. . . .

Now I say that, on the broad system of equal rights, this monstrous inequality should no longer be tolerated. If it cannot be speedily put down, not by force but by fair persuasion; if we are always to remain shackled by unjust constitutional provisions when the emergency that imposed them has long since passed away; if we must share in the guilt and danger of destroying the bodies and souls of men *as the price of our Union;* if the slave states will haughtily spurn our assistance and refuse to consult in the general welfare, then the fault is not ours if a separation eventually takes place. . . .

It may be objected that the laws of the slave states form insurmountable barriers to any interference on our part.

Answer: I grant that we have not the right, and I trust not the disposition, to use coercive measures. But do these laws hinder our prayers or obstruct the flow of our sympathies? Cannot our charities alleviate the condition of the slave, and perhaps break his fetters? Can we not operate upon public sentiment (the lever that can move the moral world) by way of remonstrance, advice, or entreaty? . . .

Suppose that, by a miracle, the slaves should suddenly become white. Would you shut your eyes upon their sufferings and calmly talk of constitutional limitations? No, your voice would peal in the ears of the taskmasters like deep thunder; you would carry the Constitution by force if it could not be taken by treaty; patriotic assemblies would congregate at the corners of every street; the old cradle of liberty would rock to a deeper tone than ever echoed therein at British aggression; the pulpit would acquire new and unusual eloquence from our holy religion. The argument that these white slaves are degraded would not then obtain. You would say: It is enough that they are white and in bondage, and they ought immediately to be set free. You would multiply your schools of instruction and your temples of worship, and rely on them for security. . . .

But the plea is prevalent that any interference by the free states, however benevolent or cautious it might be, would only irritate and inflame the jealousies of the South and retard the cause of emancipation.

If any man believes that slavery can be abolished without a struggle with the worst passions of human nature, quietly, harmoniously, he cherishes a delusion. It can never be done unless the age of miracles returns. No, we must expect a collision full of sharp asperities and bitterness. We shall have to contend with the insolence and pride and selfishness of many a heartless being. But these can be easily conquered by meekness and perseverance and prayer. . . .

If it be still objected that it would be dangerous to liberate the present race of blacks, I answer [that] the emancipation of all the slaves of this generation is most assuredly out of the question. The fabric which now towers above the Alps must be taken away brick by brick and foot by foot, till it is reduced so low that it may be overturned without burying the nation in its ruins. Years may elapse before the completion of the achievement; generations of blacks may go down to the grave, manacled and lacerated, without a hope for their children; the philanthropists who are now pleading in behalf of the oppressed may not live to witness the dawn which will precede the glori-

ous day of universal emancipation; but the work will go on, laborers in the cause will multiply, new resources will be discovered, the victory will be obtained, worth the desperate struggle of a thousand years. Or, if defeat follow, woe to the safety of this people! The nation will be shaken as if by a mighty earthquake. . . . The terrible judgments of an incensed God will complete the catastrophe of republican America.

And since so much is to be done for our country; since so many prejudices are to be dispelled, obstacles vanquished, interests secured, blessings obtained; since the cause of emancipation must progress heavily and meet with much unhallowed opposition, why delay the work? There must be a beginning and now is a propitious time, perhaps the last opportunity that will be granted us by a long-suffering God. . . . Let us not look coldly on and see our Southern brethren contending single-handed against an all-powerful foe: faint, weary, borne down to the earth. We are all alike guilty. Slavery is strictly a national sin. New England money has been expended in buying human flesh; New England ships have been freighted with sable victims; New England men have assisted in forging the fetters of those who groan in bondage. . . .

I will say, finally, that I despair of the republic while slavery exists therein. If I look up to God for success, no smile of mercy or forgiveness dispels the gloom of futurity. . . . Why should we slumber at this momentous crisis? . . . If we had any regard for our safety and happiness, we should strive to crush the vampire which is feeding upon our lifeblood. All the selfishness of our nature cries aloud for a better security. Our own vices are too strong for us and keep us in perpetual alarm. How, in addition to these, shall we be able to contend successfully with millions of armed and desperate men, as we must eventually if slavery does not cease?

66.

Catharine Beecher: The Profession of a Woman

At the beginning of the nineteenth century, female education had surmounted such early restrictions as that expressed in a 1684 school dictum to the effect that "all girls [shall] be excluded as improper and inconsistent with . . . a grammar school." Elementary education was open to all girls and secondary education to those who could afford it, but no provision had been made for higher education until Emma Willard established Troy Female Seminary (now Emma Willard School) in 1821. In 1824 Catharine Beecher, a member of an illustrious New England family, followed Mrs. Willard's lead by founding the Hartford Female Seminary. Miss Beecher explained her program for female education in the following selection from her book, Suggestions Respecting Improvements in Education, *published in 1829.*

Source: *Suggestions Respecting Improvements in Education,* Hartford, 1829, pp. 7-16.

It is to mothers and to teachers that the world is to look for the character which is to be enstamped on each succeeding generation, for it is to them that the great business of education is almost exclusively committed. And will it not appear by examination that neither mothers nor teachers have ever been properly educated for their profession? What is the *profession of a woman?* Is it not to form immortal minds, and to watch, to nurse, and to rear the bodily system, so fearfully and wonderfully made, and upon the order and regulation of which the health and well-being of the mind so greatly depends?

But let most of our sex, upon whom these arduous duties devolve, be asked: Have you ever devoted any time and study, in the course of your education, to any preparation for these duties? Have you been taught anything of the structure, the nature, and the laws of the body which you inhabit? Were you ever taught to understand the operation of diet, air, exercise, and modes of dress upon the human frame?

Have the causes which are continually operating to prevent good health and the modes by which it might be perfected and preserved ever been made the subject of any *instruction?* Perhaps almost every voice would respond, no. We have attended to almost everything more than to this; we have been taught more concerning the structure of the earth, the laws of the heavenly bodies, the habits and formation of plants, the philosophy of languages — more of *almost anything* than the structure of the human frame and the laws of health and reason.

But is it not the business, the *profession* of a woman to guard the health and form the physical habits of the young? And is not the cradle of infancy and the chamber of sickness sacred to woman alone? And ought she not to know at least some of the *general principles* of that perfect and wonderful piece of mechanism committed to her preservation and care?

The *restoration* of health is the physician's profession, but the *preservation* of it falls to other hands, and it is believed that the time will come when woman will be taught to understand something respecting the construction of the human frame; the physical results which will naturally follow from restricted exercise, unhealthy modes of dress, improper diet, and many other causes which are continually operating to destroy the health and life of the young.

Again let our sex be asked respecting the instruction they have received in the course of their education on that still more arduous and difficult department of their profession which relates to the *intellect* and the *moral susceptibilities.* Have you been taught the powers and faculties of the human mind, and the laws by which it is regulated? Have you studied how to direct its several faculties; how to restore those that are overgrown, and strengthen and mature those that are deficient? Have you been taught the best modes of *communicating* knowledge as well as of *acquiring* it? Have you learned the best mode of correcting bad *moral* habits and forming good ones? Have you made it an object to find how a selfish disposition may be made generous; how a reserved temper may be made open and frank; how pettishness and ill humor may be changed to cheerfulness and kindness? Has any woman studied her profession in this respect?

It is feared the same answer must be returned, if not from all, at least from most of our sex. No; we have acquired wisdom from the observation and experience of others on almost *all other* subjects, but the philosophy of the direction and control of the human mind has not been an object of thought or study. And thus it appears that, though it is woman's *express business* to rear the body and form the mind, there is scarcely anything to which her attention has been less directed.

But this strange and irrational neglect, may be considered as the result, of an equal neglect as it respects those whose *exclusive*

business it is, to form the mind and communicate knowledge. To the parents of a family there are many other cares committed besides the formation of the mental and moral habits of children. Indeed, the pecuniary circumstances of most parents will allow them to devote but little time to the discharge of such duties. . . .

Another defect in education is that it has not been made a *definite object* with teachers *to prepare their pupils to instruct others.* For of how comparatively little value is knowledge laid up in the mind if it is never to be imparted to others, and yet how few have ever been taught to communicate their ideas with facility and propriety. That there is a best way of *teaching* as well as of doing everything else cannot be disputed, and this can no more be learned by *intuition* than can any of the mechanical arts. This can be made an object of instruction as much as any other art, and a woman, ordinarily, might be *taught* to converse with ease and fluency, and to communicate knowledge with accuracy and perspicuity, with far less time and effort than is now given to the acquisition of *music.*

If a teacher, in communicating ideas, should make it a part of the *duty* of a scholar to communicate the same to a third person, either to a child already ignorant or to some friend who would give a listening ear, much would be accomplished in this way. During many recitations it is desirable to induce the pupils to ask questions and express opinions with this object in view. Nothing aids more in this art than attempting to *teach others,* and all who become teachers will probably find that in this and various other ways they *receive* almost as much benefit as they *confer.*

If all females were not only well educated themselves but were prepared to communicate in an easy manner their stores of knowledge to others; if they not only knew how to regulate their own minds, tempers, and habits but how to effect improvements in those around them, the face of society would speedily be changed. The time *may* come when the world will look back with wonder to behold how much time and effort have been given to the mere cultivation of the memory, and how little mankind have been aware of what every teacher, parent, and friend could accomplish in forming the social, intellectual, and moral character of those by whom they are surrounded.

67.

PHILIP LINDSLEY: The Dangers of a Sectarian College

The Jacksonian Era saw the reexamination of many traditional practices and values; an issue of particular concern was whether institutions of higher education ought to be church affiliated and controlled, or free of church influence. Liberal educators like Philip Lindsley desired to make American colleges more secular and scientific, more general and practical, than they thought the atmosphere of sectarian institutions would permit. In fact, however, the trend was the other way — the majority of American colleges were church affiliated in the 1820s. Lindsley expressed concern over the situation in his baccalaureate address at Cumberland College in 1829.

Source: *The Works of Philip Lindsley*, Le Roy J. Halsey, ed., Philadelphia, 1866, Vol. I, pp. 254-263.

A PRINCIPAL CAUSE of the excessive multiplication and dwarfish dimensions of Western colleges is, no doubt, the diversity of religious denominations among us. Almost every sect will have its college, and generally one at least in each state. Of the score of colleges in Ohio, Kentucky, and Tennessee, all are sectarian except two or three; and of course few of them are what they might and should be; and the greater part of them are mere impositions on the public. This is a grievous and growing evil. Why colleges should be sectarian, any more than penitentiaries or than bank, road, or canal corporations, is not very obvious.

Colleges are designed for the instruction of youth in the learned languages, in polite literature, in the liberal arts and sciences, and not in the dogmatical theology of any sect or party. Why then should they be baptized with sectarian names? Are they to inculcate sectarian Greek, sectarian mathematics, sectarian logic, history, rhetoric, philosophy? Must every state be divided and subdivided into as many college associations as there are religious sects within its limits, and, thus, by their mutual jealousy and distrust, effectually prevent the usefulness and prosperity of any one institution? Why does any sect covet the exclusive control of a college, if it be not to promote party and sectarian purposes?

I am aware that as soon as any sect succeeds in obtaining a charter for a *something* called a college, they become, all of a sudden, wondrously liberal and catholic. They forthwith proclaim to the public that their college is the best in the world, and, withal, perfectly free from the odious taint of sectarianism; that youth of all religions may come to it without the slightest risk of being proselyted to the faith of the governing sect. This is very modest and very specious and very hollow and very hypocritical.

They hold out false colors to allure and to deceive the incautious. Their college *is* sectarian and they know it. It is established by a party, governed by a party, taught by a party, and designed to promote the ends of a party. Else why is it under the absolute and perpetual management and control of a party? They very eagerly and very naturally desire the patronage of other sects for the double purpose of receiving pecuniary aid and of adding to their numbers and strength from the ranks of other denominations.

Let any religious sect whatever obtain the absolute direction of a college, located in a small village or retired part of the country, where their religious influence is paramount, perhaps exclusive; where the youth must necessarily attend upon such religious instructions and exercises and ceremonies as they shall prescribe; where, in fact, they can witness no other; where every sermon and prayer and form, where all private conversation and ministerial services proceed from, or are directed by, the one sect — and, is it possible that youth, at the most susceptible period of their lives, should not be operated on by such daily influences during a period of two, four, or six years? How long will the people be gulled by such barefaced impudence, by such unreasonable and monstrous pretensions?

I do not object to any sect's being allowed the privilege of erecting and maintaining, at their own expense, as many schools, colleges, and theological seminaries as they please. But, then, their sectarian views should be openly and distinctly avowed. Their purpose should be specified in their charters. And the legislature should protect the people from imposition by the very act which invests them with corporate powers. Hitherto, almost every legislature has pursued an opposite policy and has aided the work of deception by enacting that, in the said sectarian institution, youth of all sects should be entitled to equal privileges. Thus the sectarian manufactory goes into

operation under the smiles, patronage, and recommendation of the people's representatives.

Its friends puff it off and laud it as the people's school, and plead their liberal charter as the talisman that is to guard the people against every insidious attempt at proselytism; and urge the people to contribute their money to build up their promising and most catholic seminary. The bait is seized, the people are cheated, and the sect has its college. Students of all denominations frequent it. And no man of sense and reflection can doubt the consequences.

There are sects in our country who have succeeded in this way, who never permit their own children to attend any schools but such as they exclusively control, who profess the greatest liberality to the public on all occasions, and who boast among themselves of the converts which they have made from their dissenting pupils. I could specify names and places, and adduce proof positive of all the facts asserted, were it necessary. Let the people see to it, or the remedy will soon be beyond their reach.

A *public* college, that is, a literary and scientific college designed for the public generally, ought to be independent of all religious sectarian bias, or tendency, or influence. And it ought, when practicable, to be situated in a town or city where the several sects, composing the body of the people, have their own places of public worship, to which their sons may have free access; and where the public eye may be constantly fixed on the conduct of the trustees and faculty; and where every artful attempt at proselytism would be instantly detected and exposed. Some men are so constituted that they cannot help being partisans and bigots. Such men are not fit to be the instructors of youth except where it is intended that the dogmas of a sect shall be inculcated.

Science and philosophy ought to know no party in church or state. They are degraded by every such connection. Christianity, indeed, if rightly interpreted, breathes a pure, angelic charity, and is as much a stranger to the strife, and intrigue, and rancor, and intolerance, and pharisaism of party as science and philosophy can be. But so long as men are not content to be honest Christians, but will be zealous Presbyterians, Episcopalians, Methodists, Baptists, Quakers, or Romanists, we must so organize our *public* seminaries of learning as that all may entrust their sons to them without fear of danger to their religious faith.

It has been objected to Nashville as the site of a university for the purposes of general education: that it is the center of too much dissipation, extravagance, and vice; that a residence here might endanger the morals and virtue of youth, and lead them to ruinous indulgence and prodigality. This is a specious objection; but it is merely specious. Small towns and villages are generally more objectionable, in these respects, than cities containing from 5,000 to 50,000 inhabitants. Experience has fully proved in Europe, and in the older states of this Union, that large towns or cities are greatly preferable to small ones for such institutions. All the capitals and most of the second-rate cities of Europe have their universities. And wherever they have been established in small towns, the students are proverbially more riotous and ungovernable in their conduct, more boorish and savage in their manners, and more dissolute and licentious in their habits.

A large town, moreover, always affords greater advantages and facilities for the acquisition of liberal knowledge than a small village. It has comparatively more literary and scientific men, more individuals skilled in various languages, more eminent professional characters, larger libraries, more ample cabinets and collections of natural curiosities and specimens of the arts, a more enlightened and refined society to polish and restrain youth from vulgar practices and indulgences, a greater variety of churches and other religious institutions to enlarge the mind and prevent the growth of bigotry

and sectarianism, and, in general, a more powerful and salutary moral influence is exerted and felt than in a small provincial town or country village. The empire of public opinion is recognized and respected. A vigilant and energetic police is ever at hand also to check the sallies and control the renowning propensities of the thoughtless, the turbulent, the idle, the reckless, and the self-sufficient.

These and similar privileges an enlightened, judicious parent will not fail to appreciate. And in all these respects, Nashville will be every year improving. It has greatly improved within the last eight or ten years, as every citizen who has resided here long enough to judge will testify. I *know* that in Nashville, unpropitious as have been certain local and temporary circumstances, youth may be trained as safely and governed as thoroughly as in any town beyond the mountains. Youth often enter college *spoiled*; and the faculty cannot cure or reform them. But, in no instance yet has a virtuous, orderly, well-behaved youth been made *worse* at our institution.

If they come to the university with inveterate habits of idleness, vice, or insubordination, nothing more can be expected of its government than that it speedily get rid of them. And this it has seldom — without fear, partiality, or favor — failed to accomplish. The *good* have not been injured; nor are they a whit more obnoxious to evil influences *here* than in any town in Connecticut or New York. The *wicked*, if they cannot be reclaimed, are, as a matter of course, presently sent home to their parents and friends.

The good people of the Southern states generally labor under a singular delusion in regard to the benefits which their sons are supposed to enjoy at Eastern seminaries. They have heard much of the steady habits, excellent morals, and religious character of the East; and they presume that their sons, while there, will be precluded from all exposure to vicious temptation. This is a most egregious mistake. The Southern youth, at Eastern colleges, are more exposed to all manner of expensive and ruinous dissipation than they would be at home. They invariably associate together; are always presumed to have plenty of money; are solicited from every quarter to spend it freely; are trusted without hesitation to any amount by those most interested in misleading and in fleecing them; are courted and flattered and made to believe that they are superior to the natives, whose manners, customs, and maxims they affect to despise; are actuated and bound to each other by the lofty and fastidious spirit of provincial clanship, and manifest, to a most ludicrous extent, all the pride and arrogance of aristocratic exclusiveness.

Residing among strangers with whom they are never domesticated, and whose peculiarities they are accustomed to ridicule, far removed from the observation and controlling influence of that society to whose tribunal alone they feel ultimately amenable, they assume the port and bearing of independent lordlings and honorable regulators of both town and college; and, provided they manage to escape imprisonment and expulsion, they care not a rush about minor considerations or temporary consequences.

In due time, after squandering in this hopeful career some $2,000 or $3,000 each per annum, they usually succeed in obtaining what would seem to have been the sole object of their *literary* ambition: a Bachelor's diploma, certifying to the world that they are accomplished in all the liberal arts and sciences, and "adorned with every virtue under heaven." With this precious trophy of their academic achievements, they return home to gladden the hearts of doting parents and to receive the gratulations of kindred and friends; but with heads as empty as their purses, and oftentimes with broken constitutions and dissolute habits which totally unfit them for any useful vocation or honorable profession.

This is no exaggerated representation. That there are exceptions is readily granted. But, like the great prizes in a lottery, they are so few in comparison with the blanks that nice calculators, who are skilled in the doctrine of chances, would not choose to hazard much upon the issue in either case. On the contrary, at Nashville, no youth from any section of the slaveholding states will ever dream that he is superior to the common law of public sentiment, that he is above the reach of disgrace from the repulsive and frowning aspect of the society in which he lives, or that his present comfort and future respectability will not depend on the opinion which the good, the wise, the intelligent, and the influential may form of his talents, industry, morals, and gentlemanly deportment while a college student. In the metropolis of Tennessee, every son of Tennessee will look *up* with deference to the better class of citizens as models for imitation; while at an Eastern village he might look *down* with contempt upon the whole population. And the sneer of a companion at the *Yankees* is, at any time, sufficient to efface from his mind any salutary impression from the rebukes of authority or the counsels of wisdom.

Nashville has been objected to on the score of expense, and with as little reason as every other. The truth is that the cost of an education here is less by 50 and even 100 percent, all advantages considered, than at any *respectable* Northern or Southern college whatever. The price of board is $1.75 per week, and the other charges are not so high as at many of our female and classical schools. One hundred and twenty dollars defray the entire college bills for all purposes (including board) during the academic year of forty-two weeks. Contingent expenses of every kind must be regulated, of course, by parental discretion. The most rigid economy is recommended and encouraged, and, as far as practicable, enforced. It is obvious that all articles imported from abroad must be cheaper in a commercial emporium than at any remote town in the country.

Candidates for the gospel ministry are, without distinction of sect or name, admitted to all the privileges of the university at half the ordinary charges. Poor young men who desire to help themselves either by teaching in the public schools or in private families, or by laboring on the college farm or in the workshops of our mechanics, may earn more here than at any "manual labor" establishment in the country. Every possible facility is given to this species of commendable but voluntary enterprise; and no manner of disgrace attaches to the individuals who thus manfully strive to educate themselves. Every product of the garden, the field, and the workshop commands a ready and profitable market.

If it be possible for a youth to *work* his way through college in any part of the world, he can do it *here* with equal certainty and under peculiar advantages. In salubrity, also, Nashville is unrivaled; and, consequently, students are rarely subjected to any extra expense for physicians or nurses on account of ill health.

68.

Josiah Holbrook: Lyceums and Popular Education

One result of the educational reform movement of the early nineteenth century was a new interest in adult education, stimulated in part by Josiah Holbrook's 1826 proposal for the organization of "lyceums," or centers where adults might hear the best lecturers of the day. Holbrook's plan, in many ways similar to the later Chautauqua movement, quickly gained popularity; by 1834 there were more than 3,000 lyceums, spurring the hope that lyceums might develop into a nationwide system of adult education. This did not happen, but Holbrook's efforts did arouse public interest in popular education.

Source: OSL 139.

THIS INSTITUTION consists of town and county lyceums, and measures are in progress to organize state lyceums and a *general union* of the whole.

TOWN LYCEUMS

A TOWN LYCEUM is a voluntary association of individuals disposed to improve each other in useful knowledge, and to advance the interests of their schools. To gain the first object, they hold weekly or other stated meetings for reading, conversation, discussion, illustrating the sciences, or other exercises designed for their mutual benefit; and, as it is found convenient, they collect a cabinet, consisting of apparatus for illustrating the sciences, books, minerals, plants, or other natural or artificial productions.

To advance the interests of schools, they furnish teachers with a room, apparatus, and other accommodations for holding meetings and conducting a course of exercises in relation to their schools, some of the eldest members of which, with other young persons, attend the meetings of lyceums, where they are exercised and instructed in a manner fitted to their pursuits and wants. It is supposed that lyceums may aid in furnishing schools with some simple apparatus, juvenile books or other articles, fitted to awaken an interest and communicate instruction to their members.

Town lyceums have conducted their exercises in several different ways, to suit the wishes and acquirements of those who compose them. In some instances these exercises have consisted principally in reading interesting or useful articles from periodicals, a conversation on chemistry or other science, a biographical or historical sketch, communications of intelligence of improvements in education or the arts, or any other subject fitted for the entertainment or instruction of the members. The reading has frequently been accompanied or followed by questions, remarks, or conversation by any disposed to introduce them.

In other meetings the sciences have been introduced by short and very familiar illustrations by the means of simple apparatus, six or eight, or perhaps ten or twelve, taking a part in the exercises of an evening. Under this plan of exercises, nearly all the members of the lyceums which have adopted it have not only received but communicated instruction.

In some lyceums the instruction has been given principally in the form of lectures or dissertations, in which cases one or perhaps two have occupied the attention of the society during a sitting. The instruction given by lectures or dissertations, like that in a more mutual form, is intended to be of a familiar and practical character, that it may be brought within the comprehension of the most untutored minds.

Besides attending meetings of common interest to both sexes and all classes, females have conducted a course of mutual exercises among themselves by spending together, during the summer, one afternoon in a week for reading, composition, and improvement in the various branches of an accomplished and enlightened education.

Teachers have also held meetings confined to themselves in which they have introduced subjects and carried on exercises with particular reference to their schools. At these meetings they have had exercises in reading, giving an opportunity for critical remarks upon pronunciation, emphasis, inflection, modulation, and other points in good reading, all eminently calculated to improve them in this useful accomplishment. Exercises in grammar, composition, geography, arithmetic, illustrations in natural philosophy and chemistry, and sometimes discussions or dissertations upon the modes and principles of teaching have been introduced at these meetings of teachers, and uniformly and immediately for the benefit of themselves and of the schools under their charge.

Some of the eldest members of the several schools in a town, with other young persons too far advanced or too much occupied to be benefited from the daily instruction of schools within their reach, have, by the aid of professional teachers, clergymen, or other individuals (sometimes ladies) competent and disposed to guide them, carried on a course of weekly exercises, which have given them gradually, but certainly and permanently, a development and expansion of mind, and a refined and elevated taste.

Some of the advantages which have already arisen from the lyceums which have gone into operation are the following, viz.:

1. *The improvement of conversation.* An immediate and uniform effect of a lyceum, wherever it has been established and whatever the mode of conducting its exercises, is the introduction of good topics of conversation into the daily intercourse of families, neighbors, and friends, and that not among the members merely but among all who come within the circle of its influence. Subjects of science, or other topics of useful knowledge, take the place of frivolous conversation or petty scandal, frequently indulged, and uniformly deplored, in our country villages. When it is considered that conversation is a constant and an exhaustless source of information, either good or bad,

"Lyceum Lecturer and His Audience at Clinton Hall"

in every town and among the whole race of mankind, it cannot but be evident that any measures which can give it an intellectual, moral, and, of course, an elevated character must confer a distinguished benefit upon society.

2. *Directing amusements.* Few subjects are more important, and none perhaps so much neglected, as amusements. Young people always have had, and, it is believed and hoped, they always will have, places of resort for social enjoyment. From the neglect of parents, and other persons of influence, to furnish them with occasions and opportunities to meet for exercises calculated for the instruction and improvement of each other, as well as for the enjoyment of social affections of a generous and elevated character, they resort to those calculated to corrupt and debase their minds, while they afford them no pleasures but those of the most groveling character.

Instead of having placed before them at their meetings books, apparatus, minerals, plants, and other objects calculated to acquaint them with the works and the laws of their Creator, and to lead them to admire the extent, the variety, the richness, and the grandeur of His creation, all designed and fitted for their immediate use and elevated enjoyment, they are presented with shelves of loaded decanters and sparkling glasses, so

richly filled and so neatly arranged, and for *their* enjoyment, too, that to neglect them would be vulgar and unmanly. Experiments are, of course, made upon their contents, not, however, for their mutual entertainment in conversation and reflection upon the works and the goodness of their Creator, but in the merry song, the vulgar wit, and the loud laugh.

Parents and others to whom the rising generation look, and upon whom they depend for guidance and support, will you be offended at the question whether your children are most to blame for resorting to such places, and engaging in such exercises, or yourselves for neglecting to furnish them with better?

On the influence of amusements and conversation, always governing and partaking of the character of each other, and always determining the character of villages, communities, and the world, volumes might be written, but the occasion forbids enlarging.

3. *Saving of expense.* No principle in political economy is better established by experience than that a liberal support of religious and literary institutions is calculated to promote the pecuniary as well as the intellectual and moral prosperity of the community. Nor is there any mystery in this uniform result from the unerring hand of experiment. It has already been observed

that young people must have occasions for social enjoyment and for recreation; and everyone is familiar with the fact that the least useful and most pernicious amusements are the most expensive.

The expense of a year's entertainment and instruction at the meetings and exercises of a lyceum is from 50 cents to $2. The expense of one quarter's instruction in a dancing school, including extra clothes, pocket money, etc., cannot be estimated at less than $10 for each pupil. The expense of one evening's entertainment at a ball or assembly is from two to ten times the expense of a year's entertainment at the meetings of a lyceum. Many young men have paid $2 for a horse and chaise to ride upon the Sabbath, with too manly a spirit to mention it as an expense, who would be ready to confess themselves too poor to pay the same sum for a weekly course of the most useful instruction through the year. Military exercises, which can hardly be considered in any other light than as amusements for young men, cost, upon an average, everyone who engages in them in the Commonwealth of Massachusetts, not less than $10 annually. The average expense for a town is over $2,000 a year. All these amusements are attended with an expense of time which it is difficult to calculate, an expense of money for articles which it is impossible to name, and with an expense of intellects and morals which is truly appalling. These expenses it is the tendency of lyceums to prevent.

4. *Calling into use neglected libraries, and giving occasion for establishing new ones.* It has been a subject of general regret that public libraries, after a short time, fall into neglect and disuse. Where a course of weekly or other stated exercises has been carried on in connection or in the vicinity of a library, an occasion for this regret has never been known to exist. But, on the contrary, the demands immediately and uniformly created for books by the meetings and exercises of lyceums have led to the enlargement of public libraries, and induced individuals to procure private libraries for their own use.

5. *Providing a seminary for teachers.* In the United States, more than 50,000 daily teachers, and from 150 to 200,000 weekly teachers of Sabbath schools, are engaged in forming the character of the rising generation and molding the destiny of our nation. Raising the qualifications of this responsible and important class of the community is an object of such vast moment to the prosperity of our country that for several years past it has been the frequent theme of conversation, addresses, sermons, and messages and speeches to legislatures. In many places this object has already been attained in a very efficient manner by weekly or other stated meetings of teachers for the improvement of each other. And at a very trifling expense for providing them with a room, apparatus, and other accommodations for holding their meetings and conducting their exercises, every town in the United States may enable their teachers *immediately* and *constantly* to raise their own characters, and in such a way as *immediately* and *constantly* to raise the characters of their schools. If so, can anyone conceive of a more powerful or more efficient seminary to qualify teachers than an institution which shall organize and direct a system of exercises by which they shall be enabled to qualify themselves, and that universally, immediately, and constantly?

6. *Benefiting academies.* Many academies, young ladies' seminaries, and other institutions of a similar character have been greatly benefited by the exercises of lyceums. Regular courses of experimental lectures, procured from experienced teachers, and the weekly courses of mutual exercises conducted by lyceums, have usually been offered as a gratuity, or at a small consideration, to the members of academies and similar institutions for daily instruction. The opportunities of these pupils are consequently increased, not only by providing them with a

greater amount of instruction to be received from others but by leading them to engage in new exercises to instruct themselves. In very many instances, members of academies have interested others at the meeting of lyceums; and, in affording an intellectual entertainment to their friends, they have received a tenfold benefit by instructing and improving themselves.

7. *Increasing the advantages and raising the character of district schools.* Public schools have been benefited, not only by the facilities offered by lyceums for the improvement of their teachers but by the opportunities they present directly to some of the eldest members of these schools to receive a course of weekly instruction of a higher character and under better advantages than can be given among the promiscuous assemblage of children, and the great variety of objects which these schools usually embrace. A weekly meeting of a few pupils from all the schools in a town, to be instructed and examined by several teachers and by their parents or others interested in their welfare, acts almost with the rapidity and the power of electricity on all the teachers and all their schools. They immediately leave the dull, monotonous circle in which they have been traveling for years, and commence an onward and upward course. Their energies are awakened and invigorated, their minds are expanded, and they begin in earnest to lay broad and strong a foundation for their future characters and respectability.

8. *Compiling of town histories.* Several lyceums have undertaken to procure histories of the towns where they are placed. In almost every town there remain a few of those patriots who purchased at so dear a rate the independence we now enjoy. And it would perhaps be difficult to determine to whom it would afford the purest and richest entertainment, to themselves in relating the tales of their wrongs, their battles, and their successes, or to their children and grandchildren in listening to them. But that

it would afford a mutual entertainment to the old and young to hold a few meetings, to recount and to learn the most interesting incidents in the history of the place of their residence or their birth, especially at this most interesting period in the history of our country, no one can deny or doubt. Nor can it be doubted that a historical sketch of every town would furnish interesting and important documents to be preserved for the generations that are to follow.

9. *Town maps.* A few lyceums are taking measures to procure maps of their towns. To procure surveys for the purpose has been proposed as an exercise in the art of surveying to those who wish to acquire it. After a survey and draft are made, it is ascertained from artists that 200 lithographic prints can be procured for $25. And what family would not be willing to pay 12½ cents for a correct map of the town where they reside?

10. *Agricultural and geological surveys.* Many lyceums have explored, thoroughly and minutely, the mineral productions, not only of the towns where they are placed but of the surrounding country. Numerous interesting and useful minerals have been discovered, large collections have been made, and, consequently, new sources of industry and of wealth have been laid open, and the treasures of science have been enriched. And, when it is considered that the geology and mineralogy of our country are intimately connected with agriculture and internal improvements, the importance of having them fully and minutely explored must appear too great and too manifest to require one word to explain or enforce it. And, if time would permit, it might be easily shown that our resources in the mineral kingdom can be more fully and minutely explored, and the consequent knowledge placed more generally and directly in the possession of those who need it, through the agency of lyceums than by any other method which can be devised.

11. *State collections of minerals.* Some of

the states have commenced collections of minerals deposited in their capitols. When towns or counties are making surveys and collections for their own use, it will be easy to furnish specimens for a general collection, which might be arranged according to towns or geological divisions. These measures would furnish each state with a complete suite of its own minerals and a general collection of foreign specimens. Such collections would be useful, not only to science but to agriculture and internal improvements, by placing before legislators and others specimens of their own productions, and a knowledge of their own resources in the mineral kingdom, by which industry would be encouraged and individual and public wealth and prosperity increased.

Such are some of the advantages which have already, either partially or fully, arisen from the mutual efforts of individuals in numerous towns for the improvement of themselves and the advancement of popular education.

COUNTY LYCEUMS

A county lyceum is a Board of Delegates, consisting of one or more from each town society, who meet semiannually, and adopt measures to aid the efforts and forward the interests of the several branches which they represent. At their semiannual meetings, public addresses are delivered and committees appointed to inquire how books, apparatus, and instruction by lectures, or otherwise, can be procured by the several town lyceums; and to learn the state of the schools in the several towns where they are placed, and what measures can be taken to improve them. Some of the county lyceums have proposed owning some articles of apparatus too expensive to be owned by each branch, such as a telescope, galvanic apparatus, etc.; and to employ a lecturer who should give lectures to the several town lyceums in succession, and aid them in making geological and agricultural surveys, and

in their other efforts for their mutual improvement. They have also proposed to procure maps of the several counties where they are organized, including the topography, geology, etc.

STATE LYCEUMS

To render the efforts of town and county lyceums still more efficient, successful, and uniform, they have proposed the formation of state lyceums to consist of one or more representatives sent from each county society. A state lyceum would be a *Board of Education* for the state where it should be organized, and, by the appointment of committees for several specific objects, would provide means for advancing the various interests of a popular education. One important object designed to be effected by a state lyceum is the introduction of a uniform system of books and instruction into our public schools.

The frequent change and the great diversity of books in our district schools have so long been subjects of general and bitter complaints among parents and teachers that no words are necessary to convince them of the evil or of the importance of providing a remedy. But there is another evil in our public schools, still greater than the variety and change of books; it is the want of a proper selection of branches introduced into our system of popular education, and of uniform and judicious modes of teaching them. Some branches absolutely essential in the ordinary concerns of life are wholly neglected, while others, almost wholly useless, are dwelt upon year after year by numerous children in most of our public schools. A knowledge of the proper mode of writing letters of friendship or business is essential to enable a person to be decent in the social and business relations of life. But it is scarcely introduced in any of our district schools in New England. The theory of grammar, as it is frequently taught in our public schools, is not only useless but there is too much reason to believe that it is an absolute injury to the intellects of children, by forcing into their minds words which they cannot understand, and consequently giving them a disrelish, not only for the study of grammar but of other subjects which might otherwise interest them, expand their minds, and fit them for usefulness. A general remedy for this and similar evils cannot be provided except by a general society.

Infant schools. The success of infant schools has been uniform and almost miraculous. They are to form the closing scene in the great and animating drama of the benevolent operations now going on to rid the world of crime and to fill it with knowledge. They need not be confined to children of the poor and to large cities, but the heavenly blessings which they bestow may be enjoyed by all classes and in every village and neighborhood, and even in every family of our race. The principles and management which give these schools of infants such distinguished success may, and eventually must, be introduced into all public and other schools, when their success will be equally great and the results equally animating and sublime. But to carry to the door of every mother a school for her infant, as well as to change and elevate the character of all the schools now in operation, a Board of Education seems highly important, if not indispensable. The blessings of infant schools, and the extension of those principles and that management which render them the most sublime objects at present upon the earth, a state lyceum, with the cooperation of county and town lyceums, would have great power to hasten in every town, village, and neighborhood.

Agricultural seminaries. The importance of institutions which shall at once present opportunities for a *liberal,* a *practical,* and an *economical* education is extensively and sensibly felt, where by the aid of the plow, the hoe, the turning lathe, the plane and saw, young men may not only fix more deeply

in their minds the science acquired in their studies and lecture rooms, and more fully learn its use, but by the practical operations which it directs may *educate themselves.*

The occasion will not permit to enlarge upon the plan or the importance of such institutions, but it may be remarked that, if they should go into operation under the patronage of lyceums, there could not fail to arise between them a reciprocal, a salutary, and a powerful action. The members and friends of lyceums would furnish pupils to the seminaries, and the seminaries would furnish teachers with science and apparatus for illustrating it to lyceums. The manufactory of apparatus of a simple and practical character, fitted for familiar illustrations in schools, academies, and lyceums would furnish a most interesting and useful employment for the members of practical seminaries. It would make them familiar with the principles of science which the various instruments were designed to illustrate, furnish them with an agreeable and healthful exercise, and enable them either partially or wholly to defray the expenses of their education.

GENERAL UNION

As "UNION IS STRENGTH," no one can doubt the importance of several state lyceums uniting to forward the great and numerous purposes of a *popular* and a *national education.* Numerous advantages might be expected to arise from an American Lyceum, which time will not permit to mention. But the publication of a *Journal of Education,* numerous cheap, familiar, and practical tracts on the sciences, the arts, biography, history, etc., to be circulated to the branch lyceums, schools, academies, taverns, steamboats, and private families would be an object worthy of the united efforts of individuals and societies in different parts of the country who wished for a *universal diffusion of knowledge.*

69.

John Neal: American Painters and Painting

Americans in the first few decades of the nineteenth century went through a great deal of self-examination. What did it mean to be American? What was unique or different about the United States? What was the potential of American civilization? These questions resulted in part from the self-consciousness of new nationhood and in part from the need to answer frequent European criticisms of cultural shortcomings. The following editorial by John Neal, editor of The Yankee; *and Boston Literary Gazette, evaluates the quality of American painting from a nationalistic point of view. Neal was a professional author and critic whose position as an editor enabled him to express himself on a wide variety of issues.*

Source: *The Yankee; and Boston Literary Gazette*, No. 79, July 1829, New series, No. 1.

WE HAVE CERTAINLY, EITHER BY NATURE, which is not very probable, or by accident something that appears like a decided predisposition for painting in this country. At this moment there are more distinguished American painters than are to be found in any one of what are called the modern schools of Europe. Our headmakers are without number, and some without price, our historical by the acre, our portrait, our landscape, and our still-life painters, if not too numerous to mention, are much too numerous to particularize. They are better than we deserve, and more than we know what to do with. Their progress, too, is altogether astonishing if we consider the disadvantages under which they have labored, with no models, no casts, no academy figures, and little or no opportunity for them ever to see the old masters gathered together, where they could either be copied or studied with impunity.

But astonishing as their progress may have been, it is nothing to what it should be, and *will* be, if they are diligent and faithful for the next half a dozen years. The whole country is on their side now. Pictures of worth are beginning to be relished — by

and by they will be understood; after that, they will soon become not merely an article for the rich, a luxury for the few, but things for everybody, familiar household furniture. Already are they quite as *necessary* as the chief part of what goes to the embellishment of a house, and far more beautiful than most of the other furniture.

If you cannot believe this, you have but to look at the multitude of portraits, wretched as they generally are, that may be found in every village of our country. You can hardly open the door of a best room anywhere without surprising, or being surprised by, the picture of somebody plastered to the wall and staring at you with both eyes and a bunch of flowers. And the fashion once set, even for bad pictures, there is a certain market for good ones in embryo. Virtuosi abound everywhere; critics in the farthest off and most unheard of country villages — people who are not to be satisfied with the skill and taste of their doer of tavern signs, Jersey wagons, chairs, and cradles. And is nothing to come of this? Will not vanity, the love of distinction, the pride of wealth, travel, to say nothing of taste or knowledge, tend to improve the condition of painters and the quality of painting throughout our whole country, in a geometrical ratio hereafter? They certainly will. Of this, our artists may be assured; and for this, if they are prudent, they will prepare themselves, by devout study and zealous labor.

The day is near at hand — we speak in the spirit of allowed prophecy — when pictures that are now thought well of, by good judges, will not be tolerated by the multitude; when such portraits as we see covering the walls, not only of our academies and exhibitions but those of our mother country, would not be allowed to show their face in the dwelling of a tolerably educated man. This may appear extravagant to those who have not considered the matter much, nor observed the wonderful changes that have been wrought in Philadelphia, where the first annual exhibition appeared; in New York, where the next had place; in Baltimore and Boston, where they have now been repeated several years running, since our painters and the public have had an opportunity of meeting together face to face in a body. How many pictures, how many painters that were spoken well of by those who were allowed to occupy the judgment seat among the people are now forgotten, or remembered only for the purpose of registering the growth and improvement of public opinion?

We can remember when the wretched landscapes of Mr. West, done before he knew his right hand from his left in painting, were treated as prodigies for a boy. Now they would be laughed at were they shown as the early productions of an apprentice to a painter of fire buckets, looking-glass tablets, or militia standards. Ten or twelve years ago, Copley was a high standard — perhaps the highest we knew, for Stewart was then alive — in portraiture. Now the very multitude see that his portraits are colored porcelain — polished marble — smoothed over with oil and rottenstone. So with a number more, whom we

may refer to hereafter, to say nothing of the Capitol pictures by Mr. Trumbull, which have undergone the strangest apotheosis ever heard of, within six or eight years.

Meanwhile, it may not be labor wasted to review, in the lump as it were, three or four of the late exhibitions of our country, limiting our remarks to a part of those only which we have had an opportunity of seeing with our own eyes.

In 1827, the New York American Academy of Fine Arts, of which Mr. Trumbull was president and George IV and the Emperor Napoleon are honorary members, had a *thirteenth exhibition*. There were a few, and but a few, good pictures in it, many as wretched as we ever saw at Somerset House or Suffolk Street, and few which, if they had not been painted by Mr. Trumbull, the president of that association, or Mr. Morse, the president of the National Academy of Design — both men of decided strength by nature, though the strength of one has departed and that of the other is dormant — would have been thought detestable. There were two or three Holy Families — nay, five, as we find on reference to the published catalog . . . no one of which was worth picking up in the street for a cover to a tea chest, and the whole of which, multiplied into each other, were not equal in merit to the little finger of the meanest figure (except that of Sir Thomas Lawrence) in the celebrated "Sortie of Gibraltar"; a picture, by the way, which, notwithstanding his obligations to Copley in the array, management, and costume, really deserves more reputation by far than it enjoys. (What we said a moment ago of Copley was concerning his portraits; in his dealing with history and character, in a small way, he is sometimes very clever, strong, and spirited.) Yet there was one picture by Mr. Trumbull, even here, which we find marked in the catalog as bearing the proportion of seven-tenths to a great picture. It was called "Maternal Affection."

Just so was it with the work of Mr. President Morse. He had a full length of Lafayette on show; it . . . purported to belong to the corporation of New York. We were glad of it on several accounts, grieved on others; for Mr. M., who is really a man of genius and power, might have made a much better picture of anything or anybody. Perhaps, however — and we rather incline to the belief that such is the fact — perhaps, however, Mr. M. had been led astray by the coloring and chopstick handling of Sir Thomas Lawrence in his portrait of Sir Benjamin West, exhibited at the same time.

Among other old acquaintances we saw was that everlasting picture of "Lear in the Storm," by far the most gorgeous, lofty, and powerful of West's workmanship, though crowded to death, and as full of cant as a melodrama. Then followed his "Ophelia," containing the nearest approach to tenderness he ever made. A notice in the following language — "It is particularly requested *not to injure* any of the paintings or sculptures, especially by fingering *of* them." — Think of putting up such a notice in the National Academy of Fine Arts? What barbarians a stranger must think us, whether it was or was not necessary.

We shall say nothing more of the rest of the collection, save that "Orlando and Oliver," by Raphael West, ought never to appear this side of Philadelphia, where it was hung up years and years ago for the study and admiration of such as knew no better than to study and admire it; that Vanderlyn's portrait of a lady . . . was not by any means worthy of his reputation, so far as the portrait, or flesh, or drapery, or drawing was concerned, though the reflection in the glass (for the lady was before a mirror in such a way as to give two views of her head) was the best thing of the sort we ever saw; that the "Lioness in the Toils," by Rubens, was a veritable Rubens, and absolutely unmatchable even by that chief among animal painters, for strength, nature, and life; that the landscapes from the collection of the Count de Survellier (Joseph Bo-

naparte) by Salvator Rosa were not like Salvator Rosa, in any of his highest or boldest characteristics, and ought therefore to be studied with caution; that the portrait of a gentleman, by T. Frothingham . . . was, take it as a whole, a very fine picture. . . .

Having now disposed of the American Academy of Fine Arts for 1827, let us run through the National Academy of Design, at New York, for the same year.

The portrait by Morse of Lafayette we have already had up, and shall therefore pass on to the others, mentioning those, and those only, which have a pencil mark to them in the catalog — a mark, by the way, which was put to them at full speed and almost on horseback, nearly three years ago, the meaning of which is nearly forgotten at this time. . . .

The portrait of a lady . . . by S. F. B. Morse, P. N. A., was among the very worst pictures in the collection. At this we were astonished, for the painter has thrown off some heads of extraordinary power; and his portrait of Mr. Monroe, notwithstanding the fervor and wildness of the eye, was a masterly work. But he is a man who only requires to be told of a fault. He may be yet — and he will be — we think, all that he promised to be ten years ago. And that should satisfy even the aspirations of a painter.

There was a portrait of Governor Clinton, by Dunlap, which deserved considerable praise; and a cattle piece . . . by that clever but overpraised artist Fisher, not worth mentioning, though people regard it as a phenomenon.

The portrait of Mr. Maverick, by Neagle, was a very bold, straightforward, generous picture; and that of Professor Ware, by Harding, about the best he ever painted — full of the artist and strong with individuality. . . .

We shall conclude by observing that, if we take the two exhibitions in the lump, they were not worthy of New York, while those of the same year, at Boston (the catalog of which we have mislaid), was altogether superior to what a stranger would have expected in this country; and it would have done credit to the metropolis of Great Britain.

Let the public bear in mind, however, that a taste for the fine arts is no plant of the desert that will shoot forth unheeded, and spread its blossoms where there are none to enjoy their fragrance; nor a sturdy weed that can struggle into vigor through rubbish and neglect. It is a plant whose seeds will remain inert until called into life by culture, and will spread into luxuriance exactly in proportion to the care taken of it. We require no other reason to account for its languor or disappearance than the withdrawing of this culture by the cessation of encouragement. Where honor or reward fail to attend any pursuit, there will be few found to follow it.

70.

Edgar Allan Poe: "To Science"

The ornate grotesqueries of Edgar Allan Poe's poetry and fiction often concealed the precise methods he employed to achieve his fantastic effects; similarly, his deprecation of scientific inquiry and law in "To Science" obscures the fact that Poe was knowledgeable in the science of his day and was peculiarly proud of his adeptness at "scientific reasoning." Poe intended "To Science" as both a preface and a key to his longer work, "Al Aaraaf," an allegorical tale depicting man's inadequate appreciation of God and of beauty. Poe was only twenty years old when the two poems were published in 1829 as part of his second collection, Al Aaraaf, Tamerlane and Minor Poems.

Source: *Poems,* New York, 1831.

TO SCIENCE

Science! true daughter of Old Time thou art!
   Who alterest all things with thy peering eyes.
Why preyest thou thus upon the poet's heart,
   Vulture, whose wings are dull realities?
How should he love thee? or how deem thee wise,
   Who wouldst not leave him in his wandering
To seek for treasure in the jeweled skies,
   Albeit he soared with an undaunted wing?
Hast thou not dragged Diana from her car,
   And driven the Hamadryad from the wood
To seek a shelter in some happier star?
   Hast thou not torn the Naiad from her flood,
The Elfin from the green grass, and from me
The summer dream beneath the tamarind tree?

71.

A Plea for Manhood Suffrage

A significant characteristic of the Jacksonian Era was the movement to expand the base of popular power by extending the right to vote to those who did not own property. The Virginia Convention of 1829, called to revise the state's constitution of 1776, was divided on the question. James Monroe and John Randolph were opposed to any extension of the suffrage, fearing that it would erode the rights of property. Others argued that failure to liberalize the constitution would betray fundamental American principles. The following Memorial of the Non-Freeholders of Richmond, Virginia, urging expanded suffrage, was presented to the convention by John Marshall, chief justice of the Supreme Court. In the end, James Madison negotiated a compromise by which general manhood suffrage was rejected, but property qualifications for voting were relaxed.

Source: *Proceedings and Debates of the Virginia State Convention, of 1829-30,* Richmond, 1830, pp. 25-31.

YOUR MEMORIALISTS, as their designation imports, belong to that class of citizens who, not having the good fortune to possess a certain portion of land, are, for that cause only, debarred from the enjoyment of the right of suffrage. . . .

Comprising a very large part, probably a majority, of male citizens of mature age, they have been passed by, like aliens or slaves, as if destitute of interest, or unworthy of a voice, in measures involving their future political destiny; while the freeholders, sole possessors, under the existing Constitution, of the elective franchise have, upon the strength of that possession alone, asserted and maintained in themselves the exclusive power of new-modeling the fundamental laws of the state: in other words, have seized upon the sovereign authority. . . .

Among the doctrines inculcated in the great charter handed down to us as a declaration of the rights pertaining to the good people of Virginia and their posterity, "as the basis and foundation of government," we are taught,

That all men are by nature equally free and independent, and have certain inherent rights, of which, when they enter into a state of society, they cannot, by any compact, deprive or divest their posterity: namely, the enjoyment of life and liberty, with the means of acquiring and possessing property, and pursuing and obtaining happiness and safety.

That all power is vested in, and consequently derived from, the people.

That a majority of the community hath an indubitable, unalienable, and indefeasible right to reform, alter, or abolish the government.

That no man, nor set of men, are entitled to exclusive or separate emoluments or privileges, but in consideration of public services.

That all men, having sufficient evidence of permanent common interest with and attachment to the community have a right of suffrage, and cannot be taxed or deprived of their property without their consent, or that of their representative, nor bound by any law to which they have not, in like manner, assented, for the public good.

How do the principles thus proclaimed accord with the existing regulation of suffrage? . . .

Surely it were much to be desired that every citizen should be qualified for the proper exercise of all his rights and the due performance of all his duties. But the same qualifications that entitle him to assume the management of his private affairs and to claim all other privileges of citizenship equally entitle him, in the judgment of your memorialists, to be entrusted with this, the dearest of all his privileges, the most important of all his concerns. But if otherwise, still they cannot discern in the possession of land any evidence of peculiar merit or superior title. . . .

Virtue, intelligence are not among the products of the soil. Attachment to property, often a sordid sentiment, is not to be confounded with the sacred flame of patriotism. The love of country, like that of parents and offspring, is engrafted in our nature. It exists in all climates, among all classes, under every possible form of government. Riches more often impair it than poverty. Who has it not is a monster.

Your memorialists feel the difficulty of undertaking calmly to repel charges and insinuations involving in infamy themselves and so large a portion of their fellow citizens. To be deprived of their rightful equality, and to hear as an apology that they are too ignorant and vicious to enjoy it, is no ordinary trial of patience. Yet they will suppress the indignant emotions these sweeping denunciations are well calculated to excite. The freeholders themselves know them to be unfounded. Why else are arms placed in

the hands of a body of disaffected citizens, so ignorant, so depraved, and so numerous?

In the hour of danger, they have drawn no invidious distinctions between the sons of Virginia. The muster rolls have undergone no scrutiny, no comparison with the land books, with a view to expunge those who have been struck from the ranks of freemen. If the landless citizens have been ignominiously driven from the polls, in time of peace, they have at least been generously summoned, in war, to the battlefield. Nor have they disobeyed the summons, or, less profusely than others, poured out their blood in the defense of that country which is asked to disown them. Will it be said they owe allegiance to the government that gives them protection?

Be it so; and if they acknowledge the obligation; if privileges are really extended to them in defense of which they may reasonably be required to shed their blood, have they not motives, irresistible motives, of attachment to the community? Have they not an interest, a deep interest, in perpetuating the blessings they enjoy, and a right, consequently, to guard those blessings, not from foreign aggression merely but from domestic encroachment?

But, it is said, yield them this right and they will abuse it. Property, that is, landed property, will be rendered insecure, or at least overburdened by those who possess it not. The freeholders, on the contrary, can pass no law to the injury of any other class which will not more injuriously affect themselves. The alarm is sounded, too, of danger from large manufacturing institutions, where one corrupt individual may sway the corrupt votes of thousands. It were a vain task to attempt to meet all the flimsy pretexts urged, to allay all the apprehensions felt or feigned by the enemies of a just and liberal policy. The danger of abuse is a dangerous plea. Like *necessity*, the detested plea of the tyrant, or the still more detestable plea of the Jesuit, *expediency*, it serves as an ever-ready apology for all oppression. . . .

To deny to the great body of the people all share in the government on suspicion that they may deprive others of their property; to rob them in advance of their rights; to look to a privileged order as the fountain and depository of all power is to depart from the fundamental maxims, to destroy the chief beauty, the characteristic feature, indeed, of republican government.

Nor is the danger of abuse thereby diminished, but greatly augmented. No community can exist, no representative body be formed, in which some one division of persons or section of country, or some two or more combined, may not preponderate and oppress the rest. The East may be more powerful than the West, the lowlanders than the highlanders, the agricultural than the commercial or manufacturing classes. To give all power, or an undue share, to one is obviously not to remedy but to ensure the evil. Its safest check, its best corrective is found in a general admission of all upon a footing of equality. So intimately are the interests of each class in society blended and interwoven, so indispensible is justice to all, that oppression in that case becomes less probable from any one, however powerful. Nor is this mere speculation. . . .

What security . . . is there against the injustice of the freeholders? How is the assertion made good that they can pass no law affecting the rights of others without more injuriously affecting their own? They cannot do this, it is said, because they possess, in common with other citizens, all personal rights, and, in addition, the rights pertaining to their peculiar property. And if this be a satisfactory reason, then one landholder in each county or district would suffice to elect the representative body; or, the impossibility of injuring others being shown, a single landholder in the commonwealth might still more conveniently exercise the sovereign power.

But, is not the proposition obviously false? What is there to prevent their imposing upon others undue burdens, and conferring on themselves unjust exemptions? Supplying the public exigencies by a capitation or other tax exclusively or oppressively operating on the other portions of the community? Exacting from the latter, in common with slaves, menial services? Placing around their own persons and property more efficient guards? Providing for their own injuries speedier remedies? Denying to the children of all other classes admission to the public seminaries of learning? Interdicting to all but their own order, indeed, the power to elect, and the right to be elected, are most intimately if not inseparably united; all offices of honor or emolument, civil or military? Why can they not do all this, and more? Where is the impossibility? It would be unjust: admirable logic! Injustice can be predicated only of nonfreeholders.

Still, it is said the nonfreeholders have no just cause of complaint. A freehold is easily acquired. The right of suffrage, moreover, is not a natural right. Society may grant, modify, or withhold it as expediency may require. Indeed, all agree that certain regulations are proper; those, for example, relating to age, sex, and citizenship. At best, it is an idle contest for an abstract right whose loss is attended with no practical evil.

If a freehold be, as supposed, so easily acquired, it would seem highly impolitic, to say no more, to insist on retaining an odious regulation, calculated to produce no other effect than to excite discontent. But the fact is not so. The thousands expelled from the polls too well attest the severity of its operation. It is by no means easy or convenient for persons whom fortune or inclination have engaged in other than agricultural pursuits to withdraw from those pursuits, or from the support of their families, the amount requisite for the purchase of a freehold. To compel them to do this, to vest that sum in unproductive property, is to subject them, over and above the original cost, the assessments upon it, and the probable loss by deterioration, to an annual tax, equivalent to the profits they might have derived from the capital thus unprofitably expended.

What would be thought of a tax imposed, or penalty inflicted, upon all voters for exercising what should be the unbought privilege of every citizen? How much more odious is the law that imposes this tax, or rather, it may be said, inflicts this penalty, on one portion of the community, probably the larger and least able to encounter it, and exempts the other?

The right of suffrage, however, it seems, is not a natural right. If by natural is meant what is just and reasonable, then nothing is more reasonable than that those whose purses contribute to maintain, whose lives are pledged to defend the country, should participate in all the privileges of citizenship. But say it is not a natural right. Whence did the freeholders derive it? How become its exclusive possessors? Will they arrogantly tell us they own the country because they hold the land? The right by which they hold the land is not itself a natural right, and, by consequence, nothing claimed as incidental to it. . . .

Let us concede that the right of suffrage is a social right; that it must of necessity be regulated by society. Still the question recurs, is the existing limitation proper? For obvious reasons, by almost universal consent, women and children, aliens and slaves are excluded. It were useless to discuss the propriety of a rule that scarcely admits of diversity of opinion. What is concurred in by those who constitute the society, the body politic, must be taken to be right. But the exclusion of these classes, for reasons peculiarly applicable to them, is no argument for excluding others to whom no one of those reasons applies.

It is said to be *expedient,* however, to exclude nonfreeholders also. Who shall judge of this expediency? The society. And does that embrace the proprietors of certain portions of land only? Expedient, for whom? For the freeholders. A harsh appelation would he deserve who, on the plea of expediency, should take from another his property. What, then, should be said of him who, on that plea, takes from another his rights, upon which the security, not of his property only but of his life and liberty depends?

But the nonfreeholders are condemned for pursuing an abstract right, whose privation occasions no practical injury. . . .

Never can your memorialists agree that pecuniary burdens or personal violence are the sole injuries of which men may dare to complain. It may be that the freeholders have shown no disposition greatly to abuse the power they have assumed. They may have borne themselves with exemplary moderation; but their unrepresented brethren cannot submit to a degrading regulation which takes from them, on the supposition of mental inferiority or moral depravity, all share in the government under which they live. They cannot yield to pretensions of political superiority founded on the possession of a bit of land, of whatever dimensions. They cannot acquiesce in political bondage, because those who affect to sway over them the rod of empire treat them leniently. The privilege which they claim, they respectfully insist, is theirs as of right; and they are under no obligation to assign any reason whatever for claiming it but that it is their own.

Let the picture be for a moment reversed. Let it be imagined that the nonfreeholders, possessing the physical superiority which alone can cause their political influence to be dreaded, should at some future day, *after the manner of the freeholders,* take the government into their own hands and deal out to the latter the same measure of justice they have received at their hands. It is needless to inquire into the equity of such a proceeding; but would they not find for it in the example set them at least a plausible excuse, and to the freeholders' remonstrance retort the freeholders' argument? That argument your memorialists will not now recapitulate; they leave it to others to make the application.

72.

On the Degradation Caused by Universal Suffrage

Debate on the extension of the suffrage occurred not only in constitutional conventions in New York, Virginia, and Massachusetts during the years 1820-1830 but also in the popular press. Hezekiah Niles used his newspaper, the Weekly Register, *to urge more liberal voting laws and to expound his faith in the popular will. Other newspapers reflected more conservative opinions, such as those in the following editorial from the November 7, 1829, issue of the* New York Journal of Commerce, *which in general supported the view that men of property must retain control of the government in order to prevent "the utter extinction of the Republic."*

Source: *New York Journal of Commerce*, November 7, 1829 [Commons, V, pp. 154-155].

OUR CITIZENS WHO HAVE NOT YET VOTED have one day more in which they may exercise the privilege of determining whom they will have for their rulers. The old party lines are nearly obliterated, but there has sprung up a new interest which is formidable, both for the number of its adherents and the disorganizing purposes by which they are actuated. By throwing open the polls to every man that walks, we have placed the power in the hands of those who have neither property, talents, nor influence in other circumstances, and who require in their public officers no higher qualifications than they possess themselves. It would be a disgrace to the city and to republicanism if a ticket so utterly unworthy as theirs should succeed. New York has not always had her just share of influence in the national and state legislatures, on account of the character of her representatives; but never was she reduced to such an extreme of degradation as she will be should the Agrarian Party succeed.

Such a result we cannot believe is possible, notwithstanding the melancholy forebodings of one of our contemporaries. We cannot believe that we are so soon reduced to the condition of the Romans, when the popular voice was raised against every honorable distinction: a voice which finally prevailed, to the utter extinction of the republic.

73.

ANDREW JACKSON: First Annual Message to Congress

The election of Andrew Jackson in 1828 marked several important changes in American political life. Traditionally, the President had been a member of a previous President's Cabinet, and what is more a man who had made a career of national affairs; but Jackson, although he enjoyed national support, had never held a prominent governmental position. His predecessors had come from aristocratic families and had been inclined to scorn or at least distrust the common people; but Jackson brought with him the frontier faith that most men could do most things with reasonable competence. "In a country where offices are created solely for the benefit of the people," he could declare, "no one man has any more intrinsic right to official station than another." And he probably summed up his political philosophy when he asserted: "Never for a moment believe that the great body of citizens of any state can deliberately intend to do wrong." If the Jacksonian Democrats did not always agree about what was right, they at least were consistent in their opposition to certain tendencies that they considered to be wrong: for example, entrenched power in public office, traditional economic privilege, and limited voting rights. In his first annual message to Congress, December 8, 1829, Jackson outlined the policies that were to characterize his administration and earn it the name of "the age of the common man."

Source: Richardson, II, pp. 442-462.

I CONSIDER IT one of the most urgent of my duties to bring to your attention the propriety of amending that part of our Constitution which relates to the election of President and Vice-President. Our system of government was by its framers deemed an experiment, and they, therefore, consistently provided a mode of remedying its defects.

To the people belongs the right of electing their chief magistrate; it was never designed that their choice should in any case be defeated, either by the intervention of electoral colleges or by the agency confided, under certain contingencies, to the House of Representatives. Experience proves that in proportion as agents to execute the will of the people are multiplied there is danger of their wishes being frustrated. Some may be unfaithful; all are liable to err. So far, therefore, as the people can with convenience speak, it is safer for them to express their own will.

The number of aspirants to the presidency and the diversity of the interests which may influence their claims leave little reason to expect a choice in the first instance, and in that event the election must devolve on the House of Representatives, where it is obvious the will of the people may not be always ascertained or, if ascertained, may not be regarded. From the mode of voting by states the choice is to be made by twenty-four votes, and it may often occur that one of these will be controlled by an individual representative. Honors and offices are at the disposal of the successful candidate. Repeated ballotings may make it apparent that a single individual holds the cast in his hand. May he not be tempted to name his reward?

But even without corruption, supposing the probity of the representative to be proof against the powerful motives by which it may be assailed, the will of the people is still constantly liable to be misrepresented. One may err from ignorance of the wishes of his constituents; another from a conviction that it is his duty to be governed by his own judgment of the fitness of the candidates; finally, although all were inflexibly honest, all accurately informed of the wishes of their constituents, yet under the present mode of election a minority may often elect a President, and when this happens it may reasonably be expected that efforts will be made on the part of the majority to rectify this injurious operation of their institutions. But although no evil of this character should result from such a perversion of the first principle of our system — *that the majority is to govern* — it must be very certain that a President elected by a minority cannot enjoy the confidence necessary to the successful discharge of his duties.

In this, as in all other matters of public concern, policy requires that as few impediments as possible should exist to the free operation of the public will. Let us, then, endeavor so to amend our system that the office of chief magistrate may not be conferred upon any citizen but in pursuance of a fair expression of the will of the majority.

I would therefore recommend such an amendment of the Constitution as may remove all intermediate agency in the election of the President and Vice-President. The mode may be so regulated as to preserve to each state its present relative weight in the election, and a failure in the first attempt may be provided for by confining the second to a choice between the two highest candidates. In connection with such an amendment it would seem advisable to limit the service of the chief magistrate to a single term of either four or six years. If,

however, it should not be adopted, it is worthy of consideration whether a provision disqualifying for office the representatives in Congress on whom such an election may have devolved would not be proper.

While members of Congress can be constitutionally appointed to offices of trust and profit, it will be the practice, even under the most conscientious adherence to duty, to select them for such stations as they are believed to be better qualified to fill than other citizens; but the purity of our government would doubtless be promoted by their exclusion from all appointments in the gift of the President, in whose election they may have been officially concerned. The nature of the judicial office and the necessity of securing in the cabinet and in diplomatic stations of the highest rank the best talents and political experience should, perhaps, except these from the exclusion.

There are, perhaps, few men who can for any great length of time enjoy office and power without being more or less under the influence of feelings unfavorable to the faithful discharge of their public duties. Their integrity may be proof against improper considerations immediately addressed to themselves, but they are apt to acquire a habit of looking with indifference upon the public interests and of tolerating conduct from which an unpracticed man would revolt. Office is considered as a species of property, and government rather as a means of promoting individual interests than as an instrument created solely for the service of the people. Corruption in some and in others a perversion of correct feelings and principles divert government from its legitimate ends and make it an engine for the support of the few at the expense of the many. The duties of all public officers are, or at least admit of being made, so plain and simple that men of intelligence may readily qualify themselves for their performance; and I cannot but believe that more is lost by the long continuance of men in office than is generally to be gained by their experience. I submit, therefore, to your consideration whether the efficiency of the government would not be promoted and official industry and integrity better secured by a general extension of the law which limits appointments to four years.

In a country where offices are created solely for the benefit of the people, no one man has any more intrinsic right to official station than another. Offices were not established to give support to particular men at the public expense. No individual wrong is, therefore, done by removal, since neither appointment to nor continuance in office is matter of right. The incumbent became an officer with a view to public benefits, and when these require his removal they are not to be sacrificed to private interests. It is the people, and they alone, who have a right to complain when a bad officer is substituted for a good one. He who is removed has the same means of obtaining a living that are enjoyed by the millions who never held office. The proposed limitation would destroy the idea of property now so generally connected with official station, and although individual distress may be sometimes produced, it would, by promoting that rotation which constitutes a leading principle in the republican creed, give healthful action to the system.

No very considerable change has occurred during the recess of Congress in the condition of either our agriculture, commerce, or manufactures. The operation of the tariff has not proved so injurious to the two former or as beneficial to the latter as was anticipated. Importations of foreign goods have not been sensibly diminished, while domestic competition, under an illusive excitement, has increased the production much beyond the demand for home consumption. The consequences have been low prices, temporary embarrassment, and partial loss. That such of our manufacturing establishments as are based upon capital and are prudently managed will survive the shock and be ultimately profitable there is no good reason to doubt.

To regulate its conduct so as to promote equally the prosperity of these three cardinal interests is one of the most difficult tasks of government; and it may be regretted that the complicated restrictions which now embarrass the intercourse of nations could not by common consent be abolished, and commerce allowed to flow in those channels to which individual enterprise, always its surest guide, might direct it. But we must ever expect selfish legislation in other nations and are therefore compelled to adapt our own to their regulations in the manner best calculated to avoid serious injury and to harmonize the conflicting interests of our agriculture, our commerce, and our manufactures. Under these impressions, I invite your attention to the existing tariff, believing that some of its provisions require modification.

The general rule to be applied in graduating the duties upon articles of foreign growth or manufacture is that which will place our own in fair competition with those of other countries; and the inducements to advance even a step beyond this point are controlling in regard to those articles which are of primary necessity in time of war. When we reflect upon the difficulty and delicacy of this operation, it is important that it should never be attempted but with the utmost caution. Frequent legislation in regard to any branch of industry, affecting its value and by which its capital may be transferred to new channels, must always be productive of hazardous speculation and loss.

In deliberating, therefore, on these interesting subjects, local feelings and prejudices should be merged in the patriotic determination to promote the great interests of the whole. All attempts to connect them with the party conflicts of the day are necessarily injurious and should be discountenanced.

Our action upon them should be under the control of higher and purer motives. Legislation subjected to such influences can never be just and will not long retain the sanction of a people whose active patriotism is not bounded by sectional limits nor insensible to that spirit of concession and forbearance which gave life to our political compact and still sustains it. Discarding all calculations of political ascendency, the North, the South, the East, and the West should unite in diminishing any burden of which either may justly complain.

The agricultural interest of our country is so essentially connected with every other and so superior in importance to them all that it is scarcely necessary to invite to it your particular attention. It is principally as manufactures and commerce tend to increase the value of agricultural productions and to extend their application to the wants and comforts of society that they deserve the fostering care of government.

Looking forward to the period, not far distant, when a sinking fund will no longer be required, the duties on those articles of importation which cannot come in competition with our own productions are the first that should engage the attention of Congress in the modification of the tariff. Of these, tea and coffee are the most prominent. They enter largely into the consumption of the country and have become articles of necessity to all classes. A reduction, therefore, of the existing duties will be felt as a common benefit, but like all other legislation connected with commerce, to be efficacious and not injurious it should be gradual and certain.

The public prosperity is evinced in the increased revenue arising from the sales of the public lands and in the steady maintenance of that produced by imposts and tonnage, notwithstanding the additional duties imposed by the act of May 19, 1828, and the unusual importations in the early part of that year.

The balance in the treasury on January 1, 1829, was $5,972,435.81. The receipts of the current year are estimated at $24,602,230 and the expenditures for the same time at $26,164,595, leaving a balance in the treasury on the 1st of January next of $4,410,070.81.

There will have been paid on account of the public debt during the present year the sum of $12,405,005.80, reducing the whole debt of the government on the 1st of January next to $48,565,406.50, including $7,000,000 of 5 percent stock subscribed to the Bank of the United States. The payment on account of public debt made on the 1st of July last was $8,715,462.87. It was apprehended that the sudden withdrawal of so large a sum from the banks in which it was deposited, at a time of unusual pressure in the money market, might cause much injury to the interests dependent on bank accommodations. But this evil was wholly averted by an early anticipation of it at the treasury, aided by the judicious arrangements of the officers of the Bank of the United States.

This state of the finances exhibits the resources of the nation in an aspect highly flattering to its industry and auspicious of the ability of government, in a very short time, to extinguish the public debt. When this shall be done, our population will be relieved from a considerable portion of its present burdens and will find not only new motives to patriotic affection but additional means for the display of individual enterprise. The fiscal power of the states will also be increased and may be more extensively exerted in favor of education and other public objects, while ample means will remain in the federal government to promote the general weal in all the modes permitted to its authority.

After the extinction of the public debt it is not probable that any adjustment of the tariff upon principles satisfactory to the people of the Union will, until a remote pe-

Andrew Jackson; portrait by Thomas Sully

riod, if ever, leave the government without a considerable surplus in the treasury beyond what may be required for its current service. As, then, the period approaches when the application of the revenue to the payment of debt will cease, the disposition of the surplus will present a subject for the serious deliberation of Congress; and it may be fortunate for the country that it is yet to be decided. Considered in connection with the difficulties which have heretofore attended appropriations for purposes of internal improvement, and with those which this experience tells us will certainly arise whenever power over such subjects may be exercised by the general government, it is hoped that it may lead to the adoption of some plan which will reconcile the diversified interests of the states and strengthen the bonds which unite them.

Every member of the Union, in peace and in war, will be benefited by the improvement of inland navigation and the construction of highways in the several states. Let us, then, endeavor to attain this

benefit in a mode which will be satisfactory to all. That hitherto adopted has by many of our fellow citizens been deprecated as an infraction of the Constitution, while by others it has been viewed as inexpedient. All feel that it has been employed at the expense of harmony in the legislative councils.

To avoid these evils it appears to me that the most safe, just, and federal disposition which could be made of the surplus revenue would be its apportionment among the several states according to their ratio of representation; and should this measure not be found warranted by the Constitution that it would be expedient to propose to the states an amendment authorizing it. I regard an appeal to the source of power in cases of real doubt, and where its exercise is deemed indispensable to the general welfare, as among the most sacred of all our obligations.

Upon this country more than any other has, in the providence of God, been cast the special guardianship of the great principle of adherence to written constitutions. If it fail here, all hope in regard to it will be extinguished. That this was intended to be a government of limited and specific, and not general, powers must be admitted by all, and it is our duty to preserve for it the character intended by its framers. If experience points out the necessity for an enlargement of these powers, let us apply for it to those for whose benefit it is to be exercised, and not undermine the whole system by a resort to overstrained constructions. The scheme has worked well. It has exceeded the hopes of those who devised it and become an object of admiration to the world. We are responsible to our country and to the glorious cause of self-government for the preservation of so great a good. The great mass of legislation relating to our internal affairs was intended to be left where the Federal Convention found it — in the state governments. Nothing is clearer, in my view, than that we are chiefly indebted for the success of the Constitution under which we are now acting to the watchful and auxiliary operation of the state authorities. This is not the reflection of a day but belongs to the most deeply rooted convictions of my mind. I cannot, therefore, too strongly or too earnestly, for my own sense of its importance, warn you against all encroachments upon the legitimate sphere of state sovereignty. Sustained by its healthful and invigorating influence the federal system can never fall. . . .

The condition and ulterior destiny of the Indian tribes within the limits of some of our states have become objects of much interest and importance. It has long been the policy of government to introduce among them the arts of civilization, in the hope of gradually reclaiming them from a wandering life. This policy has, however, been coupled with another wholly incompatible with its success. Professing a desire to civilize and settle them, we have at the same time lost no opportunity to purchase their lands and thrust them farther into the wilderness. By this means they have not only been kept in a wandering state but been led to look upon us as unjust and indifferent to their fate. Thus, though lavish in its expenditures upon the subject, government has constantly defeated its own policy, and the Indians, in general, receding farther and farther to the west, have retained their savage habits. A portion, however, of the Southern tribes, having mingled much with the whites and made some progress in the arts of civilized life, have lately attempted to erect an independent government within the limits of Georgia and Alabama. These states, claiming to be the only sovereigns within their territories, extended their laws over the Indians, which induced the latter to call upon the United States for protection.

Under these circumstances the question presented was whether the general government had a right to sustain those people in their pretensions. The Constitution declares that "no new state shall be formed or erected within the jurisdiction of any other state" without the consent of its legislature. If the general government is not permitted to tolerate the erection of a confederate state within the territory of one of the members of this Union against her consent, much less could it allow a foreign and independent government to establish itself there.

Georgia became a member of the Confederacy, which eventuated in our federal Union as a sovereign state, always asserting her claim to certain limits, which, having been originally defined in her colonial charter and subsequently recognized in the treaty of peace, she has ever since continued to enjoy, except as they have been circumscribed by her own voluntary transfer of a portion of her territory to the United Sates in the articles of cession of 1802. Alabama was admitted into the Union on the same footing with the original states, with boundaries which were prescribed by Congress. There is no constitutional, conventional, or legal provision which allows them less power over the Indians within their borders than is possessed by Maine or New York. Would the people of Maine permit the Penobscot tribe to erect an independent government within their state? And unless they did would it not be the duty of the general government to support them in resisting such a measure? Would the people of New York permit each remnant of the Six Nations within her borders to declare itself an independent people under the protection of the United States? Could the Indians establish a separate republic on each of their reservations in Ohio? And if they were so disposed would it be the duty of this government to protect them in the attempt?

If the principle involved in the obvious answer to these questions be abandoned, it will follow that the objects of this government are reversed, and that it has become a part of its duty to aid in destroying the states which it was established to protect. Actuated by this view of the subject, I informed the Indians inhabiting parts of Georgia and Alabama that their attempt to establish an independent government would not be countenanced by the executive of the United States, and advised them to emigrate beyond the Mississippi or submit to the laws of those states.

Our conduct toward these people is deeply interesting to our national character. Their present condition, contrasted with what they once were, makes a most powerful appeal to our sympathies. Our ancestors found them the uncontrolled possessors of these vast regions. By persuasion and force they have been made to retire from river to river and from mountain to mountain, until some of the tribes have become extinct and others have left but remnants to preserve for awhile their once terrible names. Surrounded by the whites with their arts of civilization, which by destroying the resources of the savage doom him to weakness and decay, the fate of the Mohegan, the Narragansett, and the Delaware is fast overtaking the Choctaw, the Cherokee, and the Creek. That this fate surely awaits them if they remain within the limits of the states does not admit of a doubt. Humanity and national honor demand that every effort should be made to avert so great a calamity. It is too late to inquire whether it was just in the United States to include them and their territory within the bounds of new states, whose limits they could control. That step cannot be retraced. A state cannot be dismembered by Congress or restricted in the exercise of her constitutional power. But the people of those states and of every state, actuated by feelings of justice and a regard for our national honor, submit to you the interesting question whether something cannot be done, consistently with the rights of the states, to preserve this much injured race.

As a means of effecting this end, I suggest for your consideration the propriety of setting apart an ample district west of the Mississippi, and without the limits of any state or territory now formed, to be guaranteed to the Indian tribes, as long as they shall occupy it, each tribe having a distinct control over the portion designated for its use. There they may be secured in the enjoyment of governments of their own choice, subject to no other control from the United States than such as may be necessary to preserve peace on the frontier and between the several tribes. There the benevolent may endeavor to teach them the arts of civilization and, by promoting union and harmony among them, to raise up an interesting commonwealth, destined to perpetuate the race and to attest the humanity and justice of this government.

This emigration should be voluntary, for it would be as cruel, as unjust to compel the aborigines to abandon the graves of their fathers and seek a home in a distant land. But they should be distinctly informed that if they remain within the limits of the states they must be subject to their laws. In return for their obedience as individuals, they will without doubt be protected in the enjoyment of those possessions which they have improved by their industry. But it seems to me visionary to suppose that in this state of things claims can be allowed on tracts of country on which they have neither dwelt nor made improvements, merely because they have seen them from the mountain or passed them in the chase. Submitting to the laws of the states and receiving, like other citizens, protection in their persons and property, they will ere long become merged in the mass of our population.

"William C. Macready as Macbeth," by Henry Inman

NEW LIFE IN THE ARTS

In the 1820s the sense of limitless potential and self-confidence that characterized American economic expansion and political life began to be reflected in a conscious search for an authentic artistic response to the American experience.

The older painters, trained in Europe or influenced by European traditions, continued to work primarily in portraiture. Theirs was the last reigning generation in this field. Although Gilbert Stuart died in 1828, others, such as Sully and Jarvis, carried on the tradition for many years. Portraitists such as Chester Harding and John Neagle gained immense popularity, but a younger generation of painters was emerging in the late 1820s, those that looked more closely at the country and responded to its life and landscape.

The theater grew in popularity, with well-known English actors competing for American audiences at new theaters in New York and Philadelphia.

The two early heroes of American literature, Washington Irving and James Fenimore Cooper, achieved wide popularity in work based on American folk legend and frontier tales. Numerous literary periodicals were founded during the period, further stimulating literary consciousness.

The Theater

Macready as King Lear, by John Neagle

The American theater was finding increasing success in the 1820s. The large cities were building new and larger theaters. Traveling companies were penetrating as far west as St. Louis. English actors, such as Edmund Kean and William Macready, toured in Shakespearean roles. But the American stage was beginning to assert its independence. In 1826, Edwin Forrest, the first great American actor, had his first major success as Othello. In 1829, "Metamora," a romantic Indian tale by John A. Stone, was produced at the Park Theatre in New York.

(Above) Interior of the Park Theatre in New York, 1822; (right) a scene from "The Spy," based on Cooper's novel, painted by Dunlap

The second Chestnut Street Theatre in Philadelphia, 1822, designed by William Strickland

(Above) The Lafayette Theatre in New York; (below) the interior of the Chatham Theatre, New York

Portrait of Edmund Kean in the role of Shylock from the "Merchant of Venice," by John Neagle

A National Literature

By the 1820s, a native American literature had begun to emerge from more than a decade of discussion and criticism on the subject. Washington Irving and James Fenimore Cooper were the first "giants" of this literary consciousness and gained a wide audience from their treatments of popular legend or frontier romance. James Kirke Paulding, a poet and novelist, who collaborated with Irving on a literary journal in 1807, discussed a national literature in a series of criticisms of English conventions. William Cullen Bryant and Fitz-Greene Halleck were popular poets, but Bryant's major contribution was his magazine, the New York Review. More than a dozen other literary periodicals appeared during the period. Noah Webster's American Dictionary, published in 1828, expressed his wish for a national literature and language.

(Above) Thomas Cole's representation of a scene from "The Last of the Mohicans"; Cora pleads to be saved from marriage to Le Renard Subtil; ". . . the sun was seen climbing above the mountain against whose bosom the Delawares had constructed their encampment." (Left) James Fenimore Cooper, by Jarvis

(Above) Irving in London, 1830; (below) "The Return of Rip Van Winkle" by John Quidor; (top left to bottom right) James K. Paulding by Jarvis; Noah Webster; Fitz-Greene Halleck by Henry Inman; William Cullen Bryant by S. F. B. Morse

Architecture

With the completion of the Capitol in 1825, Washington occupied the center of the Greek revival movement in American architecture. The style remained the dominant mode until the Civil War in spite of continuing interest in Gothic styles and a growing taste for eccentric embellishment. The Greek forms appeared in wholly integrated plans, such as Jefferson's design for the University of Virginia, or as ornamentation on otherwise simple buildings as in the townhouses at the right.

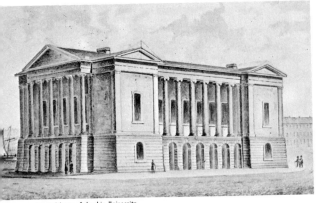

(Above left) Proposal for the Boston Customs House, by Richard Upjohn; (above right) New York townhouse by Martin Thompson, 1829; (below) Greek and Gothic revival buildings in New York, 1830

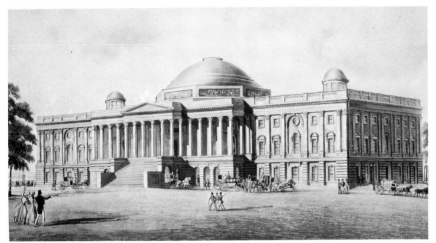

(Top) The Capitol, 1825; (center) the University of Virginia, 1826; (bottom left) Charles Bulfinch, architect of the Capitol, 1817-30, presided over the building's completion; (right) William Strickland, the leading Greek revival architect of the period; portrait by John Neagle

Thomas Sully

Thomas Sully (1783-1872) achieved great popularity as a portraitist when that field still dominated American painting. He had fully assimilated the flattering styles of English portrait painting that pleased his patrons. He painted more than 2,000 portraits in his long life. The emergence of new movements in American art in the 1820s pushed portraiture from its central position, but neither Sully's basic style nor his stature in his limited field were affected. While his portraits of Jefferson were central to artistic achievement at the time, his portraits of Lincoln were a footnote to political success.

Yale Art Gallery

Yale Art Gallery

Yale Art Gallery

White House; photo, National Geographic Society

S. F. B. Morse

The painting career of Samuel F. B. Morse (1791-1872) seems to chart the course of portraiture in his time. He was trained in France and was skilled at incisive characterization or dramatization of his subjects. He also experimented with large compositions, such as "The House of Representatives" (see page 243). But, like Fulton before him, Morse gave up painting for other interests, in his case the telegraph. Apparently, portrait painting paled beside the challenge and potential reward of invention. In 1839, shortly after he stopped painting, Morse began experimenting with photography. The photograph, as much as anything else, was responsible for the decline of portrait painting.

Paintings by Samuel F. B. Morse: (top left) "Judgment of Jupiter"; (top right) Rev. and Mrs. Hiram Bingham; (bottom) President James Monroe in 1819; (center) portrait of Morse by Oliver W. Stone

(OPPOSITE PAGE: top left to bottom right) All by Thomas Sully: Miss Eliza Ridgely; George Mifflin Dallas, 1810; Samuel Coates, director of the first U.S. Bank, manager of the Pennsylvania Hospital, and overseer of the Philadelphia Quaker schools; Sully's self-portrait as a young man

(Above) **Mrs. Daniel Webster** and (below) **Chief Justice John Marshall, by Chester Harding;** (above right) **Gilbert Stuart by John Neagle, 1825;** (below right) **Henry Clay by Charles Bird King (1785-1862),** noted for his Indian portraits

Of the popular painters of the "Golden Age" of American portraiture, Chester Harding (1792-1866) and John Neagle (1796-1865) are of particular interest. Harding was a cabinet-maker and sign painter who began doing portraits, including one of Daniel Boone, after moving to Kentucky. Returning East, his innate talent for making likenesses brought him almost instant popularity. Neagle, similarly untrained, also began painting in Kentucky, in 1818. By 1830 he was director of the Pennsylvania Academy of the Fine Arts.

1830

74.

Daniel Webster: Liberty and Union, Now and Forever, One and Inseparable

In December 1829, Senator Samuel Foote of Connecticut, reflecting the views of Eastern industry, placed before the Senate a resolution to restrict for a time the sale of public lands. Thereby was touched off one of the great debates in American political history, and one that ranged far beyond the issues raised by the resolution that was its occasion. A number of senators participated in the debate, but the two main speakers were Robert Y. Hayne of South Carolina and Daniel Webster of Massachusetts. Hayne spoke first, on January 19, 1830, upholding the strict constructionism that was characteristic of the South, and asserting that "there is no evil more to be deprecated than the consolidation of this government." Webster replied the next day, taking to task Hayne and the Southerners generally for disparaging the Union. Hayne then spoke again, and advanced the doctrine of state sovereignty and nullification. Webster's second reply, made on January 26 and 27, was one of the most eloquent orations ever delivered in the Senate. He denied Hayne's main contention, the absolute sovereignty of the states, and instead affirmed the ultimate sovereignty of the Constitution and the national government over the states and the people. His closing paragraphs, including the famous phrase, "Liberty and Union, now and forever, one and inseparable," were memorized by hundreds of thousands of schoolboys in the years before 1860, and helped to give the idea of the Union its almost sacred character in the minds of Northern soldiers in the Civil War. Portions of Webster's second reply are reprinted below.

Source: *The Writings and Speeches of Daniel Webster*, Boston, 1903, Vol. VI, pp. 3-75.

THERE YET REMAINS to be performed, Mr. President, by far the most grave and important duty which I feel to be devolved on me by this occasion. It is to state, and to defend, what I conceive to be the true principles of the Constitution under which we are here assembled. I might well have desired that so weighty a task should have fallen into other and abler hands. I could have wished that it should have been executed by those whose character and experience give weight and influence to their opinions, such as cannot possibly belong to mine. But, sir, I have met the occasion, not sought it; and I shall proceed to state my own sentiments, without challenging for them any particular regard, with studied plainness, and as much precision as possible.

I understand the honorable gentleman from South Carolina to maintain, that it is a right of the state legislatures to interfere whenever, in their judgment, this government transcends its constitutional limits and to arrest the operation of its laws.

I understand him to maintain this right as a right existing *under* the Constitution, not as a right to overthrow it on the ground of extreme necessity, such as would justify violent revolution.

I understand him to maintain an authority, on the part of the states, thus to interfere for the purpose of correcting the exercise of power by the general government, of checking it, and of compelling it to conform to their opinion of the extent of its powers.

I understand him to maintain that the ultimate power of judging of the constitutional extent of its own authority is not lodged exclusively in the general government, or any branch of it; but that, on the contrary, the states may lawfully decide for themselves, and each state for itself, whether, in a given case, the act of the general government transcends its power.

I understand him to insist that if the exigency of the case, in the opinion of any state government, require it, such state government may, by its own sovereign authority, annul an act of the general government which it deems plainly and palpably unconstitutional. . . .

What he contends for is that it is constitutional to interrupt the administration of the Constitution itself, in the hands of those who are chosen and sworn to administer it, by the direct interference, in form of law of the states, in virtue of their sovereign capacity. The inherent right in the people to reform their government I do not deny; and they have another right, and that is to resist unconstitutional laws without overturning the government. It is no doctrine of mine that unconstitutional laws bind the people. The great question is — Whose prerogative is it to decide on the constitutionality or unconstitutionality of the laws? On that, the main debate hinges.

The proposition that, in case of a supposed violation of the Constitution by Congress, the states have a constitutional right to interfere and annul the law of Congress is the proposition of the gentleman. I do not admit it. If the gentleman had intended no more than to assert the right of revolution for justifiable cause, he would have said only what all agree to. But I cannot conceive that there can be a middle course, between submission to the laws, when regularly pronounced constitutional, on the one hand, and open resistance, which is revolution or rebellion, on the other.

I say, the right of a state to annul a law of Congress cannot be maintained but on the ground of the inalienable right of man to resist oppression; that is to say, upon the ground of revolution. I admit that there is an ultimate violent remedy, above the Constitution and in defiance of the Constitution, which may be resorted to when a revolution is to be justified. But I do not admit that, under the Constitution and in conformity with it, there is any mode in which a state government, as a member of the Union, can interfere and stop the progress of the general government, by force of her own laws, under any circumstances whatever.

This leads us to inquire into the origin of this government and the source of its power. Whose agent is it? Is it the creature of the state legislatures, or the creature of the people? If the government of the United States be the agent of the state governments, then they may control it, provided they can agree in the manner of controlling it; if it be the agent of the people, then the people alone can control it, restrain it, modify, or reform it. It is observable enough that the doctrine for which the honorable gentleman contends leads him to the necessity of maintaining, not only that this general government is the creature of the states but that it is the creature of each of the states severally, so that each may assert the power for itself of determining whether it acts within the limits of its authority. It is the servant of four-and-twenty masters, of different wills and different purposes, and yet bound to obey all.

This absurdity (for it seems no less) arises from a misconception as to the origin of this government and its true character. It is, sir, the people's Constitution, the people's government, made for the people, made by the people, and answerable to the people. The people of the United States have declared that this Constitution shall be the supreme law. We must either admit the proposition or dispute their authority. The states are, unquestionably, sovereign, so far as their sovereignty is not affected by this supreme law. But the state legislatures, as political bodies, however sovereign, are yet not sovereign over the people. So far as the people have given power to the general government, so far the grant is unquestionably good, and the government holds of the people and not of the state governments. We are all agents of the same supreme power, the people. The general government and the state governments derive their authority from the same source. Neither can, in relation to the other, be called primary, though one is definite and restricted, and the other general and residuary. The national government possesses those powers, which it can be shown the people have conferred on it, and no more. All the rest belongs to the state governments, or to the people themselves. So far as the people have restrained state sovereignty, by the ex-

pression of their will, in the Constitution of the United States, so far, it must be admitted, state sovereignty is effectually controlled.

I do not contend that it is, or ought to be, controlled farther. The sentiment to which I have referred propounds that state sovereignty is only to be controlled by its own "feeling of justice"; that is to say, it is not to be controlled at all, for one who is to follow his own feelings is under no legal control. Now, however men may think this ought to be, the fact is that the people of the United States have chosen to impose control on state sovereignties. There are those, doubtless, who wish they had been left without restraint; but the Constitution has ordered the matter differently. To make war, for instance, is an exercise of sovereignty; but the Constitution declares that no state shall make war. To coin money is another exercise of sovereign power; but no state is at liberty to coin money. Again, the Constitution says that no sovereign state shall be so sovereign as to make a treaty. These prohibitions, it must be confessed, are a control on the state sovereignty of South Carolina, as well as of the other states, which does not arise "from her own feelings of honorable justice." The opinion referred to, therefore, is in defiance of the plainest provisions of the Constitution. . . .

I must now beg to ask, sir, whence is this supposed right of the states derived? Where do they find the power to interfere with the laws of the Union? Sir, the opinion which the honorable gentleman maintains is a notion founded in a total misapprehension, in my judgment, of the origin of this government, and of the foundation on which it stands. I hold it to be a popular government, erected by the people; those who administer it, responsible to the people; and itself capable of being amended and modified, just as the people may choose it should be. It is as popular, just as truly emanating from the people, as the state governments.

Robert Y. Hayne, senator from South Carolina, who argued for states' rights in his debate with Webster

It is created for one purpose; the state governments for another. It has its own powers; they have theirs. There is no more authority with them to arrest the operation of a law of Congress than with Congress to arrest the operation of their laws.

We are here to administer a Constitution emanating immediately from the people, and trusted by them to our administration. It is not the creature of the state governments. It is of no moment to the argument that certain acts of the state legislatures are necessary to fill our seats in this body. That is not one of their original state powers, a part of the sovereignty of the state. It is a duty which the people, by the Constitution itself, have imposed on the state legislatures; and which they might have left to be performed elsewhere, if they had seen fit. So they have left the choice of President with electors; but all this does not affect the proposition that this whole government, President, Senate, and House of Representatives, is a popular government. It leaves it still all its popular character. The governor of a state (in some of the states) is chosen, not directly by the people but by those who are chosen by the people, for the pur-

pose of performing, among other duties, that of electing a governor. Is the government of the state, on that account, not a popular government?

This government, sir, is the independent offspring of the popular will. It is not the creature of state legislatures; nay, more, if the whole truth must be told, the people brought it into existence, established it, and have hitherto supported it for the very purpose, among others, of imposing certain salutary restraints on state sovereignties. The states cannot now make war; they cannot contract alliances; they cannot make, each for itself, separate regulations of commerce; they cannot lay imposts; they cannot coin money. If this Constitution, sir, be the creature of state legislatures, it must be admitted that it has obtained a strange control over the volitions of its creators.

The people, then, sir, erected this government. They gave it a Constitution, and in that Constitution they have enumerated the powers which they bestow on it. They have made it a limited government. They have defined its authority. They have restrained it to the exercise of such powers as are granted; and all others, they declare, are reserved to the states or the people. But, sir, they have not stopped here. If they had, they would have accomplished but half their work. No definition can be so clear as to avoid possibility of doubt; no limitation so precise as to exclude all uncertainty. Who, then, shall construe this grant of the people? Who shall interpret their will, where it may be supposed they have left it doubtful? With whom do they repose this ultimate right of deciding on the powers of the government? Sir, they have settled all this in the fullest manner. They have left it with the government itself, in its appropriate branches.

Sir, the very chief end, the main design, for which the whole Constitution was framed and adopted was to establish a government that should not be obliged to act through state agency or depend on state opinion and state discretion. The people had had quite enough of that kind of government under the Confederation. Under that system, the legal action, the application of law to individuals belonged exclusively to the states. Congress could only recommend; their acts were not of binding force till the states had adopted and sanctioned them. Are we in that condition still? Are we yet at the mercy of state discretion and state construction? Sir, if we are, then vain will be our attempt to maintain the Constitution under which we sit.

But, sir, the people have wisely provided, in the Constitution itself, a proper, suitable mode and tribunal for settling questions of constitutional law. There are in the Constitution grants of powers to Congress, and restrictions on these powers. There are, also, prohibitions on the states. Some authority must, therefore, necessarily exist, having the ultimate jurisdiction to fix and ascertain the interpretation of these grants, restrictions, and prohibitions. The Constitution has itself pointed out, ordained, and established that authority. How has it accomplished this great and essential end? By declaring, sir, that *the Constitution, and the laws of the United States made in pursuance thereof, shall be the supreme law of the land, anything in the constitution or laws of any state to the contrary notwithstanding.*

This, sir, was the first great step. By this, the supremacy of the Constitution and laws of the United States is declared. The people so will it. No state law is to be valid which comes in conflict with the Constitution, or any law of the United States passed in pursuance of it. But who shall decide this question of interference? To whom lies the last appeal? This, sir, the Constitution itself decides also, by declaring, *that the judicial power shall extend to all cases arising under the Constitution and laws of the United States.* These two provisions cover the whole ground. They are, in truth, the key-

stone of the arch! With these it is a government; without them it is a confederation. In pursuance of these clear and express provisions, Congress established, at its very first session, in the judicial act, a mode for carrying them into full effect, and for bringing all questions of constitutional power to the final decision of the Supreme Court. It then, sir, became a government. It then had the means of self-protection; and but for this, it would, in all probability, have been now among things which are past.

Having constituted the government and declared its powers, the people have further said that, since somebody must decide on the extent of these powers, the government shall itself decide; subject, always, like other popular governments, to its responsibility to the people. And now, sir, I repeat, how is it that a state legislature acquires any power to interfere? Who, or what, gives them the right to say to the people, "We, who are your agents and servants for one purpose, will undertake to decide that your other agents and servants, appointed by you for another purpose, have transcended the authority you gave them!" The reply would be, I think, not impertinent — "Who made you a judge over another's servants? To their own masters they stand or fall."

Sir, I deny this power of state legislatures altogether. It cannot stand the test of examination. Gentlemen may say that, in an extreme case, a state government might protect the people from intolerable oppression. Sir, in such a case, the people might protect themselves, without the aid of the state governments. Such a case warrants revolution. It must make, when it comes, a law for itself. A nullifying act of a state legislature cannot alter the case, nor make resistance any more lawful. In maintaining these sentiments, sir, I am but asserting the rights of the people. I state what they have declared and insist on their right to declare it. They have chosen to repose this power in the general government, and I think it my duty to support it, like other constitutional powers. . . .

To avoid all possibility of being misunderstood, allow me to repeat again, in the fullest manner, that I claim no powers for the government by forced or unfair construction. I admit that it is a government of strictly limited powers; of enumerated, specified, and particularized powers; and that whatsoever is not granted, is withheld. But notwithstanding all this, and however the grant of powers may be expressed, its limit and extent may yet, in some cases, admit of doubt; and the general government would be good for nothing, it would be incapable of long existing, if some mode had not been provided in which those doubts, as they should arise, might be peaceably but authoritatively solved.

And now, Mr. President, let me run the honorable gentleman's doctrine a little into its practical application. Let us look at his probable *modus operandi*. If a thing can be done, an ingenious man can tell *how* it is to be done, and I wish to be informed *how* this state interference is to be put in practice, without violence, bloodshed, and rebellion. . . .

Direct collision . . . between force and force is the unavoidable result of that remedy for the revision of unconstitutional laws which the gentleman contends for. It must happen in the very first case to which it is applied. Is not this the plain result? To resist by force the execution of a law, generally, is treason. Can the courts of the United States take notice of the indulgence of a state to commit treason? The common saying that a state cannot commit treason herself is nothing to the purpose. Can she authorize others to do it? If John Fries [leader of a 1799 rebellion, indicted for treason] had produced an act of Pennsylvania annulling the law of Congress, would it have helped his case? Talk about it as we will, these doctrines go the length of revolution. They are incompatible with any peaceable

administration of the government. They lead directly to disunion and civil commotion; and, therefore, it is that at their commencement, when they are first found to be maintained by respectable men, and in a tangible form, I enter my public protest against them all.

The honorable gentleman argues that if this government be the sole judge of the extent of its own powers, whether that right of judging be in Congress or the Supreme Court, it equally subverts state sovereignty. This the gentleman sees, or thinks he sees, although he cannot perceive how the right of judging, in this matter, if left to the exercise of state legislatures, has any tendency to subvert the government of the Union. The gentleman's opinion may be that the right *ought not* to have been lodged with the general government; he may like better such a constitution as we should have under the right of state interference. But I ask him to meet me on the plain matter of fact. I ask him to meet me on the Constitution itself. I ask him if the power is not found there, clearly and visibly found there?

But, sir, what is this danger, and what are the grounds of it? Let it be remembered that the Constitution of the United States is not unalterable. It is to continue in its present form no longer than the people who established it shall choose to continue it. If they shall become convinced that they have made an injudicious or inexpedient partition and distribution of power between the state governments and the general government, they can alter that distribution at will. If anything be found in the national Constitution, either by original provision or subsequent interpretation, which ought not to be in it, the people know how to get rid of it. If any construction, unacceptable to them, be established, so as to become practically a part of the Constitution, they will amend it, at their own sovereign pleasure.

But while the people choose to maintain it as it is, while they are satisfied with it

"Webster Speaking in Reply to Hayne" depicts Daniel Webster's
defense of constitutional supremacy during the Senate debate

and refuse to change it, who has given, or who can give, to the state legislatures a right to alter it, either by interference, construction, or otherwise? Gentlemen do not seem to recollect that the people have any power to do anything for themselves. They imagine there is no safety for them, any longer than they are under the close guardianship of the state legislatures. Sir, the people have not trusted their safety, in regard to the general Constitution, to these hands. They have required other security, and taken other bonds. They have chosen to trust themselves, first, to the plain words of the instrument, and to such construction as the government themselves, in doubtful cases, should put on their own powers, under their oaths of office, and subject to their responsibility to them; just as the people of a state trust their own state governments with a similar power. Second, they have reposed their trust in the efficacy of frequent elections, and in their own power to remove their own servants and agents whenever they see cause. Third, they have re-

posed trust in the judicial power, which, in order that it might be trustworthy, they have made as respectable, as disinterested, and as independent as was practicable. Fourth, they have seen fit to rely, in case of necessity, or high expediency, on their known and admitted power to alter or amend the Constitution, peaceably and quietly, whenever experience shall point out defects or imperfections. And, finally, the people of the United States have at no time, in no way, directly or indirectly, authorized any state legislature to construe or interpret *their* high instrument of government, much less to interfere, by their own power, to arrest its course and operation.

If, sir, the people in these respects had done otherwise than they have done, their Constitution could neither have been preserved, nor would it have been worth preserving. And if its plain provisions shall now be disregarded, and these new doctrines interpolated in it, it will become as feeble and helpless a being as its enemies, whether early or more recent, could possibly desire. It will exist in every state but as a poor dependent on state permission. It must borrow leave to be; and will be no longer than state pleasure, or state discretion, sees fit to grant the indulgence and to prolong its poor existence.

But, sir, although there are fears, there are hopes also. The people have preserved this, their own chosen Constitution, for forty years and have seen their happiness, prosperity, and renown grow with its growth, and strengthen with its strength. They are now, generally, strongly attached to it. Overthrown by direct assault, it cannot be; evaded, undermined, *nullified* it will not be if we, and those who shall succeed us here, as agents and representatives of the people, shall conscientiously and vigilantly discharge the two great branches of our public trust, faithfully to preserve and wisely to administer it.

Mr. President, I have thus stated the reasons of my dissent to the doctrines which have been advanced and maintained. I am conscious of having detained you and the Senate much too long. I was drawn into the debate with no previous deliberation, such as is suited to the discussion of so grave and important a subject. But it is a subject of which my heart is full, and I have not been willing to suppress the utterance of its spontaneous sentiments. I cannot, even now, persuade myself to relinquish it without expressing once more my deep conviction that, since it respects nothing less than the Union of the States, it is of most vital and essential importance to the public happiness.

I profess, sir, in my career hitherto, to have kept steadily in view the prosperity and honor of the whole country, and the preservation of our federal Union. It is to that Union we owe our safety at home, and our consideration and dignity abroad. It is to that Union that we are chiefly indebted for whatever makes us most proud of our country — that Union we reached only by

the discipline of our virtues in the severe school of adversity. It had its origin in the necessities of disordered finance, prostrate commerce, and ruined credit. Under its benign influences, these great interests immediately awoke, as from the dead, and sprang forth with newness of life. Every year of its duration has teemed with fresh proofs of its utility and its blessings. And although our territory has stretched out wider and wider, and our population spread farther and farther, they have not outrun its protection or its benefits. It has been to us all a copious fountain of national, social, and personal happiness.

I have not allowed myself, sir, to look beyond the Union, to see what might lie hidden in the dark recess behind. I have not coolly weighed the chances of preserving liberty when the bonds that unite us together shall be broken asunder. I have not accustomed myself to hang over the precipice of disunion, to see whether, with my short sight, I can fathom the depth of the abyss below; nor could I regard him as a safe counselor in the affairs in this government whose thoughts should be mainly bent on considering, not how the Union may be best preserved but how tolerable might be the condition of the people when it should be broken up and destroyed. While the Union lasts, we have high, exciting, gratifying prospects spread out before us, for us and our children. Beyond that I seek not to penetrate the veil.

God grant that in my day, at least, that curtain may not rise! God grant that on my vision never may be opened what lies behind! When my eyes shall be turned to behold for the last time the sun in heaven, may I not see him shining on the broken and dishonored fragments of a once glorious Union; on states dissevered, discordant, belligerent; on a land rent with civil feuds, or drenched, it may be, in fraternal blood! Let their last feeble and lingering glance rather behold the gorgeous ensign of the republic, now known and honored throughout the earth, still full high advanced, its arms and trophies streaming in their original luster, not a stripe erased or polluted, nor a single star obscured, bearing for its motto, no such miserable interrogatory as "What is all this worth?" nor those other words of delusion and folly, "Liberty first and Union afterwards"; but everywhere, spread all over in characters of living light, blazing on all its ample folds, as they float over the sea and over the land, and in every wind under the whole heavens, that other sentiment, dear to every true American heart — Liberty *and* Union, now and forever, one and inseparable!

75.

ZELOTES FULLER: The Tree of Liberty

The line of separation between church and state has always been hard to draw in the United States. Most public officials, at all times, have been members of one or another of the many Christian denominations, and it has therefore always been easy to accept the notion that the nation is essentially a Christian one — even apart from the Puritan belief, which survives to this day, in the idea of a Christian Commonwealth. At various times during the nineteenth century, religious pressure groups sought to make the government formally "Christian" by demanding the election of only church members and by calling for an amendment to the Constitution. Opposition to such attempts to deny constitutional guarantees of religious freedom was always vehement. One of the many men who spoke out against what he considered to be an attack on the First Amendment was Zelotes Fuller, a Philadelphia Universalist, who delivered this Washington's Birthday Address in 1830 (the speech was actually given on February 28).

Source: *The Tree of Liberty*, Philadelphia, 1830.

SOMETHING MORE than half a century gone by, a numerous widespread and happy nation was given to the world. Great has been our prosperity. Under the mild, liberal, and wise government of our choice, we have flourished as a nation beyond all others. Witness our fruitful fields, our flocks and herds upon a thousand hills, our commerce floating in every breeze of heaven, our homes and storehouses filled with plenty, our colleges and seminaries of learning, and our temples and altars of religion. We have covered the seas with our ships; yea, we have rivaled Britain in her commerce, in mechanical ingenuity, and in every species of internal improvement. We are protected by just and equal laws, are blest with ample means of support for ourselves and families, the means of charity for our poor and aged, and the means of instruction for our children. Many learned institutions have grown up among us, that are in their nature powerful but rigorous, free but not licentious, and equal without removing those distinctions necessary to the order and subordination of society.

By the generous system of laws we have adopted, all religions are tolerated and protected. We enjoy the exalted privilege of worshiping Almighty God agreeably to the dictates of our own consciences, and there is no one to molest or to make us afraid. We can sit down under our own vine and fig tree and enjoy the life that was made for man. Surely this is a boon worthy the holy religion of Jesus, yea, worthy an infinitely merciful God — worthy of Him who has created all men free and the lawful proprietors of equal rights.

Ours is the only government under heaven where liberty can, in truth, be said to dwell; and the numberless advantages of such a government, for moral, religious, and intellectual improvement, may be learnt from the prosperous state of our country since the time she assumed her just and proper station among the nations of the earth. Contrast the situation of America with those nations where tyranny reigns in all its cruelty, degrading millions of wretched subjects almost to a level with the overladen brute which cringes beneath the cruel lash of his more brutish and unfeeling master; and the superiority of our government over all others will, *must*, be apparent. . . .

Wisely did the framers of the Constitution of our government, after defining with unexampled accuracy the rights of the citizens and limiting the authority of Congress, expressly prohibit the latter from interfering with the religious opinions of the people. There has been no change as yet in this particular, and we most sincerely pray that there never may be. Every species of creeds and varieties of faith receive equal toleration and protection. The freedom of inquiry and the right of private judgment, the freedom of the press and of public speech are still our rich inheritance — they are privileges which the laws of our common country guarantee to every citizen. This is as it should be. These privileges are just and unalienable; they originate in perfect equity; they are the birthright of every individual, and should not be infringed by any one; nor will they be, willingly or designedly, by any *real* friend to the peace and happiness of human kind.

No government under heaven affords such encouragement as that of America to genius and enterprise, or promises such rich rewards to talent and industry. Here, if a man rise to eminence, he rises by merit and not by birth, nor yet by mammon. This is as it ought to be — this is perfect justice. By the liberal government of our country, ample provision is made for the encouragement of the honest and ingenious artist, and due support is given to every laudable undertaking. Here, talent is not frowned into silence or trampled in the dust for the want of gold to support its dignity, nor for the want of noble parentage but commands the respectful attentions of all the truly wise and candid, however obscure the corner from whence it emanates, and receives that encouragement and support from a generous government to which it is justly and lawfully entitled.

Here, every man labors for himself, and not to pamper the pride of royalty, not to support kingly pomp, luxury, and dissipation! Here, no ghostly priest stalks forth, and by virtue of prerogative seizes upon a tenth of the hard earnings of the industrious poor, leaving them in a state of want and wretchedness; but they may apply their little all to the conveniences of themselves and families. He who toils and labors in the field or in the shop or in whatever employment he may engage has the high satisfaction to reflect that it is wholly for the comfort and happiness of himself or family, if he so please, and that he is not bound by law to contribute to the support of an artful, tyrannical, and corrupted priesthood.

No country could possibly possess greater advantages and facilities for continuing free and independent than what is possessed by America. We are as a nation enlightened, well informed, too much so, we think, ever to be duped or imposed upon. Nor are we wanting in zeal, neither do we believe that our courage will be called in question. We possess a vast extent of fruitful country which yields a rich and beautiful variety, not only for the convenience, but also for the luxury of its inhabitants. Such is the state of our country, such the state of our agricultural and manufacturing departments that it is not necessary, in order to obtain all the needed blessings and most of the luxuries of life, that we should leave our own native shores. Such is the flourishing state of our country that there is no real necessity, whatever may be the policy, of our going abroad for a single article that is absolutely requisite for comfort or happiness; we have all that we really need at home. From Maine to Mexico, and from the Atlantic to the Western wilderness is exhibited one continued scene of peace and plenty.

Our means of defense are in every respect ample; we have, therefore, nothing to fear from foreign invasion. So long as we are true to ourselves, we have nothing to fear from any quarter whatever.

Our schools, colleges, and universities are not surpassed by any in the known world, so that there is no necessity of our going abroad in order to receive a complete education in any branch of erudition, or in order to be fitted to practise any of the learned professions known to the present age.

Though young, yet we are a numerous, wealthy, popular, and powerful nation. Our flag is everywhere respected. In our country is found all that is grand, rich, and beautiful — and in the Constitution of our government, all that is truly wise, just, and righteous. Our means of peace, safety, plenty, and happiness are abundant. We have enough and to spare. Our resources in every respect are, as it were, without limit. Nothing is wanting but industry and faithfulness to ourselves to secure every rational enjoyment, and to perpetuate the glory and happiness of our nation. If we do our duty, all will, *must* be well. We fear not that the rights and privileges guaranteed to us by our most excellent Constitution will be infringed by those abroad, but they may be by a certain class at home if no precaution be taken to prevent it.

Brethren and friends of America! Something more than half a century ago, Washington and his distinguished companions nobly asserted, and more nobly defended, the rights and privileges we have been considering. The names of these men and their unwearied exertions in the cause of freedom are worthy of our highest admiration, and deserve to pass down the current of time to other generations, that they may live forever in the grateful recollections of all the most virtuous of the human race. May we and our children rise up and call them blest — rise up and rally round the institutions they have given us, and prove ourselves worthy to be called their sons. May we preserve these rights and privileges, and hand them unimpaired down to the generation that shall come after us as a priceless inheritance, yea, the richest earthly boon to man.

If that was a righteous cause in which the fathers of our liberty bled, and who can doubt it, then does not justice demand that we who now live and enjoy the glorious fruits of their toil and patriotic exertions should be ready and willing to support and defend with our property, and if need there should be with our lives, the rich inheritance they have left us!

If such be the feelings of our fellow countrymen, if such be the full purpose of their souls, if such their steadfast resolution; if the principles and feelings which led the heroes of '76 to declare themselves indepen-

The Tree of Liberty celebrates the birth of Washington

dent of the British Crown continue to cheer and warm the hearts of each succeeding generation of the happy sons of America, which may God send, then will it be safe to predict that long shall she remain in the sanctuary of liberty and the dwelling place of millions of happy freemen. Then will it be safe to say of America that —

> The *union* of her states in rapture shall run,
> Till nature shall freeze at the death of the sun!

Fifty-three years have we been in possession of national independence and political freedom. Our fathers willed themselves free and independent, and behold, liberty followed the sun in his path! *To continue free, we have but to will it!* And will you not do it, O people of America — ye who know the sweets of liberty? To support the liberties of your country, as did your fathers, so have ye pledged your lives, your fortunes, and your sacred honor. And are ye not ready to make good the pledge? Ye who are the friends of American freedom and of humankind have but one answer to give, and that answer is yea! Ye will duly honor the cause that is committed to your keeping. Ye will never prove false to the liberties of your country, nor violate the pledge of your fathers, the pledge of yourselves as Americans.

Remember that the civil and religious liberty which ye enjoy, and which ye hold to be the birthright of every man, was purchased with toil, and blood, and suffering. Dear was the price which it cost — precious the lives that were sacrificed. Never, O never, suffer yourselves to be robbed of such an invaluable heritage, nor quietly submit to any infringement of the rights and privileges which it confers.

I have said we fear not that the civil and religious rights and privileges which our excellent Constitution guarantees will be infringed by those abroad, but they may be by a certain class at home, if no precaution be taken to prevent it. Yea, we deem it a truth, too evident to admit of doubt, and too generally conceded to require proof on the present occasion, that it is the intention of a certain religious sect in our country to bring about, if possible, a union of church and state. To effect this purpose, a deep and artful scheme has been laid, and which may ultimately be consummated, unless it is speedily and vigorously opposed. Yea, the declaration has gone forth that in ten years, or certainly in twenty, the political power of our country will be in the hands of those who shall have been educated to believe in, and probably *pledged* to support, a certain creed. Merciful God! forbid the fulfillment of the prophecy! Forbid it all ye who have at heart the prosperity and happiness of our nation!

People of this free and happy land! We ask, will you give your consent to the political dominancy of any one religious sect and the establishment of their religious creed by law? Will you in any way encourage certain popular religious measures got up by a certain popular religious sect, in our humble opinion, for a very *unpopular* object, but which in the view of many is very popular to approve? Be assured, whatever may be the *ostensible* objects of these measures, if they should be generally adopted they will tend to infuse the spirit of religious intolerance and persecution into the political institutions of our country, and in the end, completely to annihilate the political and religious liberty of the people. Are you willing that a connection should be formed between politics and religion, or that the equal rights of conscience should in any degree be mutilated? Are ye prepared to bow your necks to an intolerant and persecuting system of religion, for instance, like that of England? Are ye prepared to submit to such an unrighteous system of tithes, taxa-

tions, and exactions, for the support of a *national religion,* as the great mass of her people are compelled to submit to? Are ye prepared to debase yourselves, like so many beasts of burden, before a dissipated nobility and an intolerant corrupted priesthood? It cannot be. . . .

Never, I beseech of you, encourage a certain "Christian party in politics," which under moral and religious pretenses is officiously and continually interfering with the religious opinions of others, and endeavoring to effect by law and other means, equally exceptionable, a systematic course of measures evidently calculated to lead to a union of church and state. If a union of church and state should be effected, which may God avert, then will the doctrines of the prevailing sect become the creed of the country, to be enforced by fines, imprisonment, and doubtless death! Then will superstition and bigotry frown into silence everything which bears the appearance of liberality; the hand of genius will be palsied, and a check to all further improvements in our country will be the inevitable consequence. If we now permit the glorious light of liberty to be extinguished, it may never more shine to cheer a benighted world with the splendor of its rays.

Was it, may we ask, for a *few* years only of freedom and independence that our fathers raised the standard of rebellion? Was it for no more than this they braved an empire's power, endured the toil, hardships, and suffering of an unequal and bloody warfare; that they closed their unarmed ports against the navies of Britain, and bid defiance to the authorities of ancient days and the threats of parliaments and thrones? It is for you to say, O people of America. The destinies of your country are in your own hands. They are committed to your own keeping. It is for you to say which ye will have, liberty or slavery, knowledge or ignorance, happiness or misery. I have said: *to continue free you have but to will it.*

If we do not choose the wiser and the better part; if by our negligence or want of zeal, we suffer the liberties of our country to be subverted; if we permit a corrupted priesthood to gain ascendancy in the civil government, then shall the like direful fate of other countries, where this has been and is still the case, be the fate of ours. The abuses which have been practised, the hellish cruelties which have been perpetrated, and the immense amount of suffering which has been inflicted under governments where the clergy have borne rule cannot easily be described. Youth and beauty, age and virtue, genius and rank were equally unable to relax the iron grasp of clerical tyranny. Even now there are regions where the infuriated demon of persecution unfurls her bloodstained banner and demands that unnumbered victims should bleed at the foot of her unrighteous throne! The past history of the Christian Church should be a solemn warning to us never to permit an alliance to be formed between the priesthood and the civil magistracy — between church and state powers.

To perpetuate our excellent government and to defend it from the attacks of its enemies is a duty we owe to ourselves, to our children, and to succeeding generations. It is what we owe to those who, fleeing from persecution, from slavery and wretchedness, in the land of their nativity, have here sought refuge, as the only country under heaven where freedom and equality, peace and plenty, can be said to dwell — as the only genuine republic on the face of the whole earth. To perpetuate our excellent government is a duty we owe to the whole world. It was long since predicted that the fate of other republics, ere this, would have been the fate of ours.

O people of America! weighty is your responsibility! The destinies of mankind hang upon *your* breath. The fate of all the nations of the earth is entrusted to *your* keeping. On you devolves the task of vindicating our human nature from the slanders heaped on it by superstitious ignorance and the libels imagined by designing ambition. With you rests the duty, for with you is the power to disprove the blasphemies of temporal tyrants and spiritual craftsmen. On you the whole family of human kind turns the eye of expectation. From the Hellespont to the icy sea, from the Don to the Atlantic, suffering Europe hopes in your liberty and waits for the influence of the virtue she dreams must be yours. On the shores of the ravaged Tagus, the ruined Tiber, the barbarous Tanais and Danube, the palace-crowned Thames, and luxurious Seine where wealth displays its splendor and poverty its wretchedness; there, in each varied realm and distant region does the oft-defeated patriot and oft-disappointed believer in the latent excellence and final enfranchisement of trampled humanity breathe his sighs and wing his hopes to the far off land which annually celebrates, not only its own, but the world's festival, and renews in the name of human kind the declaration of human independence.

Say, will you disappoint these high expectations? Will ye prove false to the cause ye have espoused? Will ye belie the sacred pledge ye have made? It *cannot* be that ye will.

Proud, happy, thrice happy America! the home of the oppressed, the asylum of the emigrant where the citizens of every clime and the child of every creed roam free and untrammeled as the wild winds of heaven, baptized at the font of liberty in fire and blood; cold must be the heart that thrills not at the mention of thy name! Search creation around, my countrymen, and where do you find a land that presents such a glorious scene for contemplation! Look at our institutions, our seminaries, our agricultural and commercial interests, and above all, and more than all, look at the gigantic strides we are making in all that ennobles humankind! When the old world with its pride, pomp, and circumstance shall be covered with the mantle of oblivion; when thrones shall have crumbled, and dynasties shall have been forgotten; then will our happy America, we trust, stand amid regal ruin and national desolation, towering sublime like the last mountain in the deluge; majestic, immutable, and magnificent, in the midst of blight, ruin, and decay — the last remnant of earth's beauty — the last resting place of liberty and the light of heaven!

76.

GEORGE McDUFFIE: Defense of a Government Bank

The Jacksonian Democrats' campaign against concentrated power was focused in the years 1829-1835 on the Second Bank of the United States and its president, Nicholas Biddle. A direct descendant of Hamilton's National Bank, the Second Bank was chartered in 1816 as a corporation with a capitalization of $35 million and with twenty-nine branches in various states. Biddle used the vast reserves of federal funds to create the strong central banking system required by a rapidly expanding commercial economy. In the process, however, he made enemies: merchants, brokers, and private bankers could not compete with the Second Bank for the lucrative domestic and foreign exchange business; Western farmers and businessmen objected to the pressure on local credit reserves; state banks resented the Second Bank's intrusion into their mortgage and loan business; and vast numbers of Americans objected to the Bank simply because they found it too big, too efficient, and therefore undemocratic. The Bank's defenders had their own enemy — Andrew Jackson — who, they claimed, was impeding commercial growth and ruining the economy with his "pet banks." The issue came to a head in 1829 when Jackson appended to his first annual message a request that Congress begin considering renewal of the Bank's charter, due to expire in 1836. The House of Representatives referred the President's request to its Ways and Means Committee, of which George McDuffie of South Carolina was chairman. The Committee submitted the following report to the House on April 13, 1830, effectively stating the most popular economic and constitutional arguments used in defense of the Bank.

Source: 21 Congress, 1 Session, House Report No. 358.

THE COMMITTEE OF WAYS AND MEANS, to whom was referred so much of the message of the President as relates to the Bank of the United States, beg leave to report that they have bestowed upon the subject all the attention demanded by its intrinsic importance, and now respectfully submit the result of their deliberations to the consideration of the House.

There are few subjects having reference to the policy of an established government so vitally connected with the health of the body politic, or in which the pecuniary interests of society are so extensively and deeply involved. No one of the attributes of sovereignty carries with it a more solemn responsibility, or calls in requisition a higher degree of wisdom than the power of regulating the common currency, and thus fixing the general standard of value for a great commercial community composed of confederated states.

Such being, in the opinion of the Committee, the high and delicate trust exclusively committed to Congress by the federal Constitution, they have proceeded to discharge the duty assigned to them, with a corresponding sense of its magnitude and difficulty.

The most simple and obvious analysis of the subject, as it is presented by the message of the President, exhibits the following questions for the decision of the national legislature:

1. Has Congress the constitutional power to incorporate a bank such as that of the United States?

2. Is it expedient to establish and maintain such an institution? . . .

I. If the concurrence of all the departments of the government, at different periods of our history, under every administration, and during the ascendancy of both the great political parties into which the country was divided soon after the adoption of the present Constitution, shall be regarded as having the authority ascribed to such sanctions by the common consent of all well-regulated communities, the constitutional power of Congress to incorporate a bank may be assumed as a postulate no longer open to controversy. . . .

It is to be remarked, in the first place, that since the adoption of the Constitution, a bank has existed under the authority of the federal government for thirty-three out of forty years; during which time public and private credit have been maintained at an elevation fully equal to what has existed in any nation in the world; whereas, in the two short intervals during which no national bank existed, public and private credit were greatly impaired and, in the latter instance, the fiscal operations of the government were almost entirely arrested. In the second place, it is worthy of special notice that in both the instances in which Congress has created a bank it has been done under circumstances calculated to give the highest authority to the decision.

The first instance, as has been already remarked, was in the primitive days of the republic, when the patriots of the Revolution and the sages of the Federal Convention were the leading members both of the executive and legislative councils; and when General Washington, who, at the head of her armies, had conducted his country to independence, and, as the head of the Convention, had presided over those deliberations which resulted in the establishment of the present Constitution, was the acknowledged President of a people undistracted by party divisions. The second instance was under circumstances of a very different but equally decisive character. We find the very party which had so recently defeated the proposition to renew the charter of the old bank, severely schooled both by adversity and experience, magnanimously sacrificing the pride of consistency and the prejudices of party at the shrine of patriotism.

It may be said without disparagement that an assembly of higher talent and purer patriotism has never existed since the days of the Revolution than the Congress by which the present bank was incorporated. If ever a political party existed of which it might be truly said that "all the ends they aimed at were their country's," it was the Republican Party of that day. They had just conducted the country through the perils of a war, waged in defense of her rights and honor, and, elevating their views far above the narrow and miserable ends of party strife, sought only to advance the permanent happiness of the people. It was to this great end that they established the present bank. . . .

The earliest and the principal objection urged against the constitutionality of a national bank was that Congress had not the power to create corporations. That Congress has a distinct and substantive power to create corporations, without reference to the objects entrusted to its jurisdiction, is a proposition which never has been maintained within the knowledge of the Committee; but that any one of the powers expressly conferred upon Congress is subject to the limitation that it shall not be carried into effect by the agency of a corporation is a proposition which cannot be maintained, in the opinion of the Committee.

If Congress, under the authority to pass *all laws*, necessary and proper for carrying into effect the powers vested in all or any of the departments of the government, may rightfully pass a law inflicting the punishment of death, *without any other authority*, it is difficult to conceive why it may not pass a law, under the same authority, for the more humble purpose of creating a corporation. The power of creating a corporation is one of the lowest attributes, or more properly speaking, incidents of sovereign power.

The chartering of a bank, for example, does not authorize the corporation to do anything which the individuals composing it might not do without the charter. It is the right of every individual of the Union to give credit to whom he chooses, and to obtain credit where he can get it. It is not the policy of any commercial country to restrict the free circulation of credit, whether in the form of promissory notes, bills of exchange, or bank notes. The charter of the Bank of the United States, therefore, merely enables the corporation to do, in an artificial capacity and with more convenience, what it would be lawful for the individual corporators to do without incorporation. . . .

The power to "coin money and fix the value thereof" is expressly and exclusively vested in Congress. This grant was evidently intended to invest Congress with the power of regulating the circulating medium. "Coin" was regarded, at the period of framing the Constitution, as synonymous with "currency"; as it was then generally believed that bank notes could only be maintained in circulation by being the true representative of the precious metals. The word "coin," therefore, must be regarded as a particular term, standing as the representative of a general idea.

No principle of sound construction will justify a rigid adherence to the letter in opposition to the plain intention of the clause. If, for example, the gold bars of Ricardo should be substituted for our present coins, by the general consent of the commercial world, could it be maintained that Congress would not have the power to *make* such money and fix its value because it is not "coined"? This would be sacrificing sense to sound and substance to mere form. This clause of the Constitution is analogous to that which gives Congress the power "to establish post roads."

Giving to the word "establish" its restricted interpretation as being equivalent to "fix" or "prescribe," can it be doubted that Congress has the power to establish a canal or a river as a post route, as well as a road? Roads were the ordinary channels of conveyance, and the term was, therefore, used as synonymous with "routes," whatever might be the channel of transportation, and in like manner, "coin," being the ordinary and most known form of a circulating medium, that term was used as synonymous with "currency."

An argument in favor of the view just taken may be fairly deduced from the fact that the states are expressly prohibited from "coining money or emitting bills of credit," and from "making anything but gold and silver a lawful tender in payment of debts." This strongly confirms the idea that the subject of regulating the circulating medium, whether consisting of coin or paper, was, at the same time that it was taken from the control of the states, vested in the only depository in which it could be placed, consistently with the obvious design of having a common measure of value throughout the Union. . . .

II. The next question proposed for consideration is the expediency of establishing an incorporated bank, with a view to promote the great ends already indicated. In discussing the constitutionality of such a measure, some of the considerations which render it expedient have been slightly unfolded. But these require a more full and complete development, while others remain to be presented.

It must be assumed as the basis of all sound reasoning on this subject that the existence of a paper currency issued by banks deriving their charters from the state governments cannot be prohibited by Congress. Indeed, bank credit and bank paper are so extensively interwoven with the commercial operations of society that, even if Congress had the constitutional power, it would be utterly impossible to produce so entire a change in the monetary system of the country as to abolish the agency of banks of discount, without involving the community in all the distressing embarrassments usually attendant on great political revolutions, subverting the titles to private property. The sudden withdrawal of some hundred millions of bank credit would be equivalent, in its effects, to the arbitrary and despotic transfer of the property of one portion of the community to another, to the extent, probably, of half that amount.

Whatever, therefore, may be the advantages of a purely metallic currency, and whatever the objections to a circulating medium partly composed of bank paper, the Committee consider that they are precluded, by the existing state of things, from instituting a comparison between them with a view to any practical result. If they were not thus precluded, and it were submitted

to them as an original question, whether the acknowledged and manifold facilities of bank credit and bank paper are not more than counterbalanced by the distressing vicissitudes in trade incident to their use, they are by no means prepared to say that they would not give a decided preference to the more costly and cumbersome medium.

But the question . . . is not between a metallic and a paper currency but between a paper currency of uniform value, and subject to the control of the only power competent to its regulation, and a paper currency of varying and fluctuating value, and subject to no common or adequate control whatever. On this question it would seem that there could scarcely exist a difference of opinion; and that this is substantially the question involved in considering the expediency of a national bank will satisfactorily appear by a comparison of the state of the currency previous to the establishment of the present bank and its condition for the last ten years.

Soon after the expiration of the charter of the First Bank of the United States, an immense number of local banks sprang up under the pecuniary exigencies produced by the withdrawal of so large an amount of bank credit as necessarily resulted from the winding up of its concerns — an amount falling very little short of $15 million. These banks, being entirely free from the salutary control which the Bank of the United States had recently exercised over the local institutions, commenced that system of imprudent trading and excessive issues which speedily involved the country in all the embarrassments of a disordered currency. The extraordinary stimulus of a heavy war expenditure, derived principally from loans, and a corresponding multiplication of local banks, chartered by the double score in some of the states, hastened the catastrophe which must have occurred at no distant period without these extraordinary causes. The last year of the war presented the singular and melancholy spectacle of a nation abounding in resources, a people abounding in self-devoting patriotism, and a government reduced to the very brink of avowed bankruptcy, solely for the want of a national institution which, at the same time that it would have facilitated the government loans and other treasury operations, would have furnished a circulating medium of general credit in every part of the Union.

In this view of the subject, the Committee are fully sustained by the opinion of Mr. Dallas, then secretary of the treasury, and by the concurring and almost unanimous opinion of all parties in Congress; for, whatever diversity of opinion prevailed as to the proper basis and organization of a bank, almost every one agreed that a national bank, of some sort, was indispensably necessary to rescue the country from the greatest of financial calamities. . . .

A very serious evil, already hinted at, which grew out of the relative depreciation of bank paper, at the different points of importation, was its inevitable tendency to draw all the importations of foreign merchandise to the cities where the depreciation was greatest, and divert them from those where the currency was comparatively sound. If the Bank of the United States had not been established and the government had been left without any alternative but to receive the depreciated local currency, it is difficult to imagine the extent to which the evasion of the revenue laws would have been carried.

Every state would have had an interest to encourage the excessive issues of its banks and increase the degradation of its currency with a view to attract foreign commerce. Even in the condition which the currency had reached in 1816, Boston and New York and Charleston would have found it advantageous to derive their supplies of foreign merchandise through Baltimore; and commerce would undoubtedly have taken that direction had not the currency been corrected. To avoid this injurious diversion of foreign imports, Massachusetts and New York and South Carolina would have been driven, by all the motives of self-defense and self-interest, to degrade their respective currencies at least to a par with the currency of Baltimore; and thus a rivalry in the career of depreciation would have sprung up to which no limit can be assigned.

As the tendency of this state of things would have been to cause the largest portion of the revenue to be collected at a few places, and in the most depreciated of the local currency, it would have followed that a very small part of that revenue would have been disbursed at the points where it was collected. The government would consequently have been compelled to sustain a heavy loss upon the transfer of its funds to the points of expenditure. The annual loss which would have resulted from these causes alone cannot be estimated at a less sum than $2 million.

But the principal loss which resulted from the relative depreciation of bank paper at different places, and its want of general credit, was that sustained by the community in the great operations of commercial exchange. The extent of these operations annually may be safely estimated at $60 million. Upon this sum, the loss sustained by the merchants and planters and farmers and manufacturers was not probably less than an average of 10 percent, being the excess of the rate of exchange between its natural rate in a sound state of the currency and beyond the rate to which it has been actually reduced by the operations of the Bank of the United States.

It will be thus perceived that an annual tax of $6 million was levied from the industrious and productive classes by the large monied capitalists in our commercial cities who were engaged in the business of brokerage. A variously depreciated currency and a fluctuating state of the exchanges open a wide and abundant harvest to the money brokers; and it is not, therefore, surprising that they should be opposed to an institution which, at the same time that it has relieved the community from the enormous tax just stated, has deprived them of the enormous profits which they derived from speculating in the business of exchange. . . .

In addition to the losses sustained by the community in the great operations of exchange, extensive losses were suffered throughout the interior of the country, in all the smaller operations of trade, as well as by the failure of the numerous paper banks, puffed into a factitious credit by fraudulent artifices, and having no substantial basis of capital to ensure the redemption of their bills. . . .

But it is impossible to exhibit anything like a just view of the beneficial operations of the bank without adverting to the great reduction it has effected and the steadiness it has superinduced in the rate of the commercial exchanges of the country. Though this branch of the business of the bank has been the subject of more complaint, perhaps, than any other, the Committee have no hesitation in saying it has been productive of the most signal benefits to the community and deserves the highest commendation.

It has been already stated that it has saved the community from the immense losses resulting from a high and fluctuating state of the exchanges. It now remains to show its effect in equalizing the currency. In this respect, it has been productive of results more salutary than were anticipated by the most sanguine advocates of the policy of establishing the bank. *It has actually furnished a circulating medium more uniform than specie.*

This proposition is susceptible of the clearest demonstration. If the whole circulating medium were specie, a planter of Louisiana, who should desire to purchase merchandise in Philadelphia, would be obliged to pay 1 percent, either for a bill of exchange on this latter place or for the transportation and insurance of his specie. His specie at New Orleans, where he had no present use for it, would be worth 1 percent less to him than it would be in Philadelphia, where he had a demand for it. But, by the aid of the Bank of the United States, one-half of the expense of transporting specie is now saved to him. The bank, for one-half of 1 percent, will give him a draft upon the mother bank at Philadelphia with which he can draw either the bills of that bank or specie, at his pleasure. In like manner, the bank and its branches will give drafts from any point of the Union to any other where offices exist, at a percentage greatly less than it would cost to transport specie, and, in many instances, at par.

If the merchant or planter, however, does not choose to purchase a draft from the bank, but prefers transmitting the bills of the office where he resides to any distant point, for commercial purposes, although these bills are not strictly redeemable at the point to which they are transmitted, yet, as they are receivable in payment of all dues to the government, persons will be generally found willing to take them at par; and if they should not, the bank will receive them frequently at par, and always at a discount much less than would pay the expense of transporting specie. The fact that the bills of the bank and its branches are indiscriminately receivable at the custom houses and land offices, in payment of duties, and for the public lands, has an effect in giving uniformity to the value of these bills, which merits a more full and distinct explanation.

For all the purposes of the revenue, it gives to the national currency that perfect uniformity, that ideal perfection to which a currency of gold and silver, in so extensive a country, could have no pretensions. A bill issued at Missouri is of equal value with specie at Boston in payment of duties; and the same is true of all other places, however distant, where the bank issues bills and the government collects its revenue. When it is, moreover, considered that the bank performs with the most scrupulous punctuality the stipulation to transfer the funds of the government to any point where they may be wanted, free of expense, it must be apparent that the Committee are correct, to the very letter, in stating that the bank has furnished, both to the government and to the people, *a currency of absolutely uniform value in all places, for all the purposes of paying the public contributions and disbursing the public revenue.* And when it is recollected that the government annually collects and disburses more than $23 million, those who are at all familiar with the subject will at once perceive that bills, which are of absolutely uniform value for this vast operation, must be very nearly so for all the purposes of general commerce. . . .

But the salutary agency of the Bank of the United States in furnishing a sound and uniform currency is not confined to that portion of the currency which consists of its own bills. One of the most important purposes which the bank was designed to accomplish, and which, it is confidently believed, no other human agency could have effected under our federative system of government, was the enforcement of specie payments on the part of numerous local banks, deriving their charters from the several states, and whose paper, irredeemable in specie and illimitable in its quantity, constituted the almost entire currency of the country. Amidst a combination of the greatest difficulties, the bank has almost completely succeeded in the performance of this arduous, delicate, and painful duty.

With exceptions too inconsiderable to merit notice, all the state banks in the Union have resumed specie payments. Their bills, in the respective spheres of their circulation, are of equal value with gold and silver; while, for all the operations of commerce beyond that sphere, the bills or the checks of the Bank of the United States are even more valuable than specie.

And even in the very few instances in which the paper of state banks is depreciated, those banks are winding up their concerns; and it may be safely said that no citizen of the Union is under the necessity of taking depreciated paper because a sound currency cannot be obtained. North Carolina is believed to be the only state where paper of the local banks is irredeemable in specie, and consequently depreciated. Even there, the depreciation is only 1 or 2 percent; and, what is more important, the paper of the Bank of the United States can be obtained by all those who desire it and have an equivalent to give for it. . . .

Although the expediency of renewing the charter of the present bank is not a question now submitted for the decision of Congress, the Committee consider it so far involved in the matter referred to them as to render it their duty to present some considerations bearing on that question, in addition to what they have said on the general expediency of maintaining such an institution. If a national bank, similar to the present, be a necessary and proper agent for the accomplishment of the great purposes heretofore indicated, the only remaining question would seem to be whether the charter of the present stockholders should be renewed, or a new set of stockholders incorporated.

In considering this question, Congress will, of course, be governed in some degree by the terms on which the present stockholders will agree to accept a renewal of their charter. But, as the committee have satisfactory reasons for believing that terms eminently advantageous to the government can be obtained, they will proceed to some other inquiries. What, then, would be the effect of refusing to renew the present charter? And, in the first place, what are the inducements for pursuing that course?

It is sometimes alleged that the present stockholders are large capitalists and, as the stock of the bank is some 20 percent above par, that a renewal of the charter would be equivalent to a grant to them of 20 percent upon their capital. It is true that a small proportion of the capital of the company belongs to very wealthy men. Something more than $2 million of that owned in the United States belongs to persons holding upward of $100,000 each. It is also true that foreigners own $7 million, or one-fifth of the capital.

But, on the other hand, it is to be remarked that the government, in trust for the people of the United States, holds $7 million; that persons owning less than $5,000 each hold $4,682,000; and that persons owning between $5,000 and $10,000 each hold upward of $3 million. It is also worthy of remark that a very considerable portion of the stock — very nearly $6 million — is held by trustees and guardians for the use of females and orphan children, and charitable and other institutions. Of the $28 million of the stock which is owned by individuals, only $3,453,000 is now held by the original subscribers. All the rest has been purchased at the market prices; a large portion of it, probably, when those prices were higher than at present. Most of the investments made by wills and deeds and decrees in equity, for the use of females and minors, are believed to have been made when the stock was greatly above par.

From this brief analysis, it will appear that there is nothing in the character or situation of the stockholders which should make it desirable to deprive them of the advantage which they have fairly gained by an application of their capital to purposes highly beneficial, as the Committee have attempted to show to the government and people of the United States.

If foreigners own $7 million of the stock of the bank, our own government owns as much; if wealthy men own more than $2 million, men in moderate circumstances own between $7 million and $8 million; and widows, orphans, and institutions devoted to charitable and other purposes own nearly $6 million.

But the objection that the stock is owned by men of large capital would apply with equal if not greater force to any bank that could be organized. In the very nature of things, men who have large surplus capitals are the principal subscribers at the first organization of a bank. Farmers and planters, merchants and manufacturers, having an active employment for their capitals, do not choose to be the first adventurers in a bank project. . . . The large amount of stock now held in trust for females and minors has been principally if not entirely purchased since the bank went into operation; and the same remark is generally applicable to the stock in the hands of small holders. It is only when the character of a bank is fully established, and when its stock assumes a steady value, that these descriptions of persons make investments in it.

It is morally certain, therefore, that if another distinct institution were created on the expiration of the present charter, there would be a much greater portion of its capital subscribed by men of large fortunes than is now owned by persons of this description of the stock of the United States' Bank. Indeed, it might be confidently predicted that the large capitalists who now hold stock in that bank would, from their local position and other advantages, be the first to forestall the subscriptions to the new bank, while the small stockholders, scattered over the country, would be probably excluded, and the females and minors, and others interested in trust investments made by decrees in equity, would be almost necessarily excluded, as the sanction of a court could scarcely be obtained after the passage of the new act of incorporation in time to authorize a subscription.

To destroy the existing bank, therefore, after it has rendered such signal services to the country, merely with a view to incorporate another, would be an act rather of cruelty and caprice than of justice and wisdom as it regards the present stockholders. It is no light matter to depreciate the property of individuals, honestly obtained and usefully employed, to the extent of $5,600,000, and the property of the government to the extent of $1,400,000, purely for the sake of change. It would indicate a fondness for experiment which a wise government will not indulge upon slight considerations. . . .

If the Bank of the United States were destroyed and the local institutions left without its restraining influence, the currency would almost certainly relapse into a state of unsoundness. The very pressure which the present bank, in winding up its concerns, would make upon the local institutions would compel them either to curtail their discounts when most needed, or to suspend specie payments.

It is not difficult to predict which of these alternatives they would adopt under the circumstances in which they would be placed. The imperious wants of a suffering community would call for discounts, in language which could not be disregarded. The public necessities would demand, and public opinion would sanction, the suspension, or at least an evasion, of specie payments.

But, even if this desperate resort could be avoided in a period of peace and general prosperity, neither reason nor experience will permit us to doubt that a state of war would speedily bring about all the evils which so fatally affected the credit of the government and the national currency during the late war with Great Britain. We should be again driven to the same miserable round of financial expedients which, in little more than two years, brought a wealthy community almost to the very brink of a declared national bankruptcy and placed the government completely at the mercy of speculating stockjobbers.

77.

Anonymous: Corporate Power

In 1800 America's economy was primarily agrarian, but the first decades of the nineteenth century saw the beginning of the change to a mercantile and manufacturing economy. The base of political power was broadened at the same time, with the result that more people than ever were able to express their opinions on complex political and economic issues. However, the two changes often ran counter to each other, for the average voter continued to think politically in terms of the Jeffersonian ideals that became more and more irrelevant as the century wore on. The corporation especially came under attack as a bastion of entrenched wealth and special privilege in an otherwise democratic society. The following article containing relatively restrained criticism of business corporations appeared in October 1830, when the controversy over the Second Bank of the United States was just getting under way.

Source: *American Jurist and Law Magazine*, October 1830.

In this country, a corporation is a community of men possessing, in conformity to constitutional or legislative provision, certain property, income, or rights, and subject to certain burdens distinct from other men.

The objects in the creation of corporations were to perpetuate succession, without submitting to the embarrassing forms of administration and guardianship, on the decease of incorporators, and to enable numerous bodies of men, acting under a charter, as municipal, pecuniary, or other associations, to negotiate as an individual. . . .

The doctrine of corporations, in this country, on account of their extent as well as the defective state of their existence and operation, presents a most interesting field of inquiry to American jurists, and demands that their best energies should be applied to the subject, that corporations may be protected and wisely directed in effecting the great public and private good of which they are capable, and restrained from inflicting the public and private evils within their power, and to which they are often tempted by their own views of interest.

Among the incidents of a corporation at common law, unless restrained by their charter, are:

To have perpetual succession; to have a common seal; to make bylaws; to sue and be sued; and to purchase, take, hold, manage, grant, and dispose of lands and personal property. Such is the language of the English common law, and if it be here in force, it follows, that if A, B, and C, and their associates are, by a legislative act, by a single section, created a corporation without declaring or limiting their operations, they have the power to organize, to perpetuate their existence by receiving new members who shall have all the rights of the original corporators, and be considered associates (for they can have no successors) to trade, buy, hold, manage, and sell any and all estates to an indefinite extent, to make and enforce contracts, all of which they do as an individual, in their corporate name. In fine, they have collectively all the rights and powers of individuals, excepting those of a political and moral character. With the want of political and moral powers, they are of course exempted from corresponding responsibilities.

The quaint language of Lord Coke, and other venerable ancient luminaries of the law, describing corporations as having no souls or consciences, as mere capacities to sue and be sued, has been productive of much mischief and led to many judicial decisions, which the enlightened reason of this age cannot but deplore. From such doctrines, the managers of corporations have sometimes been led to forget that *they* had souls and moral responsibility; and in the performance of what they deemed their duty, in the corporate name, they have done such things as, on their individual responsibility, they would never have ventured to do.

Such are some of the features of corporate being and rights at common law. In Massachusetts they remain generally unqualified; but in England and some of the states these powers have been greatly restrained and limited by legislative enactment. The time was when it was the generally received doctrine that corporations could contract and act only by their common seal. They were considered incapable of committing crimes, doing moral or personal acts of any kind. They became liable for nothing by implication, and had more capacity to acquire and hold than liability to yield to the just claims of others.

Experience and the wisdom of modern times have demonstrated the necessity of regulating the rights and liabilities of corporations, so far as the condition of their being permitted, by the same principles of law that govern individuals. To effect this the judicial tribunals of our age have labored with an honest and not unfruitful zeal. The barriers of irresponsibility by which corporations were formerly surrounded have been successfully invaded and partially broken down; but much yet remains to be done to secure to the public all the benefits that these bodies are calculated to give, and protect individuals from the evils which they have the power to inflict. The boldest and most effectual step in this career of improvement was the judicial decision that corporations are liable in *indebitatus assumpsit.*

It is now the settled law in this country established by the Supreme Court of the United States and by the highest judicial tribunals in many of the states, that corporations can establish rights and incur liabilities by implication. This principle was fully settled in the case of the *United States Bank* v. *Dandridge.* . . . In this case, which was decided in 1827, Chief Justice Marshall dissented from the court and gave his opinion at length. As was natural to expect, when the decision of the court was opposed by so great an authority, the whole strength of both sides was put forth. Every authority and argument, for and against the position, are there presented; and few more elaborate and satisfactory reports can be found.

Chief Justice Marshall said he believed that his opinion, which had been declared in the court below, gave general surprise to the profession, and was generally condemned; still he adhered to it. The case is now before the nation, and Judge Marshall, great as the authority of his opinion is, will have increasing cause to find that in this case he is disapproved. . . .

Although now corporations are more subject than formerly to the laws that govern individuals, and thereby much of their irresponsibleness is taken away, yet they have advantages over individuals in the great capitals with which they usually operate, and the enduring quality of their being; which enable them to persevere in their objects for ages with a steady aim and undiminished capital, free from the paralyzing effects of inexperienced youth or superannuated age, and the distribution of estates, which occur in the succession of generations, and frequently check individual operations both by want of capacity and capital.

It is the opinion of many that individuals without more protection cannot maintain a fair competition with corporations, if here they have all the English common law incidents attached to them. And in England and some of the states they have been subjected to various restraints.

In England, corporations, unless it is expressly otherwise provided by the charter, are now limited and rendered incapable of taking lands without the king's license. This has been effected by a series of statutes, called the statutes of mortmain. They were at first designed to restrain the accumulations of ecclesiastical corporations. But the statute declared that civil or lay corporations were within the mischief, and it brought them within the prohibition. The common law capacity of taking and holding lands by corporations is now, in that country, wholly taken away by statute.

The statutes of mortmain are in force in Pennsylvania; and, there, they hold all deeds and devises of lands to corporations void, unless sanctioned by their charters.

In New York the statutes of mortmain are not in force, but there they hold that by force of their statutes, no religious corporation can sell without an order from the chancellor. The evils felt by the power and growing number of corporations in New York induced them, on the amendment of their constitution made in 1821, to provide that in future no corporation should be created or renewed without the consent of two-thirds of the members elected to each branch of the legislature. By their general statute of wills, now in force, they withhold from corporations the power to become devisees of real estate, and in their grants of charters for private benefit they now usually insert a clause empowering the legislature to alter, modify, or repeal the charter at pleasure. And yet, with all these guards against the power and multiplication of corporations, the ablest jurists in New York speak of them as growing evils.

In Massachusetts, where probably there is a greater propensity to multiply corporations than anywhere else, they have all the incidental powers, unrestrained by statutes of mortmain or wills; and generally they are granted without a clause reserving to the legislature the power to repeal or modify them. We can look for restrictions only to the charters, or the general statutes regulating and prescribing the powers and duties of particular classes of corporations, which are referred to in the particular charters and made a part of them. And it has been determined in that state that a corporation can take devises and bequests in trust for pious and charitable uses.

With these broad powers existing in the great and rapidly increasing numbers of corporations, this branch of jurisprudence assumes an importance in Massachusetts, and a few other states, greater than it possesses elsewhere; and the Union may look to the profession in this part of the republic for a just exposition of the rise, progress, power, liability, decline, and dissolution of corporations.

It seems to be clear that we have no corporations but such as refer their existence to legislative grant. But when created, unless their powers are limited in the charter, they must be possessed of all the acknowledged common law incidents to them. Some are created for limited purposes. These have been called quasi-corporations. That means that they are beings of legislative creation, resembling corporations. But they must, in truth, be corporations, or they are nothing.

It is common, in making grants by our legislatures, to provide that the companies may do certain things mentioned in the charters; and that they may purchase, manage, and hold real and personal estate, to a specified amount. At common law, by being made corporations, they acquired these rights without limitation. Such language in the charters, although in the form of granting privileges and clothing the grantees with powers, is wholly inoperative, as all those powers are incident to their being, unless it be judicially determined to be language of limitation and restraint. By determining such language in the grants to have that ef-

fect, many, if not most, of the evils to be apprehended from the exercise of corporate powers will be avoided. And such may well be considered the meaning of the legislatures which made the grants, unless it be assumed that they were well versed in the rules of common law. and knew that the powers they carefully and specifically provided for the corporation were theirs as incidents to their becoming corporations without further legislative provision.

And such appears to be the view of the subject taken by the Supreme Judicial Court of Massachusetts. They have decided that towns, parishes, and school districts have powers only sufficient to effect the purposes and perform the duties assigned to them by the legislature; and when they attempt to exceed these powers, their acts are void. And in *The First Parish in Sutton* v. *Cole,* the court said, although the statutes of mortmain were not in force,

> still it might be inferred from the special power given to various corporations by acts of the legislature, to hold real and personal estate to a limited extent, that corporations created for specific objects would not have the power to take and hold real estate for purposes wholly foreign to those objects.

It is difficult to discover the reason why the common law clothed corporations on the moment of their springing into being with so many important rights. It vested equal power in all, though the objects for which they were created were almost as various as human operations, some being extremely limited in their objects, and affecting the interests of but few individuals, and others operating on the most valuable rights of large communities. These cannot require prerogatives and privileges of equal extent; and in this respect the common law seems to have failed of its usual excellence in its adaptation to the wants of society.

A sounder rule seems to be that every corporation should be considered as invest ed with all the powers necessary to effect the legal purposes for which it was created, and no more. Whether the establishment of such a rule requires legislative provision, or may be achieved by judicial construction, depends on the question whether the English common law relative to corporations has been adopted in its full extent in the several states, or whether it remains unsanctioned, or has become obsolete. In many parts of the country the common law doctrine has been questioned, and in some distinctly denied. The author of the *Commentaries on American Law* says that the modern doctrine is to consider corporations as possessing only such powers as are specifically granted in the act of incorporation, or are necessary for carrying into effect the powers expressly granted. . . .

The courts in Massachusetts have made many decisions from which it must be inferred that they favor the doctrine, and are inclined to adopt it, that corporations have no powers but such as are plainly granted in their charters, or are clearly necessary to effect the useful purposes for which they were created. Such rules of construction can hardly yet be considered as established anywhere in their full extent. In the courts above referred to, the common-law incidents to corporations are sometimes cited with approbation, and in other state courts they are generally referred to without qualification. The evident utility of the new construction will probably soon recommend it to general adoption.

When such becomes the declared law of the states, and when it shall become the law that corporations are generally liable for the acts of their authorized agents; for contracts by implication; for all wrongs and injuries that they are capable of inflicting; and for all injurious omissions to perform their duties, there will be no longer need of statutes of mortmain and wills; or constitutional impediments or restraints to the multiplication of corporate charters. It might still, however, be wise for legislatures to reserve more

direct control over corporations of future creation than they are accustomed to do in most of the states. The enjoyment of a corporate franchise is not of common right. It is the grant of the whole people of certain powers to a few individuals, to enable them to effect some specific benefit, or promote the general good. When the corporation fails to produce the expected benefit, and far more when its charter is perverted to injurious purposes, the whole people ought to have the power to control the operations, and even to revoke the charter.

When these doctrines shall become fully established, and legislatures grow careful to reserve visitatorial powers in granting charters for civil corporations, the fear and apprehension of corporations now existing, and too justly forced by experience into the public mind, will probably subside. Such fears have induced the legislatures in some of the states to adopt measures which should, and to a great extent do, deter the public from encountering the perils resulting from the ownership of the corporate stocks.

The making of every corporator liable in all events for every debt of the company may tend to protect the individuals who deal with them from danger of loss, but it will rob the public of many of the benefits that should result from the exercise of corporate charters. Prudent men will not take stock, if thereby they must become general copartners with all the other stockholders, who may become their associates without their consent, and in defiance of their opposition to such fellowship. Such a provision has heretofore been introduced in the grant of charters for manufacturing purposes in Massachusetts. The effect has been to drive millions of capital into the neighboring states for investment. And there it will remain. It is questionable whether the recent alleviating act is an adequate remedy. True policy requires that charters of corporations should be well guarded, carefully adapted to their objects, and kept under wholesome legislative and judicial control. But they should be made entirely free from onerous and appalling liabilities, the tendency of which is to drive prudent men from them, and to leave them in the hands of desperate speculators.

Another quality ascribed in the ancient books to aggregate corporations is immortality. And on this incident many curious and whimsical theories have been built. This position is as false as it is absurd. The most striking practical comment on it is that a large proportion of those that have been created in Europe, and many in this country, have ceased to exist, their immortality notwithstanding. It is only true to this extent: that when their duration is not limited in the grant, they are capable of being made to endure indefinitely, provided from time to time the necessary measures are taken to continue their succession, and provided they continue to effect the objects for which they were made, and refrain from violating the laws. They may be dissolved in various ways, as by the limitation of time contained in the acts establishing them, by surrendering their charters, by the death of all the members, and by forfeiture of charter through negligence or abuse of its franchises.

Since so great a portion of our national wealth is held and managed by corporations, the laws applicable to them ought to be very diligently studied by American lawyers. The growing importance of the subject demands, and it is hoped it may ere long receive, increased attention.

78.

Andrew Jackson: Veto of Maysville Road Bill

President Jackson's views concerning federal grants for internal improvements were similar to those of President James Monroe, who had told Congress in 1822 that while it could appropriate money for such projects, it could only do so when they were for the common defense or for the commercial or other benefit of the entire nation, not of one locality or state. Jackson applied this narrow construction of the Constitution in his May 27, 1830, veto message on the Maysville Road Bill, parts of which appear here. The bill appropriated federal funds for a branch of the Cumberland Road, a national highway authorized by Congress in 1806. Work on the road continued until 1838, by which time it extended from the Potomac River to Vandalia, Illinois, but Jackson's 1830 veto halted further federal road construction projects for fifty years.

Source: Richardson, II, pp. 483-493.

I HAVE MATURELY CONSIDERED the bill proposing to authorize "a subscription of stock in the Maysville, Washington, Paris, and Lexington Turnpike Road Company," and now return the same to the House of Representatives, in which it originated, with my objections to its passage.

Sincerely friendly to the improvement of our country by means of roads and canals, I regret that any difference of opinion in the mode of contributing to it should exist between us; and if in stating this difference I go beyond what the occasion may be deemed to call for, I hope to find an apology in the great importance of the subject, an unfeigned respect for the high source from which this branch of it has emanated, and an anxious wish to be correctly understood by my constituents in the discharge of all my duties. . . .

In the message which was presented to Congress at the opening of its present session, I endeavored to exhibit briefly my views upon the important and highly interesting subject to which our attention is now 'to be directed. . . . In that document the following suggestions will be found:

> After the extinction of the public debt, it is not probable that any adjustment of the tariff upon principles satisfactory to the people of the Union will, until a remote period, if ever, leave the government without a considerable surplus in the treasury beyond what may be required for its current service. . . . It appears to me that the most safe, just, and federal disposition which could be made of the surplus revenue would be its apportionment among the several states according to their ratio of representation; and, should this measure not be found warranted by the Constitution, that it would be expedient to propose to the states an amendment authorizing it.

The constitutional power of the federal government to construct or promote works of internal improvement presents itself in two points of view: the first as bearing upon the sovereignty of the states within whose limits their execution is contemplated, if jurisdiction of the territory which they may occupy be claimed as necessary to their preservation and use; the second as asserting the simple right to appropriate money from the national treasury in aid of such works when undertaken by state authority, surrendering the claim of jurisdiction. In the first view the question of power is an open one, and can be decided without the embarrassments attending the other, arising from the practice of the government. Although frequently and strenuously attempted, the

power to this extent has never been exercised by the government in a single instance. It does not, in my opinion, possess it; and no bill, therefore, which admits it can receive my official sanction.

But in the other view of the power the question is differently situated. The ground taken at an early period of the government was "that whenever money has been raised by the general authority and is to be applied to a particular measure, a question arises whether the particular measure be within the enumerated authorities vested in Congress. If it be, the money requisite for it may be applied to it; if not, no such application can be made." . . .

In the administration of Mr. Jefferson, we have two examples of the exercise of the right of appropriation, which, in the considerations that led to their adoption and in their effects upon the public mind, have had a greater agency in marking the character of the power than any subsequent events. I allude to the payment of $15 million for the purchase of Louisiana and to the original appropriation for the construction of the Cumberland Road, the latter act deriving much weight from the acquiescence and approbation of three of the most powerful of the original members of the Confederacy, expressed through their respective legislatures. Although the circumstances of the latter case may be such as to deprive so much of it as relates to the actual construction of the road of the force of an obligatory exposition of the Constitution, it must, nevertheless, be admitted that so far as the mere appropriation of money is concerned they present the principle in its most imposing aspect.

No less than twenty-three different laws have been passed, through all the forms of the Constitution, appropriating upward of $2,500,000 out of the national treasury in support of that improvement, with the approbation of every President of the United

States, including my predecessor, since its commencement. . . .

This brief reference to known facts will be sufficient to show the difficulty, if not impracticability, of bringing back the operations of the government to the construction of the Constitution set up in 1798, assuming that to be its true reading in relation to the power under consideration, thus giving an admonitory proof of the force of implication and the necessity of guarding the Constitution with sleepless vigilance against the authority of precedents which have not the sanction of its most plainly defined powers; for although it is the duty of all to look to that sacred instrument instead of the statute book, to repudiate at all times encroachments upon its spirit, which are too apt to be effected by the conjuncture of peculiar and facilitating circumstances, it is not less true that the public good and the nature of our political institutions require that individual differences should yield to a well-settled acquiescence of the people and confederated authorities in particular constructions of the Constitution on doubtful points. Not to concede this much to the spirit of our institutions would impair their stability and defeat the objects of the Constitution itself.

The bill before me does not call for a more definite opinion upon the particular circumstances which will warrant appropriations of money by Congress to aid works of internal improvement, for although the extension of the power to apply money beyond that of carrying into effect the object for which it is appropriated has . . . been long claimed and exercised by the federal government, yet such grants have always been professedly under the control of the general principle that the works which might be thus aided should be "of a general, not local, national, not state," character. A disregard of this distinction would of necessity lead to the subversion of the federal system. That even this is an unsafe one, ar-

bitrary in its nature, and liable, consequently, to great abuses, is too obvious to require the confirmation of experience.

It is, however, sufficiently definite, and imperative to my mind to forbid my approbation of any bill having the character of the one under consideration. I have given to its provisions all the reflection demanded by a just regard for the interests of those of our fellow citizens who have desired its passage, and by the respect which is due to a coordinate branch of the government, but I am not able to view it in any other light than as a measure of purely local character; or, if it can be considered national, that no further distinction between the appropriate duties of the general and state governments need be attempted, for there can be no local interest that may not with equal propriety be denominated national. It has no connection with any established system of improvements; is exclusively within the limits of a state, starting at a point on the Ohio River and running out sixty miles to an interior town; and, even as far as the state is interested, conferring partial instead of general advantages.

Considering the magnitude and importance of the power, and the embarrassments to which, from the very nature of the thing, its exercise must necessarily be subjected, the real friends of internal improvement ought not to be willing to confide it to accident and chance. What is properly *national* in its character or otherwise is an inquiry which is often extremely difficult of solution.

The appropriations of one year for an object which is considered national may be rendered nugatory by the refusal of a succeeding Congress to continue the work on the ground that it is local. No aid can be derived from the intervention of corporations. The question regards the character of the work, not that of those by whom it is to be accomplished. Notwithstanding the union of the government with the corporation, by whose immediate agency any work of internal improvement is carried on, the inquiry will still remain — Is it national and conducive to the benefit of the whole, or local and operating only to the advantage of a portion of the Union?

But although I might not feel it to be my official duty to interpose the executive veto to the passage of a bill appropriating money for the construction of such works as are authorized by the states and are national in their character, I do not wish to be understood as expressing an opinion that it is expedient at this time for the general government to embark in a system of this kind. . . .

If it is expected that the people of this country, reckless of their constitutional obligations, will prefer their local interest to the principles of the Union, such expectations will in the end be disappointed; or, if it be not so, then indeed has the world but little to hope from the example of free government. When an honest observance of constitutional compacts cannot be obtained from communities like ours, it need not be anticipated elsewhere; and the cause in which there has been so much martyrdom, and from which so much was expected by the friends of liberty, may be abandoned, and the degrading truth that man is unfit for self-government admitted.

And this will be the case if *expediency* be made a rule of construction in interpreting the Constitution. Power in no government could desire a better shield for the insidious advances which it is ever ready to make upon the checks that are designed to restrain its action. But I do not entertain such gloomy apprehensions.

If it be the wish of the people that the construction of roads and canals should be conducted by the federal government, it is not only highly expedient but indispensably necessary that a previous amendment of the Constitution, delegating the necessary power and defining and restricting its exercise

with reference to the sovereignty of the states, should be made. Without it, nothing extensively useful can be effected.

A supposed connection between appropriations for internal improvement and the system of protecting duties, growing out of the anxieties of those more immediately interested in their success, has given rise to suggestions which it is proper I should notice on this occasion. My opinions on these subjects have never been concealed from those who had a right to know them. Those which I have entertained on the latter have frequently placed me in opposition to individuals as well as communities whose claims upon my friendship and gratitude are of the strongest character; but I trust there has been nothing in my public life which has exposed me to the suspicion of being thought capable of sacrificing my views of duty to private considerations, however strong they may have been or deep the regrets which they are capable of exciting.

As long as the encouragement of domestic manufactures is directed to national ends, it shall receive from me a temperate but steady support. There is no necessary connection between it and the system of appropriations. On the contrary, it appears to me that the supposition of their dependence upon each other is calculated to excite the prejudices of the public against both. The former is sustained on the grounds of its consistency with the letter and spirit of the Constitution, of its origin being traced to the assent of all the parties to the original compact, and of its having the support and approbation of a majority of the people on which account it is at least entitled to a fair experiment.

The suggestions to which I have alluded refer to a forced continuance of the national debt by means of large appropriations as a substitute for the security which the system derives from the principles on which it has hitherto been sustained. Such a course would certainly indicate either an unreasonable distrust of the people or a consciousness that the system does not possess sufficient soundness for its support if left to their voluntary choice and its own merits. Those who suppose that any policy thus founded can be long upheld in this country have looked upon its history with eyes very different from mine. This policy, like every other, must abide the will of the people, who will not be likely to allow any device, however specious, to conceal its character and tendency.

79.

Labor Parties in New York

The main weakness of the New York Workingmen's Party was its inability to agree either on programs or on candidates for office. The party had relatively few members, but even these few were divided on almost every question. Factions lined up behind various of the party's leaders — Thomas Skidmore, Robert Owen, Frances Wright, George Henry Evans, and others — and their constant conflict helped bring about the party's decline. Some of the reasons for this situation were explained in the following editorial, which appeared shortly before the election in 1830.

Source: *New-York Sentinel and Working Man's Advocate,* July 28, 1830.

THE FOLLOWING APPEARS in a late number of the *National Intelligencer.*

To all persons within the bounds of the state, the parties and politics of New York are as puzzling as were the enigmas of the ancient Sphinx. After some fifteen years study, people abroad had begun to get some insight into the mystery of party denominations there; when, on a sudden, a year or so ago, a host of new sects sprung up, almost swallowing the old, and, like the shaking of a kaleidoscope, presenting an aspect totally different, though composed of materials identically the same. This sudden change was enough to puzzle the great magician himself (and one object of his present visit may be, for aught we know, to study the new state of things, and ascertain how the elements of old parties have combined in forming the new — this, however, by the way).

For our own parts, if anybody this side of Communipaw can tell what are the distinguishing principles, objects, characters, or affinities of the Agrarians, the Workies, the Regulars, the Regency, the Infidels, so called, the Mechanic Working, the Wrightsmen, the Radicals, the Skeletons, not to mention the more familiar Tammanies, Bucktails, etc., it is more than we can do, and we fairly "give it up." In fact, on this subject, we find ourselves in the predicament of certain worthy members of Congress, who, when a question is put which they do not understand or have not attended to, look round to see whether others, in whom they have confidence, rise or sit.

We doubt not New York politics are puzzling enough to strangers. Even our own citizens — so industrious have intriguing politicians been in casting dust in their eyes — find it no easy matter to solve the modern political riddles of our city.

We happen to have been eyewitnesses of the last year's affray since its very commencement; and having, during that time, had no interest to serve, except what we believed to be "the greatest good of the greatest number," if the *Intelligencer* will receive at our hands a plain statement of facts, it is at his service.

He needs not to be informed who the Tammany-men, Regulars, Regency, or by whatever name friends or foes designate them, are. If a name can give a character, they are "Democratic Republicans." If deeds, not words, are to be the test, they are the party in office, enjoying what they have got and casting about to see how they shall keep it and get more; fattening on the loaves and fishes, and becoming lazy and saucy in proportion as they get fat. They are the political descendants of those men who thirty years ago rallied at the cry of "Jefferson and Democracy!" — who supported the patriot-statesman through good and through bad report and gave to this republic, in the person of him whom the rich and the proud denounce as a leveller and an infidel, a chief magistrate such as we may never see again.

But if you seek in modern Tammany the likeness of their political fathers, you will lose your time and your pains. Throughout the country, indeed, you will still find attached to the party a remnant of the original stock. But look to the regular leaders — the mill-horse nomination men — and you will find them just what all *mere* political men are — scramblers for office and men who talk of public good as a bore or a chimera.

To the corruptions of this once democratic and now venal party, the so-called Working Men's Party owes its origin. We were tired of hearing empty professions yearly repeated, tired of seeing political harpies make sale of public offices, tired of having the shadow for the reality, and of witnessing the interests of the industrious many shamelessly sacrificed for the exalting and false advantaging of the indolent few. We longed to see a "Nation's Party" — a party that should embrace the honest of all political sects — that should bear for its motto "Principles not men," and act up to the motto it bore.

Universal and equal education is the first great object for which the "Working Men's Party" contends. We see in equal education the only effective and peaceful means to secure the exercise of equal rights and the chance of equal enjoyment to every citizen of the republic; and we perceive that freedom and equality are, to the mass of the people, but empty sounds until both are planted there, where alone they can grow, in the human mind.

For the nicknames which our enemies have chosen to attach to us — Agrarians, Workies, Wrightsmen, Radicals, Levellers, and half a dozen more — they are but the second edition of those that were put forth in 1801 to cheat the people into the belief that those who spoke of liberty and equality meant atheistical persecution and licentiousness.

There is, however, an Agrarian Party in this city — a very small one, but still a party — who tell us very honestly that they wish to see a general "ripping up" (as they call it), to have all the property of the state sold at a national auction, and an equal portion dealt out to every man and woman.

These are — and call themselves — Agrarians; by which term is now understood in this city those who desire an equal division of property among all adults. Their organ is the *Friend of Equal Rights*, edited by Messrs. Ming and Skidmore; and they are very bitter against all who will not swallow their political creed entire, without scruple or hesitation, especially against the "Education men," as they commonly call us.

One other party — or rather hodgepodge of parties — still remains to be spoken of.

It is easier to say what *it is not* than what it is. It is *not* the Tammany Party and *not* the Working Men's Party; and *everything except these* (if we may judge by the late ward election) it is. Its leaders compose about as motley a group as might be found in the political ranks from Maine to Missouri. The "Working Men" was a popular name; so they got hold of it; and have contrived, by its help, and by dint of great professions of horror for infidelity and agrarianism, to tack together, for the moment, the patchwork of a party, in which Stone of the *Commercial,* Charles King of the *American,* Dwight of the *Daily Advertiser,* Arthur Tappan of Church and State notoriety, and all their aiders and abettors figure by the side of a few honest mechanics (too easy tempered and shortsighted to suspect the cheat) as the real, genuine "Working Men" of the city of New York!

And so ends our catalog. We do not think the *Intelligencer* will obtain a more honest or correct one.

80.

GEORGE BANCROFT: The Importance of a University for New York City

Dissatisfaction with existing American colleges and universities became widespread in the early nineteenth century, and leading educators like George Ticknor, Joseph Cogswell, and George Bancroft determined to try to raise the level of American higher education to that of the model German universities, by broadening the curriculum, improving library facilities, and encouraging freedom of research. Many American institutions resisted such change, as evidenced by the Yale Report of 1828. A number of educational innovators met at New York City in October 1830 to discuss the problems of education and how best to overcome them in a new university for that city. George Bancroft, the eminent historian, was a contributor to the discussions, which eventually led to the founding of New York University, and was the author of the following statement on the purposes and advantages of an urban academic community.

Source: *Journal of the Proceedings of a Convention of Literary and Scientific Gentlemen,* New York, 1831, pp. 45-52.

A UNIVERSITY, IN ITS PERFECT EXTENT, is one of the noblest results of human intelligence. It aims at nothing less than to furnish a concentration of all useful knowledge; to collect, to digest, to diffuse all the learning which can in any manner be made the fit subject of public instruction and promote the honor and advantage of the nation. An individual is plainly incompetent to fulfill any but a small part of such a purpose. It requires joint action; it requires that which, more than anything else, constitutes the happiness of liberal minds — the extensive cooperation of good men in furthering good designs. To such an institution belong a library, collections in natural history, hospitals; men learned in the professions and in the arts; the inquisitive and ambitious of the young.

A university is not devoted exclusively to any one department of knowledge. It opens its gates wide to the reception of all valuable truth; and sustaining no particular branch of science by the sanction of prescription, by the continuance of favoritism, or by the dead letter of intellectual mortmains, it allows to each division of human knowledge that degree of prominence which its intrinsic merits can obtain. In the true social spirit, it receives and takes an interest in everything that belongs to the human understanding.

Neither is it a mere system of lectures adapted to the curious and the idle. It is designed not to afford pastime but to excite and encourage severe industry; not to furnish amusement but to diffuse and also to advance science.

Nor does it attach itself to any sect in religion. God forbid that the day should ever arrive when there should be a separation of pure morality and deep religious conviction from our public places of education; but the character of a university requires that it should be subordinate to no religious party, subservient to no religious sect. It must be established independently, on its own merits.

Finally, the question recurs whether the country in its present condition demands a university, and whether any responsibility rests upon New York with relation to it.

With respect to the wants of the country, the answer must be found in the *numbers of our people*, already surpassing that of any Protestant kingdom or state in the world, excepting England; in the *character of our government*, which can never interfere with free inquiry and the pursuit of truth; in the *relative age of our population*, which in its rapid increase furnishes a larger proportion of persons to be educated than is found in older countries; in the *basis of our social sys-*

tem, which regards intelligence as a conservative not less than as a productive principle in the body politic; in the *forming character of all our institutions*, which are as yet hardly fixed, but remain yet to receive the impress which they are to bear forever; in the *period of our history*, when the old states are in truth rapidly becoming the mothers of new ones; in the *condition of our strength*, since the weakness of today becomes tomorrow the confidence and admiration of the world; and, lastly, in the *character of our population*, proverbially ambitious and inquisitive, where elementary education is already universally diffused, and where, under the auspices of our political equality, the public walks of honor and emulation are crowded with throngs from every class of society.

If attention recurs to New York, the mind readily recalls the extended relations of this city with the foreign world. Where can the wisdom of former generations, the intellectual inheritance bequeathed by the Old World to the New, where can it so readily be gathered and received as in the city, which has its agents under every zone and is connected by the closest bonds with every part of the civilized world?

The subject gains a deeper interest when we consider the influence which New York must necessarily exert upon the country. The emigrant in the remotest settlements looks to this city as the place that connects him with the active world. Whether we give attention to it or not, New York, the mistress of the sea, holding also in her hands the keys of the interior, is the very heart of the business community; and its pulsations are felt throughout the land. The Christian philanthropist, the advocates of religious liberty, and the advocates of intelligence have to decide whether this extensive power shall be felt only through the markets and the exchange, or whether it shall be the means of fostering that great communion which exists among all the friends of humanity.

On New York itself a successful university might not only reflect a brilliancy of reputation but also confer inestimable benefits. It might assist in giving an honorable direction to the destinies of the city, and might aid in developing the talent required for the wisest and noblest employment of the vast material wealth which is so rapidly increasing.

On men of letters the great commercial city would exert a favorable influence. The habit of the place is industry; and the literary man, partaking of the general excitement, is led to form habits of profound application. So, too, the varied intercourse with men of all nations stirs the stagnant pool of superstition and prejudice. The immense movements in business, the daily spectacle of crowds of sail from every quarter of the world, the frequent presence of minds which have been developed in the most different pursuits or ripened under every sky, gradually yet surely tend to promote intellectual freedom, and to do away that narrowmindedness which is the worst enemy of improvement.

The idea of a university, liberally constructed, precludes rivalry or jealousy. Competition between literary corporations does not produce the same excellent results as competition between literary men. The very nature of a university implies, as we have seen, so extensive cooperation, so enlarged a liberality, that it cheerfully receives within itself all the genuine friends of science.

But as between man and man there is nothing so salutary as that healthful competition which ensures the greatest success to the most industrious and most powerful efforts, in a university, a *career* must be opened, not *places* established. Things must be so arranged as to have exertion a natural result of causes always in operation. No board of directors, no examining committee, no legislative precautions can effect the results, which come spontaneously from the free development of talent under the excitement of emulation, and stimulated by the prospect of emolument and fame. The scholar should, indeed, himself prefer his vocation to everything, and will never attain eminence unless his unbiased inclinations are heartily engaged in his pursuit. But the interest of the public requires that honors and rewards should be commensurate with practical exertions; for the public in its nurseries of science needs to foster not the indolent gratification of a favorite taste but a hardy perseverance in a course of active usefulness.

The establishment of a university calls for an effort proportioned to the dignity and importance of the design. Its perfect results can at best be realized but slowly. . . .

In New York there is no public library of any very considerable value; no scientific collections in the various departments which need them. But the study of medicine and surgery is favored by the very condition of being in a metropolis; and a learned, intelligent, and active bar, courts of all kinds, the natural attractions of a large city, and a lucrative profession would seem suited to invite the youthful aspirants after eminence in the law. At Göttingen, 700 is no unusual number to belong to the law department alone. And the profession is with us a more crowded one than it is in Europe. The pursuits of philosophy and the arts, on the contrary, may have a harder struggle. Our countrymen profess, many of them, to strive to see how much of the learning of former ages may be dispensed with, rather than how much may be retained. In the absurdly boasted march of mind, they would propose to throw away the accumulated stores of preceding ages as useless baggage, forgetting that all knowledge is but an accumulation of facts and of reasonings based upon them. The rejection of the wisdom of the past does not awaken originality, but produces poverty of intellect by the loss of the materials on which originality should be exercised.

81.

Anne Royall: A Tennessee Revival

The growing sectionalism of the nineteenth century was reflected not only in political views and economic arrangements, but also in social customs and values and educational and religious practices. Descriptions by contemporary travelers pointed out these differences as characteristic of the increasing divergence between Northern and Southern ways of life. The following account of a Tennessee revival meeting is typical of the blunt style that made Anne Royall's travel books popular in her own day. Mrs. Royall was tried in Washington in 1829 on the charge of being a "common scold," but she was a tireless researcher and a careful and accurate reporter.

Source: *Letters from Alabama,* Washington, 1830, pp. 122-125.

THIS COUNTRY IS RUN MAD after preaching. Here is a new sect called Cumberland Presbyterians; and between these, the Baptists and Methodists, the woods resound. As they have no churches, they preach out-of-doors mostly. I have just returned from preaching, where I remained about two hours; and the parson, when I left him, appeared to be only about midway through his sermon. He ought to have a patent right, for he certainly has the strongest voice in the state.

I have met with several excellent orators since I have been in the country — the best I ever heard. Parson Burress, formerly of Virginia, is, doubtless, the finest public speaker in the Union. I have seen no parallel for him. The Reverend Mr. Butler and McMahon, the latter of Nashville, Tennessee, are also men of handsome delivery. These are Methodists. I was truly astonished at this, as I never saw one of the sect before hardly worth hearing. The Baptists and the Cumberland Presbyterians are continually preaching and *covaulting* [cavorting].

Mr. Porter, a most amiable man, also a Mr. Madden, preached in Mr. B.'s house since I was here, and that busybody Mr. *They say* reported Mr. B. was to preach here today; that is, out at the stand in the woods. I observed, "I will go and hear Mr. Porter." "Oh," said a bystander, "it is another preacher than Mr. Porter that preaches today — there is not such another preacher in the known world — he's a monstrous fine preacher." As I had heard some fine preaching, for the oratory I went to hear this nonesuch. But never was I so disappointed.

I placed myself in front of the preacher (a great, rough-looking man), and the congregation sat — some on fallen timber, some on benches carried there for the purpose, some sat flat on the ground, and many stood up — about 500 in all. His text was, "He that hath ears to hear, let him hear." The people must have been deaf indeed that could not have heard him. He neither made division nor subdivision. He is one of the Cumberland Presbyterians. They are Calvinists, it is said, but do not deem education a necessary qualification to preach the Gospel.

But to the sermon. He began low but soon bawled to deafening. He spit in his hands, rubbed them against each other, and then would smite them together, till he made the woods ring. The people now began to covault and dance and shout, till they fairly drowned the speaker. Many of the people, however, burst out into a laugh. Seeing this, the preacher cried out, pointing to them with his finger, "Now look at them sinners there. You'll see how they will come tumbling down presently. I'll bring them down." He now redoubled his strength; spit in his hands and smote them together, till he made the forest resound, and took a fresh start; and sure enough the sinners came tumbling down.

The scene that succeeded baffles description. Principally confined to women and children, the young women had carefully taken out their combs from their hair, and laid them and their bonnets in a place of safety, as though they were going to set in for a fight; and it was much like a battle. After tumbling on the ground and kicking sometime, the old women were employed in keeping their clothes civil, and the young men (never saw an old man go near them) would help them up; and taking them by each hand, by *their* assistance and their own agility, they would spring nearly a yard from the ground at every jump, one jump after another, crying out, "Glory, glory," as loud as their strength would admit. Others would be singing a lively tune to which they kept time; hundreds might be seen and heard going on in this manner at once.

Others, again, exhausted by this jumping, would fall down, and here they lay cross and pile, heads and points, yelling and screaming like wild beasts of the forest, rolling on the ground like hogs in a mire — very much like they do at camp meetings in our country, but more shameless. Their clothes were the color of the dirt; and, like those who attend the camp meetings, they were all of the lower class of the people. I saw no genteel person among them.

Are not people of education answerable for this degradation of society? It appears to me, since I have had opportunities of mixing with the world, that there are a certain class of citizens whose interest it is to keep their fellowmen in ignorance. I am very sure half a dozen words of common sense, well applied, would convince those infatuated young women that they were acting like fools. In fact, a fool is more rational. Not one of those but would think it a crying sin to dance.

The noise of the preacher was effectually drowned at length, and a universal uproar succeeded louder than ever. While this was going on, I observed an old woman near me, sniveling and turning up the whites of her eyes (she was a widow — all the widows, old and young, covaulted), and often applying her handkerchief to her eyes, and throwing herself into contortions; but it would not do; she could not raise the steam.

I pointed to one young woman with a red scarf, who had tired down several young men and was still covaulting, and seeing she jumped higher than the rest, I asked who she might be. One of the gentlemen, a Mr. Gallagher, who was standing near, gave such an account of her (men know these things) as would shock a modest ear. "D —— n her, she gets converted every meeting she goes to." How much better had she been at a ball (if they must dance) where they would be obliged to behave decent, and where vile characters dare not appear.

Shortly after they began to rear and covault, a daughter of Mr. B.'s began too. He walked up to her and led her off some distance, and sat her down at the root of a tree. When he returned, I inquired if she was sick. "No," he answered, "but she was beginning to go on as the rest, and I told her if she wished to worship God to do it there, and not to expose herself before faces."

The preacher, having spent all his ammunition, made a pause, and then called upon all the sinners to approach and be prayed for. Numbers went forward, all women and children (children of ten years old get religion!), and the priest began to pray, when a decent-looking man approached the stand and took a female by the arm and led her away. As he walked along, the preacher pointed to him and said, "God, strike that sinner down!" The man turned around, and in an angry tone said, "God has more sense than to mind such a d ——— d fool as you are!" and resumed his course. He was one of the brave Tennesseeans, and the lady was his wife.

Being tired of such an abominable scene, I proposed returning home; and, taking a near cut through a slip of woodland, we surprised the red-scarf lady in a manner that gave us no favorable opinion of her piety.

82.

Public Schools for Philadelphia

The new labor organizations of the early nineteenth century sought more for their members than improved wages and hours; they also wanted improved educational opportunities for adults and free public schools for children. In line with these aims, the Philadelphia Workingmen's Party appointed a committee to study local systems of public instruction. The following report of the committee was adopted by the "friends of general and equal education," at meetings on February 4, 8, and 11, 1830. The second selection is a reply to the workingmen's proposals, published as a letter to the editor in the August 19 issue of the National Gazette. *The anonymous author of the letter reflected contemporary opposition to free public education in his arguments that such a system would destroy the incentive for the lower classes to improve themselves, and that government had no right to expect individuals to pay for the education of children other than their own.*

Source: *Working Man's Advocate*, March 6, 1830 [Commons, V, pp. 94-107].
 Philadelphia National Gazette, August 19, 1830 [Commons, V, pp. 110-112].

I.

Equal Knowledge for Equal Liberty

REPORT OF THE JOINT COMMITTEES of the city and county of Philadelphia, appointed September 1829, to ascertain the state of public instruction in Pennsylvania, and to digest and propose such improvements in educa-

tion as may be deemed essential to the intellectual and moral prosperity of the people. . . .

With the exception of this city and county, the city and incorporated borough of Lancaster, and the city of Pittsburgh, erected into "school districts" since 1818, it appears that the entire state is destitute of any provisions for public instruction, except those furnished by the enactment of 1809.

This law requires the assessors of the several counties to ascertain and return the number of children whose parents are unable, through poverty, to educate them; and such children are permitted to be instructed at the most convenient schools at the expense of their respective counties.

The provisions of this act, however, are incomplete and frequently inoperative. They are, in some instances, but partially executed; in others, perverted and abused and in many cases entirely and culpably neglected. The funds appropriated by the act have, in some instances, been embezzled by fraudulent agents; and in others, partial returns of the children have been made, and some have been illegally and intentionally excluded from participating in the provisions of the law. From a parsimonious desire of saving the county funds, the cheapest and consequently the most inefficient schools have been usually selected by the commissioners of the several counties.

The elementary schools throughout the state are irresponsible institutions, established by individuals from mere motives of private speculation or gain, who are sometimes destitute of character, and frequently, of the requisite attainments and abilities. From the circumstance of the schools being the absolute property of individuals, no supervision or effectual control can be exercised over them; hence, ignorance, inattention, and even immorality prevail to a lamentable extent among their teachers.

In some districts no schools whatever exist! No means whatever of acquiring education are resorted to; while ignorance and its never failing consequence, crime, are found to prevail in these neglected spots to a greater extent than in other more favored portions of the state.

The "three school districts," however, which have been alluded to, are not liable to these objections. Much good, in particular, has resulted from the establishment of the first of these, comprising this city and county, and which owes its establishment to the persevering efforts of a few individuals who, in order to succeed even so far, were compelled to combat the ignorance, the prejudices, and the pecuniary interests of many active and hostile opponents.

But the principles on which these "school districts" are founded are yet, in the opinion of the committees, extremely defective and inefficient. Their leading feature is pauperism! They are confined exclusively to the children of the poor, while there are, perhaps, thousands of children whose parents are unable to afford for them a good private education, yet whose standing professions or connections in society effectually exclude them from taking the benefit of a poor law. There are great numbers, even of the poorest parents, who hold a dependence on the public bounty to be incompatible with the rights and liberties of an American citizen, and whose deep and cherished consciousness of independence determines them rather to starve the intellect of their offspring than submit to become the objects of public charity.

There are also many poor families who are totally unable to maintain and clothe their children while at the schools; and who are compelled to place them, at a very early age, at some kind of labor that may assist in supporting them, or to bind them out as apprentices to relieve themselves entirely of the burden of their maintenance and education, while the practice formerly universal of schooling apprentices has, of late years, greatly diminished and is still diminishing.

Another radical and glaring defect in the existing public school system is the very limited amount of instruction it affords, even to the comparatively small number of youth who enjoy its benefits. It extends in no case further than a tolerable proficiency in reading, writing, and arithmetic, and sometimes to a slight acquaintance with geography. Besides these, the girls are taught a few simple branches of industry. A great proportion of scholars, however, from the causes already enumerated, acquire but a very slight and partial knowledge of these branches.

The present public school system, limited as it is to three solitary school districts, makes no provision for the care and instruction of children under five years old. This class of children is numerous, especially among the poor, and it frequently happens that the parents, or parent (perhaps a widow), whose only resource for a livelihood is her needle or wash tub, is compelled to keep her elder children from the school to take charge of the younger ones, while her own hands are industriously employed in procuring a subsistence for them. Such instances are far from being rare, and form a very prominent and lamentable drawback on the utility of the schools in these districts. The care thus bestowed on infants is insufficient and very partial. They are frequently exposed to the most pernicious influences and impressions. The seeds of vice, thus early scattered over the infant soil, are too often permitted to ripen as life advances, till they fill society with violence and outrage, and yield an abundant harvest for magdalens and penitentiaries.

An opinion is entertained by many good and wise persons, and supported to a considerable extent by actual experiment, that proper schools for supplying a judicious infant training would effectually prevent much of that vicious depravity of character which penal codes and punishments are vainly intended to counteract. Such schools would, at least, relieve in a great measure many indigent parents from the care of children, which in many cases occupies as much of their time as would be necessary to earn the children a subsistence. They would also afford many youth an opportunity of participating in the benefits of the public schools who otherwise must of necessity be detained from them.

From this view of the public instruction in Pennsylvania, it is manifest that even in "the school districts," to say nothing of the remainder of the state, a very large propor-

tion of youth are either partially or entirely destitute of education.

It is true the state is not without its colleges and universities, several of which have been fostered with liberal supplies from the public purse. Let it be observed, however, that the funds so applied have been appropriated exclusively for the benefit of the wealthy, who are thereby enabled to procure a liberal education for their children upon lower terms than it could otherwise be afforded them. Funds thus expended may serve to engender an aristocracy of talent, and place knowledge, the chief element of power, in the hands of the privileged few; but can never secure the common prosperity of a nation nor confer intellectual as well as political equality on a people.

The original element of despotism is a monopoly of talent which consigns the multitude to comparative ignorance and secures the balance of knowledge on the side of the rich and the rulers. If then the healthy existence of a free government be, as the committee believe, rooted in the will of the American people, it follows as a necessary consequence of a government based upon that will, that this monopoly should be broken up, and that the means of equal knowledge (the only security for equal liberty) should be rendered by legal provision the common property of all classes.

In a republic the people constitute the government, and by wielding its powers in accordance with the dictates, either of their intelligence or their ignorance, of their judgment or their caprices, [they] are the makers and the rulers of their own good or evil destiny. They frame the laws and create the institutions that promote their happiness or produce their destruction. If they be wise and intelligent, no laws but what are just and equal will receive their approbation or be sustained by their suffrages. If they be ignorant and capricious, they will be deceived by mistaken or designing rulers into the support of laws that are unequal and unjust.

It appears, therefore, to the committees that there can be no real liberty without a wide diffusion of real intelligence; that the members of a republic should all be alike instructed in the nature and character of their equal rights and duties as human beings and as citizens; and that education, instead of being limited as in our public poor schools to a simple acquaintance with words and ciphers, should tend, as far as possible, to the production of a just disposition, virtuous habits, and a rational self-governing character.

When the committees contemplate their own condition and that of the great mass of their fellow laborers; when they look around on the glaring inequality of society, they are constrained to believe that until the means of equal instruction shall be equally secured to all, liberty is but an unmeaning word, and equality an empty shadow, whose substance to be realized must first be planted by an equal education and proper training in the minds, in the habits, in the manners, and in the feelings of the community.

While, however, the committees believe it their duty to exhibit, fully and openly, the main features and principles of a system of education which can alone comport with the spirit of American liberty and the equal prosperity and happiness of the people, they are not prepared to assert that the establishment of such a system in its fullness and purity, throughout the state, is by any means attainable at a single step. While they maintain that each human being has an equal right to a full development of all his powers, moral, physical, and intellectual; that the common good of society can never be promoted in its fullness till all shall be equally secured and protected in the enjoyment of this right, and that it is the first great duty of the state to secure the same to all its members; yet, such is now the degraded state of education in Pennsylvania (compared with what, in the opinion of the committees, education for a free people

should be) that they despair of so great a change as must be involved in passing from one to the other being accomplished suddenly throughout the state. No new system of education could probably be devised with consequences so manifestly beneficial as to awaken at once in the public mind a general conviction and concurrence in the necessity of its universal adoption.

The committees are aware, also, that it is their duty to consult the views, the feelings, and the prejudices, not of a single district or county merely, but of the state in general. The measure which it is their business to propose is one designed to be of universal extent and influence and must, to be successful, be based upon the manifest wishes of nearly the whole commonwealth. It is not, therefore, to what would constitute a perfect education only, but also, to what may be rendered practicable; it is not with a view, exclusively, to the kind of education every child of Pennsylvania ought to have, but likewise to what it is possible, under existing circumstances, views, and prejudices, every child of Pennsylvania may and can have, that they have drawn up a bill or outline of what they deem a system of public education adapted to the present condition and necessities of the state in general.

The principal points in which the bill for establishing common schools, accompanying this report, differs from the existing system of free schools are as follows:

1. Its provisions, instead of being limited to three single districts, are designed to extend throughout the commonwealth. 2. It places the managers of the public schools immediately under the control and suffrage of the people. 3. Its benefits and privileges will not, as at present, be limited as an act of charity to the poor alone, but will extend equally and of right to all classes, and be supported at the expense of all. 4. It lays a foundation for infantile as well as juvenile instruction. And lastly, it leaves the door open to every possible improvement which

human benevolence and ingenuity may be able to introduce.

While, however, the committees would urge the establishment of common elementary schools throughout the state as comprising, perhaps, the best general system of education which is at present attainable, it is but just to exhibit also some of the defects as well as the advantages of such schools; and to suggest such further measures as appear calculated to obviate such defects.

The instruction afforded by common schools, such as are contemplated in the bill for a general system of education, being only elementary must of necessity produce but a very limited development of the human faculties. It would indeed diminish, but could not destroy, the present injurious monopoly of talent. While the higher branches of literature and science remain accessible only to the children of the wealthy, there must still be a balance of knowledge, and with it a "balance of power," in the hands of the privileged few, the rich, and the rulers.

Another radical defect in the best system of common schools yet established will be found in its not being adapted to meet the wants and necessities of those who stand most in need of it. Very many of the poorest parents are totally unable to clothe and maintain their children while at school, and are compelled to employ their time, while yet very young, in aiding to procure a subsistence. In the city of New York, a much more efficient system of education exists than in this city, and common schools have been in successful operation for the last ten or twelve years; yet there are at the present time upwards of 24,000 children between the ages of five and fifteen years, who attend no schools whatever, and this apparently criminal neglect of attending the schools is traced chiefly to the circumstance just mentioned. It is evidently, therefore, of no avail how free the schools may be, while those children who stand most in need of them are, through the necessity of their par-

ents, either retained from them altogether or withdrawn at an improper age to assist in procuring a subsistence.

The constitution of this state declares that "the legislature shall provide schools in which the poor may be taught gratis." If this signifies that the poor shall have an opportunity afforded for instruction, it must involve means equal to the end. The poverty of the poor must be no obstruction, otherwise the constitution is a dead letter — nay, worse, an insult on their unfortunate condition and feelings.

The committees, therefore, believe that one school at least should be established in each county, in which some principle should be adopted calculated to obviate the defects that have been alluded to, and by which the children of all who desire it may be enabled to procure, at their own expense, a liberal and scientific education. They are of the opinion that a principle fully calculated to secure this object will be found in a union of agricultural and mechanical with literary and scientific instruction; and they have therefore, in addition to a plan of common elementary schools, drawn up and appended to this report the substance of a bill providing for the establishment of high schools, or model schools, based upon this principle, which they also present for public deliberation.

Believing as the committees do that upon an equal education and proper training to industry, sobriety, and virtue hangs the liberty and prosperity of the new world and, perhaps, the ultimate emancipation of the old; and believing as they do that the union of industry with literature and science constitutes the only desideratum by which an equal education can be supplied and secured to all classes, they experience the most sincere pleasure in discovering that this good and great principle is gaining in popularity and dominion throughout the world. Not only are institutions of this kind established in France, Prussia, Germany, and Great Britain, in imitation of the original Hofwyl institutions in Switzerland, but in the United States also there are several. At Whitesborough, N.Y., there is one with from thirty to forty pupils; at Princeton, Ky., another containing eighty; a third exists at Andover, Mass., that accommodates sixty pupils; a fourth at Maysville, Tenn.; and a fifth has recently been established at Germantown, in this county. At Monmouth, N. J., and at Cincinnati, Ohio, very extensive establishments, based upon this principle, have been or are about [to be begun].

The Germantown establishment had been commenced only seven months when its first report was made in November last. The pupils are instructed in literature, the sciences, languages, morals, and manual labor. The latter consists of agriculture, gardening, and some mechanic arts. They are permitted to labor little or much, as their dispositions may incline them or their necessities dictate. The institution, at its commencement, on May 1, 1829, had but four pupils — at the date of the report it had twenty-five. By an estimate made by the board of managers, as early as July last, it appeared that the balances against several of them for board and tuition were but very small, and that some of them, by their labor, had almost cleared their expenses. They generally work from two to five hours per day.

The first institution in which manual labor appears to have been combined with literature and science was established many years since by Fellenberg, at Hofwyl, in the canton of Bern, Switzerland. . . .

There is one point in which the committees believe that the gradual extension and ultimate universal adoption of this system of education will produce a benefit, the value of which no human calculation can ascertain. It is but too well known that the growing effects of intemperance, that assassinator of private peace and public virtue, are in this country terrific; and that this fearful pestilence, unless checked in its career by some more efficient remedy than

has yet been resorted to, threatens to annihilate not only the domestic peace and prosperity of individuals, but also the moral order and political liberties of the nation. No people can long enjoy liberty who resign themselves to the slavery of this tyrant vice. Yet does it appear to the committees that all efforts to root this moral poison from the constitution of society will prove futile until the trial shall be made upon our youth.

When we behold the hundreds, perhaps thousands of youth who, between the ages of fourteen and twenty-one, are daily and nightly seduced around or into the innumerable dens of vice, licensed and unlicensed, that throng our suburbs, we are constrained to believe that in many if not in most cases, the unconquerable habit that destroys the morals, ruins the constitution, sacrifices the character, and at last murders both soul and body of its victim, is first acquired during the thoughtless period of juvenile existence. This plan of education, however, by its almost entire occupation of the time of the pupils, either in labor, study, or recreations; by the superior facilities it affords for engrossing their entire attention, and by its capability of embracing the whole juvenile population, furnishes, we believe, the only rational hope of ultimately averting the ruin which is threatened by this extensive vice.

The committee are aware that any plan of common and more particularly of equal education that may be offered to the public is likely to meet with more than an ordinary share of opposition. It is to be expected that political demagogism, professional monopoly, and monied influence will conspire as hitherto (with several exceptions more or less numerous) they ever have conspired against everything that has promised to be an equal benefit to the whole population. Nevertheless, the appearance that something will now be done for the intellectual as well as everything for the physical improvement of the state are certainly very promising. The public mind is awake and favorably excited, while the press also is somewhat active on this subject. Our present legislature and chief magistrate appear likewise earnestly desirous of producing a reform in the system of public education, and we believe they are waiting only for the public sentiment to decide on the principles and character of that reform.

When this decision shall be fully made and openly and firmly supported by the public voice, we doubt not but our representatives will cheerfully give their legislative sanction to those measures of educational reform which shall appear manifestly based upon the will of the people.

II.

Against Equal Education

WE CAN READILY PARDON the editor of the United States *Gazette* for not perceiving that the scheme of universal equal education at the expense of the state is virtually "Agrarianism." It would be a compulsory application of the means of the richer for the direct use of the poorer classes; and so far an arbitrary division of property among them. The declared object is: to procure the opportunity of instruction for the child or children of every citizen; to elevate the standard of the education of the working classes, or equalize the standard for all classes; which would doubtless be to lower or narrow that which the rich may now compass. But the most sensible and reflecting possessors of property sufficient to enable them to educate their children in the most liberal and efficacious way, and upon the broadest scale, would prefer to share their means for any other purpose, or in any other mode, than such as would injuriously affect or circumscribe the proficiency of their offspring.

A public meeting of "the mechanics and other workingmen of the city and county of New York" was held in the city, on the 17th instant, and among the principles for which they have "resolved" to contend, we find the following:

> In education — the adoption of a general system of instruction at the expense of the state, which shall afford to children, however rich or poor, equal means to obtain useful learning. To effect this, it is believed that a system of direct taxation will not be necessary, as the surplus revenue of the state and United States governments will, in a very few years, afford ample means; but even if it were necessary to resort to direct taxation to accomplish this all-important object, and the amount paid by the wealthy should be far greater than that paid by our less eligibly situated fellow citizens, an equivalent to them would be found in the increased ability and usefulness of the educated citizen to serve and to promote the best interests of the state; in the increased permanency of our institutions; and in the superior protection of liberty, person, and property.

Thus, a direct tax for "the equal means of obtaining useful learning" is not deemed improbable, and it is admitted that the amount which would be paid by the wealthy would be "far greater" than that paid by their "less eligibly situated fellow citizens." Here, we contend, would be the action, if not the name, of the agrarian system. Authority — that is, the state — is to force the more eligibly situated citizens to contribute a part (which might be very considerable) of their means for the accommodation of the rest; and this is equivalent to the idea of an actual, compulsory partition of their substance.

The more thriving members of the "mechanical and other working classes" would themselves feel the evil of the direct taxation; they would find that they had toiled for the benefit of other families than their own. One of the chief excitements to industry among those classes is the hope of earning the means of educating their children respectably or liberally. That incentive would be removed, and the scheme of state and equal education be thus a premium for comparative idleness, to be taken out of the pockets of the laborious and conscientious. . . .

We have no confidence in any compulsory equalizations; it has been well observed that they pull down what is above, but never much raise what is below, and often "depress high and low together beneath the level of what was originally the lowest." By no possibility could a perfect equality be procured. A scheme of universal equal education, attempted in reality, would be an unexampled bed of Procrustes for the understandings of our youth, and in fact, could not be used with any degree of equality of profit unless the dispositions and circumstances of parents and children were nearly the same. To accomplish which phenomenon, in a nation of many millions, engaged in a great variety of pursuits, would be beyond human power.

83.

Henry Clay: A System of Real Reciprocity

Henry Clay's American System of high protective tariffs and federally financed internal improvements, introduced in an 1824 speech, rendered the representative from Kentucky leader of the opposition to Jackson in Congress. Clay advocated federal highway programs; in 1830 Jackson vetoed the Maysville Road Bill. Clay favored a national bank; in 1832 Jackson vetoed renewal of the Second Bank's charter. In 1836 Clay proposed distribution of a treasury surplus among the states for internal improvements; the fiscal crisis of 1837 turned the surplus into a deficit. Yet Clay's programs ultimately prevailed. Within fifty years a national transportation network had been developed, a strong national economy based on industrial expansion had been established, and the new Republican Party was actively working for protective tariffs. The following speech, delivered at Cincinnati, Ohio, on August 3, 1830, is an exposition of the American System.

Source: Colton, VII, pp. 396-415.

With respect to the American System, which demands your undivided approbation and in regard to which you are pleased to estimate much too highly my service, its great object is to secure the independence of our country, to augment its wealth, and to diffuse the comforts of civilization throughout society. . . .

To the laboring classes it is invaluable, since it increases and multiplies the demands for their industry and gives them an option of employments. It adds power and strength to our Union by new ties of interest, blending and connecting together all its parts, and creating an interest with each in the prosperity of the whole. It secures to our own country, whose skill and enterprise, properly fostered and sustained, cannot be surpassed, those vast profits which are made in other countries by the operation of converting the raw material into manufactured articles.

It naturalizes and creates within the bosom of our country all the arts, and, mixing the farmer, manufacturer, mechanic, artist, and those engaged in other vocations together, admits of those mutual exchanges so conducive to the prosperity of all and everyone, free from the perils of sea and war — all this it effects while it nourishes and leaves a fair scope to foreign trade. . . .

That system has had a wonderful success. It has more than realized all the hopes of its founders. It has completely falsified all the predictions of its opponents. It has increased the wealth, and power, and population of the nation. It has diminished the price of articles of consumption and has placed them within the reach of a far greater number of our people than could have found means to command them if they had been manufactured abroad instead of at home.

But it is useless to dwell on the argument in support of this beneficent system before this audience. It will be of more consequence here to examine some of the objections which are still urged against it and the means which are proposed to subvert it. These objections are now principally confined to its operation upon the great staple of cotton wool, and they are urged with most vehemence in a particular state. If the objections are well founded, the system should be modified, as far as it can consistently with interest, in other parts of the Union. If they are not well founded, it is to be hoped they will be finally abandoned.

In approaching the subject, I have thought it of importance to inquire what was the profit made upon capital employed in the culture of cotton at its present reduced price. The result has been information that it nets from 7 to 18 percent per annum, varying according to the advantage of situation and the degree of skill, judgment, and industry applied to the production of the article. But the lowest rate of profit in the scale is more than the greatest amount which is made on capital employed in the farming portions of the Union.

If the cotton planter has any just complaint against the expediency of the American System, it must be founded on the fact that he either sells less of his staple, or sells at lower prices, or purchases for consumption articles at dearer rates, or of worse qualities, in consequence of that system than he would do if it did not exist. If he would neither sell more of his staple, nor sell it at better prices, nor could purchase better or cheaper articles for consumption, provided the system did not exist, then he has no cause on the score of its burdensome operation to complain of the system but must look to other sources for the grievances which he supposes afflict him.

As respects the sale of his staple, it would be indifferent to the planter whether one portion of it was sold in Europe and the other in America, provided the aggregate of both were equal to all that he could sell in one market, if he had but one, and provided he could command the same price in both cases. The double market would indeed be something better for him because of its greater security in time of war as well as in peace and because it would be attended with less perils and less charges. If there be an equal amount of the raw material manufactured, it must be immaterial to the cotton planter, in the sale of the articles, whether there be two theaters of the manufacture, one in Europe and the other in America, or but one in Europe; or if there be a difference, it will be in favor of the two places of manufacture instead of one. . . .

That the effect of competition between the European and American manufacture has been to supply the American consumer with cheaper and better articles, since the adoption of the American System, notwithstanding the existence of causes which have obstructed its fair operation and retarded its full development, is incontestable. Both the freeman and the slave are now better and cheaper supplied than they were prior to the existence of that system.

Cotton fabrics have diminished in price and been improved in their texture, to an extent that it is difficult for the imagination to keep pace with. Those partly of cotton and partly of wool are also better and cheaper supplied. The same observation is applicable to those which are exclusively wrought of wool, iron, or glass. In short, it is believed that there is not one item of the tariff inserted for the protection of native industry which has not fallen in price. The American competition has tended to keep down the European rival fabric, and the European has tended to lower the American.

Of what then can the South Carolina planter justly complain in the operation of this system? What is there in it which justifies the harsh and strong epithets which some of her politicians have applied to it? What is there in her condition which warrants their assertion that she is oppressed by a government to which she stands in the mere relation of a colony?

She is oppressed by a great reduction in the price of manufactured articles of consumption. She is oppressed by the advantage of two markets for the sale of her valuable staple and for the purchase of objects required by her wants. She is oppressed by better prices for that staple than she could command if the system to which they object did not exist.

She is oppressed by the option of purchasing cheaper and better articles, the produce of the hands of American freemen, instead of dearer and worse articles, the produce of the hands of British subjects.

She is oppressed by the measures of a government in which she has had for many years a larger proportion of power and influence, at home and abroad, than any state in the whole Union in comparison with the population. . . .

Yet her situation has been compared to that of a colony which has no voice in the laws enacted by the parent country for its subjection! And to be relieved from this cruel state of vassalage, and to put down a system which has been established by the united voice of all America, some of her politicians have broached a doctrine as new as it would be alarming, if it were sustained by numbers in proportion to the zeal and fervid eloquence with which it is inculcated. I call it a novel doctrine. . . .

The South Carolina doctrine . . . is that that state has the right to determine the limits of the powers granted to the general government; and that whenever any of its acts transcend those limits, in the opinion of the state of South Carolina, she is competent to annul them. If the power with which the federal government is invested by the Constitution to determine the limits of its authority be liable to the possible danger of ultimate consolidation, and all the safeguards which have been mentioned might prove inadequate, is not this power, claimed for South Carolina, fraught with infinitely more certain, immediate, and fatal danger? It would reverse the rule of supremacy prescribed in the Constitution. It would render the authority of a single state paramount to that of the whole Union. For, undoubtedly, that government, to some extent, must be supreme which can annul and set aside the acts of another. . . .

It is admitted that the South Carolina doctrine is liable to abuse; but it is contended that the patriotism of each state is an adequate security, and that the nullifying power would only be exercised "in an extraordinary case, where the powers reserved to the states, under the Constitution, are usurped by the federal government." And is not the patriotism of all the states as great a safeguard against the assumption of powers not conferred upon the general government as the patriotism of one state is against the denial of powers which are clearly granted?

But the nullifying power is only to be exercised in an extraordinary case. Who is to judge of this extraordinary case? What security is there, especially in moments of great excitement, that a state may not pronounce the plainest and most common exercise of federal power an extraordinary case? The expressions in the Constitution, "general welfare," have been often justly criticized and shown to convey, in themselves, no power, although they may indicate how the delegated power should be exercised. But this doctrine of an extraordinary case, to be judged of and applied by one of the twenty-four sovereignties, is replete with infinitely more danger than the doctrine of the "general welfare" in the hands of all.

We may form some idea of future abuses under the South Carolina doctrine by the application which is now proposed to be made of it. The American System is said to furnish an extraordinary case, justifying that state to nullify it. The power to regulate foreign commerce by a tariff, so adjusted as to foster our domestic manufactures, has been exercised from the commencement of our present Constitution down to the last session of Congress. I have been a member of the House of Representatives at three different periods, when the subject of the tariff was debated at great length, and on neither, according to my recollection, was the want of a constitutional power in Congress to enact it dwelt on as forming a serious and substantial objection to its passage. On the last occasion (I think it was) in which I participated in the debate, it was incidentally said to be against the spirit of the Constitution.

While the authority of the father of the Constitution is invoked to sanction, by a perversion of his meaning, principles of disunion and rebellion, it is rejected to sustain the controverted power, although his testimony in support of it has been clearly and explicitly rendered. This power, thus asserted, exercised, and maintained, in favor of

which leading politicians in South Carolina have themselves voted, is alleged to furnish "an extraordinary case," where the powers reserved to the states, under the Constitution, are usurped by the general government. If it be, there is scarcely a statute in our code which would not present a case equally extraordinary, justifying South Carolina or any other state to nullify it. . . .

But nullification and disunion are not the only nor the most formidable means of assailing the tariff. Its opponents opened the campaign at the last session of Congress, and, with the most obliging frankness, have since publicly exposed their plan of operations. It is to divide and conquer; to attack and subdue the system in detail. . . .

The American System of protection should be regarded as it is — an entire and comprehensive system made up of various items and aiming at the prosperity of the whole Union by protecting the interests of each part. Every part, therefore, has a direct interest in the protection which it enjoys of the articles which its agriculture produces or its manufactories fabricate, and also a collateral interest in the protection which other portions of the Union derive from their peculiar interests. Thus, the aggregate of the prosperity of all is constituted by the sums of the prosperity of each. . . .

If anything could be considered as settled, under the present Constitution of our government, I had supposed that it was its authority to construct such internal improvements as may be deemed by Congress necessary and proper to carry into effect the power granted to it. . . . Yet we are told that this power can no longer be exercised without an amendment of the Constitution. . . .

If I could believe that the executive message which was communicated to Congress upon the application of the veto to the Maysville Road really expressed the opinion of the President of the United States, in consequence of the unfortunate relations which have existed between us I would forbear to make any observation upon it. . . . It is impossible that the veto message should express the opinions of the President, and I prove it by evidence derived from himself.

Not forty days before that message was sent to Congress, he approved a bill embracing appropriations to various objects of internal improvement and, among others, to improve the navigation of Conneaut Creek. Although somewhat acquainted with the geography of our country, I declare I did not know of the existence of such a stream until I read the bill. I have since made it an object of inquiry and have been told that it rises in one corner of Pennsylvania and is discharged into Lake Erie in a corner of the state of Ohio, and that the utmost extent to which its navigation is susceptible of improvement is about seven miles. Is it possible that the President could conceive that a national object, and that the improvement of a great thoroughfare on which the mail is transported for some eight or ten states and territories, is not a national consideration? . . .

The veto message is perfectly irreconcilable with the previous acts, votes, and opinions of General Jackson. It does not express his opinions but those of his advisers and counselors, and especially those of his cabinet. If we look at the composition of that cabinet, we cannot doubt it. Three of the five who, I believe, compose it (whether the postmaster general be one or not, I do not know) are known to be directly and positively opposed to the power; a fourth, to use a term descriptive of the favorite policy of one of them, is a noncommittal; and, as to the fifth, Good Lord deliver us from such friendship as his to internal improvements!

Further, I have heard it from good authority (but I will not vouch for it, although I believe it to be true) that some of the gentlemen from the South waited upon the President while he held the Maysville Bill under consideration, and told him if he approved of that bill, the South would no longer approve of him but oppose his administration.

I cannot, therefore, consider the message as conveying the sentiments and views of the President. It is impossible. It is the work of his cabinet; and if, unfortunately, they were not practically irresponsible to the people of the United States, they would deserve severe animadversion for having prevailed upon the President, in the precipitation of business, and perhaps without his spectacles, to put his name to such a paper and send it forth to Congress and to the nation. . . .

The government of the United States at this juncture exhibits a most remarkable spectacle. It is that of a majority of the nation having put the powers of government into the hands of the minority. If anyone can doubt this, let him look back at the elements of the executive, at the presiding officers of the two houses, at the composition and the chairmen of the most important committees, who shape and direct the public business in Congress. Let him look, above all, at measures, the necessary consequences of such an anomalous state of things — internal improvements gone or going; the whole American System threatened, and the triumphant shouts of anticipated victory sounding in our ears — Georgia, extorting from the fears of an affrighted majority of Congress an Indian Bill, which may prostrate all the laws, treaties, and policy which have regulated our relations with the Indians from the commencement of our government; and politicians in South Carolina, at the same time, brandishing the torch of civil war and pronouncing unbounded eulogiums upon the President for the good he has done and the still greater good which they expect at his hands, and the sacrifice of the interests of the majority.

Another reason assigned in the Maysville

message is the desire of paying the national debt. . . . As much of the public debt as can be paid will be discharged in four years by the operation of the sinking fund. I have seen, in some late paper, a calculation of the delay which would have resulted, in its payment, from the appropriation to the Maysville Road, and it was less than one week! How has it happened that under the administration of Mr. Adams, and during every year of it, such large and liberal appropriations could be made for internal improvements without touching the fund devoted to the public debt and that this administration should find itself balked in its first year? . . .

The same scheme which has been devised and practised to defeat the tariff has been adopted to undermine internal improvements. They are to be attacked in detail. Hence the rejection of the Maysville Road, the Fredericktown Road, and the Louisville Canal. But is this fair? Ought each proposed road to be viewed separately and detached? Ought it not to be considered in connection with other great works which are in progress of execution or are projected? The policy of the foes indicates what ought to be the policy of the friends of the power.

The blow aimed at internal improvements has fallen with unmerited severity upon the state of Kentucky. No state in the Union has ever shown more generous devotion to its preservation and to the support of its honor and its interest than she has. During the late war, her sons fought gallantly by the side of the President, on the glorious 8th of January, when he covered himself with unfading laurels. Wherever the war raged, they were to be found among the foremost in battle, freely bleeding in the service of their country. They have never threatened nor calculated the value of this happy Union. Their representatives in Congress have constantly and almost unanimously supported the power, cheerfully voting for large appropriations to works of internal improvements in other states. Not one cent of the common treasure has been expended on any public road in that state. They contributed to the elevation of the President, under a firm conviction, produced by his deliberate acts and his solemn assertions, that he was friendly to the power. Under such circumstances, have they not just and abundant cause of surprise, regret, and mortification at the late unexpected decision? . . .

The present chief magistrate has done me much wrong, but I have freely forgiven him. He believed, no doubt, that I had done him previous wrong. Although I am unconscious of it, he had that motive for his conduct toward me. But others who had joined in the hue and cry against me had no such pretext. Why then am I thus pursued, my words perverted and distorted, my acts misrepresented? Why do more than a hundred presses daily point their cannon at me and thunder forth their peals of abuse and detraction? It is not against me. That is impossible. . . .

It is against the principles of civil liberty, against the tariff and internal improvements, to which the better part of my life has been devoted, that this implacable war is waged. My enemies flatter themselves that those systems may be overthrown by my destruction. Vain and impotent hope! My existence is not of the smallest consequence to their preservation. They will survive me. Long, long after I am gone, while the lofty hills encompass this fair city, the offspring of those measures shall remain; while the beautiful river that sweeps by its walls shall continue to bear upon its proud bosom the wonders which the immortal genius of Fulton, with the blessings of Providence, has given; while truth shall hold its sway among men, those systems will invigorate the industry and animate the hopes of the farmer, the mechanic, the manufacturer, and all other classes of our countrymen.

84.

James Madison: Nullification and the Rule of Law

In 1798 Madison and Jefferson had drafted the Virginia and Kentucky Resolutions (respectively), condemning the Alien and Sedition Acts of that year and hinting — though not positively asserting — that the states had the right to refuse to obey federal legislation of which they did not approve. Now, a generation later, South Carolina was pointing to the 1798 Resolutions as a precedent and using them — though with exaggerated emphasis on states' rights — as the theoretical basis of her doctrine of nullification. Jefferson was dead and could not object, but Madison, though nearly eighty, felt called upon to answer the arguments of the nullifiers. He wrote the following letter to Edward Everett in August 1830.

Source: *North American Review*, October 1830.

I HAVE DULY RECEIVED your letter, in which you refer to the "nullifying doctrine" advocated as a constitutional right by some of our distinguished fellow citizens; and to the proceedings of the Virginia legislature in 1798 and 1799, as appealed to in behalf of that doctrine; and you express a wish for my ideas on those subjects.

I am aware of the delicacy of the task in some respects, and the difficulty in every respect of doing full justice to it. But having in more than one instance complied with a like request from other friendly quarters, I do not decline a sketch of the views which I have been led to take of the doctrine in question, as well as some others connected with them; and of the grounds from which it appears that the proceedings of Virginia have been misconceived by those who have appealed to them. In order to understand the true character of the Constitution of the United States, the error, not uncommon, must be avoided, of viewing it through the medium either of a consolidated government or of a confederated government, while it is neither the one nor the other, but a mixture of both. And having, in no

model, the similitudes and analogies applicable to other systems of government, it must more than any other be its own interpreter according to its text and the facts of the case.

From these it will be seen that the characteristic peculiarities of the Constitution are: one, the mode of its formation; two, the division of the supreme powers of government between the states in their united capacity, and the states in their individual capacities.

1. It was formed, not by the governments of the component states, as the federal government for which it was substituted was formed. Nor was it formed by a majority of the people of the United States, as a single community, in the manner of a consolidated government.

It was formed by the states, that is, by the people in each of the states, acting in their highest sovereign capacity; and formed consequently by the same authority which formed the state constitutions.

Being thus derived from the same source as the constitutions of the states, it has, within each state, the same authority as the constitution of the state; and is as much a constitution, in the strict sense of the term, within its prescribed sphere, as the constitutions of the states are within their respective spheres, but with this obvious and essential difference: that being a compact among the states in their highest sovereign capacity, and constituting the people thereof one people for certain purposes, it cannot be altered or annulled at the will of the states individually, as the constitution of a state may be at its individual will.

2. And that it divides the supreme powers of government between the government of the United States and the governments of the individual states is stamped on the face of the instrument; the powers of war and of taxation, of commerce and of treaties, and other enumerated powers vested in the government of the United States being of as high and sovereign a character as any of the powers reserved to the state governments.

Nor is the government of the United States, created by the Constitution, less a government in the strict sense of the term, within the sphere of its powers, than the governments created by the constitutions of the states are within their several spheres. It is, like them, organized into legislative, executive, and judiciary departments. It operates, like them, directly on persons and things. And, like them, it has at command a physical force for executing the powers committed to it. The concurrent operation in certain cases is one of the features marking the peculiarity of the system.

Between these different constitutional governments, the one operating in all the states, the others operating separately in each, with the aggregate powers of government divided between them, it could not escape attention that controversies would arise concerning the boundaries of jurisdiction; and that some provision ought to be made for such occurrences. A political system that does not provide for a peaceable and authoritative termination of occurring controversies would not be more than the shadow of a government; the object and end of a real government being the substitution of law and order for uncertainty, confusion, and violence.

That to have left a final decision in such cases to each of the states, then thirteen and already twenty-four, could not fail to make the Constitution and laws of the United States different in different states was obvious; and not less obvious that this diversity of independent decisions must altogether distract the government of the Union and speedily put an end to the Union itself. A uniform authority of the laws is in itself a vital principle. Some of the most important laws could not be partially executed. They must be executed in all the states or they could be duly executed in none. An impost or an excise, for example, if not in force in some states, would be defeated in others. It is well known that this was among the lessons of experience which had a primary influence in bringing about the existing Constitution. A loss of its general authority would moreover revive the exasperating questions between the states holding ports for foreign commerce and the adjoining states without them; to which are now added all the inland states, necessarily carrying on their foreign commerce through other states.

To have made the decisions under the authority of the individual states coordinate in all cases with decisions under the authority of the United States, would unavoidably produce collisions incompatible with the peace of society and with that regular and efficient administration which is of the essence of free governments. Scenes could not be avoided in which a ministerial officer of the United States and the correspondent officer of an individual state would have encounters in executing conflicting decrees, the result of which would depend on the comparative force of the local posses attending them; and that a casualty depending on the political opinions and party feelings in different states.

To have referred every clashing decision under the two authorities for a final decision to the states as parties to the Constitution, would be attended with delays, with inconveniences, and with expenses amounting to a prohibiton of the expedient; not to mention its tendency to impair the salutary veneration for a system requiring such frequent interpositions, nor the delicate questions which might present themselves as to the form of stating the appeal and as to the quorum for deciding it.

To have trusted to negotiation for adjusting disputes between the government of the United States and the state governments, as between independent and separate sovereignties, would have lost sight altogether of a Constitution and government for the Union and opened a direct road from a failure of that resort to the *ultima ratio* [final reckoning] between nations wholly independent of and alien to each other. If the idea had its origin in the process of adjustment between separate branches of the same government, the analogy entirely fails. In the case of disputes between independent parts of the same government, neither part being able to consummate its will nor the government to proceed without a concurrence of the parts, necessity brings about an accommodation. In disputes between a state government and the government of the United States, the case is practically as well as theoretically different, each party possessing all the departments of an organized government, legislative, executive, and judiciary, and having each a physical force to support its pretensions. Although the issue of negotiation might sometimes avoid this extremity, how often would it happen among so many states that an unaccommodating spirit in some would render that resource unavailing! A contrary supposition would not accord with a knowledge of human nature or the evidence of our own political history.

The Constitution, not relying on any of the preceding modifications for its safe and successful operation, has expressly declared, on the one hand, (1) "that the Constitution, and the laws made in pursuance thereof, and all treaties made under the authority of the United States, shall be the supreme law of the land; (2) that the judges of every state shall be bound thereby, anything in the constitution and laws of any state to the contrary notwithstanding; (3) that the judicial power of the United States shall extend to all cases in law and equity arising under the Constitution, the laws of the United States, and treaties made under their authority, etc."

On the other hand, as a security of the rights and powers of the states in their individual capacities against an undue preponderance of the powers granted to the government over them in their united capacity, the Constitution has relied on, (1) the responsibility of the senators and representatives in the legislature of the United States to the legislatures and people of the states; (2) the responsibility of the President to the people of the United States; and (3) the liability of the executive and judicial functionaries of the United States to impeachment by the representatives of the people of the states in one branch of the legislature of the United States, and trial by the representatives of the states in the other branch; the state functionaries, legislative, executive, and judicial, being at the same time, in their appointment and responsibility, altogether independent of the agency or authority of the United States.

How far this structure of the government of the United States is adequate and safe for its objects, time alone can absolutely determine. Experience seems to have shown that whatever may grow out of future stages of our national career, there is as yet a sufficient control, in the popular will, over the executive and legislative departments of the government. When the Alien and Sedition Laws were passed in contravention to the opinions and feelings of the community, the first elections that ensued put an end to them. And whatever may have been the character of other acts, in the judgment of many of us, it is but true that they have generally accorded with the views of a majority of the states and of the people. At the present day it seems well understood that the laws which have created most dissatisfaction have had a like sanction without doors; and that, whether continued, varied, or repealed, a like proof will be given of the sympathy and responsibility of the representative body to the constituent body. Indeed the great complaint now is against the results of this sympathy and responsibility in the legislative policy of the nation.

With respect to the judicial power of the United States, and the authority of the Supreme Court in relation to the boundary of jurisdiction between the federal and the state governments, I may be permitted to refer to the thirty-ninth number of the *Federalist*, for the light in which the subject was regarded by its writer at the period when the Constitution was depending; and it is believed that the same was the prevailing view then taken of it, that the same view has continued to prevail, and that it does so at this time, notwithstanding the eminent exceptions to it.

But it is perfectly consistent with the concession of this power to the Supreme Court, in cases falling within the course of its functions, to maintain that the power has not always been rightly exercised. To say nothing of the period, happily a short one, when judges in their seats did not abstain from intemperate and party harangues, equally at variance with their duty and their dignity; there have been occasional decisions from the bench which have incurred serious and extensive disapprobation. Still it would seem that, with but few exceptions, the course of the judiciary has been hitherto sustained by the predominant sense of the nation.

Those who have denied or doubted the supremacy of the judicial power of the United States, and denounce at the same time a nullifying power in a state, seem not to have sufficiently adverted to the utter inefficiency of a supremacy in a law of the land, without a supremacy in the exposition and execution of the law; nor to the destruction of all equipoise between the federal government and the state governments if, while the functionaries of the federal government are directly or indirectly elected by and responsible to the states, and the functionaries of the states are in their appointment and responsibility wholly independent of the United States, no constitutional control of any sort belonged to the United States over the states. Under such an organization, it is evident that it would be in the power of the states individually to pass unauthorized laws, and to carry them into complete effect, anything in the Constitution and laws of the United States to the contrary notwithstanding. This would be a nullifying power in its plenary character; and whether it had its final effect through the legislative, executive, or judiciary organ of the state would be equally fatal to the constituted relation between the two governments.

Should the provisions of the Constitution as here reviewed be found not to secure the government and rights of the states against usurpations and abuses on the part of the United States, the final resort within the purview of the Constitution lies in an amendment of the Constitution according to a process applicable by the states.

And in the event of a failure of every constitutional resort, and an accumulation of usurpations and abuses rendering passive obedience and non-resistance a greater evil than resistance and revolution, there can remain but one resort, the last of all: an appeal from the canceled obligations of the constitutional compact, to original rights and the law of self-preservation. This is the *ultima ratio* under all governments, whether consolidated, confederated, or a compound of both; and it cannot be doubted that a single member of the Union, in the extremity supposed, but in that only, would have a right, as an extra and ultra-constitutional right, to make the appeal.

This brings us to the expedient lately advanced, which claims for a single state a right to appeal against an exercise of power by the government of the United States decided by the state to be unconstitutional, to the parties to the constitutional compact; the decision of the state to have the effect of nullifying the act of the government of the United States unless the decision of the state be reversed by three-fourths of the parties.

The distinguished names and high authorities which appear to have asserted and given a practical scope to this doctrine entitle it to a respect which it might be difficult otherwise to feel for it.

If the doctrine were to be understood as requiring the three-fourths of the states to sustain, instead of that proportion to reverse the decision of the appealing state, the decision to be without effect during the appeal, it would be sufficient to remark that this extra-constitutional course might well give way to that marked out by the Constitution, which authorizes two-thirds of the states to institute and three-fourths to effectuate an amendment of the Constitution, establishing a permanent rule of the highest authority in place of an irregular precedent of construction only.

But it is understood that the nullifying doctrine imports that the decision of the state is to be presumed valid, and that it overrules the law of the United States unless overruled by three-fourths of the states.

Can more be necessary to demonstrate the inadmissibility of such a doctrine than it puts it in the power of the smallest fraction over one-fourth of the United States, that is, of seven states out of twenty-four, to give the law and even the Constitution to seventeen states, each of the seventeen having as parties to the Constitution an equal right with each of the seven to expound it and to insist on the exposition? That the

seven might in particular instances be right and the seventeen wrong is more than possible. But to establish a positive and permanent rule giving such a power to such a minority over such a majority would overturn the first principle of free government, and in practice necessarily overturn the government itself.

It is to be recollected that the Constitution was proposed to the people of the states as a whole, and unanimously adopted by the states as a whole, it being a part of the Constitution that not less than three-fourths of the states should be competent to make any alteration in what had been unanimously agreed to. So great is the caution on this point that in two cases where peculiar interests were at stake, a proportion even of three-fourths is distrusted and unanimity required to make an alteration.

When the Constitution was adopted as a whole, it is certain that there were many parts which, if separately proposed, would have been promptly rejected. It is far from impossible that every part of a constitution might be rejected by a majority and yet taken together as a whole be unanimously accepted. Free constitutions will rarely if ever be formed without reciprocal concessions; without articles conditioned on and balancing each other. Is there a constitution of a single state out of the twenty-four that would bear the experiment of having its component parts submitted to the people and separately decided on?

What the fate of the Constitution of the United States would be if a small proportion of the states could expunge parts of it particularly valued by a large majority can have but one answer.

The difficulty is not removed by limiting the doctrine to cases of construction. How many cases of that sort, involving cardinal provisions of the Constitution, have occurred? How many now exist? How many may hereafter spring up? How many might be ingeniously created, if entitled to the privilege of a decision in the mode proposed?

Is it certain that the principle of that mode would not reach further than is contemplated? If a single state can of right require three-fourths of its co-states to overrule its exposition of the Constitution, because that proportion is authorized to amend it, would the plea be less plausible that, as the Constitution was unanimously established, it ought to be unanimously expounded?

The reply to all such suggestions seems to be unavoidable and irresistible; that the Constitution is a compact, that its text is to be expounded according to the provisions for expounding it, making a part of the compact; and that none of the parties can rightfully renounce the expounding provision more than any other part. When such a right accrues, as may accrue, it must grow out of abuses of the compact releasing the sufferers from their fealty to it.

In favor of the nullifying claim for the states individually, it appears, as you observe, that the proceedings of the legislature of Virginia, in 1798 and 1799, against the Alien and Sedition Acts, are much dwelt upon.

It may often happen, as experience proves, that erroneous constructions not anticipated may not be sufficiently guarded against in the language used; and it is due to the distinguished individuals, who have misconceived the intention of those proceedings, to suppose that the meaning of the legislature, though well comprehended at the time, may not now be obvious to those unacquainted with the contemporary indications and impressions.

But it is believed that by keeping in view the distinction between the governments of the states, and the states in the sense in which they were parties to the Constitution; between the rights of the parties, in their concurrent and in their individual capacities; between the several modes and objects of interposition against the abuses of power, and especially between interpositions within the purview of the Constitution, and interpositions appealing from the Constitution to the rights of nature paramount to all constitutions; with an attention, always of explanatory use, to the views and arguments which were combated, the Resolutions of Virginia, as vindicated in the report on them, will be found entitled to an exposition showing a consistency in their parts, and an inconsistency of the whole with the doctrine under consideration.

That the legislature could not have intended to sanction such a doctrine is to be inferred from the debates in the House of Delegates, and from the address of the two houses to their constituents, on the subject of the Resolutions. The tenor of the debates, which were ably conducted and are understood to have been revised for the press by most, if not all, of the speakers, discloses no reference whatever to a constitutional right in an individual state to arrest by force the operation of a law of the United States. Concert among the states for redress against the Alien and Sedition Laws, as acts of usurped power, was a leading sentiment; and the attainment of a concert, the immediate object of the course adopted by the legislature, which was that of inviting the other states "to concur, in declaring the acts to be unconstitutional, and to cooperate by the necessary and proper measures in maintaining unimpaired the authorities, rights, and liberties reserved to the states respectively and to the people." That by the necessary and proper measures to be concurrently and cooperatively taken were meant measures known to the Constitution, particularly the ordinary control of the people and legislatures of the states, over the government of the United States, cannot be doubted; and the interposition of this control, as the event showed, was equal to the occasion.

It is worthy of remark, and explanatory of the intentions of the legislature, that the words "not law, but utterly null, void, and of no force or effect," which had followed, in one of the Resolutions, the word "unconstitutional" were struck out by common consent. Though the words were in fact but synonymous with "unconstitutional"; yet to guard against a misunderstanding of this phrase as more than declaratory of opinion, the word "unconstitutional" alone was retained, as not liable to that danger.

The published *Address of the Legislature* to the people, their constituents, affords another conclusive evidence of its views. The *Address* warns them against the encroaching spirit of the general government, argues the unconstitutionality of the Alien and Sedition Acts, points to other instances in which the constitutional limits had been overleaped; dwells upon the dangerous mode of deriving power by implication; and in general presses the necessity of watching over the consolidating tendency of the federal policy. But nothing is said that can be understood to look to means of maintaining the rights of the states beyond the regular ones within the forms of the Constitution.

If any further lights on the subject could be needed, a very strong one is reflected in the answers to the Resolutions by the states which protested against them. The main objection of these, beyond a few general complaints of the inflammatory tendency of the Resolutions, was directed against the assumed authority of a state legislature to declare a law of the United States unconstitutional, which they pronounced an unwarrantable interference with the exclusive jurisdiction of the Supreme Court of the United States. Had the Resolutions been regarded as avowing and maintaining a right, in an individual state, to arrest by force, the execution of a law of the United States, it must be presumed that it would have been a conspicuous object of their denunciation.

85.

WILLIAM ELLERY CHANNING: Remarks on National Literature

William Ellery Channing wrote the essay, part of which is reprinted below, in response to Charles J. Ingersoll's Discourse Concerning the Influence of America on the Mind, *which had asserted that practicality in affairs was the distinguishing American characteristic. Channing countered that a national literature must reflect superior intellect no matter what the subject, and that American literature must free itself from English themes and models. Channing's position as a leader of the New England intellectual movement won for his* Remarks on National Literature *recognition as an important contribution to American literary development.*

Source: *The Works of William E. Channing,* 11th edition, Boston, 1849, Vol. I, pp. 243-280.

OUR PURPOSE is to treat of the importance and means of a national literature. The topic seems to us a great one and to have intimate connections with morals and religion, as well as with all our public interests. Our views will be given with great freedom, and, if they serve no other purpose than to recommend the subject to more general attention, one of our principal objects will be accomplished.

We begin with stating what we mean by national literature. We mean the expression of a nation's mind in writing. We mean the production among a people of important works in philosophy and in the departments of imagination and taste. We mean the contributions of new truths to the stock of human knowledge. We mean the thoughts of profound and original minds, elaborated by the toil of composition, and fixed and made immortal in books. We mean the manifestation of a nation's intellect in the only forms by which it can multiply itself at home and send itself abroad. We mean that a nation shall take a place, by its authors, among the lights of the world. . . .

The expression of superior mind in writing we regard, then, as a nation's literature. We regard its gifted men, whether devoted to the exact sciences, to mental and ethical philosophy, to history and legislation, or to fiction and poetry, as forming a noble intellectual brotherhood; and it is for the purpose of quickening all to join their labors for the public good that we offer the present plea in behalf of a national literature. . . . The great distinction of a country, then, is that it produces superior men. . . .

As yet the great distinction of a nation on which we have insisted has been scarcely recognized. . . .

We offer these remarks to correct what we deem a disproportioned attention to physical good, and not at all to condemn the expenditure of ingenuity and strength on the outward world. There is a harmony between all our great interests, between inward and outward improvements; and by establishing among them a wise order, all will be secured. We have no desire to shut up man in his own spiritual nature. The mind was made to act on matter, and it grows by expressing itself in material forms. We believe, too, that in proportion as it shall gain intellectual and moral power it will exert itself with increased energy and

delight on the outward creation; will pour itself forth more freely in useful and ornamental arts; will rear more magnificent structures; and will call forth new beauties in nature. . . .

The question which we most solicitously ask about this country is what race of men it is likely to produce. We consider its liberty of value only as far as it favors the growth of men. What is liberty? The removal of restraint from human powers. Its benefit is that it opens new fields for action and a wider range for the mind. The only freedom worth possessing is that which gives enlargement to a people's energy, intellect, and virtues. . . . Progress, the growth of power, is the end and boon of liberty, and, without this, a people may have the name but want the substance and spirit of freedom.

We are the more earnest in enlarging on these views because we feel that our attachment to our country must be very much proportioned to what we deem its tendency to form a generous race of men. We pretend not to have thrown off national feeling, but we have some stronger feelings. We love our country much, but mankind more. As men and Christians, our first desire is to see the improvement of human nature. . . . We love our country, but not blindly. In all nations we recognize one great family, and our chief wish for our native land is that it may take the first rank among the lights and benefactors of the human race. . . .

When a great truth is to be revealed, it does not flash at once on the race but dawns and brightens on a superior understanding from which it is to emanate and to illuminate future ages. On the faithfulness of great minds to this awful function, the progress and happiness of men chiefly depend. The most illustrious benefactors of the race have been men who, having risen to great truths, have held them as a sacred trust for their kind and have borne witness to them amid general darkness, under scorn and persecution, perhaps in the face of death. Such men, indeed, have not always made contributions to literature, for their condition has not allowed them to be authors; but we owe the transmission, perpetuity, and immortal power of their new and high thoughts to kindred spirits, which have concentrated and fixed them in books. . . .

Reading, once the privilege of a few, is now the occupation of multitudes, and is to become one of the chief gratifications of all. Books penetrate everywhere, and some of the works of genius find their way to obscure dwellings which, a little while ago, seemed barred against all intellectual light. Writing is now the mightiest instrument on earth. Through this the mind has acquired a kind of omnipresence. To literature we then look as the chief means of forming a better race of human beings. To superior minds, which may act through this, we look for the impulses by which their country is to be carried forward. We would teach them that they are the depositaries of the highest power on earth, and that on them the best hopes of society rest.

We are aware that some may think that we are exalting intellectual above moral and religious influence. . . . Religious and moral truth is indeed appointed to carry forward mankind, but not as conceived and expounded by narrow minds, not as darkened by the ignorant, not as debased by the superstitious, not as subtilized by the visionary, not as thundered out by the intolerant fanatic, not as turned into a driveling cant by the hypocrite. Like all other truths, it requires for its full reception and powerful communication a free and vigorous intellect. . . .

Religion has been wronged by nothing more than by being separated from intellect, than by being removed from the province of reason and free research into that of mystery and authority, of impulse and feeling. Hence it is that the prevalent forms or exhibitions of Christianity are comparatively inert, and that most which is written on the subject is of little or no worth. Christianity was given not to contradict and degrade the rational nature but to call it forth, to enlarge its range and its powers. It admits of endless development. It is the last truth which should remain stationary. It ought to be so explored and so expressed as to take the highest place in a nation's literature, as to exalt and purify all other literature. From these remarks it will be seen that the efficacy which we have ascribed to literary or intellectual influence in the work of human improvement is consistent with the supreme importance of moral and religious truth.

If we have succeeded in conveying the impressions which we have aimed to make, our readers are now prepared to inquire with interest into the condition and prospects of literature among ourselves. Do we possess, indeed, what may be called a national literature? Have we produced eminent writers in the various departments of intellectual effort? Are our chief resources of instruction and literary enjoyment furnished from ourselves? We regret that the reply to these questions is so obvious. The few standard works which we have produced, and which promise to live, can hardly by any courtesy be denominated a national literature. On this point, if marks and proofs of our real condition were needed, we should find them in the current apologies for our deficiencies. Our writers are accustomed to plead in our excuse our youth, the necessities of a newly settled country, and the direction of our best talents to practical life. Be the pleas sufficient or not, one thing they prove and that is our consciousness of having failed to make important contributions to the interests of the intellect.

We have few names to place by the side of the great names in science and literature on the other side of the ocean. We want those lights which make a country conspicuous at a distance. Let it not be said that European envy denies our just claims. In an age like this, when the literary world forms a great family and the products of mind are circulated more rapidly than those of machinery, it is a nation's own fault if its name be not pronounced with honor beyond itself. We have ourselves heard, and delighted to hear, beyond the Alps, our country designated as the Land of Franklin. This name had scaled that mighty barrier and made us known where our institutions and modes of life were hardly better understood than those of the natives of our forests.

We are accustomed to console ourselves for the absence of a commanding literature by urging our superiority to other nations in our institutions for the diffusion of elementary knowledge through all classes of the community. We have here just cause for boasting, though perhaps less than we imagine. That there are gross deficiencies in our common schools, and that the amount of knowledge which they communicate, when compared with the time spent in its acquisition, is lamentably small, the community begins to feel. There is a crying need for a higher and more quickening kind of instruction than the laboring part of society has yet received, and we rejoice that the cry begins to be heard. But, allowing our elementary institutions to be ever so perfect, we confess that they do not satisfy us. We want something more. A dead level of intellect, even if it should rise above what is common in other nations, would not answer our wishes and hopes for our country. We want great minds to be formed among us, minds which shall be felt afar and through which we may act on the world. We want the human intellect to do its utmost here. . . .

There is among us much superficial knowledge but little severe, persevering research; little of that consuming passion for new truth which makes outward things worthless; little resolute devotion to a high intellectual culture. There is nowhere a literary atmosphere, or such an accumulation of literary influence as determines the whole strength of the mind to its own enlargement and to the manifestation of itself in enduring forms. Few among us can be said to have followed out any great subject of thought patiently, laboriously, so as to know thoroughly what others have discovered and taught concerning it, and thus to occupy a ground from which new views may be gained.

Of course, exceptions are to be found. This country has produced original and profound thinkers. We have named Franklin, and we may name Edwards, one of the greatest men of his age, though unhappily his mind was lost, in a great degree, to literature, and we fear to religion, by vassalage to a false theology. . . . Still, we may say we chiefly prize what has been done among us as a promise of higher and more extensive effort. Patriotism, as well as virtue, forbids us to burn incense to national vanity.

The truth should be seen and felt. In an age of great intellectual activity, we rely chiefly for intellectual excitement and enjoyment on foreign minds; nor is our own mind felt abroad. While clamoring against dependence on European manufactures, we contentedly rely on Europe for the nobler and more important fabrics of the intellect. We boast of our political institutions, and receive our chief teachings, books, impressions from the school of monarchy. True, we labor under disadvantages. But, if our liberty deserves the praise which it receives, it is more than a balance for these. We believe that it is. We believe that it does open to us an indefinite intellectual progress. Did we not so regard it, we should value it little. If hereditary governments minister most to the growth of the mind, it were better to restore them than to cling to a barren freedom. Let us not expose liberty to this reproach. Let us prove, by more generous provisions for the diffusion of elementary knowledge, for the training of great minds, and for the joint culture of the moral and intellectual powers, that we are more and more instructed by freedom in the worth and greatness of human nature, and in the obligation of contributing to its strength and glory.

We have spoken of the condition of our literature. We now proceed to the consideration of the causes which obstruct its advancement; and we are immediately struck by one so prevalent as to deserve distinct notice. We refer to the common doctrine that we need, in this country, useful knowledge rather than profound, extensive, and elegant literature, and that this last, if we covet it, may be imported from abroad in such variety and abundance as to save us the necessity of producing it among ourselves. How far are these opinions just? This question we purpose to answer.

That useful knowledge should receive our first and chief care we mean not to dispute. But in our views of utility we may differ from some who take this position. There are those who confine this term to the necessaries and comforts of life, and to the means of producing them. And is it true that we need no knowledge but that which clothes and feeds us? . . .

Happily, human nature is too strong for the utilitarian. It cannot satisfy itself with the convenient. No passion unfolds itself sooner than the love of the ornamental. The savage decorates his person, and the child is more struck with the beauty than the uses of its raiment. So far from limiting ourselves to convenient food and raiment, we enjoy but little a repast which is not arranged with some degree of order and taste; and a man who should consult comfort alone in his wardrobe would find himself an unwelcome guest in circles which he would very reluctantly forgo. We are aware that the propensity to which we have referred often breaks out in extravagance and ruin-

ous luxury. We know that the love of ornament is often vitiated by vanity, and that, when so perverted, it impairs, sometimes destroys, the soundness and simplicity of the mind and the relish for true glory. Still it teaches, even in its excesses, that the idea of beauty is an indestructible principle of our nature, and this single truth is enough to put us on our guard against vulgar notions of utility.

We have said that we prize, as highly as any, useful knowledge. But by this we mean knowledge which answers and ministers to our complex and various nature; we mean that which is useful, not only to the animal man but to the intellectual, moral, and religious man, useful to a being of spiritual faculties, whose happiness is to be found in their free and harmonious exercise. . . .

In truth, we are slow to condemn as useless any researches or discoveries of original and strong minds, even when we discern in them no bearing on any interests of mankind; for all truth is of a prolific nature, and has connections not immediately perceived; and it may be that what we call vain speculations may, at no distant period, link themselves with some new facts or theories, and guide a profound thinker to the most important results. . . . For ourselves, we incline to hope much from truths which are particularly decried as useless; for the noblest and most useful truth is of an abstract or universal nature; and yet the abstract, though susceptible of infinite application, is generally, as we know, opposed to the practical. . . .

We know that it will be said that foreign scholars, bred under institutions which this country cannot support, may do our intellectual work, and send us books and learning to meet our wants. To this we have much to answer. In the first place, we reply that, to avail ourselves of the higher literature of other nations, we must place ourselves on a level with them. The products of foreign machinery we can use without any portion of the skill that produced them. But works of taste and genius, and profound investigations of philosophy, can only be estimated and enjoyed through a culture and power corresponding to that from which they sprang.

In the next place, we maintain that it is an immense gain to a people to have in its own bosom, among its own sons, men of distinguished intellect. . . .

We next observe — and we think the observation important — that the facility with which we receive the literature of foreign countries, instead of being a reason for neglecting our own, is a strong motive for its cultivation. We mean to be paradoxical, but we believe that it would be better to admit no books from abroad than to make them substitutes for our own intellectual activity. The more we receive from other countries, the greater the need of an original literature. A people into whose minds the thoughts of foreigners are poured perpetually needs an energy within itself to resist, to modify, this mighty influence, and without it will inevitably sink under the worst bondage, will become intellectually tame and enslaved. We have certainly no desire to complete our restrictive system by adding to it a literary nonintercourse law. We rejoice in the increasing intellectual connection between this country and the Old World; but sooner would we rupture it than see our country sitting passively at the feet of foreign teachers. . . .

Another view of the subject is this. A foreign literature will always in a measure be foreign. It has sprung from the soul of another people, which, however like, is still not our own soul. Every people has much in its own character and feelings which can only be embodied by its own writers, and which, when transfused through literature, makes it touching and true, like the voice of our earliest friend.

We now proceed to an argument in favor of native literature which, if less obvious, is, we believe, not less sound than those now already adduced. We have hitherto spoken of literature as the expression, the communication of the higher minds in a community. We now add that it does much more than is commonly supposed to *form* such minds, so that without it a people wants one of the chief means of educating or perfecting talent and genius. One of the great laws of our nature, and a law singularly important to social beings, is that the intellect enlarges and strengthens itself by expressing worthily its best views. In this as in other respects it is more blessed to give than to receive. Superior minds are formed, not merely by solitary thought but almost as much by communication. . . .

If we confine ourselves simply to the consideration of style, we shall have reason to think that a people among whom this is neglected wants one important intellectual aid. In this, great power is exerted, and by exertion increased. To the multitude, indeed, language seems so natural an instrument that to use it with clearness and energy seems no great effort. It is framed, they think, to the writer's hand, and so continually employed as to need little thought or skill. But in nothing is the creative power of a gifted writer seen more than in his style. True, his words may be found in the dictionary; but there they lie, disjointed and dead. . . .

The words arranged in his dictionary are no more fitted to depict his thoughts than the block of marble in the sculptor's shop to show forth the conceptions which are dawning in his mind. Both are inert materials. The power which pervades them comes from the soul; and the same creative energy is manifested in the production of a noble style as in extracting beautiful forms from lifeless stone. How unfaithful, then, is a nation to its own intellect in which grace and force of style receive no culture!

The remarks now made on the importance of literature as a means of educating talent and genius, we are aware, do not apply equally to all subjects or kinds of knowledge. In the exact or physical sciences a man may acquire much without composition and may make discoveries without registering them. Even here, however, we believe that by a systematic development of his views in a luminous style, he will bring great aid to his own faculties as well as to others. It is on the vast subjects of morals and human nature that the mind especially strengthens itself by elaborate composition; and these, let it be remembered, form the staple of the highest literature.

Moral truth, under which we include everything relating to mind and character, is of a refined and subtle, as well as elevated, nature and requires the joint and full exercise of discrimination, invention, imagination, and sensibility to give it effectual utterance. A writer who would make it visible and powerful must strive to join an austere logic to a fervent eloquence; must place it in various lights; must create for it interesting forms; must wed it to beauty; must illuminate it by similitudes and contrasts; must show its correspondence with the outward world; perhaps must frame for it a vast machinery of fiction. How invigorating are these efforts! Yet it is only in writing, in elaborate composition, that they are deliberately called forth and sustained, and without literature they would almost cease. It may be said of many truths that greater intellectual energy is required to express them with effect than to conceive them, so that a nation which does not encourage this expression impoverishes so far its own mind. . . .

We come now to our last — and what we deem a weighty — argument in favor of a native literature. We desire and would cherish it, because we hope from it important aids to the cause of truth and human nature. We believe that a literature springing up in this new soil would bear new fruits, and, in some respects, more precious fruits than are elsewhere produced. We know that our hopes may be set down to the account of that national vanity which, with too much reason, is placed by foreigners among our besetting sins. But we speak from calm and deliberate conviction. We are inclined to believe that, as a people, we occupy a position from which the great subjects of literature may be viewed more justly than from those which most other nations hold.

Undoubtedly we labor under disadvantages. We want the literary apparatus of Europe, her libraries, her universities, her learned institutions, her race of professed scholars, her spots consecrated by the memory of sages, and a thousand stirring associations which hover over ancient nurseries of learning. But the mind is not a local power. Its spring is within itself, and under the inspiration of liberal and high feeling it may attain and worthily express nobler truth than outward helps could reveal.

The great distinction of our country is that we enjoy some peculiar advantages for understanding our own nature. Man is the great subject of literature, and juster and profounder views of man may be expected here than elsewhere. In Europe political and artificial distinctions have more or less triumphed over and obscured our common nature. In Europe we meet kings, nobles, priests, peasants. How much rarer is it to meet *men;* by which we mean human beings conscious of their own nature and conscious of the utter worthlessness of all outward distinctions compared with what is treasured up in their own souls. . . .

We conceive that our position favors a juster and profounder estimate of human nature. We mean not to boast, but there are fewer obstructions to that moral consciousness, that consciousness of humanity, of which we have spoken. Man is not hidden from us by so many disguises as in the Old World. The essential equality of all human beings, founded on the possession of a spiritual, progressive, immortal nature, is, we hope, better understood; and nothing more than this single conviction is needed to work the mightiest changes in every province of human life and of human thought.

We have stated what seems to us our most important distinction. But our position has other advantages. The mere circumstance of its being a new one gives reason to hope for some new intellectual activity, some fresher views of nature and life. We are not borne down by the weight of antiquated institutions, time-hallowed abuses, and the remnants of feudal barbarism. The absence of a religious establishment is an immense gain, as far as originality of mind is in question; for an establishment, however advantageous in other respects, is by its nature hostile to discovery and progress. To keep the mind where it is, to fasten the notions of one age on all future time, is its aim and proper business; and if it happened, as has generally been the case, to grow up in an age of strife and passion, when, as history demonstrates, the church was overrun with error, it cannot but perpetuate darkness and mental bondage. Among us, intellect, though far from being free, has broken some of the chains of other countries, and is more likely, we conceive, to propose to itself its legitimate object, truth — everlasting and universal truth.

We have no thought of speaking contemptuously of the literature of the Old World. It is our daily nutriment. We feel our debt to be immense to the glorious company of pure and wise minds which in foreign lands have bequeathed us in writing their choicest thoughts and holiest feelings. Still, we feel that all existing literature has been produced under influences which have necessarily mixed with it much error and corruption; and that the whole of it ought to pass, and must pass, under rigorous review.

For example, we think that the history of the human race is to be rewritten. Men imbued with the prejudices which thrive under aristocracies and state religions cannot understand it. Past ages, with their great events and great men, are to undergo, we think, a new trial and yield new results. It is plain that history is already viewed under new aspects, and we believe that the true principles for studying and writing it are to be unfolded here, at least as rapidly as in other countries.

It seems to us that in literature an immense work is yet to be done. The most interesting questions to mankind are yet in debate. Great principles are yet to be settled in criticism, in morals, in politics; and, above all, the true character of religion is to be rescued from the disguises and corruption of ages. We want a reformation. We want a literature in which genius will pay supreme, if not undivided, homage to truth and virtue; in which the childish admiration of what has been called greatness will give place to a wise moral judgment, which will breathe reverence for the mind and elevating thoughts of God.

The part which this country is to bear in this great intellectual reform we presume not to predict. We feel, however, that, if true to itself, it will have the glory and happiness of giving new impulses to the human mind. This is our cherished hope. We should have no heart to encourage native literature did we not hope that it would become instinct with a new spirit. We cannot admit the thought that this country is to be only a repetition of the Old World. We delight to believe that God, in the fullness of time, has brought a new continent to light in order that the human mind should move here with a new freedom, should frame new social institutions, should explore new paths and reap new harvests. We are accustomed to estimate nations by their creative energies; and we shall blush for our country if, in circumstances so peculiar, original, and creative, it shall satisfy itself with a passive reception and mechanical reiteration of the thoughts of strangers.

86.

WILLIAM ELLERY CHANNING: Association and Individual Action

The formation of private associations to gain political, social, or economic ends has been traditional in America since the colonial period. During the early nineteenth century, when the nation was growing so fast that its government could not keep pace, the tendency to organize for private or public benefit became especially pronounced. Clubs and associations were formed for every conceivable purpose, and included labor unions, political parties of every stripe, social welfare groups, employers' organizations, adult education societies, religious associations, to name but a few. William Ellery Channing saw in this tendency a threat to the integrity and the development of individuals and wrote an essay in 1830 pointing out the potential dangers in social and political conformity.

Source: *The Works of William E. Channing*, 11th edition, Boston, 1849, Vol. I, pp. 281-332: "Remarks on Associations."

ONE OF THE MOST REMARKABLE circumstances or features of our age is the energy with which the principle of combination, or of action by joint forces, by associated numbers, is manifesting itself. It may be said without much exaggeration that everything is done now by societies. Men have learned what wonders can be accomplished in certain cases by union, and seem to think that union is competent to everything. You can scarcely name an object for which some institution has not been formed. Would men spread one set of opinions, or crush another? They make a society. Would they improve the penal code or relieve poor debtors? They make societies. Would they encourage agriculture, or manufactures, or science? They make societies. Would one class encourage horse racing, and another discourage traveling on Sunday? They form societies. We have immense institutions spreading over the country combining hosts for particular objects. We have minute ramifications of these societies, penetrating everywhere except through the poorhouse, and conveying resources from the domestic, the laborer, and even the child to the central treasury. . . .

It is very easy, we conceive, to explain this great development of the principle of cooperation. The main cause is the immense facility given to intercourse by modern improvements, by increased commerce and traveling, by the post office, by the steamboat, and especially by the press, by newspapers, periodicals, tracts, and other publications. Through these means, men of one mind through a whole country easily understand one another and easily act together. . . .

Those who have one great object find one another out through a vast extent of country, join their forces, settle their mode of operation, and act together with the uniformity of a disciplined army. So extensive have coalitions become through the facilities now described, and so various and rapid are the means of communication that when a few leaders have agreed on an object, an impulse may be given in a month to the whole country. Whole states may be deluged with tracts and other publications, and a voice like that of many waters be called forth from immense and widely separated multitudes. Here is a new power brought to bear on society; and it is a great moral question, how it ought to be viewed and what duties it imposes.

That this mode of action has advantages and recommendations is very obvious. The principal arguments in its favor may be stated in a few words. Men, it is justly said, can do jointly what they cannot do singly. The union of minds and hands works wonders. Men grow efficient by concentrating their powers. . . .

Nor is this all. Men not only accumulate power by union, but gain warmth and earnestness. The heart is kindled. An electric communication is established between those who are brought nigh and bound to each other in common labors. Man droops in solitude. No sound excites him like the voice of his fellow creature. The mere sight of a human countenance brightened with strong and generous emotion gives new strength to act or suffer. Union not only brings to a point forces which before existed, and which were ineffectual through separation, but, by the feeling and interest which it rouses, it becomes a creative principle, calls forth new forces, and gives the mind a consciousness of powers which would otherwise have been unknown.

We have here given the common arguments by which the disposition to association is justified and recommended. They may be summed up in a few words; namely, that our social principles and relations are the great springs of improvement, and of vigorous and efficient exertion. That there is much truth in this representation of the influences of society, we at once feel; that without impulses and excitements from abroad, without sympathies and communication with our fellow creatures, we should gain nothing and accomplish nothing, we mean not to deny. . . .

On these topics, then, we propose first to give our views; and, in so doing, we shall allow ourselves a considerable latitude because, in our judgment, the influences of society at present tend strongly to excess, and especially menace that individuality of character for which they can yield no adequate compensation.

The great principle from which we start in this preliminary discussion, and in which all our views of the topics above proposed are involved, may be briefly expressed. It is this: Society is chiefly important as it ministers to and calls forth intellectual and moral energy and freedom. Its action on the individual is beneficial in proportion as it awakens in him a power to act on himself and to control or withstand the social influences to which he is at first subjected. . . . Our social nature and connections are means. Inward power is the end — a power which is to triumph over and control the influence of society. . . .

Let the judgment of others be our trust so that we cease to judge for ourselves and the intellect is degraded into a worthless machine. The dignity of the mind is to be estimated by the energy of its efforts for its own enlargement. It becomes heroic when it reverences itself and asserts its freedom in a cowardly and servile age; when it withstands society through a calm but invincible love of truth and a consciousness of the dignity and progressiveness of its powers.

The indispensable necessity of instruction from our fellow creatures we in no degree question. But perhaps few are aware how imperfect are the conceptions received from the best instructor, and how much must be done by our own solitary thinking to give them consistency and vividness. . . .

Our daily intercourse is with fallible beings, most of whom are undisciplined in intellect, the slaves of prejudice, and unconscious of their own spiritual energies. The essential condition of intellectual progress in such a world is the resistance of social influences or of impressions from our fellow beings.

What we have said of intellectual is still

Portrait of William Ellery Channing (1780-1842) by S. Gambardella

more true of moral progress. No human being exists whose character can be proposed as a faultless model. . . . No process is so fatal as that which would cast all men into one mold. Every human being is intended to have a character of his own, to be what no other is, to do what no other can do. Our common nature is to be unfolded in unbounded diversities. It is rich enough for infinite manifestations. It is to wear innumerable forms of beauty and glory. Every human being has a work to carry on within, duties to perform abroad, influences to exert, which are peculiarly his, and which no conscience but his own can teach. Let him not, then, enslave his conscience to others, but act with the freedom, strength, and dignity of one whose highest law is in his own breast.

We know that it may be replied to us that Providence, by placing us at birth in entire subjection to social influences, has marked out society as the great instrument of determining the human mind. The child, it is said, is plainly designed to receive pas-

sively and with unresisting simplicity a host of impressions, thoughts, and feelings from those around him. This we know. But we know, too, that childhood is not to endure forever. We know that the impressions, pleasures, pains, which throng and possess the infant mind are intended to awaken in it an energy by which it is to subject them to itself; by which it is to separate from the crude mass what is true and pure; by which it is to act upon, and modify, and throw into new combinations the materials forced upon it originally by sensation and society. It is only by putting forth this inward and self-forming power that we emerge from childhood. He who continues to be passively molded prolongs his infancy to the tomb. . . .

The common opinion is that our danger from society arises wholly from its bad members, and that we cannot easily be too much influenced by the good. But, to our apprehension, there is a peril in the influence both of good and bad. What many of us have chiefly to dread from society is not that we shall acquire a positive character of vice but that it will impose on us a negative character, that we shall live and die passive beings, that the creative and self-forming energy of the soul will not be called forth in the work of our improvement. Our danger is that we shall substitute the consciences of others for our own; that we shall paralyze our faculties through dependence on foreign guides; that we shall be molded from abroad instead of determining ourselves.

The pressure of society upon us is constant and almost immeasurable; now open and direct in the form of authority and menace, now subtle and silent in the guise of blandishment and promise. What mighty power is lodged in a frown or a smile, in the voice of praise and flattery, in scorn or neglect, in public opinion, in domestic habits and prejudices, in the state and spirit of the community to which we belong! Nothing escapes the cognizance of society. Its legislation extends even to our dress, movements, features; and the individual bears the traces, even in countenance, air, and voice, of the social influences amidst which he has been plunged. We are in great peril of growing up slaves to this exacting, arbitrary sovereign; of forgetting or never learning our true responsibility; of living in unconsciousness of that divine power with which we are invested over ourselves, and in which all the dignity of our nature is concentrated; of overlooking the sacredness of our minds and laying them open to impressions from any and all who surround us.

Resistance of this foreign pressure is our only safeguard and is essential to virtue. All virtue lies in individual action, in inward energy, in self-determination. There is no moral worth in being swept away by a crowd, even toward the best objects. . . .

Our great and most difficult duty as social beings is to derive constant aid from society without taking its yoke; to open our minds to the thoughts, reasonings, and persuasions of others, and yet to hold fast the sacred right of private judgment; to receive impulses from our fellow beings, and yet to act from our own souls; to sympathize with others and yet to determine our own feelings; to act with others and yet to follow our own consciences; to unite social deference and self-dominion; to join moral self-subsistence with social dependence; to respect others without losing self-respect; to love our friends and to reverence our superiors, while our supreme homage is given to that moral perfection which no friend and no superior has realized, and which, if faithfully pursued, will often demand separation from all around us. . . .

We now pass to our principal subject; to the associations for public purposes, whether benevolent, moral, or religious, which are so multiplied in the present age. . . . We should beware of confounding together, as of equal importance, those associations which are formed by our Creator, which spring from our very Constitution and are inseparable from our being, and those of which we are now treating, which man invents for particular times and exigencies. . . .

But when we speak thus of society, we mean chiefly the relations in which God has placed us; we mean the connections of family, of neighborhood, of country, and the great bond of humanity, uniting us with our whole kind, and not missionary societies, peace societies, or charitable societies which men have contrived. These last have their uses and some do great good; but they are no more to be compared with the societies in which nature places us than the torches which we kindle on earth in the darkness of night are to be paralleled with the all-pervading and all-glorifying light of the sun. . . .

We now proceed . . . to suggest a principle by which the claims of different associations may be estimated. It is this: The value of associations is to be measured by the energy, the freedom, the activity, the moral power which they encourage and diffuse. In truth, the great object of all benevolence is to give power, activity, and freedom to others. We cannot, in the strict sense of the word, *make* any being happy. We can give others the *means* of happiness, together with motives to the faithful use of them; but on this faithfulness, on the free and full exercise of their own powers, their happiness depends. There is thus a fixed, impassable limit to human benevolence. It can only make men happy through themselves, through their own freedom and energy.

We go further. We believe that God has set the same limit to His own benevolence. He makes no being happy in any other sense than in that of giving him means, powers, motives, and a field for exertion. We have here, we think, the great consideration to guide us in judging of associations. Those are good which communicate power, moral and intellectual action, and the capacity of useful efforts to the persons who form them or to the persons on whom they act. On the other hand, associations which in any degree impair or repress the free and full action of men's powers are so far hurtful.

On this principle, associations for restoring to men health, strength, the use of their limbs, the use of their senses, especially of sight and hearing, are highly to be approved, for such enlarge men's powers; while charitable associations, which weaken in men the motives to exertion, which offer a bounty to idleness, or make beggary as profitable as labor are great calamities to society and peculiarly calamitous to those whom they relieve. On the same principle, associations which are designed to awaken the human mind, to give to men of all classes a consciousness of their intellectual powers, to communicate knowledge of a useful and quickening character, to encourage men in thinking with freedom and vigor, to inspire an ardent love and pursuit of truth are most worthy of patronage; while such as are designed or adapted to depress the human intellect, to make it dependent and servile, to keep it where it is, to give a limited amount of knowledge, but not to give impulse and an onward motion to men's thoughts, all such associations, however benevolent their professions, should be regarded as among the foes and obstructions to the best interests of society.

On the same principle, associations aiming to purify and ennoble the character of a people, to promote true virtue, a rational piety, a disinterested charity, a wise temperance, and especially aiming to accomplish these ends by the only effectual means, that is, by calling forth men's own exertions for a higher knowledge of God and duty, and for a new and growing control of themselves — such institutions are among the noblest; while no encouragement is due to such as aim to make men religious and virtuous by paralyzing their minds through terror, by fastening on them a yoke of opinions or practices, by pouring upon them influences from abroad which virtually annihilate their power over themselves and make them instruments for others to speak through and to wield at pleasure. . . .

Associations often injure free action by a very plain and obvious operation. They accumulate power in a few hands, and this takes place just in proportion to the surface over which they spread. In a large institution, a few men rule, a few do everything; and if the institution happens to be directed to objects about which conflict and controversy exist, a few are able to excite in the mass strong and bitter passions, and by these to obtain an immense ascendancy. Through such an association, widely spread yet closely connected by party feeling, a few leaders can send their voices and spirit far and wide, and, where great funds are accumulated, can league a host of instruments, and by menace and appeals to interest can silence opposition. Accordingly, we fear that in this country an influence is growing up through widely spread societies, altogether at war with the spirit of our institutions, and which, unless jealously watched, will gradually but surely encroach on freedom of thought, of speech, and of the press. It is very striking to observe how, by such combinations, the very means of encouraging a free action of men's minds may be turned against it. . . .

It is now discovered that the way to rule in this country is by an array of numbers which a prudent man will not like to face. Of consequence, all associations aiming or tending to establish sway by numbers ought to be opposed. They create tyrants as effectually as standing armies. Let them be withstood from the beginning. No matter whether the opinions which they intend to put down be true or false. Let no opinion be put down by such means. Let no error be suppressed by an instrument which will be equally powerful against truth, and which must subvert that freedom of thought on which all truth depends. Let the best end fail if it cannot be accomplished by right and just means. . . .

From the nature of things, public opinion is often unjust; but when it is not embodied and fixed by pledged societies, it easily relents, it may receive new impulses, it is open to influences from the injured. On the contrary, when shackled and stimulated by vast associations, it is in danger of becoming a steady, unrelenting tyrant, browbeating the timid, proscribing the resolute, silencing free speech, and virtually denying the dearest religious and civil rights. We say not that all great associations *must* be thus abused. We know that some are useful. We know, too, that there are cases in which it is important that public opinion should be condensed, or act in a mass. We feel, however, that the danger of great associations is increased by the very fact that they are sometimes useful. They are perilous instruments. They ought to be suspected. They are a kind of irregular government created within our constitutional government. Let them be watched closely. As soon as we find them resolved or disposed to bear down a respectable man or set of men, or to force on the community measures about which wise and good men differ, let us feel that a dangerous engine is at work among us and oppose to it our steady and stern disapprobation. . . .

Individual action is the highest good. What we want is that men should do right more and more from their own minds and less and less from imitation, from a foreign impulse, from sympathy with a crowd. This is the kind of action which we recommend. Would you do good according to the Gospel? Do it secretly, silently; so silently that the left hand will not know what the right hand doeth. This precept does not favor the clamorous and far-published efforts of a leagued multitude.

We mean not to sever men from others in well-doing, for we have said there are many good objects which can only be accomplished by numbers. But generally speaking, we can do most good by individual action, and our own virtue is incomparably more improved by it. It is vastly better, for example, that we should give our own money with our own hands, from our own judgment, and through personal interest in the distresses of others than that we should send it by a substitute. Secondhand charity is not as good to the giver or receiver as immediate. There are, indeed, urgent cases where we cannot act immediately, or cannot alone do the good required. There let us join with others; but where we can do good secretly and separately, or only with some dear friend, we shall almost certainly put forth in this way more of intellect and heart, more of sympathy and strenuous purpose, and shall awaken more of virtuous sensibility in those whom we relieve than if we were to be parts of a multitude in accomplishing the same end. Individual action is the great point to be secured. . . .

In truth, associations are chiefly useful by giving means and opportunities to gifted individuals to act out their own minds. A missionary society achieves little good, except when it can send forth an individual who wants no teaching or training from the society, but who carries his commission and chief power in his own soul. We urge this, for we feel that we are all in danger of sacrificing our individuality and independence to our social connections. We dread new social trammels. They are too numerous already. From these views we learn that there is cause to fear and to withstand great associations, as far as they interfere with or restrain individual action, personal independence, private judgment, free, self-originated effort. We do fear, from not a few associations which exist, that power is to be accumulated in the hands of a few, and a servile, tame, dependent spirit to be generated in the many. Such is the danger of our times, and we are bound as Christians and freemen to withstand it.

87.

Andrew Jackson: On Indian Removal

Westward expansion brought the United States into contact with numerous Indian nations and the admission of new states brought certain Native American lands within the national boundaries. In the following message to Congress of December 6, 1830, President Jackson inaugurated the policy of extinguishing all Indian title to such lands and removing the Native Americans to an area beyond the Mississippi River. The President asserted that such a policy would avoid a "collision" between federal authority over Native Americans and state jurisdiction of their lands, and that it would open to "dense and civilized population" areas previously occupied only by "a few savage hunters." The policy was upheld by the Supreme Court in the case of Cherokee Nation v. State of Georgia, *but when Chief Justice John Marshall ruled in* Worcester v. Georgia *that Native Americans retained certain rights in their own lands, Jackson is said to have retorted, "John Marshall has made his decision, now let him enforce it."*

Source: Richardson, II, pp. 500-529.

IT GIVES ME PLEASURE to announce to Congress that the benevolent policy of the government, steadily pursued for nearly thirty years, in relation to the removal of the Indians beyond the white settlements is approaching to a happy consummation. Two important tribes have accepted the provision made for their removal at the last session of Congress, and it is believed that their example will induce the remaining tribes also to seek the same obvious advantages.

The consequences of a speedy removal will be important to the United States, to individual states, and to the Indians themselves. The pecuniary advantages which it promises to the government are the least of its recommendations. It puts an end to all possible danger of collision between the authorities of the general and state governments on account of the Indians. It will place a dense and civilized population in large tracts of country now occupied by a few savage hunters. By opening the whole territory between Tennessee on the north and Louisiana on the south to the settlement of the whites it will incalculably strengthen the southwestern frontier and render the adjacent states strong enough to repel future invasions without remote aid. It will relieve the whole state of Mississippi and the western part of Alabama of Indian occupancy, and enable those states to advance rapidly in population, wealth, and power.

It will separate the Indians from immediate contact with settlements of whites; free them from the power of the states; enable them to pursue happiness in their own way and under their own rude institutions; will retard the progress of decay, which is lessening their numbers, and perhaps cause them gradually, under the protection of the government and through the influence of good counsels, to cast off their savage habits and become an interesting, civilized, and Christian community. These consequences, some of them so certain and the rest so probable, make the complete execution of the plan sanctioned by Congress at their last session an object of much solicitude.

Toward the aborigines of the country no one can indulge a more friendly feeling than myself, or would go further in attempting to reclaim them from their wandering habits and make them a happy, prosperous people. I have endeavored to impress upon them my own solemn convictions of the duties and powers of the general government in relation to the state authorities. For the justice of the laws passed by the states within the scope of their reserved powers they are not responsible to this government. As individuals we may entertain and express our opinions of their acts, but as a government we have as little right to control them as we have to prescribe laws for other nations.

With a full understanding of the subject, the Choctaw and the Chickasaw tribes have with great unanimity determined to avail themselves of the liberal offers presented by the act of Congress, and have agreed to remove beyond the Mississippi River. Treaties have been made with them, which in due season will be submitted for consideration. In negotiating these treaties, they were made to understand their true condition, and they have preferred maintaining their independence in the Western forests to submitting to the laws of the states in which they now reside. These treaties, being probably the last which will ever be made with them, are characterized by great liberality on the part of the government. They give the Indians a liberal sum in consideration of their removal, and comfortable subsistence on their arrival at their new homes. If it be their real interest to maintain a separate existence, they will there be at liberty to do so without the inconveniences and vexations to which they would unavoidably have been subject in Alabama and Mississippi.

Humanity has often wept over the fate of the aborigines of this country, and philanthropy has been long busily employed in devising means to avert it, but its progress has never for a moment been arrested, and one by one have many powerful tribes disappeared from the earth. To follow to the tomb the last of his race and to tread on the graves of extinct nations excite melancholy reflections. But true philanthropy reconciles the mind to these vicissitudes as it does to the extinction of one generation to make room for another. In the monuments and fortresses of an unknown people, spread over the extensive regions of the West, we behold the memorials of a once powerful race, which was exterminated or has disappeared to make room for the existing savage tribes. Nor is there anything in this which, upon a comprehensive view of the general interests of the human race, is to be regretted. Philanthropy could not wish to see this continent restored to the condition in which it was found by our forefathers. What good man would prefer a country covered with forests and ranged by a few thousand savages to our extensive republic, studded with cities, towns, and prosperous farms, embellished with all the improvements which art can devise or industry execute, occupied by more than 12 million happy people, and filled with all the blessings of liberty, civilization, and religion?

The present policy of the government is but a continuation of the same progressive change by a milder process. The tribes which occupied the countries now constituting the Eastern states were annihilated or have melted away to make room for the whites. The waves of population and civilization are rolling to the westward, and we now propose to acquire the countries occupied by the red men of the South and West by a fair exchange, and, at the expense of the United States, to send them to a land where their existence may be prolonged and perhaps made perpetual.

Doubtless it will be painful to leave the graves of their fathers; but what do they more than our ancestors did or than our children are now doing? To better their condition in an unknown land our forefathers left all that was dear in earthly objects. Our children by thousands yearly leave the land of their birth to seek new homes in distant regions. Does humanity weep at these painful separations from everything, animate and inanimate, with which the young heart has become entwined? Far from it. It is rather a source of joy that our country affords scope where our young population may range unconstrained in body or in mind, developing the power and faculties of man in their highest perfection. These remove hundreds and almost thousands of miles at their own expense, purchase the lands they occupy, and support themselves at their new homes from the moment of their arrival. Can it be cruel in this government when, by events which it cannot control, the Indian is made discontented in his ancient home to purchase his lands, to give him a new and extensive territory, to pay the expense of his removal, and support him a year in his new abode? How many thousands of our own people would gladly embrace the opportunity of removing to the West on such conditions? If the offers made to the Indians were extended to them, they would be hailed with gratitude and joy.

And is it supposed that the wandering savage has a stronger attachment to his home than the settled, civilized Christian? Is it more afflicting to him to leave the graves of his fathers than it is to our brothers and children? Rightly considered, the policy of the general government toward the red man is not only liberal but generous. He is unwilling to submit to the laws of the states and mingle with their population. To save him from this alternative, or perhaps utter annihilation, the general government kindly offers him a new home, and proposes to pay the whole expense of his removal and settlement.

In the consummation of a policy originating at an early period, and steadily pursued by every administration within the present century — so just to the states and so generous to the Indians — the executive feels it has a right to expect the cooperation of Congress and of all good and disinterested men. The states, moreover, have a right to demand it. It was substantially a part of the compact which made them members of our Confederacy. With Georgia there is an express contract; with the new states an implied one of equal obligation. Why, in authorizing Ohio, Indiana, Illinois, Missouri, Mississippi, and Alabama to form constitutions and become separate states, did Congress include within their limits extensive tracts of Indian lands, and, in some instances, powerful Indian tribes? Was it not understood by both parties that the power of the states was to be coextensive with their limits, and that, with all convenient dispatch, the general government should extinguish the Indian title and remove every obstruction to the complete jurisdiction of the state governments over the soil? Probably not one of those states would have accepted a separate existence — certainly it would never have been granted by Congress — had it been understood that they were to be confined forever to those small portions of their nominal territory the Indian title to which had at the time been extinguished.

It is, therefore, a duty which this government owes to the new states to extinguish as soon as possible the Indian title to all lands which Congress themselves have included within their limits. When this is done the duties of the general government in relation to the states and the Indians within their limits are at an end. The Indians may leave the state or not, as they choose. The purchase of their lands does not alter in the least their personal relations with the state government. No act of the general government has ever been deemed necessary to give the states jurisdiction over the persons of the Indians. That they possess by virtue of their sovereign power within their own limits in as full a manner before as after the purchase of the Indian lands; nor can this government add to or diminish it.

May we not hope, therefore, that all good citizens, and none more zealously than those who think the Indians oppressed by subjection to the laws of the states, will unite in attempting to open the eyes of those children of the forest to their true condition, and by a speedy removal to relieve them from all the evils, real or imaginary, present or prospective, with which they may be supposed to be threatened.

88.

"Shenandoah"

"Shenandoah" has been traced back to the first third of the nineteenth century; it seems fairly well established that it originated in the Missouri River Valley. The story of a white trader who fell in love with the daughter of an Indian chief followed the rivers to the ocean, where it became a capstan chantey; and at the same or a slightly later time, the U.S. Cavalry adopted the song under the name "The Wild Mizzourye." This rich and varied history is fitting for one of the most enduringly popular, and also one of the most genuine, of American folk songs.

❧ SHENANDOAH

Oh, Shenandoah, I long to hear you —
Away, you rolling river;
Oh, Shenandoah, I long to hear you —
Away, I'm bound away
'Cross the wide Missouri.

This white man loves your Indian maiden —
Away, you rolling river;
In my canoe with notions laden —
Away, I'm bound away
'Cross the wide Missouri.

Oh, Shenandoah, I love your daughter —
Away, you rolling river;
I'll take her 'cross that rolling water —
Away, I'm bound away
'Cross the wide Missouri.

Farewell, goodbye, I shall not grieve you —
Away, you rolling river;
Oh, Shenandoah, I'll not deceive you —
Away, I'm bound away
'Cross the wide Missouri.

The ship sails free, a gale is blowing —
Away, you rolling river;
The braces taut, the sheets aflowing —
Away, I'm bound away
'Cross the wide Missouri.

1831

89.

William Lloyd Garrison: For Immediate Abolition

Sometime during the year 1829, William Lloyd Garrison changed his mind about slavery. He had always advocated its abolition, but he had been a gradualist, holding that a slow, steady movement in the direction of freedom would be better for whites and blacks alike. But now he rejected this position, which he came to condemn; for "has not the experience of two centuries," he would say with his new understanding, "shown that gradualism in theory is perpetuity in practice?" The change of heart would not be important if it had not, for all practical purposes, launched the movement known as militant Abolitionism. Probably the most influential organ of this movement was the Liberator, *the Boston weekly that Garrison edited from its first issue, in January 1831, to its last, in December 1865 — the month that saw the ratification of the Thirteenth Amendment outlawing slavery. Portions of the famous salutatory of the* Liberator's *first issue are reprinted below.*

Source: *Liberator*, January 1, 1831.

In the month of August I issued proposals for publishing the *Liberator* in Washington City; but the enterprise, though hailed in different sections of the country, was palsied by public indifference. Since that time, the removal of the *Genius of Universal Emancipation* to the seat of government has rendered less imperious the establishment of a similar periodical in that quarter.

During my recent tour for the purpose of exciting the minds of the people by a series of discourses on the subject of slavery, every place that I visited gave fresh evidence of the fact that a greater revolution in public sentiment was to be effected in the free states — *and particularly in New England* — than at the South. I found contempt more bitter, opposition more active, detraction more relentless, prejudice more stubborn, and apathy more frozen than among slaveowners themselves. Of course, there were individual exceptions to the contrary. This state of things afflicted but did not dishearten me. I determined, at every hazard, to lift up the standard of emancipation in the eyes of the nation, *within sight of Bun-*

ker Hill and in the birthplace of liberty. That standard is now unfurled; and long may it float, unhurt by the spoliations of time or the missiles of a desperate foe — yea, till every chain be broken and every bondman set free! Let Southern oppressors tremble; let their secret abettors tremble; let their Northern apologists tremble; let all the enemies of the persecuted blacks tremble.

I deem the publication of my original prospectus unnecessary, as it has obtained a wide circulation. The principles therein inculcated will be steadily pursued in this paper, excepting that I shall not array myself as the political partisan of any man. In defending the great cause of human rights, I wish to derive the assistance of all religions and of all parties.

Assenting to the "self-evident truth" maintained in the American Declaration of Independence, "that all men are created equal and endowed by their Creator with certain inalienable rights, among which are life, liberty, and the pursuit of happiness," I shall strenuously contend for the immediate enfranchisement of our slave population. In Park Street Church, on the Fourth of July, 1829, in an address on slavery, I unreflectingly assented to the popular but pernicious doctrine of *gradual* abolition. I seize this opportunity to make a full and unequivocal recantation, and thus publicly to ask pardon of my God, of my country, and of my brethren, the poor slaves, for having uttered a sentiment so full of timidity, injustice, and absurdity. A similar recantation from my pen was published in the *Genius of Universal Emancipation* at Baltimore, in September 1829. My conscience is now satisfied.

I am aware that many object to the severity of my language; but is there not cause for severity? I *will be* as harsh as truth and as uncompromising as justice. On this subject I do not wish to think, or speak, or write with moderation. No! No! Tell a man whose house is on fire to give a moderate alarm; tell him to moderately rescue his wife from the hands of the ravisher; tell the mother to gradually extricate her babe from the fire into which it has fallen — but urge me not to use moderation in a cause like the present. I am in earnest; I will not equivocate; I will not excuse; I will not retreat a single inch — AND I WILL BE HEARD. The apathy of the people is enough to make every statue leap from its pedestal and to hasten the resurrection of the dead.

It is pretended that I am retarding the cause of emancipation by the coarseness of my invective and the precipitancy of my measures. *The charge is not true.* On this question my influence, humble as it is, is felt at this moment to a considerable extent, and shall be felt in coming years — not perniciously but beneficially: not as a curse but as a blessing — and posterity will bear testimony that I was right. I desire to thank God that He enables me to disregard "the fear of man which bringeth a snare," and to speak His truth in its simplicity and power.

Our Federal Union! It must and shall be preserved!

ANDREW JACKSON, toast, Jefferson Birthday banquet, 1830. John C. Calhoun rose after this toast and, his hand shaking so that the wine ran down the side of his glass, proposed: "The Union, *next to our liberty*, most dear! May we all remember that it can only be preserved by respecting the rights of the States and by distributing equally the benefits and burdens of the Union." Jackson's is the one that was remembered.

90.

An African American View of Civil Rights

While the Abolitionist movement dedicated its efforts to freeing slaves in the South, free blacks in the North found that in most states they were regarded as second-class citizens. Gustave de Beaumont, who toured America with Alexis de Tocqueville, noted in his novel Marie, *published in 1835, that free blacks throughout most of the states were prohibited from voting; from serving as judge, juror, or constable; from entering theaters, hotels, or public dining rooms (except as servants); from enrolling in schools; and in some states from reading or teaching their children to read. In response to such restrictions on their civil rights, an African American convention met in Philadelphia, June 6–11, 1831, and issued the following address to the nation.*

Source: *Liberator,* October 22, 1831.

Respected Brethren and Fellow Citizens:

In accordance with a resolution of the last Convention, we have again assembled in order to discharge those duties which have devolved upon us by your unanimous voices.

Our attention has been called to investigate the political standing of our brethren, wherever dispersed, but more particularly the situation of those in this great republic.

Abroad, we have been cheered with pleasant views of humanity and the steady, firm, and uncompromising march of equal liberty to the human family. Despotism, tyranny, and injustice have had to retreat in order to make way for the inalienable rights of man. Truth has conquered prejudice, and mankind are about to rise in the majesty and splendor of their native dignity.

The cause of general emancipation is gaining powerful and able friends abroad. Britain and Denmark have performed such deeds as will immortalize them for their humanity in the breasts of the philanthropists of the present day; while, as a just tribute to their virtues, after ages will yet erect imperishable monuments to their memory. (Would to God we could say thus of our own native soil!)

And it is only when we look to our own native land, to the birthplace of our *fathers,* to the land for whose prosperity their blood and our sweat have been shed and cruelly extorted, that the Convention has had cause to hang its head and blush. Laws, as cruel in themselves as they were unconstitutional and unjust, have in many places been enacted against our poor, unfriended, and unoffending brethren; laws (without a shadow of provocation on our part) at whose bare recital the very savage draws him up for fear of the contagion — looks noble and prides himself because he bears not the name of a Christian.

But the Convention would not wish to dwell long on this subject, and it is one that is too sensibly felt to need description.

We would wish to turn you from this

scene with an eye of pity and a breast glowing with mercy, praying that the recording angel may drop a tear which shall obliterate forever the remembrance of so foul a stain upon the national escutcheon of this great republic.

This spirit of persecution was the cause of our Convention. It was that first induced us to seek an asylum in the Canadas; and the Convention feel happy to report to their brethren that our efforts to establish a settlement in that province have not been made in vain. Our prospects are cheering; our friends and funds are daily increasing; wonders have been performed far exceeding our most sanguine expectations; already have our brethren purchased 800 acres of land — and 2,000 of them have left the soil of their birth, crossed the lines, and laid the foundation for a structure which promises to prove an asylum for the colored population of these United States. They have erected 200 log houses and have 500 acres under cultivation.

And now it is to your fostering care the Convention appeal, and we appeal to you as to men and brethren yet to enlarge their borders.

We therefore ask of you, brethren, we ask of you, philanthropists, of every color and of every kindred, to assist us in this undertaking. We look to a kind Providence and to you to say whether our desires shall be realized and our labors crowned with success.

The Convention has done its duty, and it now remains for you, brethren, to do yours. Various obstacles have been thrown in our way by those opposed to the elevation of the human species; but, thanks to an all-wise Providence, His goodness has yet cleared the way, and our advance has been slow but steady. The only thing now wanted is an accumulation of funds, in order to enable us to make a purchase agreeably to the direction of the first Convention; and, to effect that purpose, the Convention has recommended to the different societies engaged in that cause to persevere and prosecute their designs with doubled energy; and we would earnestly recommend to every colored man (who feels the weight of his degradation) to consider himself in duty bound to contribute his mite toward this great object. We would say to all that the prosperity of the rising generation mainly depends upon our active exertions.

Yes, it is with us to say whether they shall assume a rank and standing among the nations of the earth, as men and freemen, or whether they shall still be prized and held at market price. Oh, then, by a brother's love, and by all that makes man dear to man — awake in time! Be wise! Be free! Endeavor to walk with circumspection; be obedient to the laws of our common country; honor and respect its lawmakers and lawgivers; and, through all, let us not forget to respect ourselves.

During the deliberations of this Convention, we had the favor of advising and consulting with some of our most eminent and tried philanthropists — men of unblemished character and of acknowledged rank and standing. Our sufferings have excited their sympathy; our ignorance appealed to their humanity; and, brethren, we feel that gratitude is due to a kind and benevolent Creator, that our excitement and appeal have neither been in vain.

A plan has been proposed to the Convention for the erection of a college for the instruction of young men of color, on the manual labor system, by which the children of the poor may receive a regular classical education, as well as those of their more opulent brethren, and the charge will be so regulated as to put it within the reach of all. In support of this plan, a benevolent individual has offered the sum of $1,000, provided that we can obtain subscriptions to the amount of $19,000 in one year. The Convention has viewed the plan with considerable interest, and, after mature deliberation, on a candid investigation, feel strictly justified in recommending the same to the liberal patronage of our brethren, and respectfully solicit the aid of those philanthropists who feel an interest in sending light, knowledge, and truth to all of the human species.

To the friends of general education, we do believe that our appeal will not be in vain; for the present ignorant and degraded condition of many of our brethren in these United States (which has been a subject of much concern to the Convention) can excite no astonishment (although used by our enemies to show our inferiority in the scale of human beings); for, what opportunities have they possessed for mental cultivation or improvement? Mere ignorance, however, in a people divested of the means of acquiring information by books, or an extensive connection with the world, is no just criterion of their intellectual incapacity; and it has been actually seen, in various remarkable instances, that the degradation of the mind and character, which has been too hastily imputed to a people kept, as we are, at a distance from those sources of knowledge which abound in civilized and enlightened communities, has resulted from no other causes than our unhappy situation and circumstances.

True philanthropy disdains to adopt those prejudices against any people which have no better foundation than accidental diversities of color, and refuses to determine without substantial evidence and incontestable fact as the basis of her judgment. And it is in order to remove these prejudices, which are the actual causes of our ignorance, that we have appealed to our friends in support of the contemplated institution.

The Convention has not been unmindful of the operations of the American Colonization Society, and it would respectfully suggest to that august body of learning, talent, and worth that, in our humble opinion, strengthened, too, by the opinions of eminent men in this country as well as in Europe, that they are pursuing the direct road to perpetuate slavery, with all its unchristianlike concomitants, in this boasted land of freedom; and as citizens and men whose best blood is sapped to gain popularity for that institution, we would, in the most feeling manner, beg of them to desist, or, if we must be sacrificed to their philanthropy, we would rather die at home. Many of our fathers, and some of us, have fought and bled for the liberty, independence, and peace which you now enjoy and, surely, it would be ungenerous and unfeeling in you to deny us a humble and quiet grave in that country which gave us birth!

In conclusion, the Convention would remind our brethren that knowledge is power, and to that end we call on you to sustain and support by all honorable, energetic, and necessary means those presses which are devoted to our instruction and elevation; to foster and encourage the mechanical arts and sciences among our brethren; to encourage simplicity, neatness, temperance, and economy in our habits, taking due care always to give the preference to the production of freemen wherever it can be had. Of the utility of a general fund, the Convention believes there can exist but one sentiment, and that is for a speedy establishment of the same. Finally, we trust our brethren will pay due care to take such measures as will ensure a general and equal representation in the next Convention.

91.

John Marshall: *Cherokee Nation v. State of Georgia*

President Andrew Jackson's policy of extinguishing Native American title to ancestral lands, employed with success against the Choctaws and Chickasaws, was seriously challenged in Cherokee Nation v. State of Georgia. *In 1828 the government of Georgia declared null all laws, titles, and customs of the Cherokee Indians inhabiting the northwest portion of that state. The Cherokees, having previously declared themselves an independent nation, appealed to the U.S. Supreme Court to restrain the Georgia government. Though he was sympathetic to the plight of the Cherokees, Chief Justice John Marshall led the Court in refusing to grant such an injunction and, in the following opinion, delivered in 1831, declared that the Cherokee nation was not a foreign government but a domestic dependent nation in pupilage to the state.*

Source: 5 Peters 1.

Mr. Chief Justice Marshall delivered the opinion of the Court:

This bill is brought by the Cherokee Nation, praying an injunction to restrain the state of Georgia from the execution of certain laws of that state, which as is alleged, go directly to annihilate the Cherokees as a political society, and to seize, for the use of Georgia, the lands of the nation which have been assured to them by the United States in solemn treaties repeatedly made and still in force.

If courts were permitted to indulge their sympathies, a case better calculated to excite them can scarcely be imagined. A people once numerous, powerful, and truly independent, found by our ancestors in the quiet and uncontrolled possession of an ample domain, gradually sinking beneath our superior policy, our arts, and our arms, have yielded their lands by successive treaties, each of which contains a solemn guarantee of the residue, until they retain no more of their formerly extensive territory than is deemed necessary to their comfortable subsistence. To preserve this remnant the present application is made.

Before we can look into the merits of the case, a preliminary inquiry presents itself. Has this Court jurisdiction of the cause?

The 3rd Article of the Constitution describes the extent of the judicial power. The 2nd Section closes an enumeration of the cases to which it is extended, with "controversies" "between a state or the citizens thereof, and foreign states, citizens, or subjects." A subsequent clause of the same section gives the Supreme Court original jurisdiction in all cases in which a state shall be a party. The party defendant may then unquestionably be sued in this Court. May the plaintiff sue in it? Is the Cherokee Nation a foreign state in the sense in which that term is used in the Constitution?

The counsel for the plaintiffs have maintained the affirmative of this proposition with great earnestness and ability. So much of the argument as was intended to prove the character of the Cherokees as a state, as a distinct political society separated from others, capable of managing its own affairs

Chief Justice John Marshall by Robert Sully

and governing itself, has, in the opinion of a majority of the judges, been completely successful. They have been uniformly treated as a state from the settlement of our country. The numerous treaties made with them by the United States recognize them as a people capable of maintaining the relations of peace and war, of being responsible in their political character for any violation of their engagements, or for any aggression committed on the citizens of the United States by any individual of their community. Laws have been enacted in the spirit of these treaties. The acts of our government plainly recognize the Cherokee Nation as a state, and the courts are bound by those acts.

A question of much more difficulty remains. Do the Cherokees constitute a foreign state in the sense of the Constitution?

The counsel have shown conclusively that they are not a state of the Union, and have insisted that individually they are aliens, not owing allegiance to the United States. An aggregate of aliens composing a state must, they say, be a foreign state. Each individual being foreign, the whole must be foreign.

This argument is imposing, but we must examine it more closely before we yield to it. The condition of the Indians in relation to the United States is perhaps unlike that of any other two people in existence. In the general, nations not owing a common allegiance are foreign to each other. The term "foreign nation" is, with strict propriety, applicable by either to the other. But the relation of the Indians to the United States is marked by peculiar and cardinal distinctions which exist nowhere else.

The Indian Territory is admitted to compose part of the United States. In all our maps, geographical treatises, histories, and laws, it is so considered. In all our intercourse with foreign nations, in our commercial regulations, in any attempt at intercourse between Indians and foreign nations, they are considered as within the jurisdictional limits of the United States, subject to many of those restraints which are imposed upon our own citizens. They acknowledge themselves in their treaties to be under the protection of the United States; they admit that the United States shall have the sole and exclusive right of regulating the trade with them and managing all their affairs as they think proper; and the Cherokees in particular were allowed by the Treaty of Hopewell, which preceded the Constitution, "to send a deputy of their choice, whenever they think fit, to Congress." Treaties were made with some tribes by the state of New York under a then unsettled construction of the Confederation, by which they ceded all their lands to that state, taking back a limited grant to themselves in which they admit their dependence.

Though the Indians are acknowledged to have an unquestionable and, heretofore, unquestioned right to the lands they occupy until that right shall be extinguished by a voluntary cession to our government, yet it may well be doubted whether those tribes which reside within the acknowledged boundaries of the United States can, with strict accuracy, be denominated foreign nations. They may more correctly, perhaps, be denominated domestic dependent nations. They occupy a territory to which we assert a title independent of their will, which must take effect in point of possession when their right of possession ceases. Meanwhile, they are in a state of pupilage. Their relation to the United States resembles that of a ward to his guardian.

They look to our government for protection; rely upon its kindness and its power; appeal to it for relief to their wants; and address the President as their "great father." They and their country are considered by foreign nations, as well as by ourselves, as being so completely under the sovereignty and dominion of the United States that any attempt to acquire their lands or to form a political connection with them would be considered by all as an invasion of our territory and an act of hostility.

These considerations go far to support the opinion that the framers of our Constitution had not the Indian tribes in view when they opened the courts of the Union to controversies between a state or the citizens thereof and foreign states.

In considering this subject, the habits and usages of the Indians in their intercourse with their white neighbors ought not to be entirely disregarded. At the time the Constitution was framed, the idea of appealing to an American court of justice for an assertion of right or a redress of wrong had perhaps never entered the mind of an Indian or of his tribe. Their appeal was to the tomahawk, or to the government. This was well understood by the statesmen who framed the Constitution of the United States, and might furnish some reason for omitting to enumerate them among the parties who might sue in the courts of the Union. Be this as it may, the peculiar relations between the United States and the Indians occupying our territory are such that we should feel much difficulty in considering them as designated by the term "foreign state" were there no other part of the Constitution which might shed light on the meaning of these words. But we think that in construing them, considerable aid is furnished by that clause in the 8th Section of

the 3rd Article, which empowers Congress to "regulate commerce with foreign nations, and among the several states, and with the Indian tribes."

In this clause they are as clearly contradistinguished by a name appropriate to themselves from foreign nations as from the several states composing the Union. They are designated by a distinct appellation; and as this appellation can be applied to neither of the others, neither can the appellation distinguishing either of the others be in fair construction applied to them. The objects to which the power of regulating commerce might be directed are divided into three distinct classes: foreign nations, the several states, and Indian tribes. When forming this article, the Convention considered them as entirely distinct. We cannot assume that the distinction was lost in framing a subsequent article, unless there be something in its language to authorize the assumption. . . .

"Foreign nations" is a general term, the application of which to Indian tribes, when used in the American Constitution, is at best extremely questionable. In one article in which a power is given to be exercised in regard to foreign nations generally, and to the Indian tribes particularly, they are mentioned as separate in terms clearly contradistinguishing them from each other. We perceive plainly that the Constitution in this article does not comprehend Indian tribes in the general term "foreign nations"; not, we presume, because a tribe may not be a nation but because it is not foreign to the United States. When, afterward, the term "foreign state" is introduced, we cannot impute to the Convention the intention to desert its former meaning and to comprehend Indian tribes within it, unless the context force that construction on us. We find nothing in the context and nothing in the subject of the article which leads to it.

The Court has bestowed its best attention on this question and, after mature deliberation, the majority is of opinion that an Indian tribe or nation within the United States is not a foreign state in the sense of the Constitution, and cannot maintain an action in the courts of the United States.

A serious additional objection exists to the jurisdiction of the Court. Is the matter of the bill the proper subject for judicial inquiry and decision? It seeks to restrain a state from the forcible exercise of legislative power over a neighboring people, asserting their independence; their right to which the state denies. On several of the matters alleged in the bill, for example on the laws making it criminal to exercise the usual powers of self-government in their own country by the Cherokee Nation, this Court cannot interpose, at least in the form in which those matters are presented.

That part of the bill which respects the land occupied by the Indians, and prays the aid of the Court to protect their possession, may be more doubtful. The mere question of right might perhaps be decided by this Court in a proper case with proper parties. But the Court is asked to do more than decide on the title. The bill requires us to control the legislature of Georgia, and to restrain the exertion of its physical force. The propriety of such an interposition by the Court may be well questioned. It savors too much of the exercise of political power to be within the proper province of the Judicial Department. But the opinion on the point respecting parties makes it unnecessary to decide this question.

If it be true that the Cherokee Nation have rights, this is not the tribunal in which those rights are to be asserted. If it be true that wrongs have been inflicted and that still greater are to be apprehended, this is not the tribunal which can redress the past or prevent the future.

The motion for an injunction is denied.

92.

Thomas Hart Benton: The Mischiefs of a National Bank

President Jackson's request in 1829 that Congress begin considering renewal of the charter of the Second Bank of the United States opened the way for the "Bank War." The Ways and Means Committee of the House of Representatives reported favorably on renewing the charter in April 1830. Senator Thomas Hart Benton of Missouri, a spokesman for Western interests, attacked the Bank in the following speech of February 2, 1831. Benton voiced all the objections repeated again and again during the Bank War; his speech typified the Jacksonian attitude, which ascribed to the Bank's influence a growing disregard for the Constitution, and the pernicious increase of national power, of class privilege, and of financial control.

Source: *Debates*, VII, pp. 46-78.

First, Mr. President, I object to the renewal of the charter of the Bank of the United States, because I look upon the bank as an institution too great and powerful to be tolerated in a government of free and equal laws. Its power is that of a purse, a power more potent than that of the sword; and this power it possesses to a degree and extent that will enable this bank to draw to itself too much of the political power of this Union and too much of the individual property of the citizens of these states. The money power of the bank is both direct and indirect. . . .

The direct power of the bank is now prodigious and, in the event of the renewal of the charter, must speedily become boundless and uncontrollable. The bank is now authorized to own effects, lands inclusive, to the amount of $55 million, and to issue notes to the amount of $35 million more; this makes $90 million. And, in addition to this vast sum, there is an opening for an unlimited increase; for there is a dispensation in the charter to issue as many more notes as Congress, by law, may permit. This opens the door to boundless emissions; for what can be more unbounded than the will and pleasure of successive Congresses?

The indirect power of the bank cannot be stated in figures; but it can be shown to be immense. In the first place, it has the keeping of the public moneys, now amounting to $26 million per annum (the Post Office Department included), and the gratuitous use of the undrawn balances, large enough to constitute, in themselves, the capital of a great state bank. In the next place, its promissory notes are receivable, by law, in purchase of all property owned by the United States and in payment of all debts due them; and this may increase its power to the amount of the annual revenue by creating a demand for its notes to that amount. In the third place, it wears the name of the United States and has the federal government for a partner; and this name and this partnership identifies the credit of the bank with the credit of the Union. In the fourth place, it is armed with authority to disparage and discredit the notes of other banks by excluding them from all payments to the United States; and this, added to all its other powers, direct and indirect, makes this institution the uncontrollable monarch of the moneyed system of the Union.

To whom is all this power granted? To a company of private individuals, many of them foreigners, and the mass of them residing in a remote and narrow corner of the Union, unconnected by any sympathy with the fertile regions of the Great Valley in which the natural power of this Union — the power of numbers — will be found to reside long before the renewed term of a second charter would expire.

By whom is all this power to be exercised? By a directory of seven (it may be), governed by a majority of four (it may be); and none of these elected by the people or responsible to them. Where is it to be exercised? At a single city, distant a thousand miles from some of the states, receiving the produce of none of them (except one); no interest in the welfare of any of them (except one); no commerce with the people; with branches in every state; and every branch subject to the secret and absolute orders of the supreme central head: thus constituting a system of centralism hostile to the federative principle of our Union, encroaching upon the wealth and power of the states, and organized upon a principle to give the highest effect to the greatest power. This mass of power, thus concentrated, thus ramified, and thus directed, must necessarily become, under a prolonged existence, the absolute monopolist of American money, the sole manufacturer of paper currency, and the sole authority (for authority it will be) to which the federal government, the state governments, the great cities, corporate bodies, merchants, traders, and every private citizen must, of necessity, apply for every loan which their exigencies may demand. . . .

Second: I object to the continuance of this bank because its tendencies are dangerous and pernicious to the government and the people.

What are the tendencies of a great moneyed power connected with the government and controlling its fiscal operations? Are they not dangerous to every interest, public and private, political as well as pecuniary? I say they are, and briefly enumerate the heads of each mischief.

1. Such a bank tends to subjugate the government. . . .

2. It tends to collusions between the government and the bank in terms of the loans. . . .

3. It tends to create public debt by facilitating public loans and substituting unlimited supplies of paper for limited supplies of coin. . . .

4. It tends to beget and prolong unnecessary wars by furnishing the means of carrying them on without recurrence to the people. . . .

5. It tends to aggravate the inequality of fortunes; to make the rich richer and the poor poorer; to multiply nabobs and paupers; and to deepen and widen the gulf which separates Dives from Lazarus. . . .

6. It tends to make and to break fortunes by the flux and reflux of paper. Profuse issues and sudden contractions perform this operation, which can be repeated, like planetary and pestilential visitations, in every cycle of so many years; at every periodical return transferring millions from the actual possessors of property to the Neptunes who preside over the flux and reflux of paper. . . .

Third: I object to the renewal of the charter on account of the exclusive privileges and antirepublican monopoly which it gives to the stockholders. . . .

1. The name, the credit, and the revenues of the United States are given up to the use of this company and constitute in themselves an immense capital to bank upon. The name of the United States, like that of the king, is a tower of strength; and this strong tower is now an outwork to defend the citadel of a moneyed corporation. The credit of the Union is incalculable; and, of this credit, as going with the name and being in partnership with the United States, the same corporation now has possession.

The revenues of the Union are $26 million, including the Post Office; and all this is so much capital in the hands of the bank, because the revenue is received by it and is payable in its promissory notes.

2. Other banks depend upon their credit for the receivability of their notes; but this favored institution has law on its side, and a chartered right to compel the reception of its paper by the federal government. The immediate consequence of this extraordinary privilege is that the United States becomes virtually bound to stand security for the bank, as much so as if she had signed a bond to that effect; and must stand forward to sustain the institution in all emergencies in order to save her own revenue. This is what has already happened, some ten years ago, in the early progress of the bank and when the immense aid given it by the federal government enabled it to survive the crisis of its own overwhelming mismanagement.

3. To hold the moneys of the United States in deposit without making compensation for the use of the undrawn balances. . . .

4. To discredit and disparage the notes of all other banks by excluding them from the collection of the federal revenue. This results from the collection — no, not the collection but the receipt of the revenue having been committed to the bank, and, along with it, the virtual execution of the joint resolution of 1816 to regulate the collection of the federal revenue. The execution of that resolution was intended to be vested in the secretary of the treasury — a disinterested arbiter between rival banks; but it may be considered as virtually devolved upon the Bank of the United States, and powerfully increases the capacity of that institution to destroy or subjugate all other banks.

The notes of the state banks excluded from revenue payments are discredited and disparaged and fall into the hands of brokers at all places where they are not issued and payable. They cease to insulate at all the points to which the exclusion extends. I am informed that the notes of the banks south of the Potomac and Ohio, even those of the Lower Mississippi, are generally refused at the United States' Branch Bank in St. Louis, and, in consequence, are expelled from circulation in Missouri and Illinois and the neighboring districts. . . . This power to disparage the notes of all other banks is a power to injure them; and, added to all the other privileges of the Bank of the United States, is a power to destroy them! . . .

Policy may restrain the destroying faculties for the present; but they exist and will come forth when interest prompts and policy permits. They have been exercised; and the general prostration of the Southern and Western banks attests the fact. They will be exercised (the charter being renewed), and the remaining state banks will be swept with the besom of destruction. Not that all will have their signs knocked down and their doors closed up; far worse than that to many of them. Subjugation, in preference to destruction, will be the fate of many. . . .

The state banks, spared by the sword, will be passed under the yoke. They will become subordinate parts in the great machine. Their place in the scale of subordination will be one degree below the rank of the legitimate branches; their business, to perform the work which it would be too disreputable for the legitimate branches to perform. This will be the fate of the state banks which are allowed to keep up their signs and to set open their doors; and thus the entire moneyed power of the Union would fall into the hands of one single institution, whose inexorable and invisible mandates, emanating from a center, would pervade the Union, giving or withholding money according to its own sovereign will and absolute pleasure.

To a favored state, to an individual, or a class of individuals, favored by the central power, the golden stream of Pactolus would flow direct. To all such the munificent mandates of the high directory would come, as the fabled god made his terrestrial visit of love and desire, enveloped in a shower of gold. But to others — to those not favored and to those hated — the mandates of this same directory would be as "the planetary plague which hangs its poison in the sick air." Death to them! Death to all who minister to their wants! What a state of things! What a condition for a confederacy of states! What grounds for alarm and terrible apprehension, when in a confederacy of such vast extent, so many independent states, so many rival commercial cities, so much sectional jealousy, such violent political parties, such fierce contests for power, there should be but one moneyed tribunal before which all the rival and contending elements must appear! But one single dispenser of money to which every citizen, every trader, every merchant, every manufacturer, every planter, every corporation, every city, every state, and the federal government itself must apply, in every emergency, for the most indispensable loan! And this in the face of the fact that in every contest for human rights the great moneyed institutions of the world have uniformly been found on the side of kings and nobles, against the lives and liberties of the people.

5. To hold real estate, receive rents, and retain a body of tenantry. This privilege is hostile to the nature of our republican government and inconsistent with the nature and design of a banking institution. Republics want freeholders, not landlords and tenants. . . . No one, when this charter was granted, presumed to speak in favor of incorporating a society of landlords, especially foreign landlords, to buy lands, build houses, rent tenements, and retain tenantry. Loans of money was the object in view, and the purchase of real estate is incompatible with that object. Instead of remaining bank-

ers, the corporators may turn land speculators; instead of having money to lend, they may turn you out tenants to vote. To an application for a loan, they may answer, and answer truly, that they have no money on hand; and the reason may be that they have laid it out in land. . . .

The bank is now the greatest moneyed power in the Union; in the event of the renewal of its charter, it will soon be the sole one. Sole dispenser of money, it will soon be the chief owner of property. To unlimited means of acquisition would be united perpetuity of tenure, for a corporation never dies and is free from the operation of the laws which govern the descent and distribution of real estate in the hands of individuals. . . .

Monopolies and perpetual succession are the bane of republics. Our ancestors took care to provide against them by abolishing entails and primogeniture. Even the glebes of the church, lean and few as they were in most of the states, fell under the republican principle of limited tenures. All the states abolished the antirepublican tenures; but Congress reestablishes them, and in a manner more dangerous and offensive than before the Revolution. They are now given, not generally but to few; not to natives only but to foreigners also; for foreigners are large owners of this bank. And thus the principles of the Revolution sink before the privileges of an incorporated company. . . .

6. To deal in pawns, merchandise, and bills of exchange. . . . Thus the bank is an incorporated company of pawnbrokers and merchants, as well as an incorporation of landlords and land speculators; and this derogatory privilege, like the others, is copied from the old Bank of England charter of 1694.

Bills of exchange are also subjected to the traffic of this bank. It is a traffic unconnected with the trade of banking, dangerous for a great bank to hold, and now operating most injuriously in the South and West. It is the process which drains these quarters of the Union of their gold and silver and stifles the growth of a fair commerce in the products of the country. The merchants, to make remittances, buy bills of exchange from the branch banks instead of buying produce from the farmers. The bills are paid for in gold and silver; and, eventually, the gold and silver are sent to the mother bank, or to the branches in the Eastern cities, either to meet these bills or to replenish their coffers and to furnish vast loans to favorite states or individuals. The bills sell cheap, say a fraction of 1 percent; they are, therefore, a good remittance to the merchant. To the bank the operation is doubly good; for even the half of 1 percent on bills of exchange is a great profit to the institution which monopolizes that business, while the collection and delivery to the branches of all the hard money in the country is a still more considerable advantage.

Under this system, the best of the Western banks — I do not speak of those which had no foundations and sank under the weight of neighborhood opinion, but those which deserved favor and confidence — sank ten years ago. Under this system, the entire West is now undergoing a silent, general, and invisible drain of its hard money; and, if not quickly arrested, these states will soon be, so far as the precious metals are concerned, no more than the empty skin of an immolated victim.

7. To establish branches in the different states without their consent and in defiance of their resistance. No one can deny the degrading and injurious tendency of this privilege. It derogates from the sovereignty of a state, tramples upon her laws, injures her revenue and commerce, lays open her government to the attacks of centralism, impairs the property of her citizens, and fastens a vampire on her bosom to suck out her gold and silver.

a. It derogates from her sovereignty, because the central institution may impose its intrusive branches upon the state without her consent and in defiance of her resistance. The state of Alabama, but four years ago, by a resolve of her legislature, remonstrated against the intrusion of a branch upon her. She protested against the favor. Was the will of the state respected? On the contrary, was not a branch instantaneously forced upon her, as if, by the suddenness of the action, to make a striking and conspicuous display of the omnipotence of the bank and the nullity of the state?

b. It tramples upon her laws because, according to the decision of the Supreme Court, the bank and all its branches are wholly independent of state legislation; and it tramples on them again because it authorizes foreigners to hold lands and tenements in every state, contrary to the laws of many of them; and because it admits of the mortmain tenure, which is condemned by all the republican states in the Union.

c. It injures her revenue because the bank stock, under the decision of the Supreme Court, is not liable to taxation. And thus, foreigners and nonresident Americans, who monopolize the money of the state, who hold its best lands and town lots, who meddle in its elections, and suck out its gold and silver, and perform no military duty, are exempted from paying taxes in proportion to their wealth for the support of the state whose laws they trample upon and whose benefits they usurp.

d. It subjects the state to the dangerous maneuvers and intrigues of centralism by means of tenants, debtors, bank officers, and bank money which the central directory retain in the state and may embody and direct against it in its elections and in its legislative and judicial proceedings.

e. It tends to impair the property of the citizens and, in some instances, that of the states by destroying the state banks in which they have invested their money.

f. It is injurious to the commerce of the states (I speak of the Western states) by substituting a trade in bills of exchange for a trade in the products of the country.

g. It fastens a vampire on the bosom of the state, to suck away its gold and silver and to cooperate with the course of trade, of federal legislation, and of exchange, in draining the South and West of all their hard money. The Southern states, with their $30 million of annual exports in cotton, rice, and tobacco, and the Western states, with their $12 million of provisions and tobacco exported from New Orleans, and $5 million consumed in the South and on the Lower Mississippi — that is to say, with three-fifths of the marketable productions of the Union — are not able to sustain 30 specie paying banks; while the minority of the states north of the Potomac, without any of the great staples for export, have above 400 of such banks. These states, without rice, without cotton, without tobacco, without sugar, and with less flour and provisions to export, are saturated with gold and silver; while the Southern and Western states, with all the real sources of wealth, are in a state of the utmost destitution. . . .

8. Exemption of the stockholders from individual liability on the failure of the bank. . . .

9. To have the United States for a partner. . . . Disadvantageous as this partnership must be to the United States in a moneyed point of view, there is a far more grave and serious aspect under which to view it. It is the political aspect resulting from the union between the bank and the government. This union has been tried in England and has been found there to be just as disastrous a conjunction as the union between church and state. It is the conjunction of the lender and the borrower, and Holy Writ has told us which of these categories will be master of the other. But suppose they agree to drop rivalry and unite their resources, suppose they combine and make a push for political power; how great

is the mischief which they may not accomplish! . . .

10. To have foreigners for partners. This, Mr. President, will be a strange story to be told in the West. The downright and upright people of that unsophisticated region believe that words mean what they signify, and that "the Bank of the United States" is the Bank of the United States. How great then must be their astonishment to learn that this belief is a false conception, and that this bank (its whole name to the contrary notwithstanding) is just as much the bank of foreigners as it is of the federal government. . . .

It is no purpose to say that the foreign stockholders cannot be voters or directors. The answer to that suggestion is this: The foreigners have the money; they pay down the cash, and want no accommodations; they are lenders, not borrowers; and, in a great moneyed institution, such stockholders must have the greatest influence. The name of this bank is a deception upon the public. It is not the bank of the federal government, as its name would import, nor of the states which compose this Union; but chiefly of private individuals, foreigners as well as natives, denizens, and naturalized subjects.

They own $28 million of the stock, the federal government but $7 million; and these $7 million are precisely balanced by the stock of the aliens. The federal government and the aliens are equal, owning one-fifth each; and there would be as much truth in calling it the English Bank as the Bank of the United States. Now mark a few of the privileges which this charter gives to these foreigners. To be landholders, in defiance of the state laws which forbid aliens to hold land; to be landlords by incorporation and to hold American citizens for tenants; to hold lands in mortmain; to

be pawnbrokers and merchants by incorporation; to pay the revenue of the United States in their own notes; in short, to do everything which I have endeavored to point out in the long and hideous list of exclusive privileges granted to this bank.

If I have shown it to be dangerous for the United States to be in partnership with its own citizens, how much stronger is not the argument against a partnership with foreigners? What a prospect for loans when at war with a foreign power, and the subjects of that power large owners of the bank here, from which alone, or from banks liable to be destroyed by it, we can obtain money to carry on the war! What a state of things if, in the division of political parties, one of these parties and the foreigners, coalescing, should have the exclusive control of all the money in the Union, and, in addition to the money, should have bodies of debtors, tenants, and bank officers stationed in all the states, with a supreme and irresponsible system of centralism to direct the whole! Dangers from such contingencies are too great and obvious to be insisted upon. . . .

11. Exemption from due course of law for violations of its charter. This is a privilege which affects the administration of justice and stands without example in the annals of republican legislation. . . .

12. To have all these unjust privileges secured to the corporators as a monopoly, by a pledge of the public faith to charter no other bank. This is the most hideous feature in the whole mass of deformity. If these banks are beneficial institutions, why not several? One, at least, and each independent of the other, to each great section of the Union? If malignant, why create one? The restriction constitutes the monopoly and renders more invidious what was sufficiently hateful in itself.

93.

Francis Patrick Kenrick: Episcopal Rights and Parish Autonomy

Church polity in most Protestant denominations had come to be based on parish autonomy, with each congregation conducting its own affairs and owning its own property. By contrast, the Roman Catholic Church had brought with it from Europe the hierarchical structure by which its affairs had been conducted for centuries. But in a democratic society this structure was threatened for a time by the desire of laymen to conduct their parish affairs on the Protestant pattern. A case in point is the power struggle that occurred in Philadelphia in 1830 and 1831, with the bishop on one side, and the Reverend William Hogan and the trustees of St. Mary's congregation on the other. To resolve the situation the Reverend Francis Kenrick was appointed coadjutor of the diocese. He used his full episcopal authority to oppose the trustees of the parish. On April 22, 1831, Kenrick delivered the following pastoral address to the diocese, outlining Catholic principles of church government. Within a month St. Mary's parish had acquiesced in his demands.

Source: Joseph L. J. Kirlin, *Catholicity in Philadelphia*, Philadelphia, 1909, pp. 270-273.

Beloved Children in Christ:

With much anguish of heart we have, through the deepest sense of duty, ordered the cessation from all sacred functions in the Church and cemeteries of St. Mary's, under penalty of the ecclesiastical censure of suspension, to be incurred by any clergyman attempting the exercise of any such function. Of the cause which led to the adoption of this painful measure you are already apprised; yet we deem it expedient to state the events that led to it, clearly and distinctly, lest any amongst you should imagine that we had in any degree ceased to cherish that tender affection and zeal for your happiness and salvation which, from our first coming amongst you, we invariably manifested. Though discharging the duties of the sublime office originally committed to the apostles of Christ, we became little ones in the midst of you, as a nurse should cherish her children. So desirous of you, we would gladly have imparted to you not only the gospel of God but also our own souls, because you were become most dear to us.

At an early period, after we had made the episcopal visitation of the diocese and promulgated the Jubilee throughout the churches of the city, namely, on the 27th day of December last, we resolved to devote ourselves to the discharge of the pastoral duties amongst you, and we officially communicated to the Board of Trustees our determination, which sprang only from the sincerest zeal for your spiritual welfare. To our astonishment and affliction, the lay trustees made the communication a matter

Portrait of Archbishop Francis P. Kenrick (1796-1863)

of deliberation instead of simply recording it on their books and even expressed to us their dissatisfaction, though the charter of incorporation gives them no right whatever of interference under any shape or form in pastoral appointments, and though the discipline of the Catholic Church does not allow such interference. Having complained in a solemn and paternal manner, nowise unworthy the sanctity of the pulpit or the meekness of the prelacy, of this attempt to impede the conscientious exercise of our episcopal authority, we received from the lay trustees a letter dated the 12th of January, wherein, in terms not usually employed by the faithful to the bishops of the Church, they expressed their determination to persevere in their resistance. We patiently bore their opposition in the hope that our untiring efforts for the instruction and sanctification of our flock would convince them of the justice of our views and induce them spontaneously to desist from a course directly opposed to the principles of church government and the provisions of the char-

ter; and we carefully abstained from all attempts to influence the election, avowing, nevertheless, publicly in our pastoral address, our unchangeable resolution to maintain, at every risk and sacrifice, the spiritual rights with whose guardianship we have been entrusted.

More than three months having passed, and the lay trustees after their reelection having proved their determination to persist in disregarding our corporate rights as chief pastor by assembling a board without our participation, though the charter declares the three pastors of St. Mary's members of the board by their office, we could no longer tolerate this violation of our chartered rights which implied manifestly the denial of our pastoral office. We therefore, in a circular letter of the 12th of April, apprised the pewholders of the illegal course of the lay trustees and of the penalty decreed by the Provincial Council and Apostolic See against such interference in pastoral appointments.

On the 15th we received a letter signed by seven of their number, the other having refused to persevere with them in their resistance to the episcopal authority. In this communication they denied having assumed or asserted the right of choosing their own pastors; but they did not venture to deny that they had indirectly (as we had charged them in our circular) asserted and assumed it by rejecting the pastors duly appointed, and especially by violating our corporate rights as chief pastor. We called on them for a formal and explicit disclaimer of all right of interfering, directly or indirectly, in the appointment, rejection, or dismissal of pastors, and for a pledge that they would henceforward act according to the provisions of the charter. But they explicitly declined that disclaimer and pledge, and six of them merely offered to subscribe a memorandum declaring that they agreed to recognize us and the Rev. Jeremiah Keilly as clerical members of the Board of Trustees.

Such an agreement, so far from being a practical proof of their adherence to the Catholic principles of church government and of their respect for the provisions of the charter, was a measure calculated to confirm and establish the assumed right of agreeing to or dissenting from the episcopal appointments.

The letter which accompanied the memorandum contained still further evidence that the lay trustees claimed and attempted to exercise in our regard this power, since they grounded their assent to our future exercise of the pastoral office on the actual want of another pastor; thereby intimating that, though we had since the 27th of December declared our determination to act thenceforward as chief pastor of St. Mary's, and though we had since that time constantly performed all the duties of that office, yet we were not in reality chief pastor hitherto because the lay trustees had withheld their assent and approbation.

Under such circumstances we could not, consistently with our attachment to Catholic principles and the rights of our office, recall the order for the cessation from sacred functions in St. Mary's Church and cemeteries, which we had on the preceding evening issued when the receipt of the letter of the seven trustees had convinced us of their determination to persevere in eluding episcopal authority. We did indeed abstain from issuing the more solemn sentence of interdict, which the Provincial Council authorizes us to pronounce, though we well knew that the evil which called for this severity was not of recent growth but had originated and been matured in times of schism and confusion and had long since defied every mild remedy.

We still hope that the speedy acknowledgment of the Catholic principles of church government may enable us not only to abstain from any more painful exercise of authority but even to restore to our beloved children in Christ the consolation of worshiping in the splendid edifice in which you and your fathers worshiped, and which your and their generous piety erected, and the legislative authority of this state secured for the exercise of the Roman Catholic religion. We willingly persuade ourselves that those who have hitherto resisted the conscientious and mild exercise of episcopal authority acted under misconception; and we indulge the hope that they will soon render us that rational and Christian obedience and subjection which the apostle requires of the faithful to the prelates of the Church, whom the Holy Ghost has placed bishops to rule the Church of God purchased with His blood. We shall hail with joy and thanksgiving to God their return to duty and endeavor by all the exhibitions of paternal tenderness and affection to obliterate from their minds, and from yours, the remembrance of these days of affliction wherein the Church sits solitary that was full of people.

May the God of peace crush Satan speedily under your feet. The grace of our Lord Jesus Christ be with you.

94.

Emma Hart Willard: "Rocked in the Cradle of the Deep"

Emma Hart Willard is best known as an educational innovator who was influential in the nineteenth-century movement to provide higher education for women. But she also wrote poetry on occasion and published one slim volume, The Fulfillment of a Promise, *in 1831. Most of the poems were very bad and have been totally forgotten; but one of them, "Rocked in the Cradle of the Deep," may be as widely known as any poem ever written in America. It was set to music by Joseph Philip Knight, who composed many fine sea songs.*

Source: *Famous Songs and Those Who Made Them,* Helen K. Johnson and Frederic Dean, eds., New York, 1895, pp. 52-54.

ROCKED IN THE CRADLE OF THE DEEP

Rocked in the cradle of the deep
I lay me down in peace to sleep;
Secure I rest upon the wave,
For Thou, O Lord! hast power to save.
I know Thou wilt not slight my call,
For Thou dost mark the sparrow's fall!
And calm and peaceful is my sleep,
Rocked in the cradle of the deep.

When in the dead of night I lie
And gaze upon the trackless sky,
The star-bespangled heavenly scroll,
The boundless waters as they roll —
I feel Thy wondrous power to save
From perils of the stormy wave.
Rocked in the cradle of the deep,
I calmly rest and soundly sleep.

And such the trust that still were mine,
Though stormy winds swept o'er the brine,
Or though the tempest's fiery breath
Roused me from sleep to wreck and death!
In ocean cave, still safe with Thee,
The germ of immortality!
And calm and peaceful is my sleep,
Rocked in the cradle of the deep.

95.

FREDERICK ROBINSON: A Brief Exposure of Bar Associations

The Jacksonian Era's emphasis on the rights of the "common man" provided fertile ground for native American distrust of any "privileged" groups. In the following letter of June 25, 1831, to attorney Rufus Choate, Frederick Robinson attacked the bar associations as "monopolies in the practice of law." Although most bar associations of the time were little more than social clubs, Robinson saw them as "secret, powerfully organized fraternities" determined to control lawmaking, prevent justice, and prey upon the average citizen.

Source: *A Letter to the Hon. Rufus Choate, Containing a Brief Exposure of Law Craft, and Some of the Encroachments of the Bar Upon the Rights and Liberties of the People,* n.p., 1832.

Sir:

I told you yesterday that it was cowardly in you to pursue the course which you did toward me. I have had a night to reflect on your proceedings, and I now assert that it was cowardly in the extreme not only in you but in the whole "brotherhood of the bar" to postpone the question of power and privilege, which you know is odious to the people, until the court was ready to rise and until the jury had been dismissed and all the spectators had retired.

I asked you then, sir, and I ask you now, again, why, if you have the right, as you say you have, to demand the authority by which I appear to do business in our public courts, you did not demand it when the actions which I entered were called? The reason to my mind is obvious. You feared that all in the court who had not sworn allegiance to the bar would express in their countenances, at least, sympathy for a man contending for one of *their* rights, and disapprobation toward a secret, powerfully organized fraternity determined to crush him. You therefore supposed it would be more prudent to consult with the court and your secret bar association, and proceed accord-

ing to the dictation of their united wisdom and courage. But you must have thought me blind indeed if you suppose that I should not see that your proceeding toward me was the result of a preconcerted arrangement between the court and the bar. How else can I account for your conduct? When my actions were called, you suffered one of them to be defaulted and asked for leave for the other to remain open on the docket. Why did you not then call for the power? You looked around the courthouse, and you saw it filled with people who you know are jealous of their rights and liberties, and you feared to do it.

The same day, I asked you what you would do with the action of Wyman and Marshall, did you say a word then about a power? You know that, instead of intimating the course which you intended to pursue, you requested me to wait; that you said you would attend to it, by and by. I saw you again about the middle of the week and told you that I would call up the case and have it disposed of. You then said that you intended to pay money into court, and would attend to it as soon as you could, and seemed to intimate that you had not received it from your *client*. I was therefore willing to subject myself to much inconvenience because I supposed you meant to dispose of the case as soon as you had the money. You know that had I supposed you intended to pursue any other than an honorable course toward me, I should have taken an opportunity to have the action disposed of in a public and manly way.

But when the business of the court was nearly ended, I began to discover the plot. I began to observe an uncommon solicitude among the "brotherhood of the bar," by drawing themselves up around the bench. Notice was given that public business was ended; the spectators retired and the judge dismissed the jury. Then it was, sir, for the first time, you gave me notice that you were ready to pay money into the court. Then, for the first time, you told me you meant to make me produce my power of attorney, and when I remonstrated to you against the *double* course which you had pursued toward me during the term, and against the cowardliness of waiting, before you proposed this measure, until all had retired except the "secret brotherhood of the bar," then it was for the first time you said that if I attempted "to practise the law without being regularly admitted to the bar we'll put you down." I told you I feared you not, not all your secret fraternity; that I was standing on broad constitutional ground, and no power on earth should put me down until it put me in the grave.

You called for my power, and I demanded by what authority. I said that I claimed every right and every privilege in our country which any other individual can enjoy; that I claimed the same facility of doing business in our public courts which any other man can have; that if there be any laws which contravene the rights of my appearing as an attorney on terms of equality with other men, I protested against such laws as unconstitutional and void; but that I could easily conceive how such laws have been forced through our legislature, by a secret, interested, organized body within the legislature. I therefore protested against the operation of such laws on me. You know, the judge then said that the laws to which I referred were of too long standing for him to decide unconstitutional (as if any length of time can render unconstitutional laws constitutional), but that he gave me liberty to carry the question up to the S. J. Court. But did you ever know a judge in this commonwealth who was not also a member of your "secret bar association?" . . .

But what was still more dishonorable in you was your attempt to make me prove my power of attorney, when you knew that all had retired from the court except your own brotherhood and the officers of the court. To the practice of what miserable lawcraft are you compelled, by the rules of your "privileged order," to resort when a man attempts to do business in our public courts with a special power of attorney in his hands. In the first place, you tell him that if he attempts to practise the law without being regularly admitted to the bar that your "holy alliance" will declare a perpetual war against him and "put him down." If he is not intimidated with this threat, you make him produce his power of attorney. You then object to his appearance, for the want "of a decent and good moral character," and are permitted by the court to abuse him with the most scandalous Billingsgate scurrility.

He is then obliged to send home and get witnesses to prove the decency and morality of his character. If he pass through the ordeal unscathed, your fraternity fall to caviling with his power. You object to its formality; he shows that it is sufficiently formal. You object to its execution; he shows that it is executed according to law. You object to the signature; he produces a witness. You object to the witness and require subscribing witnesses. If all this infamous subterfuge arouse his indignation and he retort with severity, you represent it as a contempt of court, and require the judge to exercise his arbitrary, unconstitutional, British power of commitment.

After you have exhausted yourselves in this way without success, according to "your bar rules" to "put him down," you add to the persecution of *him* the persecution of his *employer*. You have recourse to every dilatory measure in order to harass and perplex him, and put him to unnecessary costs. You excite vexatious lawsuits against him, and practise every other art, within the reach of a numerous and powerful association, to teach him the danger of employing any other person than one of your fraternity. . . .

Now, sir, the law, which you say compels me to produce a power of attorney, was enacted for the express purpose of preventing the exercise of this scandalous lawcraft in the courts. It would seem that previous to the passage of this law the brotherhood of the bar had been accustomed to treat their fellow citizens who attempted to do business in the courts in the manner I have described. And in order to show the intention of the legislature and put it out of the power of a corrupt nest of pettifoggers, any longer, to defraud and abuse their honest neighbors, the legislature began the statute with the following Preamble:

> Whereas it has been represented to this legislature that doubts have arisen in some of the courts of judicature within this Commonwealth respecting the right of persons to constitute attorneys in certain cases, other than those which have been admitted in the usual form prescribed by law; for the removal of which doubts: *Be it enacted,* that any person of decent and good moral character who shall produce in court a power or letter of attorney specially for that purpose shall have full authority, though his principal be absent, to prosecute and defend any suit or matter, *as fully* as if such person, so authorized, was an attorney of such court.

The object of this statute, then, is clearly to secure to the citizens a right which they always possessed but which your fraternity had usurped. This right is also secured by the constitution and it is provided by a previous statute, "that the parties may plead and manage their own causes personally, or by the assistance of *such* counsel as they may *see fit* to engage." Now, can anyone believe, when he reads the Preamble to this statute, which you say compels me to produce a power of attorney, that it was the intention of the legislature to obstruct the citizen in the enjoyment of one of his natural, constitutional, and lawful rights? Could the legislature have supposed that the citizens who attempted to take advantage of this law would be perplexed and abused, both by the courts and the bar, in the way described?

The Preamble to our constitution declares, "that the end of the institution, maintenance, and administration of government is to furnish the individuals who compose it with the power of enjoying in safety and tranquillity their natural rights." But it is the "natural right" of everyone to enter into that business or to be engaged in that employment which he judges himself qualified to perform. And every constitution and every law and every rule and regulation either of the courts or "the bar" which counteracts this privilege, is an encroachment on the natural rights of man.

Our constitution also provides for the freedom and equality of all the citizens, and declares that no man nor association of men shall be possessed of exclusive privileges. But at the time of the enactment of this law, it was represented by the members of your fraternity, in the legislature, that its provisions were in exact accordance to these great natural and constitutional principles. For previously it had been the custom for "the members of the bar," in order to tax the parties with the price of a power of attorney, to appear in the courts with this qualification, and, therefore, it seemed equal and reasonable to the unsuspecting members of the legislature, who were not of your "privileged order," to require of others the same qualification. But afterward, in order to have it in your power still to practise the same lawcraft and to secure to your "secret bar association" the same monopoly in your trade, you dispensed, by a court and "bar rule," with *your* powers of attorney. So that the law which appeared equal and constitutional at the time of its enactment is now clearly unequal and therefore unconstitutional.

And now, sir, I ask what right have you to enforce the rules of your association on me? You told the judge that I was not "a member of the bar," and therefore you demanded by what authority I appeared to do business in the court. Is the court and the bar one and the same thing? The people do not so understand it, I believe; though I am well convinced that there is a close copartnership between them. I am more disposed to believe that such a partnership exists, because I cannot conceive how the bar, a secret society unknown in the law, could deprive me of my rights by any rules or by laws of the association, did not the court adopt and enforce the rules of the bar. In this way your fraternity has been enabled by little and little to entrench itself behind an impassable barrier. And the only access now is by a single door, which gives admittance only to him who has been led on by the most *lengthy* process, with the most costly formality.

In the first place, he must be regularly admitted into one of our aristocratic, incorporate colleges or universities. He must there spend at least four years, either in study or at his election, in a kind of costly, monastic idleness. He is then, wise or foolish, learned or ignorant, admitted to a *degree*, and honored with a *title*. His name is then admitted to be enrolled on the archives of the bar, and, after spending at least three years more in idleness or study, under the nominal tuition of a member of the bar to whom he must pay at least $150 annually, he is then admitted, wise or foolish, learned or ignorant, without examination, into the secret fraternity of the bar.

And no person can be admitted into "the holy alliance" of the court and the bar, even if he be more learned than Johnson, a greater lawyer than Bacon, more eloquent than Cicero, if he has devoted his time till old age with the most intense application to study, under the most learned instructors, unless he go step by step through all the formality which I have described. Now, sir, can you say that this is not a true description of "the rules of the court and the bar" with respect to the admission of attorneys? Who, then, cannot see that the object of these rules is to keep out of the profession every man of self-education, to exclude every such man as Patrick Henry, Roger Sherman, and Benjamin Franklin, whose names are now the boast, the honor, and ornament of our country? But if they were alive now, in Massachusetts, could they be admitted to "the bar"? Would they be suffered to do business in our public courts? Can you suppose then that the people who, like me, are jealous of their rights and liberties will any longer countenance a society whose object is to discourage self-education?

Do you think that they will suffer such an association to "put me down" a person who has been laboring many years, with more than common zeal, against obstacles which to most men would have been considered insuperable, to prepare myself for the practice of the law? I have a right, I think, at least to expect that my fellow citizens, who are equally interested with me in the preservation of all our common rights and privileges, will stand by and see "fair play" while you are "putting me down."

You demanded by what authority I appeared to do business in the courts, because

I was not "a member of the bar." But what right have the courts to adopt and enforce "the rules of the bar?" The courts ought to be governed by the laws of the land, and these on the subject of admission of attorneys are very different from "the rules of the bar." . . .

When I attempted a few days since to defend my own cause, and when a friend of mine attempted to render me some assistance, was he not threatened, in my hearing, with expulsion from the bar? And was he not obliged immediately to desist, fearing lest he should be deprived, by your unfeeling fraternity, of his only means of gaining a livelihood for himself and family? And this threat was made by a man who had violated the laws of the land and outraged the feelings of civilized society. Yet none can be members of your bar association but men of good moral character. When a citizen comes into the public courts to transact business according to the laws of the land, what right have you to throw obstacles in his way? What right have you to make rules that no lawyer shall advise him or render him any assistance on pain of excommunication from the bar? What right have you to attempt to "put him down"? What right to try to perplex him, to abuse him, to laugh him down, to drive him out of court? What right has the judge to sneer at him, and say, "you might as well come and take my bench"? Do you not in this way and by such rules set yourselves up in opposition to the will of the people, and attempt by every means to invalidate the acknowledged laws of the land? . . .

The right of appearing as an attorney I will never relinquish. It is a right which I mean to transmit to my children, untrammeled, if possible, by the rules of your "privileged order." And for this reason you are determined to destroy me. You think, no doubt, that the people will look on with indifference while you are "putting me down," and although it is an acknowledged

common right of us all which I am defending, yet, as but few are desirous at present of exercising the right, the people will not trouble themselves about it. But, sir, I do not believe that there is such an astonishing apathy in the great body of our citizens with respect to their rights.

The time was never yet known in our country, and I hope the time will never arrive, when they will not be ready to sacrifice much, and make every exertion in defense of their rights. And when they understand that I am contending for one of our common rights, do you believe that the great body of the people are possessed of such shortsightedness, such narrow selfishness as to see me crushed, without the expression of any sympathy for me and disapprobation toward you, merely because they do not want to exercise the right at present? Have they not the same feelings for their children which I have for mine? And are not all equally interested with me to transmit every employment to posterity, freed from the shackles of monopolies?

I know, sir, with whom I have to deal. I have weighed the matter well, and I am determined to assert and to defend the right which I claim, or to be forcibly put down, totally crushed, by "the gentlemen of the bar."

I know that my chance of success is small. I know that the fraternity of the bar which has waged war against me is powerful beyond what is commonly conceived. I know that you have fortified yourselves by alliance with the other learned professions. I know that you have interested every rich and powerful family in your favor. And I know that you have in this way established a proud, haughty, overbearing, fourfold aristocracy in our country.

The root of this aristocracy, which saps the liberties of the people and has branched out and covered the land, is in our colleges. Into these you are initiated in infancy; your seclusion from the world and your pursuits being different from the rest of society naturally excites your vanity, ambition, and pride; and even in infancy you look upon yourselves as a "superior order," as the future lawyers, doctors, priests, judges, and governors of mankind; and you look upon the rest of the world as inferior — plebeians, laborers, educated only for manual employment. You are there permitted even in infancy to form secret associations, "Phi Beta Kappa Societies," etc., in which you are taught to recognize each other by signs and grips and passwords, and swear to stand by each other through life. Does not this sufficiently account for the alliance which I have mentioned of the learned professions?

But what induces the rich also, who are not of these "liberal orders," to join this "holy alliance?" Who are the parents, generally, of the youth who fill our colleges and incorporate learned institutions? Is there a rich man in the land, the father of three booby boys, that does not, at least in his imagination, discern a regular-bred scrawler of writs at the bar, an administrator of doses to the sick, and an expounder of mysteries in the church? I know that the most of the offices of government are in your hands. Who are the presidents, the governors, the justices, the sheriffs, the judges, the solicitors and attorneys of the state? I know that the press is generally under your dictation and control, that the rich, the powerful and the learned are in your favor, yet with but truth, law, and justice on my side, I dare in our country to stand up, to assert and to defend my rights. And when the great disinterested body of the people hesitate to protect each other in their common rights and privileges, they are gone forever, and nothing but revolutions can redeem them. If the people have become careless of their rights and refuse assistance when they see them invaded in others, let them rest assured that their turn will come by and by. If such is the remissness of the people with respect to our common rights and privileges, it is time for everyone who is determined to live free and equal to seek another country. Ours can be the abode only of the master and slave.

You say that the bar is a "necessary evil." I know that it is an evil; that it is necessary I deny. I know of no good resulting to the community from the existence of your secret bar association. Public good was not the object of your combination. It is a conspiracy against the rights and liberties of the people. The same motives influence you to associate together into a fraternity denominated "the bar," which induce robbers to constitute a society called "a banditti," and one of these societies is as much "a necessary evil" as the other. And the *bar rules* of "these privileged orders" are not very dissimilar. The object of them both is to protect each other in their robberies and extortions, and to "put down" and destroy everyone who will not submit to their "rules and regulations," and become sworn brothers of the banditti, or the bar. Of these secret societies, however, the bar is the most to be feared. The one robs us of our purse, openly and honorably in comparison, in the highway, against law and at the risk of life. The other robs us, not of our purse alone but of our rights also, in the sanctuary and under the semblance of the law.

The 7th Article of our Bill of Rights declares that "government is instituted for the protection, safety, prosperity, and happiness of the people; and not for the profit, honor, or interest of any one man, family, or class of men." But let anyone now look into our judicial courts and ask himself for whose "interest, honor, and profit" do they seem to be instituted, and he cannot help answering — for the bar's. Annihilate the fraternity of the bar, and lay your trade open to universal competition, and all the evils of lawcraft would come to an end. Every citizen would then be enabled, in the language of the constitution, "to obtain right and justice freely and without being obliged to purchase it; completely and without any denial; promptly and without delay." There would then be no powerful interested "class of men," always ready to deprive him of his constitutional rights, to perplex him with the quibbles of lawcraft if he attempted to appear for himself, and to laugh him out of the courts.

96.

TIMOTHY WALKER: Defense of Mechanical Philosophy

In 1829 Thomas Carlyle published a vehement attack on the pernicious influence, as he viewed it, of what he called "mechanism" — i.e., technology — on civilization. In America, where pride in practicality, technical ingenuity, and progress had already become almost a national dogma, such an attack could hardly go unanswered. Timothy Walker, a New England scholar whose distinguished career in the law lay ahead of him, published a "Defence of Mechanical Philosophy" in reply to Carlyle in July 1831.

Source: *North American Review*, July 1831.

THE ARTICLE which we have just named ["Signs of the Times" by Thomas Carlyle] raises the grave and solemn question, whether mankind are advancing or not in moral and intellectual attainments. The writer expresses his opinion with sufficient distinctness in the following words: "In whatever respects the pure moral nature, in true dignity of soul and character, we are, *perhaps,* inferior to most civilized ages." If this be true, it is a truth of deep and melancholy import. But is it true? Well may we pause and ponder the matter carefully. What are the petty controversies which agitate sects, parties, or nations compared with one which concerns the destinies of the whole human race? . . .

Are we, then, in fact degenerating? Has the hand been moved backward on the dial-plate of Time? Has the human race, comet-like, after centuries of advancement, swept suddenly round its perihelion of intelligence and commenced its retrogradation? The author of the article before us, as we have seen, expresses, though with a *perhaps,* his belief of the affirmative. Throughout the whole article, with the exception of the last paragraph or two of which the complexion is somewhat more encouraging, he draws most cheerless conclusions from the course which human affairs are taking. If the writer does not, as he humanely assures us in the end, ultimately despair of the destinies of our ill-starred race, he does, nevertheless, perceive baleful influences hanging over us. Noxious ingredients are working in the caldron. He has detected the "midnight hag" that threw them in, and her name is Mechanism. A more malevolent spirit, in his estimation, does not come from the hateful abodes. The fated inhabitants of this planet are now under her pernicious sway, and she is most industriously plotting against their weal. To countervail her malignant efforts, the author invokes a spirit of a character most unlike the first. Her real name, as we shall see, is Mysticism, though this is not pronounced in the incantations.

Now we cannot help thinking that this brilliant writer has conjured up phantoms for the sake of laying them again. At all events, we can see nothing but phantoms in what he opposes. In plain words, we deny the evil tendencies of Mechanism, and we doubt the good influences of his Mysticism. We cannot perceive that Mechanism, as such, has yet been the occasion of any injury to man. Some liberties, it is true, have been taken with Nature by this same presumptuous intermeddler. Where she denied us rivers, Mechanism has supplied them. Where she left our planet uncomfortably rough, Mechanism has applied the roller. Where her mountains have been found in the way, Mechanism has boldly leveled or cut through them. Even the ocean, by which she thought to have parted her quarrelsome children, Mechanism has encouraged them to step across.

As if her earth were not good enough for wheels, Mechanism travels it upon iron pathways. Her ores, which she locked up in her secret vaults, Mechanism has dared to rifle and distribute. Still further encroachments are threatened. The terms uphill and downhill are to become obsolete. The horse is to be unharnessed, because he is too slow; and the ox is to be unyoked, because he is too weak. Machines are to perform all the drudgery of man, while he is to look on in self-complacent ease.

But where is the harm and danger of this? Why is every lover of the human race called on to plant himself in the path and oppose these giant strides of Mechanism? Does this writer fear that Nature will be dethroned and Art set up in her place? Not exactly this. But he fears, if we rightly apprehend his meaning, that mind will become subjected to the laws of matter; that physical science will be built up on the ruins of our spiritual nature; that in our rage for machinery, we shall ourselves become machines. . . .

On the face of the matter, is it likely that mechanical ingenuity is suicidal in its efforts? Is it probable that the achievements of mind are fettering and enthralling mind? Must the proud creator of Mechanism stoop to its laws? By covering our earth with unnumbered comforts, accommodations, and delights, are we, in the words of this writer, descending from our "true dignity of soul and character?" Setting existing facts aside, and reasoning in the abstract, what is the fair conclusion? To our view, directly the contrary. We maintain that the more work we can compel inert matter to do for us, the better will it be for our minds, because the more time shall we have to attend to them. So long as our souls are doomed to inhabit bodies, these bodies, however gross and unworthy they may be deemed, must be taken care of. Men have animal wants which must and will be gratified at all events; and their demands upon time are imperious and peremptory. A certain portion of labor, then, must be performed expressly for the support of our bodies.

But at the same time, as we have a higher and nobler nature which must also be cared for, the necessary labor spent upon our bodies should be as much abridged as possible in order to give us leisure for the concerns of this better nature. The smaller the number of human beings, and the less the time it requires to supply the physical wants of the whole, the larger will be the number and the more the time left free for nobler things. Accordingly, in the absolute perfection of machinery, were that attainable, we might realize the absolute perfection of mind. In other words, if machines could be so improved and multiplied that all our corporeal necessities could be entirely gratified without the intervention of human labor, there would be nothing to hinder all mankind from becoming philosophers, poets, and votaries of art. The whole time and thought of the whole human race could be given to inward culture, to spiritual advancement.

But let us not be understood as intimating a belief that such a state of things will ever exist. This we do not believe, nor is it necessary to our argument. It is enough, if there be any approach thereto. And this we do believe is constantly being made. Every sober view of the past confirms us in this belief. . . .

There has never been a period when so large a number of minds, in proportion to the whole, were left free to pursue the cultivation of the intellect. This is altogether the result of Mechanism, forcing inert matter to toil for man. And had it been reached gradually, commencing at the Creation and continuing until now, the blessing would have been without alloy. But, unhappily, the progress has not been gradual. Of late, Mechanism has advanced *per saltum*, and the world has felt a temporary inconvenience from large numbers being thrown suddenly out of employment while unprepared to embark in anything else. But this evil must be from its nature temporary, while the advantage resulting from a release of so large a proportion of mankind from the thralldom of physical labor will be as lasting as the mind.

And hence it is that we look with unmixed delight at the triumphant march of Mechanism. So far from enslaving, it has emancipated the mind in the most glorious sense. From a ministering servant to matter, mind has become the powerful lord of matter. Having put myriads of wheels in motion by laws of its own discovering, it rests, like the Omnipotent Mind of which it is the image, from its work of creation, and pronounces it good. . . .

Before we conclude that man's dignity is depreciated in the contrivance and use of this machinery, let us remember that a precisely analogous course of reasoning must conduct us to the conclusion that the act of Creation subtracted from the glory of the Creator; that the Infinite Mind, as it brooded from eternity over chaos, was more transcendently glorious than when it returned from its six days' work to contemplate a majestic world. We accordingly believe there is nothing irreverent in the assertion that the finite mind in no respect approximates so nearly to a resemblance of the Infinite Mind as in the subjugation of matter, through the aid of Mechanism, to fixed and beneficial laws — to laws ordained by God but discovered and applied by man.

If the views now presented be correct, it follows that the mechanical enterprise with which our age is so alive, far from being unfavorable to our spiritual growth, is the one thing needful to furnish the freedom and leisure necessary for intellectual exercises — to establish man in the *otium cum dignitate* [leisure with dignity] in a higher sense than even Cicero conceived it. . . .

Now if we are willing to recur to that barbarous principle that one nation may purchase itself leisure, as the Greeks did, by aggressions upon the rest, and if all other nations can be persuaded to submit to the experiment, we may no doubt behold a people, spurning all mechanical improvements, and yet attaining to a surprising "dignity of soul and character." But so long as it continues to be settled by compact among the nations that each shall produce the means of subsistence within itself, or else an equivalent to exchange with others; and so long as the balance of power continues to be so adjusted as to prevent anyone from living upon the rest through the force of superior numbers, we see not how we can avoid the conclusion that that nation will make the greatest intellectual progress in which the greatest number of labor saving machines has been devised. It may not produce a Newton, Milton, or Shakespeare, but it will have a mass of thought, reflection, study, and contemplation perpetually at work all over its surface, and producing all the fruits of mental activity.

But this writer has not confined his warfare to the world as a whole. He has divided mankind into classes and attacked them in detail. We shall try to follow him through his campaign. One remark, however, upon the name which he has given to the age. "It is not a Heroical, Devotional, Philosophical, or Moral Age, but, above all others, the Mechanical Age. It is the Age of Machinery, in every outward and inward sense of that word." It may puzzle our readers as much as it does ourselves to understand what is meant by the "inward sense" of machinery. We are still more perplexed to understand how the following charge, which seems intended as unusually severe, can be construed by thinking men into anything else than substantial eulogy. "With its whole, undivided might, it [this age] forwards, teaches, and practises *the great art of adapting means to ends.* Nothing is now done directly or by hand; all is by rule and calculated contrivance. For the simplest operation, some helps and accompaniments, some cunning, abbreviating process is in readiness." Now take away the lurking sneer with which this is said, and we see not how it would be possible to crowd more praise into a smaller compass. It is no small part of wisdom to possess the capacity "of adapting means to ends." What would the writer have us do? Pursue ends without regard to means?

But to the specific charges. And first, the world is full of literary, scientific, and religious associations. It is one of the mechanical features of the age that large numbers of men are in the habit of combining together to effect those objects which no individual could accomplish alone. Now we have been accustomed to consider this prevailing tendency as one of the greatest modern improvements. In no propensity do we discover *a more prudent adaptation of means to ends.* We employ the mechanical lever to lift weights which our unassisted strength could not lift. Why not employ the *social lever* in the same way?

We are aware that some great and good men have expressed apprehensions that the individual is in danger of being lost in the mass. But, for aught we can perceive, the individual is as free as ever, and his influence is even greater. Let him unite with those whose opinions agree with his, and he adds another unit to the sum. Let him stand out alone, and he must be transcendently gifted if he does not lose his unit of influence. And as to his freedom, there is no reason why he should part with that when he joins himself to a society. He may act with it so long as he approves its course. When he disapproves it, he may attempt a change; and if he cannot prevail, he may separate, and, at worst, he will stand in the position in which he was placed before he joined the society.

The writer next indulges in pleasantry at the expense of physical science and its votaries. "No Newton, by silent meditation, now discovers the system of the world from the falling of an apple; but some quite other than Newton stands in his museum, his scientific institution, and, behind whole batteries of retorts, digesters, and galvanic piles, imperatively interrogates nature; who, however, shows no haste to answer." If this means anything, it is to cast ridicule upon the universal practice of demonstrating and illustrating scientific truths by actual experiments. And in what school has the writer been brought up if he really needs to be reminded that Nature does answer, and hastily too, when thus interrogated? Again and again did she make haste to answer to Franklin, Priestley, Black, Lavoisier, Davy, and a host of other imperative interrogators. Where was this writer when she was questioned as to the cause of lightning, the composition of water, the nature of heat, the mode of guarding against the firedamp of the mine, and a hundred other equally momentous secrets?

The mathematics are next subjected to our author's criticism. "Its calculus, differential and integral, is little else than a more cunningly constructed arithmetical mill, where the factors being put in are, as it were, ground into the true product under cover, and without other effort on our part than steady turning of the hand. We have more mathematics, certainly, than ever; but less *mathesis*. Archimedes and Plato could not have read the *Mécanique Céleste;* but neither would the whole French Institute see aught in that saying, 'God geometrizes!' but a sentimental rodomontade."

Now we are much in the same predicament with regard to this passage as the French Institute with regard to that saying. We can see naught in it but rodomontade. We learn from it that Newton, Leibnitz, and Laplace were nothing more than millwrights, and that their work was very easy. Indeed, the author had just before asserted that to excel in the higher departments of mathematics required no great natural gifts. . . . It is true that Plato had the honor of *saying* "God geometrizes!" But to *prove* it was reserved for the mechanicians above mentioned.

The next thrust is made at metaphysics. And here we are informed that nobody has gone to work right. The whole world are now, and always have been, totally in the wrong. Even Locke, the great master, was at fault in the outset. . . . So because Locke confined his inquiries to what can be known instead of meddling with "grand secrets" and "mysterious relations," he is a mere mechanic. Commend us to such mechanics. Give us Locke's Mechanism and we will envy no man's Mysticism. Give us to know the "origin of our ideas," to comprehend the phenomena "which we see in the mind," and we will leave the question of the mind's essence to transcendental speculators. So of necessity and free will;

mechanical as the age is, we have heard of no machinery which can be brought to bear upon their explanation. And as to "the mind's vital or nonvital dependence upon matter," we are compelled to plead ignorance of what it means. . . .

On the whole, we have no wish to disguise the feeling of strong dissatisfaction excited in us by the article under consideration. We consider its tendency injurious and its reasoning unsound. That it has some eloquent passage must be admitted. But when we hear distinguished philosophers spoken of as "logic-mills," the religion of the age as "a working for wages," our Bible societies as "supported by fomenting of vanities, by puffing, intrigue, and chicane," and all descriptions of men "from the cartwright up to the codemaker" as mere "mechanists"; when we further hear "the grand secrets of necessity and free will," "our mysterious relations to time and space," and "the deep, infinite harmonies of Nature and man's soul," brought repeatedly forward under the most varied forms of statement as the legitimate objects of philosophical inquiry, and the most illustrious of the living and the dead, men whom we never think of but as benefactors of our race, made the objects of satire and ridicule because they have preferred the *terra firma* of mechanical philosophy to the unstable quagmire of mystic conjecture, we find it difficult not to regard the essay rather as an effort of paradoxical ingenuity — the sporting of an adventurous imagination with settled opinions — than as a serious inquiry after truth.

Indeed the writer himself seems to think, toward the end, that he has gone too far; and deems it prudent . . . to insert the following saving clause: "It seems a well-ascertained fact that in all times, reckoning even from those of the Heraclides and Pelasgi, *the happiness and greatness of mankind at large have been continually progressive.*"

This is one of the few assertions in the article in which we altogether agree with the author. We do entertain an unfaltering belief in the permanent and continued improvement of the human race, and we consider no small portion of it, whether in relation to the body or the mind, as the result of mechanical invention. It is true that the progress has not always been regular and constant. In happy times it has been so rapid as to fill the benevolent with inexpressible joy. But anon, clouds have gathered over the delightful prospect — evil influences, but not mechanical, have operated; evil times have succeeded; and human nature has undergone a disastrous eclipse. But it has been only an eclipse, not an extinguishment of light. And frequent as these alternations have been, mankind are found to have been constant gainers. The flood has always been greater than the ebb. Each great billow of time has left men further onward than its predecessor. This could be proved, if necessary, by a thousand references.

Darkness has indeed given a name to some ages, but light on the whole has immensely preponderated; and it is this conviction which nerves the heart and invigorates the arm of philanthropy. They who feel this divine impulse know that the labors of kindred spirits in past ages have not been in vain. They see Atlantis, Utopia, and the Isles of the Blest nearer than those who first descried them. These imaginary abodes of pure and happy beings, which have been conceived by the most ardent lovers of their kind, we delight to contemplate; for we regard them as types and shadows of a higher and better condition of human nature, toward which we are surely though slowly tending.

But let us not be misunderstood. The condition we speak of is not one of perfection. This we neither believe in nor hope for. Supposing it possible in the nature of things, it would be anything but desirable; for with nothing left to achieve or gain, existence would become empty and vapid. But if, with this explanation, our views should pass for visionary, we cannot help it. We cannot go back to the origin of mankind and trace them down to the present time without believing it to be a part of the providence of God that His creatures should be perpetually advancing. The first men must have been profoundly ignorant except so far as the Supreme Being communicated with them directly. But with them commenced a series of inventions and discoveries which have been going on up to the present moment. Every day has beheld some addition to the general stock of information. When the exigency of the times has required a new truth to be revealed, it has been revealed.

Men gifted beyond the ordinary lot have been raised up for the purpose: witness Cadmus, Socrates, and the other sages of Greece; Cicero and the other sages of Rome; Columbus, Galileo, Bacon, Newton, and the other giant spirits of modern times. We cannot regard it as an abuse of language to call such men inspired, that is, preeminently endowed beyond all their contemporaries and moved by the invisible agency of God to enlighten the world on subjects which had never, till they spoke, occupied the minds of men. In other words, we believe that the appearance of such men, at the exact times when all things were ready for the disclosures they were to make, was not the result of accident but the work of an overruling Providence. And if such has been the beneficent operation of Providence upon the minds of men in all past times — if whenever a revelation was needed, He has communicated it, and in the exact measure in which it was needed — how can we, without irreverence, adopt any other conclusion than that He, who changes not, will still continue, through all future time, to make known through gifted men, as fast as the world is prepared to receive them, new truths from His exhaustless store?

War Eagle, front, with Omaha, Little Missouri and Pawnee braves. Painted by Charles B. King, 1821

"THE TRAIL OF TEARS"

During the two decades after the War of 1812, almost all the Indian tribes east of the Mississippi were confined to reservations or moved to lands west of the river. American victories over British and Indian forces during the war had ended effective resistance to white migration into the Northwest Territory. Removal of British influence in the area and the death of Tecumseh in 1813 deprived the Indians of outside assistance and caused the collapse of Tecumseh's Indian confederation. With American superiority obvious and the tribes disunited, the Indians began to sign away their land east of the Mississippi. In 1819 the Kickapoos agreed to a treaty that relinquished their land in Illinois. One by one, the other tribes in the Midwest and South were forced into negotiations with government agents. Only a few minor uprisings, of which the Black Hawk War was the most important, disturbed the removal program. The process was more difficult in the South, since many of the tribes had assimilated a large measure of white culture. As the states of the deep South entered the Union, they passed legislation encouraging encroachment on Indian lands, a direct violation of federal law. The government and the federal courts refused to interfere with state policies and, in 1830, Congress passed its own Indian removal act. This law authorized Jackson to exchange land in Oklahoma for that ceded by the Indians. Federal troops were used to facilitate prompt removal to the designated territory.

Throughout this period the government's removal policy was dignified by negotiations and treaties formalizing each cession. As the momentum of growth carried Americans westward again in the 1840s almost none of these treaties was honored by the United States. This second great migration brought new violence and new treaties.

(Top) Buffalo hunting in the summer; (left) inside an Indian tent; (below left) Indian returning from the war; watercolors by Peter Rindisbacher

Government Treaties with the Indians

Under the supervision of government agents, most of the northern and western tribes met at Prairie du Chien, Wisconsin, in 1825 to sign a treaty among themselves and with the United States. The terms of the treaty sought to define the territorial boundaries of the various tribes. This was particularly important in the areas west of the Mississippi where the tribes were being resettled. For the Indians, particularly the Plains tribes, signing the treaty was a concession which would force a change in their way of life or a move farther west. The treaty threatened to upset the rough territorial alignments that had been worked out through centuries of conflict over the available supply of buffalo and other game. Several local treaties followed, reconfirming the initial concession made at Prairie du Chien.

(Above) Signing the treaty at Prairie du Chien, 1825; (below) Butte des Morts treaty ground, 1827

(Right) "Wi-Jun-Jon to and from Washington"; painted by George Catlin; (below) war dance in an Indian lodge

Catlin's Indian Gallery

(Above) Keokuk, the Sauk chief who signed away tribal lands in Wisconsin; (top right) Big Wave, Ko-man-i-kin, chief of the Menomini Indians

Most of the pictures in this section were painted by George Catlin (1796-1872). Educated as a lawyer, Catlin painted portraits in Philadelphia for a few years before deciding that "the history and customs of the Indian people are themes worthy the lifetime of one man, and nothing shall prevent me . . . becoming their historian." From 1830 to 1837, he traveled throughout the West on that mission, assembling a gallery of over 500 scenes and portraits. The paintings on these two pages are of various Midwestern tribes that were in the process of removal when Catlin painted them.

Discovery Dance, ritual of the Sauk and Fox tribes, 1836

John W. Quinney, Indian missionary preacher near Green Bay, Wisconsin

(Above) Cah-be-mub-bee, brave of the Ojibwa tribe; (left) two "Chippeway" dances painted by J. V. Lewis for his "Aboriginal Portfolio" at Prairie du Chien, 1825; (below) Ah-ton-we-tuck, with prayer stick, Kickapoo tribe, Illinois

Black Hawk War

Following the War of 1812 the Sauk Indians signed a treaty ceding their land in northwest Illinois and south Wisconsin to the government. The treaty was signed by Keokuk, since the head chief, Black Hawk, was opposed to it. By 1830, most of the Sauks had been relocated in Iowa. Black Hawk, finding the new farmland inferior, led a band back to plant crops in the old fields. The white settlers resisted. Federal troops defeated the Indians at a battle on the Bad Axe River in 1832.

(Top) Indian land in the Northwest Territory, 1835; (above) Battle of Bad Axe, 1832; (below) Black Hawk and his son, Whirling Thunder; (right) Keeokuk

ᏣᎳᎩ ᏚᎳᏚᎥᎢ.
CHEROKEE PHŒNIX,

VOL. I.   NEW ECHOTÁ, THURSDAY FEBRUARY 21, 1828.   **NO. 1.**

EDITED BY ELIAS BOUDINOTT.
PRINTED WEEKLY BY
ISAAC H. HARRIS,
FOR THE CHEROKEE NATION.

At $2.50 if paid in advance, $3 in six months, or $3.50 if paid at the end of the year.

To subscribers who can read only the Cherokee language the price will be $2.00 in advance, or $2.50 to be paid within the year.

Every subscription will be considered as continued unless subscribers give notice to the contrary before the commencement of a new year.

The Phœnix will be printed on a Super-Royal sheet, with type entirely new procured for the purpose. Any person procuring six subscribers, and becoming responsible for the payment, shall receive a seventh gratis.

Advertisements will be inserted at seventy-five cents per square for the first insertion, and thirty-seven and a half cents for each continuance; longer ones in proportion.

☞ All letters addressed to the Editor, post paid, will receive due attention.

CONSTITUTION OF THE CHEROKEE NATION,

Formed by a Convention of Delegates from the several Districts, at New Echota, July 1827.

WE, THE REPRESENTATIVES of the people of the CHEROKEE NATION in Convention assembled, in order to establish justice, ensure tranquility, promote our common welfare, and secure to ourselves and our posterity the blessings of liberty; acknowledging with humility and gratitude the goodness of the sovereign Ruler of the Universe, in offering us an opportunity so favorable to the design, and imploring his aid and direction in its accomplishment, do ordain and establish this Constitution for the Government of the Cherokee Nation.

ARTICLE I.

Sec. 1. THE BOUNDARIES of this nation, embracing the lands solemnly guarantied and reserved forever to the Cherokee Nation by the Treaties concluded with the United States, are as follows; and shall forever hereafter remain unalterably the same—to wit—Beginning on the North Bank of Tennessee River at the upper part of the Chickasaw old fields; thence along the main channel of said river, includ-

readmission. *Moreover*, the Legislature shall have power to adopt such laws and regulations, as its wisdom may deem expedient and proper, to prevent the citizens from monopolizing improvements with the view of speculation.

ARTICLE II.

Sec. 1. THE POWER of this Government shall be divided into three distinct departments;—the Legislative, the Executive, and the Judicial.

Sec. 2. No person or persons, belonging to one of these Departments, shall exercise any of the powers properly belonging to either of the others, except in the cases hereinafter expressly directed or permitted.

ARTICLE III.

Sec. 1. THE LEGISLATIVE POWER shall be vested in two distinct branches; a Committee, and a Council; each to have a negative on the other, and both to be styled, the General Council of the Cherokee Nation; and the style of their acts and laws shall be,

"RESOLVED by the Committee and Council in General Council convened."

Sec. 2. The Cherokee Nation, as laid off into eight Districts, shall so remain.

American Antiquarian Society

In the South

The land hunger behind the Indian removal process was most obvious in the expulsion of the civilized tribes in the South: the Choctaw, Chickasaw, Creek, and Cherokee nations. Many of these tribes were leaving established farms and plantations, as well as schools and churches they had built. Only the Seminoles in Florida successfully resisted. In a protracted conflict that lasted off and on until 1842, the Seminoles earned a treaty that allowed them to remain, for the time being. For the others, the trek to Oklahoma, supervised by government troops, was called "the trail of tears."

Library of Congress, Map Division

(Above) First issue of the "Cherokee Phoenix" published by Sequoia; (below) Ben Perryman, Creek Indian; (right) lands assigned to the Indians west of the Mississippi River

National Collection of Fine Arts, Smithsonian

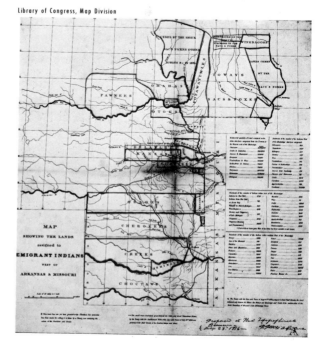

MAP
SHOWING THE LANDS
assigned to
EMIGRANT INDIANS
WEST OF
ARKANSAS & MISSOURI

The Plains Indians

The Plains Indians were largely nomadic peoples, migrating with the buffalo herds that were their primary source of food, clothing, and shelter. At the same time, centuries of conflict over hunting rights had made them warriors with elaborate rituals to signify bravery. The established way of life of these Indians was disrupted by the influx of tribes from the East. Fighting among them often erupted as new allocations of the available land and game were worked out in the most direct way.

(Top) "Halcyon Days," Sioux Indians; (left) **Dog Dance by the Dakota Indians,** an Eastern Sioux tribe; (below left) Sioux moving their tents; (below right) Stan-au-pat, the Bloody Hand, chief of the Arikara tribe which lived along the Upper Missouri River. All paintings by George Catlin

(Top) Archery contest, Mandan tribe; (left) Four Bears, chief of the Mandans; (above) back of a Mandan village on the Upper Missouri River showing their mode of depositing their dead, on scaffolds, enveloped in skins and of preserving and feeding the skulls; (below) view of a Mandan village. All paintings by Catlin

(Left) Cler-mont, head chief of the Osage Indians; (center) Buffalo's Back Fat, member of the Blackfoot tribe; (right) Horse Chief, head chief of the Grand Pawnee tribe

All: National Collection of Fine Arts, Smithsonian

(Left) Wun-nee-tou, the White Buffalo, a medicine man with his mystery shield, member of the Blackfoot tribe; (above) Pipe dance, Assineboins; (below) scene in a Comanche village. All paintings by George Catlin

97.

Stephen Simpson: Political Economy and the Producers of Wealth

Stephen Simpson, Philadelphia journalist, was a strong supporter of Andrew Jackson and an advocate of the rights of labor. Influenced by such disparate figures as Adam Smith, Robert Owen, and Frances Wright, Simpson developed an economic theory that anticipated Karl Marx. As an unsuccessful candidate for Congress in 1830, Simpson wrote much of the material that was later, in 1831, included in his main work, The Working Man's Manual, *from which the following "Preliminary Dissertation" is taken.*

Source: *The Working Man's Manual: A New Theory of Political Economy, on the Principle of Production the Source of Wealth,* Philadelphia, 1831, pp. 5-50.

A NEW THEORY OF POLITICAL ECONOMY at the present day, and from the pen of an American, may by some be considered as a bold and hazardous undertaking. Adventure and peril, however, are the characteristics of our country. Its physical features are stamped with an energy and grandeur that invite to imitation. Its moral history and its political career are equally distinguished for peril of achievement and novelty of execution. We are confessed to have achieved, as a nation, what no other people would ever have attempted. The career of intellect, of science, and of arts lies in broad characters before us; and it may surely be permitted to the most humble aspirant to add to the common stock of knowledge and of happiness.

It has been left to the people of the United States, to present to the world, for the first time, a self-formed government, whose basis was established in the equal rights of man, civil equality, and common privileges; and whose end was the general prosperity, virtue, and happiness of the people. The Declaration of (American) Independence was the first formal annunciation to the world that all men were born equally free — with equal claims to the pursuit of hap-

piness — and with inalienable rights to self-government. This truth once proclaimed flashed conviction on every mind. It became an obvious and self-evident axiom the moment it was uttered; it was received by all, disputed by none; and now constitutes a maxim in government, as well as philosophy, which every people pant to reduce to practice, as the only road to liberty, reason, affluence, and felicity. . . .

With such a Declaration of Independence, with such constitutions, formed on principles purely identical and theoretically imparting to the heart the fondest dreams of perfect liberty — blessed with a fertile soil, a frugal government, and a disposition to cultivate happiness, or bow down into content — it is not surprising that a long period should elapse ere the inconsistencies and discrepancies between our theoretical constitutions and feudal laws and customs should be discovered, exposed, and resisted. The mere acquisition of independence — the novelty of an untried condition — the glow of fervid patriotism, and the heats of party conflicts would long engross attention, and keep it from too close a scrutiny into the actual condition of the great mass of the community. It was natural that joy and satisfaction should be inspired, upon having escaped some of the intense oppressions of European systems, without feeling a restless curiosity to ascertain whether the abstract doctrines of government had actually been reduced to practice, so as to secure the *happiness of the many, instead of ministering to the benefit of the few!*

All advantages and situations are comparative; all advances to knowledge are progressive; and all changes leave the mind in tranquillity and repose long after their occurrence. But acquisitions soon grow familiar, and, when enjoyed, speedily satiate. We desire to go forward in the race of human destiny, and realize the full conception of happiness that we deem attainable to our nature; but this desire can only arise after the flush of conquest and liberty has passed over the heart, leaving it cooled, composed, and refreshed by the breezes of reflection and philosophy. . . .

It must ever form a subject of amazement and regret to succeeding generations that at the era of the Declaration of Independence, or at that of the adoption of the federal Constitution, the common law of England and the royal grants and titles to land were not instantly and totally abolished, as of no force and virtue, under the new government. Such a measure, more than all others now in the power of the people, would have established society on the true basis of merit and labor in the citizen, and tended, by its own weight, to equalize property on a scale of equity and comfort, and to adjust the wages of labor in a manner conducive to the general happiness.

Next in magnitude, as one of the parents of that unequal distribution of property and that unjust principle of distribution which now prevail, was the establishment of the *funding system* — another fungus of the corrupt institutions of a kingdom from which we had declared a *nominal* independence, at the same time that we retained, with obsti-

nate infatuation, all her moral, civil, and political cancers, under the false impression that descent, propinquity, a common origin, and a common language ought to excite a sympathy and an emulation that would blind us to their vices, and so consecrate their errors as to make it the duty of a kind of filial affection to adopt them without examination — resting satisfied with the uncontested fact, that their *English character* alone fully entitled them to our implicit approbation. . . .

In itself or its consequences, the *funding system,* of all the perversions of this equitable government, is especially oppressive to the children of labor. If it did not create a fiscal necessity, it at least afforded a plausible pretext for the *banking system* — that fruitful mother of unutterable affliction to the sons of industry — which brought us, at one fatal step, into the vortex of English aristocracy — overgrown fortunes and hopeless poverty; taxation through all the elements of existence; and speculation to the utter grinding down of the *producer,* to pamper the fortunes of the rich and swell the hoard of the speculator.

The *banking system* and the *funds* are, in the fiscal world, precisely what the royal grants were in the landed interest. They created even a greater inequality of fortune, by means more nefarious, as well as more pernicious; for they levied a tax directly upon every commodity produced by labor, which tax became immediately absorbed into the pocket of the *capitalist.* So that what England did through her royal charters and grants, antecedent to the Revolution, our own aristocracy deliberately committed through the *funding* and *banking* systems; whose results upon the happiness and comfort of an industrious and free people must be estimated fully as calamitous in respect to labor as the consequences that would attend the subjugation of the country by a foreign king, who should partition the property of the conquered people among his chiefs and followers, in large and princely domains; thus creating a monopoly of land and capital which would extort labor upon their own terms of bare subsistence.

Thus far, then, we perceive our constitution of *equal rights* to be the merest untenanted skeleton of liberty that the imagination of man can conceive; which, by its *operation,* creates aristocracy, privileges, extortion, monopoly, and overgrown fortunes; and which, by its *letter,* declares that equality of rights shall be guaranteed to all, and the pursuit of happiness be a common boon secured to industry by the equity of her principles and the simplicity of her laws.

Such are the defects of organic law, practical government, and property, which are thrown as obstacles into the path of the working man. In themselves these are formidable enough to intimidate the most intrepid champion of reform. But when are superadded to these the obstacles of *opinion,* prejudice — the long descended prejudice of antiquity, flinging the odium of servility upon the head of labor — it extorts a doubt of success, even in the very moment it excites the soul to dare all perils in so laudable a task. *Antiquity!* The word excites the most pleasing and sublime associations; but on this subject it gives rise to the most humiliating and degrading thoughts. Happily, Aristotle knew little of the true principles of political economy; and we may pardon the ignorance of a people on that score, whose occupation was war, and whose recreation was pleasure; who spent their hours in alternate devotion to the Muses, or sacrifices to their gods! . . .

To labor for another, even among us of the nineteenth century, is held as disreputable; while to labor for ourselves wipes away the stigma of reproach. In this distinction, we behold the cause and origin of that ignominy and depression which has been cast upon the working classes. . . .

As it appears indubitably to be owing to the existence of slavery combined with la-

bor, from the earliest to the latest ages of the world, that industry and toil have become associated with baseness and degradation, it would seem that nothing more was necessary to reverse the character of the productive classes, in public estimation, than to confine labor to a community of *freemen,* and abolish every vestige of bondage and servitude. This, it must be acknowledged, is an indispensable prerequisite to divesting labor of disgrace, and investing it with ideas of honor and merit; but it cannot be deemed entirely efficient in itself. Other causes must combine to produce this salutary revolution, previous to considering which, however, let us return to that auspicious feature in our Constitution to which I alluded at the commencement of this essay.

This is the only free government whose organic laws are sustained by the mixture of slavery and labor. Here, for the first time, we behold a country whose mechanics, laborers, farmers, and operatives are all eligible to the highest posts of power; where they may claim equality with kings and emperors; and for a time be equally as absolute and mighty in wielding the engines of human destiny. Labor brings neither disqualification nor stigma upon the citizen of the United States, in a political capacity. His rights are confessed, recorded, and practised; honor may be his, if genius seconds his efforts; and fame may be won by him without restriction of law.

On the part of political right, then, the *producer* suffers no disparagement from our free constitutions, whose efficiency is allowed to be complete, both in theory and practice.

Another question, however, arises. Did the Constitution intend to provide for nothing beyond *mere political right?* Does not the political embrace, necessarily, the *moral equality?* Does it not declare that equality is the basis of the whole social compact, and that all laws and regulations, customs and usages, shall bear equally upon all the members of the community? Hence, the remarks of a celebrated writer upon the principles of our constitutions:

> The idle, who seek for wealth by chartering laws, are wiser than their equalizing brethren. Law has never been able to produce an equality of property where industry exists, but it can produce its monopoly. Our policy rejects its application to both objects, and our constitutions unequivocally disclose an opinion that civil liberty depends UPON LEAVING THE DISTRIBUTION OF PROPERTY TO INDUSTRY; hence, laws for this end are as unconstitutional as those for reestablishing king, lords, and commons. LEGAL WEALTH AND HEREDITARY POWER ARE TWIN PRINCIPLES. These frauds beget all the parties or factions of civil society, such as patrician and plebian, military, civil, stock, and landed. The enmity and contrast in all these cases arise from a legal difference of interest, and the active and passive members of this fraudulent system are distinctly designated by the WEALTH AND POVERTY it diffuses. . . .

Independent, however, of this conclusive authority upon the subject, it is obvious, on the very face of our organic laws, that it was never designed by the people who framed this government, to grant the power, that law should regulate the distribution of wealth instead of industry. I use the term "law" as a generic word, embracing all the details that affect the distribution of wealth, such as monied corporations, chartered monopolies, and that endless chain of levers which move industry to empty her gains into the lap of capital; and which effectually frustrate and defeat the grand object of rational self-government, on the basis of individual freedom and personal merit.

The distinctive features of the feudal systems of Europe, which we have in form and in fact essentially repudiated are those of entails, nobility, hierarchy, monopolies, which are synonymous to the distribution of wealth by law, instead of its distribution by the same power, which is alone active in its production, industry and labor. Having shaken off, renounced, and branded those systems of antiquated barbarism and monkish superstition, by all the great leading documents of our national existence, we are bound by the highest and most sacred ties of moral, religious, and political obligation to bring the condition of the people, in respect to the wages of labor and the enjoyment of competence, to a level with their abstract political rights, which rights imply necessarily the possession of the property they may produce, on principles of equity, congenial to the equal rights guaranteed by the organic law. To substitute law for the distribution of labor is to introduce the chief feature of the feudal systems of Europe into the free, self-formed, and equitable republic of this country, and amounts to a virtual repeal of the very first principle of the Declaration of Independence and the constitutions of the Union and the states.

Happily, however, for the integrity of these institutions, and the perpetuity of the great doctrines upon which they are based, we possess a redeeming trait in our government, which opens wide the channels through which the people may enter to produce a conformity of practice to principle. Legislative abuses are never beyond the corrective control of a people whose suffrages properly directed, by a judicious concentration, can periodically annul, remove, and recreate the power that is above the laws, and mold the popular sovereignty to its own will and pleasure. Let the producers of labor but once fully comprehend their injuries and fully appreciate their strength at the polls, and the present oppressive system will vanish like the mists of the morning before the rising sun. The power to remedy the evil is unquestionable; it resides in the producers of wealth, who constitute so overwhelming a majority of the people, when not carried away by the infatuation of faction, the delusion of personal allegiance, and the vain pursuit of phantoms of liberty;

which are no sooner touched, than they melt into air, leaving the wretched follower to bewail his disappointment and execrate his fatuity.

Nothing of a public nature, at the present era, is so worthy of the attention of the people as the fallacious structure and pernicious tendency of the parties now in vogue, whose foundations are as futile as their results are nugatory to the great body of the people; neither advancing the good of the nation nor the prosperity of her citizens; but blindly ministering to the avarice, ambition, or pride of some temporary idol, who is worshiped one day and immolated on the next. A party grafted purely *on principle* has never yet engrossed the ardent people of this excited country; that of 1798 approximated nearer to such a party than any other, but its principles were so soon perverted, its object so soon merged into mere personal views, and the honest people were so soon duped by unprincipled leaders that it could scarcely lay a claim to purity of feeling or soar to patriotism of purpose. Since that era, faction has rapidly generated faction of groveling views and unholy ends, so as to cause political collisions to fester into mere cancers upon the body politic, eating into their vitality, and spreading disease and death over the whole face of our institutions.

Yet have the people been enticed into their support by plausible professions of leaders and the wheedling arts of insincere demagogues, to the detriment of their best interests, the sacrifice of their time, and the loss of their character. Lured on by the cant of party, the slang of affected patriotism, and the hollow promise of patronage, men have closed their eyes, as well as their understandings, to the deception of the game, which made use of them and their interests for the sheer and exclusive benefit of an aspiring demagogue, who, when his purpose was obtained, cast the squeezed orange from him with undissembled contempt. It is

to be hoped this epoch of delusion is rapidly passing into the waste of oblivion, never to be recalled; and that the producers of wealth will now be reinforced by the former deluded followers of faction, to second their reforms and aid them in their labors. A little reflection and inquiry cannot fail to produce this highly desirable result. Let us progress a little further in this investigation.

Personal parties are at all times, and under all circumstances, highly dangerous, and often prove fatal to the liberties of a free people. They are founded on selfishness, and terminate in usurpation and abuses. They first lead to the obscurity of principles, and gradually produce a total obliteration of all the great landmarks, which are founded on the fundamental differences of government, and engraven on the inalienable rights of man. After confounding, in this manner, all distinctions between right and wrong, justice and oppression, freedom and bondage, they soon tend to beget in the popular mind a total apathy or indifference to whatever relates to political affairs. What is radically erroneous or pernicious is often glossed over as right, and adopted by affection or reverence for a *name*; what is nefarious in principle, and even frightful in its consequences, is often welcomed, cherished, and promoted, without reflection, or inquiry, because a voice gilded with popularity has suggested its performance. Men of conflicting views, irreconcilable principles, and incompetent minds are huddled together in personal parties for a moment, until some shock of interest severs them wider than ever, with embittered animosity and aggravated feelings; or, if they cohere after the first collision, it is at the increased expense of all that is worthy of esteem and admiration in the human character. Honesty is sacrificed to expediency, truth to self-interest, patriotism to ambition, and public virtue to private aggrandizement. Honor and right can never tolerate such heterogeneous associations. The most callous and adroit knaves, in such parties, smile at the hypocrisy of one another. Mutual distrust, suspicion, and contempt sit upon the face of every thinking man of the ill-assorted group.

Yet nothing discomposes the complacency of these venal spirits; and acquiescence in the ruin of their country is purchased by a bribe, a commission, or a promise of patronage, hid in the mists of the indefinite future. The *mere animals* disport with their wonted glee under the shadow of any power, however corrupt, as there are some birds that can live even upon the gum and berries of the upas tree. A wise, prudent, and virtuous people, therefore, in order to continue free, will never lose sight of PRINCIPLE; and as parties never can be wholly demolished in a country where government is founded on *equality of rights,* it well deserves its attention whether that party ought not to be embraced and cherished, which is built upon the grand fundamental doctrines of INDUSTRY, MERIT, GENERAL HAPPINESS, *the distribution of property on the principle of the* WORTH OF LABOR, *and the intelligence, virtue, and comfort of the whole people?*

Parties of interest, however, though some of them are not much better in principle, are less noxious, because one party may be brought to check or control another, as the party of stockholders and capitalists may be met and counteracted by the *party of the producers;* which is a real party of *general interest,* whose ascendency could not fail to shed a genial and prosperous beam upon the whole society. Such a party would merely exhibit the *interest of society,* concentrating for the true fulfillment of the original terms of the social compact, the happiness and comfort of the whole. This we now behold in those parties of the workingmen, who, resisting the seductions of fanatics on the one hand and demagogues on the other, steadily follow in the path of science and justice, under the banner of *labor, the source of wealth,* and *industry,* the arbiter of its distribution.

It must be accounted a most calamitous circumstance for the sons of labor that, at the period of their emancipation from the rigors of feudal servitude in all countries, there should have arisen, at the same time, to distract their attention and entice them from their rights and their happiness, the turmoil, tumult, and collision of political excitement, to lead them, still in manacles, at the heels of ambitious demagogues; and as effectually blast their hopes of competence as the old system from which they had just emerged. This untoward event, however, is rather to be ascribed to their former ignorance of their rights than to a willful neglect of them. The specious colors with which capital invests her extortions; the appearance of justice, when protected by law, in which she envelops her oppressions, all tend to blind the uninformed multitude, and even perplex the intelligent and scientific. But that era of darkness has happily passed away, and regenerated man is slowly progressing to the recovery of his violated rights, in defiance of all the formidable obstructions of pride, prejudice, wealth, rank, and intellect. . . .

It is a perversion of the aims of the enlightened advocates of labor to represent that they are contending for an *equality of wealth* or a community of property. Our object is as remote from that as the existing system of extortion is from justice. Aware that there exists in nature no equality of industry, skill, strength, talent, wit, or any of the attributes which are essential to production, we could not advocate an equality of possessions without committing an infraction of the rights of others — and being guilty of that very injustice of which we now accuse *capital.* Equality of rights to what we produce is not equality of possession, for some will produce more than others. As this is one of the great perversions of our enemies, to bring odium and opposition upon our cause, it is necessary here to mark a distinction. . . .

It is a common and sound objection to

all preexisting parties that they are mercenary, personal, and selfish — hinging entirely upon the exchange of places by successful, overdefeated politicians; not only without regard to merit in men, or truth and justice in principles but most frequently in utter defiance of all the usual causes of rational preference of men and public tests of benefit to the commonwealth. What a splendid contrast does the party of the working men present to such groveling and besotted factions! It must be matter of astonishment to a mind divested of the yoke and harness of party that even one solitary workingman should be found among those who drag the car of faction for the exclusive benefit of a few interested leaders and inane demagogues; patricians in spirit if not in fortune, and to their own detriment, their own disadvantage, their own oppression — it is indeed marvelous, and not less lamentable than marvelous.

The inequality of property in this country has chiefly arisen from two causes: first, the *monopoly of land;* second, the monopoly of stock, or *public funded debt!* Let us examine into these sources of fortune!

By what title, founded in justice, did William Penn and the other original proprietors of land in the United States obtain possession of princely dominions? By the gift of the British king; by royal grants and imperial charters! What right had he to give that which the God of nature had bestowed upon another? Was the land untenanted, was it without proprietors, and did it not furnish nourishment, shelter, and home to thousands of great nature's unsophisticated children? The land thus given was the property of another; the gift, therefore, was null and void, as was subsequently confessed by the proprietary again becoming *a purchaser* from him who held it in possession — the hapless, deluded, and defrauded Indian.

But even the second purchase from the ignorant savage was still less valid and binding; and while it strikingly illustrates the extortion and guile of one party, it shows in strong colors the unhallowed means which cupidity adopts to impose on ignorance, and make that very ignorance the foundation of a title which it presumes to style just. For, is it within the scope of human reason, and the instincts and principles of our nature, that a few tinsel beads and burnished trinkets should form a just purchase money for the state of Pennsylvania? But even that frail tenure was nominal until the acquisition had been sealed by the blood of those proprietors, the hapless Indians, whose tenure was the gift of God, consecrated by the fiat — the sacred fiat — and the bleeding necessities of nature. Nation after nation of defenseless Indians must be immolated before even the gift of the king was worth a groat. Yet this is the foundation of most of our inequality of fortune — this, and the public funded debt.

Of a character even more unjust is the funded debt of this perverted country and its abused institutions. The funding of the poor soldier's pay, earned during the horrible trials of our Revolution, could scarcely have been expected to contribute to the detriment of labor, and erect customs, privileges, and classes, subversive of liberty. Yet so it proved. Did it go to the poor veteran — his helpless widow — his shivering orphans? No! It was diverted from its pure channel by the patrician officers, and greedy capitalists, and hungry speculators of the army, and of the government. It was adopted with a full knowledge that it never could reach the soldier, but must immediately go to form a monied aristocracy; and the funded debt was created by those immediately interested in its creation — by those who had bought up the soldier's certificates for a song!

Here, then, we behold the origin of the landed and funded wealth of this country; of what we denominate capital! What labor or industry could ever come in competition with such enemies? The land in fee simple to those who never, perhaps, saw it; and the funded debt to those who never paid for it, in sums too enormous for industry to equal, and too tempting either for the practice of virtue, the observance of justice, or even the abstinence from oppression. Here we have a double burden upon industry — a ground rent to the proprietor, forever, by the laborer; and a tax, or duty, to pay the stockholder his interest, paid by every workingman, from the time of the Revolution to the present day. And yet we are told, and gravely told, that capital is the best friend of industry; and that capitalists, merchants, stockholders, gentlemen, and lottery brokers produce their portion of the wealth of the nation — always giving a due share of credit to those highly meritorious characters, beggars and misers! And yet these latter characters are made by the operation of the corrective principle of vicissitudes, by the spending of the prodigals and the economy of the beggars. This system of social economy, I must confess, appears to me not less a strange one than it is utterly inconsistent with the spirit of the age, and repugnant to the dictates of a liberal and unaffected philanthropy. . . .

The Revolution of 1776, therefore, is, I contend, not yet fully accomplished; and all that part which relates to a moral change remains to be effectuated, that of 1776 merely being a *political* one — a separation of governments without such a separation of manners as is necessary to give the former permanence and full effect.

To come down to particulars, let us begin with *law and local politics.* The retention of the *common law system* of Great Britain was a vital error in our infant jurisprudence, being a *Gothic* system of crude and barbarous customs, as inconsistent with the equality of our government as the creation of an *order of nobility.* To this error was added the still greater one of the adoption of the *statute laws* of that realm, so far as to admit them as *conclusive precedents* in our courts. In local

polity, our error was still greater. Several of the states adopted the old royal charters of Elizabeth, Charles I, and Charles II as state constitutions; many of which remain to this day, a stigma on our reason and a sarcasm upon our liberty.

We fell into the same fatal delusions in respect to *education and literature.* Nothing *new* was suggested; or if suggested, never allowed to take root. Oxford and Cambridge, in England, were the models of our literary institutions; and a system of education devised in the midnight of the Dark Ages was adopted as the routine of instruction for a *free people,* in a boundless range of country sparsely populated, in the meridian era of the nineteenth century, when science and intellect had outrun the sublimest conceptions of the greatest geniuses of half an age ago! In minor seminaries — in those schools where the *great body of the people* receive their knowledge and form their principles — the *schoolbooks of London* constituted the sole fountain of instruction, a fountain tainted with lessons that inculcated a love of the *king,* or reverence for the *nobility,* and a passion for pomp, show, and regality. Of late years, this blemish has happily been removed; and in our popular seminaries, always the most important, an American system of *school literature* has been successfully introduced, congenial to the free spirit of our institutions. This reformation was long resisted by prejudice and aristocracy; and nothing but time, enterprise, and perseverance have succeeded in superseding so irrational a system, a system equally at war with knowledge and liberty; for of what use is a genealogy of kings, lords, and dukes to an American; or how can it conduce to his happiness, or his freedom?

The same prejudice now operates against a reform, equally desirable, in our *general literature,* which is still *imported* exclusively from England, as if she only possessed a climate formed by nature for the happy development of intellect and taste — a climate peculiar to herself and denied to all other nations. The prejudice against American authors and their productions is but a part of that great infirmity which has stigmatized us by the inconsistencies and contradictions already alluded to. A partiality for our own offspring is a natural affection and a laudable weakness; and in relation to the literature of nations, the same preferences ought to be cherished as the means of happiness and the safeguards of liberty. Whoever contemplates the load of trash that inundates this country from the bookshops of England, and reflects upon the fact that when a neglected American author transports himself to London his works are sought with eagerness and devoured with avidity, will confess to the truth that it is the *place* where he writes, and not the *quality* of his writings, that stamps him with genius or gives sterling currency to his wit. The prodigious influence of literature upon the minds and manners of people makes it of incalculable importance that it should emanate from *American minds* — minds imbued with the love of liberty, and animated by a spirit *congenial* to that which pervades our Constitution, and is calculated to advance our glory!

The importance of having the habits and manners of a people correspond to their government has never been duly appreciated by American statesmen; for it extends even to that *system of manufactures* which receives the name of *American* as a sign of preeminence. Our manners and habits should all conduce to happiness, simplicity, and independence! *Titles* should be totally abolished, and personal distinctions reduced so as to admit of easy access to all. Forms, pomp, grandeur, luxury, and expense, on a magnificent scale, ought to be discouraged. What is called "good society" is a *regal* fungus upon our social system, engendered by a desire to imitate foreign luxuries. In this regard, we have not yet commenced our *American Revolution*. The whole field lies widespread before us.

Let it not be imagined that I am inimical to good breeding, refinement, literature, taste, all that ease and polish which renders social intercourse the charm of life. I am only inimical to the exclusive assumption of "good society" by the rich and the vain, the stockholders and the idle. It should be the aim of a genuine philanthropy to impart the benefits of good breeding to all the members of the human family, if practicable. This may be done by diffusing the blessings of education; by qualifying the working classes to mix with and converse with the more cultivated, polished, and refined. If ignorance and rudeness are made the pretext for a separation of classes and a distinction of ranks, remove the causes and let the barriers of separation be broken down by the omnipotent lever of intellect; at least so far as congenial knowledge spreads her influence over the mind of the community, and assimilates in a bond of brotherhood those now repellent prejudices which sunder man from man, as if an animal of another species whose approach was incompatible with honor, safety, happiness, and even existence. . . .

THE WORKING MAN OF THE UNITED STATES, placed by nature in a moral and physical attitude, which conspire to carry to perfection all the attributes that ennoble his mind and procure happiness to his being, presents to the world the imposing spectacle of Liberty and Reason combining to consummate Justice. For the first time, since the origin of government, he presents the instance of the sovereign power, residing in the producer of labor, to be exercised at his pleasure and discretion. HOLDING THIS WEAPON OF SELF-DEFENSE, HE CANNOT BE OPPRESSED BUT THROUGH THE CONCURRENCE AND ACTION OF THOSE TOUCHED WITH HIS OWN CONDITION.

98.

Nat Turner: Confession

Nat Turner led the best known of all Southern slave revolts, which occurred on August 21, 1831, and climaxed a three-year period of unrest among the slaves during which time Turner had been successful in convincing his followers that he was divinely appointed to lead them from bondage. The statistics of the revolt were themselves sufficient to alarm the whole South: sixty whites killed by Turner's men, and at least one hundred African Americans killed in suppressing the revolt. But the details of the episode as Turner described it in the following confession struck the slaveholding South with even greater fear and put an end to the work of the emancipation societies there. Of the sixty or seventy men and one woman involved in the revolt, twenty-eight were convicted, thirteen (including Turner and the woman) were hanged, and the rest deported. The confession was dictated to Turner's attorney Thomas R. Gray, who asked the questions in the text and included an occasional comment of his own.

Source: *Anglo-African Magazine*, December 1859.

AGREEABLE TO HIS OWN APPOINTMENT, on the evening he was committed to prison, with permission of the jailer, I visited Nat on Tuesday the 1st of November, when, without being questioned at all, he commenced his narrative in the following words:

Sir, you have asked me to give a history of the motives which induced me to undertake the late insurrection, as you call it. To do so I must go back to the days of my infancy, and even before I was born. I was thirty-one years of age the 2nd of October last and born the property of Benj. Turner, of this county. In my childhood a circumstance occurred which made an indelible impression on my mind and laid the groundwork of that enthusiasm which has terminated so fatally to many both white and black, and for which I am about to atone at the gallows. It is here necessary to relate this circumstance, trifling as it may seem; it was the commencement of that belief which has grown with time, and even now, sir, in this dungeon, helpless and forsaken as I am, I cannot divest myself of. Being at play with other children, when three or four years old, I was telling them something, which my mother overhearing, said it had happened before I was born; I stuck to my story, however, and related some things which went in the opinion to confirm it; others being called on were greatly astonished, knowing that these things had happened, and caused them to say in my hearing, I surely would be a prophet, as the Lord had shown me things that had happened before my birth. And my father and mother strengthened me in this my first impression, saying in my presence, I was intended for some great purpose, which they had always thought from certain marks on my head and breast [a parcel of excrescences which I believe are not at all uncommon, particularly among Negroes, as I have seen several with the same. In this case he has either cut them off, or they have nearly disappeared].

My grandmother, who was very religious and to whom I was much attached, my master, who belonged to the church, and other religious persons who visited the house, and whom I often saw at prayers, noticing the singularity of my manners, I suppose, and my uncommon intelligence for a child, remarked I had too much sense to be raised and if I was, I would never be of any service to anyone as a slave. To a mind like mine, restless, inquisitive and observant of everything that was passing, it was easy to suppose that religion was the subject to which it would be directed, and although this subject principally occupied my thoughts, there was nothing that I saw or heard of to which my attention was not directed. The manner in which I learned to read and write not only had great influence on my own mind — as I acquired it with the most perfect ease; so much so, that I have no recollection whatever of learning the alphabet — but to the astonishment of the family, one day, when a book was shown to me to keep me from crying, I began spelling the names of different objects. This was a source of wonder to all in the neighborhood, particularly the blacks; and this learning was constantly improved at all opportunities. When I got large enough to go to work, while employed, I was reflecting on many things that would present themselves to my imagination, and, whenever an opportunity occurred of looking at a book, when the school children were getting their lessons, I would find many things that the fertility of my own imagination had depicted to me before; all my time not devoted to my master's service was spent either in prayer, or in making experiments in casting different things in molds made of earth, in attempting to make paper, gunpowder, and many other experiments that, although I could not perfect, yet convinced me of its practicability if I had the means.

I was not addicted to stealing in my youth, nor have ever been. Yet such was the confidence of the Negroes in the neighborhood, even at this early period of my life, in my superior judgment, that they would often carry me with them when they were going on any roguery, to plan for them. Growing up among them, with this confidence in my superior judgment, and when this, in their opinions, was perfected by Divine inspiration, from the circumstances already alluded to in my infancy, and which belief was ever afterwards zealously inculcated by the austerity of my life and manners, which became the subject of remark with white and black.

Having soon discovered to be great, I must appear so and, therefore, studiously avoided mixing in society and wrapped myself in mystery, devoting my time to fasting and prayer. By this time, having arrived to man's estate and hearing the Scriptures commented on at meetings, I was struck with that particular passage which says: "Seek ye the kingdom of Heaven and all things shall be added unto you." I reflected much on this passage and prayed daily for light on this subject: As I was praying one day at my plow, the Spirit spoke to me, saying "Seek ye the kingdom of Heaven and all things shall be added unto you."

Question: What do you mean by the Spirit?

Answer: The Spirit that spoke to the prophets in former days.

And I was greatly astonished and for two years prayed continually, whenever my duty would permit. And then again I had the same revelation, which fully confirmed me in the impression that I was ordained for some great purpose in the hands of the Almighty.

Several years rolled round, in which many events occurred to strengthen me in this belief. At this time I reverted in my mind to the remarks made of me in my childhood, and the things that had been shown me, and as it had been said of me in my childhood by those by whom I had been taught to pray, both white and black, and in whom I had the greatest confidence, that I had too much sense to be raised, and if I was I would never be of any use to anyone as a slave. Now finding I had arrived to man's estate and was a slave, and these revelations being made known to me, I began to direct my attention to this great object, to fulfill the purpose for which, by this time, I felt assured I was intended. Knowing the influence I had obtained over the minds of my fellow servants, (not by the means of conjuring and such like tricks, for to them I always spoke of such things with contempt) but by the communion of the Spirit whose revelations I often communicated to them, and they believed and said my wisdom came from God. I now began to prepare them for my purpose, by telling them something was about to happen that would terminate in fulfilling the great promise that had been made to me.

About this time I was placed under an overseer, from whom I ran away; and after remaining in the woods thirty days, I returned, to the astonishment of the Negroes on the plantation, who thought I had made my escape to some other part of the country, as my father had done before. But the reason of my return was, that the Spirit appeared to me and said I had my wishes directed to the things of this world, and not to the kingdom of Heaven, and that I should return to the service of my earthly master, "For he who knoweth his Master's will, and doeth it not, shall be beaten with many stripes, and thus have I chastened you." And the Negroes found fault, and murmured against me, saying that if they had my sense they would not serve any master in the world. And about this time I had a vision, and I saw white spirits and black spirits engaged in battle, and the sun was darkened, the thunder rolled in the heavens, and blood flowed in streams, and I heard a voice saying, "Such is your luck, such you are called to see, and let it come rough or smooth, you must surely bear it."

I now withdrew myself as much as my situation would permit from the intercourse of my fellow servants, for the avowed purpose of serving the Spirit more fully, and it appeared to me, and reminded me of the things it had already shown me, and that it would then reveal to me the knowledge of the elements, the revolution of the planets, the operation of tides, and changes of the seasons. After this revelation in the year 1825 and the knowledge of the elements being made known to me, I sought more than ever to obtain true holiness before the great day of judgment should appear, and then I began to receive the true knowledge of faith. And from the first steps of righteousness until the last, was I made perfect; and the Holy Ghost was with me, and said "Behold me as I stand in the Heavens," and I looked and saw the forms of men in different attitudes, and there were lights in the sky to which the children of darkness gave other names than what they really were, for they were the lights of the Savior's hands, stretched forth from east to west, even as they were extended on the cross on Calvary for the redemption of sinners. And I wondered greatly at these miracles, and prayed to be informed of a certainty of the meaning thereof, and shortly afterwards, while laboring in the field, I discovered drops of blood on the corn, as though it were dew from heaven, and I communicated it to many, both white and black in the neighborhood; and I then found on the leaves in the woods hieroglyphic characters and numbers, with the forms of men in different attitudes, portrayed in blood, and representing the figures I had seen before in the heavens. And now the Holy Ghost had revealed itself to me and made plain the miracles it had shown me. For as the blood of Christ had been shed on this earth, and had ascended to heaven for the salvation of sinners, and was now returning to earth again in the form of dew, and as the leaves on the trees bore the impression of the figures I had seen in the heavens, it was plain to me that the Savior was about to lay down the yoke He had borne for the sins of men, and the great day of judgment was at hand.

About this time, I told these things to a white man (Etheldred T. Brantley) on whom it had a wonderful effect, and he ceased from his wickedness and was attacked immediately with a cutaneous eruption, and blood oozed from the pores of his skin, and after praying and fasting nine days, he was healed, and the Spirit appeared to me again and said, as the Savior had been baptized, so should we be also; and when the white people would not let us be baptized by the church, we went down into the water together, in the sight of many who reviled us, and were baptized by the Spirit. After this I rejoiced greatly, and gave thanks to God. And on May 12, 1828, I heard a loud noise in the heavens, and the Spirit instantly appeared to me and said the Serpent was loosened, and Christ had laid down the yoke He had borne for the sins of men, and that I should take it on and fight against the Serpent, for the time was fast approaching, when the first should be last and the last should be first.

Question: Do you not find yourself mistaken now?

Answer: Was not Christ crucified?

And by signs in the heavens that it would make known to me when I should commence the great work, and until the first sign appeared, I should conceal it from the knowledge of men. And on the appearance of the sign, (the eclipse of the sun last February) I should arise and prepare myself and slay my enemies with their own weapons. And immediately on the sign appearing in the heavens, the seal was removed from my lips, and I communicated the great work laid out for me to do, to four in whom I had the greatest confidence (Henry, Hark, Nelson, and Sam). It was intended by us to have begun the work of death on the 4th of

July last. Many were the plans formed and rejected by us, and it affected my mind to such a degree that I fell sick, and the time passed without our coming to any determination how to commence; still forming new schemes and rejecting them, when the sign appeared again, which determined me not to wait longer.

Since the commencement of 1830, I had been living with Mr. Joseph Travis, who was to me a kind master and placed the greatest confidence in me; in fact, I had no cause to complain of his treatment to me. On Saturday evening, the 20th of August, it was agreed between Henry, Hark and myself, to prepare a dinner the next day for the men we expected, and then to concert a plan, as we had not yet determined on any. Hark on the following morning brought a pig, and Henry brandy, and being joined by Sam, Nelson, Will, and Jack, they prepared in the woods a dinner, where, about three o'clock, I joined them.

Question: Why were you so backward in joining them?

Answer: The same reason that had caused me not to mix with them for years before.

I saluted them on coming up and asked Will how came he there; he answered, his life was worth no more than others, and his liberty as dear to him. I asked him if he thought to obtain it? He said he would, or lose his life. This was enough to put him in full confidence. Jack, I knew, was only a tool in the hands of Hark, it was quickly agreed we should commence at home (Mr. J. Travis') on that night, and until we had armed and equipped ourselves and gathered sufficient force, neither age nor sex was to be spared (which was invariably adhered to).

We remained at the feast until about two hours in the night, when we went to the house and found Austin; they all went to the cider press and drank, except myself. On returning to the house, Hark went to the door with an axe, for the purpose of breaking it open, as we knew we were strong enough to murder the family, if they were awaked by the noise; but, reflecting that it might create an alarm in the neighborhood, we determined to enter the house secretly and murder them while sleeping. Hark got a ladder and set it against the chimney on which I ascended and, hoisting a window, entered and came down stairs, unbarred the door, and removed the guns from their places. It was then observed that I must spill the first blood. On which, armed with a hatchet and accompanied by Will, I entered my master's chamber. It being dark, I could not give a death blow; the hatchet glanced from his head; he sprang from the bed and called his wife. It was his last word. Will laid him dead with a blow of his axe, and Mrs. Travis shared the same fate, as she lay in bed.

The murder of this family, five in number, was the work of a moment, not one of them awoke; there was a little infant, sleeping in a cradle, that was forgotten until we had left the house and gone some distance, when Henry and Will returned and killed it; we got here four guns that would shoot and several old muskets, with a pound or two of powder. We remained some time at the barn, where we paraded; I formed them in a line as soldiers and, after carrying them through all the maneuvers I was master of, marched them off to Mr. Salathul Francis', about 600 yards distant. Sam and Will went to the door and knocked. Mr. Francis asked who was there; Sam replied it was him and he had a letter for him, on which he got up and came to the door; they immediately seized him, and dragging him out a little from the door, he was dispatched by repeated blows on the head; there was no other white person in the family.

We started from there for Mrs. Reese's, maintaining the most perfect silence on our march, where finding the door unlocked, we entered and murdered Mrs. Reese in her bed, while sleeping; her son awoke, but it was only to sleep the sleep of death. He

had only time to say who is that, and he was no more. From Mrs. Reese's we went to Mrs. Turner's, a mile distant, which we reached about sunrise on Monday morning. Henry, Austin, and Sam went to the still, where, finding Mr. Peebles, Austin shot him, and the rest of us went to the house; as we approached, the family discovered us and shut the door. Vain hope! Will, with one stroke of his axe, opened it, and we entered and found Mrs. Turner and Mrs. Newsome in the middle of a room almost frightened to death. Will immediately killed Mrs. Turner with one blow of his axe. I took Mrs. Newsome by the hand, and with the sword I had when I was apprehended, I struck her several blows over the head, but not being able to kill her, as the sword was dull. Will turning around and discovering it, dispatched her also.

A general destruction of property and search for money and ammunition always succeeded the murders. By this time my company amounted to fifteen, and nine men mounted, who started for Mrs. Whitehead's (the other six were to go through a by way to Mr. Bryant's and rejoin us at Mrs. Whitehead's). As we approached the house we discovered Mr. Richard Whitehead standing in the cotton patch, near the lane fence; we called him over into the lane, and Will, the executioner, was near at hand, with his fatal axe, to send him to an untimely grave. As we pushed on to the house, I discovered some one run round the garden, and, thinking it was some of the white family, I pursued them, but finding it was a servant girl belonging to the house, I returned to commence the work of death, but they whom I left had not been idle; all the family were already murdered but Mrs. Whitehead and her daughter Margaret. As I came round to the door I saw Will pulling Mrs. Whitehead out of the house, and at the step he nearly severed her head from her body with his broad axe. Miss Margaret, when I discovered her, had concealed herself in the corner formed by the projection of the cellar cap from the house; on my approach she fled, but was soon overtaken, and after repeated blows with a sword, I killed her by a blow on the head with a fence rail. By this time, the six who had gone by Mr. Bryant's rejoined us and informed me they had done the work of death assigned them.

We again divided, part going to Mr. Richard Porter's, and from thence to Nathaniel Francis', the others to Mr. Howell Harris' and Mr. T. Doyle's. On my reaching Mr. Porter's, he had escaped with his family. I understood there, that the alarm had already spread, and I immediately returned to bring up those sent to Mr. Doyle's and Mr. Howell Harris'; the party I left going on to Mr. Francis', having told them I would join them in that neighborhood. I met these sent to Mr. Doyle's and Mr. Harris' returning, having met Mr. Doyle on the road and killed him; and learning from some who joined them that Mr. Harris was from home, I immediately pursued the course taken by the party gone on before; but knowing they would complete the work of death and pillage at Mr. Francis' before I could get there, I went to Mr. Peter Edwards', expecting to find them there, but they had been here also. I then went to Mr. John T. Barrow's; they had been here and murdered him. I pursued on their track to Capt. Newit Harris', where I found the greater part mounted and ready to start; the men, now amounting to about forty, shouted and hurrahed as I rode up; some were in the yard, loading their guns, others drinking. They said Captain Harris and his family had escaped, the property in the house they destroyed, robbing him of money and other valuables. I ordered them to mount and march instantly, this was about nine or ten o'clock Monday morning.

I proceeded to Mr. Levi Waller's, two or three miles distant. I took my station in the rear, and as it was my object to carry terror and devastation wherever we went, I placed fifteen or twenty of the best mounted and most to be relied on in front, who generally approached the houses as fast as their horses could run; this was for two purposes, to prevent their escape and strike terror to the inhabitants; on this account I never got to the houses, after leaving Mrs. Whitehead's until the murders were committed, except in one case. I sometimes got in sight in time to see the work of death completed, viewed the mangled bodies as they lay, in silent satisfaction, and immediately started in quest of other victims.

Having murdered Mrs. Waller and ten children, we started for Mr. William Williams'; having killed him and two little boys that were there; while engaged in this, Mrs. Williams fled and got some distance from the house, but she was pursued, overtaken, and compelled to get up behind one of the company, who brought her back, and after showing her the mangled body of her lifeless husband, she was told to get down and lay by his side, where she was shot dead. I then started for Mr. Jacob Williams', where the family were murdered. Here we found a young man named Drury, who had come on business with Mr. Williams; he was pursued, overtaken and shot. Mrs. Vaughan's was the next place we visited, and, after murdering the family here, I determined on starting for Jerusalem. Our number amounted now to fifty or sixty, all mounted and armed with guns, axes, swords, and clubs.

On reaching Mr. James W. Parker's gate, immediately on the road leading to Jerusalem and about three miles distant, it was proposed to me to call there, but I objected, as I knew he was gone to Jerusalem, and my object was to reach there as soon as possible; but some of the men having relations at Mr. Parker's, it was agreed that they might call and get his people. I remained at the gate on the road with seven or eight; the others going across the field to the house about half a mile off. After waiting some time for them, I became impatient and started to the house for them, and on our return we were met by a party of white men, who had pursued our bloodstained track, and who had fired on those at the gate and dispersed them, which I knew nothing of, not having been at that time rejoined by any of them.

Immediately on discovering the whites, I ordered my men to halt and form, as they appeared to be alarmed. The white men, eighteen in number, approached us in about one hundred yards, when one of them fired (this was against the positive orders of Captain Alexander P. Peete, who commanded, and who had directed the men to reserve their fire until within thirty paces). And I discovered about half of them retreating. I then ordered my men to fire and rush on them; the few remaining stood their ground until we approached within fifty yards, when they fired and retreated. We pursued and overtook some of them who we thought we left dead (they were not killed); after pursuing them about two hundred yards and rising a little hill, I discovered they were met by another party, and had halted and were reloading their guns. (This was a small party from Jerusalem who knew the Negroes were in the field and had just tied their horses to await their return to the road knowing that Mr. Parker and family were in Jerusalem, but knew nothing of the party that had gone in with Captain Peete. On hearing the firing they immediately rushed to the spot and arrived just in time to arrest the progress of these barbarous villains and save the lives of their friends and fellow citizens.)

Thinking that those who retreated first, and the party who fired on us at fifty or sixty yards distant, had all only fallen back to meet others with ammunition. As I saw them reloading their guns, and more coming up than I saw at first, and several of my bravest men being wounded, the others became panic struck and scattered over the field; the white men pursued and fired on us several times. Hark had his horse shot under him, and I caught another for him as it was running by me; five or six of my men were wounded, but none left on the field; finding myself defeated here I instantly determined to go through a private way and cross the Nottoway River at the Cypress Bridge, three miles below Jerusalem, and attack that place in the rear, as I expected they would look for me on the other road, and I had a great desire to get there to procure arms and ammunition. After going a short distance in this private way, accompanied by about twenty men, I overtook two or three who told me the others were dispersed in every direction. After trying in vain to collect a sufficient force to proceed to Jerusalem, I determined to return, as I was sure they would make back to their old neighborhood, where they would rejoin me, make new recruits, and come down again. On my way back, I called at Mrs. Thomas', Mrs. Spencer's, and several other places, the white families having fled; we found no more victims to gratify our thirst for blood. We stopped at Maj. Ridley's quarter for the night, and being joined by four of his men, with the recruits made since my defeat, we mustered now about forty strong.

After placing out sentinels, I laid down to sleep, but was quickly roused by a great racket; starting up, I found some mounted and others in great confusion; one of the sentinels having given the alarm that we were about to be attacked, I ordered some to ride around and reconnoiter, and on their return the others being more alarmed, not knowing who they were, fled in different ways, so that I was reduced to about twenty again, with this I determined to attempt to recruit, and proceed on to rally in the neighborhood I had left. Dr. Blunt's was the nearest house, which we reached just before day; on riding up the yard, Hark fired a gun. We expected Dr. Blunt and his family were at Maj. Ridley's, as I knew there was a company of men there; the gun was fired to ascertain if any of the family were at home; we were immediately fired upon and retreated leaving several of my men. I do not know what became of them, as I never saw them afterwards.

Pursuing our course back and coming in sight of Captain Harris', where we had been the day before, we discovered a party of white men at the house, on which all deserted me but two (Jacob and Nat). We concealed ourselves in the woods until near night, when I sent them in search of Henry, Sam, Nelson, and Hark, and directed them to rally all they could at the place we had had our dinner the Sunday before, where they would find me, and I accordingly returned there as soon as it was dark and remained until Wednesday evening, when discovering white men riding around the place as though they were looking for some one, and none of my men joining me, I concluded Jacob and Nat had been taken and compelled to betray me.

On this I gave up all hope for the present; and on Thursday night, after having supplied myself with provisions from Mr. Travis', I scratched a hole under a pile of fence rails in a field, where I concealed myself for six weeks, never leaving my hiding place but for a few minutes in the dead of night to get water, which was very near. Thinking by this time I could venture out, I began to go about in the night and eavesdrop the houses in the neighborhood; pursuing this course for about a fortnight and gathering little or no intelligence, afraid of speaking to any human being, and returning every morning to my cave before the dawn of day. I know not how long I might have led this life, if accident had not betrayed me. A dog in the neighborhood, passing by my hiding place one night while I was out, was attracted by some meat I had in my cave, and crawled in and stole it, and was coming out just as I returned. A few nights after, two Negroes having started to go hunting with the same dog, and passed that way, the dog came again to the place, and having just gone out to walk about, discovered me and barked, on which thinking myself discovered, I spoke to them to beg concealment. On making myself known, they fled from me. Knowing then they would betray me, I immediately left my hiding place and was pursued almost incessantly until I was taken a fortnight afterwards by Mr. Benjamin Phipps, in a little hole I had dug out with my sword, for the purpose of concealment, under the top of a fallen tree. On Mr. Phipps discovering the place of my concealment, he cocked his gun and aimed at me. I requested him not to shoot, and I would give up, upon which he demanded my sword. I delivered it to him, and he brought me to prison. During the time I was pursued, I had many hairbreadth escapes, which your time will not permit you to relate. I am here loaded with chains, and willing to suffer the fate that awaits me.

I here proceeded to make some inquiries of him, after assuring him of the certain death that awaited him, and that concealment would only bring destruction on the innocent as well as guilty, of his own color, if he knew of any extensive or concerted plan. His answer was, I do not. When I questioned him as to the insurrection in North Carolina happening about the same time, he denied any knowledge of it; and when I looked him in the face as though I would search his inmost thoughts, he replied, "I see sir, you doubt my word; but can you not think the same ideas and strange appearances about this time in the heavens might prompt others, as well as myself, to this undertaking." I now had much conversation with and asked him many questions, having forborne to do so previously, except in the cases noted in parentheses; but during his statement, I had, unnoticed by him, taken notes as to some particular circumstances, and, having the advantage of his statement before me in writing, on the evening of the third day that I had been with him, I began a cross examination and found his statement corroborated by every circumstance coming within my own knowledge, or the confessions of others who had been either killed or executed and whom he had not seen or had any knowledge since 22nd of August last. He expressed himself fully satisfied as to the impracticability of his attempt.

It has been said he was ignorant and cowardly, and that his object was to murder and rob for the purpose of obtaining money to make his escape. It is notorious, that he was never known to have a dollar in his life, to swear an oath, or drink a drop of spirits. As to his ignorance, he certainly never had the advantages of education, but he can read and write (it was taught him by his parents) and for natural intelligence and quickness of apprehension is surpassed by few men I have ever seen. As to his being a coward, his reason as given for not resisting Mr. Phipps shows the decision of his character. When he saw Mr. Phipps present his gun, he said he knew it was impossible for him to escape, as the woods were full of men; he therefore thought it was better to surrender and trust to fortune for his escape. He is a complete fanatic, or plays his part most admirably.

On other subjects he possesses an uncommon share of intelligence, with a mind capable of attaining anything; but warped and perverted by the influence of early impressions. He is below the ordinary stature, though strong and active, having the true Negro face, every feature of which is strongly marked. I shall not attempt to describe the effect of his narrative, as told and commented on by himself, in the condemned hole of the prison. The calm, deliberate composure with which he spoke of his late deeds and intentions, the expression of his fiendlike face when excited by enthusiasm, still bearing the stains of the blood of helpless innocence about him; clothed with rags and covered with chains; yet daring to raise his manacled hands to heaven, with a spirit soaring above the attributes of man; I looked on him and my blood curdled in my veins.

I will not shock the feelings of humanity, nor wound afresh the bosoms of the disconsolate sufferers in this unparalleled and inhuman massacre, by detailing the deeds of their fiendlike barbarity. There were two or three who were in the power of these wretches, had they known it, and who escaped in the most providential manner. There were two whom they thought they had left dead on the field at Mr. Parker's, but who were only stunned by the blows of their guns, as they did not take time to reload when they charged on them.

The escape of a little girl who went to school at Mr. Waller's, and where the children were collecting for that purpose, excited general sympathy. As their teacher had not arrived, they were at play in the yard, and, seeing the Negroes approach, she ran up on a dirt chimney (such as are common to log houses) and remained there unnoticed during the massacre of the eleven that were killed at this place. She remained on her hiding place till just before the arrival of a party, who were in pursuit of the murderers, when she came down and fled to a swamp, where, a mere child as she was, with the horrors of the late scene before her, she lay concealed until the next day, when seeing a party go up to the house, she came up and, on being asked how she escaped, replied with the utmost simplicity: The Lord helped her. She was taken up behind a gentleman of the party and returned to the arms of her weeping mother.

Miss Whitehead concealed herself between the bed and the mat that supported it, while they murdered her sister in the same room, without discovering her. She was afterwards carried off and concealed for protection by a slave of the family, who gave evidence against several of them on their trial. Mrs. Nathaniel Francis, while concealed in a closet heard their blows and the shrieks of the victims of these ruthless savages; they then entered the closet where she was concealed, and went out without discovering her. While in this hiding place, she heard two of her women in a quarrel about the division of her clothes. Mr. John T. Baron, discovering them approaching his house, told his wife to make her escape and, scorning to fly, fell fighting on his own threshold. After firing his rifle, he discharged his gun at them and then broke it over the villain who first approached him, but he was overpowered and slain. His bravery, however, saved from the hands of these monsters his lovely and amiable wife, who will long lament a husband as deserving of her love. As directed by him, she attempted to escape through the garden, when she was caught and held by one of her servant girls, but another coming to her rescue, she fled to the woods and concealed herself. Few indeed, were those who escaped their work of death. But fortunate for society, the hand of retributive justice has overtaken them; and not one that was known to be concerned has escaped.

The Commonwealth v. *Nat Turner:* Charged with making insurrection, and plotting to take away the lives of divers free white persons, etc., on the 22nd of August, 1831. The court composed of ———, having met for the trial of Nat Turner, the prisoner was brought in and arraigned, and upon his arraignment pleaded *not guilty;* saying to his counsel, that he did not feel so.

On the part of the Commonwealth, Levi Waller was introduced, who being sworn, deposed as follows: (*agreeably to Nat's own Confession*). Col Trezvant [the committing magistrate] was then introduced, who being sworn, numerated Nat's Confession to him, as follows: (*his Confession as given to Mr. Gray*). The prisoner introduced no evidence, and the case was submitted without argument to the court, who having found him guilty, Jeremiah Cobb, Esq., chairman, pronounced the sentence of the court, in the following words: "Nat Turner! Stand up. Have you anything to say why sentence of death should not be pronounced against you?"

Answer: I have not. I have made a full confession to Mr. Gray, and I have nothing more to say.

"Attend then to the sentence of the court. You have been arraigned and tried before this court, and convicted of one of the highest crimes in our criminal code. You have been convicted of plotting in cold blood the indiscriminate destruction of men, of helpless women, and of infant children. The evidence before us leaves not a shadow of doubt, but that your hands were often imbrued in the blood of the innocent; and your own confession tells us that they were stained with the blood of a master, in your own language, too indulgent. Could I stop here, your crime would be sufficiently aggravated. But the original contriver of a plan, deep and deadly, one that never can be effected, you managed so far to put it into execution, as to deprive us of many of our most valuable citizens; and this was done when they were asleep, and defenseless, under circumstances shocking to humanity. And while upon this part of the subject, I cannot but call your attention to the poor misguided wretches who have gone before you. They are not few in number; they were your bosom associates; and the blood of all cries aloud, and calls upon you, as the author of their misfortune. Yes! You forced them unprepared, from Time to Eternity. Borne down by this load of guilt, your only justification is, that you were led away by fanaticism. If this be true, from my soul I pity you; and while you have my sympathies, I am, nevertheless, called upon to pass the sentence of the court. The time between this and your execution will necessarily be very short; and your only hope but must be in another world. The judgment of the court is, that you be taken hence to the jail from whence you came, thence to the place of execution, and on Friday next, between the hours of 10 A.M. and 2 P.M., be hung by the neck until you are dead! dead! dead! and may the Lord have mercy upon your soul."

1831-1832

99.

Alexis de Tocqueville: American Notes

Charles Alexis Henri Maurice Clérel de Tocqueville arrived in New York on May 11, 1831, and spent the next nine months traveling about the country, ostensibly to study the American prison system. But his interests were much wider than that, and he kept a series of notebooks in which he recorded his impressions of everything he saw and of everyone he talked to. In this day-to-day account one can see the substance of Democracy in America, *Tocqueville's classic work, taking shape. Although it has been in English editions for more than a century, the notebooks were not translated until 1959. We reprint here a number of journal entries, all but one from the year 1831; and, at the end of the selection, several short essays, some of them probably written in early 1832, to which Tocqueville did not affix dates. The latter are of special interest, for they deal with subjects on which he wrote at much greater length in* Democracy in America.

Source: *Journey to America*, translated by George Lawrence, J. P. Mayer, ed., New Haven, 1962.

Sing Sing, May 29

When one reflects on the nature of this society here, one sees to some extent the explanation of what I have . . . written — American society is composed of a thousand different elements recently assembled.

The men who live under its laws are still English, French, German, and Dutch. They have neither religion, morals, nor ideas in common; up to the present one cannot say that there is an American character, at least unless it is the very fact of not having any. There is no common memory, no national attachments here. What then can be the only bond that unites the different parts of this huge body? *Interest.*

Conversation with Mr. Livingston, June 7

I: It seems to me that American society suffers from taking too little account of intellectual questions.

He: I agree. Far from improving, we get daily worse in this respect.

I: Why do you think that happens?

He: Chiefly because of the law of inheritance. When I was young I remember the country peopled by rich landowners who lived on their estates as the English gentry do, and who used their minds, and had, too, a sense of tradition in their thoughts and manners. Then there was distinction in the behavior and turn of mind of one class in the nation. The law making shares equal has worked continually to break up fortunes and form them anew; our former standards and conceptions have been lost and this process goes on from day to day. Land changes hands incredibly quickly, nobody has time to strike root in one place, and everybody must turn to some practical work to keep up the position his father held. Almost all families disappear after the second or third generation.

I: Is there anything analogous to the influence, the patronage of large landowners?

He: No. Only individual merit counts here.

I: How do the wealthy classes put up with such a state of affairs?

He: They put up with it as something inevitable since there is nothing whatsoever to be done about it.

I: But is there nonetheless some resentment between them and the common people?

He: None. All classes joined together in the Revolution. Afterward, the strength of democracy was so paramount that no one attempted to struggle against it. Generally speaking the people show no distaste for electing the very rich or well-educated.

I: I am very struck by what seems an extreme equality in American social relations. The richest of men and the poorest artisan will shake hands in the street.

He: There is a great deal of equality. Less, however, than a foreigner supposes. The manners which strike you often count for no more than such a formula as "your humble servant" at the end of a letter. Here we have to be polite to everybody as everyone has political rights. There is much pride of wealth among the new-rich of New York. Like the rest of the world we have our moneyed aristocracy, if one can use the word aristocracy of an ever changing class which makes its pretensions but has no power.

I: In general what type of men hold positions in public service?

He: Generally they are held by men whose abilities and characters put them in the second rank. Such places do not carry sufficient pay, social consideration, or power to attract men of distinction. But that was not so in the first years of independence. Now we have no great men in politics. They use their energy and their resources in other careers.

Mr. Livingston has been in Europe. He comes from a very old family and seems a man of culture.

Conversation with Mr. Gallatin (who has spent several years as American minister in France and in England), New York, June 10

He: We have no villages in America, that is to say, none inhabited by people who cultivate the land. A landowner lives on his estate and the houses are scattered all over the country. What you take for villages had better be called towns as they are inhabited by shopkeepers, craftsmen, and lawyers.

I: I take you up on the last word; so you have a great many lawyers?

He: Many more, I think, than anywhere in Europe.

I: What is their social standing and character?

He: The one explains the other. Lawyers count among the top ranks of society and have much influence; so instead of having bustling, restless characters as in Europe, they tend to stability. Without the lawyers we should by now have revised our civil law, but they defend the abuses and ambiguities from which they profit.

I: Do they play a great part in elected bodies?

He: They form the majority of members of such bodies; but it has been noticed that the most distinguished speakers and, still more, the greatest statesmen have not been lawyers.

I: How are your judges chosen? What is their position and character?

He: The judges are all chosen from among the lawyers and, bar the authority of the bench, remain on a footing of equality with them. Our judges are held in very high esteem. Being entirely dependent on public opinion, they need to make continual efforts to keep this esteem. Their integrity is unquestioned. I look on the judges, supported as they always are by the lawyers as a body, as the regulators of the irregular movements of our democracy, and as those who maintain the equilibrium of the system. Note that having the power to refuse to enforce an unconstitutional law, the judges are in some sort a political force.

I: Is it true, as I am told, that morals are chaste?

He: Conjugal fidelity is admirably secure; there is not always the same chastity before marriage. It very often happens in our country districts (not in the towns) that the extreme liberty enjoyed by young people of both sexes leads to trouble. The savage tribes that surround us go even further in this disregard of chastity before marriage. They do not see it as a moral duty.

Conversation with Mr. Spencer, Canandaigua, July 17-18

Mr. Spencer is a distinguished man of law. He has been successively a lawyer, district attorney, and a member of Congress, and is at the moment a member of the New York legislature. He has been one of the editors of the *Revised Statutes.* Clearness and perspicacity seem to be the guiding lights of his spirit.

Question: Are the members of the two chambers of the various legislatures chosen in the same way and according to the same rules of eligibility?

Answer: Yes. In the state of New York in particular there is just the same type of man filling both chambers.

Question: But what then is the point of having two chambers?

Answer: It is immensely useful and so well appreciated that now everyone in America accepts it as an axiom that a single legislative body is a detestable institution. Pennsylvania, which began by making the mistake of having only one assembly, has had to give it up. Here are the chief advantages of a legislative body with two houses. The first and most important is to make a resolution pass two tests; between the two discussions time passes to the advantage of good sense and moderation. It is continually happening that the Senate, although composed of similar elements and moved by the same spirit as the legislature, sees the matter in a different light and corrects mistakes which the former, prejudiced as it is by a first vote, would not be able to correct. The second advantage which I see in the institution of our Senate is that the senators hold office for longer than the representatives, and, since they are replaced in batches, always form a body of men within the legislature who are knowledgeable about precedents and have already been through their political education. They give our legislative assemblies a practical skill and a sense of continuity which without them would often be lacking.

Question: What, generally speaking, is the corporate attitude of the lawyers?

Answer: People complain that it is conservative. I know that the opposite complaint is made in France. I see these reasons for the difference. First, the body of lawyers in America have no interest in change. Our social organization, as it now is, is the best possible one for them. Besides, I think our civil laws have a different general principle from yours and that should give our lawyers an opposite turn of mind. Our civil law is entirely founded on precedents. A judge is completely bound by what another has decided before. As a result one can almost say that there are no arguments about law with us; everything reduces itself in some sort to a question of fact. One has to know what was decided in a similar case and argue for or against the application of that example. You can see that work of that sort is not apt to develop a taste for theories. Often it even narrows the mind. Your lawyers, on the other hand, if I can judge by the reports of proceedings, feel they must delve down to the basis of society even in respect of a hole in a dunghill.

Question: Have the judges any disciplinary powers over them?

Answer: Yes. They can reprimand them, fine them, strike them off the roll, and even in extreme cases send them to prison. Otherwise the judges have no superior standing. Out of court they are on a footing of complete equality.

Question: What criticism is made of your judges?

Answer: The only criticism which I should feel able to make is that they are a little too fond of flattering the people, and that they will not fight courageously against a view that they believe is shared by the masses. We have seen some examples of that in cases with a political side to them. Usually and in ordinary cases they are inclined to leniency for this reason and not from their own convictions.

Question: What influence has the press on public opinion?

Answer: It has great influence, but it is not exercised in the same way as in France. For instance, we attach very little importance to the opinions of journalists. They only gain influence by the facts they make known and the turn they give to them. Thus they sometimes manage to mislead public opinion about a man or a measure. To sum up, in all countries and under all

governments the press will always be a formidable weapon.

Question: What limits do you impose on its freedom?

Answer: We have a very simple principle in this matter. Everything which is a question of opinion is perfectly free. One could go to print daily in America saying that monarchy is the best of all forms of government. But when a paper publishes libelous facts, when it gratuitously suggests culpable motives, then it is prosecuted and generally punished with a heavy fine. I recently had experience of an example. At the time of the case in connection with the disappearance of Morgan (a Masonic affair) a newspaper printed that the jurors had pronounced their verdict of guilty from motives of "party spirit." I prosecuted the writer of the article and had him punished.

Question: What in your view is the way to diminish the power of journalism?

Answer: I am completely convinced that the most effective way is to increase the number of newspapers as much as possible and not to prosecute them except in extreme cases. Their power gets less as their number gets greater, a fact which experience has incontrovertibly proved to us. I have heard it said that in France there were only two or three newspapers that carried weight. I should suppose that in such a situation the press is an agent of destruction. Besides I think your social situation will always make the action of the press more to be feared with you than with us. Paris will always exercise immense influence over the rest of the kingdom. With us there are an immense number of factors dividing our interests. There is no great center of activity; it is almost impossible to get public opinion excited over a large area. New York papers have no more influence over us than those of the nearest village. Another reason why the personal opinions of journalists carry very little weight is the bad use they made of them in the first years of independence. It was then proved that most of them were sold to England. Since then they have lost public confidence.

Question: Are there influential men who write in your newspapers?

Answer: Party leaders often do, but they do not sign their articles.

Question: What causes the religious tolerance prevailing in the United States?

Answer: Principally the extreme diversity of sects (there is almost no end to it). If two religions faced each other, we should be cutting each others' throats. But as none has as much as a majority, all need toleration. Besides there is a general belief among us, a belief which I share, that some religion or other is needed by man as a social being. And all the more the freer he is. I have heard it said that in France there has been an attempt to dispense with all definite religion. If that is so, in spite of all your feeling for liberty, you will not quickly see free institutions firmly established, and you must rest your hopes on the next generation.

Question: What do you think can be done so that religion should regain its natural sway?

Answer: I think the Catholic religion less suited than the Protestant to come to terms with ideas of liberty. But if the clergy were completely cut off from all worldly concern, I think that in time they would win back the power over the mind which naturally belongs to them. I think that to seem to forget about the church without being hostile to it is the best and perhaps the only way of serving it. If you act so, little by little you will see public education falling into its hands, and in time young people will have a different turn of mind.

Question: Do the clergy control public education with you?

Answer: Completely. I know of only two exceptions in the state of New York. That seems to me nature's way.

Question: What about your poor law?

Answer: In that as in many other matters we long followed the English example. We have ended by giving up their system which we thought too costly. This is the new system introduced in the last few years in the state of New York. Every county has an almshouse to which vagabonds are forced by court orders to go, and which are also bound to receive those whom an official, called the overseer of the poor, sends as having no means of subsistence. A piece of land is attached to the almshouse, which the vagabonds and the local people shut up there have to cultivate. The object of the law is that this farmland should in time cover the expenses of the institution. We have great hopes of succeeding in this. It is not the place of birth but the place of residence which is taken to decide where the pauper should be sent.

Question: How do you manage about public education?

Answer: The state has special funds . . . set aside for this purpose. It makes grants from this fund to the local authorities who need them, in proportion to the efforts they promise to make on their own behalf. For it is generally accepted among us that the state should always help and never do everything. It is felt that people who give their money and who are on the spot can and will give more careful attention to the way money is spent than is possible for a central administration. Moreover, one wants to create as many local interests as possible. This combination of money from the state with money from the locality serves both these aims admirably. Here education rouses universal concern. The populace being really king, everyone feels the need to enlighten it.

Question: Have you noticed ill effects from the recent law abolishing all property qualification for electors?

Answer: No, just the opposite. The people, being completely satisfied, disregard the schemes of agitators.

July 19, on Lake Erie, on board the Ohio

Sometimes one sees, even among those Indians who are encircled now by European possessions, men whose better intelligence foresees the destiny of the Indian race and whose savage energy still seeks to fight against a future from now on inevitable. Red Jacket, who died in 1829 in the village of Senecas near Buffalo, was one of those whom one might call the last of the Indians.

Mr. Spencer told me (July 18, 1831) the following stories about him. Red Jacket had been in our time in the New World the greatest enemy of the whites and, from hatred of them, of the Christian religion. Feeling that the time had passed for struggling with open force against the Europeans, he at least made use of all the moral power which he enjoyed among his compatriots to prevent them from becoming fused in the midst of us. Red Jacket knew our ways and understood English; but he did not condescend to speak it. His influence over his compatriots was immense. It would be difficult, added Mr. Spencer, to imagine a man whose eloquence was more natural and captivating, or who could handle irony more skillfully.

I remember that ten years ago an Indian from the neighborhood of Buffalo was accused of having killed an American. He was arrested and brought before one of our juries. I was then district attorney and had to conduct the case against him. Red Jacket appeared for the defense, and though he had to use an interpreter, he won his case. After the hearing he came up to me and said, apparently with great simplicity, "No doubt my brother (he meant the accused) formerly did you a great injury." I answered that before his crime I did not know that he existed. "I understand," Red Jacket answered. "The white man whom he killed was your brother, and you wanted to avenge him." I tried again to get that idea out of his head and make him understand the nature of my duties. Red Jacket, after

listening attentively to me, asked whether the ancients of my people paid me for what I had just explained that I was doing. I said yes. Then, pretending to be moved by the most lively indignation, he cried out: "What! Not only do you want to kill my brother who has never done you any harm but you have sold his blood in advance!"

I confess, Mr. Spencer added, that I stood aghast at that apostrophe. . . .

Many years ago now the Presbyterians in Boston sent a missionary to the Mohawk Indians who then lived in the valley which still bears their name. Red Jacket was among them. The tribe assembled to hear the missionary. After which, according to their custom, there was a general debate and Red Jacket, having obtained a decision to send back the Presbyterian minister, was appointed to inform him of this resolution. Red Jacket said: "My father has spoken well, but my brothers have a doubt which they wish cleared up. Our ancestors have told our fathers that they had seen the Great Spirit, and we believe our fathers. It is said that the white men believe a book which the Great Spirit has given them; but it is added that each of the innumerable tribes of white men puts a different meaning to this book. Have my brothers been given a false report?" The missionary was obliged to say that there was some truth in what Red Jacket was saying, and the latter went on with an air of humility: "If the white men to whom the Great Spirit has been at pains to open knowledge of everything, and to whom he has given this book, are not sure of understanding it, how can my father expect poor savages to succeed in that?"

The missionary strove to explain that Christians only differed about certain points, and agreed about all the rest. Red Jacket, having let him talk as much as he wanted, ended the interview by saying: "These things are difficult for the red men to understand. But if my father would go and repeat them to our nearest neighbors, the white men, and if the results of his preaching is to prevent the white men from stealing our land and our herds as they are doing every day, my father can come back to the red men and will find their ears ·more open."

July 26

Saginaw: an area of cultivation in the midst of savage tribes and impenetrable forest. Beauty of the lonely stream that runs at its foot. We go to see Mr. Williams. He trades with the Indians. He shows us a quantity of little objects intended for their use, for which they pay with the money given to them by the United States as the price of their land and with furs. Clearly he robs them. What he and all the other Europeans say about the savages: excellent folk. Good and gentle. More reliable than the whites. Universal testimony. Coming back I go into the house of one of the French people. His wife like an Indian woman, working at a mat. A red child by her side. I ask her if she is French. No. English? No. What blood? She answers me lowering her head: *a savage*. The Frenchman was her husband and she had already given him several children. Extraordinary race; mixture of the savage and the civilized man; does not know any language well; speaks English, French, and Indian. Has a taste for the wilds, but is still attached to the towns. A common case, they say, among the French. Go duck shooting with the young man in an Indian canoe. Ducking, we go up the Saginaw through impenetrable forests. Some savages come up to us. Envy of my gun which, they say, is fired by the rain. Where are guns like that made? In the land where the fathers of the French Canadians live. Beavers. Sort of insects. . . .

In the evening, toward sunset, we come back alone in the canoe and go down a branch of the Saginaw. Such an evening as one hardly ever sees. Still air, cloudless sky. Our canoe glides without making the slightest noise. We paddle gently and enjoy the sight. Still, transparent water. Wonderful vegetation on the banks. Immense forests reflected in the water, setting sun shining through and casting its light on the undergrowth. In twenty years all this will be replaced by villages, a change in the near future which makes the present sight still more impressive. Echo of a gunshot. We come back at nightfall. Our efforts to keep safe from the mosquitoes.

September 18

Today Mr. Clay (Mr. Clay is a planter from Georgia; I have seldom met a more likeable or better informed man) pointed out to me several of the beautiful houses in Boston and told me that most of those who had built these sumptuous dwellings had made their fortunes themselves and had risen from very low down. He added: Fortunes change hands here at an incredible rate. It has been noted that a poor son almost always succeeds a rich father and that a family only stays down for one generation.

"How does that happen?" I ask. "I understand that your law of inheritance tends to break up fortunes. But a still more democratic law is in force in France. Fortunes no doubt get smaller little by little, but they do not collapse like ₍yours." Mr. Clay answered: "The reason for the difference is that great fortunes in France are landed, and in New England they are all trading fortunes. You know that in general in America one cannot find tenants. The opposite is an exception; land costs too little and its products are too cheap for anyone to want to cultivate it unless he is the owner. Without tenants, no great territorial fortunes. Now great commercial fortunes are won and preserved by industry and skill, things which cannot be bequeathed like dollars and seldom pass from father to son. In the South, on the other hand, where our slaves take the place of your tenants, fortunes do not disappear faster than with you."

That led us to talk about the slaves. Mr. Clay said to me: "In our Southern states there are a great many districts where white people cannot get acclimatized and where the blacks live and prosper. I imagine that in time the black population of the South, as it becomes free, will concentrate in that portion of the American territory, and the white population, on the other hand, will gradually move out. In that way a population will be formed entirely descended from the Africans, which will be able to have its own nationality and to enjoy its own laws. I can see no other solution to the great question of slavery. I do not think that the blacks will ever mingle sufficiently completely with the white to form a single people with them. The introduction of this foreign race is anyhow the one great plague of America."

Note: Must not this impossibility of which Mr. Clay speaks, of forming great territorial fortunes in the North of the United States (one cannot doubt that it is an impossibility), be an important contributory factor in shaping the commercial, manufacturing, restless state of mind which is so extraordinarily prominent among the men of this part of the states? In New England the urge to grow rich can only find satisfaction through trade and industry.

September 20
Mr. Quincy, president of Cambridge University [Harvard], said to me today: "The state of Massachusetts is a union of little republics who appoint their magistrates and manage their own affairs."
"But," said I, "what is the central tie?"
"The legislature," Mr. Quincy answered. "These little republics have a sphere of action fixed by the law, and outside that they become completely dependent on the great political body which represents the people. When individual communities break the law, they are prosecuted in the courts by the state attorney general. They can also be sued by anyone who has been harmed by them. Such-and-such a town is bound to repair a road, neglects it and I break my carriage there. I bring an action for damages at once against the town."

Mr. Quincy also said to me: "I think our present happy state is even more due to circumstances outside our control than to our Constitution. Here all a man's material needs are satisfied, and, furthermore, we are born in freedom, knowing no other state. Massachusetts was very, very nearly as free before the Revolution as it is now. We have put the people's name in place of that of the king. For the rest one finds nothing changed among us."

Note: One of the happiest consequences of the absence of government (when a people is happy enough to be able to do without it, a rare event) is the ripening of individual strength which never fails to follow therefrom. Each man learns to think and to act for himself without counting on the support of any outside power which, however watchful it be, can never answer all the needs of man in society. The man thus used to seeking his well-being by his own efforts alone stands the higher in his own esteem as well as in that of others. He grows both stronger and greater of soul. Mr. Quincy gave an example of that state of things when he spoke of the man who sued the town that had let the public road fall into disrepair; the same goes for all the rest.

If a man gets the idea of any social improvement whatsoever, a school, a hospital, a road, he does not think of turning to the authorities. He announces his plan, offers to carry it out, calls for the strength of other individuals to aid his efforts, and fights hand to hand against each obstacle. I admit that in fact he often is less successful than the authorities would have been in his place, but, in the total, the general result of all these individual strivings amounts to much more than any administration could undertake; and, moreover, the influence of such a state of affairs on the moral and political character of a people would more than make up for all the inadequacies if there were any.

But one must say it again, there are but few peoples who can manage like that without government. Such a state of affairs can only exist at the two extremes of civilization. The savage with nought but his physical needs to satisfy, he too relies only on himself. For the civilized man to be able to do the same, he must have reached that state of society in which knowledge allows a man to see clearly what is useful for him and in which his passions do not prevent him carrying it out. The most important care of a good government should be to get people used little by little to managing without it.

September 30

The two great social principles which seem to me to rule American society, and to which one must always return to find the reason for all the laws and habits which govern it, are as follows:

First, the majority may be mistaken on some points, but finally it is always right and there is no moral power above it.

Second, every individual, private person, society, community, or nation is the only lawful judge of its own interest, and, provided it does not harm the interests of others, nobody has the right to interfere. I think that one must never lose sight of this point.

Boston, October 1

Interview with Mr. Adams (the former President). We met him when we were dining with Mr. Everett. He was received with great politeness, as an honored guest, but that was all. Most of those present called him "Sir." Some gave him the courtesy title of "President." Mr. Adams is a man sixty-two years old who seems still to enjoy full strength of mind and body. He speaks French with ease and elegance. I was put next to him at table and we had a long conversation together.

I told him how surprised I was to see how far the American people were able to get along without government. I commented, among other things, on the way any group of opinion was allowed to send representatives to an agreed rendezvous and so form a convention.

Mr. Adams answered: "The practice of having these conventions is only five or six years old. Now we have them for all sorts of things. But to tell you frankly what I think, I find these assemblies dangerous. They usurp the place of political bodies and could end by completely thwarting their action."

We spoke of the character of Americans in general and he said: "There are two facts which have had a great influence on our character. In the North the political and religious doctrines of the founders of New England; in the South, slavery."

Question: Do you look on slavery as a great plague for the United States?

Answer: Yes, certainly. That is the root of almost all the troubles of the present and fears for the future.

Question: Do the Southerners realize that state of affairs?

Answer: Yes, at the bottom of their hearts. But it is a truth that they will not admit, although they are clearly preoccupied about it. Slavery has altered the whole state of society in the South. There the whites form a class to themselves which has all the ideas, all the passions, all the prejudices of an aristocracy. But do not be mistaken; nowhere is equality between the whites so complete as in the South. Here we have great equality before the law, but it simply does not affect our ways of life. There are upper classes and working classes. Every white man in the South is an equally privileged being whose destiny it is to make the

Negroes work without working himself. You cannot conceive how far the idea that work is shameful has entered into the spirit of the Americans of the South. Any undertaking in which the Negroes cannot serve in a subordinate role is sure not to succeed in that part of the Union. All those who trade in a large way in Charleston and the towns have come from New England.

I remember a Southern congressman who was dining with me in Washington, and who could not conceal his surprise at seeing white servants serving us at table. He said to Mrs. Adams: "I feel that it is degrading the human race to have white men for servants. When one of them comes to change my plate, I am always tempted to offer him my place at table." From the idleness in which the whites in the South live spring great differences in their character. They devote themselves to bodily exercises, to hunting and races. They are strongly built, brave, and very honorable; they are more touchy about "points of honor" than people anywhere else; duels are frequent.

Question: Do you think that actually it is impossible to do without Negroes in the South?

Answer: I am convinced to the contrary. Europeans cultivate the land in Greece and in Sicily; why should they not do so in Virginia or the Carolinas? It is not hotter there.

Question: Is the number of slaves increasing?

Answer: It is diminishing in all the provinces to the east of the Delaware because there wheat and tobacco are grown, and for those crops Negroes are more hindrance than help. So they are sent from there to the provinces where cotton and sugar are grown; in those provinces their numbers increase. In the states of the West where they have been introduced, their numbers remain small. I know nothing more insolent than a black when he is not speaking to his master and is not afraid of a beating. It is not rare

even to see Negroes treating their master very badly when they have to do with a weak man. The Negro women especially very often take advantage of their mistresses' kindness. They know that it is not the custom to inflict corporal punishment on them.

We spoke of religion, which Mr. Adams seemed to consider as one of the principal guarantees of American society. I asked him whether he thought that religious feeling was on the decline in the United States.

"If one compares the present with the state of affairs a century ago," he answered, "yes; but if one compares things as they are today with how they were forty years ago, I think religion has gained, not lost, ground with us. Forty years ago the philosophy of Voltaire in France and the school of Hume in England had shaken all the beliefs of Europe. The rebound was felt in America. Since then the crimes of the French Revolution have made a profound impression on us; there was a spiritual reaction, and one feels the effect of it still."

"But consider," I said to him, "the road which men's minds have traveled since their point of departure in Catholicism. Do you not think that this progress is continuing, and do you not see the Unitarianism of this country as the last link in a chain leading from Christianity to natural religion?"

Mr. Adams agreed that that was his view. He added: "Nevertheless, all the Boston Unitarians protest strongly against this consequence of their doctrine, and firmly stick to the extreme position they have taken up."

Mr. Adams appeared to think that one of the greatest guarantees of order and internal security in the United States was found in the movement of the population toward the West. "Many more generations yet will pass," he added, "before we feel that we are overcrowded."

I then spoke to him about the more immediate dangers to the Union and the causes which might lead to its dissolution. Mr. Adams did not answer at all, but it was easy to see that in this matter he felt no more confidence than I did in the future.

Mr. Adams has just been elected to Congress. Many people are surprised that he accepted. He is the first President who has reentered public affairs.

October 2

Mr. Sparks said to me today: "Landed estates in Massachusetts are no longer being divided up. The eldest almost always inherits the whole of the land."

"And what happens to the other children?" I asked.

"They emigrate to the West."

Note: The bearings of this fact are immense.

October 10

The power of the association has reached its highest degree in America. Associations are made for purposes of trade, and for political, literary, and religious interests. It is never by recourse to a higher authority that one seeks success, but by an appeal to individual powers working in concert.

The last word in the way of an association seems to me to be the temperance societies, that is to say, an association of men who mutually agree to abstain from a vice, and find in collective power an aid in resisting what is most intimate and personal to each man, his own inclinations. The effect of temperance societies is one of the most notable things in this country.

Philadelphia, October 25

When the detractors of popular governments claim that in many points of internal administration the government of one man is better than the government of all, they are, in my view, incontestably right. It is in fact rare for a strong government not to show more consistency in its undertakings, more perseverance, more sense of the

whole, more accuracy in detail, and more discretion even in the choice of men than the multitude. So a republic is less well administered than an enlightened monarchy; republicans who deny that miss the point; but if they said that it was not there that one must look for the advantages of democracy, they would win back the initiative. The wonderful effect of republican governments (where they can subsist) is not in presenting a picture of *regularity* and *methodical order* in a people's administration but in the *way of life*. Liberty does not carry out each of its undertakings with the same perfection as an intelligent despotism, but in the long run it produces more than the latter. It does not always and in all circumstances give the peoples a more skillful and faultless government; but it infuses throughout the body social an activity, a force, and an energy which never exist without it, and which bring forth wonders. It is there that one must look for its advantages.

Conversation with Mr. Duponceau,
October 27

Mr. Duponceau is an old man, the author of several well-considered books, and well known for his learning. He is French, but has lived in this country for nearly sixty years. He said to us, discussing France as if she were still the same as he remembered her: "One thing that goes to the shaping of your morality in France is that, with you each man is shut in in a certain sphere from which he does not hope to escape. Here, on the contrary, since the road to riches and fortune is open to everybody no matter from where they start, there is a restlessness of spirit and a greed for wealth which it would be hard for you to understand. You must appreciate that everybody here wants to grow rich and rise in the world, and there is no one but believes in his power to succeed in that. From that there springs a wearisome social activity, ever changing intrigues, continual excitement, and an uncontrolled desire of each to outdo the others."

"But in all this frenzy," said I, "what becomes of equality?"

"Equality only exists in the marketplace," answered Mr. Duponceau. "Money makes extreme inequalities in society. No doubt an able man, whatever his fortune, is received everywhere; but people are at pains to make him realize that he is not rich, and his wife and children are not received. 'We cannot go visiting those people there,' say the women, 'they have an income of only 2,000 francs and we have 10,000.' It is this uncontrolled wish to shine that drives many families into luxurious habits and spoils life's simplicity. One sees the same wish to shine between state and state. What a lot of money vanity has made us throw out of the window."

"I have heard it asserted," said I, "that in general you have appointed incompetent people to run your undertakings."

"That is true," answered Mr. Duponceau. "Seldom does the choice fall on an able man. All official positions are given for political reasons; the spirits of faction and intrigue grow here as they do under monarchies. Only the master is different."

Another time Mr. Duponceau said: "How strangely blind men can be to the effects of what they themselves have caused! I am sure that if England had not conquered Canada in 1763, the American Revolution would not have taken place. We should still be English. The need to resist French power in the North and the Indians, natural allies of the French in the West, would have kept the colonies in dependence on Great Britain. If they had attempted to throw off the yoke, France, for fear of insurrection in Canada, would not have dared to take their side. Nevertheless no nation has ever been more drunk with triumph than the English at the time of which I speak."

He also said: "The great plague of the United States is slavery. It does nothing but get worse. The spirit of the times works toward granting liberty to the slaves. I do not doubt that the blacks will all end by being free. But I think that one day their race will disappear from our land."

"How will that be?" I asked.

"Never will white and black blood mix among us. The two races abhor each other and yet are obliged to live in the same land. That state is contrary to nature. It must end in the destruction of the weaker of the two enemy peoples. Now the white race, supported as it is in the West and North, cannot go to destruction in the South. The blacks will arm against them and will be exterminated. We will not get out of the position in which our fathers put us by introducing slavery, except by massacres."

Conversation with Mr. Latrobe, a very distinguished lawyer from Baltimore, October 30

He said to us: "I think the constitution of Maryland is the most democratic in America. No property qualification is demanded for the electors. Any man who is a citizen of the United States and has been living for a year in the republic is an elector."

"Do you not find," I said, "that this universal suffrage has disadvantages?"

"There are some," said Mr. Latrobe. "The choices are not always good. It has been noticed that we have fewer able men in our legislature than the Virginians have in theirs."

"But," I answered, "since your legislature is so democratic, is it not true then that Maryland is the place in the United States where the spirit of aristocracy is most in evidence?"

Mr. Latrobe answered: "Our outward habits have indeed kept an aristocratic cast which is found neither in our laws nor in our political practice. So there is more luxury here than anywhere else. In the streets you see four-horse carriages, *jackets,* something like liveries; the members of different families are distinguished by names of estates."

"Formerly your laws, like your manners, were aristocratic?"

"Yes, Maryland was founded by English nobles, and, moreover, the first emigrants professed the Catholic religion, which itself is favorable to aristocracy. So they divided the territory into great estates; but America does not at all favor the existence of great landed fortunes, and the landowners were never able to get large incomes from their lands. Up to the Revolution, however, Maryland had the appearance of an English county; birth was as much valued there as on the other side of the Atlantic; all the power was in the hands of the great families."

"What changed this state of affairs?"

"The law of inheritance. With equal shares, fortunes were quickly divided up. Some families, that of Charles Carroll, for instance, having only one representative during several generations, kept their fortunes, but in general the great estates have been divided into a thousand fragments. With the small landowners and commercial industry, democracy was born. You see what progress it has made."

"But how have the members of the great families put up with this change? What is their position over against the people, and what do the people think of them?"

"The people have not, as you seem to think, any hostility against the members of the old families. It shows no discrimination against them in appointments to all the offices. On their side the members of the old families do not *show* any hostility against the present order. This state of affairs is due to two circumstances. When war broke out with Great Britain, the great families of Maryland zealously supported the cause of independence. They shared the passion of the people and led them on the field of battle. After the War of Independence the political question dividing people was concerned with the Constitution. The nation was split between the Federalists, who wanted to give the Union a very strong central power, and the Democrats, or Republicans, who wanted to keep almost complete independence for the states. The latter party, which won in the end, was the most popular.

"Now it happened that the Maryland aristocrats, from love of power and a wish to keep their local importance, almost all supported it. So these were two great occasions on which they went with the people and won rights for them. I was speaking just now of Federalists and Republicans and told you that in the end the Republicans carried off the victory. That is to say that they came to power in the end. For the rest, once in charge of the government, they managed things in almost all respects in the same way as their adversaries would have done. They allowed a central power, a standing army, a navy. . . . Oppositions never can govern with the principles that have brought them to power. Now, to put the matter truthfully, there are no parties in the United States; everything turns on questions of personalities. There are those who have got power and those who want to have it: the 'ins and outs'."

"What class is most usually elected by the people?"

"Lawyers. The United States are ruled by lawyers. It is they who hold almost all the offices. The President is a military man, but look at all his ministry; there is not one minister who is not a lawyer. The lawyers here have even more preponderance than in the rest of the Union, because here it is the custom before an election for the candidates to address the people. We often see the eloquence of one of them carry an election by surprise against an opponent whose real merit should have decided the matter."

"Is there still slavery in Maryland?"

"Yes. But we are making great efforts to get rid of it. The law allows the export of slaves and does not allow their import. Cultivating wheat we can very easily do without the blacks. It is perhaps even an economy."

"Is enfranchisement allowed?"

"Yes, but we often find that enfranchisement brings great evil in its train, and that the freed Negro finds himself more unhappy and unable to help himself than the slave. One odd thing is that west of the Chesapeake, the Negro population is increasing faster than the white, whereas to the east of that bay the opposite is true. I think the reason is that the west is divided into great estates which have no attraction for the hard-working, free population.

"Baltimore, which now has a population of 80,000, did not have thirty houses at the time of the Revolution."

"What then has made that city grow so fast?"

"First, as a result of our Revolution; then the ruin of Santo Domingo, which sent many French families as refugees to us and gave us the victualing of the colony; and finally the wars of the French Revolution in Europe. England was at war with the whole Continent and ruled the seas; we became Europe's manufacturers."

"Is it true that there are great differences between Americans of the North and those of the South?"

"Yes, at Baltimore we think we can recognize a Yankee in the street, and even an inhabitant of New York or of Philadelphia."

"But what are the principal traits that distinguish the North from the South?"

"I would express the difference like this: what distinguishes the North is the *spirit of enterprise;* what distinguishes the South is the *spirit of chivalry.* The manners of a Southerner are frank and open; he is excitable, even irritable, and very ticklish on a point of honor. The New Englander is cold, calculating, and patient. As long as you are staying with a Southerner, you are made

French National Museums

Portrait of Alexis de Tocqueville

welcome, and he shares all the pleasures of his house with you. The Northerner, when he has received you, begins to think whether he can do business with you."

(Having painted this spirited portrait, Mr. Latrobe seemed to be afraid that he had been talking too frankly to us, and he added several details to diminish the effect.)

"But your present legislation, your law of inheritance among other things, should change the look of your society?"

"Yes, we used to have a race of landowners living on their estates. In general those were the most distinguished people in the country. They had received an excellent education, and had the manners and standards of the English upper classes. We still have a certain number of these gentleman farmers; but the law of inheritance and democracy are killing them. In two or three generations they will have disappeared."

"Do you not regret that it should be so?"

"Yes, from some points of view. In general that class was a seedbed of distinguished people for the legislature and the army. They were our best statesmen and our finest characters. All the great men of the Revolution came, in the South, from that class. But, nonetheless, I am inclined to think that, all things considered, the new order is better. Our upper classes now are less remarkable, but the people is more enlightened; there are fewer distinguished men, but more general happiness. In a word, we are daily getting more like New England. Now New England, in spite of all I was saying to you about it, is well ahead of us in everything to do with the economy of society. I think that the whole American continent must model itself one day on New England. What hastens this tendency is the perpetual flow of people from the North to the South. Their will to grow rich and their spirit of enterprise are continually driving them among us. Little by little all trade and control over society is falling into their hands."

"Do you think you could do without slaves in Maryland?"

"Yes, I am convinced of it. Slavery is in general an expensive way of farming, and it is more so with certain crops. Thus wheat farming requires many laborers, but only twice in the year, at sowing time and at harvest. Slaves are useful at those two seasons. For the rest of the year they must be fed and kept without, one may say, employing them. Besides, on a farm with slaves there are always a multitude of women and children who must be fed without being employed. So generally speaking slavery is worth nothing in wheat-growing country. And that applies to the greater part of Maryland. In the South, where the crop from the plantations is very large, one can employ slaves."

"But if sugar and coffee are more profitable crops than corn, and if slave labor for agriculture is more expensive than free, it surely follows that the Southerners *can* keep their slaves, but it also follows that they would get a better return from their lands if they cultivated them themselves or employed free labor?"

"No doubt, but in the South the white man cannot, without getting ill or dying, do what the black does easily. Besides there are certain crops that are raised much more economically by slaves than by free workers. Tobacco, for instance. Tobacco needs continual attention; one can employ women and children in cultivating it. In a country where labor is as expensive as it is in America, it would be difficult to grow tobacco without slaves. It is a crop admirably suited for slave labor. Tobacco is the only Southern crop grown in Maryland. People will end by giving up growing it in proportion as slavery disappears. It would be better to lose that source of income than to keep it. All that I have been telling you just now is not only my own opinion, it is an expression of public opinion. Over the last fifteen years there has been a complete revolution in people's attitude to this matter. Fifteen years ago one was not allowed to say that slavery could be abolished in Maryland; now no one disputes that."

"Do you not think that the law of inheritance should have a great influence on the existence of slavery?"

"Yes, immense. The division of properties multiplies small fortunes and quickly creates a class of white laborers who start competing with the slaves. Everywhere in Maryland where properties have been divided up, slavery has disappeared and the white population has developed extraordinarily."

"In Maryland do you have a code for the blacks?"

"No. The penal code applies to both races. There are, however, some offenses which can only be committed by a black. A black, for instance, even if free, cannot carry arms. A black slave cannot buy or sell on his own account without the written permission of his master. Free blacks cannot come together for meetings."

"Do enfranchised blacks have political rights?"

"None. The law gives them them in Pennsylvania, but in practice they do not use them any more than with us."

"Is it true that public education in Maryland is infinitely less advanced than in New England?"

"Yes. We have only just set out on the road along which the Northerners have been going for 200 years. We find the chief obstacle in the sentiments of the people themselves. A curious thing has long happened and still happens with us: the enlightened classes of the population feel the need for public education and work ceaselessly to spread it. But the people, who still do not see the need to give their money to attain this object, does not reelect to office those who thus work for their welfare in spite of themselves."

"Do you realize that what you are saying is a very strong argument against the principle of the sovereignty of the people?"

"No, at least not in my view. The people is often blind and falls into incredible mistakes. But I have always found that it ends up by understanding its own interests. And then it does more than the strongest power could do. So in public education it has long been impossible for us to do anything; but now public opinion begins to turn to our side. The impulse has been given and nothing will now stop it."

"How do the Catholics in America prosper?"

"They are increasing extraordinarily and are pursuing a very skillful policy. The Catholics are the only congregation that is never divided about doctrine. They march united like a single man. For the last twenty years they have very skillfully diverted all their efforts toward education. They have established seminaries and colleges. The best educational institutions in Maryland are Catholic. They have even colleges in other states. These colleges are full of Protestants. There is perhaps no young man in Maryland who has received a good education who has not been brought up by the Catholics. Although they are very careful not to speak of their beliefs to their pupils, you realize that they always exercise a certain influence. They have also very cleverly directed their chief attention to the education of women. They think that where the mother is Catholic, the children will almost always become such. Generally their bishops in America are able men."

"What are the doctrines of the American Catholics about the question of church government?"

"They recognize the pope's right to appoint the bishops, and the bishops' right to appoint the parish priests. As to matters of faith they think that only an Ecumenical Council presided over by the pope has a right to pronounce."

November 5

This evening we paid a visit to Charles Carroll.

Charles Carroll is the last survivor of the signatories of the Declaration of Independence. He is descended from a very ancient English family. He owns the most huge domain in America now. The estate on which he lives comprises 13,000 acres and 300 Negro slaves. He has married his granddaughter to the Duke of Wellesley. He is a Catholic. Charles Carroll is ninety-five years old. He holds himself very erect, has no infirmity, his memory is rather uncertain. Nonetheless he still talks very well as an informed and likeable man. He was educated in France. He welcomed us with great kindness and friendliness. Conversation turned on the great time of his life, that is the Revolution. He reminded us with very natural pride that he had signed the Declaration of Independence, and that by doing so he risked, together with his life, the most considerable fortune that there was in America. I ventured to ask him whether from the beginning of the quarrel the colonies had had the idea of separating from Great Britain.

"No," Charles Carroll answered me, "we were strongly attached in our hearts to the motherland. But she forced us by degrees to cut ourselves off from her." He added with much warmth: "No, doubtless we did not believe that things would go so far. Even after we signed the Declaration of Independence, we thought that Great Britain, frightened by that, would seek to get closer to us, and that we could be good friends. But the English pressed their point of view, and we ours."

We talked of the government of the United States. Charles Carroll showed that he regretted the old aristocratic institutions of Maryland. The general tone and content of his conversation breathed the spirit of the English aristocracy, mingled sometimes in a peculiar way with the habits of the democratic government under which he lived and the glorious memories of the American Revolution. He ended by saying to us: "A mere democracy is but a mob. The English form of government is the only one suitable for you; if we tolerate ours, that is because every year we can push our innovators out West."

The whole way of life and turn of mind of Charles Carroll make him just like a European gentleman. Probably the great Southern landowners at the time of the Revolution were very much after this fashion. This race of men is disappearing now, after having provided America with her greatest spirits. With them the tradition of cultivated manners is lost; the people is becoming enlightened, attainments spread, and a middling ability becomes common. The striking talents, the great characters are rare. Society is less brilliant and more prosperous. These various effects of the progress of civilization and enlightenment, which are only hinted at in Europe, appear in the clear light of day in America. From what first cause do they derive? I do not yet see clearly.

Philadelphia, November 18

Mr. Biddle, president of the Bank of the United States, is one of the most distinguished men in this country. I said to him today: "What I least understand in America is the nature and ways of activity of the political parties. In France, and elsewhere in Europe, society is divided by two or three important conceptions round which definite interests and emotions group themselves. In America I see nothing like that; one might say that there are nothing but coteries here and no parties properly so called. Personalities are everything, and principles of little account."

Mr. Biddle answered me: "I can believe that you find it difficult to understand the nature and activity of parties in America, for we get lost ourselves in just the same way. There has been a mixup of all the old parties and today it would be impossible to say what is the political belief of those who support the administration, or of those who attack it."

"But it has not always been like that?" I asked.

"No, certainly not," replied Mr. Biddle, "this is something quite new with us. For a long time we were divided between Federalists and Republicans. Those two parties were very like what you have in Europe; they had political doctrines to which interests and emotions were attached. They fought bitterly until the Federalist Party, always short in numbers, was completely crushed by its adversary. Tired of their vanquished position, the Federalists ended by giving up their own cause; they either merged in the successful party, or rallied, under other names, about questions of detail. But the party standard has really been knocked down for good and all. This revolution finally worked itself out when General Jackson came on the scene; he claimed to make no distinction between the old parties in his choice. Since then there have been people who support the administration and people who attack it; people who extol a measure and people who abuse it. But there are no parties, properly so called, opposed one to the other and adopting a contrary political faith. The fact is that there are not two practicable ways of governing this people now, and political emotions have scope only over the details of administration and not over its principles."

"With you the head of state can have the majority of Congress against him without public business suffering?"

"Yes, certainly. Our political machine is organized so that it can work by itself. The situation of which you speak has already come about several times; even now the President has lost the confidence of Congress and of informed opinion. His proposals are not adopted and his selections are turned down by the Senate; nonetheless public business is carried on just as well as before and no one has any fears for the future. I regard as one of the severest tests of the excellence of our institutions this ease with which we succeed in getting along without government or going upstream against it."

Conversations with Mr. Poinsett, January 12-17 (1832)

Question: In America are morals really as good as is said?

Answer: There is laxity in the lower classes of society, but otherwise morals are excellent everywhere. I have never seen anything that one can compare to this state of affairs in any of my travels. There is nothing like it in England. The people and the upper classes in England are very disorderly in their morals; morality is only found in the middle classes. There is such a prodigious respect for the marriage tie among us

that the lover of a married woman disgraces himself even more surely than she who yields to him. The road to honors is shut to him; even that to wealth becomes difficult for him; he has to count himself very lucky if he dies otherwise than by assassination. The woman's relations often feel bound to revenge the honor of the family on the man.

Question: But to what, according to you, is this extreme chastity of morals due? I tell you frankly that I cannot look on you as a *virtuous* people.

Answer: Neither do I think that we are more virtuous than many other peoples. The chastity of our morals is due more to particular circumstances and especially to the complete absence of a class of men with the time and means to attack women's virtue. Besides I think that the race of women is very remarkable in America. I find them much superior to our men.

Question: Do you think this state of morals reacts on the political state of society?

Answer: Certainly, very much. It gives us habits of order and morality which serve powerfully to bridle our political passions.

Question: What do you think of the influence of religion on politics?

Answer: I think that the state of religion in America is one of the things that most powerfully helps us to maintain our republican institutions. The religious spirit exercises a direct power over political passions, and also an indirect power by sustaining morals. It is because many enlightened Americans are convinced of this truth that not only do they not show the doubts they may have about the reality of Christianity but even hesitate to join new sects such as the Unitarians. They are afraid that they may lead indirectly to the destruction of the Christian religion, which would be an irreparable ill for humanity.

Question: What do they mean in the South by the procedure of nullification? It seems to me that the procedure amounts purely and simply to annulment of the Union.

Answer: No doubt it would come to that indirectly; but the nullificators deny that. They only claim that the separate states have the right to *suspend* the laws of Congress and to call for the convocation of a convention.

Question: Does that doctrine make you afraid for the future of the Union?

Answer: No. The nullificators only form a party in South Carolina; even there their majority is doubtful. And even if they had the whole state with them, what can the 700,000 whites who live there do against the forces of the Union? This party, like so many others, owes its existence to the personal ambitions of a few citizens, particularly Mr. Calhoun and Mr. Duke. The doctrine of nullification has in the past been preached without conviction; now it has believers. (Mr. Poinsett comes from South Carolina and is a member of the legislature.)

Question: Is the difference as real as they say between the social state of the South and that of the North?

Answer: Yes. The difference is evident and all in favor of the North.

Question: What are the reasons for it?

Answer: The first is slavery; the second the climate. The South, however, is progressing, though it seems to go back because the North and West go so fast. Every ten years the South loses some proportion of its representation; the West and North, on the other hand, keep increasing their votes. Power is quickly shifting from these old centers. Soon the thirteen original states will not have the majority in Congress.

Question: It is impossible that this state of affairs should not create a state of jealousy and suspicion in the South. The weak do not generally believe in the fairness of the strong.

Answer: That is true.

Question: Has the South got ships to carry its produce?

Answer: It has none. It is the North that goes to fetch the produce of the South and carry it all over the world.

Question: How did this strange state of affairs arise?

Answer: Partly because in the South there is still no lower class. One would not know where to find a population of sailors.

Question: But why not employ the Negroes?

Answer: That would be taking a chance of losing them; they would desert. Besides, there is no industry in the South.

Question: Do you see any means of getting rid of the slaves?

Answer: No. The plan which consists in buying them up at the expense of the state and transporting them elsewhere seems to me extravagant. The wealth of the whole Union would not be enough. In proportion as the number of slaves diminished, their price would become exorbitant. Besides, the need felt for them would lead to their being introduced again by the slave trade. I do not share the fears born of the increasing numbers of the blacks as far as the safety of the white race is concerned. A slave revolt would never succeed. If they ever became enlightened enough to combine their forces and form a formidable league, they would be wise enough to see that, placed as they are, they could never hope for final success.

Question: Do the half-castes make common cause with the blacks?

Answer: No. They treat them with disdain, and the latter hate them. They think they are much closer to the whites than to the blacks. The most dangerous men are the emancipated blacks. Their presence makes the slaves restless and long for freedom. I think it is indispensable to take away from the masters the right to free their slaves and especially the right to free them by will. Washington gave a very bad example by freeing his slaves at his death. It is an extraordinary thing how far public opinion is becoming enlightened about slavery. The idea that it is a great evil and that one could do without it is gaining ground more and more. I hope that the natural course of things will rid us of the slaves. I know people still who have seen slavery in New England. In our time we have seen it abolished in the state of New York, then in Pennsylvania; it only holds on to a precarious existence in Maryland; there is already talk against it in the legislature of Virginia. The black race is continually retreating toward the South, pushed by the emigration of men of the white race.

Question: Do you think that slaves are smuggled into the territory of the Union?

Answer: Hardly at all. But the slave trade nonetheless exists on an immense scale. Last year the English House of Commons made an inquiry into the matter, and I read myself in its report that the number of blacks carried off each year from Africa amounts to 300,000.

Question: What do you think of the Indians of the United States?

Answer: I think that it is a race which will perish without the wish to become civilized. One could only succeed in that with the help of the half-castes. Besides, I think that the civilized man has the right to take the land of savages from which the latter do not know how to profit, and where the white man flourishes and increases rapidly.

ALMOST ALL POLITICAL PRECEPTS have in the way they are announced something so generalized, so theoretical, and so vague that it is difficult to derive the least advantage from them in practice. There are almost always so many remedies whose usefulness depends even more on the temperament of the patient than on the nature of the illness. I only know of one means of increasing the prosperity of a people whose application

is infallible and on which I think one can count in all countries and in all places. That means is none other than increasing the facility of communication between men. On this point what can be seen in America is both strange and instructive.

The roads, the canals, and the post play a prodigious part in the prosperity of the Union. It is good to examine their effects, the value attached to them, and the way they are obtained.

America, which is the country which enjoys the greatest sum of prosperity that has ever yet been vouchsafed to any nation, is also that which, in proportion to its age and means, has made the greatest effort to supply itself with the free communications of which I was speaking above.

In France there are a great number of very crowded centers of population through which no road passes, in such a way that they are more separated from the rest of the nation than half the world has been in time past. I have no doubt that it would take longer and be more expensive to have ten sacks of wheat sent from some village in Lower Brittany to Paris than to have all the sugar of the colonies sent to the same place.

In America one of the first things done in a new state is to make the post go there; in the forests of Michigan there is no cabin so isolated, no valley so wild but that letters and newspapers arrive at least once a week; we have seen that. It is especially in these conditions that I felt the difference between our own social state and that of the American people. There are few rural districts in France in which, proportionately speaking, as many letters and newspapers are received as in these still savage lands where man still fights against all the miseries of life and only has glimpses of society at long intervals.

When it seems that the population is turning toward a certain part of the country, there is a hurry to open a road thither.

The road almost always comes before those whom it is intended to serve, but it encourages them to move; we have several times seen main roads opened up literally in the middle of the wilderness.

America has undertaken and finished the construction of some immense canals. It already has more railways than France. No one fails to see that the discovery of steam has incredibly increased the power and prosperity of the Union; and that is because it facilitates speedy communications between the different parts of that immense land. The states of the South, where communications are less convenient, are those which languish compared to the rest.

Of all the countries in the world, America is that in which the spread of ideas and of human industry is most continual and most rapid. There is not an American but knows the resources of all the parts of the vast land that he inhabits; all the able men in the Union know each other by reputation, many of them personally. I have often been struck by astonishment to find how far that is the case. I can say that it has never happened to me to speak to an American about one of his compatriots without finding that he was up-to-date in knowing both how he was now placed and the story of his life.

I know that this intense industrial and intellectual movement is particularly encouraged by education, by the sort of government America enjoys, and by the altogether special situation in which the Americans find themselves. In America populations are not at all sedentary, even in the old established parts; almost all of them are real industrial entrepreneurs who feel the need for means of communication with a liveliness and use them with a zeal which one could never expect from the routine and lazy spirit of our peasants. The effect of a road or a canal is therefore more noticeable and above all more immediate in America than it would be in France.

So we ought to act as the Americans do in the new districts of the West; open the road before the travelers in the certainty that they will come along sooner or later to use it.

As to the means employed to open up communications in America, this is what I have noticed about the matter.

It is generally believed in Europe that the great maxim of government in America is that of laissez-faire, of standing by as a simple spectator of the progress of society, of which individual interest is the prime mover; that is a mistake.

The American government does not interfere in everything, it is true, as ours does. It makes no claim to foresee everything and carry everything out; it gives no subsidies, does not encourage trade, and does not patronize literature or the arts. But where great works of public utility are concerned, it but seldom leaves them to the care of private persons; it is the state itself that carries them out. The great canal joining the Hudson to Lake Erie was made at the expense of the state of New York; that joining Lake Erie to the Mississippi is the work of the state of Ohio; the canal joining the Delaware to Chesapeake Bay is an undertaking of the state. The main roads which lead to distant places are usually planned and carried out by the states and not by companies.

But it is important to observe that there is no rule about the matter. The activity of companies, of parishes, and of private people is in a thousand ways in competition with that of the state. All undertakings of moderate extent or limited interest are the work of parishes or companies. Turnpikes or toll roads often run parallel to those of the state. In some parts of the country, railways built by companies fulfill the functions of the canals as main thoroughfares. The local roads are maintained by the districts through which they pass. So then no exclusive system is followed; in nothing does America exemplify a system of that uniformity that delights the superficial and metaphysical minds of our age.

In institutions, laws, government of society, and everyday life, everything, on the contrary, is different and various.

Everything adapts itself to the nature of men and places without any pretension to bend them to the strictness of an inflexible rule. From this variety springs a universal prosperity spread throughout the whole nation and over each of its parts.

To return to roads and all the other means of bringing the achievements of industry or of thought quickly from one place to another, I make no claim to have discovered that they contributed to the prosperity of a people; it is a truth universally felt and recognized. I only say that America illustrates this truth most palpably, makes it stand out more clearly than any other country in the world, and that it is impossible to travel through this Union without being convinced, not by argument but by the evidence of all the senses, that the most powerful and the most infallible means of increasing the prosperity of a country is in every possible way to encourage easy exchanges between those who live there.

The spirit of association, as I have already remarked . . . is one of the distinctive characteristics of America; it is by this means that a country where capital is scarce and where absolutely democratic laws and habits hinder the accumulation of wealth in the hands of a few individuals has already succeeded in carrying out undertakings and accomplishing works which the most absolute kings and the most opulent aristocracies would certainly not have been able to undertake and finish in the same time.

RESTLESSNESS OF CHARACTER seems to me to be one of the distinctive traits of this people. The American is devoured by the longing to make his fortune; it is the unique passion of his life; he has no memory that attaches him to one place more than another, no inveterate habits, no spirit of routine; he is the daily witness of the swiftest changes of fortune, and is less afraid than any other inhabitant of the globe to risk what he has gained in the hope of a better future, for he knows that he can without trouble create new resources again. So he enters the great lottery of human fate with the assurance of a gambler who only risks his winnings. The same man, we were told, has often tried ten occupations. He has been seen successively a trader, lawyer, doctor, and minister of the gospel.

In one word, men do not have habits here, and what they see under their eyes prevents them from forming any. First, many have come from Europe and have left behind their habits and their memories there. Second, even those who have long been established in this country have kept this difference of habits. As yet there is no American outlook. Each takes from the association what suits him and remains as he was.

He has inhabited twenty different places and has nowhere formed ties that hold him; and how could it not be so? Here laws are continually changing and magistrates succeeding one another; systems of administration triumph turn by turn; nature herself changes more quickly than man.

By a strange inversion of the ordinary order of things, it is nature that changes, while man is unchanging. The same man may give his name to wilds that none has traversed before him; he has been able to fell the first tree in the forest, and build in the midst of the solitude a planter's house round which first a hamlet has formed, and which is now surrounded by a huge city. In the short space between birth and death he has seen all these changes, and a thousand others like him have been able to do so. In his youth he has lived among tribes who now live only in history; during his life rivers have changed or diminished their course, the climate is different from what it was before, and all that is still in his imagination only a first step in an endless career.

Howsoever powerful and impetuous the course of history is here, imagination always goes in advance of it, and the picture is never large enough. There is not a country in the world where man more confidently takes charge of the future, or where he feels with more pride that he can fashion the universe to please himself. It is a movement of the mind which can only be compared with that which brought about the discovery of the New World three centuries ago. And in fact one might say that America has been discovered for the second time. And one must not imagine that such thoughts only take shape in a philosopher's head; the artisan thinks them as much as the speculator, the peasant as much as the town dweller. They belong to every object. They form a part of all feelings; they are palpable, visible, felt, and, in some sort, strike all the senses.

Often born under another sky, placed in the middle of an ever moving picture, driven himself by the irresistible torrent that carries all around him along, the American has no time to attach himself to anything. He is only accustomed to change and ends by looking on it as the natural state of man. Much more, he feels the need of it, he loves it; for instability, instead of causing disasters for him, seems only to bring forth wonders around him. (The idea of a possible improvement, of a successive and continuous betterment of the social condition, that idea is ever before him in all its facets.)

The relationship between the different social positions in America is rather difficult to understand, and foreigners make one or the other of these two mistakes. Either they suppose that in the United States there is no distinction between man and man except that of personal merit, or else, struck by the high standing accorded to wealth here, they come to think that in several of our European monarchies, in France for instance, we enjoy a more real and more complete equality than that of the American republics. I hold . . . that both these ways of seeing the matter are exaggerated.

First, let us get the ground clear. Equality before the law is not at the moment in question, for that is complete in America; it is not only a right but a fact. One might even say that for whatever inequality exists elsewhere, the world of politics makes ample compensation in favor of the middle and lower classes who, with the inheritors of historic names, hold almost all the elected offices.

I am talking of equality in the exchanges of social life; the equality which draws certain individuals to come together in the same places, to share their views and their pleasures, and to join their families in marriage. It is in that that one must make distinctions between France and America. The differences turn out to be essential.

In France, whatever one says, prejudices of birth still hold very great sway. Birth still puts an almost insurmountable barrier between men. In France the profession a man exercises still to a certain extent places him socially. These prejudices are the most fatal of all to equality because they make permanent and almost indelible distinctions, even when wealth and time are against them. Such prejudices do not exist at all in America. Birth is a distinction, but it does not in the least place a man socially; it carries with it no right and no disability, no obligation toward the world or toward oneself. Class structure by professions is also almost unknown; it certainly does make a definite difference to the position of individuals, a difference of wealth rather than of standing, but it does not create any radical inequality, for it by no means prevents the intermarriage of families (that is the great touchstone).

However, one must not suppose that in America all classes of society mix in the same drawing rooms; that is not so. People in the same profession, with the same views and the same education, seek each other out by a sort of instinct and come together to the exclusion of others. The difference is that no arbitrary, inflexible rule prescribes this arrangement. So there is little offensive in it. There is nothing final about it for anybody, and no one can be hurt by it. So in America, less than anywhere else, does one see that burning desire of one class to share not only the political rights but also the pleasures of the others.

That is the difference for the better between American society and our own.

This is the difference for the worse.

The first of all social distinctions in America is *money*. Money makes a real privileged class in society, which keeps itself apart and rudely makes the rest conscious of its preeminence.

This preeminence of wealth in society has less fatal consequences for equality than those which spring from prejudices of birth and profession. It is not at all permanent; it is within the reach of all. It is not radical, but it is perhaps even more offensive still. It is paraded in America much more impudently than with us; talent, merit, which in France decidedly outweigh it when the two are in competition, are here obliged to give place to it. One can give several reasons for this state of affairs.

In France, inequality of rank was extreme. To compensate for imaginary distinctions it was necessary to have recourse to the only reasonable distinction, that of merit. In France, intellectual pleasures and gifts of the mind have always been held in high esteem.

In America, in the absence of all material and external distinctions, wealth appeared as the natural test to measure men's merit. Besides, the Americans are a people with very little feeling for the pleasures of the mind. Exclusively occupied in making their fortunes, they must naturally have a sort of veneration for wealth. It arouses their envy, but tacitly they recognize it as the chief advantage.

To summarize, then, men in America, as with us, are ranked according to certain categories by the give and take of social life. Common habits, education, and especially wealth establish these classifications; but these rules are neither absolute, nor inflexible, nor permanent. They establish passing distinctions and by no means form classes properly so called; they give no superiority, even in thought, to one man over another. So that although two men may never see each other in the same drawing rooms, if they meet outside, they meet without pride on one side or envy on the other. At bottom they feel themselves to be, and they are, equal.

When one wants to judge the equality between the different classes of a people, one always comes to the question how marriages are made. That is the root of the matter. A certain equality, the result of necessity, politeness, or policy, can appear to exist and deceive the eye. But when one wants to take practical advantage of this equality for the intermarriage of families, then one puts one's finger on the wound.

One cannot know exactly how much energy and how great power of self-control American democracy could show in time of crisis. So far it has not experienced a crisis.

What is certain is that every time the central government has tried to impose direct taxes it has not succeeded, and that even in the fervor of political passions stirred by the Revolution, it was never without the greatest difficulty that it succeeded in collecting men or money; even then always in insufficient quantity.

So then one must wait for the time when the nation will have recourse to conscription and to heavy taxes to be able to judge what sacrifices democracies can impose on themselves.

1832

100.

THOMAS R. DEW: Pro-Slavery Arguments

Virginia's Constitutional Convention of 1829, moved both by scruple and by the declining economic value of slaves, argued seriously a proposal to abolish slavery in the state. In 1831–1832 the legislature debated the same question, inspired largely by Nat Turner's slave rebellion of 1831, which cast doubt on the safety of the institution. Shortly afterward, in a critique of this debate, Thomas R. Dew, professor of political economy at the College of William and Mary, published a defense of the slave economy that stiffened sentiment in its favor. Dew's book became a major source for pro-slavery argument throughout the South. A part of it is reprinted here.

Source: *The Pro-Slavery Argument*, Philadelphia, 1853, pp. 451-462.

IT IS SAID SLAVERY IS WRONG, in the *abstract* at least, and contrary to the spirit of Christianity. To this we answer . . . that any question must be determined by its circumstances, and if, as really is the case, we cannot get rid of slavery without producing a greater injury to both the masters and slaves, there is no rule of conscience or revealed law of God which *can* condemn us. The physician will not order the spreading cancer to be extirpated although it will eventually cause the death of his patient, because he would thereby hasten the fatal issue.

So, if slavery had commenced even contrary to the laws of God and man, and the sin of its introduction rested upon our heads, and it was even carrying forward the nation by slow degrees to final ruin — yet, if it were *certain* that an attempt to remove it would only hasten and heighten the final catastrophe — that it was, in fact, a *vulnus immedicabile* on the body politic which no legislation could safely remove, then we would not only not be found to attempt the extirpation but we would stand guilty of a high offense in the sight of both God and man if we should rashly make the effort. But the original sin of introduction rests not on our heads, and we shall soon see that all those dreadful calamities which the false prophets of our day are pointing to will never, in all probability, occur.

With regard to the assertion that slavery is against the spirit of Christianity, we are ready to admit the general assertion, but deny most positively that there is anything in the Old or New Testament which would go to show that slavery, when once introduced, ought at all events to be abrogated, or that the master commits any offense in holding slaves. The children of Israel themselves were slaveholders and were not condemned for it. All the patriarchs themselves were slaveholders; Abraham had more than 300; Isaac had a "great store" of them; and even the patient and meek Job himself had "a very great household." When the children of Israel conquered the land of Canaan, they made one whole tribe "hewers of wood and drawers of water," and they were at that very time under the special guidance of Jehovah; they were permitted expressly to purchase slaves of the heathen and keep them as an inheritance for their posterity; and even the children of Israel might be enslaved for six years.

When we turn to the New Testament, we find not one single passage at all calculated to disturb the conscience of an honest slaveholder. No one can read it without seeing and admiring that the meek and humble Savior of the world in no instance meddled with the established institutions of mankind; he came to save a fallen world, and not to excite the black passions of men and array them in deadly hostility against each other. From no one did he turn away; his plan was offered alike to all — to the monarch and the subject, the rich and the poor, the master and the slave. He was born in the Roman world, a world in which the most galling slavery existed, a thousand times more cruel than the slavery in our own country; and yet he nowhere encourages insurrection; he nowhere fosters discontent; but exhorts *always* to implicit obedience and fidelity.

What a rebuke does the practice of the Redeemer of mankind imply upon the conduct of some of his nominal disciples of the day, who seek to destroy the contentment of the slaves, to rouse their most deadly passions, to break up the deep foundations of society, and to lead on to a night of darkness and confusion! "Let every man" (says Paul) "abide in the same calling wherein he is called. Art thou called *being* a servant? Care not for it; but if thou mayest be made free, use *it* rather" (I Cor.

7:20,21). Again: "Let as many servants as are under the yoke count their own masters worthy of all honor, that the name of God and His doctrines be not blasphemed; and they that have believing masters, let them not despise *them,* because they are brethren, but rather do them service, because they are faithful and beloved partakers of the benefit. These things teach and exhort" (I Tim. 6:1,2). Servants are even commanded in Scripture to be faithful and obedient to unkind masters. "Servants," (says Peter) "be subject to your masters with all fear; not only to the good and gentle but to the froward. For what glory is it if when ye shall be buffeted for your faults ye take it patiently; but if when ye do well and suffer for it, ye take it patiently, this is acceptable with God" (I Pet. 2:18,20). These and many other passages in the New Testament most convincingly prove that slavery in the Roman world was nowhere charged as a fault or crime upon the holder, and everywhere is the most implicit obedience enjoined.

We beg leave . . . to address a few remarks to those who have conscientious scruples about the holding of slaves, and therefore consider themselves under an obligation to break all the ties of friendship and kindred — dissolve all the associations of happier days to flee to a land where this evil does not exist. We cannot condemn the conscientious actions of mankind, but we must be permitted to say that if the assumption even of these pious gentlemen be correct, we do consider their conduct as very unphilosophical. And we will go further still — we look upon it as even immoral upon their own principles.

Let us admit that slavery is an evil; and what then? Why, it has been entailed upon us by no fault of ours, and must we shrink from the charge which devolves upon us, and throw the slave, in consequence, into the hands of those who have no scruples of conscience — those who will not perhaps treat him so kindly? No! This is not philos-

Portrait of Thomas R. Dew (1802-1846)

ophy, it is not morality; we must recollect that the unprofitable man was thrown into utter darkness. To the slaveholder has truly been entrusted the five talents. Let him but recollect the exhortation of the apostle — "Masters, give unto your servants that which is just and equal; knowing that ye also have a Master in heaven"; and in the final day he shall have nothing on this score with which his conscience need be smitten, and he may expect the welcome plaudit— "Well done thou good and faithful servant, thou hast been faithful over a few things, I will make thee ruler over many things; enter thou into the joy of thy Lord." . . .

It is further said that the moral effects of slavery are of the most deleterious and hurtful kind. And as Mr. Jefferson has given the sanction of his great name to this charge, we shall proceed to examine it with all that respectful deference to which every sentiment of so pure and philanthropic a heart is justly entitled.

The whole commerce between master and slave . . . is a perpetual exercise of the most boisterous passions; the most unremitting despotism on the one part, and degrading submission on the other. Our children see this and learn to imitate it, for man is an imitative animal — this quality is the germ of education in him. From his cradle to his grave, he is learning what he sees others do. If a parent had no other motive, either in his own philanthropy or self-love, for restraining the intemperance of passion toward his slave, it should always be a sufficient one that his child is present. But generally it is not sufficient. The parent storms, the child looks on, catches the lineaments of wrath, puts on the same airs in the circle of smaller slaves, gives a loose to his worst of passions, and thus nursed, educated, and daily exercised in the worst of tyranny, cannot but be stamped by it with odious peculiarities.

Now we boldly assert that the fact does not bear Mr. Jefferson out in his conclusions. He has supposed the master in a continual passion — in the constant exercise of the most odious tyranny — and the child, a creature of imitation, looking on and learning. But is not this master sometimes kind and indulgent to his slaves? Does he not mete out to them, for faithful service, the reward of his cordial approbation? Is it not his interest to do it? And when thus acting humanely and speaking kindly, where is the child, the creature of imitation, that he does not look on and learn? We may rest assured, in this intercourse between a good master and his servant, more good than evil *may* be taught the child; the exalted principles of morality and religion may thereby be sometimes indelibly inculcated upon his mind, and instead of being reared a selfish, contracted being, with nought but self to look to, he acquires a more exalted benevolence, a greater generosity and elevation of soul, and embraces for the sphere of his generous actions a much wider field.

Look to the slaveholding population of our country and you everywhere find them characterized by noble and elevated sentiments, by humane and virtuous feelings. We do not find among them that cold, contracted, calculating selfishness, which withers and repels everything around it, and lessens or destroys all the multiplied enjoyments of social intercourse. Go into our national councils and ask for the most generous, the most disinterested, the most conscientious, and the least unjust and oppressive in their principles, and see whether the slaveholder will be passed by in the selection. . . .

Is it not a fact known to every man in the South that the most cruel masters are those who have been unaccustomed to slavery. It is well known that Northern gentlemen who marry Southern heiresses are much severer masters than Southern gentlemen. And yet, if Mr. Jefferson's reasoning were correct, they ought to be milder; in fact, it follows from his reasoning that the authority which the father is called on to exercise over his children must be seriously detrimental; and yet we know that this is not the case; that, on the contrary, there is nothing which so much humanizes and softens the heart as this *very authority*. And there are none, even among those who have no children themselves, so disposed to pardon the follies and indiscretion of youth as those who have seen most of them and suffered greatest annoyance. There may be many cruel masters, and there are unkind and cruel fathers too; but both the one and the other make all those around them shudder with horror. We are disposed to think that their example in society tends rather to strengthen than weaken the principle of benevolence and humanity.

Let us now look a moment to the slave and contemplate his position. Mr. Jefferson has described him as hating rather than loving his master, and as losing, too, all that *amor patriae* which characterizes the true patriot. We assert again that Mr. Jefferson is not borne out by the fact. We are well convinced that there is nothing but the mere relations of husband and wife, parent

and child, brother and sister which produce a closer tie than the relation of master and servant. We have no hesitation in affirming that, throughout the whole slaveholding country, the slaves of a good master are his warmest, most constant, and most devoted friends; they have been accustomed to look up to him as their supporter, director, and defender.

Everyone acquainted with Southern slaves knows that the slave rejoices in the elevation and prosperity of his master; and the heart of no one is more gladdened at the successful debut of young master or miss on the great theater of the world than that of either the young slave who has grown up with them and shared in all their sports, and even partaken of all their delicacies, or the aged one who has looked on and watched them from birth to manhood, with the kindest and most affectionate solicitude, and has ever met from them all the kind treatment and generous sympathies of feeling, tender hearts. Judge Smith, in his able speech on Foote's Resolutions in the Senate, said, in an emergency he would rely upon his own slaves for his defense — he would put arms into their hands, and he had no doubt they would defend him faithfully. In the late Southampton insurrection, we know that many actually convened their slaves and armed them for defense, although slaves were here the cause of the evil which was to be repelled.

We have often heard slaveholders affirm that they would sooner rely upon their slaves' fidelity and attachment in the hour of danger and severe trial than on any other equal number of individuals; and we all know that the son or daughter who has been long absent from the parental roof, on returning to the scenes of infancy, never fails to be greeted with the kindest welcome and the most sincere and heartfelt congratulations from those slaves among whom he has been reared to manhood. . . .

In the debate in the Virginia legislature, no speaker *insinuated even*, we believe, that the slaves in Virginia were not treated kindly; and all, too, agree that they were most abundantly fed; and we have no doubt but that they form the happiest portion of our society. A merrier being does not exist on the face of the globe than the Negro slave of the United States. Even Captain Hall himself, with his thick "crust of prejudice," is obliged to allow that they are happy and contented, and the master much less cruel than is generally imagined. Why, then, since the slave is happy, and happiness is the great object of all animated creation, should we endeavor to disturb his contentment by infusing into his mind a vain and indefinite desire for liberty — a something which he cannot comprehend, and which must inevitably dry up the very sources of his happiness.

The fact is that all of us, and the great author of the Declaration of Independence is like us in this respect, are too prone to judge of the happiness of others by ourselves — we make *self* the standard and endeavor to draw down everyone to its dimensions — not recollecting that the benevolence of the Omnipotent has made the mind of man pliant and susceptible of happiness in almost every situation and employment. We might rather die than be the obscure slave that waits at our back — our education and our habits generate an ambition that makes us aspire at something loftier, and disposes us to look upon the slave as unsusceptible of happiness in his humble sphere, when he may indeed be much happier than we are, and have his ambition too; but his ambition is to excel all his other slaves in the performance of his servile duties, to please and to gratify his master, and to command the praise of all who witness his exertions.

Let the wily philanthropist but come and whisper into the ears of such a slave that his situation is degrading and his lot a miserable one; let him but light up the dungeon in which he persuades the slave that he is caged, and that moment, like the serpent that entered the Garden of Eden, he destroys his happiness and his usefulness. We cannot, therefore, agree with Mr. Jefferson in the opinion that slavery makes the unfeeling tyrant and ungrateful dependent. And in regard to Virginia, especially, we are almost disposed, judging from the official returns of crimes and convictions, to assert . . . "that the whole population of Virginia, consisting of three *castes* — of free white, free colored, and slave colored population, is the soundest and most moral of any other, according to numbers, in the whole world, as far as is known to me."

It has been contended that slavery is unfavorable to a republican spirit; but the whole history of the world proves that this is far from being the case. In the ancient republics of Greece and Rome, where the spirit of liberty glowed with most intensity, the slaves were more numerous than the freemen. Aristotle and the great men of antiquity believed slavery necessary to keep alive the spirit of freedom. In Sparta the freemen were even forbidden to perform the offices of slaves, lest [they] might lose the spirit of independence. In modern times, too, liberty has always been more ardently desired by slaveholding communities. "Such," says Burke, "were our Gothic ancestors; such, in our days, were the Poles; and such will be all masters of slaves who are not slaves themselves." "These people of the southern (American) colonies are much more strongly, and with a higher and more stubborn spirit, attached to liberty than those of the northward." And from the time of Burke down to the present day, the Southern states have always borne the same honorable distinction. Burke says, "it is because freedom is to them not only an enjoyment but a kind of rank and privilege." Another, and perhaps more efficient cause of this is the perfect spirit of equality so prevalent among the whites of all the slaveholding states. Jack Cade, the English reformer, wished all mankind to be brought to one common level.

We believe slavery in the United States has accomplished this, in regard to the whites, as nearly as can be expected or even desired in this world. The menial and low offices being all performed by the blacks, there is at once taken away the greatest cause of distinction and separation of the ranks of society. The man to the North will not shake hands familiarly with his servant, and converse and laugh and dine with him, no matter how honest and respectable he may be. But go to the South, and you will find that no white man feels such inferiority of rank as to be unworthy of association with those around him. Color alone is here the badge of distinction, the true mark of aristocracy, and all who are white are equal in spite of the variety of occupation. . . . And it is this spirit of equality which is both the generator and preserver of the genuine spirit of liberty.

101.

David Moulton and Mordecai Myers: Against Appointing Chaplains to the Legislature

The 1777 constitution of the state of New York and its 1821 revision attempted to insure freedom of worship by excluding ministers and priests from all civil and military offices. The 1829 Revised Statutes, however, authorized the employment of chaplains for the state legislature. That body was soon besieged with memorials and petitions protesting the law, but the records do not show whether the protests were against having chaplains or paying them with state funds. A special committee was appointed to study the question and, in 1832, issued the following recommendation against the use of chaplains and prayers in public assemblies. In the next session of the legislature the Revised Statutes were amended to prohibit payment of chaplains, but the issue of the constitutionality of the chaplaincy as such was never resolved.

Source: *Documents of the Assembly of the State of New-York*, 55 Session, 1832, Vol. IV, No. 298.

Mr. Moulton, from the select committee to whom were referred twenty-six memorials from the inhabitants of various towns and counties in this state against appointing chaplains to the legislature, and against the law by which money is drawn from the public treasury to pay for religious services, respectfully reports: That they have taken the subject matter of the said memorials into their serious consideration and given to it that attentive examination to which its great importance eminently entitles it.

Knowing that a great contrariety of opinions are entertained, and that numerous and conflicting prejudices exist in the minds of many honest and zealous religious sectarians on the subject treated on in the said memorials; and being aware that the due discharge of the duties assigned to the committee requires them to explore ground which by some persons is deemed *holy*, and to disturb questions which by many have long been regarded as fully and righteously settled; the committee have examined the subjects referred to them with all that candor and circumspection which they deem consistent with their duties to their constituents: the due exercise of their own rights of conscience and their disposition to treat the opinions of their fellowmen with all that deference and respect to which, by the law of equal rights and the provisions of the constitution of the civil government of the state, they are entitled.

Your committee have not deemed it necessary or useful on the present occasion to grope amidst the ignorance and superstition of the darker ages, to discover the origin or utility of legislative prayers, nor to learn what nations *have*, or what have *not* practised them; nor to ascertain whether the custom was derived from human or divine authority. The "march of mind" must have progressed to a very limited extent and to very little useful purpose, if the civil and religious liberties of the people of this country were to be ascertained and measured by the opinions and customs of mankind in remote ages and in other nations, and under governments as dissimilar in their principles and character to those of our own country as they were incompatible with the equal rights of man.

Yet, amidst all the heterogeneous details of falsehood, fable and fact, which constitute the history of man, of nations and of governments, there are no truths more clearly illustrated by historic record and the concurrent testimony derived from the present state of the civilized world than that no nation was ever free, or could be so, while subjected to a government constituted of a union of political and ecclesiastical powers; that no political despotism ever did or could long exist unsustained by clerical influence; that no religion could be "pure and undefiled" when perverted to political purposes; and that no people could escape being depraved and miserable when subjected to the double tyranny of spiritual and political power. Nor can a different result

be rationally expected from the combined operation of church and state machinery; for it has generally happened that when political authority has been given to men who believe themselves to be elected ministers of a power above the people and to possess authority "beyond the civil law," who are prone to regard their own will and opinions as the will and word of their master, and whose interest and business calling is to propagate their own religious creeds, they have ever been disposed to render their political influence subservient to their own views of religious duty, and have always exercised their political power to sustain their own particular church and faith, to the detriment and exclusion of all others.

"In *some* instances," says the venerable and patriotic Madison, in his remonstrance to the legislature of Virginia against a bill establishing a provision for teachers of the Christian religion, "they (ecclesiastical establishments) have been seen to erect a spiritual tyranny on the ruins of the civil authority: in *more* instances they have been seen upholding the thrones of political tyranny; and in *no instance* have they been seen the guardians of the liberties of the people."

It was doubtless these truths, attested by historic evidence and the observation of the American people, that induced them to hold as political axioms that the union of church and state is incompatible with free government and destructive to the moral influence of all statutory religion; and that to vest with political power those who claim to possess authority paramount to that derived from man is dangerous or destructive to the civil and religious liberties of the people.

That the patriots of the American Revolution, who adopted the state constitution of 1777, recognized the aforementioned evils and intended to guard against them is proved by the unequivocal phraseology of those provisions of that instrument which were intended to sever the union of church and state powers, and to protect the civil and religious liberties of their country; the 38th Article of which said constitution, is in the words following, viz.:

And whereas we are required by the benevolent principles of rational liberty, not only to expel civil tyranny but also to guard against that spiritual oppression and intolerance wherewith the bigotry and ambition of weak and wicked priests and princes have scourged mankind; this convention doth further, in the name of the good people of this state, ordain, determine, and declare, that the free exercise and enjoyment of religious profession and worship, without discrimination or preference, shall forever hereafter be allowed within this state to all mankind: Provided, that the liberty of conscience hereby granted shall not be so construed as to excuse acts of licentiousness or justify practices inconsistent with the peace and safety of this state.

It was unquestionably with the same view that the convention when about to revive a portion of the laws of England and of the late province of New York, all of which were effectually nullified by virtue of the Declaration of Independence, expressly excepted from such revival all laws by which church and state had been leagued together. Accordingly they declared, in the 35th Article of the constitution,

That all such parts of the said common law, and all such of the statutes and acts aforesaid or parts thereof as may be construed to establish or maintain any particular denomination of Christians or their ministers, or are repugnant to this constitution, be, and they are hereby abrogated and rejected.

Thereby expressly confirming the logical and legal effect of the Declaration of Independence, to destroy all laws tending to an alliance of ecclesiastical and political powers, and also all laws by which ministers of religion could be maintained from the public treasury, or receive .pay for their religious services, but from the private purse and voluntary contributions of those who chose to employ them. . . .

In the same spirit and with the same view to religious liberty, it is declared in the first and the present constitution that "no minister of the gospel or priest of any denomination whatsoever shall at any time hereafter under any pretense or description whatever be eligible to or capable of holding any civil or military office or place within this state."

Yet, notwithstanding so much care had been taken to guard against ecclesiastical encroachments, we find, in a very few years after the adoption of the first constitution of this state, priests were ushered into the halls of political legislation, not only (as we shall show) without legal authority but in direct opposition to the spirit and express provisions of that instrument. . . . Nor was it ever based on higher authority than the naked resolutions of the two branches of the legislature, each acting independently of the other, until the year 1829, when by the revised statutes, first part, page 161, Section 7, Chapter 7, Title 6, the pay of chaplains was first prescribed by law, and priests thus recognized as if they were legitimate and necessary appurtenances to the legislative department of the state. . . .

The adoption and continuance of the practice under consideration, after the nullification of all laws uniting church and state, "and after the adoption of a constitution of civil government repugnant to it, both in its spirit and provisions, is no sufficient reason for its further continuance; proof of its harmless influence on the religious liberties of the people. So intimate an association of official legislative duties with religious forms and ceremonies is a practical approximation to a union of church and state. The facility which it affords for the exercise of clerical influence in the legislative department of the government" militates against the equal rights of conscience, and also accounts for the existence and continuance of several

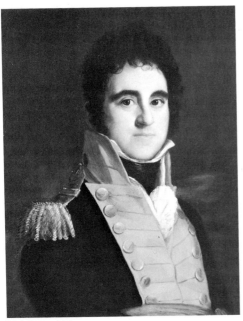

Major Mordecai Myers; portrait by J. W. Jarvis

other laws on our statute books which actually trench on religious liberty, in contravention to those provisions of the constitution which were intended to repress the evil spirit of religious intolerance and persecution.

Your committee will now proceed to show that the legislature possess no legitimate authority to associate religious prayers with legislative proceedings, nor to appoint legislative chaplains, nor to appropriate the public money to pay for any religious service; and because, first, no such authority has been delegated to them; and, second, because the exercise of such powers is not only repugnant to the constitution but expressly interdicted by it.

It will not be denied, and hence not necessary to prove that the legislature is vested with civil powers *only*, and have not been clothed with spiritual jurisdiction. Nor will it be requisite to inquire into the utility of religious prayers or the obligation to pray as a religious duty. "Religion is a concern between a man's conscience and his God,

with which no human tribunal has a right to meddle." If prayer be deemed an act of religious devotion, the legislature have no authority officially to perform it, nor to require others to do so or to attend its performance. The people have not delegated power to the legislature to perform religious worship of any kind . . . and legislative acts which transcend the powers delegated by the people to the legislature are an official exercise of "power beyond the law." . . .

But the absence of legal authority is not the only objection to which the practice under consideration is obnoxious. It often interferes with the legitimate business of the legislature, and thus operates unpropitiously to the public interest. Some members of the legislature, like many of their constituents, conscientiously disapprove of prayers altogether; others are adverse to *legislative* prayers; others again do not hold to prayers in *public places*; and amidst the congregated assembly of persons of various religious sects and adverse religious opinions, and who are elected without reference to their religious creeds, there are but few who can at any one time join heartily in the service. And the effect produced in the minds of such as are induced by courtesy, or are constrained by a species of legal coercion to attend legislative *prayer meetings*, is anything but piety or "a praying spirit."

Mankind are generally averse to associate in religious devotion with any but those whose feelings and faith accord with their own. And although regard to the opinions of others may often induce some occasionally to listen with respectful attention to a sincere supplicant, yet being, as many of the members of the legislature frequently are, annoyed by the repeated annunciation of sentiments out of harmony with their own, and finding at length their courtesy greatly overtaxed, their feeling constantly disobliged, and their convictions as often counteracted by attending prayers in which they have no faith, and with those with whom they cannot, consistently with their own creeds, have any religious communion or fellowship, they usually absent themselves from the legislative chambers until after the ecclesiastical business of the house shall have been concluded. Hence it is that during prayer time there is seldom more than a lean quorum in attendance, and often less. . . .

The exercise of power by the legislature, to employ priests to perform religious worship, not being authorized by the constitution or constitutional law is altogether an *assumed* power. Originating in the bare *will* of the legislature, it has no limit of time, place nor extent. Dependent alone on the legislative will, it is as uncertain and unstable as the fluctuating opinions of mankind, and as undefined and undefinable as the future opinions of different men at different times, who might in their turn assume authority to legislate on religious matters. . . .

If the right of the legislature to appoint chaplains to pray were to be admitted, the right to employ them to preach and sing psalms could not be denied. All are religious services, and are deemed by many to be religious duties. By the like assumed authority by which the legislature employ chaplains to pray at one time, they could employ them to do the like, or any other religious service at any other time; on Sunday as well as on any other day; and at one place as well as another. If in the halls of legislation, why not out of them? If in the form of prayer, why not in any other manner? What then could prevent their assuming authority to direct and regulate religious worship throughout the state? The precedent for such a measure is before them; and can be followed as legally, and with as much propriety as that which attaches to the example set by the state executive, who, under his official proclamation, with the air of legality, the apparent forms of law, and the language of recommendation, prescribes the performance of religious worship on fast and thanksgiving days throughout the state. . . .

It is no sufficient apology for the official employment of priests by the legislature, that the clergy of all sects in the city of Albany, "without discrimination or preference," are appointed to the office of legislative chaplains. The words "without discrimination or preference" are used in the provision of the constitution, which interdicts legislative interference with the religious concerns of their constituents, and guarantees the freedom of religious opinion, "without discrimination or preference to all mankind within this state," and affords no justification for the appointment of priests to civil or ecclesiastical office "without discrimination or preference." Having no constitutional authority to appoint *any*, they can have no right to appoint *all* or any portion of the clergy to any office; nor in fact are chaplains appointed "without discrimination or preference."

It is true that on the face of the resolutions by which the clergy in Albany are called to officiate in the legislature, no discrimination appears to be made among the various sects. But can any person who knows the true meaning of those resolutions believe, that were there a Shaker society in Albany, they would be considered as included in those resolutions, or their ministering elder be permitted to perform any of his religious duties in the legislature? Can it be imagined that the legislature meant under any circumstances to give a call to Shaker chaplains, and to join in the devotions of that humble sect, whose faith and trust in God is such, they have no fear that He will do them any wrong, and therefore never pray to have Him do as He or they think right; but with hearts inspired with gratitude and joy, they hymn His praise in music's moving strains, and perform with measured steps, as pious David did, a solemn "dance before the Lord."

But the proof that a discrimination is made, and intended to be made, by which all the clergy in Albany have not been permitted to officiate even in prayer, at the instance of the legislature, does not rest alone on hypothetical data. The committee are credibly informed and think, as the circumstance was noticed in the public prints, it may still be in the recollection of some of the members of this house, that some three or four years since, a respectable, regular, orthodox clergyman, who has the pastoral charge of a colored flock in this city, knowing that the resolutions by which chaplains were appointed to make legislative prayers made no discrimination which excluded him from participating with his professional brethren in offering praise and supplication to an almighty and just God who is "no respecter of persons," nor the color of "the outward man," he claimed his equal right to pray and to be paid. The dilemma thus produced was the subject of negotiation which resulted in a compromise by which the sable pastor was paid from the public purse, *not* for saying prayers for the legislature as other chaplains did, but for *not* saying them; and thus obtained "the penny without the *pater noster*." Whether it is true, as is said, that a similar arrangement is yearly made, your committee have not been able fully to ascertain, but believe the fact is so. . . .

The office of chaplain to the legislature is a civil or an ecclesiastical office. Prayer is not a civil but religious duty. To appoint priests or others to do religious service is to appoint them to ecclesiastical office. Were the office of chaplain a civil office, the appointment of a priest to perform the duties connected with it would be, as has been already proved, a palpable violation of the above recited provision of the constitution: and there being no ecclesiastical authority vested in the legislature, they are as totally destitute of legitimate power to create an ecclesiastical office, or to appoint priests to

perform any religious duty or service whatever, as if the official employment of chaplains for such purpose by the legislature were in express terms prohibited by the constitution.

After showing that the legislature possess no legitimate power to associate religious devotion with legislative business proceedings nor to appoint others to do so; it would seem to be superfluous to prove that it follows, as a necessary consequence, that they have no better warrant to take money from the public treasury to pay officers whom they have no right to appoint. . . .

It is well said, in several of the memorials on this subject, that "the laborer is worthy of his hire"; and that when priests or other persons are hired to do religious duty or to render any other service, they ought, in justice, to be paid if they require it; but justice also requires that they should be paid by those at whose instance and for whose benefit their services may be rendered, and not from the public purse, nor from the pockets of individuals who neither require nor approve public prayers, nor any hired religious devotion. No person of mature understanding who is acquainted with the principles of our government and the provisions of the constitution will contend that the legislature have a right to enact a law, expressly for the purpose of levying a direct tax on the people to pay the wages of priests appointed to say prayers, or to perform any other kind of religious service for the legislature. Equally certain is it that they have no better right to take money which has been paid by the people for legitimate objects, and apply it to purposes for which the legislature have no constitutional right to impose a tax. . . .

Your committee would be willing here to close their remarks, were they not aware that there is an evil spirit abroad, seeking to infuse its baleful influence among the people, to obtain a dominant power in the civil government, through which to manage all the political concerns of the nation, and thus to establish ecclesiastical dominion on the ruins of our free republican institutions and the civil and religious liberties of our country.

To stifle thought, to suppress the exercise of human reason, and to prevent the use of argument, the name of God and of religion have often been profanely used to excite hostility and denunciation against *all* who oppose clerical domination or any measures tending to a union of church and state, or who dare evince moral courage sufficient to exercise the rights of conscience and maintain the freedom of opinion and the right of free discussion.

In opposition to the view which your committee have taken of the subject of the present report, it may again, as with like intent it often has been said, "that the United States are a nation of Christians; that Christianity is the law of the land, and that all are infidels who disbelieve this doctrine or oppose it."

Were it true that Christianity, as such, is the law of the land, because a majority of the people are professing Christians, it would be indispensable that every citizen should know what Christianity is; because *all* ought to know the law who are required to obey it. It would become essential then to ascertain which particular creed, of the seventy different Christian sects, is to be respected as the law of the land, and by which the other sixty-nine would be held as illegal. If a majority can arbitrarily violate the provisions of the Constitution by which the rights of the minority were intended to be secured, on the same principle then, Methodism, which is as much entitled to the name of Christianity as the creed of any other sect, and the professors of which possess as much intelligence, integrity, and sincere religious faith as any other, and are far more numerous than any other Christian sect in this country, would be justly deemed "the law of the land"; and the creed and worship of the minor Christian sects would

be adjudged illegal. And when we consider that all may be wrong, and only one can be right, it might become highly important, in order to know what kind of Christianity is "the law of the land," to ascertain whether the religious faith of St. Paul or St. Peter, Martin Luther or John Calvin, would be considered as the law of the state; and which two or three of these would be denounced as illegal. Equally requisite would it be, in order to know "the law of the land," to understand whether modern or primitive Christianity is such.

To settle all these questions or any of them would require the united effort of church and state. A religious inquisition would thence be indispensable; and all the horrid scenes of the darker ages, when ecclesiastical power reigned triumphant, would be again reacted. Our "happy land" would be as other nations have been, the bloody arena of religious strife and church and state contention. . . .

But to many honest and sincere professors of Christianity it ought to be a source of felicitation that "the kingdom of Christ is not of this world"; and that the precepts and doctrines of Jesus are not "the law of the land"; for were they so, "prayers in public places" would be by law interdicted and suppressed; and men would be obliged, "when they pray, to go into their closets and shut the doors and pray in secret." And those who profess to be sent by God, to "go throughout all the earth and teach the gospel to every creature, without money and without price," would not be allowed by law to take pay for preaching or for prayers, nor would the people be taxed to pay hire for the performance of any religious duty. . . .

But it is not true that Christianity as such is the law of the land. The Constitution is the supreme law of the land by virtue of which the mosque, the synagogue, the Christian church, and all other churches and religions are placed on equal grounds. It makes no discrimination between them, nor allows any preference to be given by law to any or either of them. It prohibits none, protects all, but permits no religious creed to be enforced as the law of the land. Hence the law of the land is that no religious creed as such can be recognized as the law of the state; that "all mankind," and therefore every individual "within this state," have an equal and inalienable right to "believe according to the dictates of their understanding," and no person, nor "human tribunal," has a right to use the name of God or religion to make men afraid to avow their honest and conscientious opinions, or in any way to coerce them to act the hypocrite, with a view to escape the wrath, or to propitiate the evil spirit of religious intolerance and persecution, which is denounced in the Christian books and interdicted by the constitution of this state, both of which place clergymen precisely in that situation which was recognized and approved by their great and acknowledged Master. Neither He nor His apostles . . . sought nor received political aid, nor the pecuniary emoluments attached to services unknown to them, but which, in the revolution of time and events, have been sought and obtained by their successors.

The result of all the foregoing facts and arguments is that your committee have arrived to the most satisfactory conclusion; that the association of ecclesiastical duties with political legislative proceedings is unauthorized by any power delegated by the people, is incompatible with the character of a free government predicated on the principle of equal rights, uncongenial with the spirit and provisions of the constitution of this state, and that the practice ought therefore to be abolished. . . .

And your committee further report that in several of the memorials referred to their consideration, there are other laws which are represented to infringe the civil and religious liberties of your constituents; the alleged unconstitutionality of which is sustained by such facts and arguments as leave no doubt on the minds of the committee that the exceptions of the memorialists to the several subjects of complaint are well taken. But your committee not having time to draw up a detailed report on all the matters contained in the said memorials, and not being willing that the memorialists should be misled to believe that their petitions have been neglected, their complaints disregarded or treated with any disrespect, and thus their grievances remain unredressed, your committee have deemed it proper to recommend the adoption of the following resolutions.

Resolved, that all legislation on religion, other than pursuant to the Constitution, to secure to "all mankind within this state without discrimination or preference" the free and unmolested enjoyment of the rights of opinion and free discussion, is unjust, unauthorized and unconstitutional.

Resolved, that all existing laws by which any person within this state is coerced against his conscientious opinions to conform to the religious creeds or doctrines of others, are unjust, unconstitutional, nugatory, and ought to be repealed.

Resolved, that to obstruct the public streets or highways with iron chains or other impediments to the free use thereof on Sunday or any other day is an exercise of power without right and ought to be interdicted under proper and effectual penalties.

102.

William Cullen Bryant: Songs of the City

The best known of Bryant's poems celebrate the country, especially the Berkshire Hills of Massachusetts, his boyhood home; and they did much to awaken his contemporaries to the natural beauty that surrounded them in America. Yet Bryant was not unaware of the beauty and interest to be found in other settings, too, even the most common; as he had declared in a lecture in 1826, "if . . . our poetry should finally fail of rivaling that of Europe, it will be because Genius sits idle in the midst of its treasures." Among these poetic treasures was New York City itself, where Bryant found fame and fortune and of which he sang in the two lyrics reprinted below.

Source: *Poetical Works*, Household Edition, New York, 1905.

HYMN OF THE CITY

Not in the solitude
Alone may man commune with Heaven, or see,
  Only in savage wood
And sunny vale, the present Deity;
  Or only hear His voice
Where the winds whisper and the waves rejoice.

  Even here do I behold
Thy steps, Almighty! — here, amid the crowd
  Through the great city rolled,
With everlasting murmur deep and loud —
  Choking the ways that wind
'Mong the proud piles, the work of humankind.

  Thy golden sunshine comes
From the round heaven, and on their dwelling lies
  And lights their inner homes;
For them thou fill'st with air the unbounded skies,
  And givest them the stores
Of ocean, and the harvests of its shores.

  Thy Spirit is around,
Quickening the restless mass that sweeps along;
  And this eternal sound —
Voices and footfalls of the numberless throng —
  Like the resounding sea,
Or like the rainy tempest, speaks of Thee.

And when the hour of rest
Comes, like a calm upon the mid-sea brine,
Hushing its billowy breast —
The quiet of that moment too is Thine;
It breathes of Him who keeps
The vast and hapless city while it sleeps.

SPRING IN TOWN

The country ever has a lagging Spring,
Waiting for May to call its violets forth,
And June its roses — showers and sunshine bring,
Slowly, the deepening verdure o'er the earth;
To put their foliage out, the woods are slack,
As one by one the singing-birds come back.

Within the city's bounds the time of flowers
Comes earlier. Let a mild and sunny day,
Such as full often, for a few bright hours,
Breathes through the sky of March the airs of May,
Shine on our roofs and chase the wintry gloom
And lo! our borders glow with sudden bloom.

For the wide sidewalks of Broadway are then
Gorgeous as are a rivulet's banks in June,
That overhung with blossoms, through its glen,
Slides soft away beneath the sunny noon,
And they who search the untrodden wood for flowers
Meet in its depths no lovelier ones than ours.

For here are eyes that shame the violet,
Or the dark drop that on the pansy lies,
And foreheads white, as when in clusters set,
The anemones by forest mountains rise;
And the spring-beauty boasts no tenderer streak
Than the soft red on many a youthful cheek.

103.

George Catlin: Letter from the Yellowstone River

The American fascination with the wilderness infected painter George Catlin during his days as a student in Philadelphia. Impressed by the "silent and stoic dignity" of a group of Native Americans he chanced to observe, Catlin decided to devote himself to recording the appearance and customs of American Indians in a series of paintings. In the following letter, written at the beginning of an eight-year western journey that resulted in more than 500 paintings, Catlin explained his interest in the primitive.

Source: *The Manners, Customs, and Condition of the North American Indians*, London, 1841, Vol. I, pp. 14-16.

I ARRIVED AT THIS PLACE yesterday in the steamer *Yellow Stone* after a voyage of nearly three months from St. Louis, a distance of 2,000 miles, the greater part of which has never before been navigated by steam; and the almost insurmountable difficulties which continually oppose the *voyageur* on this turbid stream have been by degrees overcome by the indefatigable zeal of Mr. Chouteau, a gentleman of great perseverance and part proprietor of the boat. To the politeness of this gentleman I am indebted for my passage from St. Louis to this place, and I had also the pleasure of his company, with that of Major Sanford, the government agent for the Missouri Indians.

The American Fur Company have erected here, for their protection against the savages, a very substantial fort, 300 feet square, with bastions armed with ordnance; and our approach to it under the continued roar of cannon for half an hour, and the shrill yells of the half-affrighted savages who lined the shores, presented a scene of the most thrilling and picturesque appearance. A voyage so full of incident, and furnishing so many novel scenes of the picturesque and romantic as we have passed the numerous villages of the "astonished natives," saluting

them with the puffing of steam and the thunder of artillery, would afford subject for many epistles; and I cannot deny myself the pleasure of occasionally giving you some little sketches of scenes that I have witnessed, and *am witnessing;* and of the singular feelings that are excited in the breast of the stranger traveling through this interesting country. Interesting (as I have said) and *luxurious,* for this is truly the land of epicures; we are invited by the savages to feast of *dog's meat,* as the most honorable food that can be presented to a stranger, and glutted with the more delicious food of beavers' tails and buffaloes' tongues.

You will, no doubt, be somewhat surprised on the receipt of a letter from me, so far strayed into the Western world; and still more startled when I tell you that I am here in the full enthusiasm and practice of my art. That enthusiasm alone has brought me into this remote region, 3,500 miles from my native soil, the last 2,000 of which have furnished me with almost unlimited models, both in landscape and the human figure, exactly suited to my feelings. I am now in the full possession and enjoyments of those conditions on which alone I was induced to pursue the art as a profession;

Mandan Indian brave demonstrating endurance through self-torture; painting by George Catlin

and in anticipation of which, alone, my admiration for the art could ever have been kindled into a pure flame. I mean the free use of nature's undisguised models, with the privilege of selecting for myself. If I am here losing the benefit of the fleeting fashions of the day and neglecting that elegant polish which the world says an artist should draw from a continual intercourse with the polite world, yet have I this consolation — that in this country I am entirely divested of those dangerous steps and allurements which beset an artist in fashionable life, and have little to steal my thoughts away from the contemplation of the beautiful models that are about me. If, also, I have not here the benefit of that feeling of emulation which is the life and spur to the arts where artists are associates together, yet am I surrounded by living models of such elegance and beauty that I feel an unceasing excite-

ment of a much higher order — the certainty that I am drawing knowledge from the true source.

My enthusiastic admiration of man in the honest and elegant simplicity of nature has always fed the warmest feelings of my bosom, and shut half the avenues to my heart against the specious refinements of the accomplished world. This feeling, together with the desire to study my art independently of the embarrassments which the ridiculous fashions of civilized society have thrown in its way, has led me to the wilderness for a while, as the true school of the arts.

I have for a long time been of the opinion that the wilderness of our country afforded models equal to those from which the Grecian sculptors transferred to the marble such inimitable grace and beauty; and I am now more confirmed in this opinion, since I have immersed myself in the midst of thousands and tens of thousands of these knights of the forest, whose whole lives are lives of chivalry, and whose daily feats, with their naked limbs, might vie with those of the Grecian youths in the beautiful rivalry of the Olympian games.

No man's imagination, with all the aids of description that can be given to it, can ever picture the beauty and wildness of scenes that may be daily witnessed in this romantic country; of hundreds of these graceful youths, without a care to wrinkle or a fear to disturb the full expression of pleasure and enjoyment that beams upon their faces — their long black hair mingling with their horses' tails, floating in the wind, while they are flying over the carpeted prairie and dealing death with their spears and arrows to a band of infuriated buffaloes; or their splendid procession in a war parade, arrayed in all their gorgeous colors and trappings, moving with most exquisite grace and manly beauty, added to that bold defiance which man carries on his front, who acknowledges no superior on earth and who is amenable to no laws except the laws of God and honor.

In addition to the knowledge of human nature and of my art which I hope to acquire by this toilsome and expensive undertaking, I have another in view which, if it should not be of equal service to me, will be of no less interest and value to posterity. I have, for many years past, contemplated the noble races of red men who are spread over these trackless forests and boundless prairies, melting away at the approach of civilization. Their rights invaded, their morals corrupted, their lands wrested from them, their customs changed, and therefore lost to the world; and they at last sunk into the earth, and the plow share turning the sod over their graves, and I have flown to their rescue — not of their lives or of their race (for they are *doomed* and must perish) but to the rescue of their looks and their

modes, at which the acquisitive world may hurl their poison and every besom of destruction, and trample them down and crush them to death; yet, phoenixlike, they may rise from the "stain on a painter's palette" and live again upon canvas, and stand forth for centuries yet to come, the living monuments of a noble race. For this purpose I have designed to visit every tribe of Indians on the continent, if my life should be spared, for the purpose of procuring portraits of distinguished Indians, of both sexes in each tribe, painted in their native costume; accompanied with pictures of their villages, domestic habits, games, mysteries, religious ceremonies, etc., with anecdotes, traditions, and history of their respective nations.

If I should live to accomplish my design, the result of my labors will doubtless be interesting to future ages, who will have little else left from which to judge of the original inhabitants of this noble race of beings who require but a few years more of the march of civilization and death to deprive them of all their native customs and character. I have been kindly supplied by the commander in chief of the army and the secretary of war with letters to the commander of every military post and every Indian agent on the Western frontier, with instructions to render me all the facilities in their power which will be of great service to me in so arduous an undertaking. The opportunity afforded me by familiarity with so many tribes of human beings in the simplicity of nature, devoid of the deformities of art, of drawing fair conclusions in the interesting sciences of physiognomy and phrenology, of their manners and customs, rites, ceremonies, etc., and the opportunity of examining the geology and mineralogy of this Western and yet unexplored country, will enable me occasionally to entertain you with much new and interesting information, which I shall take equal pleasure in communicating by an occasional letter in my clumsy way.

104.

For and Against the Bank Renewal Bill

A bill to renew the charter of the Second Bank of the United States passed the Senate on June 11 and the House on July 3, 1832. President Jackson returned the bill on July 10, along with a strong veto message. The veto brought the "Bank War" to a head. Nicholas Biddle, the Bank's president, called the veto message "a manifesto of anarchy"; and Daniel Webster rose in the Senate the next day to deliver a speech in which he charged that the veto usurped congressional prerogatives established by the Constitution. Nevertheless, Congress was unable to repass the bill with the necessary two-thirds majority in both chambers, and Jackson's victory over Bank advocate Henry Clay in the fall elections dashed any remaining hopes of rechartering the Bank. Webster's protest summarized the arguments for the Bank, as the veto message summarized those against it; taken together, they defined the issues of the 1832 campaign and, to a great extent, of the whole Jacksonian Era. Both are reprinted here.

Source: Richardson, II, pp. 576-591.
  The Works of Daniel Webster, 16th edition, Boston, 1872, Vol. III, pp. 416-447.

I.

ANDREW JACKSON: Veto Message

THE BILL "TO MODIFY AND CONTINUE" the act entitled "An act to incorporate the subscribers to the Bank of the United States" was presented to me on the 4th July instant. Having considered it with that solemn regard to the principles of the Constitution which the day was calculated to inspire, and come to the conclusion that it ought not to become a law, I herewith return it to the Senate, in which it originated, with my objections.

A bank of the United States is in many respects convenient for the government and useful to the people. Entertaining this opinion, and deeply impressed with the belief that some of the powers and privileges possessed by the existing bank are unauthorized by the Constitution, subversive of the rights of the states, and dangerous to the liberties of the people, I felt it my duty at an early period of my administration to call the attention of Congress to the practicability of organizing an institution combining all its advantages and obviating these objections. I sincerely regret that in the act before me I can perceive none of those modifications of the bank charter which are necessary, in my opinion, to make it compatible with justice, with sound policy, or with the Constitution of our country.

The present corporate body, denominated the president, directors, and company of the Bank of the United States, will have existed at the time this act is intended to take effect twenty years. It enjoys an exclusive privilege of banking under the authority of the general government, a monopoly of its favor and support, and, as a necessary consequence, almost a monopoly of the foreign and domestic exchange. The powers, privileges, and favors bestowed upon it in the original charter, by increasing the value of the stock far above its par value, operated as a gratuity of many millions to the stockholders.

An apology may be found for the failure to guard against this result in the consideration that the effect of the original act of incorporation could not be certainly foreseen at the time of its passage. The act before me proposes another gratuity to the holders of the same stock, and in many cases to the same men, of at least $7 million more. This donation finds no apology in any uncertainty as to the effect of the act. On all hands it is conceded that its passage will increase at least 20 or 30 percent more the market price of the stock, subject to the payment of the annuity of $200,000 per year secured by the act, thus adding in a moment one-fourth to its par value. It is not our own citizens only who are to receive the bounty of our government. More than $8 million of the stock of this bank are held by foreigners. By this act the American republic proposes virtually to make them a present of some millions of dollars. For these gratuities to foreigners and to some of our own opulent citizens the act secures no equivalent whatever. They are the certain gains of the present stockholders under the operation of this act, after making full allowance for the payment of the bonus.

Every monopoly and all exclusive privileges are granted at the expense of the public, which ought to receive a fair equivalent. The many millions which this act proposes to bestow on the stockholders of the existing bank must come directly or indirectly out of the earnings of the American people. It is due to them, therefore, if their government sell monopolies and exclusive privi-

leges, that they should at least exact for them as much as they are worth in open market. The value of the monopoly in this case may be correctly ascertained. The $28 million of stock would probably be at an advance of 50 percent and command in market at least $42 million, subject to the payment of the present bonus. The present value of the monopoly, therefore, is $17 million, and this the act proposes to sell for $3 million, payable in fifteen annual installments of $200,000 each.

It is not conceivable how the present stockholders can have any claim to the special favor of the government. The present corporation has enjoyed its monopoly during the period stipulated in the original contract. If we must have such a corporation, why should not the government sell out the whole stock and thus secure to the people the full market value of the privileges granted? Why should not Congress create and sell $28 million of stock, incorporating the purchasers with all the powers and privileges secured in this act and putting the premium upon the sales into the treasury?

But this act does not permit competition in the purchase of this monopoly. It seems to be predicated on the erroneous idea that the present stockholders have a prescriptive right not only to the favor but to the bounty of government. It appears that more than a fourth part of the stock is held by foreigners and the residue is held by a few hundred of our own citizens, chiefly of the richest class. For their benefit does this act exclude the whole American people from competition in the purchase of this monopoly and dispose of it for many millions less than it is worth. This seems the less excusable because some of our citizens not now stockholders petitioned that the door of competition might be opened and offered to take a charter on terms much more favorable to the government and country.

But this proposition, although made by

men whose aggregate wealth is believed to be equal to all the private stock in the existing bank, has been set aside, and the bounty of our government is proposed to be again bestowed on the few who have been fortunate enough to secure the stock and at this moment wield the power of the existing institution. I cannot perceive the justice or policy of this course. If our government must sell monopolies, it would seem to be its duty to take nothing less than their full value, and, if gratuities must be made once in fifteen or twenty years, let them not be bestowed on the subjects of a foreign government nor upon a designated and favored class of men in our own country. It is but justice and good policy, as far as the nature of the case will admit, to confine our favors to our own fellow citizens and let each in his turn enjoy an opportunity to profit by our bounty. In the bearings of the act before me upon these points I find ample reasons why it should not become a law.

It has been urged as an argument in favor of rechartering the present bank that the calling in its loans will produce great embarrassment and distress. The time allowed to close its concerns is ample, and, if it has been well managed, its pressure will be light, and heavy only in case its management has been bad. If, therefore, it shall produce distress, the fault will be its own; and it would furnish a reason against renewing a power which has been so obviously abused. But will there ever be a time when this reason will be less powerful? To acknowledge its force is to admit that the bank ought to be perpetual, and as a consequence the present stockholders and those inheriting their rights as successors be established a privileged order, clothed both with great political power and enjoying immense pecuniary advantages from their connection with the government.

The modifications of the existing charter proposed by this act are not such, in my view, as make it consistent with the rights of the states or the liberties of the people. The qualification of the right of the bank to hold real estate, the limitation of its power to establish branches, and the power reserved to Congress to forbid the circulation of small notes are restrictions comparatively of little value or importance. All the objectionable principles of the existing corporation, and most of its odious features, are retained without alleviation. . . .

By documents submitted to Congress at the present session it appears that on the 1st of January, 1832, of the $28 million of private stock in the corporation, $8,405,500 were held by foreigners, mostly of Great Britain. The amount of stock held in the nine Western and Southwestern states is $140,200, and in the four Southern states is .$5,623,100, and in the Middle and Eastern states is about $13,522,000. The profits of the bank in 1831, as shown in a statement to Congress, were about $3,455,598; of this there accrued in the nine Western states about $1,640,048; in the four Southern states about $352,507, and in the Middle and Eastern states about $1,463,041. As little stock is held in the West, it is obvious that the debt of the people in that section to the bank is principally a debt to the Eastern and foreign stockholders; that the interest they pay upon it is carried into the Eastern states and into Europe, and that it is a burden upon their industry and a drain of their currency, which no country can bear without inconvenience and occasional distress.

To meet this burden and equalize the exchange operations of the bank, the amount of specie drawn from those states through its branches within the last two years, as shown by its official reports, was about $6 million. More than $500,000 of this amount does not stop in the Eastern states but passes on to Europe to pay the dividends of the foreign stockholders. In the principle of taxation recognized by this act the Western states find no adequate compensation for this perpetual burden on their industry and drain of their currency. The branch bank at Mobile made last year $95,140, yet under the provisions of this act the state of Alabama can raise no revenue from these profitable operations, because not a share of the stock is held by any of her citizens. Mississippi and Missouri are in the same condition in relation to the branches at Natchez and St. Louis, and such, in a greater or less degree, is the condition of every Western state. The tendency of the plan of taxation which this act proposes will be to place the whole United States in the same relation to foreign countries which the Western states now bear to the Eastern. When by a tax on resident stockholders the stock of this bank is made worth 10 or 15 percent more to foreigners than to residents, most of it will inevitably leave the country.

Thus will this provision in its practical effect deprive the Eastern as well as the Southern and Western states of the means of raising a revenue from the extension of business and great profits of this institution. It will make the American people debtors to aliens in nearly the whole amount due to this bank, and send across the Atlantic from $2 million to $5 million of specie every year to pay the bank dividends.

In another of its bearings this provision is fraught with danger. Of the twenty-five directors of this bank, five are chosen by the government and twenty by the citizen stockholders. From all voice in these elections the foreign stockholders are excluded by the charter. In proportion, therefore, as the stock is transferred to foreign holders the extent of suffrage in the choice of directors is curtailed. Already is almost a third of the stock in foreign hands and not represented in elections. It is constantly passing out of the country, and this act will accelerate its departure. The entire control of the institution would necessarily fall into the hands of a few citizen stockholders, and the

ease with which the object would be accomplished would be a temptation to designing men to secure that control in their own hands by monopolizing the remaining stock. There is danger that a president and directors would then be able to elect themselves from year to year and, without responsibility or control, manage the whole concerns of the bank during the existence of its charter. It is easy to conceive that great evils to our country and its institutions might flow from such a concentration of power in the hands of a few men irresponsible to the people.

Is there no danger to our liberty and independence in a bank that in its nature has so little to bind it to our country? The president of the bank has told us that most of the state banks exist by its forbearance. Should its influence become concentered, as it may under the operation of such an act as this, in the hands of a self-elected directory whose interests are identified with those of the foreign stockholders, will there not be cause to tremble for the purity of our elections in peace and for the independence of our country in war? Their power would be great whenever they might choose to exert it; but if this monopoly were regularly renewed every fifteen or twenty years on terms proposed by themselves, they might seldom in peace put forth their strength to influence elections or control the affairs of the nation. But if any private citizen or public functionary should interpose to curtail its powers or prevent a renewal of its privileges, it cannot be doubted that he would be made to feel its influence.

Should the stock of the bank principally pass into the hands of the subjects of a foreign country, and should we unfortunately become involved in a war with that country, what would be our condition? Of the course which would be pursued by a bank almost wholly owned by the subjects of a foreign power and managed by those whose interests, if not affections, would run in the same direction, there can be no doubt. All its operations within would be in aid of the hostile fleets and armies without. Controlling our currency, receiving our public moneys, and holding thousands of our citizens in dependence, it would be more formidable and dangerous than the naval and military power of the enemy.

If we must have a bank with private stockholders, every consideration of sound policy and every impulse of American feeling admonishes that it should be *purely American.* Its stockholders should be composed exclusively of our own citizens, who at least ought to be friendly to our government and willing to support it in times of difficulty and danger. So abundant is domestic capital that competition in subscribing for the stock of local banks has recently led almost to riots. To a bank exclusively of American stockholders, possessing the powers and privileges granted by this act, subscriptions for $200 million could be readily obtained. Instead of sending abroad the stock of the bank in which the government must deposit its funds and on which it must rely to sustain its credit in times of emergency; it would rather seem to be expedient to prohibit its sale to aliens under penalty of absolute forfeiture.

It is maintained by the advocates of the bank that its constitutionality in all its features ought to be considered as settled by precedent and by the decision of the Supreme Court. To this conclusion I cannot assent. Mere precedent is a dangerous source of authority and should not be regarded as deciding questions of constitutional power except where the acquiescence of the people and the states can be considered as well settled. So far from this being the case on this subject, an argument against the bank might be based on precedent. One Congress in 1791 decided in favor of a bank; another in 1811 decided against it. One Congress in 1815 decided against a bank; another in 1816 decided in its favor. Prior to the present Congress,

therefore, the precedents drawn from that source were equal. If we resort to the states, the expressions of legislative, judicial, and executive opinions against the bank have been probably to those in its favor as four to one. There is nothing in precedent, therefore, which, if its authority were admitted, ought to weigh in favor of the act before me.

If the opinion of the Supreme Court covered the whole ground of this act, it ought not to control the coordinate authorities of this government. The Congress, the executive, and the court must each for itself be guided by its own opinion of the Constitution. Each public officer who takes an oath to support the Constitution swears that he will support it as he understands it and not as it is understood by others. It is as much the duty of the House of Representatives, of the Senate, and of the President to decide upon the constitutionality of any bill or resolution which may be presented to them for passage or approval as it is of the supreme judges when it may be brought before them for judicial decision. The opinion of the judges has no more authority over Congress than the opinion of Congress has over the judges, and on that point the President is independent of both. The authority of the Supreme Court must not, therefore, be permitted to control the Congress or the executive when acting in their legislative capacities, but to have only such influence as the force of their reasoning may deserve.

But in the case relied upon, the Supreme Court have not decided that all the features of this corporation are compatible with the Constitution. It is true that the Court have said that the law incorporating the bank is a constitutional exercise of power by Congress; but, taking into view the whole opinion of the court and the reasoning by which they have come to that conclusion, I understand them to have decided that, inasmuch as a bank is an appropriate means for carrying into effect the enumerated powers of the general government, therefore the law incorporating it is in accordance with that provision of the Constitution which declares that Congress shall have power "to make all laws which shall be necessary and proper for carrying those powers into execution." Having satisfied themselves that the word "necessary" in the Constitution means "needful," "requisite," "essential," "conducive to," and that "a bank" is a convenient, a useful, and an essential instrument in the prosecution of the government's "fiscal operations," they conclude that to "use one must be within the discretion of Congress" and that "the act to incorporate the Bank of the United States is a law made in pursuance of the Constitution"; "but," say they, *where the law is not prohibited and is really calculated to effect any of the objects entrusted to the government, to undertake here to inquire into the degree of its necessity would be to pass the line which circumscribes the judicial department and to tread on legislative ground."*

The principle here affirmed is that the "degree of its necessity," involving all the details of a banking institution, is a question exclusively for legislative consideration. A bank is constitutional, but it is the province of the legislature to determine whether this or that particular power, privilege, or exemption is "necessary and proper" to enable the bank to discharge its duties to the government, and from their decision there is no appeal to the courts of justice. Under the decision of the Supreme Court, therefore, it is the exclusive province of Congress and the President to decide whether the particular features of this act are necessary and proper in order to enable the bank to perform conveniently and efficiently the public duties assigned to it as a fiscal agent, and therefore constitutional, or unnecessary and improper, and therefore unconstitutional.

Without commenting on the general principle affirmed by the Supreme Court, let us examine the details of this act in accordance with the rule of legislative action which they had laid down. It will be found that many of the powers and privileges conferred on it cannot be supposed necessary for the purpose for which it is proposed to be created and are not, therefore, means necessary to attain the end in view, and consequently not justified by the Constitution.

The original Act of Incorporation, Section 21, enacts that "no other bank shall be established by any future law of the United States during the continuance of the corporation hereby created, for which the faith of the United States is hereby pledged: *Provided,* Congress may renew existing charters for banks within the District of Columbia not increasing the capital thereof, and may also establish any other bank or banks in said District with capitals not exceeding in the whole $6 million if they shall deem it expedient." This provision is continued in force by the act before me fifteen years from the 3rd of March, 1836.

If Congress possessed the power to establish one bank, they had power to establish more than one if in their opinion two or more banks had been "necessary" to facilitate the execution of the powers delegated to them in the Constitution. If they possessed the power to establish a second bank, it was a power derived from the Constitution to be exercised from time to time, and at any time when the interests of the country or the emergencies of the government might make it expedient. It was possessed by one Congress as well as another, and by all congresses alike, and alike at every session. But the Congress of 1816 have taken it away from their successors for twenty years, and the Congress of 1832 proposes to abolish it for fifteen years more. It cannot be "necessary" or "proper" for Congress to barter away or divest themselves of any of the powers vested in them by the Constitution to be exercised for the public good. It is not "necessary" to the efficiency of the bank, nor is it "proper" in relation to themselves and their successors. They may *properly* use the discretion vested in them, but they may not limit the discretion of their successors. This restriction on themselves and grant of a monopoly to the bank is therefore unconstitutional.

In another point of view this provision is a palpable attempt to amend the Constitution by an act of legislation. The Constitution declares that "the Congress shall have power to exercise exclusive legislation in all cases whatsoever" over the District of Columbia. Its constitutional power, therefore, to establish banks in the District of Columbia and increase their capital at will is unlimited and uncontrollable by any other power than that which gave authority to the Constitution. Yet this act declares that Congress shall *not* increase the capital of existing banks, nor create other banks with capitals exceeding in the whole $6 million.

The Constitution declares that Congress *shall* have power to exercise exclusive legislation over this District *"in all cases whatsoever,"* and this act declares they shall not. Which is the supreme law of the land? This provision cannot be *"necessary"* or *"proper"* or *constitutional* unless the absurdity be admitted that whenever it be "necessary and proper" in the opinion of Congress they have a right to barter away one portion of the powers vested in them by the Constitution as a means of executing the rest.

On two subjects only does the Constitution recognize in Congress the power to grant exclusive privileges or monopolies. It declares that "Congress shall have power to promote the progress of science and useful arts by securing for limited times to authors and inventors the exclusive right to their respective writings and discoveries." Out of this express delegation of power have grown our laws of patents and copyrights. As the Constitution expressly delegates to Congress the power to grant exclusive privileges in these cases as the means of executing the substantive power "to promote the progress of science and useful arts," it is

consistent with the fair rules of construction to conclude that such a power was not intended to be granted as a means of accomplishing any other end. On every other subject which comes within the scope of congressional power there is an ever living discretion in the use of proper means, which cannot be restricted or abolished without an amendment of the Constitution. Every act of Congress, therefore, which attempts by grants or monopolies or sale of exclusive privileges for a limited time, or a time without limit, to restrict or extinguish its own discretion in the choice of means to execute its delegated powers is equivalent to a legislative amendment of the Constitution and palpably unconstitutional.

This act authorizes and encourages transfers of its stock to foreigners and grants them an exemption from all state and national taxation. So far from being *"necessary and proper"* that the bank should possess this power to make it a safe and efficient agent of the government in its fiscal operations, it is calculated to convert the Bank of the United States into a foreign bank, to impoverish our people in time of peace, to disseminate a foreign influence through every section of the republic, and in war to endanger our independence.

The several states reserved the power at the formation of the Constitution to regulate and control titles and transfers of real property, and most, if not all, of them have laws disqualifying aliens from acquiring or holding lands within their limits. But this act, in disregard of the undoubted right of the states to prescribe such disqualifications, gives to aliens stockholders in this bank an interest and title, as members of the corporation, to all the real property it may acquire within any of the states of this Union. This privilege granted to aliens is not *"necessary"* to enable the bank to perform its public duties, nor in any sense *"proper,"* because it is vitally subversive of the rights of the states.

The government of the United States have no constitutional power to purchase lands within the states except "for the erection of forts, magazines, arsenals, dockyards, and other needful buildings," and even for these objects only "by the consent of the legislature of the state in which the same shall be." By making themselves stockholders in the bank and granting to the corporation the power to purchase lands for other purposes, they assume a power not granted in the Constitution and grant to others what they do not themselves possess. It is not *necessary* to the receiving, safekeeping, or transmission of the funds of the government that the bank should possess this power, and it is not *proper* that Congress should thus enlarge the powers delegated to them in the Constitution. . . .

The government is the only "proper" judge where its agents should reside and keep their offices, because it best knows where their presence will be "necessary." It cannot, therefore, be "necessary" or "proper" to authorize the bank to locate branches where it pleases to perform the public service, without consulting the government and contrary to its will. The principle laid down by the Supreme Court concedes that Congress cannot establish a bank for purposes of private speculation and gain, but only as a means of executing the delegated powers of the general government. By the same principle a branch bank cannot constitutionally be established for other than public purposes. The power which this act gives to establish two branches in any state, without the injunction or request of the government and for other than public purposes, is not "necessary" to the due execution of the powers delegated to Congress.

The bonus which is exacted from the bank is a confession upon the face of the act that the powers granted by it are greater than are "necessary" to its character of a fiscal agent. The government does not tax its officers and agents for the privilege of serving it. The bonus of $1,500,000 required by the original charter and that of $3 million proposed by this act are not exacted for the privilege of giving "the necessary facilities for transferring the public funds from place to place within the United States or the territories thereof, and for distributing the same in payment of the public creditors without charging commission or claiming allowance on account of the difference of exchange," as required by the act of incorporation, but for something more beneficial to the stockholders.

The original act declares that it (the bonus) is granted "in consideration of the exclusive privileges and benefits conferred by this act upon the said bank," and the act before me declares it to be "in consideration of the exclusive benefits and privileges continued by this act to the said corporation for fifteen years, as aforesaid." It is therefore for "exclusive privileges and benefits" conferred for their own use and emolument and not for the advantage of the government, that a bonus is exacted. These surplus powers for which the bank is required to pay cannot surely be "necessary" to make it the fiscal agent of the treasury. If they were, the exaction of a bonus for them would not be "proper."

It is maintained by some that the bank is a means of executing the constitutional power "to coin money and regulate the value thereof." Congress have established a mint to coin money and passed laws to regulate the value thereof. The money so coined, with its value so regulated, and such foreign coins as Congress may adopt are the only currency known to the Constitution. But if they have other power to regulate the currency, it was conferred to be exercised by themselves and not to be transferred to a corporation. If the bank be established for that purpose, with a charter unalterable without its consent, Congress have parted with their power for a term of years, during which the Constitution is a dead letter. It is neither necessary nor proper to transfer its legislative power to such a bank, and therefore unconstitutional.

By its silence, considered in connection with the decision of the Supreme Court in the case of M'Culloch against the state of Maryland, this act takes from the states the power to tax a portion of the banking business carried on within their limits, in subversion of one of the strongest barriers which secured them against federal encroachments. Banking, like farming, manufacturing, or any other occupation or profession, is a business, the right to follow which is not originally derived from the laws. Every citizen and every company of citizens in all of our states possessed the right until the state legislatures deemed it good policy to prohibit private banking by law. If the prohibitory state laws were now repealed, every citizen would again possess the right. The state banks are a qualified restoration of the right which has been taken away by the laws against banking, guarded by such provisions and limitations as in the opinion of the state legislatures the public interest requires. These corporations, unless there be an exemption in their charter, are, like private bankers and banking companies, subject to state taxation. The manner in which these taxes shall be laid depends wholly on legislative discretion. It may be upon the bank, upon the stock, upon the profits, or in any other mode which the sovereign power shall will.

Upon the formation of the Constitution the states guarded their taxing power with peculiar jealousy. They surrendered it only as it regards imports and exports. In relation to every other object within their jurisdiction, whether persons, property, business, or professions, it was secured in as ample a manner as it was before possessed. All persons, though United States officers, are liable to a poll tax by the states within which they reside. The lands of the United States are liable to the usual land tax, except in the new states, from whom agreements that they will not tax unsold lands are exacted when they are admitted into the Union. Horses, wagons, any beasts or vehicles, tools, or property belonging to private citizens, though employed in the service of the United States, are subject to state taxation. Every private business, whether carried on by an officer of the general government or not, whether it be mixed with public concerns or not, even if it be carried on by the government of the United States itself, separately or in partnership, falls within the scope of the taxing power of the state. Nothing comes more fully within it than banks and the business of banking, by whomsoever instituted and carried on. Over this whole subject matter it is just as absolute, unlimited, and uncontrollable as if the Constitution had never been adopted, because in the formation of that instrument it was reserved without qualification.

The principle is conceded that the states cannot rightfully tax the operations of the general government. They cannot tax the money of the government deposited in the state banks nor the agency of those banks remitting it; but will any man maintain that their mere selection to perform this public service for the general government would exempt the state banks and their ordinary business from state taxation? Had the United States, instead of establishing a bank at Philadelphia, employed a private banker to keep and transmit their funds, would it have deprived Pennsylvania of the right to tax his bank and his usual banking operations? It will not be pretended. Upon what principle, then, are the banking establishments of the Bank of the United States and their usual banking operations to be exempted from taxation?

It is not their public agency or the deposits of the government which the states claim a right to tax, but their banks and their banking powers, instituted and exercised within state jurisdiction for their private emolument — those powers and privileges for which they pay a bonus, and which the states tax in their own banks. The exercise of these powers within a state, no matter by whom or under what authority, whether by private citizens in their original right, by corporate bodies created by the states, by foreigners or the agents of foreign governments located within their limits, forms a legitimate object of state taxation. From this and like sources, from the persons, property, and business that are found residing, located, or carried on under their jurisdiction, must the states, since the surrender of their right to raise a revenue from imports and exports, draw all the money necessary for the support of their governments and the maintenance of their independence. There is no more appropriate subject of taxation than banks, banking, and bank stocks, and none to which the states ought more pertinaciously to cling.

It cannot be "necessary" to the character of the bank as a fiscal agent of the government that its private business should be exempted from that taxation to which all the state banks are liable, nor can I conceive it "proper" that the substantive and most essential powers reserved by the states shall be thus attacked and annihilated as a means of executing the powers delegated to the general government. It may be safely assumed that none of those sages who had an agency in forming or adopting our Constitution ever imagined that any portion of the taxing power of the states not prohibited to them nor delegated to Congress was to be swept away and annihilated as a means of executing certain powers delegated to Congress.

If our power over means is so absolute that the Supreme Court will not call in question the constitutionality of an act of Congress the subject of which "is not prohibited, and is really calculated to effect any of the objects entrusted to the government," although, as in the case before me, it takes away powers expressly granted to Congress and rights scrupulously reserved to the states, it becomes us to proceed in our leg-islation with the utmost caution. Though not directly, our own powers and the rights of the states may be indirectly legislated away in the use of means to execute substantive powers.

We may not enact that Congress shall not have the power of exclusive legislation over the District of Columbia, but we may pledge the faith of the United States that as a means of executing other powers it shall not be exercised for twenty years or forever. We may not pass an act prohibiting the states to tax the banking business carried on within their limits, but we may, as a means of executing our powers over other objects, place that business in the hands of our agents and then declare it exempt from state taxation in their hands. Thus may our own powers and the rights of the states, which we cannot directly curtail or invade, be frittered away and extinguished in the use of means employed by us to execute other powers. That a bank of the United States, competent to all the duties which may be required by the government, might be so organized as not to infringe on our own delegated powers or the reserved rights of the states I do not entertain a doubt. Had the executive been called upon to furnish the project of such an institution, the duty would have been cheerfully performed. In the absence of such a call it was obviously proper that he should confine himself to pointing out those prominent features in the act presented which in his opinion make it incompatible with the Constitution and sound policy. A general discussion will now take place, eliciting new light and settling important principles; and a new Congress, elected in the midst of such discussion, and furnishing an equal representation of the people according to the last census, will bear to the Capitol the verdict of public opinion, and, I doubt not, bring this important question to a satisfactory result.

Under such circumstances the bank comes forward and asks a renewal of its charter for a term of fifteen years upon conditions which not only operate as a gratuity to the stockholders of many millions of dollars but will sanction any abuses and legalize any encroachments.

Suspicions are entertained and charges are made of gross abuse and violation of its charter. An investigation unwillingly conceded and so restricted in time as necessarily to make it incomplete and unsatisfactory discloses enough to excite suspicion and alarm. In the practices of the principal bank partially unveiled, in the absence of important witnesses, and in numerous charges confidently made and as yet wholly uninvestigated there was enough to induce a majority of the committee of investigation — a committee which was selected from the most able and honorable members of the House of Representatives — to recommend a suspension of further action upon the bill and a prosecution of the inquiry. As the charter had yet four years to run, and as a renewal now was not necessary to the successful prosecution of its business, it was to have been expected that the bank itself, conscious of its purity and proud of its character, would have withdrawn its application for the present and demanded the severest scrutiny into all its transactions. In their declining to do so there seems to be an additional reason why the functionaries of the government should proceed with less haste and more caution in the renewal of their monopoly.

The bank is professedly established as an agent of the executive branch of the government, and its constitutionality is maintained on that ground. Neither upon the propriety of present action nor upon the provisions of this act was the executive consulted. It has had no opportunity to say that it neither needs nor wants an agent clothed with such powers and favored by such exemptions. There is nothing in its legitimate functions which makes it necessary or proper. Whatever interest or influence, whether public or private, has given birth to this act, it cannot be found either in the wishes or necessities of the Executive Department, by which present action is deemed premature, and the powers conferred upon its agent not only unnecessary but dangerous to the government and country.

It is to be regretted that the rich and powerful too often bend the acts of government to their selfish purposes. Distinctions in society will always exist under every just government. Equality of talents, of education, or of wealth cannot be produced by human institutions. In the full enjoyment of the gifts of Heaven and the fruits of superior industry, economy, and virtue, every man is equally entitled to protection by law; but when the laws undertake to add to these natural and just advantages artificial distinctions, to grant titles, gratuities, and exclusive privileges, to make the rich richer and the potent more powerful, the humble members of society — the farmers, mechanics, and laborers — who have neither the time nor the means of securing like favors to themselves, have a right to complain of the injustice of their government. There are no necessary evils in government. Its evils exist only in its abuses. If it would confine itself to equal protection, and, as Heaven does its rains, shower its favors alike on the high and the low, the rich and the poor, it would be an unqualified blessing. In the act before me there seems to be a wide and unnecessary departure from these just principles.

Nor is our government to be maintained or our Union preserved by invasions of the rights and powers of the several states. In thus attempting to make our general government strong, we make it weak. Its true strength consists in leaving individuals and states as much as possible to themselves — in making itself felt, not in its power, but in its beneficence; not in its control, but in its protection; not in binding the states more closely to the center, but leaving each to move unobstructed in its proper orbit.

Experience should teach us wisdom. Most of the difficulties our government now encounters and most of the dangers which impend over our Union have sprung from an abandonment of the legitimate objects of government by our national legislation and the adoption of such principles as are embodied in this act. Many of our rich men have not been content with equal protection and equal benefits but have besought us to make them richer by act of Congress. By attempting to gratify their desires, we have in the results of our legislation arrayed section against section, interest against interest, and man against man, in a fearful commotion which threatens to shake the foundations of our Union.

It is time to pause in our career to review our principles and, if possible, revive that devoted patriotism and spirit of compromise which distinguished the sages of the Revolution and the fathers of our Union. If we cannot at once, in justice to interests vested under improvident legislation, make our government what it ought to be, we can at least take a stand against all new grants of monopolies and exclusive privileges, against any prostitution of our government to the advancement of the few at the expense of the many, and in favor of compromise and gradual reform in our code of laws and system of political economy.

II.

DANIEL WEBSTER: Reply to Jackson

I HESITATE NOT TO SAY THAT, as this *veto* travels to the West, it will depreciate the value of every man's property from the Atlantic states to the capitol of Missouri. Its effects will be felt in the price of lands, the great and leading article of Western property, in the price of crops, in the products of labor, in the repression of enterprise, and in embarrassment to every kind of business

and occupation, I state this opinion strongly because I have no doubt of its truth, and am willing its correctness should be judged by the event. Without personal acquaintance with the Western states, I know enough of their condition to be satisfied that what I have predicted must happen. The people of the West are rich, but their riches consist in their immense quantities of excellent land, in the products of these lands, and in their spirit of enterprise.

The actual value of money, or rate of interest, with them is high because their pecuniary capital bears little proportion to their landed interest. At an average rate, money is not worth less than 8 percent per annum throughout the whole Western country, notwithstanding that it has now a loan or an advance from the bank of $30 million at 6 percent. To call in this loan, at the rate of $8 million a year, in addition to the interest on the whole, and to take away, at the same time, that circulation which constitutes so great a portion of the medium of payment throughout that whole region, is an operation which, however wisely conducted, cannot but inflict a blow on the community of tremendous force and frightful consequences. The thing cannot be done without distress, bankruptcy, and ruin to many. . . .

Although, sir, I have spoken of the effects of this *veto* in the Western country, it has not been because I considered that part of the United States exclusively affected by it. Some of the Atlantic states may feel its consequences, perhaps, as sensibly as those of the West, though not for the same reasons. The concern manifested by Pennsylvania for the renewal of the charter shows her sense of the importance of the bank to her own interest and that of the nation. That great and enterprising state has entered into an extensive system of internal improvements, which necessarily makes heavy demands on her credit and her resources; and by the sound and acceptable currency which the bank affords, by the stability which it gives to private credit, and by occasional advances made in anticipation of her revenues and in aid of her great objects, she has found herself benefited, doubtless, in no inconsiderable degree. Her legislature has instructed her senators here to advocate the renewal of the charter, at this session. They have obeyed her voice, and yet they have the misfortune to find that, in the judgment of the President, *the measure is unconstitutional, unnecessary, dangerous to liberty, and is, moreover, ill-timed.*

But, Mr. President, it is not the local interest of the West, nor the particular interest of Pennsylvania, or any other state, which has influenced Congress in passing this bill. It has been governed by a wise foresight and by a desire to avoid embarrassment in the pecuniary concerns of the country; to secure the safe collection and convenient transmission of public moneys; to maintain the circulation of the country, sound and safe as it now happily is, against the possible effects of a wild spirit of speculation. Finding the bank highly useful, Congress has thought fit to provide for its continuance. . . .

Before proceeding to the constitutional question, there are some other topics treated in the message which ought to be noticed. It commences by an inflamed statement of what it calls the "favor" bestowed upon the original bank by the government, or, indeed, as it is phrased, the "monopoly of its favor and support"; and through the whole message all possible changes are rung on the "gratuity," the "exclusive privileges," and "monopoly" of the bank charter. Now, sir, the truth is that the powers conferred on the bank are such, and no others, as are usually conferred on similar institutions. They constitute no monopoly, although some of them are of necessity, and with propriety, exclusive privileges.

"The original act," says the message, "operated as a gratuity of many millions to the stockholders." What fair foundation is there for this remark? The stockholders received their charter, not gratuitously but for a valuable consideration in money prescribed by Congress and actually paid. At some times the stock has been above par, at other times below par, according to prudence in management, or according to commercial occurrences. But if, by a judicious administration of its affairs, it had kept its stock always above par, what pretense would there be, nevertheless, for saying that such augmentation of its value was a "gratuity" from government?

The message proceeds to declare that the present act proposes another donation, another gratuity, to the same men, of at least $7 million more. It seems to me that this is an extraordinary statement and an extraordinary style of argument for such a subject and on such an occasion. In the first place, the facts are all assumed; they are taken for true without evidence. There are no proofs that any benefit to that amount will accrue to the stockholders, nor any experience to justify the expectation of it. It rests on random estimates or mere conjecture.

But suppose the continuance of the charter should prove beneficial to the stockholders; do they not pay for it? They give twice as much for a charter of fifteen years as was given before for one of twenty. And if the proposed bonus, or premium, be not, in the President's judgment, large enough, would he, nevertheless, on such a mere matter of opinion as that, negative the whole bill? May not Congress be trusted to decide even on such a subject as the amount of the money premium to be received by government for a charter of this kind?

But, sir, there is a larger and a much more just view of this subject. The bill was not passed for the purpose of benefiting the present stockholders. Their benefit, if any, is incidental and collateral. Nor was it passed on any idea that they had a *right* to a renewed charter, although the message argues against such a right, as if it had been somewhere set up and asserted. No such right has been asserted by anybody. Congress passed the bill, not as a bounty or a favor to the present stockholders, nor to comply with any demand of right on their part, but to promote great public interests, for great public objects. Every bank must have some stockholders, unless it be such a bank as the President has recommended, and in regard to which he seems not likely to find much concurrence of other men's opinions; and if the stockholders, whoever they may be, conduct the affairs of the bank prudently, the expectation is always, of course, that they will make it profitable to themselves as well as useful to the public. If a bank charter is not to be granted because, to some extent, it may be profitable to the stockholders, no charter can be granted. The objection lies against all banks.

Sir, the object aimed at by such institutions is to connect the public safety and convenience with private interests. It has been found by experience that banks are safest under private management and that government banks are among the most dangerous of all inventions. Now, sir, the whole drift of the message is to reverse the settled judgment of all the civilized world, and to set up government banks independent of private interests or private control. For this purpose the message labors, even beyond the measure of all its other labors, to create jealousies and prejudices, on the ground of the alleged benefit which individuals will derive from the renewal of this charter. Much less effort is made to show that government, or the public, will be injured by the bill than that individuals will profit by it.

Following up the impulses of the same spirit, the message goes on gravely to allege that the act as passed by Congress proposes to make a *present* of some millions of dollars to foreigners because a portion of the stock is held by foreigners. Sir, how would this sort of argument apply to other cases? The President has shown himself not only willing but anxious to pay off the 3 percent stock of the United States at par, notwith-standing that it is notorious that foreigners are owners of the greater part of it. Why should he not call that a donation to foreigners of many millions? . . .

From the commencement of the government, it has been thought desirable to invite rather than to repel the introduction of foreign capital. Our stocks have all been open to foreign subscriptions; and the state banks, in like manner, are free to foreign ownership. Whatever state has created a debt has been willing that foreigners should become purchasers, and desirous of it. How long is it, sir, since Congress itself passed a law vesting new powers in the President of the United States over the cities in this District for the very purpose of increasing their credit abroad, the better to enable them to borrow money to pay their subscriptions to the Chesapeake and Ohio Canal? It is easy to say that there is danger to liberty, danger to independence, in a bank open to foreign stockholders, because it is easy to say anything. But neither reason nor experience proves any such danger. The foreign stockholder cannot be a director. He has no voice even in the choice of directors. His money is placed entirely in the management of the directors appointed by the President and Senate and by the American stockholders. So far as there is dependence or influence either way, it is to the disadvantage of the foreign stockholder. He has parted with the control over his own property, instead of exercising control over the property or over the actions of others. . . .

I now proceed, sir, to a few remarks upon the President's constitutional objections to the bank; and I cannot forbear to say, in regard to them, that he appears to me to have assumed very extraordinary grounds of reasoning. He denies that the constitutionality of the bank is a settled question. If it be not, will it ever become so, or what disputed question ever can be settled? . . .

As early as 1791, after great deliberation, the First Bank charter was passed by Congress and approved by President Washington. It established an institution, resembling, in all things now objected to, the present bank. . . . That bank continued twenty years. In 1816, the present institution was established and has been ever since in full operation.

Now, sir, the question of the power of Congress to create such institutions has been contested in every manner known to our Constitution and laws. The forms of the government furnish no new mode in which to try this question. It has been discussed over and over again in Congress; it has been argued and solemnly adjudged in the Supreme Court; every President, except the present, has considered it a settled question; many of the state legislatures have instructed their senators to vote for the bank; the tribunals of the states, in every instance, have supported its constitutionality; and, beyond all doubt and dispute, the general public opinion of the country has at all times given, and does now give, its full sanction and approbation to the exercise of this power as being a constitutional power. . . .

But if the President thinks lightly of the authority of Congress in construing the Constitution, he thinks still more lightly of the authority of the Supreme Court. He asserts a right of individual judgment on constitutional questions, which is totally inconsistent with any proper administration of the government, or any regular execution of the laws. Social disorder, entire uncertainty in regard to individual rights and individual duties, the cessation of legal authority, confusion, the dissolution of free government — all these are the inevitable consequences of the principles adopted by the message whenever they shall be carried to their full extent.

Hitherto it has been thought that the final decision of constitutional questions belonged to the supreme judicial tribunal. The very nature of free government, it has been supposed, enjoins this; and our Constitution, moreover, has been understood so to provide, clearly and expressly. It is true that each branch of the legislature has an undoubted right, in the exercise of its functions, to consider the constitutionality of a law proposed to be passed. This is naturally a part of its duty; and neither branch can be compelled to pass any law, or do any other act, which it deems to be beyond the reach of its constitutional power. The President has the same right, when a bill is presented for his approval; for he is, doubtless, bound to consider, in all cases, whether such bill be compatible with the Constitution, and whether he can approve it consistently with his oath of office.

But when a law has been passed by Congress and approved by the President, it is now no longer in the power, either of the same President or his successors, to say whether the law is constitutional or not. He is not at liberty to disregard it; he is not at liberty to feel or to affect "constitutional scruples," and to sit in judgment himself on the validity of a statute of the government and to nullify it, if he so chooses. After a law has passed through all the requisite forms; after it has received the requisite legislative sanction and the executive approval, the question of its constitutionality then becomes a judicial question, and a judicial question alone. In the courts that question may be raised, argued, and adjudged; it can be adjudged nowhere else. . . .

It is to be remembered, sir, that it is the present law, it is the Act of 1816, it is the present charter of the bank, which the President pronounces to be unconstitutional. It is no bank *to be created*, it is no law proposed to be passed which he denounces; it is the *law now existing*, passed by Congress, approved by President Madison, and sanctioned by a solemn judgment of the Supreme Court which he now declares unconstitutional, and which, of course, so far as it may depend on him, cannot be executed. If these opinions of the President be maintained, there is an end of all law and all judicial authority. Statutes are but recommendations, judgments no more than opinions. Both are equally destitute of binding force. Such a universal power as is now claimed for him, a power of judging over the laws and over the decisions of the judiciary, is nothing else but pure despotism. If conceded to him, it makes him at once what Louis XIV proclaimed himself to be when he said, "I am the State."

The Supreme Court has unanimously declared and adjudged that the existing bank *is* created by a constitutional law of Congress. . . . This bank, so far as the present question is concerned, is like that which was established in 1791 by Washington and sanctioned by the great men of that day. In every form therefore, in which the question can be raised, it has been raised and has been settled. Every process and every mode of trial known to the Constitution and laws have been exhausted, and always and without exception the decision has been in favor of the validity of the law. But all this practice, all this precedent, all this public approbation, all this solemn adjudication directly on the point is to be disregarded and rejected and the constitutional power flatly denied. . . .

Hitherto it has always been supposed . . . that the policy of granting a particular charter may be materially dependent on the structure and organization and powers of the proposed institution. But its general constitutionality has never before been understood to turn on such points. This would be making its constitutionality depend on subordinate questions; on questions of expediency and questions of detail; upon that which one man may think necessary and another may not. If the constitutional question were made to hinge on matters of this kind, how could it ever be decided? All would depend on conjecture; on the complexional feeling, on the prejudices,

on the passions, of individuals; on more or less practical skill or correct judgment in regard to banking operations among those who should be the judges; on the impulse of momentary interests, party objects, or personal purposes. Put the question in this manner to a court of seven judges, to decide whether a particular bank was constitutional, and it might be doubtful whether they could come to any result, as they might well hold very various opinions on the practical utility of many clauses of the charter. . . .

One man may think the granted powers not indispensable to the particular bank; another may suppose them injudicious or injurious; a third may imagine that other powers, if granted in their stead, would be more beneficial; but all these are matters of expediency, about which men may differ; and the power of deciding upon them belongs to Congress.

I again repeat, sir, that if, for reasons of this kind, the President sees fit to negative a bill on the ground of its being inexpedient or impolitic, he has a right to do so. But remember, sir, that we are now on the constitutional question; remember that the argument of the President is that, because powers were given to the bank by the charter of 1816 which he thinks unnecessary, that charter is unconstitutional. . . .

This power, if constitutional at all, is only constitutional in the hands of Congress. Anywhere else its exercise would be plain usurpation. If, then, the authority to decide what powers ought to be granted to a bank belong to Congress, and Congress shall have exercised that power, it would seem little better than absurd to say that its act, nevertheless, would be unconstitutional and invalid if, in the opinion of a third party, it had misjudged, on a question of expediency, in the arrangement of details. According to such a mode of reasoning, a mistake in the exercise of jurisdiction takes away the jurisdiction. If Congress decide right, its decision may stand; if it decide wrong, its decision is nugatory; and whether its decision be right or wrong, another is to judge, although the original power of making the decision must be allowed to be exclusively in Congress. . . .

If the reasoning of the message be well founded, it is clear that the charter of the existing bank is not a law. The bank has no legal existence; it is not responsible to government; it has no authority to act; it is incapable of being an agent. The President may treat it as a nullity tomorrow, withdraw from it all the public deposits, and set afloat all the existing national arrangements of revenue and finance. It is enough to state these monstrous consequences to show that the doctrine, principles, and pretensions of the message are entirely inconsistent with a government of laws. If that which Congress has enacted, and the Supreme Court has sanctioned, be not the law of the land, then the reign of law has ceased, and the reign of individual opinion has already begun. . . .

Mr. President, I have understood the true and well-established doctrine to be that, after it has been decided that it is competent for Congress to establish a bank, then it follows that it may create such a bank as it judges in its discretion to be best, and invest it with all such power as it may deem fit and suitable; with this limitation, always, that all is to be done in the bona fide execution of the power to create a bank. . . .

What is called the "monopoly" is made the subject of repeated rehearsal, in terms of special complaint. By this "monopoly," I suppose, is understood the restriction contained in the charter that Congress shall not, during the twenty years, create another bank. Now, sir, let me ask — Who would think of creating a bank, inviting stockholders into it, with large investments, imposing upon it heavy duties, as connected with the government, receiving some millions of dollars as a bonus or premium, and yet retaining the power of granting, the next day, an-

other charter, which would destroy the whole value of the first? If this be an unconstitutional restraint on Congress, the Constitution must be strangely at variance with the dictates both of good sense and sound morals. Did not the First Bank of the United States contain a similar restriction? And have not the states granted bank charters with a condition that, if the charter should be accepted, they would not grant others? States have certainly done so; and, in some instances, where no bonus or premium was paid at all, but from the mere desire to give effect to the charter by inducing individuals to accept it and organize the institution.

The President declares that this restriction is not necessary to the efficiency of the bank; but that is the very thing which Congress and his predecessor in office were called on to decide, and which they did decide, when the one passed and the other approved the act. And he has now no more authority to pronounce his judgment on that act than any other individual in society. It is not his province to decide on the constitutionality of statutes which Congress has passed and his predecessors approved.

There is another sentiment in this part of the message which we should hardly have expected to find in a paper which is supposed, whoever may have drawn it up, to have passed under the review of professional characters. The message declares that this limitation to create no other bank is unconstitutional because, although Congress may use the discretion vested in them, "they may not limit the discretion of their successors." This reason is almost too superficial to require an answer. Everyone at all accustomed to the consideration of such subjects knows that every Congress can bind its successors to the same extent that it can bind itself. . . . Any Congress may repeal the act or law of its predecessor if, in its nature, it be repealable, just as it may repeal its own act; and if a law or an act be irrepealable in its nature, it can no more be repealed by a subsequent Congress than by that which passed it. All this is familiar to everybody. And Congress, like every other legislature, often passes acts which, being in the nature of grants or contracts, are irrepealable ever afterward. . . .

As to the taxing power of the states, about which the message says so much, the proper answer to all it says is that the states possess no power to tax any instrument of the government of the United States. It was no part of their power before the Constitution, and they derive no such power from any of its provisions. It is nowhere given to them. Could a state tax the coin of the United States at the Mint? Could a state lay a stamp tax on the process of the courts of the United States, and on customhouse papers? Could it tax the transportation of the mail, or the ships of war, or the ordnance, or the muniments of war of the United States? The reason that these cannot be taxed by a state is that they are means and instruments of the government of the United States. The establishment of a bank exempt from state taxation takes away no existing right in a state. . . .

I beg leave to repeat, Mr. President, that what I have now been considering are the President's objections, not to the policy or expediency but to the constitutionality of the bank; and not to the constitutionality of any new or proposed bank but of the bank as it now is and as it has long existed. If the President had declined to approve this bill because he thought the original charter unwisely granted and the bank, in point of policy and expediency, objectionable or mischievous, and in that view only had suggested the reasons now urged by him, his argument, however inconclusive, would have been intelligible and not, in its whole frame and scope, inconsistent with all well-established first principles. His rejection of the bill, in that case, would have been, no doubt, an extraordinary exercise of power; but it would have been, nevertheless, the exercise of a power belonging to his office and trusted by the Constitution to his discretion.

But when he puts forth an array of arguments such as the message employs, not against the expediency of the bank but against its constitutional existence, he confounds all distinctions, mixes questions of policy and questions of right together, and turns all constitutional restraints into mere matters of opinion. As far as its power extends, either in its direct effects or as a precedent, the message not only unsettles everything which has been settled under the Constitution but would show, also, that the Constitution itself is utterly incapable of any fixed construction or definite interpretation, and that there is no possibility of establishing, by its authority, any practical limitations on the powers of the respective branches of the government.

105.

Frances Trollope: The American Poor

Thomas and Frances Trollope, parents of novelist Anthony Trollope, joined the wave of English emigrants to America in 1827 and settled in Cincinnati, where they opened a fancy-goods shop. The business failed three years later, and the Trollopes returned to England, in 1831, where Mrs. Trollope published a caustic criticism of American life, Domestic Manners of the Americans *(1832), that included the following commentary on the American poor. Mrs. Trollope's emphasis on the rudeness of American frontier society, and her notion that its more grotesque features were typical of all American life in general, provoked widespread indignation. American journalist Calvin Colton attempted to answer these charges in his* Manual for Emigrants to America, *also published in 1832.*

Source: *Domestic Manners of the Americans,* 4th edition, London, 1832, Vol. I, pp. 159-178.

MOHAWK, AS OUR LITTLE VILLAGE WAS called, gave us an excellent opportunity of comparing the peasants of the United States with those of England, and of judging the average degree of comfort enjoyed by each. I believe Ohio gives as fair a specimen as any part of the Union; if they have the roughness and inconveniences of a new state to contend with, they have higher wages and cheaper provisions; if I err in supposing it a mean state in point of comfort, it certainly is not in taking too low a standard.

Mechanics, if good workmen, are certain of employment and good wages, rather higher than with us; the average wages of a laborer throughout the Union is $10 a month, with lodging, boarding, washing, and mending; if he lives at his own expense he has $1 a day. It appears to me that the necessaries of life, that is to say, meat, bread, butter, tea, and coffee (not to mention whiskey), are within the reach of every sober, industrious, and healthy man who chooses to have them; and yet I think that an English peasant, with the same qualifications, would, in coming to the United States, change for the worse. He would find wages somewhat higher and provisions in western America considerably lower; but this statement, true as it is, can lead to nothing but delusion if taken apart from other facts, fully as certain and no less important, but which require more detail in describing, and which perhaps cannot be fully comprehended except by an eyewitness.

The American poor are accustomed to eat meat three times a day; I never inquired into the habits of any cottagers in western America where this was not the case. I found afterwards in Maryland, Pennsylvania, and other parts of the country, where the price of meat was higher, that it was used with more economy; yet still a much larger portion of the weekly income is thus expended than with us. Ardent spirits, though lamentably cheap, still cost something, and the use of them among the men, with more or less of discretion according to the character, is universal. Tobacco also grows at their doors and is not taxed; yet this too costs something, and the air of heaven is not in more general use among the men at America than chewing tobacco.

I am not now pointing out the evils of dram-drinking, but it is evident that where this practice prevails universally, and often to the most frightful excess, the consequence must be that the money spent to obtain the dram is less than the money lost by the time consumed in drinking it. Long, disabling, and expensive fits of sickness are incontestably more frequent in every part of America than in England, and the sufferers have no aid to look to but what they have saved or what they may be enabled to sell. I have never seen misery exceed what I have witnessed in an American cottage where disease has entered.

But if the condition of the laborer be not superior to that of the English peasant, that of his wife and daughters is incomparably worse. It is they who are indeed the slaves of the soil. One has but to look at the wife of an American cottager and ask her age to be convinced that the life she leads is one of hardship, privation, and labor. It is rare to see a woman in this station who has reached the age of thirty without losing every trace of youth and beauty. You continually see women with infants on their knee that you feel sure are their grandchildren till some convincing proof of the contrary is displayed.

Even the young girls, though often with lovely features, look pale, thin, and haggard. I do not remember to have seen in any single instance among the poor a specimen of the plump, rosy, laughing physiognomy so common among our cottage girls. The horror of domestic service, which the reality of slavery and the fable of equality have generated, excludes the young women from that sure and most comfortable resource of de-

cent English girls; and the consequence is that with a most irreverent freedom of manner to the parents, the daughters are, to the full extent of the word, domestic slaves.

This condition, which no periodical merrymaking, no village *fete* ever occurs to cheer, is only changed for the still sadder burdens of a teeming wife. They marry very young; in fact, in no rank of life do you meet with young women in that delightful period of existence between childhood and marriage, wherein, if only tolerably well spent, so much useful information is gained, and the character takes a sufficient degree of firmness to support with dignity the more important parts of wife and mother. The slender, childish thing, without vigor of mind or body, is made to stem a sea of troubles that dims her young eye and makes her cheek grow pale, even before nature has given it the last beautiful finish of the full-grown woman.

"We shall get along," is the answer in full for all that can be said in way of advice to a boy and girl who take it into their heads to go before a magistrate and "get married." And they do get along till sickness overtakes them, by means perhaps of borrowing a kettle from one and a teapot from another; but intemperance, idleness, or sickness will, in one week, plunge those who are even getting along well into utter destitution; and where this happens, they are completely without resource.

The absence of poor laws is, without doubt, a blessing to the country, but they have not that natural and reasonable dependence on the richer classes which, in countries differently constituted, may so well supply their place. I suppose there is less almsgiving in America than in any other Christian country on the face of the globe. It is not in the temper of the people either to give or to receive.

I extract the following pompous passage from a Washington paper of February 1829 (a season of uncommon severity and distress), which, I think, justifies my observation.

Among the liberal evidences of sympathy for the suffering poor of this city, two have come to our knowledge which deserve to be especially noticed: the one a donation by the President of the United States to the committee of the ward in which he resides of $50; the other, the donation by a few of the officers of the War Department to the Howard and Dorcas Societies, of $72.

When such mention is made of a gift of about £9 sterling from the sovereign magistrate of the United States and of £13 sterling as a contribution from one of the state departments, the inference is pretty obvious that the sufferings of the destitute in America are not liberally relieved by individual charity.

I had not been three days at Mohawk Cottage before a pair of ragged children came to ask for medicine for a sick mother; and when it was given to them, the eldest produced a handful of cents and desired to know what he was to pay. The superfluous milk of our cow was sought after eagerly, but every newcomer always proposed to pay for it. When they found out that "the English old woman" did not sell anything, I am persuaded they by no means liked her the better for it; but they seemed to think that if she were a fool it was no reason they should be so too, and accordingly the borrowing, as they called it, became very constant, but always in a form that showed their dignity and freedom. One woman sent to borrow a pound of cheese; another, half a pound of coffee; and more than once an intimation accompanied the milk jug that the milk must be fresh and unskimmed; on one occasion the messenger refused milk and said, "Mother only wanted a little cream for her coffee."

I could never teach them to believe, during above a year that I lived at this house, that I would not sell the old clothes of the family; and so pertinacious were they in bargain making that often, when I had given them the articles which they wanted to purchase, they would say, "Well, I expect I shall have to do a turn of work for this; you may send for me when you want me." But as I never did ask for the turn of work, and as this formula was constantly repeated, I began to suspect that it was spoken solely to avoid uttering that most un-American phrase "I thank you."

There was one man whose progress in wealth I watched with much interest and pleasure. When I first became his neighbor, himself, his wife, and four children were living in one room, with plenty of beefsteaks and onions for breakfast, dinner, and supper, but with very few other comforts. He was one of the finest men I ever saw, full of natural intelligence and activity of mind and body, but he could neither read nor write. He drank but little whiskey and but rarely chewed tobacco and was therefore more free from that plague spot of spitting which rendered male colloquy so difficult to endure. He worked for us frequently, and often used to walk into the drawing room and seat himself on the sofa and tell me all his plans. He made an engagement with the proprietor of the wooded hill . . . by which half the wood he could fell was to be his own.

His unwearied industry made this a profitable bargain, and from the proceeds he purchased the materials for building a comfortable frame (or wooden) house; he did the work almost entirely himself. He then got a job for cutting rails, and, as he could cut twice as many in a day as any other man in the neighborhood, he made a good thing of it. He then let half his pretty house, which was admirably constructed, with an ample portico that kept it always cool. His next step was contracting for the building a wooden bridge, and when I left Mohawk he had fitted up his half of the building as a hotel and grocery store; and I have no doubt that every sun that sets sees him a richer man than when it rose. He hopes to make his son a lawyer, and I have little doubt that he will live to see him sit in Congress. When this time arrives, the woodcutter's son will rank with any other member of Congress, not of courtesy but of right, and the idea that his origin is a disadvantage will never occur to the imagination of the most exalted of his fellow citizens.

This is the only feature in American society that I recognize as indicative of the equality they profess. Any man's son may become the equal of any other man's son, and the consciousness of this is certainly a spur to exertion. On the other hand, it is also a spur to that coarse familiarity, untempered by any shadow of respect, which is assumed by the grossest and the lowest in their intercourse with the highest and most refined. This is a positive evil and, I think, more than balances its advantages.

And here again it may be observed that the theory of equality may be very daintily discussed by English gentlemen in a London dining room, when the servant, having placed a fresh bottle of cool wine on the table, respectfully shuts the door and leaves them to their walnuts and their wisdom; but it will be found less palatable when it presents itself in the shape of a hard, greasy paw and is claimed in accents that breathe less of freedom than of onions and whiskey. Strong, indeed, must be the love of equality in an English breast if it can survive a tour through the Union.

Sketch of the Trollope family made in Cincinnati in 1829

106.

Calvin Colton: Manual for Emigrants to America

Immigration in the early nineteenth century pushed the American frontier beyond the Alleghenies and helped open the West, as well as supplying workers for the growing manufacturing interests in the East. After a pause during the War of 1812, the flow of immigrants increased once again through the 1820s, culminating in the tremendous influx of new settlers from England, Ireland, and Germany in the 1830s and 1840s. American journalist and historian Calvin Colton published his Manual for Emigrants to America *in 1832 while employed as British correspondent for the* New York Observer. *In this work he defended America against the criticisms of some European writers and specifically answered the charges made by Frances Trollope in her* Domestic Manners of the Americans, *published the same year.*

Source: *Manual for Emigrants to America,* London, 1832, pp. 120-149.

The importance of a nation is *physical* and *moral.* Its physical importance consists generally in the extent and resources of its soil, and its commercial advantages. The moral power of a nation is estimated by the amount and character of the population, and by the nature of its institutions. Population is also a component element of the physical power of a community.

The number of square miles in all Europe is about 3,400,000, Russia claiming nearly half of this. The territorial jurisdiction of the United States is equal to *three-fourths* of all Europe. And the resources of its soil, and its commercial advantages, all things considered, cannot be considered inferior to Europe. Each of the twenty-four United States, on an average, is nearly as large as the whole of England proper. And the territory not yet organized into states is vastly larger than that which is.

The present actual population of the United States will only compare with some of the individual states of Europe. It is less than half of the population of France, and about two-thirds of the population of Great Britain and Ireland. But the past and prospective increase of population in the United States is prodigious. It doubles at least once in twenty-five years. By this rule, the present population being assumed as 13,000,000, in 1857 it will be 26,000,000; in 1882 it will be 52,000,000; in 1907 it will be 104,000,000; and, in 1932, or in one hundred years from this time, it will be 208,000,000! In one hundred and fifty years, it will be 832,000,000 — equal to the present population of the globe!

Assuming the permanency of the government of the United States in the maintenance of the integrity of the Union, on the ground of the federal compact, with an ordinary degree of prosperity, however amazing these results may seem, a large moiety of them may be set down as *probable* against all contingencies. Bating the effects of foreign war and of internal and violent disruptions, a growth of this kind would seem to be a physical certainty; the former of which is hardly to be expected, so as to afford a serious check to such advancement, inasmuch as there is no rival power on the continent of America, and the republic is too remote to be reduced by invasion from another continent. And as to internal disruption, it is possible, but not probable to occur, with such calamity in its train, as to disappoint a destiny sufficiently bright and cheering to satisfy any reasonable ambition.

The destiny of the United States is reasonably rescued from the ordinary calculations of historical data, inasmuch as the providence of God never yet set up a nation of a like character in like circumstances. It is thrown completely without the pale of ordinary political prognostication. There are no premises in the history of nations bearing resemblances sufficient to found a prediction of overthrow in the present instance, within the scope of a statesman's ken — unless it be, that which has not been, cannot be — which is disproved in the threshold, that that which has not been, already *is; viz.*, a nation without a type in character and circumstance.

Those who deal so generously in their predictions of a disastrous issue to the republic of the United States, only show their ignorance of the nature of its government and of the moral character of the community. Every severe test, as yet, has only contributed to cement and consolidate the Union. And whatever doubt there may have been of the perpetuity of the government in all its purity and energy, there is less doubt now than ever. The world at a distance, witnessing the occasional violent irruptions of party feeling in the United States from a particular quarter, and on some local, or even general question, and listening to the stormy rancor of some newspaper declaimers, and perhaps of parliamentary debates, might imagine that the republic was in jeopardy, and the Union about to be dissolved; whereas, all these agitations, instead of disjointing the general fabric of the community, only settle it down more firmly on its own proper foundations.

Take, for instance, the recent public agitations respecting the rights of the aboriginal tribes. The state of Georgia, in violation of the Constitution of the United States, assumed jurisdiction over the Cherokees. The question was brought before the Supreme Court of the United States, and that Court, on the 3rd of March, 1832, decreed all the legislation of Georgia over the Indians *unconstitutional* and, consequently, null and void. And three days after this decision, a Georgia member of Congress rose in his place and declared that his state would never submit; and the state herself, anticipating this decree, had also made the same declaration beforehand. And will the Union therefore be dissolved? Why, it is a mere wordy quarrel of one member of a numerous family against all the rest. It will only confirm the Union. And the rights of the Indians thus vindicated and asserted will never again be invaded. With the people of the United States as a *body*, law is supreme, and they know how to respect it.

And as to the *capabilities* of the United States, both physical and moral, such as they are now, in fact, and such as they are in prospect — there is no arithmetic of man that can estimate them.

And the great bulk of these capabilities prospectively lie in the valley of the Mississippi. It is there they are to be developed and demonstrated. In twenty years the bulk of the population will be there. In half a century the *nation* will be there; so that everything found on the Atlantic declivity, east of the Alleghenies, although it was originally itself the nation, and although it shall still be growing in the meantime, will notwithstanding be left only a skirt. There, in the Mississippi Valley, beyond a question, and in a very brief time, will be cities and towns to rival any in the world in population, in commercial enterprise, in the productions of art, in the refinements of cultivated life and manners, and, I fear, in luxury. There, in that vast region, compared with which, in geographical extent, the whole of Europe on this side of Russia is no more than equal, will be found within half a century a teeming, active, industrious population, themselves a *world!* Still increasing with unexampled rapidity, and crowding still more densely the place, which shall have become too strait for them, and sending out their swarms toward the shores of the Pacific. Then, instead of 300 steamboats, more or less, now in active employment, will be thousands, shooting up and down the channels of its rivers; and where the natural channels fail, canals and railways will supply their place, to connect every smaller and more remote district with every other, and to bring the market of the world near to every point.

There is nothing visionary, or improbable in all this. It is even now as certain as that the world shall endure and the family of man multiply upon the face of it. Nor need we trouble ourselves at present to bring in the benefit of Mr. Malthus' theory to save this valley from being deluged with a population beyond its physical resources to sustain. Much more would it be a premature anxiety and a rare waste of benevolence, to contrive to bring in war, and famine, and pestilence, and earthquake, to assist the High Providence above in maintaining His own offspring, and in keeping their increase within just limits, as to save them from starvation, and leave them place to set a foot upon. We hope mankind will yet become too good to kill one another, too temperate and virtuous to fall victims of vice, and so observant of the precepts of Heaven as not to provoke Heaven's exterminating judgments; and that that period is not far distant.

And as to the earth's being *overrun,* He who made and peopled it will take care of that; and, if necessary, will, peradventure, anticipate such a catastrophe by some change in the economy of His providence; such, for example, as the conflagration of the world, and the introduction of the human family, when they shall have become worthy, to a higher and nobler state of existence. It is to be hoped that all this reasoning, predicated on the vices of mankind, in its prophecies of the future, will yet find

reason to shift its ground, and assume for its premises the virtues of a better era of the world.

And, for one, I have no objection that America should present the first example, the first array of facts in the economy of human society, to dissolve this dark and gloomy spell of evil boding to man. It is unnecessary to my present purpose, however, that I should prove all this. It is enough to have shown that America presents an open field for a mighty and an incalculable population; that it is evidently destined to such importance; that the providence of God has set up a state of society and a government there of hopeful and high promise; that from the peculiarity of its institutions, and in consideration of its remoteness from rival interests, it is not likely soon to be shaken or disturbed in its foundations; and, above all, if, from the gleamings and faith of divine prophecy, it may be hoped that the world is on the eve of a better state, that the American government and institutions shall *never* be overthrown, but still be improved in their forms, and ultimately arrive at the perfection of the constitution of human society. That those who have been used only to a government of physical force should reason differently is not strange.

WE ALL KNOW there are such things as romance and poetry getting a place in and stealing upon the human mind; and such a thing as the *beau ideal* of society, and of life and manners; and the beau ideal of being *alone:*

Oh, lost virtue — lost to manly thought,
  Who think it solitude to be *alone.*

Now, any person looking at this couplet, whether he regards its construction and measure, or its sentiment, if he is not very stupid, will see that it is poetry. But is it *truth?* Yes; it may be so, if one does not get too much of it. But he who forgets that man was made for society, and adopts the opposite as his moral creed, and follows it up, makes a mistake. It will do well enough for those who can afford it, and who have nothing else to do — who are so fenced in by wealth and circumstance as not to be obliged to feel the common thorns of life, and the many "ills that flesh is heir to." For such it may be convenient to luxuriate in the speculative regions of poetry and romance. But those who meditate leaving Europe and going to America to work, and toil, and build a fortune, might as well also leave their poetry behind. It will not be supposed that I mean their books, but their poetry of expectation. Nor do I mean that there is no room for poetry in America — no material and no elements. It is as rich as any other region of the globe for such purposes, in materials of its own kind, and as naturally productive, and for this reason: that men everywhere love poetry, and because they love it, they everywhere find materials. This faculty or disposition of the human mind to invest things that *are* in agreeable forms, and to charge them with the ingredients of happiness — or to create things that are *not,* and make them the means of a fancied, and for the time being, real enjoyment, is more or less the privilege of all — and may be profitably used, if well chastened, and kept within reasonable limits. But for men to set out on a migratory enterprise, under the sole impulse and leadings of such sentiments, with reins thrown loose on the neck of imagination, whether they go to America or anywhere else, are likely to be involved in disappointment and trouble.

To the point, then, as to what may reasonably be expected in America and what ought not to be expected. Towns and cities may be found there, and all the ordinary conveniences, and privileges, and delicacies which they afford in any part of the world. But London is not there — nor Paris. Those who can be satisfied only with such a city as London, and who can command the means of living in it to their utmost gratification, had better stay in London. And yet an American city of equal magnitude does not differ very much from a European city, either in external show or in the means of enjoyment.

There is *society* in America, as good as in any part of the world. But notwithstanding all the theoretical notions of republican equality, society there has its grades, and everyone must expect to take his own proper rank. Or if rank be an obnoxious term — his proper place. Unequal relations in closest contact are always unnatural and unhappy — and it is not in man to make them otherwise. It might as well be understood beforehand, as it might reasonably be presumed, that there is no miraculous charm in republican institutions to make minds alike, or to fit them to be society for each other, which are constitutionally and by education and habit unlike. No person can conveniently have many particular friends and intimate associates; and it is not only natural but best that those who are most intimate should be equal — that they should have common sympathies. He, therefore, who aspires to a higher place in society than he is fit for, by going to America — who imagines that everybody there will make obeisance to him, or yield him the station which his own mistakes may lead him to claim, is naturally destined to the chastening of experience.

It is, however, true of society in the United States that *precedence* is not so much the award of adventitious rank and of birth as in Europe; although these considerations are not without influence. Real intrinsic worth and practical talents for usefulness are most honored there and are rarely overlooked. He who possesses and acquires these excellencies may find opportunities to demonstrate them, and is likely to be appreciated. And he who aspires to be respected and honored by the public must be content to earn his reputation by his virtues, by his industry, and by his persevering devotion to useful and honorable pursuits. And on this condition he will not fail to obtain any privileges of society to which he is fairly entitled.

Religious privileges are as abundant and the ordinances of Christianity, under all the forms of the leading Christian sects, are as well sustained in the older portions of the United States as in any part of the Christian world, and on the best foundation; because they rest solely upon the virtue of the people — having no state patronage except the protections of law for the rights of conscience, made equal to all. The first thorough experiment, since the days of Constantine, of resigning the maintenance of the ordinances and the orthodoxy of Christianity to the virtue and pious zeal of its advocates and friends, without enforcing it by state enactments upon the people, has been made in the United States and made with triumphant success. For in no part of the Christian world does religion receive a more general or more pure regard from the people; and in no part of the world have the means and the agencies of Christianity been more effectual in securing their legitimate sway over the popular mind. It is not unknown, even abroad, that Christianity in the United States has proved in a very extraordinary degree efficient in the attainment of great and notable public reformations.

In the western and new settlements of the country, it is natural to suppose the ordinances of Christianity are not so generally established and religious privileges are more rare — although great pains are taken by the benevolent efforts of the Christian public to supply this defect and to maintain religious culture, as far as possible, in an equal march with the extension and progress of population. The itinerant preacher of the gospel goes out upon his horse and endeavors to visit the remotest settlement and cabin of the wilderness. But those who emigrate to the new settlements, or who plunge into the forests, or plant themselves upon the distant rivers of the West must expect that it will take time for the best and most desirable organization of Christian society.

In the older towns and settlements of the East, places of public worship are abundant, and all the means of religion enjoyed in any part of the world are brought within everyone's reach. In the cities, in the villages, and in the country, the Christian steeple and its lofty spire may be seen in every direction, pointing the way to heaven, and the church-going bell invites the wanderer to the house and to the altars of God.

The churches (for all places of public worship in America are called *churches,* and all ministers of religion *clergymen*) are not so ancient in the United States; but they are often magnificent without and splendid within, and not unfrequently more in taste, as it seems to me, than those I generally see on this side of the Atlantic. The public taste here is reluctant, perhaps commendably so, to emerge from the somber glooms of antiquity in church architecture. It apes what is old, and often labors ineffectually to make a *new* thing old; to create an ugly feature, which was not an original stamp of the pattern, but is the effect of the wasting hand of time.

Schools and seminaries of education of every grade, for children and youth, and for every destination of life, from the infant school up to all the privileges of the university, are abundantly supplied in the older states of the Union, especially at the East and North. The people of the United States are allowed to have done more to secure the education of the common mass than any other nation and, no doubt, with justice. It is a fundamental and just political maxim that a people must be enlightened to govern themselves. And the necessity of universal education has been *imposed* upon the people of the United States from the fact that they have undertaken to support a popular government. To neglect this would be the abandonment of their dearest and most cherished hopes. It is a principle of practical policy throughout the states that the rich shall be taxed as far as is necessary to educate the children of the poor. The higher seminaries of learning in the middle grades, of which there is every variety, are supported by the patronage of those who can afford, and who desire to give their children a better education.

Of colleges and universities, which are both virtually of one class in America, being chartered in the respective states in which they are found for the purpose of conferring academical degrees, there are forty-six in all scattered over the Union, most of them in the infancy of existence. The ordinary course of an industrious student, after he has commenced his academical education, to his final graduation for the use of either of the learned professions — law, medicine, or theology — is about ten years. As good and as thorough an education may be obtained at the schools and universities of the United States as at the same institutions on this side of the Atlantic.

The emigrant from Great Britain, or from any of the states of Europe to the United States, will doubtless receive this general impression: that all things in the latter country, as created by man, are comparatively in the childhood of existence. He will find no architectural antiquities. Commercial towns and cities are equally compact, but do not ordinarily exhibit an equal degree of splendor. Agriculture, except in the vicinity of large towns, has not been carried to so great a degree of perfection; because the farmer, having more land, can obtain a greater product with a given amount of culture by spreading his labor over a larger surface. Roads are not so good; though, in the older states, improvements of this and every other kind are constantly advancing. He who has been accustomed to the excellent roads and who has seen the most cultivated parts of England would hardly know how to appreciate the modes and degrees of improvement in like things in the United States. He must recollect, however, that in a new and wide country, where land is plenty and the population sparse, the most profitable product is not by the highest degree of improvement. It is only when a country is crowded with its population that men are driven to make the most of every foot of land.

The prairie farmer of Indiana and of Illinois has no other trouble but to plant his seed corn and reap his harvest. Such a thing as the necessity and labor of tillage is hardly known to him. His cattle, and sheep, and hogs, and poultry run at large, and multiply and fatten without his care; and he has only to bring them up and drive them to market or pickle them for transportation. Ordinarily, however, and especially in the Eastern states, tillage and the care of cattle are more expensive. But still the labors of husbandry and the expense of raising cattle and sheep, etc., in America bear no comparison to the pains and labor devoted to the same objects in Europe. Everything necessary for life is obtained at a cheaper rate, and of course the general and most obvious appearances of the country exhibit less improvement. For example: the people of a country whose population averages 200 to a square mile must obviously work harder and their improvements must be of a higher character to gain sustenance from the soil than where the population is not more than ten to a mile — allowing the soil in both cases to be equally good. This example, it may be understood, is assumed merely for illustration.

The citizen who meditates a removal into the wilds of America, or into its new and more unsettled territories, should calculate the loss as well as the gain. With a given amount of money he may acquire more land, and ultimately he may expect to leave a larger estate to his children. But he should consider the sacrifices he is to make. He leaves behind him his church and his pastor; schools, roads, and all the improvements and advantages of a cultivated country, and of a well-organized and perhaps refined state of society; and besides the time which must necessarily elapse, before he can enjoy them again, he should recollect that he must bear his share of the trouble and expense of creating them. And the negative loss to himself and family, intellectually and morally, in the meantime, should also come into the reckoning. Can he well afford all this? Is the gain in expectancy tantamount to the sacrifice? And is his moral courage equal to the undertaking?

He must recollect that his destiny in such an enterprise is literally the patience of labor — and his enjoyment the pleasure of anticipation. If, after well weighing all these considerations, he can brave the disadvantages of the enterprise, his ambition will not unlikely be rewarded to his entire satisfaction. To a mind properly constituted and well adapted to such circumstances, there are a thousand cheering and animating considerations in the prospects of a new and rising country. The vast and endless susceptibilities of improvement, and the actual advances of every day — the sure reward of labor and the increasing value of every species of property — and a common sympathy with hundreds and thousands of others devoted to the same objects — sustain the mind and nourish it continually with the freshness of hope and the joy of anticipation.

Especially to be identified with the interests and prospects of such a community as that which is now organizing and spreading itself over the valley of the Mississippi is itself a powerful spring of hope and of enterprise. The mind is at once enlarged and ennobled, and becomes great by the very contemplation of such a scene. It estimates and limits its own importance only by the importance of its circumstances and relations. Who can estimate the difference between the influence of those circumstances on the mind, where a man is forever cut off from the hope of extending his relations and sphere of importance, whatever be his efforts — and of those in which he knows that every single effort of laudable ambition will not only accumulate his personal wealth but raise him to a higher sphere and advance him to more honorable relations in society? And who again can estimate the difference between being a member of a community which can only hope to maintain its present ground of relative importance, and of one whose prospects of growth are absolutely inappreciable, both for rapidity and extent? The latter are the animating prospects of him who aspires to identify himself with the people of the Mississippi Valley, however remote and wild the retreat in that vast region in which he chooses to set up his tent and fix his abode.

What has been called the republican importance of servants in the United States deserves, perhaps, a single remark by way of advice to those emigrants from Europe who have been accustomed to depend on the obsequious services and attentions of inferiors. American servants are reputed, and not, perhaps, without reason, to be very scrupulous in the observance of the scriptural maxim: Call no man master.

But, *mutato nomine* — consult the prejudice — and under different names I am not aware, from any experience or observation (and I have certainly had some of the first, and no small opportunity for the second), I am not aware that every and any convenient service which any persons can reasonably need, may not be purchased in America. Only let him who wishes to be served be kind and gracious — as in all countries and in all circumstances he ought to be — and he need not sacrifice a single feeling which a reasonable man should desire to retain. He may then be served in all that he may require as respectfully, as cheerfully, and as thoroughly in America as in any other country. But if Europeans going to America or traveling there will insist upon that obsequiousness and servility in servants which may have been rendered to them in their own country; if they can err so much as to imagine that superciliousness toward inferiors is a legitimate emanation of a proper self-respect and a necessary protection of their own importance against invasion, why, then, they must take the consequences. And those consequences will not unlikely be a perpetual annoyance — or the vexation of being served badly, if at all — at least of the perpetual change of servants.

I do not believe there is a country in the world where a reasonable and an accommodating temper may not get along well enough in matters of this kind — and for this good reason, that human nature is the same all the world over — and that those whose necessities oblige them to sell their personal services will naturally try to please, not only for their own profit, but because themselves like to be pleased. Those persons, therefore, who have found occasion to complain of the republican independence of American servants have by the same word, or by the same dash of their pen, written the severest libel against themselves — and that is that they themselves have been the aggressors — that they have been guilty of the first impropriety. They had had the indiscretion to forget that they had got into another country.

Society and manners in the United States have sometimes been complained of by transient residents or flying travelers from this side of the Atlantic. I have only to reply that *this* also is a libel against the complainants, and proves either that their own want of merit had excluded them from good society or that their own ill manners had provoked a treatment which they well deserved. For it is evident to all the world that the greatest portion of the people of the United States are in higher conditions of life than the greatest portion of any state in Europe. And the challenge may be extended yet farther: Select what is considered the highest and most cultivated class of society in any European community, and a greater portion of the community of the United States shall be found whose cultivation of mind and accomplishment of manners are not unequal.

If, however, the adventitious show of a court, of a titled nobility, and of enormous estates, is insisted on as an indispensable element of good society and of good manners, it must be confessed the people of the United States have slender claims of this sort to assert. But if *mind* be the measure of the man, associated with simplicity and kindness of manners; if independent wealth and well-provided mansions, and a generous hospitality, go to make up the pleasant things of life; then America has at least some claims to good society and to good manners. I would willingly submit this question to the verdict of the exact impressions and the honest convictions of those Europeans who have visited America, and whose merits entitled them to the respect and hospitality of the American public. He must be an ungrateful man, indeed, who could forget the politeness he had received and abuse the hospitality, the bounty, and grace of which he had enjoyed. It may be and doubtless is true that the habitual occupation of most of the citizens of the United States, in some avocations of business, or professional employment, and that of the highest conditions and of the most wealthy — may in some instances preclude them from that amount of devotion to strangers which they may perhaps expect. But every reasonable man can make allowance for this — and, if he is truly enlightened, he will admire rather than reprobate such a state of society.

In a word — the emigrant from Europe to the United States should be reasonable and chastened in his expectations. He should remember that he is going to another country — to a country in many respects unlike to what he has been accustomed; unlike in its physical appearances, unequal, perhaps, in those improvements which age only can create; whose government and institutions of society are somewhat diverse and peculiar; and where he will find and feel himself to be in novel and unwonted circumstances. A country, indeed, of rising and hopeful prospects, but not exempting man from inconvenience nor from the necessity of labor; a country where government and laws are as indispensable as in any other — and where prosperity is ordinarily the reward of virtue, and ruin the consequence of vice. And he who is honest and industrious in America may do well — well enough to satisfy any reasonable expectations. But he who is unwilling to be *doomed* to an honest life might as well stay away. Unfortunately for America, Europe has already furnished her with too many of this character.

107.

SAMUEL FRANCIS SMITH: "America"

Samuel Francis Smith wrote "America," published in February 1832, while a student at Andover Theological Seminary. Lowell Mason, a distinguished music teacher, asked Smith to write a ballad suitable for a children's choir. Smith selected a tune from a German hymn book and within half an hour had set down the words. Apparently he did not discover until later that the tune he had selected was that of the British national anthem, since the melody in his hymn book bore a German title, but by then it was too late. The song gained immediate popularity, and during the Civil War it was sung at patriotic rallies, at meetings and funerals, in army camps, and on the battlefield.

Source: *Famous Songs and Those Who Made Them,* Helen K. Johnson and Frederic Dean, eds., New York, 1895, p. 1136.

AMERICA

My country, 'tis of thee,
Sweet land of liberty,
 Of thee I sing;
Land where my fathers died,
Land of the pilgrims' pride,
From every mountainside
 Let freedom ring.

My native country, thee,
Land of the noble free —
 Thy name I love;
I love thy rocks and rills,
Thy woods and templed hills;
My heart with rapture thrills,
 Like that above.

Let music swell the breeze,
And ring from all the trees,
 Sweet freedom's song;
Let mortal tongues awake,
Let all that breathe partake,
Let rocks their silence break, —
 The sound prolong.

Our fathers' God, to Thee,
Author of liberty,
 To Thee we sing;
Long may our land be bright
With freedom's holy light;
Protect us by thy might,
 Great God, our King.

108.

Joseph Caldwell: On the Need for Popular Education

Public support for education, which had been traditional in New England since colonial times, was not always forthcoming in some of the Southern states. There, the scattered population made locating schools a problem, and the poorer economy made taxation generally unwelcome. Joseph Caldwell, president of the University of North Carolina, outlined the problems facing popular education in his state in a series of letters to the Raleigh Register. *The letters, from which selections appear below, were published in book form in 1832.*

Source: *Letters on Popular Education, Addressed to the People of North-Carolina,* Hillsborough, 1832, Letters I, III, and VII.

There is perhaps no art or science in which greater improvement has been made than in that of education in primary schools. It has assumed a character wholly different from that of former times and from that in which it still appears among ourselves. The mode of communicating instruction, the variety of which it consists, the interest ever kept alive in the bosom of the pupil, the exclusion of corporal punishment with which it is most successfully conducted, the activity and versatility to which it trains the intellectual faculties, the life and force which it imparts to the humane affections, and the wide range of thought and knowledge which it opens before the reason and curiosity of the pupil transcend the anticipated pictures even of an indulged imagination.

Could we witness it in its processes and effects, its superior excellence would assuredly occur to us with a conviction as complete as everyone now feels in favor of the gin in preference to the fingers in the process of cleaning cotton, of the steamboat compared with sails or oars, or of a locomotive engine carrying its numerous tons at twelve miles an hour, contrasted with the labor and plodding movement of wagons and horses, of which, unhappily, to our incalculable loss, we are still fain to avail ourselves, over the sharp pinches, the floundering water pits, and jolting obstacles of highways on which the hand of improvement has never operated. Nothing certainly is wanted but this ocular demonstration, to the resolute and instant adoption of all these astonishing and inestimable improvements which distinguish the generation of men and the age to which we belong, above the bygone ages and generations of the world.

But to witness the present perfection of the schoolmaster's art is not our privilege, for its examples are too remote. And this presents an obstacle to any system of elementary schools we can recommend for the children of our state. Another obstruction meets us in our aversion to taxation beyond the bare necessities of government and the public tranquillity. Any scheme for popular education must be capable of deriving existence originally, and of maintaining it perpetually, without taxing us for the purpose, or we are well aware that we shall not, as a people, consent to its establishment.

A still further difficulty is felt in the indifference unhappily prevalent in many of our people on the subject of education. Vast numbers have grown up into life, have passed into its later years, and raised families without it; and probably there are multitudes of whose forefathers this is no less to be said. Human nature is ever apt to contract prejudices against that which has never entered into its customs. Especially is this likely to be the case if there be large numbers who have been subject in common to the same defects and privations. They sustain themselves by joint interest and feelings against the disparagements and disadvantages of their condition. It becomes even an object to believe that the want of education is of little consequence; and as they have made their way through the world without it, better than some who have enjoyed its privileges, they learn to regard it with slight if not with opposition, especially when called to any effort or contribution of funds for securing its advantages to their children.

Such are the woeful consequences to any people who, in the formation of new settlements, have not carried along with them the establishment of schools for the education of their families. So strangely may the truth be inverted in the minds of men in such circumstances that they become avowed partisans of mental darkness against light, and are sometimes seen glorying in ignorance as their privilege and boast. When a people lapse into this state, and there is reason to fear that multitudes are to be found among us of this description, it must be no small difficulty to neutralize their antipathy against education, and enlist them in support of any system for extending it to every family in the state.

I might mention further, as one of the greatest obstructions, the scattered condition of our population, over a vast extent of territory, making it difficult to embody numbers within such a compass as will make it convenient or practicable for children to attend upon instruction.

A most serious impediment is felt in our want of commercial opportunities, by which, though we may possess ample means of subsistence to our families, money is difficult of attainment to build schoolhouses and support teachers. Could the avenues of trade be opened to this agricultural people, funds would flow in from abroad, and resources would be created at home, which would make the support of schools and many other expenses to be felt as of no consequence. Excluded as we now are from the market of the world, the necessity of a rigid economy is urged against every expenditure, however small, and the first plea which meets us, when the education of children is pressed upon parents, is their inability to bear the expense. This is one principal reason why it has been thought that, among all the improvements in which we are called to engage for the benefit of the state, commercial opportunity should be the first. With the enlargement of funds, every difficulty would vanish, in the way to such improvements as are rapidly elevating other states to distinction and opulence.

It appears, then, how numerous are the discouragements we have to encounter in framing any plan for popular education. Our habits of legislation have been long established, and their uniformity has in few instances been broken, from our first existence as a state. To provide for the education of the people has unhappily never entered as a constituent part of these habits. We are wholly unaware of the immense improvements, which would render captivating to us if we could but witness them, the methods of instruction in elementary schools now practised in other parts of the world. Our aversion to taxation, even to provide for the education of our children, is invincible and extinguishes at once the hopes of any plan to the execution of which such means are necessary.

The same fate awaits every scheme of education which looks for success to the borrowing of funds. Through the influence of inveterate habit, large portions of our population have learned to look with indifference on education. But to what an appalling magnitude does this difficulty grow, when, among many, a spirit of hostility is even boasted in behalf of ignorance against knowledge! We want resources too, and must forever want them, not only for educating our children but for every other improvement, so long as we are without commercial intercourse with the world. . . .

We are a people whose habits and wishes revolt at everything that infringes upon an entire freedom of choice upon almost every subject. It would be easy to elucidate how this has come to be a trait so deeply marked in our character, but its reality is unquestionable. Provision for general instruction can scarcely be effected without some compulsory measures regulating the actions of individuals into particular channels directed upon the object. Every such measure is felt to be an entrenchment upon the indefinite discretion to which we tenaciously adhere, when a relinquishment of it is not absolutely indispensable. . . .

Two METHODS OF PROVIDING for popular education occur in ordinary practice. One is voluntary, leaving it wholly to the discretion of the people themselves, without aid by the state; the other is by the intervention of the legislature. A third will appear in a combination of both. On the two former, some explanation, as brief as I can make it, will help us to arrive at intelligent and satisfactory conclusions. . . .

The first method is the one which we now practise. It consists in the origination and maintenance of a school in any neighborhood by a voluntary combination among as many of the inhabitants as will agree. Its insufficiency is proved by all our past and present experience. A schoolhouse is to be erected at the common expense; a site for it is to be chosen with the consent of all; a master is to be found; a selection and approbation, if there be more than one, is to be discussed and settled; his compensation and support must be fixed to the general satisfaction; and the time of continuance must be stipulated.

Here are six principal points, on every one of which dissension of opinions, feelings, and interests may spring up, to produce weakness or defeat. It is unnecessary to enlarge upon the perplexities that meet us at every step, and the discouragement of failures and disappointments, until, at last, in a vast number of instances, the object is relinquished in despair.

The evil which is really the greatest of all is the want of qualified masters. It may be difficult to obtain a teacher at all, but it is pretty certain, in the present state of the country, not one is properly fitted for the occupation. Do we think that of all the professions in the world that of a schoolmaster requires the least preparatory formation? If we do, there cannot be a more egregious mistake. For, if any man arrived at years of maturity, who can read, write, and cipher, were taken up to be trained to the true methods of instructing and managing an elementary school by a master teacher who understood them well, he could scarcely comprehend them and establish them in his habits in less than two years. This is not to speak with looseness and extravagance on the subject; and we need only to examine with opportunity of information to be convinced of it as a practical truth. Yet in our present mode of popular education, we act upon the principle that schoolkeeping is a business to which scarcely anyone but an idiot is incompetent, if he only knows reading, writing, and arithmetic. If in almost every vicinage there happen to be one or a few who have more correct opinions, the numbers who think otherwise carry it over their heads, and our primary schools are kept sunk down to the lowest point of degradation, and education is disgraced by our own misconceptions and mismanagement.

In the present condition of society and of public opinion, the occupation of a schoolmaster, in comparison with others, is regarded with contempt. It would be wonderful were it otherwise, when we look at the manner in which it is very often if not most usually filled. Is a man, constitutionally and habitually indolent, a burden upon all from whom he can extract a support? Then there is one way of shaking him off — let us make him a schoolmaster. To teach a school is, in the opinion of many, little else than sitting still and doing nothing. Has any man wasted all his property or ended in debt by indiscretion and misconduct? The business of schoolkeeping stands wide open for his reception, and here he sinks to the bottom for want of capacity to support himself.

Has anyone ruined himself, and done all he could to corrupt others, by dissipation, drinking, seduction, and a course of irregularities? Nay, has he returned from a prison, after an ignominious atonement for some violation of the laws? He is destitute of character and cannot be trusted, but presently he opens a school, and the children are seen flocking into it; for if he is willing to act in that capacity, we shall all admit that as he can read and write and cipher to the square root, he will make an excellent schoolmaster. In short, it is no matter what the man is, or what his manners or principles, if he has escaped with life from the penal code, we have the satisfaction to think that he can still have credit as a schoolmaster.

Is it possible, fellow citizens, that, in such a state of things as this, education can be in high estimation among us? Is it strange that

in the eye of thousands, when education is spoken of, you can read a most distinct expression that it is a poor and valueless thing? Can we rationally hope that so long as such a method of popular education as this shall be all to which we look, the great body of the people will become enlightened and intelligent? Will they be qualified to act in all the various relations of parents and children, brothers and sisters, masters and servants, neighbors, members of the community, citizens of the state, subjects of Providence, and heirs of immortality? In all these capacities, every child that grows up into life must necessarily act; and the teacher whose habits, views, and dispositions do not qualify, and whose conscience does not urge him to instill into his pupil the principles, excite the emotions, and select the books best fitted to them all, is totally defective in the business of a schoolmaster and has need to learn the first elements of his art. . . .

Every species of business may be executed with various degrees of ability, and men may differ in their opinions of such as possess skill of a higher order in their profession. But respecting such as possess no talent, no qualification, none can mistake. All must feel one common, overpowering conviction that their pretensions are despicable. Let any profession be wholly consigned to occupants so wretchedly destitute of every qualification in skill or principle, let it be known to the people only in such defective and degrading forms, and how can it be otherwise than contemptible, and all that is connected with it of little or no worth?

It is apparent, then, that popular education cannot be efficient when left to the insignificancy into which it sinks, with no other security for its prosecution than the accidental and voluntary action to which it is now left. So unvarying and universal has been this method of educating children among us that to speak of schools and schoolmasters modeled upon other plans, as they are understood and maintained in other parts of the world, would probably expose a man to the charge of romancing, or at least as recommending something to us wholly unattainable, and fitted only to men of different attributes and capabilities from ourselves. This plan of popular schools, hitherto the only one we know, is so haggard and meager and deformed in its features, and rickety in its constitution, that its repulsiveness prevents many from the use of it, who have not a doubt that education is of the utmost importance to the young, to families, and to the population of a free state.

The mind is a proper subject of cultivation, as much, at least, as the soil which we subdue and mellow for a harvest. Its powers must be developed and its affections molded by an informing and plastic hand. It should have the knowledge of letters and the easy use of them, both in reading and with the pen. These are the portals which should be thrown open to all, that they may have free access to the information of the age. These are essential; but to know how to read and write are but a part only of the great objects of early education. Good and evil dispositions must be distinguished, and habits established of feeling and thinking and acting. Reading and writing are but instruments for forming the mind. All this would be admitted, nay, strenuously asserted, by many, if not by every individual. But when the concession is made, when the conviction is complete, and we turn to the means of securing these advantages for children, how are all our ardors suddenly arrested and congealed as soon as we turn to the only means for forming their principles and dispositions. The schoolhouse too often presents itself to the eye as a region infested with mists and noxious reptiles and poisonous plants, and among these the dearest objects of our affections must be

placed that they may have access by reading and writing to the springs of knowledge and intellectual life.

That education in our primary schools should be held in low estimation is but a natural consequence of the circumstances in which it is acquired. It never can be valued so long as they continue. The resources to which we have been left through our whole progress as a people, being of this character, the consequence is well known, that thousands, and perhaps tens of thousands, are left to grow up unable to read at all. Experience has made it indisputable that the plan which we have practised, if plan it can be called, is a total failure so far as North Carolina is concerned. Can evidence be wanting of its deplorable consequences, when it is by no means rare to hear men directing upon education a derision which would imply that they deem it a glory and a privilege to be without it?

I have been placed in circumstances, and there are few I fear who have not been similarly situated, where it would be dangerous to the election of a candidate to have it thought that he had any pretensions to information or culture, at least beyond a bare capacity to read. And some miserable being, to secure the great object of his ambition, has frontlessly presented it as a sure and glorious passport to success over the head of a rival, who was so unfortunate as to have had some education, that he belonged to the class of the ignorant, with whom the greater part considered it their glory to be ranked.

We see, then, the consequences of educating children by such wretched methods as we commonly practise. Thus it will always continue to be so long as these methods are retained. We dress up the occupation of a schoolmaster in rags. It appears in hideous deformity by our own arrangement. It is no wonder if that which we intended for the figure of a man cannot be thought of otherwise than as a laughing stock, a byword, or a scarecrow; and then education is put down as a questionable subject. Nay, it becomes a thing of scorn and reproach. The repulsive and disgraceful form in which it appears have been given to it by ourselves, in the crudity of our own misconceptions. Where is the subject or the personage that may not be exposed to derision and rejection by a similar process?

And how shall the confidence and the affections of the people be regained? It is by stripping off the offensive and contemptible disguise, and presenting education in all the beauty and excellence of her proper character. No sooner shall this be done than all will fall in love with her. Her presence will be courted as the privilege and ornament of every vicinage, and under her patronage the clouds and mists that lower upon us will be dissipated. . . .

THAT IT IS HIGH TIME for us, for the whole people of North Carolina, to look with more intentness than ever upon the subject of popular education, and to devise the means of it, is a sentiment in which surely most of us, if not all, will cordially concur. It claims from every man, especially from every head of a family, faithful and dispassionate consideration. How can it be otherwise than that a deep impression must be felt in the mind of every considerate man, of its indispensable necessity to a people who have remained to this late period destitute of its privileges. Our country presents to ourselves and to the world the spectacle of a strange abstraction from light and knowledge, impenetrable to their beams, while they are falling upon her externally with the meridian splendor of science, religion, and the arts. Can anyone who feels toward her one affectionate desire, who wishes for her respectability, who would see her raised out of the intellectual darkness and desolation that hovers over her and

settles with pervasion through the minds of her offspring, fail to be impressed with a conviction that we can no longer postpone the day of action upon the subject?

Shall we still plead that our physical ability is inadequate; that we possess not the means? To what distant period, then, are we to look, in what more auspicious condition must we be placed to be conscious of strength enough to set forth in the attempt? What future prosperity or growth is in our prospect which shall take from us all excuse for delay, and dispossess the spirit of supineness that reigns in our bosoms, of the scepter which by its torporific touch benumbs all our faculties?

We are a nation in all the vigor of early manhood. If the sound of war ever reaches our ears, it is not to afflict or even to threaten us with its ravages but only to remind us that, through forty-seven years of peace out of the last fifty of our existence, we have continued under the fostering care and protecting shield of a kind Providence, in the full opportunity of growing prosperity in our worldly condition. No taxation has weighed heavily upon us. We glory in the energies infused into the heart, the muscles, and the sinews of our popular system by the plastic force of civil liberty. A comparison with others in power and privileges would flush our cheek with disdain and indignation. We have a country inferior to none of the original states in soil; in climate it is far superior to most, in the mildness of its winters, in the diversity of its productions and in the renovation of its crops.

In the midst of all these sources of wealth and opportunity, our children are left to grow up unpruned and uncultivated as the forest or the brake which the hand of our industry has never touched. This continues to the present hour, while it implies an almost total exclusion of knowledge, like the opacity of incarcerating walls, in the last and most enlightened age of the world.

109.

Thomas Cooper: A Defense of Intellectual Freedom

Most of Thomas Cooper's political and academic career was involved in controversy. As a Jeffersonian Democrat he was convicted under the Sedition Act in 1800. As a state judge in Pennsylvania he became disillusioned with the workings of practical democracy and lost his judgeship. As a scientist he endured the hostility of the clergy for his position on religion. While serving as president of South Carolina College (now University of South Carolina), he antagonized a number of factions in the state because of his anticlerical sentiments and his states' rights position on nullification. An attempt in 1832 to remove him from office prompted him to give the following defense of intellectual freedom.

Source: *American Higher Education*, Richard Hofstadter and Wilson Smith, eds., Chicago, 1961, Vol. I, pp. 397-417.

In drawing up a brief account of this interesting trial, we have aided our own notes and recollections by consulting others who were present, as well as Dr. Cooper himself.

After a series of incessant attacks on Dr. C.'s presumed infidelity during the whole of the year 1831, this case was first brought before the Board of Trustees in December 1831. To insure a full attendance of the board, it was deferred to the 16th of May, 1832. It was then put off until the regular meeting of the board in December 1832. At the meeting of May 16, Dr. Cooper moved that his trial and the proceedings relating to the charges against him should be held in public. This was agreed to by the board.

On the 3rd of December, 1832, the trustees met, but not in full board. The trial was again put off to the evening of the 5th, and adjourned to the hall of the House of Representatives; on which, and on the succeeding evening, Dr. Cooper made and closed his defense. The proceedings occupied altogether about four hours, including both evenings.

The charges, in number three, brought against this gentleman were in substance, that by various publications, such as his *Political Economy*, his *Letter to any Member of Congress*, and his translation of *Broussais on Insanity*, he had unnecessarily advanced opinions respecting religion offensive to the parents of students committed to his care, and to large classes of citizens, and injurious to the interests of the college; and that he had at lectures and on other occasions interfered unnecessarily with the religious opinions of the students, and inculcated upon them doctrines contrary to those in which he knew they had been educated, and offensive to their parents and guardians.

In support of these charges, the books abovementioned were at a former meeting produced and passages read, and a letter also was read from one of the students containing averments of the last part of the charge. This letter was not on oath, nor was any examination had of the writers; and it was furnished by Dr. C. himself on the evening of the 5th. Dr. Thomas Taylor, who sent this information, did not make his appearance to support it, and he was positively contradicted by six several witnesses present on the occasion referred to.

The evidence of students, summoned by the trustees in support of the charges, and by Dr. Cooper in his defense, having been taken on oath before Judge Martin and Colonel Preston, and being sealed up when taken, was read on the evening of December 5, 1832. When the reading of the testimony was finished, Dr. Cooper was called on to make his defense.

He began by stating that this was a new scene in republican America — and would furnish a new page in the history of South Carolina. He stood there an accused person before a court of ecclesiastical inquisition, sitting under legislative authority, to inquire into all false doctrines, heresies, and schisms of which the president of the college might have been *vehemently suspected* (the usual expression of the courts of inquisition — prototypes of the present). This inquiry took place in the middle of the nineteenth century, in South Carolina — a state at this moment tremblingly alive to the usurpations and infractions of our national compact by Congress, and the substitution of discretionary jurisdiction, in lieu of the express authority of the Constitution, and in defiance of its wholesome limitations. The trustees (said Dr. C.) are now called on by my accusers to commit the very same usurpations that they complain of in Congress.

This was not the case 150 years ago, when John Locke of England, in 1669, was appointed to draw up a constitution for the colony of South Carolina, containing a clause "that no one should be molested on account of his religious tenets; or prohibited, on that account, from any office under the civil government of the colony." This

constitution was deliberately confirmed after 20 years experience in 1689, and declared to be the constitutional law of the colony forever. He stated that the Test Act of England had passed in 1678, and the revocation of the Edict of Nantes in 1688. The liberal constitution of South Carolina attracted hither those who revolted at religious persecution in England, as well as very many of the oppressed Huguenots of France, greatly to the advantage and prosperity of the colony. In 1690, John Archdale, a Quaker, was chosen governor of the colony and served with exemplary fidelity and reputation.

Dr. Cooper hoped that no descendant of the Huguenots, who had hitherto ranked among our most respectable citizens, would disgrace himself and his ancestors by appearing among the persecutors on the present occasion.

Far different, however, was the case now. The march of mind had been retrograde and he now appeared before a court of ecclesiastical inquiry to defend himself for holding opinions which the evidence that accompanied them had forced upon his conviction, and which the Constitution of the United States and of this state had guaranteed the right to profess and avow. He then enumerated briefly the substance of the arguments on which he proposed to rely, but which, not having time during that evening to dwell upon so fully as his case required, he craved time till the succeeding evening for that purpose, which was acceded to.

On the succeeding evening, in the hall of the House of Representatives which was crowded with members, and townsmen, and citizens from the country, Dr. Cooper about a quarter past six began his defense in chief. The arguments he dwelt upon were substantially as follows, to wit:

That the charges brought against him must be proved as laid; that accusation was of itself no proof; that, if convicted, he must be convicted on the testimony produced; that the two facts, of his opinions being offensive to large classes of people and to the parents of the young men, and that these, his opinions, had been injurious to the college, were facts not to be assumed, but to be proved. He appealed to every trustee who had heard the testimony read whether there was one syllable of evidence that had the least bearing on either of these two facts, or any attempt to show that the publications referred to had been circulated in this state. The only substantial point of inquiry for the trustees was, had Dr. Cooper's opinions lessened the number of the students? He stated it as a fact officially known to every trustee at the board that during the year 1831, when the presses teemed with pamphlets against him, and the papers throughout the state with weekly invective, a greater number of students had applied for admission into college than had ever been known before, except on one occasion. He called upon every man who had heard that testimony read to say whether it was not, in every part of it, and from every student examined without exception, one continued and ample panegyric on his caution, his impartiality, his faithful discharge of duty, and his total abstinence from all interference with the religious opinions of the young men under his care; every one of whom when examined declared upon oath that Dr. Cooper was accustomed, on all occasions, to direct the students that it was their duty, while at college, to abide by the religion of their parents; and that he never did interfere in any manner with their religion, nor had they ever heard that he had done so. He concluded this head by calling on any trustee to point out one sentence in the whole of the evidence thus taken that could be adduced in support of the accusations or any of them. He denied that any court of law would send such evidence to a jury; and he demanded of the trustees, as his matter of right, a judgment, as in case of nonsuit.

He denied the jurisdiction of the board over publications not made in South Carolina. He contended that whether these publications were issued at London, or Constantinople, or Pekin, or New York, or Washington was immaterial. The board had no jurisdiction beyond the state. And he proved from evidence formerly given before the board, coupled with the declarations of General Blair and a member of the board, that the *Letter of a Layman* and *Broussais* had never in point of fact been published by Dr. Cooper in South Carolina. As to the passages referred to in his *Political Economy,* they related not to religion but the ministers and dispensers of religion; not to doctrines but preachers; and the question was not a theological but a statistical one, connected with the subject of political economy and related to pecuniary expedience alone. At any rate, every Quaker throughout the Union had held during 150 years, and do now hold, the same opinions with Dr. Cooper on this express point.

He went on to give a history of the numerous attacks on him without the least provocation, and without reply, from the very time when he first came to South Carolina to the present day. He showed also that the present accusations had already been made before the legislature some years ago, on presentment of a grand jury; referred to a committee; considered and dismissed as without foundation. That the accusations, therefore, now prepared, had already passed *in rem judicatam,* and he was entitled to be free from them; unless it was intended to harass him with annual applications to the legislature on charges already decided.

He stated that all these attacks were manifestly and on the face of them the attempts of the Calvinistic clergy and their adherents to monopolize all the seminaries of education in the United States, and to advance beyond the power of opposition the political predominance of that class of sectarian clergy. All this was too manifest to be doubted. It was the same kind of attempt to monopolize for that sect the home market of ecclesiastical dominion over, and the supply of teachers to schools and colleges, which the manufacturing monopolists had succeeded in establishing.

He appealed to every trustee whether it was not notorious to the public that all the opinions now complained of were held and avowed by Dr. C. at the time when he was elected president. His previous publications, his connection with Dr. Priestley, and with Priestley's opinions, were known to every trustee when he came here. His defense of materialism was published as early as the year 1789.

He contended that every opinion complained of as held by the president of the college had long been held by large classes of the most respectable citizens of the United States, and were not novelties introduced by himself.

His opinions as to a salaried clergy and public prayer were held by Wm. Penn and the whole body of Quakers; by your own John Archdale, the subject of Dr. Ramsay's panegyric in the history of South Carolina.

His opinion as to materialism by all the fathers of the Christian Church, for some centuries after Christ; by all the Priestleyans and Unitarians in England and this country; some of the most eminent of modern divines of the Episcopal Church; by Law, Bishop of Carlisle; by Watson, Bishop of Llandaff; and this doctrine is, at present, a subject of controversy between Mr. Balfour, of Charlestown (Mass.) and Professor Steuart of Andover; that it is the opinion of those eminent physiologists: Cabanis and Broussais, of Paris; Lawrence, of London; and McCartney, of Dublin; that it was the opinion avowed also by Thomas Jefferson. It is known to have been held by Dr. Rush; and must of necessity in a very few years become the prevailing opinion of every physiologist, if it not be so at this moment.

That the Sabbath is not a day of religious observation under the Christian dispensation is well known to be the opinion of almost every divine of eminence in England and this country; and is so held by Dr. Paley, whose works are textbooks in this college, under direction of the trustees.

That as to the Pentateuch, of which the discussion was rendered unavoidable by Professor Silliman, no man who has duly attended to the scriptural and historical arguments on both sides of this question can possibly believe that the Pentateuch, as we now possess it, was the writing of Moses. Dr. Cooper went so far as to declare that he would scruple to give credence to the oath of any man who would, after full examination, deliberately say that it was so.

Dr. Cooper then proceeded to show that all these obnoxious opinions were, in fact, propagated by the legislature of South Carolina as well as by Dr. Cooper; inasmuch as they are all to be found in the Rev. Dr. Channing's panegyrical view of the theological tenets of the poet and republican John Milton; to be found (as it ought to be) in the legislative library.

Suppose a legislator were to ask me (said the Dr.) who propagated among the people the dangerous heresies? They are laid at your door. My reply would be *mutato nomine de te fabula narratur* [with the name changed, the story is told about you]. As Nathan said unto David, thou are the man! They are your own heresies, propagated under your authority, recommended by your sanction, found in your own library.

He then read from that review the opinions of Milton denying the creation out of nothing; denying the immateriality and separate existence of the soul; denying the propriety of a separate order of men like the clergy; denying the propriety of pecuniary pay given to the clergy; denying the obligation of public prayer, and of the modern Sabbath; insisting on the *right* of free discussion.

Dr. Cooper referred also to the very strong argument of Dr. Channing against the Calvinistic principles of the class usually styled *orthodox,* and the elaborate defense of Unitarianism in that book. He stated that Dr. Channing was, by common acknowledgment, one of the most eloquent, able, and learned divines of the United States. He asked then whether these were not accusations against Wm. Penn, John Archdale, John Milton, Benjamin Franklin, Thomas Jefferson, Dr. Rush, Dr. Priestley and Dr. Channing as much as against Dr. Cooper? And whether it was a crime in the president to hold opinions in common with such men? He declared that he did not pretend to advance his own opinions as true, but as the opinions which, whether true or false, had been forced upon him by the evidence to which he had been subjected; he had no doubt his adversaries were equally honest and justifiable in holding their own opinions, which must of course be the result of the evidence to which they had access. They had as much right to their opinions as he had to his own; but neither of them had any right to be offended with the other for opinions which did not depend upon the will, but were forced on our conviction by the evidence which accompanied them. In proportion as that evidence was complete, the decisions and the opinions would approximate to truth. If imperfect in material points, the result would be error. But every person was irresistibly compelled to decide according to the balance of evidence actually presented to his understanding. Error of opinion therefore could be no crime, for it was involuntary; and for the same reason, no cause of offense to others. If a man differs in sentiment from his neighbor, his neighbor differs from him; and it is a subject of mutual amnesty, not of mutual complaint, or anger, or hostility.

This matter (says Dr. C.) has been misunderstood. A man can utter what he pleases; his organs of speech are under his control; he can say that an apple is an oak tree, or that the propositions of Euclid are all false, but he cannot *believe* this. Belief is the result of evidence addressed to the *understanding;* the *will* has no control over it; a jury may deliver a false verdict knowing it to be so, but it is not in their power to believe it true. In belief or unbelief, therefore, there is neither merit or demerit, for no man can avoid the result of evidence actually presented.

Dr. Cooper then took occasion to descant on the charge that his opinions were offensive to large classes of the community; and on Judge Huger's assertion in the legislature that unpopularity was of itself a sufficient cause of removal from office. . . .

When I wrote and published *Consolidation* (said Dr. C.), I became so unpopular on that account that two public proposals were made to remove me from the presidency. When in my speech at the anti-tariff meeting at Columbia in June 1827, I asserted that if the system so popular at the North, of making the South a tributary, was persisted in, we should by and by be driven to calculate the value of the Union to our section of the country. You all know the torrent of abuse thrown on me for that prophetic expression, from one end of the United States to the other.

Look at your own proceedings. Is nullification even yet a popular measure? Is not the abuse thrown on you unmeasured and unqualified? Have you yet persuaded your enemies that a law enacted by incompetent authority is null and void, and is no law binding upon others? That any man may, and honest men ought to, oppose it? But will South Carolina be deterred from what is right, through dread of its being offensive or unpopular with the ignorant and interested? No. Her march is onward; and the abuse heaped on her by the men who vociferate "unpopularity" will be unneeded and forgiven; for those who abuse her, like the populace at Jerusalem, know not what they do.

I am not ignorant that cautious and experienced men of the world, who look exclusively to their own successful standing with the public, regard as imprudent, dangerous, and unwise all those persons who brave public prejudice and render themselves, by so doing, unpopular. It is a serious misfortune to run half a century ahead of the knowledge of the day; and if a man is bent on doing this, he should make up his mind to meet the consequences and count the cost. Men of moderate intellect disapprove, the timid are alarmed, foes are excited, and friends stand aloof. A man, so determined to abide by truth, through evil report and good report, must be content to brave the pity of some, the sneers of others, and the rancorous hatred of all who live and prosper by existing error. I am not blind to all this; but the prospect of becoming the instrument of good to mankind, and the cheering of a man's own conscience, are of no small value when honestly earned. The pamphlet entitled *Consolidation* was, in this point of view, an act of imprudence; an accusation which has been and still is brought against every proceeding of the State Rights Party by their more cautious opponents. This, therefore, is a dart that my political fellow laborers are not entitled to cast at me.

That no one ought to oppose existing error but those who are able to afford the risk is an established maxim of worldly prudence; most sedulously inculcated by everyone who profits by existing error, because it withdraws from opposition nineteen-twentieths of their opponents. Is it a maxim for the *people* to adopt?

Let me now suppose a case: that you have a president of the college of known talents and extensive acquirements, who possesses the difficult art of communicating knowledge to others, whose literary reputation is established, whose manners are conciliatory, whose morals are unexceptionable, and his long tried course of conduct unimpeachable — would you reject these qualifications because some of his speculative opinions were unpopular to a portion, and that not a large one, of his fellow citizens? If he has a right to claim popularity for qualifications useful and substantial, will you reject him on account of "the color of his mule, or the cut of his cravat"? I should hope the gentlemen appointed to preside over the highest literary institution of the state — whose duty it is not to follow public prejudice but to counteract the tendencies of ignorance and to lead public opinion to enlarged and liberal views of the prospect before us — would hardly condescend to make such a sacrifice on the altar of popularity.

Offensive? Who has a right to be offended at the speculative opinions of Dr. Cooper? Dr. Cooper asks such a man, "What right, sir, have you to be of a different opinion from me? By the same right, I differ from you." Offensive! Are the constitutions of the United States and of our own state to be sacrificed to the ignorant prejudices of men who have never taken the trouble to read them? Of men who know not what spirit they are of? Dr. Cooper takes no offense at their differing from him; he would feel himself degraded if he did; why should they be offended because he does not see sectarian questions in the same light that they do? Is not the press open to both sides, and is not the tribunal of the public the proper court to try these questions? Those only resort to obloquy and abuse and call in the aid of the civil power who feel themselves in the wrong — who are angry because their cause is weak; and being unable to conquer by argument, call upon the civil authority for pains and penalties on their opponents. But the public have learned at last that their own interest requires discussion, wherever there is doubt; that persecution makes no converts; and that a cause which trembles at the slightest breath of inquiry may be safely permitted to stand or fall as unworthy of support if it cannot support itself.

If I am (says Dr. C.) to avoid unpopular and offensive opinions, which change their character and costume almost every year, give me, if you please, under the authority of the board, an *index expurgatorius* for the year; furnish me with a chart of my annual voyage, so that I may avoid the rocks and shoals and breakers of what is called heterodoxy. Orthodoxy means always the opinions of those who hold their own opinions to be true. Orthodoxy, said Bishop Warburton to Lord Sandwich, is my doxy; heterodoxy is another man's doxy.

Dr. C. then proceeded to state that it was the universal law of every civilized community that all contracts deliberately settled and agreed upon should be punctually performed; that no party had a right to add clauses, conditions, or provisos of which no notice was given when the contract was entered into. No party can, at his own good will and pleasure, make a new contract in despite of the other; or add, alter, or interpolate any clause or proviso to serve his own temporary purpose, and force it on the other. . . .

Does the contract of Dr. Cooper with the trustees contain any prohibition as to uttering or publishing, or avowing, defending, or professing any speculative opinion whatever? Would the trustees have had any right, under the Constitution, to have insisted on such a condition, or to have made any discrimination or preference? Most certainly, if any such clause or condition had been proposed, Dr. Cooper would have rejected it at once. He would not, in such case, have been here now. The very proposal by the board or by any member of it would have been a crime.

To make that an offense now which was no offense when Dr. C. accepted of his present situation, amounts to the enactment of an *ex post facto* law; do the trustees claim the right of constituting new offenses at their own good will and pleasure, and of punishing them as they see fit?

Dr. Cooper then proceeded to deny the right of the board to make discriminations and differences as to the religious opinions which the faculty of the college had a right to profess and avow. If any section or description is peculiarly fostered or sanctioned, every other is prostrated and proscribed. Where can the trustees find their authority to institute in college an established religion, or to make *any* discrimination? If they had, as they have not, the right, it would be highly expedient to use it. We have, in college, sons of Calvinists and Universalists, Trinitarians and Unitarians, Arminians and Antinomians; sons of Jews, and of persons of no particular religion. What is the rule of justice and expedience in such case? Interfere with none of them; leave every opinion to fall or rise by its own value. Dr. Cooper's advice has been constant, reiterated, and uniform to the students, *as every witness examined has testified* — "follow, while at college, the religion of your parents."

It savors of unfair dealing with the students of the college to conceal from them differences of opinion which they are sure to meet when they leave it; and prohibit all insight into views and arguments which are necessary to be known and considered before any man can honestly determine where truth is to be found. This system of management, the offspring of sectarian timidity, is not to be approved. Would it not be a fraud on the students to teach them one side of a question and to prohibit or conceal all arguments on the other side? Is this the system of ethics that this board will venture to avow? Do you require a student who comes here to commence his studies under this organized plan of authorized deception?

Dr. Cooper had intended to suggest that this was, in fact, a political attack of the party who now form the minority of the state. But the voice of the people has spoken; and those who formerly doubted will be inclined to obey. For this reason, he would urge no irritating remarks or unnecessarily wound the feelings of those whom he hoped to see united with the people of this state, lending their aid to a common cause, and joining to resist a common oppression. His inclination was to convert, if possible, foes into friends.

Dr. Cooper took occasion to examine the act of 1802, which gave origin to this institution. In that act, the only cause of removal permitted to the trustees is misconduct in office. *Expressio unius, et exclusio alterius* [The enumeration of only one is the exclusion of all others]. Conduct is one thing, opinion is another thing. The usual meaning of language must not be changed, confounded, and rejected in the construction of an enacting clause. Whoever pretended before that opinion meant conduct or conduct opinion? Or how can the profession of opinion be misconduct, if the right to profess it be guaranteed (as it is) by the paramount law of the land? To convert opinion into misconduct, you must show your right to control opinion; whence do you derive it? Had the legislature committed to this board the charge of investigating whether Dr. C. had been guilty of misconduct in office (the only question which they had a right to give in charge) it might have been determined by an appeal to the testimony of witnesses; and all the rest of the present discussion saved; but, as it is, charges are brought forward which involve the religious rights of the whole community, and compel Dr. C. to feel that he is not now pleading the cause of the president of the college, but the cause of religious liberty and the rights which the Constitution has guaranteed to every citizen without exception. This cause he will defend at all risks, faithfully and fearlessly.

That the opinions objected to as used by Dr. C. in his lectures were intimately connected with the subjects treated, and the doctrines necessarily advanced, or were unavoidably elicited by the occasion, has been fully shown by the testimony. They were not extraneous to his duty or uncalled for by the subject and the occasion. They cannot therefore amount to misconduct in any possible sense of the word.

Dr. C. alluded very briefly to the very strange opinions advanced, and the objections taken, at a former meeting. But, as the gentlemen from whom they proceeded were not present, he forbore to consider them.

He then proceeded with his argument drawn from the Constitution of the United States and of this state, to establish his right to entertain, profess, and avow, and in public or private to defend, any opinion whatever on the subject of religion.

He said the liberties of the American people depend on the principles that will govern the present case. If the trustees may construe the Constitution so as to serve a present convenience, if they may substitute their own discretionary construction and indirectly contravene the plain meaning of the constitutional expressions; if they are at liberty to supply at their own will and pleasure any supposed *casus omissus* among the constitutional provisions; if they are at liberty to mold the national compact into any form that may suit the present notions of the present board and make the constitutional rights of the citizen to bow down before the decisions of a temporary tribunal; if *they* may do all this on the present occasion, why is *Congress* to be prohibited from doing the same? The same legal principles may apply to a case where a dollar is at issue, as where a million is at stake.

Let us examine then first the Constitution of the United States and next the constitution of our own state. But before I enter into detail (the doctor said) I would willingly make some preliminary remarks.

All sound politics and all sound morality, like all sound science of every kind, must be built not on any *a priori*, innate, or intuitive knowledge but on the results of actual experience. Wisdom must be bought, and sometimes at a high price. It is well founded only when it is founded on experience. But experience is not innate and intuitive. Many an experiment must be made and fail; many a fanciful and deceitful theory must be brought to the test of fact and trial before we can be convinced that it is worthless. Such is the case peculiarly with the science of government. Truth is a slow traveler. It has taken mankind 3,000 years to get a glimpse of one political conclusion which long and dear bought experience has pointed out; viz., that all governments ought to be instituted and constructed for the good of the many who are governed and not of the few who govern. Theoretical writers of modern times seem, for the most part, to adopt this conclusion; but it is a truth *practically* rejected throughout Europe, and it cannot be said to be put in practice even here.

In all the revolutions that the abuse of power has driven the people to engage in, they have changed their tyrants, but they have not changed the tyranny. Despots have been sacrificed to popular vengeance; but the despotism remained. Rays of light, gleaming through the darkness of past ages, gave birth to the Cortes of Spain, the parliaments of France, the Magna Carta of the English barons, the Bill of Rights under Charles I and the Revolution of 1688. But no great and leading principles in favor of the many were deliberately penned as the documentary charter of the *people's* rights. In England, the farce of a constitution, much talked of, nowhere to be found, has at length been reduced to one principle: the omnipotence of Parliament; a principle anxiously enforced and strenuously urged by the present abandoned majority in the Congress of the United States. This principle was distinctly laid down as constitutional law in Mr. Cooke's late speech and listened to with great complacency by the House. It is in fact based upon the doctrine of general

welfare introduced by Mr. J. Q. Adams, and received with infinite satisfaction by all the Federalists and consolidationists of the day: men with whom the government is everything, the people nothing.

The first effectual attempt to give origin to political power by express delegation, and to limit the extent and define the bounds of entrusted authority by a written constitution, was among ourselves. This was the result of reflection on past experience; and a measure it was full of wisdom and happy omen. Unluckily, as no human effort is ever perfect at the first trial, the imperfection of language has rendered our experiments defective. The ingenuity of verbal quibble has contrived to throw doubts on a part of our Constitution where common sense and plain popular feeling would see no difficulty. Moreover, instead of making all implied powers indispensable to the powers expressly delegated, we have most injudiciously admitted the words useful and proper; affording a latitude of interpretation to perversity of construction not foreseen by the men who penned our national compact. Hence the door has been thrown open for discretionary interpretation; and Congress now considers a written constitution as a nose of wax — a theory to be treated civilly but disregarded practically. Your government is now the discretion of a majority exercised under the omnipotence of Congress; and the rights of the states, as well as of the citizen, are now held by that tenure and by that alone. Discretionary construction adopted to suit temporary expedience has converted this federal union of independent states into one despotic, consolidated government, and limitations of power and jurisdiction deduced from the Constitution are openly laughed to scorn.

I ask of you, gentlemen, is it not so? I ask of you whether, at this moment, this be not the sum and substance of the complaints of South Carolina? And whether congressional discretion, usurped and enforced to promote the purposes of sectional plunder, has not prostrated the Constitution through the very men who have taken a solemn oath to preserve it inviolate? And again I appeal to you as republicans and Carolinians and I ask whether my accusers have not called upon you deliberately to commit the same grave offense on the present occasion, which you have so long complained of and so steadily opposed when committed by Congress against yourselves? You are asked, by people who pretend to take umbrage against all those who do not adopt their sectarian theology, to set aside the Constitution of the United States and your own state; to substitute your discretion, in lieu of the Constitution; and forfeit your characters for the sake of their religious prejudices. But I know you better than my accusers do; and I have no fears while I have wise and honorable men to appeal to as my judges.

Let us take up the Constitution of the United States; if not as authority strictly technical and legal, yet as demonstrative evidence of public opinion.

By Article VI, Section 2, this is made the supreme law of the land.

By Amendment I, "Congress shall make no law, respecting an establishment of religion: or prohibiting the free exercise thereof: or abridging the freedom of speech, or of the press."

Let us analyze these clauses and their expressions,

Respecting: that is, about or concerning, or relating to religious preference.

An establishment of religion: that is, giving one set of opinions respecting religion a preference, by law, over another. No such law shall be passed.

Well then, if you may not enact such a law directly, can you bring about such a result by indirect legislation, by management or implication? For instance, no tax shall be paid on any article of export; but, says the majority in Congress, we will lay such a tax on the imported article, which pays for the export, that one half of the value of the exports shall be forced into the public treasury or into the pocket of the home monopolist.

In imitation of this maneuver, my opponents say, we will not establish by law any form of religious worship; O! no! God forbid. But we will expel from office all men who express religious opinions not conformable to our own. For all such are offensive and unpopular. This may be a clerical mode of superseding the limits imposed by the Constitution; is it an honest one?

Or abridging the freedom of speech, or of the press: that is, nothing shall be punishable by law which the plain meaning of the Constitution permits. It does not permit slander or libel. Punish them. It does permit every freedom concerning religion. You cannot punish that. In my own case, whom have I libeled? The clergy? Is not the press open to them and to me? Have I libeled religion? Whose? Not my own: there *is* no true religion but mine. Every man says so of his religion; I have the same right to say so of mine. That is truth which is truth to me.

The constitutions of our sister states recently adopted may be considered as popular, constitutional comments on that of the United States. Here Dr. Cooper read and referred to the constitutions of Maine (1819), Indiana (1816), Mississippi (1817), Illinois (1818), Alabama (1819), Missouri (1820), and recently Mississippi, in all of which it is substantially declared that no man whatever shall be hurt or molested, or in any manner damnified on account of his tenets respecting religion; and presenting altogether a body of testimony conclusive against all kind of legislation respecting or concerning religion. This general, this anxious, sedulous exclusion of religion from legislation furnishes a fair comment on the part of the people of the United States on the Constitution of 1787 and a reasonable rule for construing it. Whether this prohibition to Congress is of itself a prohibition also to each particular state within its boundary may admit of a doubt; but it is important to show the perfect coincidence of opinion and feeling throughout our continent on these subjects.

From these premises Dr. Cooper deduced the conclusion that every kind of restraint on the profession, avowal, or discussion of religious tenets was in manifest hostility, not only to the letter and spirit of the Constitution of the United States, but of the people in general in every state. They had furnished a commentary on that Constitution, and a canon of construction for the amendment above quoted, by which its real meaning might be reasonably and fairly settled. If so, by what authority could the trustees, as agents of the legislature, legislate on the subject of religious opinion at this board and frame a constitution for the government of the college in direct hostility with public sentiment?

Proceed we now to the constitution of our own state (1790). It says that "The free exercise and enjoyment of religious profession and worship, without discrimination or preference, shall forever hereafter be allowed within this state to all mankind" (Const. S. C. Art. 8).

Free exercise and enjoyment: that is, unfettered, untrammeled, unchecked, uncontrolled, unlimited, unforbidden. If otherwise, is it free? Can a man be said to have the free exercise and enjoyment of his religion if he is liable to be turned out of office for professing it? Can a man have the free enjoyment of that which he is forbidden to enjoy under pain of punishment? Have the ignorant people who have instigated these accusations against me ever read the constitution of their own state; or are they aware that every legislator takes a solemn oath to protect, support, and preserve that constitution? If a choice is to be made between the college and the constitution, far better is it to prostrate the first than the last. The religionists have rights but they have no right

to ask that the constitution shall be surrendered to be mangled at their sectarian discretion. They have no right to require of their representatives to commit perjury in support of orthodoxy.

Religious profession and worship: that is open, public avowal, at all times and everywhere. What is profession but *public* avowal? Or worship but public worship?

Without discrimination or preference: so you may be a Presbyterian, Episcopalian, or Baptist; but not a Quaker, Unitarian, Jew, or Deist. You may profess with John Calvin, or John Knox, or John Wesley, but not with John Milton, John Archdale, or John Adams. You may hold with Archbishop Laud, or Bishop Horsley, but not with Benj. Franklin, or Jos. Priestley, or Thos. Jefferson. You may believe and profess that three units added together make one; but if you should miscalculate and call them three, you are a dangerous man — begone! And this is called making no discrimination, giving no preference! And your President must conform in submissive silence to this grave mockery of the Constitution or he is "turned out to grass!"

To all mankind: does all mankind include Dr. Cooper? I have heard of a classification in England of the human race, into the men, the women, and the Herveys; is it here, the men, the women, and Dr. Cooper? Is Dr. Cooper excluded from the expression, "of all mankind"?

In South Carolina: so, I may profess whatever I please in South Carolina, but not in the South Carolina College! Where is it laid down that the boundaries of South Carolina do not include the college? Or is it like the District of Columbia an extraparochial locality? The climate in this insulated district being essentially and exclusively orthodox!

Remember the great and leading truth of republican policy. All assumption of undelegated, unauthorized authority is usurpation; to enforce it is tyranny; to assume it and enforce it in plain and manifest violation of a solemn oath is — what? Not a drop in the ocean, not the small dust of the balance; it is something more weighty and more serious; something that one would suppose a religious man would not hastily rush upon, even in support of what is called orthodoxy.

Remember, this is not a country of legislative omnipotence or uncontrolled discretion but of defined and limited jurisdiction. You are not permitted to act on dubious implication or discretionary latitude of construction. The authority you assume is unjustifiable, if it be not plainly delegated, in words not to be misunderstood and void of all ambiguity. Where there is reasonable doubt — room for hesitation — you are bound not to act. *Quod dubitas ne feceris.* Is there anything like doubt, or any latent or any patent ambiguity in these liberal expressions of constitutional right? Can any honest man put two meanings upon them? If not, you are conscientiously bound by the plain words of our national compact to their fullest extent.

When the people of this state, by their constitutional representatives, met to form a political community and to make with each other a mutual compact on terms of liberal equality, they met, not as Calvinists or Arminians, as Trinitarians or Unitarians, as Christians, whether Papist or Protestant, as Jews or Deists — but as men. They met not to form a religious but a political community. They met not to regulate their expectations in another world but their interests as men and citizens in this. They purposely excluded all religious distinctions and considerations and agreed to permit full license to each other to agree or disagree on the contentious questions of theology. All this is manifest from the expressions of the Constitution. The mutual compact thus entered into is binding upon us; but if any legislature or any board of trustees can set it aside because it may be convenient to do so, a national compact of citizen with citizen is a farce; and constitutional rights are words without meaning. If the ignorance of the people will not permit you to support your college without annulling the Constitution, there is no hesitation which should be saved. But in fact your college is quite as flourishing as the difficulties of the times and surrounding competition will permit it to be. You have no reason for complaint in this respect; and I take for granted you will furnish no reason for complaint in any other.

Such is the defense on which I, for my own part, choose to rest this case. I take this ground because I am not now fighting my own battle. Every citizen of the state is as much concerned in this defense as I am. The questions are: whether the free exercise and enjoyment of religious profession and worship without discrimination or preference shall forever hereafter in South Carolina be allowed to all mankind, or shall it not? Are our religious rights in whole or in part within the power and jurisdiction of the legislature or any agent appointed by the legislature? Are we bound by the Constitution or are we not? I contend that the Constitution — that contract made on terms of perfect equality by every citizen with every other — has withdrawn from the legislature all consideration of religious questions. Is it so or not?

Compared to these great questions my office and its emoluments are the mere dust of the balance. I desire it distinctly to be understood that, having fully and faithfully performed my duty, I have no favor to ask of the legislature or of this board. I am contending for objects of higher moment than my own — for the rights of every inhabitant of South Carolina. Nor will I, from any risk of what may happen, yield one iota of the great trust which an ignorant and ill-judging coalition of politicians and religionists have thought fit to throw upon me.

I go further. If the Constitution by which

you are bound had not included one syllable touching the religious rights of the people, they would have been as sacred and as binding as they are now; for they were so before a Constitution was thought of. Can any man whatever possess the right of sacrificing to another, for any consideration under heaven, his obligations to his Creator, his rights of conscience, his duty to promulgate whatever he believes to be useful to his fellowmen and true in itself? Can any man voluntarily contract with his fellowmen, for any consideration under heaven, that he will live on, a time-serving hypocrite and a deceiver of those who put confidence in his declarations? His religious obligations are anterior to and independent of all social compact; and profligate and immoral must that contract be that would annihilate them. The declarations of the Constitution, therefore, are not enactive, but declaratory; and every honest and wise man must feel the honesty and wisdom that dictated them.

Sir, this board is acting as the agent of the legislature in this affair, and I claim from them and from you, for myself and all other citizens of this state, the right of entertaining in private, and professing and defending in public, peaceably, by all fair and reasonable argument, any opinion whatever on any subject whatever without exception, within the illimitable extent of human inquiry. I claim it as one of the *rights of man* before political constitutions were invented or proposed. I claim it as a right clearly and fully guaranteed by the Constitution of the United States and of this state in particular; a right that cannot be refused or withheld without prostituting the Constitution of the country at the foot of undelegated, discretionary authority.

Sir, this is not a day when the right of free discussion is to be submitted to a licenser. This is not a day when the human intellect may be required to bow down before the presumptuous ignorance of civil authority as the sufficient judge of all possible controversies. No, sir, the *tribunal of the public* is the only court of appeals in the last resort; and fact and argument, with full freedom of discussion to all the parties before that court, are the means by which Truth seeks to obtain its decision in her favor. The tide of public opinion, long checked by the ignorance of past ages, is returning with irresistible force toward the vast ocean of unlimited inquiry; and no puny effort of civil despotism or religious fanaticism can turn it from its course or set bounds to its progress. To this board, sir, of well informed and honorable men, I can safely state this feature of the nineteenth century; for you are well able to appreciate its correctness, and prepared to act according to your honest judgments, on these most manifest signs of the times. Experience has settled the rule: where there is doubt, let there be discussion.

I have now, in this great question, done my duty, faithfully I hope, and fearlessly, to my fellow citizens and myself. I leave you, gentlemen, to do yours.

During the course of Dr. Cooper's speech, the plaudits of the multitude who attended as auditors and spectators threatened to interrupt the business of the evening, but they were checked and silenced by a remonstrance from the president of the board.

On the evening of Saturday the 8th, the Board of Trustees met in the college library, and

Resolved, that no charge against Dr. Cooper showing that his continuance in office defeats the ends and aims of the institution or authorizing his removal has been substantiated by proof; and that the charges against him be therefore dismissed.

110.

South Carolina Ordinance of Nullification

High tariffs stirred resentment in the South during the early years of the nineteenth century. South Carolina responded to the 1828 "Tariff of Abominations" with a protest written secretly by Vice-President John C. Calhoun, stating that if Congress enacted legislation that exceeded the powers delegated to it by the states, the states could declare the legislation unconstitutional and thereby nullify it. This assertion of state sovereignty, derived in theory from the Kentucky and Virginia Resolves of 1798, received official sanction when South Carolina reacted to an 1832 tariff with the following "Ordinance of Nullification" of November 24, 1832.

Source: *The Statutes at Large of South Carolina*, Thomas Cooper, ed., Vol. I, Columbia, 1836, pp. 329-331.

An ordinance to nullify certain acts of the Congress of the United States purporting to be laws laying duties and imposts on the importation of foreign commodities.

Whereas, the Congress of the United States, by various acts purporting to be acts laying duties and imposts on foreign imports, but in reality intended for the protection of domestic manufactures and the giving of bounties to classes and individuals engaged in particular employments, at the expense and to the injury and oppression of other classes and individuals, and by wholly exempting from taxation certain foreign commodities, such as are not produced or manufactured in the United States, to afford a pretext for imposing higher and excessive duties on articles similar to those intended to be protected, has exceeded its just powers under the Constitution, which confers on it no authority to afford such protection, and has violated the true meaning and intent of the Constitution, which provides for equality in imposing the burdens of taxation upon the several states and portions of the confederacy;

And whereas, the said Congress, exceeding its just power to impose taxes and collect revenue for the purpose of effecting and accomplishing the specific objects and purposes which the Constitution of the United States authorizes it to effect and accomplish, has raised and collected unnecessary revenue for objects unauthorized by the Constitution;

We, therefore, the people of the state of South Carolina, in Convention assembled, do declare and ordain, and it is hereby declared and ordained, that the several acts and parts of acts of the Congress of the United States purporting to be laws for the imposing of duties and imposts on the importation of foreign commodities, and now having actual operation and effect within the United States, and more especially an act entitled "An Act in Alteration of the Several Acts Imposing Duties on Imports," approved on the 19th of May, 1828, and also an act entitled "An Act to Alter and Amend the Several Acts Imposing Duties on Imports," approved on the 14th day of July, 1832, are unauthorized by the Constitution of the

United States and violate the true meaning and intent thereof, and are null, void, and no law, nor binding upon this state, its officers, or citizens; and all promises, contracts, and obligations made or entered into, or to be made or entered into, with purpose to secure the duties imposed by said acts, and all judicial proceedings which shall be hereafter had in affirmance thereof, are and shall be held utterly null and void.

And it is further ordained that it shall not be lawful for any of the constituted authorities, whether of this state or of the United States, to enforce the payment of duties imposed by the said acts within the limits of this state; but it shall be the duty of the legislature to adopt such measures and pass such acts as may be necessary to give full effect to this ordinance, and to prevent the enforcement and arrest the operation of the said acts and parts of acts of the Congress of the United States, within the limits of this state, from and after the 1st day of February next; and the duty of all other constituted authorities, and of all persons residing or being within the limits of this state, and they are hereby required and enjoined to obey and give effect to this ordinance, and such acts and measures of the legislature as may be passed or adopted in obedience thereto.

And it is further ordained that in no case of law or equity decided in the courts of this state, wherein shall be drawn in question the authority of this ordinance, or the validity of such act or acts of the legislature as may be passed for the purpose of giving effect thereto, or the validity of the aforesaid acts of Congress imposing duties, shall any appeal be taken or allowed to the Supreme Court of the United States, nor shall any copy of the record be permitted or allowed for that purpose. And if any such appeal shall be attempted to be taken, the courts of this state shall proceed to execute and enforce their judgments according to the laws and usages of the state without

reference to such attempted appeal, and the person or persons attempting to take such appeal may be dealt with as for a contempt of the court.

And it is further ordained that all persons now holding any office of honor, profit, or trust, civil or military, under this state (members of the legislature excepted), shall, within such time and in such manner as the legislature shall prescribe, take an oath well and truly to obey, execute, and enforce this ordinance, and such act or acts of the legislature as may be passed in pursuance thereof, according to the true intent and meaning of the same; and on the neglect or omission of any such person or persons so to do, his or their office or offices shall be forthwith vacated and shall be filled up as if such person or persons were dead or had resigned. And no person hereafter elected to any office of honor, profit, or trust, civil or military (members of the legislature excepted), shall, until the legislature shall otherwise provide and direct, enter on the execution of his office, or be in any respect competent to discharge the duties thereof, until he shall, in like manner, have taken a similar oath. And no juror shall be empaneled in any of the courts of this state, in any cause in which shall be in question this ordinance, or any act of the legislature passed in pursuance thereof, unless he shall first, in addition to the usual oath, have taken an oath that he will well and truly obey, execute, and enforce this ordinance, and such act or acts of the legislature as may be passed to carry the same into operation and effect, according to the true intent and meaning thereof.

And we, the people of South Carolina, to the end that it may be fully understood by the government of the United States and the people of the co-states, that we are determined to maintain this, our ordinance and declaration, at every hazard, *do further declare*, that we will not submit to the application of force on the part of the federal government to reduce this state to obedience; but that we will consider the passage by Congress of any act authorizing the employment of a military or naval force against the state of South Carolina, her constituted authorities or citizens, or any act abolishing or closing the ports of this state, or any of them, or otherwise obstructing the free ingress and egress of vessels to and from the said ports, or any other act on the part of the federal government to coerce the state, shut up her ports, destroy or harass her commerce, or to enforce the acts hereby declared to be null and void, otherwise than through the civil tribunals of the country, as inconsistent with the longer continuance of South Carolina in the Union.

And that the people of this state will thenceforth hold themselves absolved from all further obligation to maintain or preserve their political connection with the people of the other states and will forthwith proceed to organize a separate government, and to do all other acts and things which sovereign and independent states may of right do.

111.

John C. Calhoun: States' Rights and Nullification

When South Carolina responded to the Tariff of 1832 by asserting the doctrine of nullification, John C. Calhoun resigned the vice-presidency to speak for his state in the Senate. He wrote the following Address to the People of the United States *to accompany the* Ordinance of Nullification *of November 24, 1832. In the address, based upon the "South Carolina Exposition" he had written secretly four years earlier, Calhoun set forth South Carolina's objections to the protective tariff and his states' rights theory of the Constitution. The latter has enjoyed lasting popularity with groups intent on defending minority and sectional interests.*

Source: *Reports and Public Letters of John C. Calhoun*, Richard K. Crallé, ed., New York, 1856, Vol. VI, pp. 193-209.

WE, THE PEOPLE OF SOUTH CAROLINA, assembled in convention in our sovereign capacity as one of the parties to the compact which formed the Constitution of the United States, have declared the act of Congress, approved the 14th of July, 1832, to alter and amend the several acts imposing duties on imports, and the acts which it alters and amends to be unconstitutional, and therefore null and void; and have invested the legislature of the state with power to adopt such measures, not repugnant to the Constitution of the United States nor of this state, as it may deem proper to carry the same into effect. In taking this step, we feel it to be due to the intimate political relations existing between the states of the Union, to make known to them, distinctly, the principles on which we have acted, with the cause and motive by which we have been influenced, to fulfill which is the object of the present communication.

For this purpose, it will be necessary to state, summarily, what we conceive to be the nature and character of the Constitution of the United States, with the rights and duties of the states — so far as they relate to the subject — in reference both to the Union and to their own citizens; and also the character and effect, in a political point of view, of the system of protective duties contained in the acts which we have declared to be unconstitutional, as far as it may be necessary, in reference to the same subject.

We, then, hold it as unquestionable that on the separation from the Crown of Great Britain, the people of the several colonies became free and independent states, possessed of the full right of self-government; and that no power can be rightfully exercised over them but by the consent and authority of their respective states, expressed or implied. We also hold it as equally unquestionable that the Constitution of the United States is a compact between the people of the several states, constituting free, independent, and sovereign communities; that the government it created was formed and appointed to execute, according to the provisions of the instrument, the powers therein granted as the joint agent of the several states; that all its acts, transcending these powers, are simply and of themselves null and void, and that in case of such infractions, it is the right of the states, in their sovereign capacity, each acting for itself and its citizens, in like manner as they adopted the Constitution to judge thereof in the last resort and to adopt such measures — not inconsistent with the compact — as may be deemed fit to arrest the execution of the act within their respective limits. Such we hold to be the right of the states in reference to an unconstitutional act of the government; nor do we deem their duty to exercise it on proper occasions less certain and imperative than the right itself is clear.

We hold it to be a very imperfect conception of the obligation which each state contracted in ratifying the Constitution and thereby becoming a member of the Union to suppose that it would be fully and faithfully discharged simply by abstaining, on its part, from exercising the powers delegated to the government of the Union, or by sustaining it in the due execution of those powers. These are, undoubtedly, important federal duties, but there is another not less important; to resist the government, should it, under color of exercising the delegated, encroach on the reserved powers. The duty of the states is no less clear in the one case than in the other; and the obligation as binding in the one as in the other; and in like manner, the solemn obligation of an oath imposed by the states through the Constitution on all public functionaries, federal and state, to support that instrument comprehends the one as well as the other duty; as well that of maintaining the government in the due exercise of its powers as that of resisting it when it transcends them.

But the obligation of a state to resist the encroachments of the government on the reserved powers is not limited simply to the discharge of its federal duties. We hold that it embraces another, if possible, more sacred — that of protecting its citizens, derived from their original sovereign character, viewed in their separate relations. There are none of the duties of a state of higher obligation. It is, indeed, the primitive duty, preceding all others, and in its nature paramount to them all; and so essential to the existence of a state that she cannot neglect or abandon it without forfeiting all just claims to the allegiance of her citizens, and with it, her sovereignty itself. In entering into the Union, the states by no means exempted themselves from the obligation of this, the first and most sacred of their duties; nor, indeed, can they without sinking into subordinate and dependent corporations. It is true that in ratifying the Constitution they placed a large and important portion of the rights of their citizens under the joint protection of all the states, with a view to their more effectual security; but it is not less so that they reserved; at the same time, a portion still larger, and not less important, under their own immediate guardianship; and in relation to which the original obligation, to protect the rights of their citizens from whatever quarter assailed, remained unchanged and unimpaired.

Nor is it less true that the general government, created in order to preserve the rights placed under the joint protection of the states, and which, when restricted to its proper sphere, is calculated to afford them the most perfect security, may become, when not so restricted, the most dangerous enemy to the rights of their citizens, including those reserved under the immediate guardianship of the states respectively as well as those under their joint protection; and thus, the original and inherent obligation of the states to protect their citizens is united with that which they have contracted to support the Constitution, thereby rendering it the most sacred of all their duties to watch over and resist the encroachments of the government; and on the faithful performance of which we solemnly believe the duration of the Constitution and the liberty and happiness of the country depend.

But, while we hold the rights and duties of the states to be such as we have stated, we are deeply impressed with the conviction that it is due to the relation existing between them, as members of a common Union, and the respect which they ought ever to entertain toward the government ordained to carry into effect the important objects for which the Constitution was formed, that the occasion to justify a state in interposing its authority ought to be one of·necessity; where all other peaceful remedies have been unsuccessfully tried; and where the only alternative is interposition on one side, or oppression of its citizens

and imminent danger to the Constitution and liberty of the country on the other; and such we hold to be the present.

That the prohibitory, or protective system, which, as has been stated is embraced in the acts which we have declared to be unconstitutional, and therefore null and void, is, in fact, unconstitutional, unequal, and oppressive in its operation on this and the other staple and exporting states and dangerous to the Constitution and liberty of the country; and that (all other peaceful remedies having been tried without success) an occasion has occurred where it becomes the right and duty of the state to interpose its authority to arrest the evil within its limits, we hold to be certain; and it is under this deep and solemn conviction that we have acted.

For more than ten years the system has been the object of continued, united, and strenuous opposition on the part both of the government of the state and its representatives in Congress, and, we may add, of the other staple and exporting states. During this long period, all the ordinary means of opposition — discussion, resolution, petition, remonstrance, and protest — have been tried and exhausted, without effect. We have, during the whole time, waited with patience under the unequal and oppressive action of the system, hoping that the final payment of the public debt, when there would be no longer a pretext for its continuance, would bring it to a termination. That period, for all practical purposes, is now passed. The small remnant of debt which now remains is amply provided for by the revenue already accrued; but the system remains in full force; its restrictive character established and openly avowed; the inequality of its action between this and other sections greatly increased; and the amount of its exertions vastly exceeding, probably doubling, the just and constitutional wants of the government.

The event which, it was hoped, would

put an end to its duration has thus but served to give it increased strength; and instead of mitigating, has aggravated its most obnoxious features. Having stood this shock, it seems almost impossible that any other within the ordinary scope of events can shake it. It now stands for the first time, exclusively on its own basis, as an independent system, having a self-existing power with an unlimited capacity of increasing, which, left unopposed, must continue to expand till it controls the entire labor and capital of the staple and exporting states; subjecting them completely, as tributaries, to the great dominant and sectional interest which has grown up at their expense. With this prospect of the indefinite extent and duration of the system, we had thus presented the alternative of silently acquiescing in its oppression and danger, or of interposing as the last peaceful measure of redress the authority of the state to arrest the evil within its limits. We did not hesitate.

When we reflect on the principle on which the system rests, and from which the government claims the power to control the labor and capital of the country, and the bitter fruits it has already produced, the decay and impoverishment of an entire section of the country, and the wide spread of discord and corruption, we cannot doubt that there is involved in the issue not only the prosperity of this and the other staple and exporting states, but also the Constitution and liberty of the country. In rearing up the system it was not pretended, nor is it now, that there is in the Constitution any positive grant of power to protect manufactures; nor can it be denied that frequent attempts were made in the Convention to obtain the power, and that they all failed. And yet, without any grant and notwithstanding the failure to obtain one, it has become one of the leading powers of the government, influencing more extensively its movements and affecting more deeply and permanently the relative interests and condition of the states and the probable fate of the government itself than any or all of the enumerated powers united.

From whatever source its advocates may derive this power, whether from the right "to lay and collect taxes, duties, imposts, and excises," or from that "to regulate commerce," it plainly rests on the broad assumption that the power to impose duties may be applied, not only to effect the original objects — to raise revenue, or regulate commerce — but also to protect manufactures; and this, not as an incidental but as a substantive and independent power, without reference to revenue or commerce; and, in this character it has been used in building up the present system.

That such a power, resting on such a principle, is unauthorized by the Constitution; that it has become an instrument in the hands of the great dominant interests of the country, to oppress the weaker; that it must ultimately concentrate the whole power of the community in the general government and abolish the sovereignty of the states; and that discord, corruption, and, eventually, despotism must follow if the system be not resisted, we hold to be certain. Already we see the commencement of this disastrous train of consequences — the oppression of the weaker; the assumption by government of the right to determine, finally and conclusively, the extent of its own powers; the denial and denunciation of the right of the states to judge of their reserved powers and to defend them against the encroachments of the government, followed by discord, corruption, and the steady advance of despotic power.

That something is wrong, all admit; and that the assumption by government of a power so extensive and dangerous, and the control which it has thereby acquired through its fiscal operations over the wealth and labor of the country, exacting, in the shape of high duties, a large portion of the annual income of our section and bestowing it in the form of monopolies and appropriations on the other, is the true cause of the existing disorder and the only adequate one that can be assigned, we cannot entertain a doubt. To this unequal and excessive fiscal action of the government may be immediately and clearly traced the growing discontent and alienation on the part of the oppressed portion of the community and the greedy pursuit of office; and with it, the increasing spirit of servility, subserviency, and corruption on the other, which all must see and acknowledge, and which every lover of the country and its institutions must deplore.

Nor is it less clear that this dangerous assumption, by which the reserved powers of the states have been transferred to the general government, is rapidly concentrating, by a necessary operation, the whole power of the government in the hands of the executive. We must be blind to the lessons of reason and experience not to see that the more a government interferes with the labor and wealth of a community, the more it exacts from one portion and bestows on another, just in the same proportion must the power of that department, which is vested with its patronage, be increased. It ought not, then, to be a subject of surprise that, with this vast increase of the power and revenues of the federal government and its unequal fiscal action, both in the collection and distribution of the latter, the power of the executive, on whose will the disposition of the patronage of the government mainly depends, and on which, in turn, depends that powerful, active, and mercenary corps of expectants, created by the morbid moneyed action of the government, should be, of late, so greatly and dangerously increased. It is indeed not difficult to see that the present state of things, if continued, must end, and that speedily, in raising this department of the government into an irresponsible and despotic power, with the ca-

pacity of perpetuating itself through its own influence; first, virtually appointing its successor, or, by controlling the presidential election, through the patronage of the government; and, finally, as the virtue and patriotism of the people decay, by the introduction and open establishment of the hereditary principle.

The federal government has, indeed, already passed through the first and most difficult part of this process, which, if permitted to proceed, must terminate, as it ever has, in the absolute and unlimited power of a single despot.

We hold it as certain that wherever the majority of a people becomes the advocate of high taxes and profuse appropriations and expenditures, there the despotic power is already, in fact, established and liberty virtually lost, be the form of government what it may; and experience has proved that the transition from this stage to the absolute power of a single individual is certain and rapid; and that it can only be arrested by the interposition of some high power out of the ordinary course. Our government has already clearly reached the first stage; and will inevitably — unless the process be arrested by some such power — speedily terminate its career in the last. In the meantime, while this train of events is consummating itself in the loss of the liberty of all, the oppression and impoverishment of this and the other staple and exporting states will necessarily advance with equal steps. The very root of the system, that from which it derives its existence and sprouts forth all its evils, is its unjust and unequal action — giving to one portion what it takes from another — and thus creating that powerful and irresistible interest in favor of high taxes and profuse expenditures, which are fast sweeping away, at the same time, the foundation of our liberty and exhausting and reducing to poverty a large portion of the community.

That such is, in truth, the real state of

things, the extraordinary spectacle which our government now exhibits to the world affords the most conclusive proof. On what other principle can it be explained that a popular government, with all the forms of freedom, after having discharged a long standing and heavy public debt, should resist every effort to make a corresponding reduction of the public burden? What other cause can be assigned for a fact so remarkable as that of a free community refusing to repeal this tax, when the proceeds are, confessedly, no longer wanted, and when the embarrassment of the government is not to find the revenue but the objects on which to expend it?

Such is the nature of the disorder which the system has engendered. Of all the diseases which can afflict the body politic, we hold it to be the most inveterate and difficult to remedy. Others, originating in ignorance, delusion, or some sudden popular impulse, yield to the influence of time and reflection; and we may, accordingly, look in such cases, with confidence, for relief to the returning good sense and feelings of the community. Not so in this. Having its source in the most powerful passions of the human heart — the love of gain and power — neither time, reflection, reason, discussion, entreaty, nor remonstrance can arrest or impede its course. Nor, if left to itself, will it stop while there is a cent to be exacted or a particle of power to be acquired. With us the disease must assume the most aggravated character. There is no country in which so many and such powerful causes exist to give to the unequal fiscal action of the government, in which it originates, so powerful an impetus, and an operation so oppressive and dangerous.

When we reflect on the extent of our country, and the diversity of its interests; on the peculiar nature of the labor and production of this and the other suffering states; with how much facility they may be made subservient to the power and wealth of the

other sections, as experience has shown, and how deep, radical, and disastrous must be the change in the social and political condition of this and the other states similarly situated in reference to pursuits and population, when the increasing pressure shall reach the point at which the exactions of the government shall not leave a sufficient amount of the proceeds of labor to remunerate the expense of maintenance and supervision; we cannot but foresee, if the system be not arrested, calamity awaiting us and our posterity, greater than ever befell a free and enlightened people. Already we perceive indications of its approach that cannot be mistaken. It appears in that quarter to which, from the nature of the disease, we would naturally look for it; that quarter where labor is the least productive and is least capable of bearing the pressure of the system.

Such we hold to be the general character of the system, viewed in its political connections and its certain effects, if left to its natural operations; to arrest the evils of which, within our limits, we have interposed the authority of the state as the only peaceful remedy that remains of defending the Constitution against its encroachments, the citizens of the state against its oppression, and the liberty of the country against its corrupting influence and danger.

In performing this high and sacred duty, our anxious desire has been to embarrass the action of the government in the smallest degree possible, consistent with the object we have in view; and had it been possible to separate the portion of duties necessary for revenue from that imposed for the purpose of protection, the action of the state would have been limited exclusively to the latter. But we could have no right to discriminate when the government had made no discrimination; and if we had, it would have been impossible, as revenue and protection are so blended throughout, and the duties, as well those included in the act of

July last, as those contained in the acts it alters and amends, comprehending the unprotected and the protected articles, are adjusted so obviously with the design to form one entire system of protection, as much so, as if the whole had been incorporated in a single act passed expressly with that intention, and without regard to revenue except as a mere incident.

The whole thus forming one system, equally contaminated throughout by the same unconstitutional principle, no alternative was left but to declare the entire system unconstitutional; and as such null and void. Anxious, however, while thus compelled to arrest an unconstitutional act, to continue in the discharge of all our constitutional obligations, and to bear our just and full share of the public burdens, we have, with a view to effect these objects, pledged the state to make good her proportional part of the revenue that would have accrued on the imports into the state, which may be exempted from duties, by the interposition of the state; calculated according to the rate per centum on the general imports which may, on a fair estimate, be considered requisite to meet the just and constitutional wants of the government; and have, accordingly, authorized the government of the state to adopt the necessary measures on its part to adjust the same on the termination of the present unhappy controversy.

That so desirable an event may be speedily brought about to the satisfaction of all is our sincere desire. In taking the stand which she has, the state has been solely influenced by a conscientious sense of duty to her citizens and to the Constitution without the slightest feeling of hostility towards the interests of any section of the country, or the remotest view to revolution, or wish to terminate her connection with the Union; to which she is now, as she ever has been, devotedly attached. Her object is not to destroy, but to restore and preserve. And, in

asserting her right to defend her reserved powers, she disclaims all pretension to control or interfere with the action of the government within its proper sphere, or to resume any powers that she has delegated to the government or conceded to the confederated states. She simply claims the right of exercising the powers which, in adopting the Constitution, she reserved to herself; and among them, the most important and essential of all, the right to judge, in the last resort, of the extent of her reserved powers, a right never delegated nor surrendered, nor, indeed, could be, while the state retains her sovereignty.

That it has not been, we appeal with confidence to the Constitution itself, which contains not a single grant that, on a fair construction, can be held to comprehend the power. If to this we add the fact, which the journals of the Convention abundantly establish, that reiterated but unsuccessful attempts were made, in every stage of its proceedings, to divest the states of the power in question, by conferring on the general government the right to annul such acts of the states as it might deem to be repugnant to the Constitution, and the corresponding right to coerce their obedience; we have the highest proof of which the subject is susceptible, that the power in question was not delegated, but reserved to the states. To suppose that a state, in exercising a power so unquestionable, resists the Union, would be a fundamental and dangerous error originating in a radical misconception of the nature of our political institutions. The government is neither the Union, nor its representative, except as an agent to execute its powers. The states themselves, in their confederated character, represent the authority of the Union; and, acting in the manner prescribed by the Constitution, through the concurring voice of three-fourths of their number, have the right to enlarge or diminish, at pleasure, the powers of the government, and to amend, alter, or even abolish the Constitution, and, with it, the government itself.

Correctly understood, it is not the state that interposes to arrest an unconstitutional act, but the government that passed it, which resists the authority of the Union. The government has not the right to add a particle to its powers; and to assume, on its part, the exercise of a power not granted, is plainly to oppose the confederated authority of the states, to which the right of granting powers exclusively belongs; and, in so doing, the Union itself, which they represent. On the contrary, a state, as a member of the body in which the authority of the Union resides, in arresting an unconstitutional act of the government, within its limits, so far from opposing, in reality supports the Union, and that in the only effectual mode in which it can be done in such cases. To divest the states of this right would be, in effect, to give to the government that authority over the Constitution which belongs to them exclusively; and which can only be preserved to them, by leaving to each state — as the Constitution has done — to watch over and defend its reserved powers against the encroachments of the government, and in performing which, it acts, at the same time, as a faithful and vigilant sentinel over the confederate powers of the states.

It was doubtless with these views that the Convention which framed the Constitution steadily resisted, as has been observed, the many attempts which were made, under the specious but fallacious argument of preserving the peace and harmony of the Union, to divest the states of this important right, which is not less essential to the defense of their joint confederate powers than to the preservation of their separate sovereignty and the protection of their citizens.

With these views — views on which the Convention acted in refusing to divest the states of this right — has this state acted in asserting it on the present occasion; and this with a full understanding of all the responsibilities attached to the position she has assumed, and with a determination as fixed as her conception of her right and duty is clear, to maintain it under every circumstance, and at every hazard. She has weighed all the consequences, and can see, in no possible result, greater disasters than those which must certainly follow a surrender of the right and an abandonment of her duty.

Having thus taken, immovably, her stand, there remain, to bring the controversy to a happy termination, but two possible courses. It may be effected by the government ceasing to exercise the unconstitutional power through which, under the name of duties, it has assumed the control over the labor and wealth of the country, and substituting for the present high rates an average ad valorem duty; or some other system of revenue equally just and fair; or by obtaining a positive grant of the power in the manner prescribed by the Constitution.

But, when we consider the great interests at stake and the number and magnitude of the questions involved in the issue, directly and indirectly, and the necessity of a full understanding on all the points, in order to a satisfactory and permanent adjustment of the controversy, we hold it difficult, if not impracticable, to bring it to a final and satisfactory close, short of convening again the body to whose authority and wisdom we are indebted for the Constitution. And under this conviction we have made it the duty of the legislature of the state to apply, in the manner prescribed by the Constitution, for a general convention of the states, as the most certain, prompt, and effectual, if not the only practicable mode of terminating the conflict and restoring harmony and confidence to the country.

If the other states of the Union be actuated by the same feelings which govern us, if their desire to maintain the Constitution, to preserve the Union, and to transmit to posterity the blessings of liberty, be as strong as ours (and we doubt not that it is), this most august of all assemblies, provided by the Constitution to meet this and similar emergencies, as a great moral substitute for revolution and force, may be convened in a few months; when the present, and every other constitutional question endangering the peace and harmony of the Union may be satisfactorily adjusted.

If there be any conceivable occasion that can justify the call of a Convention of the states, we hold the present to be that occasion; and surely the framers of the Constitution, in providing a mode for calling one, contemplated that great emergencies would arise in the course of events, in which it ought to be convened. They were not so vain as to suppose that their work was so perfect as to be too clear to admit of diversity of opinion, or too strong for passion or interest to derange. They accordingly, in their wisdom, provided a double remedy to meet the contingencies, which, if not provided for might endanger our political system: one, to meet ordinary and less pressing occurrences by vesting in two-thirds of Congress the power to propose amendments to the Constitution, to be ratified by three-fourths of the states; the other, for those of a more urgent character, when some deep derangement of the system, or some great and dangerous conflict of interests or opinion, might threaten with a catastrophe the institutions of the country.

That such a remedy is provided is proof of the profound wisdom of the great men who formed our Constitution; and entitles them to the lasting gratitude of the country. But it will be in vain that their wisdom de-

vised a remedy so admirable, a substitute so infinitely superior to the old and irrational mode of terminating such controversies as are of too high a nature to be adjusted by the force of reason, or through the ordinary tribunals, if their descendants be so blind as not to perceive its efficacy, or so intently bent on schemes of ambition and avarice as to prefer to this constitutional, peaceful, and safe remedy the wanton, hazardous, and, we may add, immoral arbitrament of force.

We hold that our country has arrived at the very point of difficulty and danger contemplated by the framers of the Constitution in providing for a General Convention of the states of the Union; and that, of course, the question now remaining to be tested is whether there be sufficient moral elevation, patriotism, and intelligence in the country to adjust, through the interposition of this highest of tribunals, whose right none can question, the conflicts which now threaten the very existence of our institutions, and liberty itself, and which, as experience has proved, there is no other body belonging to the system having sufficient weight of authority to terminate.

Such, at least, is our conviction; and we have acted accordingly. It now rests with the other states to determine whether a General Convention shall be called or not. And on that determination hangs, we solemnly believe, the future fate of the country. If it should be in favor of a call, we may, with almost perfect certainty, entertain the prospect of a speedy and happy termination of all our difficulties, followed by peace, prosperity, and lengthened political existence. But if not, we shall, by rejecting the remedy provided by the wisdom of our ancestors, prove that we deserve the fate which, in that event, will, in all probability, await the country.

112.

The Threat of Disunion

Andrew Jackson regarded the South Carolina Ordinance of Nullification of November 1832 as a clear threat to the federal union and to national authority. He reacted by submitting to Congress a Force Bill authorizing the use of federal troops in South Carolina, and by asking Secretary of State Edward Livingston to draw up the following "Proclamation to the People of South Carolina." Jackson's proclamation, delivered December 10, 1832, evoked a defiant response from South Carolina in the resolutions of December 20 that appear below. But support from other Southern states was not forthcoming, and this, coupled with Jackson's determination to employ military force if necessary, ultimately forced South Carolina to retreat. With the help of Henry Clay a moderate tariff bill more acceptable to South Carolina was passed in 1833. However, the episode had established a strategy the South would employ on the slavery issue, under weaker presidents, until the outbreak of the Civil War.

Source: Richardson, II, pp. 640-656.
The Statutes at Large of South Carolina, Thomas Cooper, ed., Vol. I, Columbia, 1836, pp. 356-357.

I.

ANDREW JACKSON: Proclamation to the People of South Carolina

Whereas, a convention assembled in the state of South Carolina have passed an ordinance by which they declare "that the several acts and parts of acts of the Congress of the United States purporting to be laws for the imposing of duties and imposts on the importation of foreign commodities and now having actual operation and effect within the United States, and more especially" two acts for the same purposes passed on the 29th of May, 1828, and on the 14th of July, 1832, are unauthorized by the Constitution of the United States, and violate the true meaning and intent thereof, and are null and void and no law, nor binding on the citizens of that state or its officers; and by the said ordinance it is further declared to be unlawful for any of the constituted authorities of the state or of the United States to enforce the payment of the duties imposed by the said acts within the same state, and that it is the duty of the legislature to pass such laws as may be necessary to give full effect to the said ordinance; and

Whereas, by the said ordinance it is further ordained that in no case of law or equity decided in the courts of said state wherein shall be drawn in question the validity of the said ordinance, or of the acts of the legislature that may be passed to give it effect, or of the said laws of the United States, no appeal shall be allowed to the Supreme Court of the United States, nor shall any copy of the record be permitted or allowed for that purpose, and that any person attempting to take such appeal shall be punished as for contempt of court; and, finally, the said ordinance declares that the people of South Carolina will maintain the said ordinance at every hazard, and that they will consider the passage of any act by Congress abolishing or closing the ports of the said state or otherwise obstructing the free ingress or egress of vessels to and from the said ports, or any other act of the federal government to coerce the state, shut up her ports, destroy or harass her commerce, or to enforce the said acts, otherwise than through the civil tribunals of the country, as inconsistent with the longer continuance of South Carolina in the Union, and that the people of the said state will thenceforth hold themselves absolved from all further obligation to maintain or preserve their political connection with the people of the other states, and will forthwith proceed to organize a separate government and do all other acts and things which sovereign and independent states may of right do; and

Whereas, the said ordinance prescribes to the people of South Carolina a course of conduct in direct violation of their duty as citizens of the United States, contrary to the laws of their country, subversive of its Constitution, and having for its object the destruction of the Union . . . to preserve this bond of our political existence from destruction, to maintain inviolate this state of national honor and prosperity, and to justify the confidence my fellow citizens have reposed in me, I, Andrew Jackson, President of the United States, have thought proper to issue this my proclamation, stating my views of the Constitution and laws applicable to the measures adopted by the convention of South Carolina and to the reasons they have put forth to sustain them, declaring the course which duty will require me to pursue, and appealing to the understanding and patriotism of the people, warn them of the consequences that must inevitably result from an observance of the dictates of the convention.

Strict duty would require of me nothing more than the exercise of those powers with which I am now or may hereafter be invested for preserving the peace of the Union and for the execution of the laws; but the imposing aspect which opposition has assumed in this case, by clothing itself with state authority and the deep interest which the people of the United States must all feel in preventing a resort to stronger measures while there is a hope that anything will be yielded to reasoning and remonstrance, perhaps demand, and will certainly justify, a full exposition to South Carolina and the nation of the views I entertain of this important question, as well as a distinct enunciation of the course which my sense of duty will require me to pursue.

The ordinance is founded, not on the indefeasible right of resisting acts which are plainly unconstitutional and too oppressive to be endured but on the strange position that any one state may not only declare an act of Congress void but prohibit its execution; that they may do this consistently with the Constitution; that the true construction of that instrument permits a state to retain its place in the Union and yet be bound by no other of its laws than those it may choose to consider as constitutional. It is true, they add, that to justify this abrogation of a law it must be palpably contrary to the Constitution; but it is evident that to give the right of resisting laws of that description, coupled with the uncontrolled right to decide what laws deserve that character, is to give the power of resisting all laws; for as by the theory there is no appeal, the reasons alleged by the state, good or bad, must prevail. If it should be said that public opinion is a sufficient check against the abuse of this power, it may be asked why it is not deemed a sufficient guard against the passage of an unconstitutional act by Congress?

There is, however, a restraint in this last case which makes the assumed power of a state more indefensible, and which does not exist in the other. There are two appeals from an unconstitutional act passed by Congress — one to the judiciary, the other to the people and the states. There is no appeal from the state decision in theory, and the practical illustration shows that the courts are closed against an application to review it, both judges and jurors being sworn to decide in its favor. But reasoning on this subject is superfluous when our social compact, in express terms, declares that the laws of the United States, its Constitution, and treaties made under it are the supreme law of the land, and, for greater caution, adds "that the judges in every state shall be bound thereby, anything in the constitution or laws of any state to the contrary notwithstanding." And it may be asserted without fear of refutation that no federative government could exist without a similar provision.

Look for a moment to the consequence. If South Carolina considers the revenue laws unconstitutional and has a right to prevent their execution in the port of Charleston, there would be a clear constitutional objection to their collection in every other port; and no revenue could be collected anywhere, for all imposts must be equal. It is no answer to repeat that an unconstitutional law is no law so long as the question of its legality is to be decided by the state itself, for every law operating injuriously upon any local interest will be perhaps thought, and certainly represented, as unconstitutional, and, as has been shown, there is no appeal.

If this doctrine had been established at an earlier day, the Union would have been dissolved in its infancy. The excise law in Pennsylvania, the embargo and nonintercourse law in the Eastern states, the carriage tax in Virginia were all deemed unconstitutional, and were more unequal in their operation than any of the laws now complained of; but, fortunately, none of those states discovered that they had the right now claimed by South Carolina. The war into which we were forced to support the dignity of the nation and the rights of our citizens might have ended in defeat and disgrace, instead of victory and honor, if the states who supposed it a ruinous and unconstitutional measure had thought they possessed the right of nullifying the act by

which it was declared and denying supplies for its prosecution. Hardly and unequally as those measures bore upon several members of the Union, to the legislatures of none did this efficient and peaceable remedy, as it is called, suggest itself. The discovery of this important feature in our Constitution was reserved to the present day. To the statesmen of South Carolina belongs the invention, and upon the citizens of that state will unfortunately fall the evils of reducing it to practice.

If the doctrine of a state veto upon the laws of the Union carries with it internal evidence of its impracticable absurdity, our constitutional history will also afford abundant proof that it would have been repudiated with indignation had it been proposed to form a feature in our government. . . .

Under the Confederation, then, no state could legally annul a decision of the Congress or refuse to submit to its execution; but no provision was made to enforce these decisions. Congress made requisitions, but they were not complied with. The government could not operate on individuals. They had no judiciary, no means of collecting revenue.

But the defects of the Confederation need not be detailed. Under its operation we could scarcely be called a nation. We had neither prosperity at home nor consideration abroad. This state of things could not be endured, and our present happy Constitution was formed but formed in vain if this fatal doctrine prevails. It was formed for important objects that are announced in the Preamble, made in the name and by the authority of the people of the United States, whose delegates framed and whose conventions approved it. The most important among these objects — that which is placed first in rank, on which all the others rest — is *"to form a more perfect union."*

Now, is it possible that even if there were no express provision giving supremacy to the Constitution and laws of the United States over those of the states, can it be conceived that an instrument made for the purpose of *"forming a more perfect union"* than that of the Confederation could be so constructed by the assembled wisdom of our country as to substitute for that Confederation a form of government dependent for its existence on the local interest, the party spirit of a state or of a prevailing faction in a state? Every man of plain, unsophisticated understanding who hears the question will give such an answer as will preserve the Union. . . .

I consider, then, the power to annul a law of the United States, assumed by one state, *incompatible with the existence of the Union, contradicted expressly by the letter of the Constitution, unauthorized by its spirit, inconsistent with every principle on which it was founded, and destructive of the great object for which it was formed.*

After this general view of the leading principle, we must examine the particular application of it which is made in the ordinance.

The Preamble rests its justification on these grounds: It assumes as a fact that the obnoxious laws, although they purport to be laws for raising revenue, were in reality intended for the protection of manufactures, which purpose it asserts to be unconstitutional; that the operation of these laws is unequal; that the amount raised by them is greater than is required by the wants of the government; and, finally, that the proceeds are to be applied to objects unauthorized by the Constitution. These are the only causes alleged to justify an open opposition to the laws of the country and a threat of seceding from the Union if any attempt should be made to enforce them. The first virtually acknowledges that the law in question was passed under a power expressly given by the Constitution to lay and collect imposts; but its constitutionality is drawn in question from the *motives* of those who passed it. However apparent this purpose may be in the present case, nothing can be more dan-

gerous than to admit the position that an unconstitutional purpose entertained by the members who assent to a law enacted under a constitutional power shall make that law void.

For how is that purpose to be ascertained? Who is to make the scrutiny? How often may bad purposes be falsely imputed, in how many cases are they concealed by false professions, in how many is no declaration of motive made? Admit this doctrine and you give to the states an uncontrolled right to decide; and every law may be annulled under this pretext. If, therefore, the absurd and dangerous doctrine should be admitted that a state may annul an unconstitutional law, or one that it deems such, it will not apply to the present case.

The next objection is that the laws in question operate unequally. This objection may be made with truth to every law that has been or can be passed. The wisdom of man never yet contrived a system of taxation that would operate with perfect equality. If the unequal operation of a law makes it unconstitutional, and if all laws of that description may be abrogated by any state for that cause, then indeed is the federal Constitution unworthy of the slightest effort for its preservation.

We have hitherto relied on it as the perpetual bond of our Union; we have received it as the work of the assembled wisdom of the nation; we have trusted to it as to the sheet anchor of our safety in the stormy times of conflict with a foreign or domestic foe; we have looked to it with sacred awe as the palladium of our liberties; and with all the solemnities of religion have pledged to each other our lives and fortunes here and our hopes of happiness hereafter in its defense and support. Were we mistaken, my countrymen, in attaching this importance to the Constitution of our country? . . .

Our Constitution does not contain the absurdity of giving power to make laws and another to resist them. The sages whose memory will always be reverenced have given us a practical and, as they hoped, a permanent constitutional compact. The father of his country did not affix his revered name to so palpable an absurdity. Nor did the states, when they severally ratified it, do so under the impression that a veto on the laws of the United States was reserved to them or that they could exercise it by implication. Search the debates in all their conventions, examine the speeches of the most zealous opposers of federal authority, look at the amendments that were proposed; they are all silent — not a syllable uttered, not a vote given, not a motion made to correct the explicit supremacy given to the laws of the Union over those of the states, or to show that implication, as is now contended, could defeat it.

No; we have not erred. The Constitution is still the object of our reverence, the bond of our Union, our defense in danger, the source of our prosperity in peace. It shall descend, as we have received it, uncorrupted by sophistical construction, to our posterity; and the sacrifices of local interests, of state prejudices, of personal animosities that were made to bring it into existence will again be patriotically offered for its support.

The two remaining objections made by the ordinance to these laws are that the sums intended to be raised by them are greater than are required, and that the proceeds will be unconstitutionally employed. . . .

The ordinance, with the same knowledge of the future that characterizes a former objection, tells you that the proceeds of the tax will be unconstitutionally applied. If this could be ascertained with certainty, the objection would with more propriety be reserved for the law so applying the proceeds, but surely cannot be urged against the laws levying the duty.

These are the allegations contained in the ordinance. Examine them seriously, my fellow citizens; judge for yourselves. I appeal to you to determine whether they are so clear, so convincing, as to leave no doubt of their correctness; and even if you should come to this conclusion, how far they justify the reckless, destructive course which you are directed to pursue. Review these objections and the conclusions drawn from them once more. What are they? Every law, then, for raising revenue, according to the South Carolina ordinance, may be rightfully annulled unless it be so framed as no law ever will or can be framed. Congress have a right to pass laws for raising revenue and each state has a right to oppose their execution — two rights directly opposed to each other; and yet is this absurdity supposed to be contained in an instrument drawn for the express purpose of avoiding collisions between the states and the general government by an assembly of the most enlightened statesmen and purest patriots ever embodied for a similar purpose.

In vain have these sages declared that Congress shall have power to lay and collect taxes, duties, imposts, and excises; in vain have they provided that they shall have power to pass laws which shall be necessary and proper to carry those powers into execution, that those laws and that Constitution shall be the "supreme law of the land, and that the judges in every state shall be bound thereby, anything in the constitution or laws of any state to the contrary notwithstanding"; in vain have the people of the several states solemnly sanctioned these provisions, made them their paramount law, and individually sworn to support them whenever they were called on to execute any office. Vain provisions! Ineffectual restrictions! Vile profanation of oaths! Miserable mockery of legislation! — if a bare majority of the voters in any one state may, on a real or supposed knowledge of the intent with which a law has been passed, declare themselves free from its operation; say, here it gives too little; there, too much, and operates unequally; here it suffers articles to be free that ought to be taxed; there it taxes those that ought to be free; in this case the proceeds are intended to be applied to purposes which we do not approve; in that, the amount raised is more than is wanted.

Congress, it is true, are invested by the Constitution with the right of deciding these questions according to their sound discretion. Congress is composed of the representatives of all the states and of all the people of all the states. But *we*, part of the people of one state, to whom the Constitution has given no power on the subject, from whom it has expressly taken it away; *we*, who have solemnly agreed that this Constitution shall be our law; *we*, most of whom have sworn to support it — *we* now abrogate this law and swear, and force others to swear, that it shall not be obeyed; and we do this not because Congress have no right to pass such laws — this we do not allege — but because they have passed them with improper views. They are unconstitutional from the motives of those who passed them, which we can never with certainty know; from their unequal operation, although it is impossible, from the nature of things, that they should be equal; and from the disposition which we presume may be made of their proceeds, although that disposition has not been declared. This is the plain meaning of the ordinance in relation to laws which it abrogates for alleged unconstitutionality.

But it does not stop there. It repeals in express terms an important part of the Constitution itself and of laws passed to give it effect which have never been alleged to be unconstitutional. The Constitution declares that the judicial powers of the United States extend to cases arising under the laws of the United States, and that such laws, the Constitution, and treaties shall be paramount to the state constitutions and laws. The judiciary act prescribes the mode by which the case may be brought before a court of the United States by appeal when a state tribunal shall decide against this provision of the Constitution. The ordinance declares there shall be no appeal — makes the state law paramount to the Constitution and laws of the United States, forces judges and jurors to swear that they will disregard their provisions, and even makes it penal in a suitor to attempt relief by appeal. It further declares that it shall not be lawful for the authorities of the United States or of that state to enforce the payment of duties imposed by the revenue laws within its limits.

Here is a law of the United States, not even pretended to be unconstitutional, repealed by the authority of a small majority of the voters of a single state. Here is a provision of the Constitution which is solemnly abrogated by the same authority.

On such expositions and reasonings the ordinance grounds not only an assertion of the right to annul the laws of which it complains but to enforce it by a threat of seceding from the Union if any attempt is made to execute them.

This right to secede is deduced from the nature of the Constitution, which, they say, is a compact between sovereign states who have preserved their whole sovereignty and therefore are subject to no superior; that because they made the compact they can break it when in their opinion it has been departed from by the other states. Fallacious as this course of reasoning is, it enlists state pride and finds advocates in the honest prejudices of those who have not studied the nature of our government sufficiently to see the radical error on which it rests. . . .

The Constitution of the United States, then, forms a *government*, not a league; and whether it be formed by compact between the states or in any other manner, its character is the same. It is a government in which all the people are represented, which operates directly on the people individually, not upon the states; they retained all the power they did not grant. But each state, having expressly parted with so many powers as to constitute, jointly with the other states, a single nation, cannot, from that period, possess any right to secede, because such secession does not break a league but destroys the unity of a nation; and any injury to that unity is not only a breach which would result from the contravention of a compact but it is an offense against the whole Union.

To say that any state may at pleasure secede from the Union is to say that the United States are not a nation, because it would be a solecism to contend that any part of a nation might dissolve its connection with the other parts, to their injury or ruin, without committing any offense. Secession, like any other revolutionary act, may be morally justified by the extremity of oppression; but to call it a constitutional right is confounding the meaning of terms, and can only be done through gross error or to deceive those who are willing to assert a right, but would pause before they made a revolution or incur the penalties consequent on a failure.

Because the Union was formed by a compact, it is said the parties to that compact may, when they feel themselves aggrieved, depart from it; but it is precisely because it is a compact that they cannot. A compact is an agreement or binding obligation. It may by its terms have a sanction or penalty for its breach, or it may not. If it contains no sanction, it may be broken with no other consequence than moral guilt; if it have a sanction, then the breach incurs the designated or implied penalty. A league between independent nations generally has no sanction other than a moral one; or if it should contain a penalty, as there is no common superior it cannot be enforced. A government, on the contrary, always has a sanction, express or implied; and in our case it is both necessarily implied and expressly given. An attempt by force of arms to destroy a government is an offense, by whatever means the constitutional compact may have been formed; and such government has the right by the law of self-defense to pass acts for punishing the offender, unless that right is modified, restrained, or re-sumed by the constitutional act. In our system, although it is modified in the case of treason, yet authority is expressly given to pass all laws necessary to carry its powers into effect, and under this grant provision has been made for punishing acts which obstruct the due administration of the laws.

It would seem superfluous to add anything to show the nature of that Union which connects us, but as erroneous opinions on this subject are the foundation of doctrines the most destructive to our peace, I must give some further development to my views on this subject. No one, fellow citizens, has a higher reverence for the reserved rights of the states than the magistrate who now addresses you. No one would make greater personal sacrifices or official exertions to defend them from violation; but equal care must be taken to prevent, on their part, an improper interference with or resumption of the rights they have vested in the nation. The line has not been so distinctly drawn as to avoid doubts in some cases of the exercise of power. Men of the best intentions and soundest views may differ in their construction of some parts of the Constitution; but there are others on which dispassionate reflection can leave no doubt.

Of this nature appears to be the assumed right of secession. It rests, as we have seen, on the alleged undivided sovereignty of the states and on their having formed in this sovereign capacity a compact which is called the Constitution, from which, because they made it, they have the right to secede. Both of these positions are erroneous, and some of the arguments to prove them so have been anticipated.

The states severally have not retained their entire sovereignty. It has been shown that in becoming parts of a nation, not members of a league, they surrendered many of their essential parts of sovereignty. The right to make treaties, declare war, levy taxes, exercise exclusive judicial and legislative powers were all of them functions of sovereign power. The states, then, for all these important purposes, were no longer sovereign. The allegiance of their citizens was transferred, in the first instance, to the government of the United States; they became American citizens and owed obedience to the Constitution of the United States and to laws made in conformity with the powers it vested in Congress. . . .

This, then, is the position in which we stand. A small majority of the citizens of one state in the Union have elected delegates to a state convention; that convention has ordained that all the revenue laws of the United States must be repealed, or that they are no longer a member of the Union. The governor of that state has recommended to the legislature the raising of an army to carry the secession into effect, and that he may be empowered to give clearances to vessels in the name of the state. No act of violent opposition to the laws has yet been committed, but such a state of things is hourly apprehended. And it is the intent of this instrument to proclaim, not only that the duty imposed on me by the Constitution "to take care that the laws be faithfully executed" shall be performed to the extent of the powers already vested in me by law, or of such others as the wisdom of Congress shall devise and intrust to me for that purpose, but to warn the citizens of South Carolina who have been deluded into an opposition to the laws of the danger they will incur by obedience to the illegal and disorganizing ordinance of the convention; to exhort those who have refused to support it to persevere in their determination to uphold the Constitution and laws of their country; and to point out to all the perilous situation into which the good people of that state have been led, and that the course they are urged to pursue is one of ruin and disgrace to the very state whose rights they affect to support. . . .

Disunion by armed force is *treason*. Are you really ready to incur its guilt? If you are, on the heads of the instigators of the act be the dreadful consequences; on their heads be the dishonor, but on yours may fall the punishment. On your unhappy state will inevitably fall all the evils of the conflict you force upon the government of your country. It cannot accede to the mad project of disunion, of which you would be the first victims. Its first magistrate cannot, if he would, avoid the performance of his duty. . . .

Fellow citizens of the United States, the threat of unhallowed disunion, the names of those once respected by whom it is uttered, the array of military force to support it, denote the approach of a crisis in our affairs on which the continuance of our unexampled prosperity, our political existence, and perhaps that of all free governments may depend. The conjuncture demanded a free, a full and explicit enunciation, not only of my intentions, but of my principles of action; and as the claim was asserted of a right by a state to annul the laws of the Union, and even to secede from it at pleasure, a frank exposition of my opinions in relation to the origin and form of our government and the construction I give to the instrument by which it was created seemed to be proper.

Having the fullest confidence in the justness of the legal and constitutional opinion of my duties which has been expressed, I rely with equal confidence on your undivided support in my determination to execute the laws, to preserve the Union by all constitutional means, to arrest, if possible, by moderate and firm measures the necessity of a recourse to force; and if it be the will of Heaven that the recurrence of its primeval curse on man for the shedding of a brother's blood should fall upon our land, that it be not called down by any offensive act on the part of the United States.

Fellow citizens, the momentous case is before you. On your undivided support of your government depends the decision of the great question it involves — whether your sacred Union will be preserved and the blessing it secures to us as one people shall be perpetuated.

II.

Reply to Jackson's Proclamation

THE COMMITTEE ON FEDERAL RELATIONS, to which was referred the proclamation of the President of the United States, have had it under consideration, and recommend the adoption of the following resolutions:

Resolved, that the power vested by the Constitution and laws in the President of the United States to issue his proclamation does not authorize him in that mode to interfere whenever he may think fit in the affairs of the respective states, or that he should use it as a means of promulgating executive expositions of the Constitution, with the sanction of force thus superseding the action of other departments of the general government.

Resolved, that it is not competent to the President of the United States to order by proclamation the constituted authorities of a state to repeal their legislation; and that the late attempt of the President to do so is unconstitutional, and manifests a disposition to arrogate and exercise a power utterly destructive of liberty.

Resolved, that the opinions of the President in regard to the rights of the states are erroneous and dangerous, leading not only to the establishment of a consolidated government in the stead of our free confederacy but to the concentration of all powers in the chief executive.

Resolved, that the proclamation of the President is the more extraordinary that he has silently and, as it is supposed, with entire approbation witnessed our sister state of Georgia avow, act upon, and carry into effect, even to the taking of life, principles identical with those now denounced by him in South Carolina.

Resolved, that each state of the Union has the right, whenever it may deem such a course necessary for the preservation of its liberties or vital interests, to secede peaceably from the Union, and that there is no constitutional power in the general government, much less in the Executive Department of that government, to retain by force such state in the Union.

Resolved, that the primary and paramount allegiance of the citizens of this state, native or adopted, is of right due to this state.

Resolved, that the declaration of the President of the United States in his said proclamation, of his personal feelings and relations toward the state of South Carolina, is rather an appeal to the loyalty of subjects than to the patriotism of citizens, and is a blending of official and individual character, heretofore unknown in our state papers and revolting to our conception of political propriety.

Resolved, that the undisguised indulgence of personal hostility in the said proclamation would be unworthy of the animadversion of this legislature, but for the solemn and official form of the instrument which is made its vehicle.

Resolved, that the principles, doctrines, and purposes contained in the said proclamation are inconsistent with any just idea of a limited government, and subversive of the rights of the states and liberties of the people, and if submitted to in silence would lay a broad foundation for the establishment of monarchy.

Resolved, that while this legislature has witnessed with sorrow such a relaxation of the spirit of our institutions that a President of the United States dare venture upon this highhanded measure, it regards with indignation the menaces which are directed against it, and the concentration of a standing army on our borders — that the state will repel force by force, and, relying upon the blessings of God, will maintain its liberty at all hazards.

Resolved, that copies of these resolutions be sent to our members in Congress, to be laid before that body.

Index of Authors

*The numbers in brackets
indicate selection numbers
in this volume*

ADAMS, JOHN QUINCY (July 11, 1767-Feb. 23, 1848), diplomat and statesman. Sixth President of the United States (1825-29); U.S. senator from Massachusetts (1803-08); minister to St. Petersburg (1809-14); minister to Great Britain (1815); secretary of state under Monroe; U.S. representative (1831-48). [3, 9, 10, 13, 29, 38, 39] See also Author Index, Vols. 4, 6.

BANCROFT, GEORGE (Oct. 3, 1800-Jan. 17, 1891), historian, diplomat, politician, and educator. Secretary of the navy (1845-46) under Polk; founded the U.S. Naval Academy, Annapolis; minister to Great Britain (1846-49); author of Andrew Johnson's first annual message; minister to Germany (1867-74); wrote *History of the United States* (10 vols., 1834-74). [80] See also Author Index, Vol. 6.

BEECHER, CATHARINE (Sept. 6, 1800-May 12, 1878), educator. Established women's colleges including a school in Hartford and the Western Female Institute (Cincinnati); opposed woman suffrage. [66]

BENTON, THOMAS HART (March 14, 1782-April 10, 1858), political leader and author. U.S. senator (1821-51) and representative (1853-55) from Missouri; known as "Old Bullion" for his views on bank and money issues; pro-slavery but against secession. [92]

BERNHARD, KARL, duke of Saxe-Weimar Eisenach (1792-July 31, 1862), soldier.

Served under Napoleon until the Battle of Waterloo; traveled in U.S.; commander of the Dutch Army. [51]

BRYANT, WILLIAM CULLEN (Nov. 3, 1794-June 12, 1878), poet, editor, and lawyer. Co-editor and co-owner (1829-78) of the *New York Evening Post;* wrote "Thanatopsis" (1817), "To a Waterfowl" (1817), "The Flood of Years" (1876). [33, 102] See also Author Index, Vol. 6.

BUEL, DAVID, JR. (fl. 1821), public official. Delegate to the New York state constitutional convention (1821). [2]

CALDWELL, JOSEPH (April 21, 1773-Jan. 27, 1835), mathematician and educator. President (1804-12, 1817-35) of the University of North Carolina. [108]

CALHOUN, JOHN C. (March 18, 1782-March 31, 1850), political philosopher, lawyer, and statesman. U.S. representative from South Carolina (1811-17); secretary of war under Monroe; Vice-President of the United States (1825-32) under J. Q. Adams and Jackson; U.S. senator (1833-43, 1845-50); secretary of state (1844-45) under Tyler. [111] See also Author Index, Vols. 4, 6, 7, 8.

CATLIN, GEORGE (July 26, 1796-Dec. 23, 1872), artist and author. Painted (1829-38) the series of Indian portraits now in the National Museum, Washington, D.C.; wrote *Life Among the Indians* (1867). [103]

CHANNING, WILLIAM ELLERY (April 7, 1780-Oct. 2, 1842), clergyman and author. Pastor (1803-42) of Boston Federal Street Church; founded (1825) the American Unitarian Association; wrote *Negro Slavery* (1835) in behalf of the Abolitionist cause, *Remarks on National Literature* (1830), *Self Culture* (1838). **[85, 86]** See also Author Index, Vols. 4, 6.

CLAY, HENRY (April 12, 1777-June 29, 1852), lawyer and statesman. U.S. senator from Kentucky (1806-07, 1810-11, 1831-42, 1849-52); U.S. representative (1811-14, 1815-21, 1823-25) and House speaker in all years but 1821; secretary of state under J. Q. Adams. **[24, 83]** See also Author Index, Vols. 4, 6, 8.

COLTON, CALVIN (Sept. 14, 1789-March 13, 1857), author, journalist, and politician. Worked for the *New York Observer* in England; wrote travel journals, political pamphlets, and biographies of Henry Clay. **[106]** See also Author Index, Vol. 7.

COOPER, JAMES FENIMORE (Sept. 15, 1789-Sept. 14, 1851), novelist. Wrote tales of the frontier, travel books, social and political criticism; author of the Leatherstocking Tales (*The Pioneers*, 1823; *The Last of the Mohicans*, 1826; *The Prairie*, 1827; *The Pathfinder*, 1840; *The Deerslayer*, 1841) and *The American Democrat* (1838). **[53]** See also Author Index, Vol. 6.

COOPER, THOMAS (Oct. 22, 1759-May 11, 1839), chemist, educator, jurist, and political philosopher. **[109]**

CORNISH, SAMUEL (fl. 1827), editor and Abolitionist spokesman. Co-founder and editor (1827-29) of *Freedom's Journal*, the first African American newspaper. **[46]**

CRAMER, JOHN (fl. 1821), public official. Delegate to the New York state constitutional convention (1821). **[2]**

DAY, JEREMIAH (Aug. 3, 1773-Aug. 22, 1867), professor of natural philosophy and mathematics, and president (1817-46) of Yale College. **[55]**

DEW, THOMAS R. (Dec. 5, 1802-Aug. 6, 1846), economist. Professor of political law and economy (1827-36) and president (1836-45) of the College of William and Mary; wrote numerous essays in defense of slavery. **[100]**

DUANE, WILLIAM (May 17, 1760-Nov. 24, 1835), journalist. Editor (1798-1822) of the *Philadelphia Aurora*; indicted (1799) under the Sedition Act for articles on the conduct of federal troops in crushing Fries's Rebellion. **[6]** See also Author Index, Vol. 4.

EVERETT, EDWARD (April 11, 1794-Jan. 15, 1865), Unitarian clergyman, orator, educator, and statesman. Pastor of the Brattle Street Church, Boston; editor (1820-24) of the *North American Review*; U.S. representative from Massachusetts (1825-35); governor (1836-40); minister to Great Britain (1841-45); president (1846-49) of Harvard College; secretary of state (1852-53) under Fillmore; U.S. senator (1853-54). **[22, 25]** See also Author Index, Vols. 6, 7.

FLINT, TIMOTHY (July 23, 1780-Aug. 16, 1840), Congregational clergyman, missionary, and author. Editor (1827-30) of the *Western Monthly Review* and (1833) of the New York *Knickerbocker Magazine*; wrote numerous accounts of Western life. **[41]**

FULLER, ZELOTES (fl. 1830), Philadelphia Universalist. **[75]**

FURMAN, RICHARD (Oct. 9, 1755-Aug. 25, 1825), Baptist minister and educator. First president (1821) of the Baptist State Convention in South Carolina; founder (1825) of Furman University; president of the Baptist Triennial Convention. **[8]**

GALLATIN, ALBERT (Jan. 29, 1761-Aug. 12, 1849), financier and diplomat. U.S. representative from Pennsylvania (1795-1801); secretary of the treasury (1801-14) under Jefferson and Madison; minister to France (1816-23); minister to Great Britain (1826-27). **[42]** See also Author Index, Vols. 4, 7.

GARRISON, WILLIAM LLOYD (Dec. 12, 1805-May 24, 1879), Abolitionist leader and journalist. Founded (1831) the *Liberator*; helped establish (1833) the American Anti-Slavery Society; its president (1843-65); advocate of immediate emancipation and of woman suffrage; opposed the

American Colonization Society; wrote *Thoughts on African Colonization* (1832). **[65, 89]** See also Author Index, Vol. 6.

GIBSON, JOHN BANNISTER (Nov. 8, 1780-May 3, 1853), jurist. Chief justice of the Pennsylvania Supreme Court. **[36]**

GRUNDY, FELIX (Sept. 11, 1777-Dec. 19, 1840), political leader, lawyer, and jurist. U.S. representative from Kentucky (1811-14); U.S. senator (1829-38, 1839-40); U.S. attorney general (1838-39) under Van Buren. **[18]** See also Author Index, Vol. 4.

HALL, JAMES (Aug. 19, 1793-July 5, 1868), author, soldier, lawyer, circuit judge, and editor. Wrote about life on the frontier; compiled *Western Souvenir* (1828), the first literary annual in the West; edited (1830-32) the *Illinois Monthly Magazine*, which became the *Western Monthly Magazine* in Cincinnati (1832-36); wrote *Letters from the West* (1828), *The Romance of Western History* (1857). **[50]**

HAWLEY, ZERAH (1781-1856), Connecticut physician. **[7]**

HOLBROOK, JOSIAH (1788-June 17, 1854), educator. Proponent of popular and adult education; editor of (1832-33) the *Family Lyceum;* encouraged the establishment of town lyceums throughout the U.S. **[68]**

INGERSOLL, CHARLES J. (Oct. 3, 1782-May 14, 1862), lawyer, public official, and author. U.S. representative from Pennsylvania (1813-15, 1841-49); U.S. district attorney for Pennsylvania (1815-29); wrote *View of the Rights and Wrongs, Power and Policy, of the United States of America* (1808). **[20]** See also Author Index, Vol. 4.

JACKSON, ANDREW (March 15, 1767-June 8, 1845), lawyer, statesman, and soldier, known as "Old Hickory." Seventh President of the United States (1829-37); U.S. representative from Tennessee (1796-97); U.S. senator (1797-98, 1823-25); justice of the Tennessee Supreme Court (1798-1804); major general of the state militia (1802); major general of the U.S. Army (1814); governor of the Florida Territory (1821). **[73, 78, 87, 104, 112]** See also Author Index, Vols. 6, 7.

JAY, PETER (Jan. 24, 1776-Feb. 20, 1843),

lawyer. Son of John Jay; member of the New York Assembly (1816-20); New York city recorder (1820); delegate to the New York state constitutional convention (1821). **[2]**

JEFFERSON, THOMAS (April 13, 1743-July 4, 1826), lawyer, architect, agriculturalist, educator, political philosopher, diplomat, and statesman. Third President of the United States (1801-09); member (1775-76) of the Continental Congress; author of the Declaration of Independence; governor of Virginia (1779-81); minister to France (1785-89); secretary of state (1790-93) under Washington; Vice-President of the United States under John Adams; founder of the University of Virginia. **[5, 12]** See also Author Index, Vols. 2, 3, 4.

JOHNSON, RICHARD M. (1780-Nov. 19, 1850), lawyer and public official. U.S. representative from Kentucky (1807-19, 1829-37); U.S. senator (1819-29); Vice-President of the United States under Van Buren. **[60]** See also Author Index, Vol. 4.

KENRICK, FRANCIS PATRICK (Dec. 3, 1796-July 8, 1863), Roman Catholic prelate, archbishop of Baltimore. **[93]**

KENT, JAMES (July 31, 1763-Dec. 12, 1847), jurist. Professor of law at Columbia College (1793-98, 1823-26); justice (1798-1804) and chief justice (1804-14) of the New York Supreme Court; chancellor (1814-23) of the New York Court of Chancery; delegate to the New York state constitutional convention (1821). **[2]**

KINGSLEY, JAMES (Aug. 28, 1778-Aug. 31, 1852), educator and historian. First professor of classical languages (1805-51) at Yale College. **[55]**

LEGARÉ, HUGH S. (Jan. 2, 1797-June 20, 1843), lawyer, diplomat, and public official. Member of the South Carolina legislature (1820-22, 1824-30); a founder (1828-32) of the *Southern Review;* state attorney general (1830-32); chargé d'affaires to Belgium (1832-36); U.S. representative (1836-38); secretary of state ad interim (1843) under Tyler. **[56]**

LINDSLEY, PHILIP (Dec. 21, 1786-May 25, 1855), Presbyterian minister and educator. Teacher, vice-president, and acting president (1823) of the College

ROYALL, ANNE (June 11, 1769-Oct. 1, 1854), traveler and writer. Founded and edited (1831-36) *Paul Pry* and (1836-54) *The Huntress.* [81]

RUSH, RICHARD (Aug. 29, 1780-July 30, 1859), lawyer, diplomat, and public official. Comptroller of the U.S. treasury (1811); U.S. attorney general (1814-17) and secretary of state (1817) under Madison; minister to Great Britain (1817-25); secretary of the treasury under J. Q. Adams; secured the Smithson bequest to found the Smithsonian Institution (1836-38); minister to France (1847-49). [11] See also Author Index, Vol. 4.

RUSSWURM, JOHN (Oct. 1, 1799-June 17, 1851), Abolitionist spokesman. First African American graduate of Bowdoin College; co-founder and editor (1827-29) of *Freedom's Journal;* superintendent of public schools (1829) in Liberia, Africa; governor of the Maryland Colony at Cape Palmas, Africa (1836-51). [46]

SANFORD, NATHAN (Nov. 5, 1777-Oct. 17, 1838), jurist and public official. U.S. district attorney for New York (1803-15); member of the state assembly (1808-09, 1811); state senator (1812-15); U.S. senator (1815-21, 1826-31); delegate to the state constitutional convention (1821). [2]

SHAW, LEMUEL (Jan. 9, 1781-March 30, 1861), jurist. Chief justice (1830-60) of the Massachusetts Supreme Court. [45] See also Author Index, Vol. 7.

SIMPSON, STEPHEN (July 24, 1789-Aug. 17, 1854), editor and author. Co-founder and editor (1816-17) of the *Portico;* contributed to the *Columbian Observer,* the *Aurora,* and *The Philadelphia Book;* wrote *The Working Man's Manual* (1831). [97]

SKIDMORE, THOMAS (?-1832), mechanic, author, and leader of the New York Workingmen's Party. Editor of the *Friend of Equal Rights* and author of *The Rights of Man to Property!* (1829). [64]

SMITH, MARGARET BAYARD (Feb. 20, 1778-June 7, 1844), Washington society leader and author. Wife of Samuel Harrison Smith; wrote articles for *Godey's Lady's Book,* the *Southern Literary Messenger,* etc.; author of *What Is Gentility?* (1828)

and letters about Washington personalities. [61]

SMITH, SAMUEL FRANCIS (Oct. 21, 1808-Nov. 16, 1895), poet, editor, and Baptist clergyman. Edited (1842-48) *The Christian Review;* wrote "America" (1832). [107]

TAYLOR, JOHN (?Dec. 19, 1753-Aug. 21, 1824), political writer and public official. Member (1779-81, 1783-85, 1796-1800) of the Virginia House of Delegates; U.S. senator (1792-93, 1803, 1822-24); author of *An Enquiry into the Principles and Policy of the Government of the United States* (1814), *Tyranny Unmasked* (1822). [19] See also Author Index, Vol. 4.

TICKNOR, GEORGE (Aug. 1, 1791-Jan. 26, 1871), educator, historian, and author. Professor of languages (1819-35) at Harvard College; a founder (1852) of the Boston Public Library. [16]

TOCQUEVILLE, ALEXIS DE (July 29, 1805-April 16, 1859), French historian and politician. Traveled in U.S. (1831-32) with Gustave de Beaumont to observe American prisons and published a report in 1832; wrote *Democracy in America* (1835-40), a classic study of the American political system. [99] See also Author Index, Vol. 6.

TROLLOPE, FRANCES (March 10, 1780-Oct. 6, 1863), English novelist and author of travel books. Mother of Anthony Trollope; wrote *Domestic Manners of the Americans* (1832). [105]

TURNER, NAT (Oct. 2, 1800-Nov. 11, 1831), religious fanatic and the leader of a slave rebellion (1831) that spread terror throughout the South, and for which he was tried and hanged. [98]

VAN BUREN, MARTIN (Dec. 5, 1782-July 24, 1862), lawyer, political leader, and public official. Eighth President of the United States (1837-41); attorney general of New York (1816-19); U.S. senator (1821-28); governor (1829); secretary of state (1829-31) and Vice-President of the United States (1833-37) under Jackson. [2] See also Author Index, Vol. 6.

WALKER, TIMOTHY (Dec. 1, 1802-Jan. 15, 1856), jurist, writer, and educator. Founded (1833) the Law School of Cincinnati College (now University); edited (from 1843) the *Western Law Journal;* wrote *Introduction to American Law* (1837). [96] See also Author Index, Vol. 7.

WEBSTER, DANIEL (Jan. 18, 1782-Oct. 24, 1852), lawyer, orator, and statesman. U.S. representative from New Hampshire (1813-17) and from Massachusetts (1823-27); U.S. senator from Massachusetts (1827-41, 1845-50); secretary of state (1841-43) under Tyler and (1850-52) under Fillmore. [23, 74, 104] See also Author Index, Vols. 4, 6, 7, 8.

WILLARD, EMMA HART (Feb. 23, 1787-April 15, 1870), educator and poetess. Pioneer in women's education; founded Waterford (N.Y.) Academy (1819) and Troy (N.Y.) Female Seminary (1821); wrote "Rocked in the Cradle of the Deep." [94] See also Author Index, Vol. 4.

WRIGHT, FRANCES (Sept. 6, 1795-Dec. 13, 1852), reformer. Toured U.S. (1818-20) and wrote *Views of Society and Manners in America* (1821); accompanied Lafayette on his visit (1824); liberal spokesman for religious, educational, and civil rights causes. [62]